EVERYTHING you need to know to create
a flourishing garden just right for your
home—step by step, season by season,
plant by plant, wherever you live.
How to grow luxuriant lawns,
flowers, shrubs, trees,
fruit, vegetables,
even if you

have never
gardened before.
A uniquely specific guide—
with 500 how-to-do-it drawings
and "idea" photographs.

McCALL'S GARDEN BOOK

Written Especially for McCall's by

Gretchen Fischer Harshbarger

SIMON AND SCHUSTER NEW YORK

Published by Simon and Schuster
Rockefeller Center, 630 Fifth Avenue
New York, New York 10020

Library of Congress Catalog Card Number: 68-11985

Manufactured in the United States of America

6 7 8 9 10 11 12 13 14 15

About the Author

GRETCHEN HARSHBARGER is a landscape architect and enthusiastic hobby-gardener. She has written and taken photographs for virtually every important garden publication, was Garden Editor of *Household Magazine* and Midwest Garden Editor of *American Home*, is a former president of the Garden Writers' Association of America, and the recipient of the "Asta" award for outstanding professional writing in horticulture, the "Garden Writer's Award" from the American Association of Nurserymen, and a "Citation" from the American Horticultural Society. Mrs. Harshbarger and her husband, Clay, who is a professor at the University of Iowa, live in Iowa City, Iowa, and have two sons.

Acknowledgments

Grateful acknowledgment is made to the following regional experts who gave much valued advice and furnished lists of recommended plants:

For the Northeast: Harold O. Perkins, landscape architect and Professor Emeritus, University of Connecticut

For the Midwest: the late E. L. Kammerer, former Curator of Collections, The Morton Arboretum, Lisle, Illinois

For the Upper South: Dr. Fred Galle, Director of Horticulture, Callaway Gardens, Pine Mountain, Georgia

For the Deep South: John V. Watkins, Professor Emeritus, University of Florida

For the Plains and Intermountain: Dr. A. C. Hildreth, Director Emeritus, Denver Botanic Garden

For the Southwest: John M. Harlow, nurseryman and landscape contractor, Tucson, Arizona

For the Northwest: Donald J. Martel, head of Department of Landscape Architecture, Oregon State University

For Northern California: P. H. Brydon, Director, Strybing Arboretum, San Francisco

For Southern California: George Spalding, Superintendent, Los Angeles State and County Arboretum, Arcadia

For Alaska: Alaska Agricultural Experiment Station, Palmer

For Hawaii: Dr. Horace Clay, Program Director, Institute for Technical Interchange, East West Center, Honolulu

Acknowledgment is also made to the following for illustrations in this book:

Drawings: John Burton Brimer

Photographs:
Molly Adams
W. Atlee Burpee Co.
Ferry-Morse Seed Co.
Florida State News Bureau
Gottscho-Schleisner
Jeannette Grossman

Gretchen Harshbarger
Inter-State Nurseries
Ray Manley
Phil Palmer
Geo. W. Park Seed Co.
John Robinson
Roche Photography

CONTENTS

1

How to Cultivate Your
Green Thumb

Approach gardening as an exhilarating adventure! You are going to create beauty with living plants that grow and change from day to day, and month to month, as you watch and aid. This is exciting, fascinating and satisfying. There are no hard and fast rules to make things difficult—just some general, helpful ones. Let this book be your friend and guide. It will introduce you to plants you should know and explain the basic hows and whys of growing them.

Think of plants as live pets to be loved, enjoyed and cared for to the best of your common-sense ability as they develop to their destined maturity. Each will have a unique personality. Most will be so sturdy and self-reliant that they can get along with minimum attention. Others will have special requirements such as a unique diet, protection from sun or cold, or annual pruning. This makes them—and gardening itself—more interesting.

Do Things the Easy, Enjoyable Way

GET YOURSELF A FEW REALLY GOOD BASIC TOOLS

With a handy supply of primary garden aids, you won't be constantly thwarted by commonplace tasks, such as digging a hole or cutting a twig. If you're in doubt as to those tools you would like, try out some of your neighbor's—temporarily. But don't be a permanent borrower; it's bad for everyone's disposition. Tools can be bought at garden supply, department or hardware stores and at lumber yards.

You'll need as a minimum:

* A spade or long-handled shovel for digging holes to place large plants.

* A spading fork for turning over and

loosening soil. (You'll find there are "ladies' sizes" available for both spade and fork.)

✳ A trowel for digging holes for small plants, mixing soil, and innumerable other small chores. My preference is for a sharp-pointed one similar to a small mason's trowel, because it's useful for cultivating, too. Those with slightly rounded sides, like miniature shovels, are excellent for digging small plants and making holes in which to place them.

✳ A rake for smoothing soil that's been dug, and tidying up messes.

✳ A hoe for cultivating and weeding.

✳ Hand pruners for pruning small size growth and picking flowers. These should be of good quality and should fit your hand and grip. Try out several at the store.

✳ A watering can and/or garden hose.

PAMPER YOURSELF WITH HANDY ACCESSORIES

A waterproof cushion is one of the gardener's best friends. It can be any old pillow wrapped in a polyethylene sack. Or it can be something fancy like a plastic-coated car cushion. Sit on it; kneel on it. You will be comfortable and relatively clean and dry as you weed, cultivate or sow tiny seeds.

A small basket in which to carry all your small tools, seed packets and other small objects is also a joy.

BE KIND TO YOUR HANDS

Before working in soil, claw your nails into a bar of soap that's been slightly moistened and softened. You'll be amazed to see how clean they emerge when you wash your hands later.

Durable work gloves, such as the relatively inexpensive leather ones farmers wear—which can be cleaned in the washing machine—save you from scratches. Use hand lotion after washing your hands.

Understand Plants' Basic Needs

LEAVES MUST HAVE LIGHT

Leaves are the plants' food factories, and light is the power that helps them manufacture food from elements of air and soil. Most plants need many hours of sunshine daily in order to grow satisfactorily. Roses, for instance, need at least six hours. Some plants, however, get along with little light, so they can grow in shade or semishade. This book will tell you which are which.

A good general rule to remember is that ordinarily the more sun a plant gets, the better it will flower. Morning sunlight is kind light, bright but relatively cool; thus the east side of your house is a favored position for plants. Afternoon sunshine is hot and harsh, so a western exposure is less versatile.

Sun touching and warming the soil is desirable in early spring, to start plants into growth. And it's good all year in cool climates. But in hot-summer areas, it can dry the earth and overheat roots, so plants often require part-time shade, or being close enough together to shade the ground, or having a protective carpet of groundcover plants.

ROOTS NEED GOOD SOIL

How well the tops of plants grow depends upon their roots, for the roots gather nutrient elements to send up to the leaves, which serve as food factories. The above-ground parts of plants usually balance their root systems exactly; if roots can't grow, tops won't either—and vice versa.

The best soil for gardens is a kind that:

Pleases *you* because it's easy to dig and cultivate.

Pleases *roots* by providing good conditions for them and the tiny soil bacteria that aid in making plant-food elements available to them.

Is loose and porous enough so that air and water can reach the roots.

Lets excess water drain away quickly so roots won't drown.

Holds considerable decomposed plant or animal material, called humus or organic matter, to act as a sponge providing space for air and water and to supply some plant food.

If your soil is like this, you're in luck! If it doesn't meet all the specifications but grows healthy and husky-looking weeds, it probably will grow a good garden. (See the chapter on soils.)

FOOD SUPPLIES SHOULD BE REPLENISHED

Nutrients in the soil provide the raw materials from which plants manufacture their true food—starches, sugars and proteins. It helps if occasionally you replenish soil nutrients by adding plant food in some form.

The best, easiest, and most common type of plant food for beginners and most gardeners to use is a "complete" fertilizer containing all the needed elements. Some of these are in dry form to be scattered on the ground and raked in. Others are used in solution. They come packaged in small or large quantities, under many brand names. Be sure to follow the instructions on the package and never use in larger amounts than advised. If you do, you'll make your plants sick! To learn about the various kinds of fertilizers, see the chapter on soils.

WATER IS ESSENTIAL AND CRUCIAL

Without water a plant will not only wilt but starve! Roots can absorb food elements only when the elements are in solution. That's why you should try to keep the soil constantly moist at root level, and one of the reasons why you should always water after applying plant food—unless rain is about to fall.

Ideally, plants should get about an inch of moisture a week during the growing season, either from rain or watering. But in parts of the country where rainfall is fairly regular, most people don't water lawns or gardens except during periods of drought—or while getting new plants established.

It is better to water thoroughly and deeply, and then let soil become dry on top before watering again, than to sprinkle a little each day. If only the top of the soil is kept moist, roots will stay in that shallow upper surface; and if you forget to water, or your plants are exposed to sunny windy weather, roots may dry and die.

LOTS OF LOVING PAYS OFF

Plants respond to affectionate and understanding care! Watch over them as you do your family; you will learn to foresee and supply their needs before emergencies occur.

🍁 Learn To Speak the Language

Botanical names of plants may sound strange, complicated, and unnecessarily fancy to you at first. But there's a good reason for them, so don't be awed but learn the language. You see, some plants tend to have many local names or nicknames. Also, the same names often are applied to different plants in various parts of the country. This tends to confuse gardeners.

Botanists through the years have assigned each plant one standard, internationally recognized name, written in Latin. Nurserymen and publishers of garden books and magazines, as well as gardeners, use these names in addition to common ones to clarify identification. You will find that using them gives you considerable satisfaction.

Names are arranged in orderly sequence, according to the plant's botanical classification. First comes the genus name (equivalent to a person's surname), then the species name (equivalent to a given name). If there's a third name, it's a special variety. For example: All lilies are *Lilium;* Tiger Lily is *Lilium tigrinum;* Double Tiger Lily is *Lilium tigrinum flore-pleno.* If *I* were a flower, my name would be: *Harshbarger gretchen brown-eyed.*

🍁 Tips to Beginners

The following conclusions and advice are based on the observations of a group of young gardeners who were beginners just a few seasons ago.

Don't get into emotional knots about gardening. Enjoy it!

Don't be too ambitious the first year or so, while you develop your skill. Take on just a little at a time.

Beware of impulse buying. Make a plan, and know why you need a plant and where you're going to put it before you start shopping.

Get the basic plants in first, working on a long-term plan. The first to go in should be your major shade trees.

Remember that plants develop rapidly. Shrubs and trees will grow large sooner than you think.

Don't plant bulbs and other flowers in a long single-file row. They'll look better in groups.

Keep a notebook of suggestions to yourself about what you want to plant where, dates to do things, and dates you have done them.

You *must* thin annuals. Otherwise they will stretch up and become lanky.

Get ideas by visiting other gardens. Drive about to see what is in bloom each week.

Learn identification of plants by sending for illustrated seed and nursery catalogues.

🍁 The Aim of This Book

I have tried to foresee your problems and provide information for solving them.

Each chapter begins by explaining general principles, then gives specific helps for gardening where you live. You will learn "why" as well as "how-to," so you can gradually trust yourself to make decisions on your own.

Since the book was planned for beginners rather than for experienced gardeners, plants are called by their common names in the general text and charts. But you will find their botanical names in the full descriptions given at the ends of chapters.

The part of the country in which you live will influence the kind of plants that you can grow successfully, and the way that you garden. In order to give you the most specific advice possible, we have divided the United States into several large regions and hardiness zones. Throughout the book, recommendations are made that refer to these divisions. Experts on plant materials have provided lists of the most satisfactory trees, shrubs, vines and groundcovers for each region. Authorities on gardening have prepared regional calendars of what to do month by month, and charts of sequence of bloom. Descriptions of plants include their zones of hardiness. The explanation of how your climate affects your garden is given in the next chapter. If you want to use this book to best advantage, read Chapter 2 now, before you dip into any other portion.

🍁 Consult the Index

If you do not find a particular plant, be sure to use the master index in the back of this book. Hundreds of plants are included there, though of course space does not permit discussing every known flower, shrub and tree.

2

Climate,
Key to What You Can Grow

There are hundreds of wonderful plants that will excel in your garden, though they may not flourish in other parts of the country, or even in different sections of your state. The unique qualities of your climate have a powerful influence on what will grow well for you. Some plants thrive only in mild-winter areas, and cannot survive freezing temperatures. Others do best where winters are cold, for they need an annual period of chilling. Some demand a great deal of moisture, including humid air, while others adapt easily to dry conditions. Many like acid soil—or the kind of climate that produces it—while others enjoy or tolerate alkalinity.

Fortunately this is not as complex as it sounds, for the main factor in determining which plants will succeed for you is the minimum winter temperature in your area.

Locate your zone on the hardiness map (next page) based on one done by the United States Department of Agriculture, and used as reference by nurserymen and garden publications. Memorize your number, for hardiness zones will be given throughout this book when plants are mentioned. The zones are arranged according to minimum winter temperatures. While these are accurate in a general way, they cannot show temperature variations between mountaintops and valleys, pavement-warmed cities and adjoining open-country suburbs, or coastal sites along large bodies of water as differing from inland properties. So, if you live in a spot that varies from most of the region around it, adjust your plant selections accordingly. The zone numbers run from 1 to 10, each indicating a difference of 10 degrees. In our text we sometimes use the letters "a" and "b" in connection with the numbers, to indicate that a plant is hardy in the colder half of the zone—"a", or the milder half—"b".

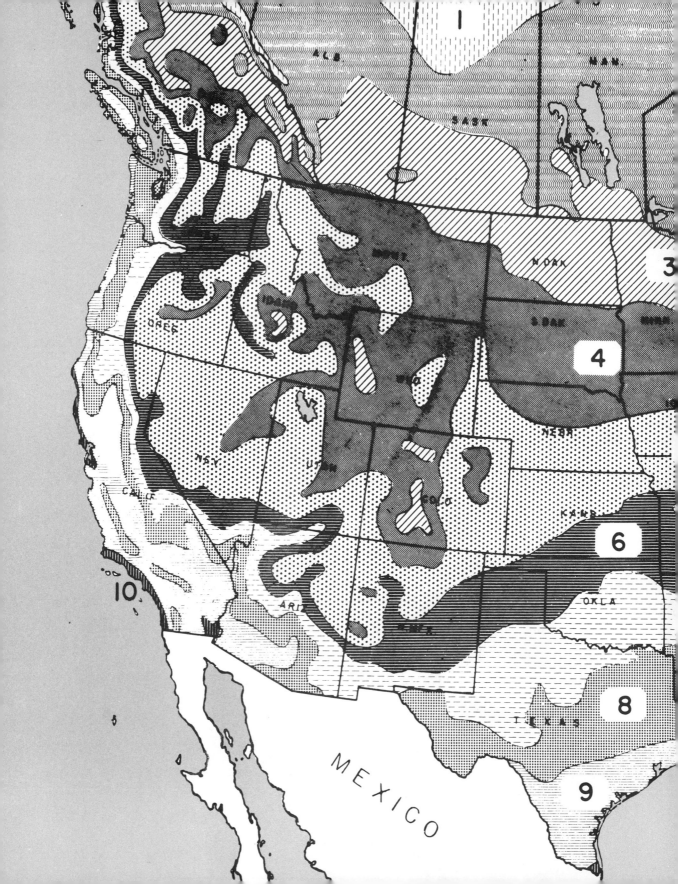

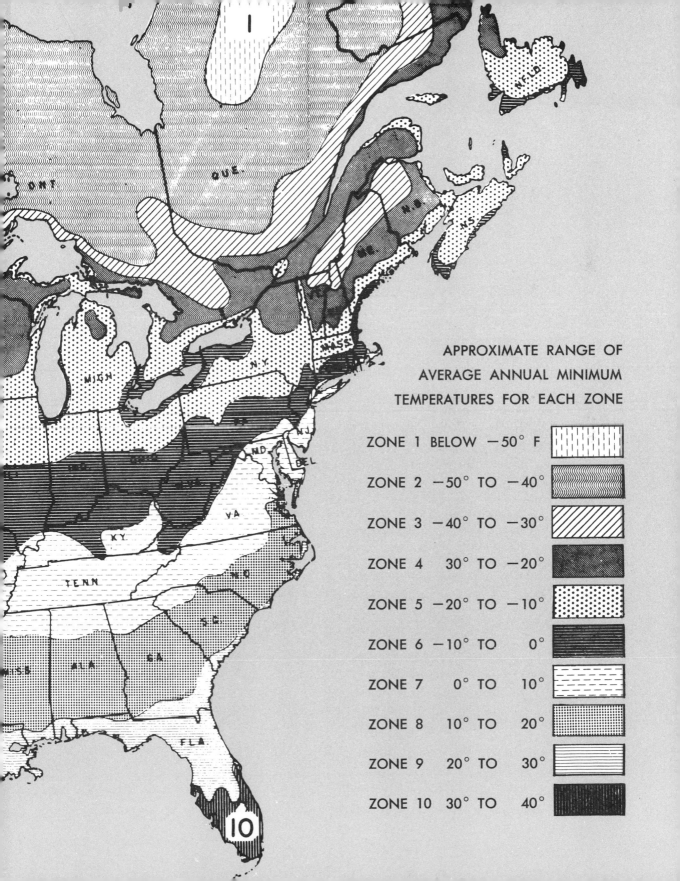

APPROXIMATE RANGE OF
AVERAGE ANNUAL MINIMUM
TEMPERATURES FOR EACH ZONE

ZONE 1 BELOW −50° F

ZONE 2 −50° TO −40°

ZONE 3 −40° TO −30°

ZONE 4   30° TO −20°

ZONE 5 −20° TO −10°

ZONE 6 −10° TO   0°

ZONE 7   0° TO 10°

ZONE 8   10° TO 20°

ZONE 9   20° TO 30°

ZONE 10 30° TO 40°

❧ Major Climate Regions and How To Garden in Each

Factors that affect the way you garden—besides temperature—include the amount of rainfall, type of soil, elevation of land, amount of wind, and, of course, sunshine. Wherever you live, it will pay to learn the quirks of your climate and site. Count your blessings and make the most of them! Undoubtedly you can grow many plants superbly—to the envy of people in other parts of the country. But, face it, you probably have some unique problems, too. Discovering what the difficulties are will aid you in finding ways to adapt to, moderate, or conquer them.

Throughout this book, references will be made to the climate regions discussed below, and recommendations will be made for plants to grow in them. In addition, at the back of the book you will find a calendar of what to do each month in your region.

Northerners Like Their Changing Seasons

When you garden in the North you are due for excitement and challenges. Seasons change dramatically. One minute it is winter; the next, spring is bursting out all over with grass instantly green, skies sunny, and bulbs and trees in bloom. You race to sow seeds and set new plants. Then it is summer. Temperatures soar except in northernmost states. Roses, perennials and annuals come into their glory. Hardy perennials do exceptionally well for they like a winter chilling and rest. A great variety of bloom is possible in summer gardens. Autumn is glorious; flowers continue to bloom until frost; foliage on deciduous trees and shrubs offers a dazzling color show as nights turn cool. Then, for winter, leafless deciduous trees take on a sculptured look. You tuck in the garden for its long winter sleep and relax, while temperatures tumble to zero.

Rains furnish fairly dependable moisture spring, summer and fall, so you may never need to do artificial watering except in times of drought or when setting out new plants. Snowfall varies from year to year.

Plants develop rapidly through the growing season, but it takes about 5 years for new shrubs to look mature; you must constantly encourage them. Winter protection is necessary for many things, especially from Zone 5 northward.

The Northeast: This part of the North has more rainfall than the Midwest. At one time, this region was entirely covered by forests. The climate is modified by large bodies of water—the Great Lakes and the Atlantic Ocean. The soil is predominantly acid and frequently rocky or shallow. Azalea, rhododendron, holly, mountain laurel and other broad-leaved evergreens thrive. So do many other plants that like ample moisture in the air as well as in the soil. Flowering dogwood trees are native to much of the area.

IMPRESSIONS OF VERMONT GARDENING

by Stella Clancy, hobby gardener of Norwich, Vermont, formerly of California and Iowa

"Stones are lovely here and are all over the place, covered with lichens in various shades of green. The woods are knee-deep in leaf mold. I have never had such a variety of annuals and perennials, with a riot of color all summer. As opposed to the Midwest and California, blooms last for weeks because the weather is more moderate and the temperature cooler at night. The big disadvantage of gardening here is the very long winter, and hence a short growing season. Trees and bushes seem to take forever to grow the tiniest bit. There is not the great variety of trees and shrubs that there is in California, but there are fewer insect pests."

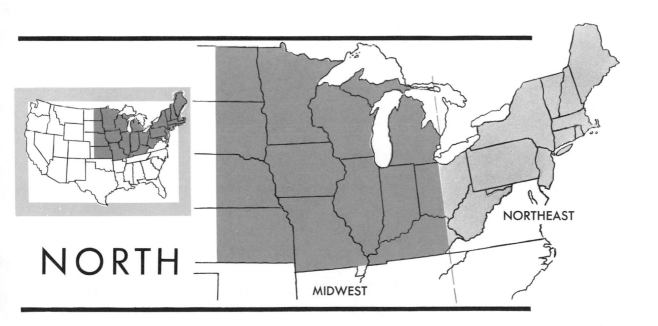

NORTH

NORTHEAST

MIDWEST

The Midwest: Most of this land has "delicious" soil, deep and fertile, slightly acid to neutral. It was formerly prairie. With ample rains, plants grow luxuriantly. However, temperatures fluctuate widely and suddenly. In summer the thermometer may register in the 90's for long periods, and occasionally top 100°. In winter temperatures may drop far below zero; there is alternate freezing and thawing accompanied by raw winds that may be deadly to some plants. Broad-leaved evergreens do not like the drying effect of sunshine coupled with these conditions; few of them are grown and they must be set in a protected spot. However, many narrow-leaved evergreens thrive.

A REPORT FROM THE SOUTHERN PART
OF THE MIDWEST

by Eleanor McClure, Editor,
The National Gardener: Horticultural Writer,
Missouri Botanical Garden Bulletin

"A wide variety of plants may be grown here. But in many areas it is difficult to grow them well for they must endure both torrid heat and bitter cold. Droughts may come at any season and plants are whipped by desiccating winds. High night temperatures in summer months make it more difficult to grow annuals, perennials and roses. Bluegrass goes on a sit-down strike, with the result that this region is often called 'the heart of the crabgrass belt.'

"Fortunately there are ways to reduce the hazards of difficult weather by selecting trees and shrubs that are reliably hardy for the area, and finding the most favorable location for each plant."

Moderate Winters Influence Southern Gardening

The South is a lovely land where camellias, jasmines and magnolias bloom. Winters are moderate to mild; rainfall is plentiful; soil varies in type but is primarily acid, so azaleas and hollies excel. Horticulturally the region is divided into the Upper South [Zones 7 and 8] and the Deep South [Zones 9 and 10]. In the Upper South, one can grow an intermingling of northern and southern plants, because winters are cold enough to give hardy things a beneficial chilling and period of dormancy. In the Deep South, which is mostly lowland, tidewater and Gulf Coast, winters are mild and summers long and hot; the southern part of Florida is subtropical. Rains average 50 in. a year coming mostly from June to October.

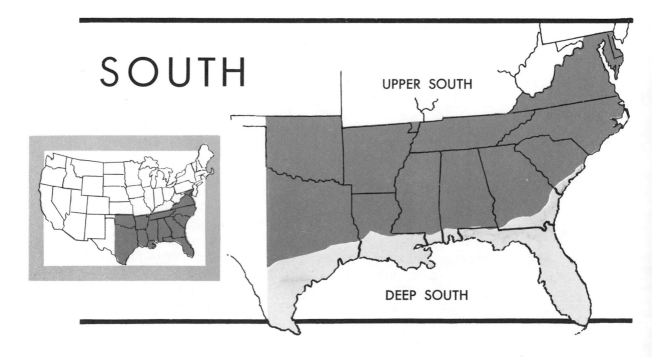

SOUTH

UPPER SOUTH

DEEP SOUTH

TIPS ON FLORIDA GARDENING

*by Olive Hindman, amateur horticulturist
of Ocala, who formerly gardened
in Kansas and Missouri*

"Our soil is mostly very sandy. I marvel that so many plants grow in it. Even after the addition of muck, peat and other humus, which is a must for successful gardening, it is easy to handle immediately after a rain.

"Types of plants are different: Few hardy perennials, shrubs or trees familiar in the North are successful here. Our kinds of oaks stay evergreen until spring, then lose leaves and immediately put out new ones. There is a wealth of subtropical woody plants, mostly evergreen. Many have spectacular bloom. In exceptionally cold winters some may be killed but most survive and grow quickly again. Annuals are planted in the fall for winter and spring bloom; they cannot be counted on for summer. Among perennials that do well are day-lilies. They should be the evergreen kinds because dormant ones simply pine away. Some roses can be grown, but varieties must be carefully selected and even then they are a bother and short-lived.

"Problems include the fact that there are more pests, insects, fungus, etc. One must do more spraying and fertilizing. Much artificial watering must be done in times of drought, because moisture soon drains away through the sandy soil. Mulch helps in most plantings —not for protection from cold but to keep the soil cooler and preserve moisture. Shade is welcome. Many plants needing full sun in colder states do well or better here with part shade."

MORE ON FLORIDA

*by Flo Beth Ehninger, hobby gardener recently
transplanted from Gainesville, Florida, to Iowa*

"You live outdoors so much that gardening and the outdoor living area are very impor-tant. You can do something in the yard every day of the year. Late winter and early spring are the showiest times for flowers because then the weather is pleasantly cool. Summers are hot, and people and gardens take a rest. Everything is lush because of ample moisture. Shrubs grow rapidly; you must keep pruning to keep them within bounds. There seem to be more insects than in the North, especially in lawns.

"Plants are seldom used indoors. They do not seem to be needed in the house when there are plentiful blooms and green leaves in the yard all winter—and when most of the types of plants that are grown inside in the North can be safely grown outdoors, here, the year around."

LOUISIANA AND SIMILAR SECTIONS

*by Mrs. U. B. Evans,
Horticulturist of Ferriday, Louisiana*

"How can we give rules for gardening in an area that has tall hills with poor, acid soil; delta soil that is very fertile with a subsurface water table that rises and falls with the rivers; and intermediate soils of heavy clay-loam filled with nutrients, but lacking in humus? You must learn what your plant requires and fill those needs by creating proper soil and drainage conditions. For instance, camellias and azaleas must have perfect drainage. When planted in delta areas they must be set at least 4 in. higher than surrounding ground. Properly mixed soil must be built up around the plants. In a few years the plants may sink and need to be lifted and replanted.

"We are short on perennials. A major reason is that a normal southern summer, with showers on hot days, is apt to cause crown rot in plants such as Shasta daisy and plantain-lily. One perennial that is dependable and a 'must' is day-lily; you can have it in bloom from the first of March until freezing weather. Bearded irises, unless varieties are carefully selected, are just not for the South."

In the West Success Depends Upon Water

Climate trademarks here are bright sunshine, warm days and cool nights, invigorating dry air, and little rainfall. These are the things that influence the type of gardening done in the Plains-Intermountain area and Southwest. Though little moisture comes as rain, the snows of the mountains provide irrigating water, and where such water is abundant, plants grow fabulously well and the colors of flowers are exceptionally brilliant. Benefits of regular irrigation are so remarkable that one feels sorry for gardeners living farther east who rely solely upon rainfall! Where water is not available, drought-resistant native plants are most reliable. As for winter temperatures—in the northernmost states and also at high elevations winters are cold and the growing season short; zones of hardiness range from 3 through 6. But lower desert areas have mild winters, and are in Zones 7 through 10.

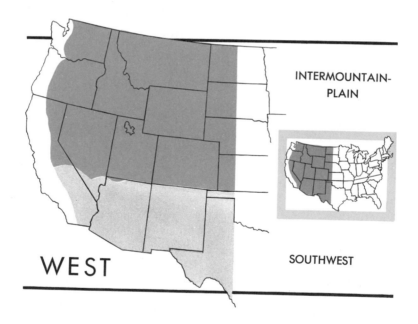

INTERMOUNTAIN-PLAIN

SOUTHWEST

WEST

IRRIGATION GARDENING IN BOISE, IDAHO
by George Fields, educator and hobby gardener, who formerly lived in the Midwest

"Here gardening activities are modified by one or more characteristics of the region: low annual rainfall which comes mostly during winter; amount and type of supplementary water available; long growing season; soil that tends toward alkaline condition on hills but is slightly acid in the river bottom; deficiency of organic matter and phosphates in the soil; hot sunny days and cool nights during the growing season.

"We irrigate by flooding. The abundant water supply tempts one to overwater, creating a build-up in alkalinity. Spring-flowering bulbs that need dry conditions during dormancy must be segregated or dug and stored. Iris also must be planted so the water supply is controlled.

"The long growing season makes it possible to raise most non-tropical plants. Even peanuts and sweet potatoes will mature. Acid-loving plants require special soil treatment and constant attention. Low humidity must be considered. There are few cloudy days during summer so flower varieties must be sun-tolerant. Shade is difficult, even on the north side of the house, and this must be considered in placement of plants. Mild winters allow insects to get an early start. The most satisfactory plants are those that like lots of sun and abundant water once a week."

ROCKY MOUNTAIN HORTICULTURE
IS DIFFERENT

by George Kelly, nurseryman and garden writer of Littleton, Colorado

"At the foot of the mountains where most people live, soil and air have little moisture because of the limited precipitation. However, snow melting in the mountains provides easily available supplemental water for gardens. We have hot sun in winter as well as summer, a generally alkaline soil, and many unseasonable changes in temperature, especially in spring and fall.

"Many plants familiar in other climates will not grow well here because of 'winter-kill.' It is not cold alone that does the damage, but hot, drying sunshine. For this reason many broad-leaved evergreens are difficult or impossible to grow, though many borderline plants survive on the east side of a building where they miss the severe northwest winds and southwest sun.

"Our type of soil is the result of scanty rainfall for thousands of years. There has been relatively little native plant growth so there is a lack of natural humus; we need to supply organic matter. Excess minerals have not been washed from the soil, so it is alkaline. To correct this we may apply limited amounts of some chemical such as iron sulfate or sulfur. We can have the soil analyzed, but this rarely tells us anything that we do not already know, and adding organic matter and digging it in deep usually does everything that a soil analysis might indicate.

"Needed additional moisture must be supplied in the most efficient way. Remember that soil around roots must be moist at all times; during open winters water may be needed several times, for we seldom have soaking fall rains or heavy winter snows; it is best to water thoroughly instead of frequently."

SUGGESTIONS FOR THE SOUTHWEST

by Mrs. Howard Kittel, of Fort Worth, past president of Texas Garden Clubs, Inc.

"The pleasures and problems of gardening in the Southwest vary enormously. The area includes deserts, lush tropical growth, arid mesquite and sage, grassy plains and deep forests, topography ranging from mile-high mountains to below sea level, and soils highly acid to highly alkaline, with some needing no additional potassium and others requiring the addition of *all* nutrients.

"In many areas the query as to whether a plant is 'hardy' does not refer to the necessity of protection from quick freezes but to the plant's ability to withstand 9 months of hot dry winds.

"It is important to know your soil, since temperature, rainfall and soil conditions vary almost from inch-to-inch rather than mile-to-mile. Check nutrient content as well as soil alkalinity or acidity."

Along the Pacific Coast the Ocean Tempers the Climate

How you garden on the West Coast depends upon the precise spot where you live and its relationship to the ocean, mountains, desert and winds. The climate changes not only north to south, but west to east and according to elevation. On the narrow strip next to the ocean, temperatures are modified by nearness to the Pacific Ocean; there is often fog that cools and humidifies the air and lessens the effect of sun. Inland, and on the east side of the mountains, there may be hot, dry deserts, or winds coming from them. Rainfall comes mainly in winter, so watering is essential through much of the growing season.

In the Pacific Northwest winters are mild and rainy, springs long, cool and moist, summers dry with cool to moderate temperatures. Northern California, especially the bay area around San Francisco and Oakland, features mild winters and cool, dry summers; inland the winter temperatures are colder and the summer temperatures hot. Southern California, near the ocean, verges on the tropical; its climate is influenced both by the ocean and the desert; inland, desert climate predominates.

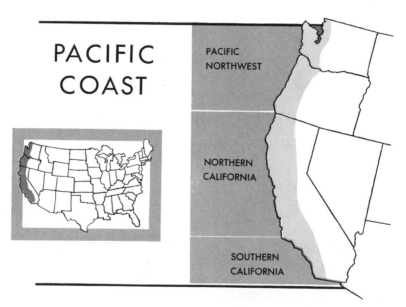

PACIFIC COAST

PACIFIC NORTHWEST

NORTHERN CALIFORNIA

SOUTHERN CALIFORNIA

IN THE NORTHWEST
PLANTS MUST FIT THE CLIMATE

by Jeannette Grossman, garden writer and horticultural photographer of Portland, Oregon

"Our geography presents a fascinating but complex challenge to the gardener.

"In the belt extending from Seattle into the Willamette Valley of Oregon, rhododendron, camellias and other choice broad-leaved evergreens thrive in the mild winters and ample rainfall. Strawberries, and cane fruits such as raspberries, are especially fine. On the other hand, fruit trees, lilacs and other deciduous trees and shrubs prefer the colder winters of the Rogue Valley area. Often gardeners in the Puget Sound and Willamette areas experience a cool summer which is referred to as 'The Year of the Green Tomato.' In the Rogue Valley crops mature more quickly, due to higher light intensity, which compensates for the shorter growing season.

"East of the Cascade Mountains winter temperatures average from 10° above zero to 30° below zero, depending on altitude and exposure.

"At the seacoast the large body of salt water keeps temperatures mild, and heavy frost is almost unknown. However, many broad-leaved evergreens should be ruled out if the garden is exposed to wind and salt spray. Escallonia is an excellent substitute for rhododendrons and camellias. Hydrangeas, fuchsias, begonias, dahlias and most bulbous plants revel in the sandy soil and moist air. Annual flowers have brilliance of color which is never as fine inland.

"Since there are few well-defined climatic boundaries in the Northwest, gardening here is an adventure. Part of the fun is finding that certain plants thrive in your garden while they sulk for your neighbor. A gentle rain may be falling on your valley garden while a few miles away hilltop gardens are blanketed in cold, wet snow. Yet in warm valley gardens a sudden spring frost may hit tender new growth while cooler hilltop gardens escape damage due to less advanced growth.

"The best way for a new gardener to start is to list the plants seen growing well in older gardens of the neighborhood. However, experienced Northwest gardeners would suggest that you gamble a bit with plants that your neighbor cannot grow; chances are good that you can grow them."

REACTIONS OF AN EX-IOWA GARDENER IN THE SANTA CLARA VALLEY OF CALIFORNIA

by Harold Crain,
college professor and garden hobbyist

"The joys of gardening out here are big. Anything grows! Put it in the ground and stand back, or at least take out the plants on either side of it. Prepare to prune it, thin it, and haul it away by the trailer load.

"You can meddle with growing conditions extravagantly. Does the plant like dryness? Do not water it so much. Does it like heat? Set it on the south side of a wall or house. Does it hate to get its head wet? Irrigate from along the ground.

"Roses! They develop trunks the size of your arm. They put out crops from April to December and have no winter die-back.

"Things are hard to get used to. In September the ground is hard, grass dead, trees wilted, even weeds brown. You think there will never be enough water to soak up all the ground. But there is. In December the place floats away on a flood.

"There is no rain in summer, and only an occasional nuisance sprinkle from April to November. Such sprinkles damage fruits and wash off costly sprays; farmers dread spring and summer rains.

"Watering does not get the same results as rain. Rain gets into corners, turns the grass greener, and rain does not produce the harmful mineral salts collecting in the soil that irrigating does.

"Nurseries and plant stores are everywhere, offering at all seasons such a profusion of materials in flats, cans, boxes, baskets and tubs that a gardener's self-control and common sense are sorely taxed.

"There are disappointments for a transplanted Midwesterner. Some old favorites perform only half-heartedly—such as peonies, tulips and lilacs; they seem homesick for a long cold spell followed by the song of meadow larks.

"Diseases and pests demand constant vigilance and determined treatment.

"Sometimes, briefly, I grow nostalgic for the blizzard season of the midwest. What I miss is not the cold, but the fun of staying indoors and poring over seed catalogues."

In Alaska, Astonishing Growth in Long Summer Days

Gardening in Alaska is not easy, but it can be one of the most rewarding of all outdoor activities in the 49th state. Since this is a vast area, as extensive as from Florida to Arizona, and the Canadian border to Texas, no single set of gardening recommendations will fit everywhere. Rainfall varies from 8 in. in the north to 200 in. in the south. Temperatures range from 70° below zero to 100° above. The practical approach as far as shrubs and trees are concerned is to use native material. If you are an avid gardener planning to move here, you should try to choose one of the climatic regions where gardening can be done quite successfully, such as Central, South Central, Southeast or Southwest.

GARDENING IN THE ANCHORAGE
AREA OF SOUTH CENTRAL ALASKA

by Louise M. Marx, garden writer, Anchorage

"This is the largest city of Alaska. Our elevation is 38 ft. Summer temperatures—June through early September—hover around 60° to 65°, with 84° as the highest ever recorded. Winter temperatures may drop to 15° below or 25° below, as contrasted with 50° below in the interior; normally the depth of snow on the ground does not exceed 15 in. Average rainfall is 14 in. The driest season of the year usually occurs during the months of May and June. During this period we also have exceptionally long days. On June 21, 22, 23, and 24, bright daylight barely fades into twilight until the sun starts its journey again. This is the time of year when plants make unbelievable growth since they are active all of the 24 hours. And they must make haste, for our growing season is short. We feel lucky, indeed, to be favored with 100 growing days.

"Local seasons vary considerably. The rainy season usually starts during the latter part of July and may continue through the remainder of the growing season. Frosts visit the area near the mountains earlier than areas near the heart of Anchorage, but heavy killing frosts can be expected about mid-September throughout the area.

"Gardeners depend on bedding plants and summer-flowering bulbs for their annual flower beds and borders. However, hardy perennials such as alyssum basket-of-gold, columbine, bellflower, delphinium, pink, peony, phlox, primrose and bleeding-heart, winter over quite successfully.

"Our growing season is too short to raise most annuals from seed started in the outdoor garden. But many people have greenhouses in which they start plants, and the rest start them on the window sill or under artificial lights. These plants are set outdoors about May 30 or about the time when young birch leaves emerge. Many gardeners move them outdoors earlier, however, and use plastic covering for protection against cool nights.

"Our chief garden invaders are aphids, red spider, mites, mealybugs and moose. The moose are very fond of the swollen buds in early spring, and especially like lilac, birch buds and young tulips.

"Roses seem to love our long cool days of summer. They produce very large blossoms, highly colored and well formed. Their foliage is positively lush—thick, waxy and rigid. While some gardeners buy bargain bare-root roses that reach our markets in spring, and treat them as annuals, rose enthusiasts buy quality bushes and attempt to winter them over. With protection, they can count on about 50% survival. Climbers are not grown too successfully though there are a few exceptions. Old-fashioned roses are gaining in popularity and produce beautiful blossoms that are almost everlasting.

"Vegetables are the same as those grown in the Pacific Northwest. They grow well and have superb flavor. Dependable small fruits are strawberries, currants, gooseberries and raspberries. Wild berries grow in abundance, particularly blueberries and lowbush cranberries. Gathering them in the fall is fun and an Alaskan tradition.

"Soil in our section varies from neighborhood to neighborhood. Topsoil on high ground measures 16 in. deep. We are able to buy topsoil, and there is an endless supply of peat moss in the area though it does not contain nutrients. Good cow manure is available about 40 miles from Anchorage in the Matanuska Valley. The farmers seem happy to share their black gold with gardeners, and sell quantities to nurseries in the area."

Hawaii Can and Does Grow Almost Anything

The Hawaiian Islands are in several zones according to altitude and rainfall. They can grow almost anything from temperate to tropical—apples at 3,000 ft. on Maui and bananas at sea level on Hawaii. In general, however, there is no frost where the bulk of urban and suburban gardens are located. Instead one finds a dry Southern Californian climate, or a rain forest a little more tropical than Southern Florida. The Oriental influence in gardens is strong; plants are rampant; people use fresh flowers; there are garden insects and diseases just as there are in other states.

HONOLULU

HAWAII

GARDENING HERE CAN BE VERY EASY

AND A LOT OF FUN

*by Dr. Horace F. Clay, Program Director,
Institute for Technical Interchange,
East-West Center, Honolulu*

"The malihini—or newcomer—to Hawaii is overwhelmed by the wide variety of tropical plants which abound. Even more startling is the fact that as one travels up into the higher parts of the hills and mountains, one finds that the unfamiliar tropical plants are less common and are intermingled with garden favorites of much cooler areas. In the cool, moist parts of the Islands, one can still find the distinctive native Hawaiian plants such as Loulu or Hawaiian fan palm, and Hapuu or Hawaiian tree fern. In the drier areas the plants that are grown in gardens are all native to some other tropical or subtropical region.

"The bewildered newcomer, with this wealth of plant material at hand for landscaping, should consult a landscape architect who can give wise counsel about garden de-sign, correct combinations of plants and proper spacing. Most plants grow easily and rapidly here, and it is often the plight of the new garden planner to accept too many mis-cellaneous plants from well-meaning friends, and then place them too close together in chop-suey fashion.

"If you are going to live in one of the beach areas, you must be satisfied at first with salt-tolerant, wind-resistant plants which succeed in alkaline coral sand. Drainage will be either too good or too poor, due to solid coral shelves which protrude here and there through the sand. Later, as the windbreak plants begin to function, more tender tropical plants may be grown in especially prepared wind-protected areas where compost, leaf mold, well-rotted manure and top soil have been incorporated into the beach sand. Daily watering will be necessary in such locations.

"If your home will be in one of the cool, wet areas of Hawaii, you will have quite a differ-ent set of problems to contend with. The an-nual rainfall at the beach is around 20 in. per year, but in the wetter areas it may aver-age around 200 in. per year. The plants which succeed best in such locations are those which like acid soil, high humidity and constant moisture. Drainage may be a problem. And here, as at the beach, the addition of organic material in the form of compost, leaf mold, etc., will help as soil conditioners.

"Pruning and controlling the growth of plants is often like attempting to hold back a jungle—a continuous chore. Hawaii's climate is like a natural outdoor greenhouse, and plants grow throughout the year without seeming to have a dormant period.

"Like the plants, insect pests and plant diseases flourish continuously.

"The present trend of landscaping is for Oriental effects in the garden. Plants with bright-colored flowers and gaudy, showy leaves are not popular now. Rocks are featured, and accenting them are shrubs, trees, and groundcovers with small rather than large leaves. As in the Oriental garden, the shape of the plant is almost more important than other features, such as attractive flowers.

"Along with the trend toward the simple, uncluttered appearance of the Oriental garden, low-maintenance gardens are stressed. Lawn areas are at a minimum, for this means less lawn mowing and more time for activities like swimming and sailing. Replacing the lawns are expanses of groundcovers which require little care.

"Many people live in apartment houses. This means gardening must be carried on in pots, tubs and other containers. This is a distinctive type of gardening and the pot gardener must know a great deal about soil mixtures, drainage and repotting techniques.

"Some gardeners like double-purpose plants. Shade trees can bear delicious fruits. Hedges and specimen shrubs can have edible berries and fruits. Herbs and salad greens can be groundcovers. By careful planning, the clever garden fancier can have all of these in Hawaii."

3

Landscaping Begins with a Plan

Planning before planting pays off. Not only will your final results be more attractive and usable, but you will save money and time. You will not have to redo or move plants. It is a situation similar to that of decorating the interior of your home. If you start buying furniture, carpets and drapes helterskelter, without knowing your basic goal and color scheme, your results will look that way! You can spend a lot of money for something you will later regret—just because you were in a hurry or bought on impulse. It is much simpler to move plants around as pencil sketches on paper, or in your mind, than in your yard after they have been solidly planted.

You can hire a professional landscape architect to draw a master plan for you, or you can prepare your own. Once you have the plan, it is easy to tackle segments bit by bit over a period of years. Then you have assurance that in the end everything will look handsomely unified.

Decide what you want. This is *your* home. Develop the grounds to fit your family's way of life, interests and preferences. Nobody but you knows what these things are. Think of the outdoors area as an extension of your house, with space to be utilized and enjoyed. If you can have a patio to walk onto from your living room or family room, it is like adding another room to the house, only better. If the lawn and garden can be viewed from your windows, hurrah! If you can achieve some privacy when you are out in the yard, marvelous!

There are no hard and fast rules for landscaping. You do not have to duplicate what the neighbors have done. Your lot may have special features that you would like to emphasize or highlight. A slight slope maybe? A lovely tree? A rocky ledge? A view? The architectural style of your house may influence the style of your streetside plantings, and the materials from which your house is built may suggest materials you can use in your patio, paths or fences, to have pleasing harmony. One thing is sure: Landscaping is much more than an attractive setting for a house. It gives you maximum *use* of your yard!

How much will it cost? This depends upon many variables. How extensive are your dreams? How much of the work will you do yourselves? Are grading and lawn-making involved? Fences? Retaining walls? Paved areas like a patio? Will you use young, small-sized plants, or will you use larger, more expensive ones? Many evergreens? A rule-of-thumb way to guess on total cost is used by professional landscape architects. They estimate that an appropriate amount for a home owner to consider budgeting for a complete landscaping—beginning with grading—is about 10% of the value of the house. Of course, you would spread planting and cost over several years.

HOW TO MAKE A SIMPLE PLAN

Start your thinking by listing your most important goals. Attractive entrance planting? Backyard privacy? Trees for shade? Outdoor eating area? Play space for the children where you can see them from the house? Vegetables? Also size up your enthusiasm for maintaining plantings, for this can have a bearing upon the design of the grounds, and what you choose to plant.

Next, discover the solid facts about what you have to work with on your property by drawing an accurately measured map of the entire lot. This should include the house and any immovable permanent features of the property that should be taken into consideration. What you discover may be quite surprising and enlightening! The easiest way to make the map is to get some graph paper (it is divided into little squares) and let each square represent 1 or 2 ft., or ¼ in. equal 1 ft.

Your map should include:

* Telephone poles and their lines. You will not want to plant a tree beneath the wire.

* Sewer and tile lines. If trees are planted near them, the roots may invade and clog the tiles.

* Septic tanks and tile fields. You must not plant anything permanent over them.

* Boundary lines.

* The direction of important good views, or bad ones you want to screen off.

* Underground gas lines or other shallow buried lines or wires.

* All paved areas, walks, drives, patios; also fences and walls.

* Directions of the compass.

* Slopes and how steep they are.

* Downspouts or other drainage outlets for whose water you must make arrangements.

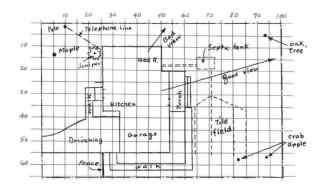

Now Start Sketching

After you know your measurements, problems and goals, you are ready to start sketching plans. Do not make marks on your precious map—save it for reference through the years—but sketch *over* the map, without touching it, by using transparent tracing paper. Draw and doodle to your heart's content, trying various arrangements of lawn areas, private areas, patios, places for flowers, trees, outside work areas, paths, etc. Do not rush, because you will be making decisions that may affect the way you and your family will live for many years.

Pay special attention to the interrelationship of house and grounds. For instance, will there be a door leading to your patio so you can serve food out there easily? Can you have privacy when you sit outdoors? Can you see your flowers from the window, or from your outdoor sitting area?

Here are suggestions that may help you with your sketching. All the basic principles of good design that you have learned in relation to interior decorating, clothes or art apply to landscape designing. Keep things simple! Simple shapes and logical layouts not only look best but are easiest to live with and maintain. Straight lines are usually easier to deal with than curves. If you choose curved lines, they will be most pleasing if they are long and flowing rather than wiggly. Where the curve ends against a straight line, it should meet it perpendicularly so that the corner forms a right angle. This, to the eye, looks secure, strong and correct.

Represent trees as circles, whose diameters are the expected spread of their branches. A dot in the center can mark the spot where the tree is to be planted. Draw shrubs, groundcovers and flower beds as grouped masses rather than separately. You can make dots within the mass to show individual plants in order to estimate the number you will need.

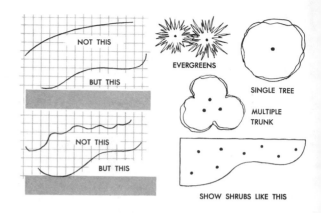

NOT THIS

BUT THIS

NOT THIS

BUT THIS

EVERGREENS

SINGLE TREE

MULTIPLE TRUNK

SHOW SHRUBS LIKE THIS

Test How Something Will Look

You can try out a certain shape or position of a flower bed, patio, etc., by staking it out on the ground with strings, or outlining it with your garden hose. Then you can move it and live with it a few days—until you are sure.

To tell whether you have chosen the right place for a tree or a group of screening shrubs, put tall stakes (or your spade stuck into the ground) at the spot. Then you can go indoors and look at the location from the window, or walk around and observe it from all angles. It helps to have an "assistant" who can move the stake to right or left as you make suggestions from a distance.

LOCATE TREES THOUGHTFULLY

You are going to live with your trees a long, long time, and cannot move them after they become established, so it behooves you to get them in the right place!

The first ones to consider should be your major shade trees. Place them so they will produce shade where you want it, at the time of day and year that is most important. Perhaps your picture window is your problem, or the kitchen or dining room. Maybe you would like to shade the roof of your house, to

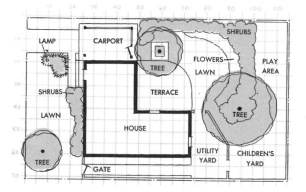

Note how each area is logically set apart, with fences or shrubs to screen and keep them separated. Curved line of terrace is echoed by flower bed and shrubbery area.

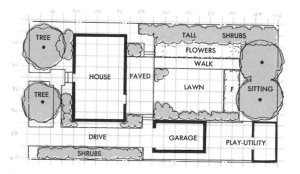

Though small, this garden plan offers the beauty of straight lines, simplicity lending a spacious feeling to the garden yet play and utility areas are not overlooked.

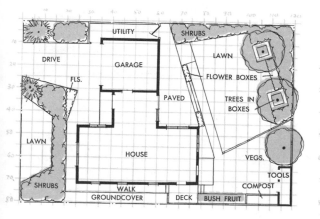

Setting the back garden on the bias gives a longer axis, adds interest to a small area. The slanting lines are echoed in the front, adding parking space to the driveway.

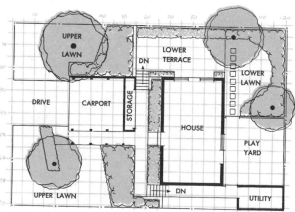

Split level houses call for split level gardens. In this case, house is set back to let carport be near the street. Therefore a simple treatment makes the restricted garden area seem larger.

Planter box along the walk guides guests to this front door. The box is made of bricks, harmonizing with those used in the front of the house and in the walk. C. Jaroe home, Austin, Texas

OPPOSITE:
Note how the lines of the wooden headers and raised planter beds lead your eye to the door of this lovely California home. Robert Babcock, landscape architect

Here is privacy for an entrance, obtained by a baffled-fence design. Steps lead to an enclosed garden. Joseph Cary home, San Jose, California. Geraldine Scott, landscape architect

When you approach this house from the driveway, steps welcome you, and a hedge of yew points to the doorway. Elmer Priebe home, Rock Island, Illinois. Elizabeth Howerton, landscape architect

EXAMPLES OF
GOOD ENTRANCE PLANNING

keep it cooler or to reduce the load on your air-conditioning system. The patio may need shade in the afternoon though not in the morning. Remember that the sun moves; its position varies during the day and also through the year. It is highest in the sky during summer. You will need to do considerable plotting in order to have shade trees in the most useful positions. Supplementary trees can be added purely for beauty, to frame your doorway, or provide a focal point in your garden.

Unless your lot is quite big, 1 or 2 shade trees may be all that are needed, and all for which you have space. Large trees become very tall and broad, and you must allow for this in your planning. For instance, a sugar maple eventually becomes 60 ft. high or more, and needs 45 ft. for its branches. Its roots will spread even farther. A sycamore is rapid-growing and within 10 years its branches may make a circle covering 25 ft. If your house is low, small-type shade trees will probably look better than tall kinds. Another thing to take into consideration is the density of the trees' foliage. Some trees cast light shade under which grass can grow, while others have such dense shade that it is difficult to have a lawn beneath them.

Trees on the street side of your house should be considered as part of the front-of-the-house planting, and located where they will attractively complement the house or entrance. Whether you want evergreen or deciduous trees depends both upon your climate and the reason for which you wish the tree. If you like shade in summer but prefer sunshine during winter, deciduous trees (that lose their leaves) are best. But if you want the tree especially to cover a window, or for all-year foliage, an evergreen has the advantage.

Be careful that you do not get so enthusiastic about planting trees that you turn your place into a young forest. Tree plants are small-appearing when young but grow and grow! This is one reason why it is important to make a plan—so you can estimate eventual sizes of things.

If having a flower garden is important to you, plant no more trees than actually needed, for flowers prefer to grow in sunshine and do not like to compete with tree roots.

For lists of trees recommended for your region and hardiness zone, see the chapter on trees.

PERSONALIZE THE STREET SIDE OF YOUR HOUSE

The portion of your home that the public and your friends glimpse from the street creates the first impression of your family. Let the landscaping be attractive and express the hospitality and personality of your home.

Accent your main door! There should be no doubt where guests are expected to enter. The approach should be not only obvious but easy. The major walk should lead directly to the door, and people should get to this walk effortlessly from the place where they park their cars.

Plantings about the door can be formal or informal (the style of your house may dictate), flowery or simple. Because this is such an important area, it should look well winters as well as summers, so probably should contain some evergreens that will remain the desired size permanently, instead of growing into giant trees. Many of the narrow-leaved (needle) evergreens grow to be very tall. Among these are spruce, fir, hemlock and most pines, except mugho. They look cute when small, but soon get out of hand as they strive to become typical forest trees. Shrub evergreens that remain permanently low are available in both needle-type and broad-leaf. See the chapter on shrubs. Plants selected for entrances should be easy to maintain.

Guests will pause here as they wait for you

Landscaping Begins with a Plan

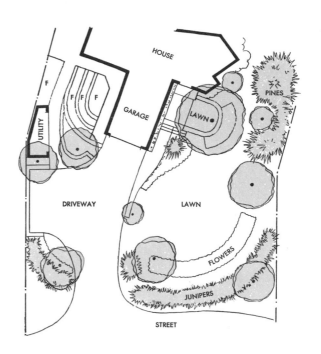

The Harshbarger yard, in Iowa, is separated from the street by a hedge of pfitzer juniper that encloses a border of day-lilies. At the front door, a gardened area features espaliered vines of purpleleaf wintercreeper. The shade tree is a thornless honey locust. Elizabeth Howerton, landscape architect

Plantings do not need to be elaborate to have charm. At this New Jersey home they are concentrated at the front entrance. Since the house faces north, the shrubs used are those that do well in shade. Note how the trees have been pruned high, so that the trunks and branches make interesting silhouettes.

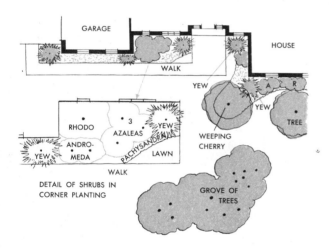

DETAIL OF SHRUBS IN CORNER PLANTING

Simplicity and easy maintenance are keynotes here. An evergreen groundcover around the base of the house is trimmed low, except for higher accents at the door. The tall shrub is a honeysuckle, and the lower one a lilac. Russel Boom residence, Bettendorf, Iowa. Elizabeth Howerton, landscape architect

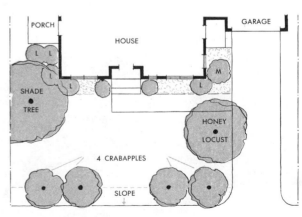

A vestibule garden, enclosed by a yew hedge, looks attractive in both winter and summer in this Massachusetts planting. A flowering dogwood tree (between the lamp and hedge) adds beauty in spring with blooms, and in autumn with colorful foliage. The tall evergreen at the left is a hemlock.

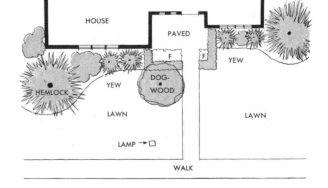

THE STREETSIDE PLANTING CAN EXPRESS YOUR HOME'S PERSONALITY

to answer the bell, so give them something to look at. If possible, plantings or ornaments should indicate the personality of your home.

There is a trend to "outdoor vestibules"—enclosed or semi-enclosed areas outside the door, often outlined by a low hedge. They aid in directing guests, and serve as an intermediate spot between outdoors and in.

"Doorstep" gardens are also delightful. They can be small, fitted within the "vestibule" area. Or they can expand to fill part or all of the front yard. Much depends upon what you like, the kind of house you have, and the nature of your lot and land.

To visualize and compare how various plantings will look, put a piece of transparent paper over a photograph of the front of your house. Sketch on this, trying shrubs of various heights in assorted positions and groupings. You do not need to know, at this stage of planning, exactly what the shrubs will be, for you are trying to decide what general type and heights you want, and can later discover what shrubs would fill that bill.

About foundation plantings: it is not necessary to have a continuous mass of shrubs around the building. If your house is attractive all the way to the ground, why hide it? Shrubs should enhance rather than smother the architecture. Old style foundation plantings were devised back in the days when houses were built on ugly, high foundations, and also when landscaping was supposed to be looked at rather than lived in.

DESIGN OUTDOOR LIVING AREAS

Just as the various parts of your house are used for different purposes, so sections of your yard can be allotted certain uses. Certainly you will want a place for sitting and eating in private. Probably you will wish some flowers and some play space for children. A utility or service area is just as necessary outdoors as indoors, and may need to be screened from view. There will need to be

a "traffic pattern"—walks or paths that get you from one place to another in the handiest and best way. All these items look most attractive when interrelated logically, practically, and according to a planned design.

Lay out your lawn so it will be easy to mow. Do not clutter your grassed area with flower beds which must be mowed around, and whose edges must be kept neat. Avoid placing shrubs in the midst of the lawn area where they will be in the way of the mower and require hand trimming around bases. Even more important than these practical considerations is the desirability of keeping the lawn space from being spotty, and the need to retain some space for vistas of flower borders.

One of the best ways to avoid having to hand-clip the edge of a lawn where it adjoins a cultivated area, or where it comes up against a vertical wall, tree trunk, etc., is to construct mowing strips. These are flat barriers, level with the soil, which can be mowed over but which grass cannot cross. They are usually made of brick, patio-type cement blocks, or concrete poured into a long, narrow, shallow form. You plan them as permanent, attractive edgings. The wheel of your mower can ride along on the paved surface, clipping the grass on the boundary line. If mowing strips are used close to the wall of a house, or around a tree trunk, they can enclose groundcovers such as pebbles or plants.

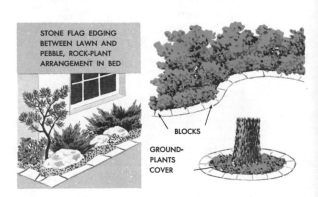
STONE FLAG EDGING BETWEEN LAWN AND PEBBLE, ROCK-PLANT ARRANGEMENT IN BED

BLOCKS

GROUND-PLANTS COVER

Here is a front-of-the-house patio where privacy is achieved with a redwood fence. Baum residence, Kentfield, California. Royston, Hanamoto, Mayes, and Beck, landscape architects

OUTDOOR LIVING AREAS
ARE PART OF THE MODERN GARDEN

Indoors, outdoors and swimming pool are interrelated at the T. C. Maino home in San Luis Obispo, California. Design by Eckbo, Dean and Williams, landscape architects

Spacious backyards can feature large lawns. Note how the hedge gives privacy and accents the design. Carbus garden, Menlo Park, California. Thomas Church and Associates, landscape architects

A small, fence-enclosed garden adjoins the brick-floored open porch at the rear of the home of Mrs. Jere Wilson in Denver, Colorado. The shade tree is a young sycamore.

If your children are young, the patio can be
a play place. The Elmer Bergers of Mansfield,
Ohio, built theirs to include a shade tree—a
pin oak. Also note the sandbox.

This small play area holds swings and a combination storage unit and sandbox that can be quickly converted into a tent. Design by Pat Gallavan for his home in Denver, Colorado.

The sandbox is an integral part of the design of this compact backyard at the home of the John Caseys in San Francisco. In future years the space may become a flower bed or small pool. The climbing logs are embedded 12 in. deep in soil, and held firm with concrete. John Vogley, landscape architect

PLAY AREAS FIT INTO YOUR OVER-ALL YARD PLAN

Have your lawn as level as possible and practical, so walking and mowing will be easy. If your yard slopes steeply, you may wish to grade it into a series of terraces. These can be connected either by low retaining walls, or by slopes covered with ground-cover plants. Mowing grass on a hillside is both difficult and dangerous.

Patios and terraces are for outdoor leisure. The design of your patio depends upon where it is going to be, how you plan to use it, and the site. It must be easy to reach from indoor living quarters, have privacy, be attractive, pleasant and easy to maintain, or it will not be used! If you live in a region where wind is a problem, you will need some sort of windbreak. On the other hand, if a breeze is essential to outdoor comfort, you must figure a way to obtain it.

The surface of the patio should be level, or nearly so—sloped just enough to shed water quickly. Otherwise your chairs and tables may tip and rock annoyingly. To achieve enough level space, you may need to do some regrading before you begin construction. This may result in expense, upheaval of your yard, and frustrating delay. However, if you do not do this you will regret it forever.

The "floor" should be firm, and as smooth as possible, at least in the area where you plan to sit, eat and walk. You do not want chair legs sinking into the ground or snagging between cracks of flagstones. If the area is to be used as play space for small children, it should not only dry quickly but be smooth enough for tricycle traffic. It is wonderful to have sidewalks that make a "circuit" for the young travelers to negotiate.

It is not necessary to pave the entire area of the patio. Portions of it can be in gravel, planting pockets, etc. However, with loose pebbles, ground bark and similar covering material, weeds may become a nuisance. There is no doubt that some type of paving is the easiest type of surface to maintain.

You will want privacy. Solid fences give immediate results. A short section or two will sometimes be enough to shield you from the neighbors. Build them to match the materials and style of your house. Or, if you choose, prefabricated units of several types are available at garden supply centers, lumber yards, and by mail order.

Rolls of woven bamboo, or reeds, can be bought and nailed along frames. They will last for several years.

Annual vines on cord, rope, fencing or plastic-coated wire, such as clothesline, will give a dense leafy screen by midsummer.

Permanent vines grown on fence, trellis or other supports are an inexpensive way to screen a large area. They do not take up as much space as tall shrubs would. It takes them at least a year to get going well.

For choices of both annual and perennial vines, and photographs showing many perennial varieties in use, see the chapter on vines.

Put play areas where you can supervise. Play places for small children should be located where you can keep an eye on things from your windows. They can fit into the design of the yard attractively. However, do not be so intent on good looks that you finish things too slickly and completely. Leave some elements that the children can rearrange and shift. They like a challenge and are bored by something that is supposed to be left exactly as it is. Some shade is desirable.

Sandboxes or wading pools made in interesting forms as part of the garden's design can be so constructed that when the children no longer need them they can become planter boxes.

The surface beneath swings and climbing equipment, where youngsters are apt to fall, should be as soft as possible, yet clean and dry. A good-looking, inexpensive, soft, quick-drying material recommended by landscape architect Jane Smith of East Lansing, Michigan, is composed of ⅔ sawdust or ground bark and ⅓ sand.

SLOPING SITES NEED SPECIAL
TREATMENT

If your lot is on a hillside, or contains even a little sloping land, you have a marvelous chance to create a uniquely attractive landscape design. You can arrange your outdoor living areas, patio, gardens, and walks or paths on different levels, possibly connecting them with steps. The structural lines of retaining walls and terraces can make interesting patterns. Plants will have interesting locations and backgrounds. Your garden can be the envy of friends who live on level ground. However, in developing your property, you will face some very challenging problems. They have to do with the comforts of living, how to hold your slope, and how to handle run-off water. The solutions are interrelated.

For ease of getting around, humans like to live and walk on level surfaces. The areas that you will use the most should not only *be* level but *look* level. Of course they must slope slightly to shed water, but this should not be conspicuous. It is especially important that the locations immediately outside of doors and at the foot of steps be level. When you step out or down, you should feel sure that you will land on something flat and solid— not on something unpredictably tipped. One way to increase the general aura of stability, visually, is to use as many truly horizontal lines as possible around your house and grounds. For instance, if your house sits on a leveled terrace that extends beyond it on either side, it will look much more secure than if the grade along its walls is sloping. Steps, with their level, horizontal lines, are pleasing and reassuring to the eye. Fences

built in horizontal sections that stair-step down a hill are more reassuring to the eye than those that follow the slope of a grade. Level tops of retaining walls or hedges are other examples.

Holding the soil, and controlling excess water both on the surface and below ground, are related problems. They are so crucial that you should consider them before anything else. Some regrading may be needed to save you from future difficulties. Water causes the worst erosion when it flows rapidly, especially if it is in a narrow channel and over soil that is not bound down by some sort of cover, such as grass. Run-off water from your property, and possibly that of your neighbors, must be safely channeled on its way to a sewer or other proper outlet.

Terracing your yard to hold your slope and to make level living space available is indirectly a form of contouring, and thus an erosion control. On leveled areas the speed of flowing water is slowed, and if the areas contain grass or other plants, these absorb a considerable percentage of the moisture.

Your various level areas can be connected either by slopes or by retaining walls. If you have slopes, they can be treated as gardened areas—especially rockeries—or they can be planted to groundcovers or grass. Grass can be mowed on slopes as steep as 3 ft. horizontal to 1 ft. vertical. For information on groundcover plants useful for holding slopes, and for photos showing several of them in use, see the chapter on groundcovers. For help on rock gardens, see the chapter on rocks and pebbles.

Retaining walls are as ornamental as they are useful. Low ones, up to 4 ft. high, can be built by do-it-yourselfers. Taller ones involve so much engineering knowledge and know-how that they should be designed and built by experienced professionals. Any retaining wall must be strong enough to withstand the weight and pressure of the soil, and also the pressure of subsurface water. These pressures are greater than you would imagine. In severe winter climates frost action is another hazard.

The easiest kinds of walls for amateurs to construct successfully are those of rock laid up dry (without mortar) and ones made of railroad ties. With both of these, water trapped in the soil can easily escape through cracks, and so does not produce the kind of pressure that can knock the wall down. A solid base is vital. With rocks, a layer of big ones can be placed below ground. With railroad ties, put the first row below ground. Either type of wall should not be vertical, but should slant 2 to 3 in. horizontally for each vertical foot. Please believe this and save yourself the nuisance and frustration of having to rebuild the wall in a few years. Vertical walls, no matter how carefully and strongly built, tend to be pushed outward from the top and eventually collapse! Build

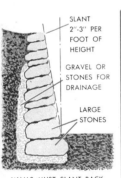

WALLS MUST SLANT BACK TO RESIST SOIL PRESSURE. GOOD DRAINAGE IS VITAL

SLANT 2"-3" PER FOOT OF HEIGHT

GRAVEL OR STONES FOR DRAINAGE

LARGE STONES

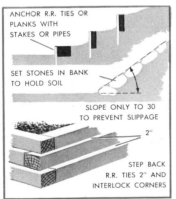

ANCHOR R.R. TIES OR PLANKS WITH STAKES OR PIPES

SET STONES IN BANK TO HOLD SOIL

SLOPE ONLY TO 30 TO PREVENT SLIPPAGE

2"

STEP BACK R.R. TIES 2" AND INTERLOCK CORNERS

	IF RISERS MEASURE	TREADS SHOULD BE
	4 INCHES	19 INCHES
	4½ INCHES	18 INCHES
	5 INCHES	17 INCHES
	5½ INCHES	16 INCHES
	6½ INCHES	13 INCHES
	7 INCHES	11 INCHES

TREAD

RISER

NARROW TREADS AND HIGH RISERS MAKE CLIMBING DANGEROUS

FOR DRAINAGE: SLOPE EACH STEP TOWARD RISER—¼ IN. TO 12 IN.

with rocks or ties so that the vertical joints in one row do not coincide with those above or below them. In other words, each rock should rest on parts of 2 below it—overlap them. This gives an interlocking and strong result.

Steps should be solid, smooth, and of a material and type of construction that harmonize with the other materials used in your house, terraces, retaining walls, etc. Each step consists of 2 parts, the treads upon which you walk and the risers which provide the height. The proportions of one to the other are important for your comfort and stride. Each tread should slope at the rate of ¼ in. to 1 ft. so water will run off quickly. Outdoor stairs usually have a wider spacing than those indoors. If the slope to be climbed extends quite a distance, and is gradual rather than steep, you may wish to alternate groups of steps with sections of walkway that are either level or slightly sloped.

Sturdy rot-resistant lumber holds the soil in this sloping flower bed at the home of the George Chapmans, Sausalito, California. Design by R. McChesney

This hill is held by a planted slope plus a planted retaining wall. At the top, a hedge of yew acts as a protective fence. W. F. Krebill home, Davenport, Iowa. Elizabeth Howerton, landscape architect

Rock walls laid without mortar can have pockets of soil for plants. The ones in this picture are sloped for strength, and the rocks tilted so water will run back to the roots of the plants.

Redwood steps lead down to an enclosed terrace in what was formerly a useless area at the Rae home in San Francisco. Eckbo, Dean and Williams, landscape architects

HERE ARE HANDSOME
WAYS TO HOLD AND LANDSCAPE
A HILLSIDE

4

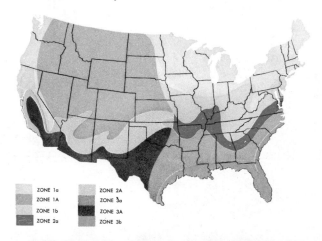

Simple Steps to a Luxuriant Lawn

by Dr. Robert Schery,

Director of The Lawn Institute

Your lawn can be the kind you dream about—lovely and lushly green—if you understand a few simple facts about how grass grows, what it needs in order to thrive, and how your climate influences the timing of the various things you do to help. Maintenance is not nearly so complicated as you might think, considering all of the products offered for use on grass these days. The main things a lawn needs are fertilization, mowing suited to the kind of grass you have, and some weed control. The best kind of grass for you, and the timing of its care, depend upon where you live. There is one set of grasses and time schedule for the northern part of the country, and a different set for the southern. In the intermediate or border zone, roughly from Washington, D.C., to Atlanta, to Nashville, to Wichita, to Albuquerque, to San Francisco, both northern and southern schemes are used. If you live in this in-between area, you should follow local preferences, and realize that since neither system fits the climate exactly, the one you choose will have to be carefully handled.

ZONE 1a		ZONE 2A	
ZONE 1A		ZONE 3a	
ZONE 1b		ZONE 3A	
ZONE 2a		ZONE 3b	

Northern grasses like cool weather. Grasses adapted to northern climates do most of their growing during autumn, winter and spring, and slow down during summer heat. The main one is Kentucky bluegrass. There are a number of varieties such as C-1, Delta, Merion, Newport, Park, Prato, Windsor, etc. Most of these do not differ much, and like moderate attention. Merion, probably the best known, needs heavy fertilization and is not suited to the southern part of the range of cool-climate grasses.

Fine fescues (such as Chewings, Illahee, Pennlawn, Creeping Red) are usually included in bluegrass lawns. If you are going to start a new lawn, it is good to have about 25% fescue in the seed mixture. Fescues sprout well, survive on dry, poorish soils under trees, and are a good companion for bluegrass since they respond to the same care.

Bentgrasses are for the fancy, more formal lawns that get a great deal of care. They are used on golf greens, where they are meticulously tended, but are ordinarily too troublesome for a home owner. However, in some favorable climates, such as around the Great Lakes, or coastal Oregon-Washington, bentgrass lawns are standard because there unpedigreed bentgrass has gained a toehold in most lawns. If you want to plant bentgrass, choose one of the less troublesome varieties such as Highland, rather than creeping sorts. However, compared to bluegrass, it will require extra feeding and watering, closer and more frequent mowing, disease prevention, and probably occasional thinning.

The best and most important time of year to handle northern lawn groundwork is in the autumn. This is when the grass plants build strength for the following spring. Early spring is the next best time—or even winter, if you live where snow is not too bothersome. When hot summer weather arrives, bluegrass does not need as much attention as in cooler months. When you fertilize in autumn and spring, all of the food goes to the grass, which is growing rapidly at that time—while weeds are not. If, on the other hand, you feed in summer, you may encourage and help weeds, because most of them do best in warm weather when bluegrass is relatively inactive.

Southern grasses thrive on warmth. In the South the seasonal approach to lawns is almost the opposite of that of the North. The growing period for grasses is from spring until autumn, with winter the season of dormancy—unless you wish to overseed your lawn each autumn with a "winter grass" to provide temporary greenness during the cooler months. You have many more choices of kinds of grass than northerners do.

In Florida and along the coast you may have St. Augustine. It is a headache these days, attacked by chinch bugs and disease. You will probably have to hire a service to keep it looking good. However, no southern grass is better adapted to shade. There is no seed available, so live starts or sod must be purchased.

In the coastal plain (southern part) from South Carolina through Georgia, Alabama, Mississippi and Louisiana into Texas, centipedegrass does well. This is a "poor-soil grass" that does not need much attention. You can start it from seed—which takes 2 years—but much is sodded or set with small divisions called sprigs. It does best where soils are acid. Though it is okay in northern Florida, do not choose it for southern or coastal parts of that state.

Throughout the South, but especially in the upper South, bermuda will probably be the main grass. It is a rampant grower, and if well tended looks good. But it does require more care than most lawn grasses. For average lawns you can start with seed; for lawns that look like golf greens, you have to buy live starts of varieties.

Zoysias make good lawns through most of

the South, and are not difficult to maintain once established. But zoysia is slow-growing, takes 2 or 3 years to fill in and make a tight cover, and is tough to mow. The best selections must be started live.

And finally, much used for the deep South (Florida especially), are seed mixtures mainly of bahiagrass. Lawns predominately bahia do not have the delicate texture of a selected bermuda. But they get along with just average care and are the least troublesome of any type for Florida.

Lawn tending in the South starts in March or April, and carries through until October or November. How much you work at it will depend upon the kind of grass you have. Bermuda requires a lot of everything; St. Augustine needs much pest control; zoysia gets along on moderate care; centipede and bahia do not need much attention.

HOW TO CARE FOR YOUR LAWN EASILY

The most important things to do for your grass are to feed it, mow it, and get rid of the weeds. All of these interrelate. Good mowing and fertilizing help with weed control because weeds cannot push into thick turf. You will have an easy time with maintenance matters if you do the basic things correctly.

When, What and How To Feed

The best time to fertilize lawns in the North is autumn; additional feeding can be done in spring and early summer. In the South, feed regularly, beginning in spring and continuing through autumn.

The best fertilizers for lawns are "complete" ones with lots of nitrogen in them. The percentage of nitrogen should be about double that of the other two main ingredients—phosphorus and potassium. Fortunately you do not have to hunt for fertilizers with such formulas, because various manufacturers prepare and package them especially for use on lawns. Their brand names indicate they are for grass. These are sold wherever garden supplies are handled, and will be prominently displayed at the time of year you should be applying them.

Each sack has instructions for applying the material, and specifies the area of lawn over which it should be spread. The label also tells the percentage of nitrogen and other major elements in the fertilizer. This sometimes affects the price, and the rate at which the material is spread. A fertilizer having 5 to 10% nitrogen is on the weak side, while one with 15 to 20% nitrogen is on the strong side and worth proportionally more in price. Some straight nitrogen plant foods have 20 to 45% nitrogen and are used at correspondingly lighter rates. (You can learn more about the make-up of fertilizers in the chapter on soils and plant foods—including an explanation of the numerals and percentages.)

It does not make much difference what kind of fertilizer you use. Some are safer because they are "non-burning." But for this convenience you may pay a bit more. As long as the fertilizer is not dusty, and is not used more heavily than about 1 pound of actual nitrogen (10 lb. of a fertilizer containing 10% nitrogen) per 1000 sq. ft., there should be no danger of injuring the grass.

Some kinds of grass need more fertilizer than others. Give heavy feeders such as bermudas, Merion bluegrass and bentgrasses a total of 8 lb. or more of actual nitrogen per 1000 sq. ft. per year. (That is, for each 1000 sq. ft. of lawn you would give an annual total feeding of 80 lb. of a complete fertilizer having a 10-6-4 analysis, or 40 lb. of one with a 20-10-5 analysis.)

Bluegrass lawns, except Merion, get by well with about 4 lb. of actual nitrogen per 1,000 sq. ft. per year (that is, a total of 40 lb. of 10-6-4, or 20 lb. of 20-10-5). Fine fescues can get along on 3 lb. or less (30 lb. of 10-6-4 or 15 lb. of 20-10-5), and this rate is usually adequate also for centipede and bahia, though these latter two may look better if fertilized more generously.

The handiest and best way to apply fertilizer is with a mechanical spreader. Often you can rent one at the store where you buy your fertilizer—or at a general rental supply store. When pushing the spreader up and down over your lawn, be sure to overlap the runs slightly so that there are no missed spots. These would show up as conspicuous streaks later—the fertilized grass would be dark green and the missed strips yellowish. If you suspect you may have overdosed, or if the fertilizer seems dusty, it is a good idea to rinse it off the grass leaves and into the ground. However, most modern fertilizers are pelleted and thus roll off grass foliage easily, at least with erect grasses such as bluegrass. With tight bentgrasses and bermudas, watering-in may be needed more.

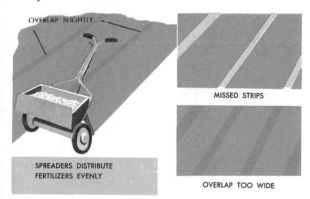

OVERLAP SLIGHTLY

MISSED STRIPS

SPREADERS DISTRIBUTE FERTILIZERS EVENLY

OVERLAP TOO WIDE

Practical Pointers on Mowing

The object of mowing is to keep the lawn neat without cutting away too much vital green grass leaf. It is the evenness of cut, not height, that is important for appearance. In fact, a low-clipped lawn may look shaggy quickly because of conspicuous weeds.

The proper height to cut depends mostly on the kind of grass. In the North, bluegrass-fescue lawns are best cut at 1½ to 2½ in., bentgrasses ½ to 1 in. In the South, bermudas can be mowed ¾ to 2 in. depending on

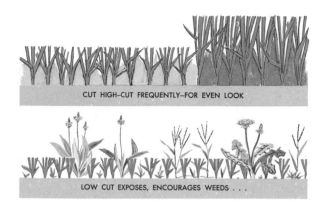

CUT HIGH-CUT FREQUENTLY-FOR EVEN LOOK

LOW CUT EXPOSES, ENCOURAGES WEEDS . . .

the fineness of the variety; St. Augustine and bahia 2 in. or so; zoysia and centipede about 1½ in. Some portion of green leaf should be left; brown stubble should not show after the lawn is cut. If you mow too close, especially with upright grasses such as bluegrass, your weed problems will increase. The more grass, the fewer weeds.

Start mowing in spring as soon as the grass begins growing and continue as long as it makes significant growth in autumn. The time to mow is any time the grass has grown enough so that it has added about 50% to its usual mowing height. It is a mistake to let it get very tall and then scalp it; this "shocks" the lawn and disrupts its growth. With bluegrass you might mow about every 4 or 5 days during the peak growing season in spring; then only every 10 or 12 days during summer —or not mow at all during drought.

Should you pick up clippings? Maybe. Clippings left to decay on the lawn return some fertility to the soil. With grasses such as Kentucky bluegrass and fine fescue, which grow in an open manner, clippings can settle into the sod—and the easiest thing to do is to leave them. Trailing grasses such as bents and bermudas weave a dense layer of stems that can prevent clippings from reaching the ground, where decay occurs. With them it might be better to collect and remove clippings. If you think clippings look unsightly, collect or sweep them. The fertility lost can easily be replaced by a single feeding. Some people think clippings left on the lawn encourage disease. Others think that leaving them on improves the soil.

Get a mower that is big enough for the job. Do not buy an insubstantial machine for economy. So much time is spent mowing the lawn that it is not a luxury to want good equipment. A mower that breaks down all the time, or is hard to start, or that will not adjust easily to the proper cutting height, can take all the fun out of your lawn life.

Rotary mowers (that cut by a horizontally whirling blade) are generally a little more economical and more versatile; they are good for lawns that are mowed above 1½ in. high. But they are more dangerous. Reel mowers (that cut with a "squirrel-cage" of blades brushing against a bedknife) do the neatest job on low-cut grasses. Either kind should be kept sharp and in good condition. Of course, riding mowers are fun but more expensive.

When Watering Is Needed

Strangely, watering is seldom vital in climates where rainfall runs upward of 25 in. per year. Of course, in arid country such as around Denver, you cannot have grass at all without irrigating. But even moist climates have occasional droughts. The only way to keep grass green during dry periods is to water it. Most lawns use 1 in. of water per week. Heavy claylike soils hold 2 to 3 in. in the root zone, enough to last a lawn for 2 weeks following a good soaking. Sandy soils hold only ½ in. or less so they need watering more frequently. On the heavier clay and silt soils, watering should be fairly slow and prolonged. It may take more than an hour of sprinkling to soak 2 in. of water deeply without any running off. On sandy soils such as occur on the Coastal Plain, water would be wasted if more than about ½ in. were applied, and this soaks in about as fast as you

can water. Because it drains so quickly, it should be rewatered every 3 or 4 days during drought.

Well-established lawns can usually become completely brown from drought yet come back green when conditions again turn favorable. So most watering is for appearance's sake rather than for the health of the grass. As a matter of fact, watering sometimes helps the weeds more than the grass, encouraging annual bluegrass, nutgrass and other water-loving weed species.

If you are interested in installing an irrigation system, select one that applies water evenly at the right rate. The Southwest in particular is turning to automatic underground irrigating systems. In most cases it is advisable to have them installed by a professional to be sure of proper coverage, correct pipe size and adequate water pressure.

HOW TO GET RID OF YOUR WEEDS

A weed, so far as a lawn is concerned, is any plant that does not blend well with grass. It sticks out like a sore thumb. A new lawn can be expected to have many—unless the soil was sterilized—for weeds arise from dormant seeds present in almost all soils. Some will disappear in time as the grass crowds them out, or because they cannot persist under regular mowing. Still others are rather easily controlled with modern weed killers. So, all in all, the situation may not be as alarming as it appears at first glance.

There are usually fewer kinds of weeds in the North than in the South, though the plants of any given kind may be more abundant. Control by use of weed killers is generally quite effective in the North.

The best time to do the killing varies somewhat with the location and kind of weed. Usually weeds are most susceptible to chemical control when they are growing vigorously. This usually means when weather is warm and there is ample moisture. Spring is a good time to go after most broad-leaved weeds in northern lawns, and autumn for those that renew their growth cycle in fall. In the South, where something is sprouting almost all the time, weed treatment may be at almost any season. In both North and South there is less chance of injuring lawn grass if a weed killer is not applied during extra hot days. Summer drought may toughen weeds, too, so they become less susceptible to regular amounts of the chemical.

Broad-leaved Weeds Most Objectionable

Fortunately broad-leaved weeds are generally controllable with the 2,4-D group of chemicals, including 2,4,5-T, Silvex (2,4,5-TP) and Dicamba (Banvel-D) without injury to grass. Some of these weeds are relatively easy to kill, while others are more stubborn.

The ones easily controlled with 2,4-D are:

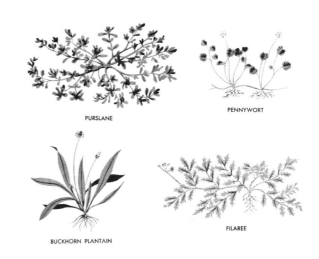

PURSLANE

PENNYWORT

BUCKHORN PLANTAIN

FILAREE

Types more difficult to kill, perhaps requiring repeat applications or Silvex formulations, are:

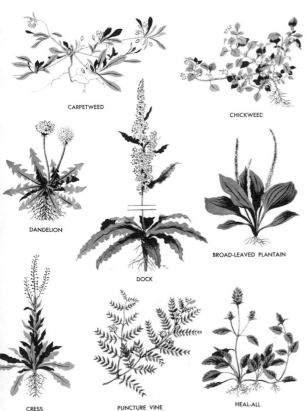

CARPETWEED

CHICKWEED

DANDELION

DOCK

BROAD-LEAVED PLANTAIN

CRESS

PUNCTURE VINE

HEAL-ALL

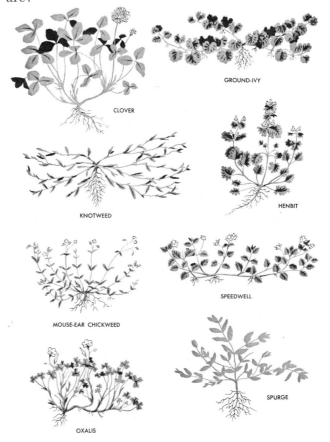

CLOVER

GROUND-IVY

KNOTWEED

HENBIT

MOUSE-EAR CHICKWEED

SPEEDWELL

OXALIS

SPURGE

The 2,4-D type of weed killers are absorbed through the leaves. The weed dies slowly, twisting and curling. Since the material affects the roots as well as the tops, there is seldom any resprouting.

Make certain that this material gets on the leaves. Sometimes granular weed killers do not stick well to foliage; you may have better results if you spread them when the leaves are moist with dew. Sprays generally stick better than dry materials, but even sprays may work better if you add a pinch of detergent to the solution. The detergent acts as a wetting agent—that is, it "makes the water wetter" so that it spreads and is absorbed more easily. CAUTION: *These 2,4-D weed killers must be used exactly as recommended in the instructions that come with the product. If you use too little you may not kill the weeds. If you use too much you can damage the grass and soil. Some products, both liquid and granular, tend to vaporize, and these vapors can injure or kill garden plants at surprising distances away. Most manufacturers of weed killers for home gardens use "low-volatile" formulas in their products. When you make your purchase of the 2,4-D types it is wise to ask for low-volatile kinds. Containers (such as sprayers) that have been used for 2,4-D and related materials are best not used for applying fertilizers, insecticides, etc. They are difficult to clean completely of the 2,4-D, and even tiny amounts can damage some plants.*

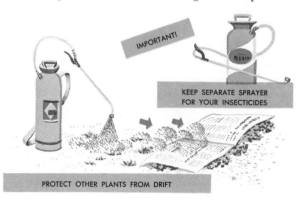

IMPORTANT!

KEEP SEPARATE SPRAYER FOR YOUR INSECTICIDES

PROTECT OTHER PLANTS FROM DRIFT

Tricky Grass Weeds

Since weed grasses grow and behave as good grasses do, they are difficult to eradicate without harming your lawn grasses.

The annual sorts include crabgrass. These start from seed anew each spring, and the weakness in their life cycle is the seedling stage. Chemicals have been found which kill them at this time without injuring established grasses. These pre-emergence or preventer weed killers are applied to blanket the soil before the seeds germinate, and kill the seedlings as they appear.

Grasses that are frequently controllable with such chemicals, or later controlled selectively with arsonates, include:

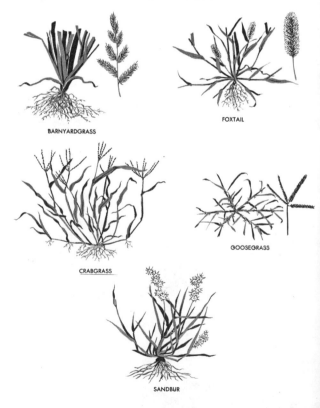

BARNYARDGRASS

FOXTAIL

CRABGRASS

GOOSEGRASS

SANDBUR

Crabgrass is the most pestiferous annual grass in most lawns. Its seed lies dormant in the soil and only a small percentage of it sprouts in any given year. A big crop of it is almost sure to result if your lawn becomes weak. Seeds sprout when the soil warms to around 60° F. You will notice the seedlings first on south-facing slopes. This may be as early as March in the South (the year-round in Florida), or as late as June and July in Minnesota.

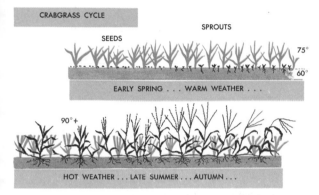

The seedlings look innocent enough—two small spear-shaped yellowish-green leaves. But with hot weather and ample rain the plant expands rapidly, with its spreading stems rooting at the joints. By August a plant may be too big to be covered with a 10-gallon hat. From middle to late summer it produces wiry "crowfoot"-shaped seedheads. Then before frost, the plant turns an unattractive yellow. Pulling up dead plants or scratching them out in autumn accomplishes little more than the threshing of the seed, thus planting it for the next year.

One of the good pre-emergent chemicals that kill crabgrass seedlings as they sprout is Dacthal. Also used are various arsenicals, Bandane, Betasan, Chlordane, and Tupersan, with new ones coming out almost yearly. Good preventers remain effective for months, controlling later sprouting seeds as well as early.

CAUTION: *Most effective preventers decimate newly sown lawn seed, so are best used on established lawns where the grass is old enough to be mowed. If you are planning to overseed a lawn that is looking sparse, do it well ahead of the time you apply a crabgrass preventer, or wait until autumn to do the new seeding.*

The time to apply the preventer is before the first crabgrass seedling makes its appearance. But there is no sense in applying it much ahead of sprouting season—which is about the time lilacs finish blooming—since it gradually loses its effectiveness. Most of the preventers are effective only a few months and in following years you will need to put on a booster treatment.

Spread the preventer uniformly over the lawn at the rate recommended on the product. The easiest way to do it is with granular materials dropped from the same sort of mechanical spreader you use to apply lawn fertilizer. You do not need to put any in shaded areas, for crabgrass will not grow in shade—as under trees.

If you miss out on killing annual grasses as they sprout, there are chemicals which will kill them selectively later. Sprays are ordinarily more effective for this, since the chemical is absorbed through the foliage, and it is easier to coat leaves with liquid than to make granular materials adhere. Arsonates (AMA and DSMA) have proven best for this type of control. Usually 2 applications about a week apart are needed. On well-established bluegrass, treatment will be completely selective, killing the crabgrass without injuring the lawn grass. In very hot weather there may be temporary discoloration, especially to bentgrasses. Arsonates should not be used on bahia, centipede and St. Augustine in the South.

Perennial Grasses Hardest To Lick

Any weed killer strong enough to kill perennial weed grasses will kill good grass along with the bad. About the only thing to do is to dig out the unwanted clumps, spot-spray them with a general weed killer, or kill everything in the lawn with a weed killer and then replant. Sometimes a lawn can be upgraded gradually, simply by overseeding with good grass and managing the lawn so as to give it every possible encouragement. For example, quackgrass may sometimes be eased out of a bluegrass lawn over a period of years just by tending the lawn well.

Grassy perennial weeds that can be spot-killed with general weed killers such as Dalapon and Amitrol include:

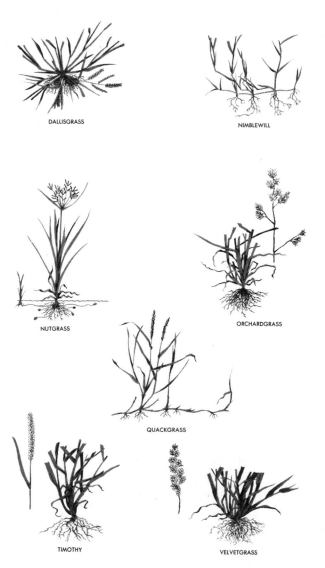

DALLISGRASS

NIMBLEWILL

NUTGRASS

ORCHARDGRASS

QUACKGRASS

TIMOTHY

VELVETGRASS

Some perennial grassy weeds, including nutgrass and dallisgrass, are inhibited and may disappear in time with repeat applications of 2,4-D and DSMA. Dalapon kills almost any grass. It is absorbed through the foliage and has a systemic effect; that is, it spreads through the plant internally. Amitrol is similar, but drift or shoe tracks can blanch any foliage it contacts. Even gasoline and kerosene can be used to paint unwanted grasses.

Chemicals that kill all vegetation are used to clean out old weedy grass before reseeding. Nothing will grow for a while so seeds should not be planted for several weeks. This is true where Dalapon or Amitrol are used to kill spots of tough grass. Cacodylic acid, which is usually the active chemical in "quick knock-down" lawn renovation products, does not harm soil, so seed can be planted within a day or two.

While general weed killers such as Dalapon, Amitrol and cacodylic acid are not quite so hazardous to use as volatile forms of 2,4-D, they should be carefully confined to the weeds being killed. A splash or drift from them will blemish other plants. Such chemicals can be purchased in aerosol "bomb" cans, "salt-shaker" dusters, or can be mixed for spraying in the familiar garden sprayers. If the sprayer is rinsed out well, there is no harmful residue left in the equipment. When a pressure sprayer is used to spot-spray the weeds, keep pressures low to reduce the mist that might drift to good plants. For small areas, the weeds could even be painted with the solution, using a dauber of any absorbent material, or even a paint brush. Since such herbicides are effective through foliage, it is not good to dowse them heavily as with a sprinkling can; most of the chemical runs through to the soil rather than adhering to the weed. The chemical may be weeks in dissipating, which would cause a delay if you plan to reseed.

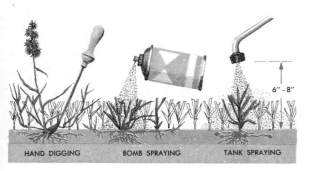

HAND DIGGING   BOMB SPRAYING   TANK SPRAYING   6" - 8"

Cautions for the South

While the weed killers listed in the charts are useful on bermudagrass and most zoysias (and 2,4-D is effective on bahia and centipede, too), they cannot be employed on all Southern grasses without danger of damaging them. Moreover, pre-emergence preventive weed control loses much of its value for the deep South, where some sort of weed is sprouting almost the year around. A pre-emergence treatment may have temporary effectiveness for a new lawn planting where the permanent grass is being started "live" rather than from seed. But it will be relatively useless for keeping established lawns clean of weeds in a subtropical climate.

A couple of special chemicals are used for certain grasses in the deep South. (Do not use these in bluegrass country.) Simazine and Atrazine seem not to injure St. Augustine, centipede or zoysia, yet control most other vegetation when used as a pre-emergent. Atrazine also works as a post-emergent —after the weed has appeared—and is useful in St. Augustine where 2,4-D is harmful.

Weed Control for Special Situations or Plants

It is possible to keep borders neat and perennial grasses out of shrub beds by careful spraying with suitable weed killers. Cacodylic acid—often used to kill back a poor lawn prior to reseeding—will edge borders quite trimly if neatly applied.

Cacodylic acid and Diquat are inactivated almost immediately when they touch the soil. These chemicals are good for keeping grass and weeds away from the base of small trees planted in the lawn, with no danger to the tree roots, though of course you must avoid letting the spray drift onto the tree foliage.

OTHER LAWN PROBLEMS

Yellowish grass: This may have several causes. If you think the lawn may suffer from lack of enough nitrogen—feed it; if from chlorosis—caused by trace elements being tied up by too much alkalinity or acidity— apply a chelated iron; if from general weakness due to disease—use fungicide; if from compacted soil—aerify it; or if from standing water—drain it.

Lawn insects: An insecticide spread uniformly is the cure. Unfortunately, some insects build resistance to an insecticide. This has happened with chinch bugs and Chlordane and Dieldrin. Much the same seems to be happening with sod web-worms. Ask your local garden center or county agent what insecticide to use locally. Alternating different insecticides helps prevent the building up of resistance against a single chemical.

Lawn disease: This is easier to prevent than to control. Almost any general-purpose fungicide (ask for one economical enough for lawn care) can help check disease if applied shortly before the trouble usually appears. For example, snow mold is almost inevitable on northern bentgrass lawns during winter; the preventive treatment should be undertaken in late autumn.

During the warm growing season, disease

prevention is difficult; new grass leaves pop out every few days and of course do not have a protective cover of fungicide unless this is applied almost weekly. You can usually help the situation by temporarily withholding water and keeping the lawn relatively dry, since disease thrives most under humid conditions. And do not fertilize heavily in hot weather, since lush grass is more susceptible.

Moles and other burrowing animals: They are looking for food and can usually be forced to go elsewhere if the grubs and other insects for which they are looking are eliminated by an insecticide. Almost any insecticide cleans up soil grubs. Chlordane and Dieldrin have been used for a long time; they remain effective in the soil for many years. Such insecticides are applied in much the same way as crabgrass preventers, and over a period of months will complete their mission.

HOW TO START A NEW LAWN

The best time to start a new lawn: In the North begin in late August or early September, but if you miss that chance, plant any time through winter or early spring. In the South, start in spring.

Whether the lawn is to be seeded, planted to sprigs or plugs, or sodded, it is worthwhile to provide the best possible soil bed. You should cultivate the soil and mix in fertilizer. In some instances the old vegetation can be burned back with a chemical such as cacodylic acid and the surface of the soil then be scuffed and reseeded. Do not cultivate the soil so much that it becomes dusty; soil lumps, in thumbnail size, make the best surface.

Advice for the North: If you are going to use seed, choose a good blend. You can tell what is in a seed mixture by looking at the listing on the outside of the package. The label groups grasses as "fine-textured" and "coarse kinds." Good blends are mainly or entirely bluegrasses and fine fescues. Do not

be fooled by tall fescue (Kentucky-31 is a variety), a coarse relative of fine fescues; it is sometimes included in inexpensive seed mixtures and can become a pest. How much seed? For new lawns a bluegrass mixture is usually spread at the rate of about 3 lb. to 1000 sq. ft., say about 15 lb. to the average lawn. To thicken old lawns, use half that rate.

Suggestions for the South: Exact directions that will cover all types of lawn are too complicated to give. If you are going to seed, buy a good mixture recommended by your garden store; Bermudas are good for the upper South, and bahia for Florida and the Gulf Coast. Otherwise, buy live starts of your favorite lawngrass.

To plant: Spread seed uniformly; covering it with a light mulch helps the grass start more quickly with less sprinkling. Keep it constantly moist until it has germinated and is growing well. With live starts, space them on equidistant centers. Do not let them lack for water until they are well established.

Sodding for extra-fast results: In this case, someone else grows the grass and sells it to you in relatively mature condition. When such sod is professionally grown, it can be excellent. But it is not as economical as your own seeding, and often you are not sure of what you are planting. Old field sod may be full of weeds and off-type grass. Sod is especially useful for slopes, even if used only in strips across the top to prevent washing away of soil. It is best laid on soil prepared just about as thoroughly as for a new seeding.

After-care for new lawns: Be sure the grass always has enough water. Do not use weed killers or apply fertilizers until the grass is old enough to have been mowed a few times. Begin mowing as soon as the grass is slightly taller than customary mowing height. Fertilize in the future according to the recommendations given earlier in this chapter.

5

Groundcovers to Clothe
and Hold Soil

Groundcovers are what their name implies—and more. They are plants which can, respectively, carpet bare earth, substitute for grass, bind sandy soils, check erosion on hillsides, underplant trees and shrubs, survive neglect, and live long with little maintenance. Some adapt to life in shady situations; others endure full sun and drought; many can live where nothing else will grow. In general, they are tough and durable, low-growing and rapid-spreading shrubs, or other perennial plants. However, annual flowers can be used to achieve immediate results that are attractive and practical.

What a boon these are to gardeners! But be warned that some of the most vigorous kinds, useful for difficult sites, can become rampant pests if they escape into the good soil of your garden. The very qualities that make them desirable are their worst faults! Bear in mind that they must be so able to take care of themselves, and so immune to hardships, that they are practically weeds. It is wise to plant such potential menaces where they can expand indefinitely without causing trouble, or to contain them within impassable barriers such as cement sidewalks or driveways. If you plant them adjoining a cultivated flower bed, they will move in and take over, and you will fight them forever. In the description of each groundcover, given in the alphabetical listing at the end of this chapter, you will be told about cautions for use.

The best plants for groundcovers are those with evergreen leaves that look handsome both winter and summer. There is a wider selection of these in mild climates than where winters have subzero temperatures. They must be rapid-spreading. Suitable vines are those whose stems develop roots wherever they touch soil. Ideal shrubs are those that extend and multiply by means of underground runners or suckers; some have branches that root when they arch over and touch earth.

On level areas, almost any plant can cover the ground attractively, even though it grows in clumps instead of spreading. But on slopes, roots or rooting stems must form a continuous network to bind the soil surface, and roots must go deep if they are to keep the ground from breaking loose during heavy rains.

PLANTING KNOW-HOW

Time to plant: Where winters are very cold, spring is best. Where winters are moderate [Zones 6 and 7], plant in fall or spring. In mild-winter climates [Zones 8, 9 and 10], plant in fall or winter.

Size of plants to get: They do not have to be large and expensive. If they are shrubs, they can be young or small, and certainly do not need to be choice specimens. If they are vines, they are often available in pots or cans, but deciduous types are sold "bare-root," often grouped in bundles of a dozen or 25. You can sometimes buy clumps—or beg them from a friend—and tear them apart into many

pieces, each of which has roots and the start of a top. Such plants as these, that root at every node, can be quickly propagated by cutting their leafy stems into sections 8 to 10 in. long. Put the lower ends into water or moist soil to induce rooting. (See the chapter on starting plants.)

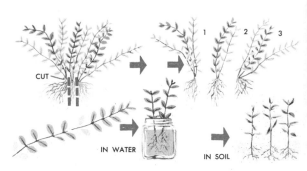

Any of your friends who have a sizeable planting of some groundcover will probably be happy to give you starts—either plants or clippings which you can root. And later on, *you* will have some plants to share!

You are asking these plants to do an important job for you, and they need your help. They cannot excel in poor, hard soil. Give them a good send-off. Prepare the ground just as you would for a bed of fine flowers. If the area is level, dig the entire space, and work in some "complete" fertilizer of a dry type, using 3 lb. per 100 sq. ft. If the area is on a hill, it may not be wise to loosen the soil for fear of erosion. You may prefer to prepare rows on contour—a series of little horizontal terraces with rims on the downhill side to hold water. If you are using shrubs, or large clumps of vines, you can prepare individual holes, staggered in checkerboard fashion, with water-holding saucers around them.

Setting plants in rows makes them easier to cultivate, and you *must* keep weeds out and provide water for the first year or two.

else your efforts will have been wasted. Controlling weeds now will give you leisure later. Plant carefully. Shrubs and clump-plants should be positioned to be at the same ground level that they were before. If you are dealing with segments of vines with roots on their ends, be sure the roots are covered with at least 2 in. of soil. If the vine has roots at a series of nodes, it can be placed in the hole or trench in a horizontal position with just the top few inches of leafy part exposed. Firm the soil about the roots, and water well.

After setting out, vinelike plants should be cut back almost to the soil. (Usually this means within 5 in., or leaving 2 or 3 nodes visible above ground.) This makes them branch rather than grow out in a single long shoot. Clippings can often be rooted.

Deciduous shrubs should be pruned, shortening branches by at least ⅓ of their height. Mulching between rows will help hold the soil and cut down on the need for watering

and weeding. Use some coarse material such as straw, grass clippings, or wood chips.

FUTURE MAINTENANCE

Do not expect instant coverage. The more plants you start with, and the more closely they are spaced, the more quickly they will touch. But ordinarily it takes 2 years to get the effect of which you dreamed—unless you use annuals, which give results at once but are not permanent. During this early period, while plants are becoming established, they are not able to fend for themselves. They are dependent upon you, and will need weed control and water.

How much you need to feed the plants depends upon your soil and climate. In most areas, after they are established, one feeding a year in early summer is enough. But in sandy soil, plants getting started will need to be fed every 2 or 3 weeks, and later be given both a spring and summer feeding.

The belief that groundcovers need absolutely no upkeep is a myth! They need occasional attention, even after they are established. Some should be sheared or pruned. Watering is often essential, not only to save plants through dry periods but also to reduce the hazard of fire, since groundcovers collect and hold an underlayer of dry leaves. Such areas should be cleaned regularly of trash and paper fragments before they become unsightly.

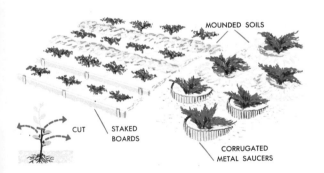

MOUNDED SOILS

CUT   STAKED BOARDS

CORRUGATED METAL SAUCERS

THE BEST GENERAL PURPOSE GROUNDCOVERS

Listed here are low-growing, neatly attractive but unassuming groundcovers, which are used where grass is difficult to maintain, beneath shrubs, on gentle slopes, etc. The top ten for each region have been included. In areas where the climate varies considerably from north to south, or by altitude, not all of the recommendations will be hardy over the entire area. To learn each plant's hardiness and other details, check the descriptions in the alphabetical listing given at the end of this chapter. In arid regions, it is assumed that water is available for the plants suggested.

NORTHEAST

Ajuga
Baltic Ivy
Creeping Thyme
Moss-Pink
Pachysandra terminalis
Purpleleaf Wintercreeper
Rockspray Cotoneaster
Vinca minor
Wilton Juniper
Yellow-Root

MIDWEST

Ajuga
Baltic Ivy
Creeping Juniper vars.
Creeping Lily-Turf
Dead Nettle
Epimedium pinnatum
Pachysandra terminalis
Purpleleaf Wintercreeper
Vinca minor
Wild Ginger

PLAINS AND INTERMOUNTAIN

Ajuga
Artemisia 'Silver Mound'
Bear-Berry
Blue Leadwort
Creeping Mahonia
English Ivy (shade)
Goldmoss Stonecrop
Purpleleaf Wintercreeper
Vinca minor (shade)
Wood Sage

UPPER SOUTH

Ajuga
Carolina Yellow Jessamine
Creeping Juniper
Ivy (self-branching)
Hypericum calycinum
Lily-Turf
Moss-Pink
Shore Juniper
Vinca minor
Wintercreeper

DEEP SOUTH

Ajuga
Dwarf Lily-Turf
English Ivy (shade)
Kalanchoe fedtschenkoi
Lily-Turf
Setcreasea 'Purple Queen'
Shore Juniper
Vinca minor
Wandering Jew
Wedelia

SOUTHWEST*

Ajuga
Blue Fescue (semi-shade)
Carissa grandiflora
    'Prostrata'
Creeping Juniper
Creeping Rosemary
Dichondra
English Ivy (shade)
Ground Morning-Glory
Hypericum calycinum
    (shade)
Vinca major

PACIFIC NORTHWEST

Ajuga
Bear-Berry
Cornish Heath
    'Mrs. D. F. Maxwell'
*Cotoneaster microphylla
    cochleata*
Hypericum calycinum
Pachysandra terminalis
Small Himalayan
    Sarcococca
Tamarix Juniper
Vinca minor 'Bowles'
Waukegan Juniper

NORTHERN CALIFORNIA

Ajuga
Bearberry Cotoneaster
Creeping Lily-Turf
Dwarf Lily-Turf
Hahn's Self-Branching Ivy
Mother-of-Thyme
Pachysandra terminalis
Roman Chamomile
Vinca minor
Wild Strawberry

SOUTHERN CALIFORNIA

Ajuga
Dwarf Lily-Turf
Hahn's Self-Branching Ivy
Hypericum calycinum
Lippia
Polygonum capitatum
Potentilla verna
Star-Jasmine
Vinca minor
Wild Strawberry

* In the Southwest, Zones 5 and 6, use Plains and Intermountain list.

HAWAII	ALASKA
Chlorophytum elatum vittatum	Bear-Berry
Dissotis rotundifolia	Bog-Rosemary
Dwarf Lily-Turf	Bunchberry
Hemigraphis colorata	Common Juniper
Ligularia kaempferi	Creeping Juniper
Pilea microphylla	Crowberry
Pilea nummulariaefolia	Dogbane
Spathiphyllum clevelandi	Goats-Beard
Syngonium auritum	Northern Bedstraw
Waipahu Fig	Twin-Flower

GROUNDCOVERS RECOMMENDED FOR HILL-HOLDING

These are toughies! They must bind soil both on the surface and as deeply as possible. In addition they must tolerate the dry conditions of their rapid-draining site. WARNING: Because effective erosion-control plants are necessarily aggressive, some of them, under good growing conditions, can become seriously invasive. Examples of these are dwarf Japanese fleece-flower, artemisia 'Silver King,' Hall's Japanese honeysuckle and matrimony-vine. Modern weed-killing sprays can come to your rescue if things get out of hand.

NORTHEAST	MIDWEST	PLAINS AND INTERMOUNTAIN
Ajuga	Akebia	Artemisia 'Silver King'
Andorra Juniper	American Bitter-Sweet	Double Creeping Buttercup
Bear-Berry	*Euonymus obovatus*	Dwarf Iris
Lowbush Blueberry	Forsythia 'Arnold Dwarf'	Dwarf Japanese Fleece-Flower
Moss-Pink	Hall's Japanese Honeysuckle	Hall's Japanese Honeysuckle
Purpleleaf Wintercreeper	Matrimony-Vine	Marine Ivy
Rockspray Cotoneaster	Memorial Rose	Matrimony-Vine
Sweet-Fern	Purpleleaf Wintercreeper	Ribbon-Grass
Vinca minor	Rose 'Max Graf'	Snow-in-Summer
Yellow-Root	Waukegan Juniper	Two-Row Stonecrop

UPPER SOUTH	DEEP SOUTH	SOUTHWEST*
Carolina Yellow Jessamine	Confederate-Jasmine	Banksia Rose
English Ivy	Coral Honeysuckle	Cats-Claw
Hall's Japanese Honeysuckle	Coromandel	Ground Cotoneaster
Hypericum calycinum	English Ivy	Hall's Japanese Honeysuckle
Junipers, creeping types	Hottentot-Fig	Mesembryanthemum, various
Rose 'Max Graf'	Japanese Honeysuckle	Primrose Jasmine
Vinca major	Primrose Jasmine	Pyracantha 'Santa Cruz Prostrate'
Vinca minor	*Vinca minor*	Rose 'Mermaid'
Wintercreeper	Wedelia	*Trachelospermum asiaticum*
Zoysia (from seed)	Weeping Lantana	Trailing Lantana

* In the Southwest, Zones 5 and 6, use Plains and Intermountain list.

Shade-loving Pachysandra terminalis *rates high as a permanent underplanting for shrubs. E. L. Wilder residence, Rochester, New York*

Ground-hugging ajuga or bugle is semi-evergreen and likes some shade. It has spikes of purplish-blue flowers in spring.

Vinca minor, *myrtle or periwinkle, has lovely blue flowers in spring. It is shown growing on the north side of a house in Oberlin, Ohio.*

Hypericum calycinum *or Aaronsbeard St. Johnswort is excellent for either level ground or hills. Photographed in Corvallis, Oregon*

THE BEST GENERAL PURPOSE GROUNDCOVERS

PACIFIC NORTHWEST	SOUTHERN CALIFORNIA	NORTHERN CALIFORNIA
Bear-Berry	Carmel Creeper	Bear-Berry
Bearberry Cotoneaster	Creeping Rosemary	Creeping Rosemary
Cotoneaster microphylla cochleata	*Delosperma alba*	English Ivy
Hypericum calycinum	Dwarf Baccharis	Hottentot-Fig
Pfitzer Juniper	*Erigeron karvinskianus*	*Hypericum calycinum*
Rock Cotoneaster	Gazania	Mock-Strawberry
Salal	*Hymenocyclus purpureo-croceus*	Necklace Cotoneaster
Virburnum davidi	Japanese Honeysuckle	Rock Cotoneaster
Vinca minor	Weeping Lantana	Tamarix Juniper
Waukegan Juniper	Woolly Thyme	Wild Strawberry

HAWAII	ALASKA
Asystasia gangetica	Bear-Berry
Clematis 'Sweet Autumn'	Common Juniper
Japanese Honeysuckle	Western Sand Cherry
Lippia	
Sweet Potato	
Taro Vine	
Variegated St. Augustine-Grass	
Walking-Iris	
Wandering Jew	
Wedelia	

❧ Alphabetical List of the Best Groundcovers

AARONSBEARD ST. JOHNSWORT, see HYPERICUM

AJUGA or BUGLE. This creeping semi-evergreen perennial grows in Zones 5 to 10, inclusive. The leaves, 4 in. long and narrow, are arranged in flat rosettes. They may be green, bronze or mottled, depending upon variety. The flowers in spring are showy 6-in.-high spikes of purplish-blue, pink or white. The plants like part shade. Space them 6 to 12 in. apart and propagate by dividing clumps.

AKEBIA. See the chapter on vines.

ARTEMISIA. See the chapter on perennials.

ASYSTASIA, see COROMANDEL

BACCHARIS, DWARF (*B. pilularis*) or DWARF CHAPARRAL BROOM. This is found in Zones 9 and 10. It has evergreen leaves 1 in. long on a prostrate shrub that grows 6 to 24 in. high and spreads to become 2 to 10 ft. across. The roots are strong and grow deep, holding soil, sand and slopes. It bears white, chaffy flowers.

BEAR-BERRY (*Arctostaphylos uva-ursi*). This native trailing evergreen thrives in Zones 2b to 9a, inclusive. It grows 6 to 12 in. high. While it prefers acid soil, it adapts to sandy or rocky conditions, sun or shade, coastal site or inland. The leaves are small and leathery; little white flowers are followed by bright red berries. Potted plants transplant most easily.

BEDSTRAW, NORTHERN (*Galium boreale*). This is native to Zones 2 through 5. The slender plants grow 1 to 2 ft. high with profuse, small, fragrant white flowers, and spread by stolons.

BISHOPS HAT, see EPIMEDIUM

BITTER-SWEET. See the chapter on vines.

BLUEBERRY, LOWBUSH (*Vaccinium angusti-folium*). This native small twiggy shrub is very cold-hardy, into Zone 3, and grows 8 in. high. It tolerates poor, rocky, acid soils; sun or shade. The flowers are small and white, followed by dark blue berries.

BOG-ROSEMARY (*Andromeda polifolia*). This low-growing native shrub is hardy north through Zone 2. It has narrow evergreen leaves 1 in. long, lighter on undersides, and pink urn-shaped flowers. The shrub spreads by creeping root stalks. It likes moist, peaty, acid soil; sun or light shade.

BROOM, DWARF CHAPARRAL, see BACCHARIS

BUNCHBERRY (*Cornus canadensis*). This is native to cool climates and mountain regions, including Zone 2. Its glossy leaves are held 4 to 8 in. high. The blooms resemble those of flowering dogwood, with 4 showy white petal like bracts. Clusters of red fruits follow. Get starts by cutting chunks from established plantings. It likes moist, acid soil rich in humus; also shade.

BUGLE, See AJUGA

BUTTERCUP. See the chapter on perennials.

CAMOMILE, ROMAN (*Anthemis nobilis*). This herb, in Zones 5a to 10, inclusive, grows 3 to 6 in. high with ferny, scented leaves and small yellow blooms. It can be walked upon and mowed. Full sun or light shade are preferred. Set the plants 1 to 2 ft. apart. They can be grown from seed or divisions.

CARISSA. See the chapter on shrubs.

CARMEL CREEPER (*Ceanothus griseus horizontalis*). One of California's wild lilacs, this can be found in Zones 8, 9 and 10. It is a low or creeping evergreen shrub 18 to 30 in. high, fast-growing and spreading to cover 6 to 12 ft. The flowers are blue, growing in clusters in spring. Space the plants 8 ft. apart. They need sun, water and good drainage.

CARPOBROTUS, see MESEMBRYANTHEMUM

CATS-CLAW. See the chapter on vines.

CHERRY, WESTERN SAND (*Prunus besseyi*). Hardy in cold climates, including Alaska, it grows 1 to 4 ft. high with a spreading or near-prostrate form. The leaves are deciduous and glossy. Profuse white flowers are followed by edible black fruit. It likes fertile soil and resists drought.

CINQUEFOIL, see POTENTILLA

CLEMATIS. See the chapter on vines.

COROMANDEL (*Asystasia gangetica*). This perennial, with trailing branches 1 to 4 ft. long, grows in Zone 10. Its flowers are purple to yellowish.

COTONEASTER. These shrubs are grown for their attractive small leaves and decorative berries. Several are particularly good for groundcovers.

Bearberry (*C. dammeri*), Zones 6 to 10a, inclusive, is a mat-forming evergreen trailer 6 to 12 in. high. The berries are red.

C. microphylla cochleata, Zones 7 to 10a, inclusive, is an evergreen, growing 1 to 2 ft. high and 15 ft. across. It has tiny leaves and red berries.

Necklace (*C. decora*), lives in Zones 7 to 10a, inclusive. It is an evergreen with arching branches up to 3 ft. high, and bears red fruit.

Rockspray (*C. horizontalis*), Zones 6 to 10a, inclusive, is a semi-evergreen with flat horizontal branches sometimes 3 ft. high. It bears red berries. The variety *perpusilla* is called ground cotoneaster.

CROWBERRY (*Empetrum nigrum*), is native to arctic and cool areas. An evergreen shrub 10 in. high, it has needlelike leaves, purplish flowers, and edible black berries. Use it for low, rough places.

DAY-LILY. See the chapter on perennials.

DEAD NETTLE (*Lamium maculatum*). This pretty mound-making perennial grows 6 to 8 in. high in Zones 5 to 8, inclusive. Its leaves are small, green with decorative silvery-white markings. It blooms in early summer, with purplish-pink or white blossoms clustered at the tips of branches. Sun or part shade are preferred. Propagate by dividing clumps, and space 10 in. apart.

DELOSPERMA, see MESEMBRYANTHEMUM

DICHONDRA (Dy-kon'drah), Zones 9 and 10, is a creeping plant with small kidney-shaped leaves, used as a grass substitute. The stems root at nodes and form sod. It likes sun or shade and tolerates walking on. It does not like alkali soils. Weed control is vital and difficult, since chemicals that kill most weeds hurt dichondra. Plant it in spring and through summer. Prepare the ground as for grass, and sow seed 4 oz. per 1000 sq. ft. Or use plugs of sod spaced 6 in. apart.

DISSOTIS ROTUNDIFOLIA. This plant is shrubby, with oval leaves. Its flowers are purplish, large and conspicuous. It grows in full sun and does well on walls.

DOGBANE (*Apocynum androsaemifolium*). This American native has pink flowers on stems 1 to 4 ft. high. It likes sun and spreads by underground shoots.

DUCHESNEA, see STRAWBERRY

EPIMEDIUM or BISHOPS HAT. These semievergreen 9-in.-high plants are found in Zones 4 to 8, inclusive. They have 2- or 3-parted glossy leaves on wiry stems rising from creeping root stalks. Their loose clusters of dainty flowers, shaped like a bishop's hat in white, yellow, lavender or pink, appear in spring. When cut, they are long-lasting in water. The plant grows in shade or semishade and likes moist, humusy, slightly acid soil. It propagates by dividing the root stalks. Varieties that are especially desirable because they multiply rapidly are *E. grandiflorum* and *E. pinnatum sulphureum*.

ERIGERON KARVINSKIANUS (Ehe-rij'-er-on). These trailing perennials do well in mild climates. They grow 12 to 18 in. high with daisylike flowers ¾ in. across in pink or white. They like sun or some shade, and bloom the first year from seed. Each year, after bloom, cut the plants back.

EUONYMUS RADICANS. See WINTERCREEPER in the chapter on vines.

FERN, LAU'A'E (*Polypodium phymatodes*). This Hawaiian native has large, broad, deeply divided fronds 1 to 3 ft. high over thick creeping root stalks.

FESCUE, BLUE (*Festuca ovina glauca*). This handsome gray-leaved perennial grass grows in tufts or clumps 8 in. high in Zones 4b to 10, inclusive. The clumps grow larger each year but, unless planted too thickly, retain their individual form. Each plant can be torn apart into many small divisions, each of which will quickly become a full-sized plant. Sun or part shade is needed. Space the plants 12 in. apart.

FIG, WAIPAHU (*Ficus tikoua*). This fast-growing vine does well in mild climates. It has large, rough leaves and likes sun or shade.

FLEECE-FLOWER, see POLYGONUM

FORSYTHIA 'ARNOLD DWARF'. This deciduous shrub grows 2 to 3 ft. high and twice that wide in Zones 5 to 8, inclusive. Its arching branches root wherever they touch moist ground. Grow it only for foliage, since blooms are scanty. These plants like sun or shade. Space them 2 ft. apart.

GAZANIA. See the chapter on perennials.

GOATS-BEARD (*Aruncus acuminata*). This perennial grows 2 to 4 ft. high with plumy white flowers. It is good for moist low places and hardy in the North, Zone 2.

GRASS, BLUE FESCUE, SEE FESCUE

GRASS, RIBBON-, see RIBBON-GRASS

GRASS, VARIEGATED ST. AUGUSTINE- (*Stenotaphrum secundatum variegatum*). This creeping grass with leaves attractively banded in white is fine for warm climates. It likes sun or shade, and tolerates salt spray. You start it from divisions.

HEATH, CORNISH (*Erica vagans*). This grows in Zones 7 and 8. It is a low-growing, broadly spreading, twiggy evergreen with needlelike leaves. Small bell-shaped flowers appear on spikes in late summer. It prefers sun but tolerates some shade. The soil should be acid and rapid-draining. Do not fertilize. The variety 'Mrs. D. F. Maxwell' has cherry-pink blooms.

HEMIGRAPHIS COLORATA. This creeper with glossy purple leaves 2 to 3 in. long and clusters of small white flowers does well in frost-free climates.

Purpleleaf wintercreeper, an evergreen vine, produces roots wherever its stems touch soil. Henry F. Kenny garden, Cincinnati, Ohio

OPPOSITE:
English ivy is both handsome and hard-working. It is shown holding a hill at the Richard Finnie home, Belvedere, California.

Ribbon-grass, tough and tenacious, tolerates heat and drought. It is shown in a Denver garden.

Hall's Japanese honeysuckle is aggressive and rugged. R. S. Allison home, Salt Lake City, Utah. B. Vorse, landscape architect

GROUND COVERS RECOMMENDED FOR HILL-HOLDING

HONEYSUCKLE. See the chapter on vines.

HOTTENTOT-FIG, see MESEMBRYANTHE-MUM RELATIVES

HYMENOCYCLUS, see MESEMBRYANTHE-MUM RELATIVES

HYPERICUM CALYCINUM or AARONSBEARD ST. JOHNSWORT. This evergreen or semi-evergreen shrub, Zones 6 to 10, inclusive, grows 1 to 1½ ft. high with leaves 4 in. long. It has bright yellow flowers 3 in. across in summer. It likes sun or part shade. It will grow in sandy soil and on steep banks—if watered—and spreads by underground runners. Set the plants 18 in. apart. Tops may winterkill but come back.

ICE-PLANT, see MESEMBRYANTHEMUM RELATIVES

IRIS, DWARF. See the chapter on perennials.

IVY, ALGERIAN, BALTIC, BULGARIAN, ENGLISH. See the chapter on vines.

IVY, MARINE or IVY TREEBINE (*Cissus*). This vine, native to Southern states, grows to 30 ft. in Zones 6 to 9, inclusive. Its leaves are light green with 3 fingerlike parts 1 in. long. Sun or shade, wet or dry soils, are equally suitable.

JACOBS-LADDER (*Polemonium*). In Alaska, *P. occidentale* and *P. lanatum* are used. They have blue bell-shaped flowers and pretty fern foliage.

JASMINE and JESSAMINE. See the chapter on vines.

JUNIPERS. See the section on narrow-leaved evergreens in the chapter on shrubs.

KALANCHOE (Kal-an-koh′-ee). These decorative succulent plants grow in Zone 10. Most popular for groundcover use in southern Florida is *K. fedtschenkoi*. It is bushy, either upright or trailing, with wiry branches and fleshy broad leaves that are notched and edged in purple. The flowers are brownish rose.

LAMIUM, see DEAD NETTLE

LANTANA. These shrubs are much used in mild climates. The weeping or trailing lantana (*L. montevidensis*) is hardiest, Zones 8 through 10. It grows to a 3-ft height with fragrant lavender flowers in small heads. Those of the goldrush group are trailers with yellow flowers. All like full sun and a yearly cutting back in early spring. Plant them 18 to 24 in. apart.

LEADWORT, BLUE. See PLUMBAGO in the chapter on perennials.

LIGULARIA KAEMPFERI. This low-growing plant has rounded leaves 6 to 10 in. wide. The variety *aureo-maculata* with white or yellow mottling is called leopard-plant. Its flowers are yellow in clusters 2 in. wide on stems 24 in. high. It grows in Southwest, mild climates from Zone 8, and likes a cool, moist, shady site.

LILY-TURFS. These have grasslike evergreen leaves 6 to 12 in. high and are especially popular in warm climates, where they are used mostly in shade. Stepping on them occasionally does no harm, but they are not for steady walking on. The flowers are lavender, held erect on a spike somewhat resembling grape-hyacinth. Creeping lily-turf (*Liriope spicata*) is hardy into Zone 5b, while big blue lily-turf (*L. muscari*) and dwarf lily-turf (*Ophiopogon japonicus*) are for warmer Zones 7 through 10. To plant them, separate the clumps and set divisions 3 to 6 in. apart.

LIPPIA or MAT GRASS (*Lippia nodiflora*). In Zones 7 to 10, inclusive, this mat-forming creeper grows 3 to 6 in. high with small graygreen leaves that can be walked upon. White or lavender flowers are clustered in small heads ½ in. across. It tolerates sun, heat, desert conditions, salt spray, and mowing, and spreads rapidly by underground runners. You should plant pieces of sod 12 in. apart and mow occasionally. It attracts bees, which may be a hazard for children.

MAHONIA, CREEPING (*Mahonia repens*). This broad-leaved evergreen or semi-evergreen shrub grows 1 ft. high in Zones 4 to 8, inclusive. It spreads by underground rooting stems.

MAT GRASS, see LIPPIA

MATRIMONY-VINE (*Lycium chinense* and *L. halimifolium*). This is a tough, coarse-growing semi-evergreen shrub with branches erect, arching or trailing. It grows in Zones 3 to 6, inclusive, to a height varying from 4 to 10 ft. The plant's suckering habit can be invasive. It has small purple flowers followed by showy orange berries 1 in. long. Though useful in difficult places, in any soil, and tolerant of salt spray, the fruits grow best in sun. It propagates by suckers or seed.

MESEMBRYANTHEMUM or ICE-PLANT RELATIVES. This large group of similar succulent plants, annual or perennial, has showy daisylike flowers in dazzling colors. It grows in Zones 9b and 10. Formerly all bore the botanical name *Mesembryanthemum*, but now they are officially in separate genera, though they continue to be called — and sold as — mesembryanthemums. They are fast-growing, sun-loving, soil-binding and are good for hillsides and dry sandy areas in full sun. They may be started from seed, or from tip cuttings which you can set out 18 in. apart. In California, do your planting during the rainy season. Among the best for groundcover use are Hottentot-fig (*Carpobrotus edulis*) with large yellow flowers, *Hymenocyclus purpureo-croceus* with purple, yellow-centered blooms, and *Delosperma alba*.

MORNING-GLORY, GROUND (*Convolvulus mauritanicus*). This prostrate perennial, Zones 7 to 10, inclusive, grows 1 to 2 ft. high, and to 3 ft. across. The flowers are blue to purplish, 1 to 1½ in. wide, lasting all summer. It likes sun and fast-draining soil. Space the plants 3 ft. apart. They are not invasive.

MOSS-PINK. See PHLOX in the chapter on perennials.

MYRTLE, see VINCA

NATAL-PLUM, CREEPING. See CARISSA in the chapter on shrubs.

PACHYSANDRA or SPURGE. These shade-loving plants in Zones 5 to 8, inclusive, grow 8 to 12 in. high with upright fleshy stems carrying decorative leaves that are 2 to 4 in. long and notched.

Japanese Spurge (*Pachysandra terminalis*) is one of the most popular groundcovers. Its leaves, evergreen and lustrous, spread rapidly by under-ground or surface runners. The plant can be propagated by rooting pieces of leaf-topped stems in water, moist sand, or wherever you want it to grow—if you keep the soil moist. It prefers slightly acid, moist ground, but tolerates dry conditions. There is a mottled variety.

Allegheny Spurge (*P. procumbens*) is deciduous in the North. Its leaves are a soft green color that harmonizes with naturalistic woodland plantings.

PERIWINKLE, see VINCA

PILEA. Two of these are popular groundcovers in Hawaii. Artillery plant (*P. microphylla*) is described and illustrated in the chapter on indoor plants. Creeping Charlie (*P. nummulariaefolia*) is a trailer with round, hairy, crinkled leaves ¾ in. wide. It roots where stems touch the soil.

PLANTAIN-LILY. See the chapter on shade.

POLYGONUM or FLEECE-FLOWER. These plants are handsome, easy to grow in tough situations and quick-spreading, with attractive flowers. They will grow in poor soil under full sun or part shade. But they have drawbacks! They spread so energetically by underground runners that the largest and most vigorous kinds are difficult to eradicate if they get out of bounds. Use them where they are contained within root barriers, or where it does not matter if they escape.

Reynoutria Fleece-Flower or Dwarf Japanese Fleece-Flower (*P. cuspidatum compactum*) lives in Zones 4b to 10, inclusive. It grows 15 to 24 in. high. The leaves are reddish in spring, green in summer, and red again in autumn. The flowers appear in pink sprays in late summer. This groundcover is invasive.

Polygonum capitatum, 'Pink Clover Blossom' or Pink Knotweed, is a trailing evergreen plant growing 6 in. high and 20 in. across. Its leaves are heart-shaped, 2 in. long, with red midrib, margin and stems. The flowers are pink, in small round heads resembling clover blossoms, and occur almost all year. Sun or shade is suitable. They are tender to frost, but when tops are killed, the plants come back either from root or from self-sown seeds. The roots develop along stems. Space these plants 12 to 18 in. apart.

POTENTILLA or CINQUEFOIL. The appearance of these plants, and the shape of their flowers, is somewhat similar to strawberry. *P. verna* is a creeper making flat mats. The leaves are 5-parted, and the flowers are yellow, in spring. Propagate by dividing.

POTHOS, see TARO VINE

PYRACANTHA (or FIRETHORN) 'SANTA CRUZ PROSTRATE' (*Pyracantha koidzumi*). This evergreen shrub, Zones 7 to 10, inclusive, spreads to 8 ft. and has shiny red berries. It is deep-rooted, good for holding fill or cuts.

RIBBON-GRASS (*Phalaris arundinacea*). In Zones 4b to 9, inclusive, this grows as decorative clumps of long leaves that are striped green and white. The plant reaches a height of 1 to 3 ft. It is very tough, and able to stand sun and drought.

ROSE. Several trailing kinds are popular for use as groundcovers on banks. All like sun, and should be spaced 4 ft. apart. The hardiest [Zones 5b through 9] are 'Max Graf' with single pink blossoms, and memorial rose (*R. wichuraiana*) with single white ones. They root along their branches. Where winters are not extremely severe, you can grow lovely 'Mermaid' with yellow single blooms 5 to 6 in. across. In the South, favorites are the banksias which bear small yellow or white flowers.

ROSEMARY, BOG-, see BOG-ROSEMARY

ROSEMARY, CREEPING or DWARF. Two prostrate forms of rosemary carry this name in Zones 8 to 10, inclusive. One is *Rosemarinus officinalis* 'Prostratus.' The other is *R. officinalis* 'Lockwood de Forest' which is sometimes sold under the names of Santa Barbara Rosemary and *R. forresti*. Both grow 1 to 2 ft. high and 4 to 8 ft. wide. They are evergreen shrubs with narrow aromatic leaves and small clusters of light blue flowers in spring. Give them sun, poor soil, good drainage. Space them 3 to 5 ft. apart.

SALAL (*Gaultheria shallon*). This plant is found in Zones 6 to 9a, inclusive. A Pacific Coast native evergreen shrub, it has a spreading shape, oval leaves 2 to 4 in. long, and pink bell-form flowers. It likes acid soil. When grown in sun

the plant is only 1 to 2 ft. high; in shade, much taller. It is used by florists as cut foliage.

SARCOCOCCA, HOOKER (*Sarcococca hookeriana humilis*). This slow-growing evergreen shrub, Zones 6 to 10a, inclusive, has narrow leaves 2 to 3 in. long. It grows 1½ ft. high and spreads 8 ft. across. The shrub is excellent in shade and bears fragrant, inconspicuous flowers.

SEDUM or STONECROP. These are low-growing, fleshy-leaved succulents, mostly perennial. Some are tender, others cold-hardy. Many are creepers that root at every node, thus excellent for groundcovers.

Goldmoss Stonecrop (*Sedum acre*), Zones 4 through 9, creeps, spreads rapidly, and has pretty bright yellow flowers. It is invasive but easy to weed out. Plants should be set 12 in. apart.

SETCREASEA. These tender trailing perennials, 8 to 12 in. high, grow in Zones 9b and 10, and somewhat resemble wandering Jew, to which they are related. The one called 'Purple Queen' has leaves of a beautiful purple color and flowers that are small, 3-petaled, inconspicuous. It will grow in sun or part shade. Space the plants 8 in. apart.

SNOW-IN-SUMMER. See the chapter on perennials.

SPATHIPHYLLUM 'CLEVELANDI.' This tropical perennial grows 1½ to 2 ft. high with white callalike blooms, broadly lance-shaped leaves and thick roots. It likes shade. Space the plants 18 in. apart and propagate by dividing roots after the flowering season. In cold climates it is a house plant.

SPURGE, see PACHYSANDRA

STAR-JASMINE. See the chapter on vines.

STONECROP, see SEDUM

STRAWBERRY and STRAWBERRY-LIKE PLANTS. Strawberries that are most popular for groundcovers are wild types: American strawberry (*Fragaria vesca americana*), Zones 2b through 10; wild or sand strawberry (*Fragaria chiloensis*), Zones 6 through 10; and ornamental hybrid 25. They all have relatively small 3-parted semi-evergreen leaves, white flowers and delicious fruits. They cover ground rapidly by putting out runner plants and like sun or part shade. Space them 1 to 2 ft. apart.

Mock-Strawberry (*Duchesnea indica*) is found in Zones 6 to 10, inclusive. It resembles true strawberries but has less tidy growth, yellow flowers, and inedible fruit.

Barren- or False-Strawberry (*Waldsteinia fragarioides*) lives in Zones 5b to 10, inclusive. It is similar to the true strawberry but has yellow blooms and inedible fruit.

SWEET-FERN (*Comptonia peregrina*) This hairy, aromatic shrub is native to eastern states, Zones 2b to 8, inclusive. It usually grows about 3 ft. high in the acid soil it needs. The leaves are narrow, 4 to 5 in. long, and deep-cut like ferns. It is excellent for steep, dry, sunny banks, also rocky, sandy, or seaside places. It spreads by underground stems, making large clumps.

SWEET POTATO (*Ipomoea batatas*). This tropical morning-glory ancestor of the modern vegetable makes a long, trailing vine.

SYNGONIUM AURITUM. This creeper or climber does well in mild climates. Its leaves are fleshy, 6 to 10 in. long, with 3 to 5 segments. (See also the chapter on indoor plants.)

TARO VINE or POTHOS (*Scindapsus aureus*). This frost-tender climbing or creeping perennial has heart-shaped leaves mottled with yellow, and grows 6 to 18 in. long. It roots along stems and may be a house plant in cold climates. (See photo and data on pothos in the chapter on indoor plants.)

THYME (*Thymus*). These low, carpet-forming fragrant-leaved plants, Zones 5 to 10a, inclusive, can stand hot, dry, sunny places and poor soil. They tolerate quite a bit of walking upon so are good to grow among stepping stones, patio paving units, and sunny strips along curbs. These are the same plants you grow and use as herbs. There are many kinds, some with green leaves and others with gray or woolly foliage. The flowers are tiny, in red, lavender or white. To plant, tear the clumps into divisions and set them 10 to 12 in. apart.

TRACHELOSPERMUM. See JASMINE and JESSAMINE in the chapter on vines.

TWIN-FLOWER (*Linnaea borealis*). This trailing evergreen shrub, native to the Far North, grows 4 in. high with small, fragrant pink blooms in bell-shaped pairs. It likes acid soil and shade.

VIBURNUM DAVIDI. This evergreen shrub, Zone 7b and warmer, grows 2 to 3 ft. high and wide. It has large oval leaves 6 in. long with decoratively indented veins; small flowers; blue berries.

VINCA, MYRTLE or PERIWINKLE. Two of these trailing plants are used as groundcovers in sun or shade.

Vinca minor or Common Myrtle is found in Zones 5 to 10, inclusive. Its slender stems are covered with small glossy evergreen leaves. The flowers, in spring, are typically vivid blue, though there are varieties with white and purple flowers. The outstanding blue type is 'Bowles.' Roots form along the stems, and pieces cut off and planted in moist soil quickly become plants. Space these, or divisions, 12 in. apart.

Vinca major or Big-Leaf Periwinkle thrives in Zones 7 to 10, inclusive. It has long trailing stems. The leaves are oval, 2 in. long, and either glossily green or variegated green and white. The plants may become 2 ft. high. Their flowers are lavender-blue, 1 in. wide. These are good on banks or naturalized under trees, and in cold climates may be used as a summer window-box plant. Space them 12 in. apart.

WALKING-IRIS (*Neomarica gracilis*). This tropical iris-like plant has sword-shaped leaves 18 in. high held in open fan form, and fragrant blue and white iris-shaped flowers 2 in. across. Young plants develop where flowers were, bend to the ground, and root.

WANDERING JEW (*Zebrina pendula*). This succulent creeper, Zones 9b and 10, grows 6 in. high. Its leaves are green or white striped above and purple below. It needs shade and moist soil, spreads quickly and is easily propagated by cuttings. Space the plants 8 in. apart. In the North this is used for window gardens. (See the photo in the chapter on indoor plants.)

WEDELIA (*W. trilobata*). This trailing perennial,

8 in. high with glossy evergreen leaves and small yellow daisylike flowers, does well in frost-free climates. It grows rapidly in sun or part shade and tolerates salt spray. Space plants 8 in. apart. A native of southern Florida, this is one of the invasive groundcovers.

WILD GINGER *(Asarum)*. These handsome native American woodland plants are hardy north through Zone 4. They grow 6 in. high, with heart-shaped leaves 2 to 5 in. across, above creeping root stalks. Their odd-shaped flowers hide beneath the leaves. They are good for shady places, preferably moist. *Asarum canadense,* native to the eastern U.S., loses its leaves in winter. British Columbia Wild Ginger *(A. caudatum)* and European Wild Ginger *(A. europaeum)* are evergreen, and thus preferable. Space the plants 8 in. apart. Propagate them by dividing clumps of root stalks.

WINTERCREEPER. See the chapter on vines.

WOOD-SAGE *(Teucrium canadense)*. This native perennial herb is hardy north through Zone 5 and grows 1 to 2½ ft. high. Its leaves are lance-shaped, 3 in. long, white beneath. The flowers, carried in 6-in. spikes, are small, tubular, cream to purplish-pink.

YELLOW-ROOT *(Xanthorhiza simplicissima)*. This 24 in.-high suckering shrub, native to the eastern U. S., is hardy as far north as Zone 4. Its foliage, composed of 5 deep-cut leaflets on a long stalk, are carried on top of erect stems. The autumn foliage color is brilliant orange-yellow. It grows in sun or shade, but is best in moist, shady places. Space the plants 18 to 24 in. apart.

ZOYSIA *(Z. japonica)*. This coarse-leaved warm-climate grass spreads by runners. These in turn bind and protect the soil.

Star-jasmine, with fragrant white flowers, may be used as vine or groundcover. Robert Jones garden, Modesto, California. Thomas Church & Associates, landscape architects

6

〰〰〰〰〰〰〰〰〰〰〰〰〰〰〰〰〰〰〰〰〰〰〰〰〰〰〰〰〰〰

Vines for Beauty and Cover-up

Vines lend a distinctive touch to your landscaping and there are types to fit many purposes. They can decorate or conceal a wall, fence or eyesore. They can provide shade, either quickly with annuals grown from seed or more slowly, but permanently, with long-lived perennials. Some vines have handsome flowers while others are grown primarily for their attractive foliage. Several are among the best groundcovers for hillsides, to stop erosion and to save you the hazard and chore of mowing grass on an incline. In small yards, where space for planting is limited, vines are especially handy because they are "airborne"; they take very little ground space and also can be trained flat. For a boundary-line planting, for instance, vines on a fence take only about 6 in. of width, while shrubs tall enough to give the same amount of privacy attain a minimum width of 4 to 6 ft.

In choosing the best vines for your yard, consider first the reasons you want to use them. Then check the vine list for your region, in this chapter, and the descriptions that follow, including hardiness zones.

How Vines Climb

The ways in which vines tend upward determine the supports you fix for them. Some have slender tendrils which coil around string, rope or wire. These include clematis, sweet pea, passion-flower and gourd. Others cling to masonry or the rough bark of trees with rootlike holdfasts along their stems, or by disks at the ends of tendrils. Among these are wintercreeper, philodendron, creeping fig, Boston ivy, climbing hydrangea, English ivy and trumpet-creeper. Twiners—whose stems go around and around a support—include wisteria, akebia, morning-glory, bittersweet, star-jasmine, honeysuckle and silver lace-vine. A few plants treated as vines have no built-in method of climbing. They have long, arching stems that must be fastened to uprights or interwoven. These include climbing roses, jasmines, creeping lantana and ivy geranium.

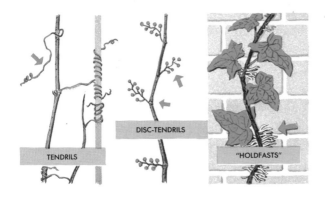

When To Plant

Seed-sowing time for annual vines, and the tender perennials grown as annuals, is given in the chart for annual vines in this chapter.

Perennial vines are set out like shrubs. Those that are container-grown may be planted at any time. Dormant, bare-root vines are generally planted in mild-winter climates during late fall, winter or early spring; in Zones 6 and 7, either during late autumn or early spring; in Zones 5 and north, in the spring.

How To Plant

Most perennial vines are deep-rooted, and since the amount and quality of top growth will depend upon the condition of the roots, it is well to make them happy. So dig a hole much larger and deeper than the plant's present root system. If your soil is not good, remove it, and as you set the plant, fill in with good topsoil, or soil into which you have mixed moist peat moss. Place the vine so its relation to ground level is the same as it was when growing in the nursery. (Any exceptions are noted in the descriptions of vines in the alphabetical listing.) Firm the earth well among and around the roots, then water. It is neither necessary nor desirable to feed at planting time. Hold off until the plant is growing actively. In later years fertilize at least annually, preferably just before the main burst of growth in spring.

Supports and Fastenings

Be sure your vine has something to climb, that this support fits the plant's method of pulling upward, and that it is sturdy enough to bear the weight of the full-grown vine.

Often young vines need to be guided toward their support, and helpfully fastened to it while they get the idea and catch hold. With tendril bearers, slender stakes or twiggy brush poked into the ground at the base of the plant, and slanted to lead to the strings or wires, will do the job. For woody perennial twiners, such as wisteria, you can tie the branches into position. Vines being trained on walls of masonry or wood need the most aid. On wood you can use screw eyes for anchor units. For concrete, stone or brick, buy small devices that can be cemented to the wall. They consist of small disks in which hairpinlike wires are imbedded. The wires are bent about the vine.

Material for tying should always be soft, such as cloth, raffia or plastic-coated wire. Never tie tightly, for as stems increase in size the binding can constrict the flow of food and cut and injure the plant. Check the ties occasionally to make sure they are not tight.

Trellises on walls should preferably be several inches out, so air can circulate behind them. It is wise to build or install them so they can be loosened at the top and folded down when necessary to get behind for painting. The more simple they are in pattern, the more quietly harmonious with the wall.

About Pruning

The best time to prune specific vines is given in the descriptive lists that follow. For general instructions and techniques, see the chapter on pruning, and treat vines as though they were a type of shrub.

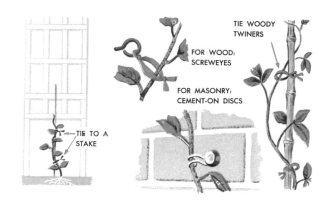

❧ Annual Vines, and Some Perennials Often Grown as Annuals

These are all easy to grow from seed. Some are dainty and grown primarily for ornament or flowers. Others will give you hurry-up shade over a window or patio, or cover a fence to give you privacy.

Name	Height	Sow Seed	Description
Balloon-Vine (*Cardiospermum*)	5-10 ft.	Outdoors, when warm	Grown primarily for ornament. Leaves oval. Flowers small, in clusters, followed by papery, puffy balloons 1″ across. Stands heat and drought.
Black-eyed Susan (*Thunbergia alata*)	8 ft.	Outdoors, when warm	Dainty twining or trailing vine. Arrow-shaped leaves. 1½″ flowers in yellow, orange, white, often with black centers. Used in window boxes; hanging baskets.
Canary-Bird-Flower (*Tropaeolum peregrinum*)	8 ft.	Outdoors, when warm	Dainty nasturtium relative with finger-like leaves. Yellow 1″ blooms resemble birds with open wings.
Cardinal-Climber (*Quamoclit sloteri*)	20 ft.	Outdoors, when warm	Trumpet-shaped 2″-long flowers, scarlet with white throat. Deep-lobed leaves. Climbs by twining. Dainty.
Cup-and-Saucer (*Cobaea scandens*)	10 ft.	Indoors, or outdoors when warm	Purple or white bell-shaped blooms 2″ across. Start indoors North, outdoors South. Climbs by tendrils arising from tips of multiparted leaves.

Name	Height	Sow Seed	Description
Cypress-Vine (*Quamoclit pennata*)	20 ft.	Outdoors, when warm	Similar to cardinal-climber (see above), but with leaves more fernlike. 1½" trumpet-shaped scarlet, orange or white flowers. Sun or part shade.
Gourd	20 ft.	Outdoors, when warm	Easiest-to-grow, large-leaved vine for quick cover. Flowers white or yellow and large. Interesting fruits develop in summer for fall decoration.
Hop, Japanese (*Humulus japonicus*)	30 ft.	Outdoors, when warm	Dense foliage for screening purposes. Leaves 5" to 7" across, lobed, rough-textured. Variegated white and green form available. Sun or part shade. Likes heat.
Morning-Glory (*Ipomoea*)	15 ft.	Outdoors, when warm	Quick-growing. Large, usually heart-shaped leaves give good cover. Flowers pink, blue, white, red; single or double. Open mornings and cloudy days.
Nasturtium (*Tropaeolum majus*)	8 ft.	Outdoors, when warm	Trailer or climber with attractive round leaves, fragrant yellow, orange or red flowers. For details see alphabetical list of annuals.
Sweet Pea (*Lathyrus odoratus*)	6 ft.	Outdoors, fall or spring	Grown primarily for its flowers, fragrant, in many colors. For details see alphabetical list of annuals.

🍂 The Best Perennial Vines, Recommended by Regions

For descriptions, hardiness ratings and culture, see alphabetical lists that follow:

Northeast	Midwest	Plains and Intermountain
Akebia	Akebia	American Bitter-Sweet
Baby Wintercreeper	Baltic Ivy	*Clematis jackmani*
Baltic Ivy	Boston Ivy	Climbing Roses, hardy kinds
Boston Ivy 'Lowi'	*Clematis lawsoniana*	Dutchmans-Pipe
Bower Actinidia	'Henryi'	Englemann Ivy
Chinese Wisteria	Climbing Hydrangea	Hall's Japanese Honeysuckle
Climbing Hydrangea	*Euonymous fortunei*	Japanese Wisteria
Euonymous fortunei	*vegetus*	Purpleleaf Wintercreeper
vegetus	Porcelain Ampelopsis	Silver Lace-Vine
Hybrid Clematis	Purpleleaf Wintercreeper	Trumpet-Vine
Sweet Autumn Clematis	Sweet Autumn Clematis	
	Trumpet-Vine	

Upper South	Deep South	Southwest*
Boston Ivy 'Lowi'	Allamanda	Algerian Ivy
Carolina Yellow Jessamine	Bougainvillea	Bougainvillea
Climbing Roses	Carolina Yellow Jessamine	Carolina Yellow Jessamine
Cross-Vine	Chinese Wisteria	Cats-Claw
English Ivy	Coral-Vine	Coral-Vine
Japanese Wisteria	Flame-Vine	Creeping Fig
Muscadine Grape	Lavender Trumpet-Vine	English Ivy
Sweet Autumn Clematis	Star-Jasmine	Hall's Japanese Honeysuckle
Trumpet-Creeper 'Madame Galen'	Trumpet Honeysuckle	Passion-Vine
Wintercreeper varieties	Trumpet-Vine	Star-Jasmine

Pacific Northwest	Northern California	Southern California
Bluecrown Passion-Flower	Akebia	Boston Ivy 'Veitchi'
Boston Ivy	Bluecrown Passion-Flower	*Bougainvillea glabra* vars.
Chinese Actinidia	Clematis, Large-Flowered	Cape-Honeysuckle
Clematis jackmani and others	Evergreen Clematis	Carolina Yellow Jessamine
Climbing Hydrangea	*Fatshedera lizei*	Chinese Wisteria
English Ivy varieties	Hall's Japanese Honeysuckle	Kangaroo-Vine
Evergreen Clematis	Japanese Wisteria	Lavender Trumpet-Vine
Japanese Wisteria	*Pileostegia viburnoides*	Passion-Vine
Silver Lace-Vine	Primrose Jasmine	Potato-Vine
Trumpet-Vine	Star- or Confederate-Jasmine	Wonga-Wonga Vine

Hawaii	Alaska
Allamanda	Annual vines such as Scarlet
Bougainvillea spectabilis	Runner Bean make fantastic
Jade-Vine	growth during the summer.
Jasminum gracillimum	
Madagascar-Jasmine	
Norantea guineensis	
Spray-of-Gold	
Tecomanthe dendrophila	
Thunbergia mysorensis	
Wax-Plant	

* In the Southwest, Zones 5 and 6, use Plains and Intermountain list.

❧ Hardy Vines You Can Grow

ACTINIDIA. These deciduous rapid-growing twiners reach 30 ft., and are used for their handsome, shade-providing foliage. They respond to sun or shade. Their flowers, borne on 2-year wood, are inconspicuous, followed by edible plum-shaped fruits 1 to 2 in. long. Male and female appear on separate plants so you must have both types to get fruit.

A. arguta, Bower Actinidia or Tara-Vine, is hardy north through Zone 6. It has glossy, oval leaves 5 in. long on red stems. The fruit is sweet.

A. chinensis, Chinese Actinidia or Yangtao, does best in mild climates but is hardy through Zone 7b. Its leaves are 5 to 7 in. long, white beneath. Young growth is covered with attractive red hairs. The fruit has a gooseberry flavor.

AKEBIA, FIVELEAF (*A. quinata*). In Zones 5b to 9, inclusive, this is a rapid-growing semi-evergreen twiner reaching 12 to 30 ft. Though dainty-looking, its vigor makes this vine useful as a groundcover. It casts light shade or makes attractive patterns on fence or wall. Leaves have 5 fingerlike parts. Small flowers, purple and fragrant, are sometimes followed by purple fruit pods 4 in. long. Sun or shade is acceptable.

ALLAMANDA (*A. cathartica* and variety *hendersoni*). This evergreen, a rapid-growing, shrubby twiner for Zones 9b and 10, reaches 10 to 40 ft. Its leaves are glossy and thick, 6 in. long; the flowers yellow, flaring, bell-shaped with white throats, bloom during summer. It likes sun and light, rich, well-drained soil. In sandy ground, feed this vine frequently. No part of the plant should be eaten.

AMPELOPSIS, PORCELAIN (*Ampelopsis brevipedunculata*). This rapid-growing vine, climbing by tendrils to 20 ft., thrives in Zones 5b to 8, inclusive. It is used for shade; also for its attractive berries, which are carried in clusters and which change color from pale lavender to green and then bright turquoise blue. The leaves are 3-lobed, 5 in. long. The flowers are inconspicuous. It will grow in either sun or shade.

BAGNIT, see SPRAY-OF-GOLD

BITTER-SWEET, AMERICAN (*Celastrus scandens*). This deciduous rapid-growing native trails or climbs 20 ft. or more by twining. It is vigorous in Zones 3 to 8, inclusive, and does well in sun or part shade. The foliage gives dense cover in summer; in autumn turns yellow and falls. Clusters of small, bright orange and red berries hang on through winter and are eaten by birds— or you can pick them for winter bouquets. To be sure to get fruit, set out several plants, because male and female flowers are usually on separate plants and you must have both. Pruning time for vines is late winter or very early spring, since flowers and fruit are produced on new growth that emerges in spring. When used as a groundcover, scythe back to 1½ ft. each year in spring. Remember, this vine is invasive, and the roots are difficult to eradicate!

BITTER-SWEET, EVERGREEN, see WINTER-CREEPER

BOUGAINVILLEA. *B. spectabilis* varieties grow in Zone 10; *B. glabra* varieties are hardier, doing well into Zone 9.

These are woody, spiny vines climbing 15 to 25 ft. by twining. Their leaves are oval, 3 in. long, and the spectacular floral display covers the plants. The true flowers are inconspicuous but are surrounded by 3 showy, petal-like bracts. Different varieties come in pink, red, purple, gold or salmon.

Give these vines sun and well-drained soil. They resent having their roots disturbed, so buy container-grown plants and set them with soil intact about the roots. These plants may delay blooming while growing vigorously. They flower best when roots are confined and growth not rampant. Prune them heavily after each period of flowering.

New dwarf varieties are excellent in containers. For instructions on growing bougainvillea as house plants, see the chapter on indoor gardens.

CAPE-HONEYSUCKLE (*Tecomaria capensis*). This vine, grown in Zones 9b and 10, is vigorous, shrubby and sprawling; it needs support and training to reach 15 to 25 ft. Its evergreen leaves are made up of pairs of leaflets along a central stem. The flowers are tubular, orange-red, 2 in. long in clusters. Give it sun and considerable space, and prune each year right after flowering. This vine is good to espalier.

CAROLINA YELLOW JESSAMINE, see JASMINE

CATS-CLAW or YELLOW TRUMPET-VINE (*Doxantha unguis-cati*). This is sometimes sold under its former name, *Bignonia tweediana*. It is a rampant fast-grower in Zones 8b and warmer; evergreen in mild-winter climates. Showy flowers blooming in spring are bright yellow tinged with orange, and shaped like flaring trumpets, 3 in. long and 4 in. across. The leaves are 2-parted with a clawlike tendril. This vine climbs 25 to 40 ft. on masonry or wood by clinging. It likes sun, heat, poor soil, and resists drought and wind. The root is tuberous; the fruit a pod 12 in. long. Prune severely each year after flowering.

CLEMATIS. These vines are grown primarily for their fabulous flowers, which may be small or large, white, pink, yellow, red, blue or purple.

They like a location in sun, except in hot climates where they need some shade. Roots should always be cool, so plan to shade the base of the vines with low-growing plants. A mulch also helps. Soil should be rich, fast-draining and neutral or alkaline. If yours is acid, work some lime into it before planting, and add a handful yearly. For suggestions, see the chapter on soils. Planting can be done in autumn or early spring. Set these so the crown (where roots and top meet) is 3 in. below soil level. Then tie the stem to a support at once, so it will not be broken from the crown. The clematis vines pull themselves upward by an unusual method, using their leaf stems as tendrils. They must have a support on which to climb, and generous watering. Do not expect much growth or flowering the first year.

Clematis armandi, Evergreen Clematis, in Zones 7b to 10, inclusive, grows 15 to 25 ft. with slender, glossy leaves 4 to 6 in. long. Early spring flowers are white, starlike, 1 to 2½ in. across and wonderfully fragrant. Prune annually right after flowering, cutting out the oldest stems, and thinning those that crowd or cover under layers. Do not let seed heads form.

Large-flowered species and hybrids include *C. jackmani, C. lanuginosa, C. lawsoniana* 'Henryi,' etc. Most of these are hardy north through Zone 4 and noted for spectacular blooms 6 to 7 in. across, wonderful in the garden and for picking. The vines are deciduous; some grow only 6 to 8 ft. high, while others extend 20 ft. In cold climates they usually die to the ground in winter. Most of them bloom on new shoots that emerge in spring, and for best results should be pruned severely each winter before new growth starts. Cut them back 2 to 3 ft. above ground or at least thin out the branches.

Sweet Autumn Clematis (*C. dioscoreifolia,* frequently sold as *C. paniculata*), thrives in Zones 4 to 9, inclusive. It is a semi-evergreen, vigorous grower to 30 ft. The fragrant, star-shaped white flowers, 1 to 1½ in. across, bloom in profusion in late summer and early autumn. Decorative, fluffy seed heads follow. Bloom is on new growth so vines can be pruned in late winter if desired.

CONFEDERATE-JASMINE, see JASMINE

CORAL-VINE or MEXICAN-CREEPER (*Antigonon leptopus*) This vine is used in Zones 9 and 10. It is favored for its prolific flowers, small and pink in trailing sprays. It grows to 40 ft., climbing by tendrils at tips of its heart-shaped evergreen leaves. The root is tuberous, and the plant fairly slow to develop. Give heat, sun, and soil that is well-drained and not very rich. Water during bloom time but not during the dormant period. Prune severely each winter. This is easy to grow from seed, and tubers can be divided.

CROSS-VINE (*Bignonia capreolata*). In Zones 7 to 10, inclusive, this rapid-growing native of southeastern states climbs 50 ft. into treetops. It is an evergreen, with leaves turning reddish in fall and winter. The flowers are tubular, red-orange, 1½ to 2 in. long, and appear in early spring. It clings to, and climbs, rough surfaces by tendrils that have adhesive disks. Though it grows in sun or shade, it prefers rich soil and moisture. Blooms come on new growth, Prune in late winter, shortening the branches.

DUTCHMANS-PIPE (*Aristolochia durior*). This vigorous twiner is a deciduous vine with huge, heart-shaped leaves (8 to 16 in.) that give dense shade. It grows to 30 ft. in Zones 5 to 9, inclusive. Inconspicuous brown flowers are shaped like little curved pipes. It is slow to start, then rapid-growing, in sun or shade.

EUONYMOUS, see WINTERCREEPER

FATSHEDERA LIZEI or BOTANICAL WONDER. This evergreen shrubby vine grows 8 to 10 ft. high in Zones 8, 9 and 10. It is a hybrid between the shrub *Fatsia japonica* and the English ivy vine. The leaves are glossy, shaped like ivy, 6 to 8 in. across. It does best in shade; tolerates heat, dry air, and brief exposure to temperatures near zero; and needs ample water. This is an excellent indoor or patio plant.

FIG, CREEPING (*Ficus pumila*). In tropical and subtropical climates, or indoors, this rapid-growing evergreen makes a quick, flat cover on masonry walls. It prefers part shade and climbs 20 to 60 ft. by roots along stems. There are two types of foliage. The juvenile leaves are dainty, heart-shaped, 1 in. long. Later, as the vine matures and branches grow out from the wall, foliage is larger and coarse. An annual shearing keeps these side branches under control.

FLAME-VINE (*Pyrostegia ignea*). This grows in tropical or warm subtropical climates, Zones 9b and warmer. It is a high-climbing (25 to 70 ft.), woody evergreen with spectacular floral display. The blossoms are orange-red, tubular, 2 to 3 in. long, in huge clusters during the winter. In some localities they bloom a second time in summer. The leaves are 2- or 3-parted with tendrils that cling to stone or wood. It likes rich soil and resents dry air and freezing. Though slow to start, it grows rapidly. Prune the vine heavily after flowering.

FLEECE-VINE, CHINA, or SILVER LACE-VINE (*Polygonum auberti*). This is a vine for quick results in Zones 5 to 10, inclusive. It is a vigorous grower, often extending 20 to 30 ft. in one season, climbing by twining. It likes sun; tolerates wind. The flowers are profuse, tiny and white, borne in showy lacey clusters. In mild-winter climates the vine is evergreen and blossoms occur almost all summer. In cold climates the tops winterkill and in spring are cut back to live wood or the ground; masses of new shoots arise from the roots and begin to bloom in late summer and continue through autumn. The leaves are heart-shaped and glossy.

GRAPE, MUSCADINE. See the chapter on fruits.

HONEYSUCKLE, CAPE-, see CAPE-HONEYSUCKLE

HONEYSUCKLE, HALL'S JAPANESE (*Lonicera japonica halliana*). In Zones 5b to 9, inclusive, this tough, vigorous, rampant vine may be used as a climber or as a groundcover for difficult hillsides. It responds to sun or shade. The leaves are evergreen in the South, semi-evergreen in the North. Flowers are white, fading to yellow, intensely fragrant. As a groundcover it roots wherever stems touch soil and can become an invasive pest. There is an attractive variegated form with yellow-netted leaves that is not as rampant as the regular form. Space plants for groundcover use (single shoots with roots) 2 ft. apart, or larger clumps 3 ft. apart.

HONEYSUCKLE, TRUMPET or CORAL (*Lonicera sempervirens*). This woody evergreen or semi-evergreen twining vine succeeds in Zones 4b to 9, inclusive, and is native to eastern states. It can grow to 40 ft. The flowers are showy, trumpet-shaped, red lined with yellow, 2 in. long, nonfragrant. It grows in sun or shade, sometimes troubled with aphids.

HYDRANGEA, CLIMBING (*Hydrangea petiolaris*). This deciduous vine climbs by rootlets along its stem and thrives in Zones 5 to 9a, inclusive. It can climb tall trees or clothe masonry walls, but should not be used on wooden structures since the rootlike holdfasts are destructive. The leaves are heart-shaped, 2 to 4 in. long. The flowers are showy white, in flat clusters 6 to 10 in. across. It is slow to establish but then durable, in sun or part shade. Do any pruning or shaping in winter or very early spring.

IVY, ALGERIAN (*Hedera canariensis*). Grown in Zones 8, 9, and 10, it looks and behaves like a giant form of English ivy. The leaves are 5 to 8 in. wide, solid green or variegated green and white. In sun, and where summers are hot, it does better than English ivy. For groundcover use, plant 15 to 18 in. apart.

IVY, BOSTON or JAPANESE CREEPER (*Parthenocissus tricuspidata*). This deciduous dense-growing vine, with glossy 3-lobed leaves 8 in. wide, grows rapidly in Zones 5 to 9, inclusive. It clings to masonry and climbs by adhesive disks at tips of tendrils. It may reach 60 ft. in length. The flowers are inconspicuous, but the bluish-black berries are attractive in autumn. Foliage turns brilliant scarlet in autumn in cold-winter climates.

Small-leaved forms are 'Lowi,' with foliage only 1½ in. across, and 'Veitchi,' whose leaves are purple when young.

IVY, ENGLEMANN (*Parthenocissus quinquefolia englemanni*). Growing in Zones 3 to 10, inclusive, this is an improved variety of the native Virginia creeper or woodbine, with similar though smaller 5-parted leaves. Its foliage turns bright red in autumn. Deciduous, vigorous, graceful, it climbs high by tendrils with adhesive tips.

IVY, ENGLISH (*Hedera helix*). Thriving in Zones 6 to 10, inclusive, this evergreen has roots along stems that cling to masonry or tree trunks. It can extend to 40 ft. The leaves, 3-lobed, may be tiny or 4 in. across, depending on the variety. Self-branching types are especially good as groundcovers. It will grow in sun where summers are cool; elsewhere plant in a shady location. One of the hardiest varieties is 'Baltic.' It will survive in Zone 5b if kept on the ground on the north side of the house, or in shade and protected from winter sun. Leaves may discolor in winter but new ones will replace them in spring; old tops can be sheared. Start from plants or rooted cuttings.

For groundcover use, space 12 to 24 in. apart. If young plants have a single stem, cut back to 3 leaves in spring or summer, to induce branching. It needs 2 years to cover and will grow 12 in. high. The foliage and berries are poisonous if eaten.

JADE-VINE (*Strongylodon macrobotrys*). This is a vigorous, tropical vine with jade-green sweet-pea-type flowers in drooping clusters through spring and summer. It likes moist, loamy soil; sun or part shade.

JAPANESE CREEPER, see IVY, BOSTON

JASMINES, JESSAMINES and JASMINE-LIKE VINES. Several flowering vines familiarly called jasmine or jessamine are not true jasmines, though they are similar in appearance and fragrance. To make it easier for you to compare them, and straighten out their names, we have grouped "true" and similarly-named kinds together here. Only one true jasmine (*Jasminum*) is included.

Carolina Yellow Jessamine (*Gelsemium sempervirens*). This graceful evergreen vine, native to the South, grows in Zones 7b to 10, inclusive. Glossy leaves 4 in. long are carried in pairs on slender, swaying branches. Flowers appear very early in spring, bright yellow, trumpet-shaped, 1 to 1½ in. long, fragrant. This vine prefers a partly shaded spot. The blossoms, leaves and root are poisonous if eaten.

Madagascar-Jasmine (*Stephanotis floribunda*) does well in frost-free climates or indoors. It is an evergreen with thick, glossy oval leaves 4 in. long, and fragrant, trumpet-shaped white flowers 1 to 2 in. long in clusters during summer.

Pinwheel Jasmine (*Jasminum gracillimum*) is for mild climates. An arching evergreen vine-shrub, it has oval leaves 2 in. long and fragrant white flowers 1 in. across in dense, hanging clusters in late winter and early spring.

Star- or Confederate-Jasmine (*Trachelospermum jasminoides*) thrives in Zones 8b to 10, inclusive. It is a slender-stemmed evergreen that climbs high by twining. The flowers are small white trumpets with twisted petals, 1 in. across, very fragrant, in loose clusters in spring. The leaves are small and waxy. This vine likes part shade and moist soil. It is slow-growing when young. You may use it as a vine, pot plant, shrub or groundcover. For the latter three it should be cut back each year right after flowering to induce branching. Yellow star- or Japanese star-jasmine (*Trachelospermum asiaticum*, often sold as *Rhynchospermum asiaticum*), grows in Zones 7 to 10, inclusive.

KANGAROO-VINE *(Cissus antarctica)*. This flourishes in frost-free climates or indoors. It is an evergreen with shiny leaves 3 to 4 in. long, climbing to 10 ft. by tendrils. It likes sun or part shade, and is grown for its attractive foliage.

MADAGASCAR-JASMINE, see JASMINE

MEXICAN-CREEPER, see CORAL-VINE

NORANTEA GUINEENSIS. This shrubby vine has spectacular clusters of orange flowers (bracts). Its leaves are leathery, 4 in. long. It likes full sun and grows rank in average soil.

PASSION-FLOWER *(Passiflora)*. These vines are fast-growing climbers using tendrils to rise 20 to 35 ft. Their flowers are intricate and fabulously beautiful. The branches are slender, with evergreen leaves. They like sun and can be grown as house plants in northern climates. If grown indoors, move them into the ground outdoors for summer. There they will grow extensively and bloom. Then when autumn nears, take stem cuttings from your vine, root them in water, and pot them for your window garden. Among the best varieties for outdoor vines are the ones listed here.

Bluecrown Passion-Flower *(P. caerulea)*. This thrives in Zones 7b and warmer. The flowers are 3 in. wide, pale pink, white or blue with a central crown tipped in blue; slightly fragrant. The leaves are 5-lobed, 4 to 7 in. wide. Its rampant growth makes it a good groundcover.

Passion-Vine *(P. alato-caerulea or P. pfordti)*. This hybrid has 3-lobed leaves and flowers 4 in. across, white with pink on inside of petals; crown white marked with purple and blue. They are slightly fragrant. This one tolerates more cold than *caerulea*, and in Columbus, Ohio is root-hardy in a protected spot.

PILEOSTEGIA VIBURNOIDES. In Zone 8 and warmer this tall evergreen vine grows to 45 ft. in a manner resembling climbing hydrangea. The leaves are 3 to 6 in. long. The flowers are white, appearing in profuse clusters in late summer and fall. It prefers shade.

POTATO-VINE *(Solanum jasminoides)*. This evergreen or semi-evergreen twiner grows rapidly to 30 ft. in Zones 9b and warmer. The leaves

are 1½ in. long, some lobed and some plain. The flowers are profuse and dainty, 1 in. wide, star-shaped, white flushed with blue, growing in clusters. It can be grown in sun or shade. Prune severely in late fall.

QUEENS WREATH *(Petrea volubilis)*. This is an evergreen, woody-stemmed twining vine, growing to 20 ft. high in Zones 9b and 10. The flowers are purple-blue, funnel-form, 1 in. across, in clusters 5 to 8 in. long, borne mostly in spring. The leaves are large and rough.

RHYNCHOSPERMUM, see JASMINE, STAR-

ROSES, CLIMBING. See the chapter on roses.

SILVER LACE-VINE, see FLEECE-VINE

SPRAY-OF-GOLD or BAGNIT *(Tristellateia australasiae)*. This long woody vine has smooth, pointed leaves 2 to 4 in. in length. Its flowers, yellow with red centers, 1 in. in diameter, are borne in clusters of 10 to 15. It grows in full sun and will withstand dry, poor soil. The vine does well on median fences on freeways in Honolulu.

STAR-JASMINE, see JASMINE

TARA-VINE, see ACTINIDIA

TECOMANTHE DENDROPHILA. This woody vine has inconspicuous foliage but good tubular rose-pink flowers 3 to 4 in. long. It is used on tree trunks in partial shade in Hawaii.

THUNBERGIA MYSORENSIS. This vine has large clusters of yellow flowers 2 in. across, with purple tubes 1½ in. long. Its leaves are 4 to 6 in. in length. It grows to 15 ft. and likes good soil with full sun.

TRUMPET-VINE *(Campsis radicans)*. In Zones 4b to 9, inclusive, this vine grows to 40 ft. or more, clinging to masonry or wood with rootlike holdfasts. It is vigorous, rampant, and difficult to control. The flowers are orange-red trumpets, 3 in. long, growing in clusters. The plant is woody and can be trained as a clipped vine, hedge or "tree." Blooms appear on new growth, and main pruning should be done immediately after flowering. Keep root suckers removed.

'Madame Galen' *(Campsis x tagliabuana)* is a

hybrid, with salmon-red flowers larger and showier than the ordinary trumpet-vine.

TRUMPET-VINE, LAVENDER or PAINTED (*Clytostoma callistegioides*). This strong, rapid-growing evergreen in Zone 9 and warmer, has lovely, profuse lavender trumpet-flowers in pairs at the ends of branches in spring. Its blooms are 2 to 5 in. long, 2 to 3 in. wide. The vine likes sun or part shade, fertile soil and heat. It climbs by leaf tendrils and twining, and roots wherever stems touch moist soil. It is sometimes sold by its former name, *Bignonia speciosa*.

TRUMPET-VINE, YELLOW, see CATS-CLAW

WAX-PLANT (*Hoya carnosa*). This evergreen is grown outdoors in tropical or subtropical climates, and as a house plant elsewhere. Outdoors it likes part shade and climbs 10 to 25 ft., either by clinging with rootlets on its stems or by twining. For description, illustration and data on how to grow indoors, see the chapter on indoor plants.

WINTERCREEPER (*Euonymus fortunei*). In Zones 5 to 9a, inclusive, these broadleaf evergreen vines will grow on the ground or cling and climb on masonry or trees. They produce roots along their stems, and are good to bind soil. They grow in sun or shade but hold foliage in winter best if out of sun. For groundcover use, space them 18 in. apart. They are slow to start, but when established grow vigorously. The plants can be clipped or sheared. They are susceptible to infestations of scale. Here are the most useful varieties.

Baby Wintercreeper (*E. fortunei minimus*) has tiny leaves ½ in. long. It is slow-growing and can be used for small spaces.

E. fortunei radicans has green leaves 1 in. long.

Evergreen Bitter-sweet or Bigleaf Wintercreeper (*E. fortunei vegetus*) has glossy, rounded leaves 1 to 1½ in. across. It is shrubby and in the fall bears colorful fruit similar to that of bitter-sweet.

Purpleleaf Wintercreeper (*E. fortunei coloratus*) has leaves 1½ in. long, dark green in summer and purplish-red autumn and winter. It is extra hardy, thriving into Zone 4b.

WISTERIA. These rampant, woody deciduous vines climb by twining to 50 ft. in Zones 5b to 9, inclusive. Trunks can become enormous and heavy, so the vines need a strong support. The fragrant flowers, shaped like pea blossoms, are grouped in long, drooping clusters. They are usually lavender, but sometimes white or pink, and come in early spring before the leaves unfurl.

There are two main kinds. Chinese wisteria (*W. sinensis*) has flower clusters 7 to 14 in. long, and all the florets open simultaneously. Japanese wisteria (*W. floribunda*) is slightly hardier, and its bloom clusters, 8 to 36 in. long, open progressively. The florets nearest the stem open first, and those at the tip are last.

Plant wisterias in a sunny place, for best bloom. While plants are young, encourage them to grow rapidly by watering generously and feeding a complete fertilizer in spring. No pruning is needed until the vine has covered the desired space. Later, feed sparingly and avoid fertilizers with a high nitrogen content that would encourage leaves instead of flowers. Water well and prune severely each year. Since the blossom clusters develop on new shoots that emerge from wood of the previous season, pruning is done just after the flowering period. Shorten new shoots—those with green rather than brown wood—so that each has 2 to 3 leaves. Continue heading back excess growth until August.

If you would like to grow a wisteria in tree form, you can buy a plant already trained. Otherwise you can develop your own tree by tying a vine to a stake, removing side branches, and cutting off the top at the desired height before growth starts in spring.

"Seeds and pods are poisonous if eaten."

WONGA-WONGA VINE (*Pandorea pandorana*). In tropical and subtropical climates this shrubby evergreen vine climbs to 30 ft. by twining. It has luxuriant foliage composed of 3 to 9 leaflets each, resembling those of roses. Flowers, carried in clusters, are ¾ in. long, trumpet-form, pale yellow with throats spotted in violet. It blooms in early spring and requires sun, except in hot areas where part shade is needed.

YANGTAO, see ACTINIDIA

OPPOSITE:
Wisteria vine is shown in the garden of
landscape architect Ethelbert Furlong
in New Jersey. Notice that it is kept off
of the house, and on strong supports.

Dutchmans-pipe is a big-leaved, vigorous, cold-hardy, fine vine with which to
get dense shade or to hide something.
Flowers are inconspicuous. Photographed in Rochester, N. Y.

English ivy can easily be trained to go
where you wish it, as in this charming
point of interest on the fence at the Bill
Wheaton home, Claremont, California.

Evergreen bittersweet or bigleaf wintercreeper climbs by root-like holdfasts
along its stems. As a groundcover, it
roots where branches touch moist soil.
Shown in Ann Arbor, Michigan

ORNAMENTAL AND USEFUL
PERENNIAL VINES

7

‧‧

Trees for Shade and Ornament

The best tree for you depends upon the purpose for which you want it, as well as climate, for different trees fill different needs. There are majestically tall trees to provide high shade, lower ones for smaller situations, flowering sorts whose blooms turn them into giant bouquets each springtime, some with leaves that turn brilliant in autumn, and many with evergreen foliage that looks handsome in winter and can provide protection from cold wind. They grow at different rates of speed. Some develop so slowly that it takes them many years to become full size, while others mature fairly rapidly.

Leaves vary in size and shape, and also in the amount of shade that they cast. Some trees have such heavy foliage that it is almost impossible to maintain a lawn beneath them, while others allow either grass or flowers. Roots may be deep, or at the soil's surface where they get into your flower beds or clog your tile lines. Since trees are such a permanent part of your planting, and will affect your way of life as well as the appearance of your property, choose each one thoughtfully and plan its placement carefully. For help on where to locate your trees, see the chapter on landscaping.

Time To Plant

In mild-winter climates, planting can be done most safely during the winter months when trees are nearly dormant, although potted or canned trees can be set out at any time.

In the mid-section of the country, Zones 6 and 7, deciduous trees may be moved bare-root, either before growth starts in the spring or after plants become more or less dormant in the late autumn. A few should be planted only in spring, including the birch, flowering dogwood, magnolia, redbud and tulip-tree. Evergreens may be moved in the spring or early autumn. Plants in containers may be set out any time.

In Zone 5 and north, spring planting is advised for all deciduous material. Evergreens may be planted in the spring, or in late August or early September. The latter gives their roots a long, cool, moist growing season before winter.

The Best Size To Buy

You do not start trees from seed, if you are in a hurry for results! You buy them well-started, from a nursery. There are several sizes that can be best buys, depending upon your hurry for results, the condition of your pocketbook, and the importance of the tree in your landscape planting. Sometimes one tree warrants practically all of your landscaping budget for the first year.

Young trees—those with well-developed but compact root systems that can be dug without much damage or loss—transplant most easily. They also start growing again rapidly with the least shock and setback. Often, within a few years, they catch up with trees that were several years older when planted. The bigger the tree, the more carefully it must be moved, and the more apt it is to "just sit" for its first year or two in the new location. The largest size trees, and all evergreens, are moved with a ball of earth in which their roots are growing.

The most economical type and size to buy in deciduous trees are young ones in dormant and leafless bare-root condition. These have been dug in late fall, soil removed from their roots, and stored in a cool, moist, dark place where they remained in sleeping condition. They are ready to awaken and grow immediately when planted. You can purchase them locally or by mail order in sizes from "whips" —which are so young that they have not de-

veloped side branches—to those around 10 ft. high. Prices increase with size of the tree, for the larger ones have been grown and tended for more years in the nursery.

If a head start of a few years of growth is quite important to you, when buying a shade tree, the best size in dormant bare-root stock is 8 to 10 ft. with a trunk diameter of 1½ in. This size is young enough to transplant fairly easily, though its trunk bark is old enough to be fairly tough and not apt to be injured.

Potted or canned trees are easy to handle and can be transplanted at almost any reasonable time of year, for you do not need to disturb their roots. They probably will be priced higher than dormant bare-root trees, for they have taken more nurseryman's time.

Large trees can be moved successfully only in big balls of earth. There must be an adequate mass of roots within the ball, and to assure this the tree must be prepared by having its roots pruned for a year or two in advance of the transplanting. This is normal procedure in nurseries, where they also have equipment for digging and moving, and the knowledge of how tops must be pruned to compensate for the loss of roots. The operation is an expensive one, but if it is important to have a good-sized tree in a hurry, I would vote for the luxury of getting it—and buying less important trees and shrubs in smaller sizes.

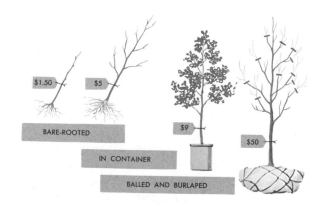

$1.50 $5

BARE-ROOTED

$9

IN CONTAINER

$50

BALLED AND BURLAPED

Digging trees from the wild is sometimes possible, but if you do it well, you will work hard for your success. Young ones, 2 to 4 ft. high, move most easily. Their roots are not extensive and can be moved bare. Be sure not to let them dry out during the transplanting. Large trees must have a ball of earth enclosing an ample root system. Trees that have grown many years in one place have surprisingly far-ranging roots, so a year ahead of the move you should select your tree or trees and prune the roots. Do this by digging a trench 18 in. deep and 6 in. wide in a circle smaller than the ball of earth you will eventually dig. Cut out all roots within this space, and refill the trench with good soil into which new fibrous roots will grow.

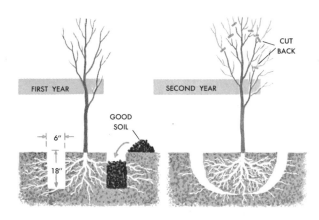

Where To Buy

You will be most satisfied if you deal with stores or nurseries, local or mail order, that specialize in plants and guarantee their product. Local firms often deliver, and frequently can be hired to do your planting if you wish.

Be cautious of surprising bargains. If you know the general standard prices for trees and suddenly see an ad for what seems to be an amazing bargain, be suspicious! It may be a bona fide excellent "leader" to attract you to the store. Possibly the store has purchased fine plants in large quantity. But if they are closing out left-over plants that have been sitting around for weeks, be cautious, for you are gambling. Do not buy trees with dried or wrinkled bark, limp or wilted leaves, or with balls of earth that have become broken and loose so that roots may have dried.

If this is a mail-order "bargain" making fantastic claims, read the fine print to discover exactly what size is being sold (height, not age), and check the botanical name to be sure that this is not some fancy improvised name for a common tree that could be purchased locally to greater advantage. If the ad says the trees have been "collected," this means that they have been dug where they grew wild, and therefore will not have as good, compact root systems as would trees of the same size that have been cultivated in nursery rows.

How To Plant

Again, while getting around to planting, make sure the tree's roots do not dry out. If the tree is a deciduous type, in dormant bare-root condition, it can be stored for several days in a cool, dark place, by covering its roots with damp material. If the delay is to be only a day, the roots could spend that time soaking in a tub of water. For a long postponement, plant the tree temporarily (called heeling-in) by laying it horizontally in a shallow trench and covering the roots with moist soil.

The hole you dig should be the best one you can possibly prepare! You will plant this tree only once, and cannot go back later to improve basic conditions, so take time to do it right. The hole should be at least 1 ft. wider and deeper than the size of the current root system, for the roots are going to grow as the tree grows, and will spread outward farther than the branches.

If your soil is heavy clay, or is underlaid with rock or hardpan, the hole that you dig may act as a water-accumulating well and drown roots. You will need to improve the drainage, not only by adding humus to the soil with which you fill the hole but also by breaking outlets through the walls and bottom so excess water can escape. You may need to lay a drain tile. If your entire soil area drains poorly because the area is lower than surrounding ground, perhaps you can have earth hauled in to raise it until the level is even with, or higher than, adjoining soil.

Loosen earth in the bottom of the hole; mix into it good topsoil and moistened peat moss. Moist peat moss absorbs and holds moisture; dry peat moss repels it. Incorporate also some complete plant food at the rate recommended on its package.

Place the tree so that the soil line (after settling) will be the same as it was when the tree was growing in the nursery row or in its container. Fill in around the roots with the best soil you have available, preferably mixing in moistened peat moss and a little complete plant food. The latter is for the future rather than immediately, for the tree needs no fertilizer while its roots are not active.

The best soil should be at the bottom of the hole where the roots will be. Firm it. When the hole is almost filled, water thoroughly. Then complete the filling. Any soil or sod left over should be mounded into a ridge or dike, making a circle around the edge of the hole to help hold water (unless your problem is to get rid of water rather than to save it).

Container-grown trees should be removed from their cans or pots before planting. Have your nurseryman cut the sides or bottom for you. Do not disturb the roots; keep them intact within their soil.

A balled-and-burlaped tree, after being lowered into its hole and placed in position, should have the burlap loosened from the top and pushed down into the sides of the hole; it will rot away.

Staking newly set trees whose trunks are 2 in. or more in diameter is important. Otherwise the tree will sway in the wind and loosen the roots. The stake should be placed while you have the hole open, so you can see where the roots are and not drive the stake through them. It should be strong enough to last about 3 years.

Be careful how you fasten trees to stakes. To avoid cutting or rubbing the bark, make sure that any supporting wires are threaded through one or more loops of old rubber hose, 6 to 8 in. long, which can be tied around the trunk before the wires are tightened and staked in place. Be sure to leave several inches in each loop for the growth of the stem. When the tree starts to grow it will expand in girth, and any tight wires—including those that attach name labels—can cut the bark, slow the flow of sap, and even kill the tree. Observe the way the experts fasten supports in planting young trees in city parks and along public sidewalks.

Pruning at planting time is needed primarily on trees that have lost considerable roots. For bare-root deciduous trees, the general recommendation is to remove ⅓ to ½ of the top growth. Perhaps the nursery will have done this for you. Do not cut the main leader or major structural branches, but do the pruning on unneeded ones, or ends of secondary branches. Of course you should also remove any broken parts of either branches or roots. On balled-and-burlaped evergreens, and trees grown in containers, little or no pruning is needed except to remove injured growth.

Wrap the trunk and major branches as high as you can reach with burlap or with the special brown corrugated paper sold for the purpose (you buy it in bandagelike rolls at garden supply stores). I cannot emphasize too strongly that this is important. It protects the tree from damage by borers that attack while the tree is not growing vigorously, and it also protects from weather damage. The latter can be more serious than you suspect, for the bark on the tree's trunk is sensitive to its changed situation. Quite likely the side that was in shade while it was growing in the nursery—protected by surrounding trees or by being on the side away from the sun—is now in sunlight. Branches removed in pruning probably left more of the trunk exposed to sunshine.

If the tree is not protected while it is recovering from its move, the sun may scald its skin, killing the bark on that side. Winter will bring more problems because the abrupt changes of temperature from sunny days to freezing nights can injure plant tissues. Also, rodents such as rabbits or mice may gnaw the tender bark of unprotected trees, girdling the tree and severely injuring or even killing it.

Mulching the ground around the base will help conserve moisture and keep the soil cooler.

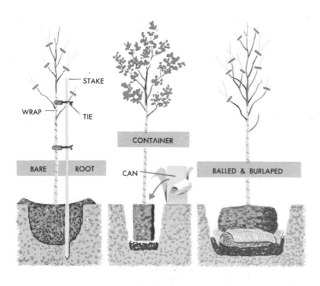

First-Year Care

This is the crucial time. The tree will be fighting to survive the shock of moving, and struggling to start new roots with which to anchor itself and provide and collect moisture and nutrients. It will need kindness and under-

standing. Hold off fertilizing until the tree is obviously established and the roots functioning well. This takes 6 months to a year.

Watering begins at once. You must provide ample moisture reliably through the first 2 or 3 years. Water slowly, thoroughly and deeply, letting the moisture soak to the bottom of the roots. Dig down and test to make sure. If you are carrying water in pails, it will take several. Then do not water again until the top inch or so of soil is dry.

The length of time between waterings will depend upon your climate and type of soil. If you have frequent rains, supplementary water may not be needed except in times of drought. Sandy soils need frequent attention. Newly set out evergreens appreciate having their foliage sprayed with water often; this helps compensate for the moisture being lost by leaves while roots are not able to replace it.

Later Care

Pruning to guide growth and make repairs on trees is taken up in detail in a later chapter. Feeding should be done annually, preferably in the spring before growth starts, or in very late autumn. In cold climates do not feed in late summer or fall, because the vigorous and succulent young growth produced would be very susceptible to damage by freezing.

Use a complete fertilizer. The amount will depend upon the general fertility of your soil, but a safe, moderate rate is 1 lb. for each 1 in. of the trunk's diameter. While the tree is small the fertilizer can be spread on top of the soil's cultivated surface; keep it at least 1 ft. from the trunk. Water it in.

As the tree grows, surface feeding is not enough. Roots become deeper and surprisingly extensive. They spread even farther than the branches. The most important feeding roots are on the outer edge of the branches, at their "drip line." The fertilizer should be placed 15 to 18 in. deep. One method is to punch holes 1½ to 2 ft. apart with crowbars, place proportioned amounts of fertilizer in them, and after watering fill the holes with moist peat moss or compost. The other is to use a device known as a deep-root waterer and feeder which is attached to the end of your garden hose. This implement is a hollow spike with holes in its bottom through which the water or liquid fertilizer squirts. It is available at most places that sell garden supplies.

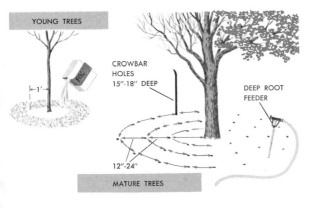

Dangers of Changing Grade Level around Trees

Changing the level of the soil around trees that have been growing in one place for a long time can sicken or kill them. So if you are building a new home on ground with trees you wish to save, or contemplate some grading to make terraces, be careful. Such work is really a job for a professional tree expert. The roots, over a period of years, grew at a level where they got just the right amount of air, water, etc. If you cover them with as much as an inch or two of additional soil, you can upset the delicate balance, or smother them. Filling over the ground with clay soil does most damage, for it packs and does not

let air and moisture through. Adding sandy or gravelly soil does least damage. Among trees most easily harmed by changing soil levels are beech, oak, sugar maple and evergreens. Cutting away earth is injurious also, though in a different manner. Some roots are destroyed, and others damaged, by exposure to air or sunshine.

If you must add "fill," building a dry well of rocks around the trunk of the tree is only a start; it helps the trunk, but not the main mass of roots which covers all the area beneath the branches and beyond. To keep roots from being smothered, and to assure that they will get air, food, and moisture, takes considerable effort. First, the present soil surface should be loosened and fertilized. Over it should go a layer of gravel, crushed rock or stones, extending beyond the farthest branch tips. Only the upper and final layer should be soil. Ideally, there should be tiles leading down into the layer of rocks through which roots can obtain air and be fed and watered.

When you change grade by lowering it, trees do not suffer as much as when soil is filled. However, strive to keep as large an area as possible at the original level around the tree. Leave it as a mound, or make some sort of terrace extending in a curve that contains most of the roots.

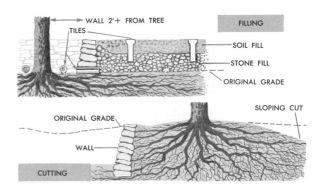

🍁 Help in Selecting Trees

In order to make the wisest choice of a shade tree, there are several things that you should know and consider. You probably want shade in a hurry, would like a tree that grows quickly, and would like to buy it in an inexpensive size. However, as a general rule, the finest, most permanent and trouble-free shade trees do not grow with magic swiftness. They tend to be relatively slow. To achieve fairly fast results with one, you should buy it in quite a large size; nurseries do wonders these days transplanting such trees with big balls of earth.

There are quick-growing shade trees, but many of them have serious faults. They may be weak-wooded so that their branches break in wind or when covered with snow or ice. They may have invasive roots that clog tile lines—poplars and willows are notorious in this regard. Perhaps they are a pleasant size in their youth but rapidly become too big for an average-sized lot and are expensive to remove. Some are susceptible to diseases or are short-lived.

This book tells you which shade trees are recommended, which are fast-growing, which have distinctive ornamental value, and which are the best flowering types. As you study the lists of the ones for your region, note that only a few of the fast-growing shade trees are on the "best" list, while several are in the group that may prove troublesome. If you decide that you are willing to put up with the problems of a quickie-type tree in order to obtain shade, why not also plant at least one of the highly recommended ones in a place where it has ample space in which to grow; later, as the slow one reaches usable size, you can remove the less desirable stand-in if you wish. Flowering trees vary in speed of growth, as well as in final size, but generally they develop fast.

TREES FOR THE NORTHEAST

The 10 Best Shade Trees

Ginkgo (*Ginkgo biloba*, male forms)
Zones 5-9. Deciduous. 40-120 ft. high.

Japanese Zelkova (*Zelkova serrata*)
Zones 5b-8. Deciduous. 50-80 ft. high.

Little-Leaf Linden (*Tilia cordata*)
Zones 3-8. Deciduous. 30-90 ft. high.

Pin Oak (*Quercus palustris*)
Zones 5-9. Deciduous. 50-75 ft. high.

Red Oak (*Quercus borealis* or *Q. rubra*)
Zones 4b-8. Deciduous. 75 ft. high.

Sugar Maple (*Acer saccharum*)
Zones 4-8. Deciduous. 40-120 ft. high.

Sweet-Gum (*Liquidambar styraciflua*)
Zones 6-10a. Deciduous. 60-100 ft. high.

Thornless Honey Locust (*Gleditsia triacanthos inermis*) Zones 4b-9. Deciduous. 50-80 ft. high.

Norway Maple (*Acer platanoides*)
Zones 4-8. Deciduous. 40-90 ft. high.

Yellow-Wood (*Cladrastis lutea*)
Zones 5b-8. Deciduous. 30-50 ft. high.

The Best Fast-growing Shade Trees

Chinese Elm (*Ulmus parvifolia*) Zones 6-9
Japanese Poplar (*Populus maximowiczi*)
Red Maple (*Acer rubrum*) Zones 3-9
Weeping Willow (*Salix babylonica*)
Wiers Cutleaf Maple (*Acer saccharinum laciniatum wieri*) Zones 4b-9

Outstanding Flowering Trees
(Described later in this chapter)

Chinese Kousa Dogwood
Crape-Myrtle
Floribunda Crab-Apple
Flowering Dogwood
Franklinia
Golden-Chain
Saucer Magnolia
Scholar-Tree
Silk-Tree or Mimosa
Weeping Higan Cherry

Ornamental Trees with Special, Distinctive Qualities

Some with interesting bark

American Beech (*Fagus grandifolia*)
Cutleaf European Birch (*Betula pendula gracilis*)
Korean Stewartia (*Stewartia koreana*)
Paperbark Maple (*Acer griseum*)
Paper or Canoe Birch (*Betula papyrifera*)

Some with colorful or cut foliage

Copper Beech (*Fagus sylvatica atropunicea*)
Crimson King Maple (*Acer platanoides* 'Crimson King')
Fernleaf Beech (*Fagus sylvatica asplenifolia*)
Newport Purpleleaf Plum (*Prunus blireiana* 'Newport')
Redleaf Japanese Maple (*Acer palmatum atropurpureum*)

Some Trees That May Prove Troublesome

American Elm ● Subject to disease
Black Locust ● Subject to borers, and must be sprayed each year to control them.
Carolina Poplar ● Roots clog drain lines and water pipes.
Silver Maple ● Large branches tend to break and fall; roots are rapid-spreading.
White Poplar ● Suckers continually invade the lawn; roots clog drain tiles.
White Willow ● Roots clog drain lines and water pipes.

TREES FOR THE MIDWEST

The 10 Best Shade Trees

Common Hackberry (*Celtis occidentalis*)
Zones 4b-9a. Deciduous. 40-100 ft. high.

Ginkgo (*Ginkgo biloba*)
Zones 5-9. Deciduous. 120 ft. high.

Norway Maple (*Acer platanoides*)
Zones 4-8. Deciduous. 30-90 ft. high.

Pin Oak (*Quercus palustris*)
Zones 5-9. Deciduous. 50-75 ft. high.

Red Maple (*Acer rubrum*)
Zones 3-9. Deciduous. 40-100 ft. high.

Red Oak (*Quercus borealis* or *Q. rubra*)
Zones 4b-8. Deciduous. 75 ft. high

Seedless Green Ash (*Frasinus lanceolata* vars.)
Zones 3-9a. Deciduous. 50-60 ft. high.

Sugar Maple (*Acer saccharum*)
Zones 4-8. Deciduous. 40-120 ft. high.

Sweet-Gum (*Liquidambar styradiflua*)
Zones 6-10a. Deciduous. 60-100 ft. high.

Thornless Honey Locust (*Gleditsia triacanthos inermis*)
Zones 4b-9. Deciduous. 50-80 ft. high.

Fast-growing Shade Trees

American Plane-Tree (*Platanus occidentalis*)
Red Oak (*Quercus borealis*) Zones 4b-8
Silver Maple (*Acer saccharinum*) Zones 4b-9
Silver Maple, Improved (var. *pyramidale*)
Thornless Honey Locust (see preceding list)
White Poplar (*Populus alba*) Zones 4-9

Outstanding Flowering Trees
(Described later in this chapter)

Apple Service-Berry
Carolina Silver-Bell
Cockspur Hawthorn
Flowering Crab-Apple
Japanese Tree-Lilac
Mayday-Tree
Redbud
Saucer Magnolia
Star Magnolia
Washington Hawthorn

Ornamental Trees with Special, Distinctive Qualities

American Maple ● Small, often multiple trunked.
Black Alder ● Attractive stems, foliage and catkins. Zones 4-8.
Paper Birch ● Bark is white and papery. Attractive grown in clumps. Zones 2-8.
River Birch ● The bark is tan and shaggy. Zones 5-9.
Sour Gum ● Picturesque habit of growth. Bright scarlet fall color. Zones 5-9.

Some Trees That May Prove Troublesome

American Elm ● Subject to disease
American Plane-Tree ● A dirty tree. Drops leaves, fruit and strips of bark.
Box-Elder, Female ● Attracts box-elder bugs, which are an autumn nuisance.
Common Horse-Chestnut ● These drop flowers and fruits messily on the lawn.
Ginkgo (female) ● Fruits drop to the ground and have a disagreeable odor.
Poplar ● Roots clog tile lines. White poplars spread by suckering.
Willow ● Their roots enter and clog drain tiles and water lines.

TREES FOR THE PLAINS AND
INTERMOUNTAIN REGION

The 10 Best Shade Trees

American Linden (*Tilia americana*)
Zones 3-8. Deciduous. 40-100 ft. high.

Arizona Ash (*Fraxinus velutina*)
Zones 6-9. Deciduous. 35-45 ft. high.

Baumann Horse-Chestnut (*Aesculus hippocastanum baumanni*)
Zones 3b-9a. Deciduous. 60 ft. high.

Cut-Leaf Weeping Birch (*Betula pendula dalecarlica*) Zones 3-8. Deciduous. 60 ft. high.

Kentucky Coffee-Tree (*Gymnocladus dioica*)
Zones 5-8. Deciduous. 50-90 ft. high.

Little-Leaf Linden (*Tilia cordata*)
Zones 3-8. Deciduous. 30-90 ft. high.

London Plane-Tree (*Platanus acerifolia*)
Zones 5b-9. Deciduous. 40-80 ft. high.

Norway Maple (*Acer platanoides*) and varieties as 'Crimson King.'
Zones 4-8. Deciduous. 30-90 ft. high.

Red Oak (*Quercus borealis* or *Q. rubra*)
Zones 5-8. Deciduous. 75 ft. high.

Thornless Honey Locust (*Gleditsia triacanthos inermis*) Zones 4b-9. Deciduous. 50-80 ft. high.

The Best Fast-growing Shade Trees

Cottonwoods: Fremont, Zones 6-9; Great Plains,
    Zones 3-8; Rio Grande, Zones 6-9
Siberian Elm *(Ulmus pumila)* Zones 3b-10
Silver Maple *(Acer saccharinum)* 4b-9
Tree-of-Heaven *(Ailanthus altissima)* Zones 5-9
Western Catalpa *(Catalpa speciosa)* Zones 5-9
White Poplar *(Populus alba)* Zones 4-9

Outstanding Flowering Trees
(Described later in this chapter)

European Mountain-Ash
Flowering Crab-Apple
Goldenrain-Tree
Japanese Pagoda-Tree
Laburnum vossi
Mayday-Tree
Ohio Buckeye
Redbud
Washington Hawthorn
Western Catalpa

Ornamental Trees with Special, Distinctive Qualities

Amur Maple ● Red winged seeds; orange fall foliage. Described in shrub chapter.
Paper Birch ● Graceful paper-white trunks. Especially attractive grown in clumps.
Russian-Olive ● Drought-tolerant small tree with distinctive silvery foliage.
Weeping Willows ● Golden weeping willow has yellow bark.
Western Yellow Pine ● Pruned high, it makes a handsome evergreen shade tree.

Some Trees That May Prove Troublesome

Black Locust and New Mexico Locust ● These locusts send up suckers over a wide
area and become a nuisance.
Flowering Dogwood, Ginkgo, Chinese Elm ● Do not plant these in areas where
cottonroot rot disease occurs; they are 100% susceptible.
Poplars and Cottonwoods ● Female trees yield "cotton" which litters grounds and
clogs screens. Plant only male trees. Roots penetrate and plug tile lines.
Silver Maple ● Wood breaks easily in storms. In highly alkaline soil the foliage
develops iron-deficiency chlorosis.
Thorny Honey Locust ● Fallen thorns puncture tires and bare feet. Plant thornless
types.
Tree-of-Heaven ● Spreads rapidly by seeds and suckers. Flowers of male trees
have an offensive odor; plant only female trees.

TREES FOR THE UPPER SOUTH

The 10 Best Shade Trees

American Plane-Tree *(Platanus occidentalis)*
Zones 5-9. Deciduous. 100 ft. or more high.

Ginkgo *(Ginkgo biloba*, male forms)
Zones 5-9. Deciduous. 40-120 ft. high.

10 Best Shade Trees (cont.)

Loblolly Pine (*Pinus taeda*)
Zones 7-10. Evergreen. 100 ft. high.

Pin Oak (*Quercus palustris*)
Zones 5-9. Deciduous. 50-75 ft. high.

Sugarberry Hackberry (*Celtis laevigata*)
Zones 6-9. Deciduous. 50-90 ft. high.

Red Maple (*Acer rubrum*)
Zones 3-9. Deciduous. 40-100 ft. high.

Southern Magnolia (*Magnolia grandiflora*)
Zones 6b-10. Evergreen. 40-75 ft. high.

Sweet-Gum (*Liquidambar styraciflua*)
Zones 6-10. Deciduous. 50-80 ft. high.

Tulip-Tree (*Liriodendron tulipifera*)
Zones 5-9. Deciduous. 75-100 ft. high.

Willow Oak (*Quercus phellos*)
Zones 6-9. Deciduous. 60 ft. high.

The Best Fast-growing Trees

American Plane-Tree (*Platanus occidentalis*)
Red Maple (*Acer rubrum*)
Silver Maple (*Acer saccharinum*)
Thornless Honey Locust (*Gleditsia triacanthos inermis*)
Wilt-resistant Silk-Tree (*Albizia julibrissin*)

Outstanding Flowering Trees
(Described later in this chapter)

Bradford Pear
Carolina Silver-Bell
Flowering Cherry
Flowering Crab-Apple
Flowering Dogwood
Goldenrain-Tree
Redbud
Saucer Magnolia
Silk-Tree or Mimosa
Sweet Bay Magnolia

Ornamental Trees with Special Distinctive Qualities

Carolina Cherry-Laurel ● Small tree with rounded head and evergreen foliage.
Corkscrew Willow ● Fast-growing small tree with twisted and contorted branches.
Downy Service-Berry ● Small multiple-trunked tree with gray bark; white flowers early spring.
River Birch ● Multiple-trunked with flaking, colorful reddish bark.
Sour-Wood ● Clusters of bell-like flowers in spring; brilliant red foliage in fall.

Some Trees That May Prove Troublesome

Common Silk-Tree ● Subject to mimosa wilt. Plant wilt-resistant types instead.
European Mountain-Ash ● Short-lived in the South and best used in cooler locations.
Ginkgo (female) ● These have foul-smelling fruits. Plant selected male forms.
Paper Birch ● It is not adaptable to southern conditions.

TREES FOR THE DEEP SOUTH

The 10 Best Shade Trees

American Holly *(Ilex opaca)*
Zones 6-10. Evergreen. 25-40 ft. high.

Black-Olive *(Bucida buceras)*
Zone 10. Evergreen. 25-40 ft. high.

Camphor-Tree *(Cinnamomum camphora)*
Zones 8b-10. Evergreen. 25-40 ft. high.

Flowering Dogwood *(Cornus florida)*
Zones 5-9. Deciduous. 20-30 ft. high.

Glossy Privet *(Ligustrum lucidum)*
Zones 7b-10. Evergreen. 25 ft. high.

Live Oak *(Quercus virginiana)*
Zones 8b-10. Evergreen. 50-75 ft. high.

Loquat *(Eriobotrya japonica)*
Zones 9-10. Evergreen. 15-25 ft. high.

Pongam *(Pongamia pinnata)*
Zone 10. Semi-evergreen. 20-40 ft. high.

Sapodilla *(Achras zapota)*
Zone 10. Evergreen. 20-40 ft. high.

Southern Magnolia *(Magnolia grandiflora)*
Zones 6b-10. Evergreen. 40-60 ft. high.

The Best Fast-growing Trees

Chinese and Siberian Elms, Zones 9-10
Glossy Privet, Zones 9-10
Maples, Zones 9-10
Royal Palm, Zone 10
Sweet-Gum, Zones 9-10

Outstanding Flowering Trees
(Described later in this chapter)

Cassia or Shower
Crape-Myrtle
Flowering Dogwood
Jacaranda
Jerusalem-Thorn
Orchid-Tree
Redbud
Royal Poinciana
Silk-Tree or Mimosa
Southern Magnolia

Four Trees with Special, Distinctive Qualities

Cabbage Palmetto ● Tall, tropical-looking and durable native palm for Zones 9 and 10.
Cajeput-Tree ● Thick, white, papery bark, and white blossoms. Zone 10.
Gumbo-Limbo ● Gnarled limbs with coppery-red glossy bark. Zone 10.
Southern Red-Cedar ● Native narrow-leaved evergreen; geometric shape. Zones 9, 10.

Some Trees That May Prove Troublesome

Dwarf Poinciana ● Self-sows annoyingly. Flower color clashes. Poisonous seeds.
Ear-Tree ● Grows fast—as much as 10 ft. per year—to great size.
Laurel Oak ● Grows rapidly to large size, but is short-lived.
Wild Cherry ● Deciduous, rapid-growing tree with weak wood that breaks.
Womans-Tongue-Tree ● It is deciduous, fast-growing with weak wood and noisy rattling pods.

TREES FOR THE SOUTHWEST—
Zones 7 through 10
If you live in Zone 5 or 6, use recommendations for the Plains and Intermountain Region

The 10 Best Shade Trees

African Sumac (*Rhus lancea*)
Zones 9b-10. Evergreen. 20-25 ft. high.

California Pepper-Tree (*Schinus molle*)
Zones 8b-10. Evergreen. 25-40 ft. high.

Carob or St.-Johns-Bread (*Ceratonia siliqua*)
Zones 9 and 10. Evergreen. 20-40 ft. high.

Chinese Elm (*Ulmus parvifolia*)
Zones 3b-10. Semi-evergreen. 40-60 ft. high.

Fruitless Mulberry (*Morus alba* 'Fruitless')
Zones 5-9. Deciduous. 20-60 ft. high.

Japanese Privet (*Ligustrum japonicum*)
Zones 7b-10. Evergreen. 8-12 ft. high.

Modesto Ash (*Fraxinus velutina* 'Modesto')
Zones 6-9. Deciduous. 40-50 ft. high.

Olive (*Olea europaea*)
Zones 8b-10. Evergreen. 25-35 ft. high.

Oriental Plane-Tree (*Platanus orientalis*)
Zones 7-9. Deciduous. 40-100 ft. high.

Red-Box Gum (*Eucalyptus polyanthemos*)
Zones 8b-10. Evergreen. 70-100 ft. high.

The Best for Hurry-up Shade

California Pepper-Tree (*Schinus molle*)
Chinese Elm (*Ulmus parvifolia*)
Eucalyptus in variety
Mapleleaf Mulberry (*Morus alba* 'Mapleleaf')
Texas Umbrella-Tree (*Melia azedarach umbraculiformis*)

Outstanding Flowering Trees
(Described later in this chapter)

Blue Palo-Verde
Chaste-Tree
Citrus in variety
Cootamundra
Crape-Myrtle
Flowering Peach
Mexican Palo-Verde
Pomegranate
Redbud
Southern Magnolia

Ornamental Trees with Special, Distinctive Qualities

Chinese Pistachio ● One of the few Southwest trees with crimson fall foliage.
Loquat ● Small tree with bold, leathery foliage.
Olive ● Picturesque, especially when allowed to grow with multiple trunks.
Silk-Tree ● Light green feathery foliage, silken flowers, horizontal branching.
Strawberry-Tree ● Develops interesting bark texture and trunk structure.

Some Trees That May Prove Troublesome

Desert Gum ● This eucalyptus is subject to a virus.
Tamarisk ● Brittle branches; irregular uninteresting growth; a soil robber.
Tree-of-Heaven ● A rank grower with brittle branches that break in the wind.

TREES FOR THE PACIFIC NORTHWEST

The 10 Best Shade Trees

Eley Crab-Apple *(Malus purpurea 'Eleyi')*
Zones 4-9a. Deciduous. 20-30 ft. high.

European Beech *(Fagus sylvatica)*
Zones 5-8. Deciduous. 90 ft. high.

Honey Locust *(Gleditsia triacanthos)*, named
kinds. Zones 4b-9. Deciduous. 50-80 ft. high.

Kwanzan Flowering Cherry *(Prunus serrulata
'Kwanzan')* Zones 5-8. Deciduous. 30-50 ft. high.

Oriental Plane-Tree *(Platanus orientalis)*
Zones 7-9. Deciduous. 40-90 ft. high.

Red Horse-Chestnut *(Aesculus carnea)*
Zones 4-9a. Deciduous. 40 ft. high.

Red Maple *(Acer rubrum)*
Zones 3-9. Deciduous. 40-100 ft. high.

Scarlet Oak *(Quercus coccinea)*
Zones 4b-9. Deciduous. 60-80 ft. high.

Washington Hawthorn *(Crataegus phaenopyrum)* Zones 5-9a. Deciduous. 25-30 ft. high.

Yellow-Wood *(Cladrastis lutea)*
Zones 5b-8. Deciduous. 30-50 ft. high.

Best Fast-growing Shade Trees

American Plane-Tree *(Platanus occidentalis)*
American Yellow-Wood *(Cladrastus lutea)*
Amur Cork-Tree *(Phellodendron amurense)*
London Plane-Tree *(Platanus acerifolia)*
Silver Maple *(Acer saccharinum)*
Thornless Honey Locust, named kinds

Outstanding Flowering Trees
(Described later in this chapter)

Alexander Saucer Magnolia
Autumn Higan Cherry
Chinese Kousa Dogwood
Flowering Cherries:
   'Shirotae' & 'Kwanzan'
Flowering Dogwood
Goldenrain-Tree
Hardy Silk-Tree
Japanese Snowbell
Pacific Dogwood
Redbud

Ornamental Trees with Special, Distinctive Qualities

Austrian Pine ● Admired for its strength in terms of landscape effect.
Autumn Glory Hawthorn ● Excellent autumn display of large bright red fruits.
Bloodleaf Japanese Maple ● Handsome foliage, especially viewed from below.
Deodar Cedar ● Recommended for its grace and the soft color of its varieties.
Sour-Wood ● Bright fall color. Interesting contrast between rather pendulous
leaves and horizontal effect of flowers and old flower parts.

Some Trees That May Prove Troublesome

American Elm ● Subject to disease.
Bigleaf Maple ● Not usually attractive as a young tree, but magnificent when old.
Garry Oak ● Too slow-growing to plant new; an excellent tree after 100 years.
Norway Maple ● Too subject to aphids. The "honey dew" drip is disagreeable.
Black Walnut ● Nuts are a nuisance in the vicinity of sidewalks and patios.
Silver Maple ● Use only in difficult climates where better trees make slow growth.

TREES FOR NORTHERN CALIFORNIA

The 10 Best Shade Trees

Chinese Pistachio (*Pistacia chinensis*)
Zones 6b-9. Deciduous. 40-60 ft. high.

Crimson King Maple (*Acer platanoides* 'Crimson King') Zones 4-8. Deciduous. 30-90 ft. high.

Ginkgo 'Autumn Gold' (*Ginkgo biloba* 'Autumn Gold') Zones 5-9. Deciduous. 40-120 ft. high.

Holly Oak (*Quercus ilex*)
Zones 9-10. Evergreen. 40 ft. high.

Japanese Zelkova (*Zelkova serrata*)
Zones 5b-8. Deciduous. 50-80 ft. high.

London Plane-Tree (*Platanus acerifolia*)
Zones 5b-9. Deciduous. 40-80 ft. high.

Magnolia 'Samuel Sommer' (*Magnolia grandiflora* 'Samuel Sommer') Zones 6b-9. Evergreen.

Modesto Ash (*Fraxinus velutina* 'Modesto')
Zones 6-9. Deciduous. 35-45 ft. high.

Moraine Honey Locust (*Gleditsia triacanthos* 'Moraine') Zones 4b-9. Deciduous. 40-80 ft. high.

Shamel or Evergreen Ash (*Fraxinus uhdei*)
Zones 9-10. Semi-evergreen. 30 ft. high.

The Best for Hurry-up Shade

Chinese Elm (*Ulmus parvifolia*)
Fruitless Mulberry (*Morus alba* 'Fruitless')
Norway Maple (*Acer platanoides*)
Sierra or White Alder (*Alnus rhombifolia*)
Tulip-Tree (*Liriodendron tulipifera*)

Outstanding Flowering Trees
(Described later in this chapter)

Blireiana Plum
Flowering Cherry
Hopa Crab-Apple
Japanese Apricot
Parkman Crab-Apple
Pink Flowering Dogwood
Ruby Horse-Chestnut
Silk-Tree or Mimosa
Weeping Flowering Cherry
Yulan Magnolia

Ornamental Trees with Special, Distinctive Qualities

European White Birch ● Lovely when grown in multiple-stemmed clumps.
Hawthorn 'Autumn Glory' ● A small tree with masses of giant red berries.
Japanese Maple ● Colorful decorative foliage and interesting branching patterns.
Mayten ● Dainty evergreen with pendulous branches similar to weeping willow.
Sweet-Gum 'Palo Alto' ● A selected form with unusually brilliant red leaves in fall.

Some Trees That May Prove Troublesome

American Elm ● Susceptible to disease and insect pests. Wood is weak and brittle.
Bigleaf Maple ● Too large. Root system is greedy. Plants do not grow under it.
Blue and Ribbon Gums ● They become too big. Roots rob soil. Falling leaves are a problem.
Lombardy Poplar ● Roots clog drains. Wood is weak and brittle.
Tree-of-Heaven ● Too vigorous and large. Limbs break easily.
Weeping Willow ● Roots clog drains. Limbs break easily.

TREES FOR SOUTHERN CALIFORNIA

The 10 Best Shade Trees

Aleppo Pine *(Pinus halepensis)*
Zones 8-10. Evergreen. 30-60 ft. high.

Brazilian Pepper-Tree *(Schinus terebinthifolius)*
Zones 9b-10. Evergreen. 15-30 ft. high.

Camphor-Tree *(Cinnamomum camphora)*
Zones 8b-10. Evergreen. 25-40 ft. high.

Carob or St.-Johns-Bread *(Ceratonia siliqua)*
Zones 9-10. Evergreen. 20-40 ft. high.

Cupaniopsis anacardioides or *Blighia sapida*
Zone 10. 40 ft. high.

European Hackberry *(Celtis australia)*
Zones 8-10. Deciduous. 35-75 ft. high.

Fruitless Mulberry *(Morus alba* 'Fruitless')
Zones 5-9. Deciduous. 20-60 ft. high.

Goldenrain-Tree or Hayata *(Koelreuteria formosana)* Zones 9b-10. Deciduous. 20-30 ft. high.

Modesto Ash *(Fraxinus velutina* 'Modesto')
Zones 6-9. Deciduous. 35-45 ft. high.

Strawberry-Tree *(Arbutus unedo)*
Zones 8-10. Evergreen. 8-20 ft. high.

The Best Fast-growing Trees

Brazilian Pepper-Tree *(Schinus terebinthifolius)*
Chinese Elm *(Ulmus parvifolia)*
Cootamundra *(Acacia baileyana)*
Eucalyptus saligna
Russian-Olive *(Elaeagnus angustifolius)*

Outstanding Flowering Trees
(Described later in this chapter)

Coral-Tree
Eucalyptus ficifolia
Floss-Silk Tree
Jacaranda
Jerusalem-Thorn
Red Bottle-Brush
Sweetshade
Southern Magnolia
Tipu-Tree
Yellow-Bells

Ornamental Trees with Special, Distinctive Qualities

California Sycamore ● Big tree with twisting branches and patchy buff bark.
Crape-Myrtle ● Bark on trunk sheds in patches to show smooth pink under layer.
Cajeput-Tree ● Attractive peeling bark and white bottle-brush type of flowers.
Lemon Gum ● Slender and graceful with white bark. 50 to 75 ft. high.
Olive ● Interesting twisting trunk and branches carrying gray-green foliage.
Weeping Acacia ● Blue-gray leaves on long pendant branches. 15 or 25 ft.
Willow Pittosporum ● Weeping form similar to weeping willow. Grows to 20 ft.

Some Trees That May Prove Troublesome

Canary Island Date Palm ● Enormous tree, suitable only for large lots.
Deodar Cedar ● Large size makes it unsuitable for typical modern lots.
Lombardy Poplar ● Its roots are invasive. It is bothered by borers and diseases.
Moreton Bay Fig ● Grows rapidly to a huge size; too big for average-size lots.
Red and Blue Gums ● Too large for small yards, and out of scale with them.
Tree-of-Heaven ● This tree spreads by suckering. Flowers have offensive odor.
Weeping Willow ● Roots get into tile lines. Borers and diseases cause trouble.

TREES FOR HAWAII

The 10 Best Shade Trees

Allspice (*Pimenta dioica*) 30 ft.
Autograph-Tree (*Clusia rosea*) 25 ft.
False Olive (*Elaeodendron orientale*) 40 ft.
Fern Tree (*Filicium decipiens*) 35 ft.
Fiddleleaf Fig (*Ficus lyrata*) 15-35 ft.
Geometry-Tree (*Bucida buceras*) 35 ft.
Mimusops (*Mimusops caffra*) 30 ft.
Monkey-Pod (*Samanea saman*) 50 ft.
Podocarpus neriifolius 30 ft.
Tulipwood (*Harpullia pendula*) 25 ft.

Five Distinctive Trees

Bauhinia blakeana
Carambola (*Averrhoa carambola*)

Lignum Vitae (*Gauicum officinale*)
Madagascar Olive (*Noronhia emarginata*)
Mei sui lan (*Aglaia odorata*)

Outstanding Flowering Trees
(Described later in this chapter)

Alibangbang
Jatropha hastata
Kou
Mock-Orange
Plumeria
Rainbow Shower
Royal Poinciana
Senegal Coral-Tree
Tabebuia argentea
Thevetia thevetioides

Flowering Crab-Apple

Mayday Tree

Saucer Magnolia

OUTSTANDING
FLOWERING TREES

OPPOSITE:
Silver-Bell

Southern Magnolia

Flowering Peach

Silk-Tree or Mimosa

Some Trees for Quick Results and Their Possible Problems

Mango ● Best to plant a named tree, and pick fruit, rather than have a poor
   variety and let fruit become a nuisance as it decays beneath the tree.
Octopus-Tree ● Roots may become troublesome because they are aggressive.
Oleander ● Somewhat difficult to maintain the desired number of trunks without
   suckers. The plant's poisonous qualities are resented by some.

Trees To Avoid in Average-sized Yards

African Tulip-Tree ● Roots invade water pipes. Branches produce litter.
Chinese Banyan ● Too large. Very aggressive root system. Seedlings come where
   unwanted.
Norfolk Island-Pine ● Too large—150 ft. Suitable when young and small only.
Silk-Oak ● Branches are brittle and break in wind.

TREES FOR ALASKA

The best-growing large trees in Alaska are those that are native to the state. Deciduous trees include poplars and birches. The most useful narrow-leaved evergreens in home yards are mountain and western hemlock, and blue and Alberta spruce.

Among flowering trees grown successfully in Anchorage are many varieties of flowering crab-apple, including 'Almey,' 'Dolgo,' 'Hopa' and Siberian; the native and European mountain-ash, Pacific service-berry and mayday-tree.

🍁 The Best Flowering Trees

ACACIA or WATTLE (*Acacia*). These can be grown in Zones 9 and 10. They are charming, fast-growing, free-flowering evergreen trees and shrubs, with fine-cut ferny foliage and myriads of tiny, fluffy yellow flowers. They tend to be short-lived and have shallow roots and brittle branches. Give them abundant water while they are young; later they will be drought-resistant.

Cootamundra Wattle (*A. baileyana*) grows 20 to 30 ft. high and 15 to 20 ft. wide. Its foliage is blue-gray in color. The blooms come in January and February.

ALIBANGBANG, see ORCHID-TREE

APRICOT, JAPANESE or FLOWERING (*Prunus mume*). In Zones 7 to 9, inclusive, this species may be used. It is a round-headed deciduous tree growing to 30 ft. high, with single, fragrant pink blooms and small, sour fruits. Named varieties come with double flowers in white, pink or crimson, grow about 20 ft. high, and bloom extremely early in spring. One of the best is 'Dawn' with double shell-pink flowers.

BAY, BULL, see MAGNOLIA

BAUHINIA, see ORCHID-TREE

BOTTLE-BRUSH. For general data and description of red bottle-brush, see the chapter on shrubs.

Weeping (*Callistemon viminalis*), for Zones 8b to 10, inclusive, is a fast-growing small evergreen tree that reaches 20 ft. high, with pendulous branches and spikes of fluffy red flowers in summer.

BUCKEYE, see HORSE-CHESTNUT

CASSIA or SHOWER (*Cassia*). Limited to Zone 10, these grow primarily in southern Florida and Hawaii. They are among the showiest flowering trees, and bloom prolifically over a long period. Foliage, fine-cut and arranged in feather-form, is usually briefly deciduous, though some varieties are evergreen. The flowers, carried in clusters or spikes, come in yellow, pink, light brown or red. The trees like full sun.

Golden-Shower (*C. fistula*) is 30 ft. high with bright yellow flowers 2 in. across in pendulous clusters, followed by long, slender seed pods. Its foliage is deciduous.

Rainbow-Shower (*C. javanica x fistula*) has pink-and-white blossoms reminding one of apple blossoms. It is a small deciduous tree, 25 to 30 ft. high, of picturesque, irregular form.

CATALPA, WESTERN or NORTHERN (*Catalpa speciosa*). This rapid-growing large tree reaches a height of from 40 to 90 ft. in Zones 5b to 9, inclusive.The leaves are heart-shaped, 8 to 12 in. long; the showy white trumpet-shaped flowers 2 in. across, carried in pyramidal clusters. They are followed by seed pods that look like giant string beans; these are woody, and 12 in. or more long. The tree stands heat and drought, but its falling flowers, leaves and pods can be an untidy nuisance.

CHASTE-TREE (*Vitex agnus-castus*). In Zones 5b to 9, inclusive, this deciduous small tree or shrub grows 8 to 25 ft. high. It has gray twigs and narrow leaves that are green above and gray below. The flowers, in late summer, are lavender-blue or white spikes, somewhat resembling the bloom of lilacs. It likes sun and heat. In the coldest part of chaste-tree's hardiness range, tops usually kill to the ground in winter and new shoots that arise in spring produce blooms the same year.

CHERRY, FLOWERING or ORIENTAL (*Prunus* species). These are ethereally lovely when covered with blossoms in early spring. They do best in Zones 6b through 9a, in areas where the temperature rarely falls below zero, yet where winters are cold enough to provide a good chilling and let the trees have a period of complete dormancy. Give them a site in full sun with fast-draining soil. Small sizes, 3 to 5 ft. high, can be handled in bare-root condition. Larger sizes should be moved in a ball of earth.

Be very kind to these choice trees during their first few years. Feed them in spring and water generously. However, do not water them during autumn—except in cases of drought—or otherwise stimulate new growth then, for the succulent new wood which results is very susceptible to winter damage by freezing temperatures. To avoid sun-scalding the tender bark on the young trunks, and to protect them from borers and rodents, wrap them with burlap or special tree-wrap paper for 2 years. For details, see how-to-plant instructions in the first part of this chapter.

There are innumerable kinds of flowering cherries. They bloom at slightly different times, have single or double flowers in white or shades of pink, and the trees may have upright, spreading or weeping form.

Higan or Rosebud (*P. subhirtella*) grows to 30 ft. and blooms very early in spring with single 1-in. pink flowers. Autumn Higan (*P. subhirtella autumnalis*) reblooms in autumn after the foliage falls. Weeping Higan has pendulous branches.

Sargent (*P. sargenti*) is the hardiest flowering cherry, Zones 5b through 8. It grows to 60 ft. high and has single pink flowers. Young leaves are copper-colored, and in autumn the foliage turns red.

P. serrulata varieties are the most popular, and include many named varieties. 'Kwanzan' is exceptionally vigorous, with double pink blooms 2½ in. across. It is an upright tree 18 to 25 ft. high. 'Sirotae' has double white 2-in. flowers in drooping clusters.

Yoshino (*P. yedoensis*) is fairly quick-growing, reaches 30 or 50 ft., and has spreading branches. It is the one planted around the tidal basin in Washington, D. C. Blooms come before the foliage and are single, pale pink or white, and fragrant. Allow them 30 ft. of space, and blooms will show to best advantage if planted where they can be seen against a dark background such as evergreens.

CHERRY, EUROPEAN BIRD, see MAYDAY-TREE

CITRUS. See the chapter on fruit.

CORAL-TREE (*Erythrina*). In Zone 10 these erect or wide-branched, deciduous or semi-evergreen trees attain a height of 12 to 40 ft., with picturesque habits of growth. The flowers are brilliant red, in modified pea bloom shapes. They are carried in large and showy clusters, mostly at a time of year when the trees are leafless. The branches are prickly; the leaves 3-parted. Seeds are borne in long pods. The trees need full sun, warmth and rapid-draining soil.

CRAB-APPLE, FLOWERING (*Malus*). These lovely spring-flowering trees are as hardy as they are beautiful. Many thrive in Alaska. They are especially useful in the northern Midwest and Plains and Intermountain areas, where it is difficult or impossible to grow flowering dogwoods and flowering cherries.

You can choose crab-apples with white, pink or rose-red flowers; there are a few with double blossoms. Foliage may be green or bronzy-red. Some of the trees grow only 8 to 10 ft. high while others become as big as regular apple trees. Their shape may be spreading, vertical or weeping. Fruits vary in color and in size from some as tiny as peas to others almost as large as eating apples. It is wise to select varieties with small fruits of a size that birds glean.

Grow these trees in full sun. Feed them in spring and water generously the first two years. Be certain to protect the trunks by wrapping them through both summer and winter the first two seasons. To learn the reasons why, and details on how to do it, see the first part of this chapter describing how to plant trees.

After the trees' babyhood, do not feed them, and do not water except in periods of serious drought, since this promotes excessive leafy growth and delays flowering. Here are some of the outstanding kinds.

'Almey,' with foliage that is bronzy when young, has crimson blossoms with white centers. It blooms when young and becomes a good-sized, spreading tree. The ½-in. bright red fruits persist after foliage falls, and are as decorative as the blossoms.

'Dorothea' is new, and excellent because of its profuse, fragrant, double pink blossoms 2 in. across. The tree is small, with a very informal, wide-spreading type of growth. It blooms when young. The fruits are small, bright yellow, and hang on all winter.

'Eleyi' has wine-red blooms and apples, and foliage that has a reddish tinge when young. It grows 20 to 30 ft. high.

'Hopa,' an old favorite, has leaves that are reddish in spring. The flowers are bright rosy-pink. The tree becomes as large as a regular apple tree. Its 1-in. dark red fruits are attractive through summer, and fall when frosts come. They are useful for making jelly.

Japanese Flowering or Floribunda is an old, beautiful, dependable favorite. The buds are red and the flowers open pale pink but become white. Its fruits are small, yellow or red. The tree grows 20 to 30 ft. high.

'Lemoine' is similar to 'Eleyi,' but smaller and later-blooming.

Redbud (*M. zumi calocarpa*) grows 25 to 30 ft. high, with profuse blooms that are pink in bud but white when open. Its fruits are small, bright red to orange, and persist through winter.

'Red Jade,' with weeping form, is a small tree 6 to 8 ft. high. Its flowers are white, followed by myriads of tiny red fruits that gleam after leaves fall in autumn.

Sargent is a pygmy, growing only 8 to 10 ft. high like a big shrub. It blooms late in crab-apple season, the pink buds opening into glistening white flowers. The foliage is green.

'Van Eseltine' is one of the few vertical-growing crabs, and is additionally distinctive in having handsome double light-pink blooms followed by ¾-in. showy yellow fruits that hang on. It grows 10 to 15 ft. high.

CRAPE-MYRTLE. See the chapter on shrubs.

DOGWOOD *(Cornus)*. These beloved trees are deciduous, put on a majestic display of long-lasting flowers, and are showy again in autumn with colorful leaves. The true flowers are tiny and inconspicuous—appearing to be stamens and pistils—surrounded by showy petal-like bracts.

Flowering *(C. florida)*, in Zones 5b to 9, inclusive, is native to Eastern and Southern states, and does best in areas with generous amounts of rainfall. It grows to a 30-ft. height. The flowers come early, before leaves in spring, and the bracts are snowy white. *C. florida rubra* is the pink variety. Its fruits are bright red, like oval berries.

In your garden these trees will like sun or part shade. The small sizes transplant easily. Those less than 4 ft. high can be transplanted bare-root but larger ones should be purchased balled-and-burlaped or growing in a container. Water copiously the first few years, and be sure to wrap the trunk with burlap or a special tree-wrap paper to protect the trunk from invasion by borers, and from winter damage.

Kousa *(C. kousa)* and its variety Chinese Kousa *(C. kousa chinensis)*, in Zones 5b to 9, inclusive, have white blooms similar to those of flowering dogwood, but considerably later in spring. These trees grow about 20 ft. high. Their rose-red fruits are clustered in a shape resembling a raspberry.

Pacific *(C. nuttalli)*, in Zones 7 to 9a, inclusive, is native to the West Coast. It is a tall, slender tree that may reach a 75-ft. height. The blooms are white, resembling those of flowering dogwood, but may have 4 to 6 bracts. It often reblooms in autumn.

EUCALYPTUS or GUM *(Eucalyptus)*. These evergreen trees with aromatic foliage grow in Zones 9 and 10. They are well adapted to semi-arid climates.

Pink Ironbark *(E. sideroxylon rosea)* is a slender, dark-trunked tree 30 to 40 ft. high, with blue-green leaves and masses of pink flowers in spring and summer.

Scarlet-Flowering *(E. ficifolia)* grows slowly to a 30- to 40-ft. height, spreading 20 to 40 ft. wide. Its flowers, 1½ in. long, are produced in July. These trees may be selected with blooms that are red, salmon or white.

FLOSS-SILK TREE *(Chorisia speciosa)*. This grows to 50 ft. high in Zones 9 and 10. The flowers are extremely showy, lilylike, 3 to 5 in. across in yellow, pink, red or purple. They come in late autumn when the tree is leafless. The foliage, composed of 5 to 7 leaflets arranged in finger fashion, provide light shade. The tree trunk may be thorny.

FRANGIPANI, see PLUMERIA

FRANKLINIA *(Franklinia alatamaha,* or *Gordonia alatamaha)* thrives in Zones 6b to 9a, inclusive. This tree, related to camellias, grows in a pyramidal form to a 25-ft. height. Its leaves, shaped like those of camellia, are bright green, 6 in. long, deciduous, and turn brilliant orange-red in autumn. The flowers bloom in late summer, August and September. They are cup-shaped, white, 3 in. across, fragrant, centered by a mass of yellow stamens. Franklinias like soil that is well-drained though fairly moist.

GEIGERTREE, see KOU

GOLDEN-CHAIN, see LABURNUM

GOLDENRAIN-TREE *(Koelreuteria)*. These trees produce clusters of small yellow blossoms that are shaped like those of peas, followed by bladderlike, puffy seed containers. Their foliage is made up of many small leaflets along a central stem, and gives light shade.

K. formosanum or Hayata is for mild-climate Zones 9b and 10, and grows 20 to 40 ft. high. Its dainty yellow flowers come in late summer, followed immediately by rosy-pink puffy pods so showy that they remind one of bougainvillea blooms.

K. paniculata is deciduous and hardy in Zones 5b through 8. It grows 15 to 20 ft. high and is wide-spreading. The flowers, held in erect clusters, come in early summer. They are followed by yellow-brown seed capsules. The tree tolerates drought and alkali soils but is weak-wooded and short-lived.

GORDONIA, see FRANKLINIA

GUM, most kinds, see EUCALYPTUS

HAWTHORN (*Crataegus*). These are found in Zones 5b to 9, inclusive. They are spiny small trees with attractive flowers—usually white—in spring, followed by showy small red fruits that resemble tiny apples. The fruits hang on into winter, or until birds eat them. The foliage is deciduous. There are several popular kinds.

'Autumn Glory' is an outstanding hybrid with showy large fruits.

Cockspur (*C. crus-galli*) grows to 30 ft., with wide-spreading branches. The flowers are white, ½ in. across in clusters; fruits are ½ in. in diameter.

Paul's Scarlet (*C. oxyacantha pauli*) grows 18 to 25 ft. high. Its flowers are double, and are usually red, though white and pink varieties are available.

Washington (*C. phaenopyrum*) grows 20 to 30 ft. high and is the latest of the hawthorns to bloom. Its flowers are white, followed by innumerable tiny jewel-like fruits that remain until spring. The foliage turns vivid orange-scarlet in autumn.

HAYATA, see GOLDENRAIN-TREE.

HORSE-CHESTNUT and BUCKEYE (*Aesculus*). These are deciduous trees with large 5-parted leaves arranged like fingers. They cast dense shade. The blooms, in late spring, are carried in showy upright clusters. Falling flowers, leaves and fruits (horse-chestnuts) tend to create litter. They grow best where there is ample moisture. Children have been poisoned by eating the seeds.

Baumann Horse-Chestnut (*A. hippocastanum baumanni*) has double white flowers that do not result in fruit. It is found in Zones 3b through 9a.

Ohio Buckeye (*A. glabra*), in Zones 5 to 8, inclusive, is a round-headed tree 30 ft. high with small greenish yellow flowers. The foliage turns orange in autumn.

Red Horse-Chestnut (*A. carnea*) grows 40 ft. high or more and 30 ft. across in Zones 4 to 9a. Its flowers are rose-red. Its variety 'Brioti,' or Ruby Horse-Chestnut, has more vivid blooms, scarlet to crimson.

JACARANDA (*Jacaranda acutifolia*). This tree is grown in Zones 9b and 10 and is especially popular in central Mexico and Southern California. It is grown for its foliage as well as its flowers. The profuse summer blooms are lavender-blue, tubular, 2 in. long in big clusters. The leaves are extremely fine-cut and ferny, giving a lacy effect and light shade. The tree likes full sun, fast-draining soil, and not much wind. It needs to be staked when young, to steady and train the trunk, and begins to bloom when about 7 years old.

JATROPHA HASTATA. This small tree with semi-penduous branches, and clusters of star-shaped scarlet flowers, is used in Zone 10.

JERUSALEM-THORN or MEXICAN PALO-VERDE (*Parkinsonia aculeata*). This deciduous tree grows in Zones 8b to 10, inclusive. It is graceful, small, spiny, with green bark, reaching a height of 15 to 25 ft. The foliage is feathery, composed of tiny 3-parted leaves. The swaying branches are covered with ½-in. yellow fragrant flowers in clusters 4 to 6 in. long during spring and summer. The fruits are pea-pod type. It grows in full sun and tolerates desert, alkaline and seaside conditions.

JESSAMINE, ORANGE-, see ORANGE-JESSAMINE

KOELREUTERIA, see GOLDENRAIN-TREE

KOU or GEIGER TREE (*Cordia sebestena*). This tropical tree is called by the first name in Hawaii, and the second in Florida. It grows 15 to 30 ft. high, with large, broad, rough evergreen leaves, and brilliant orange flowers in small clusters most of the year. It tolerates drought and salt spray; must have well-drained soil.

LABURNUM or GOLDEN-CHAIN (*Laburnum*). These are small deciduous trees with 3-parted leaves noted for their yellow pea-shaped flowers in pendulous clusters in late spring. Their seeds and foilage are poisonous if eaten.

Waterer or Vossi (*L. watereri* 'Vossi'), in Zones 5b to 8, inclusive, is the variety with the most attractive blooms in the longest clusters—sometimes 20 in. long. The flowers come at about the same time that rhododendrons bloom. This tree is upright, 12 to 20 ft. high. It grows in sun, or semishade where summers are hot.

LILAC, JAPANESE TREE, see Chapter 8.

MAGNOLIA (*Magnolia*). These trees, some deciduous and others evergreen, are known for their glamorous flowers. Many grow to unexpectedly large size. All like rich, well-drained soil and copious amounts of water, especially during summer.

The best time to plant them is in early spring, when their fleshy roots are just ready for their main spurt of growth that will help them adjust to the new situation, and also heal any possible injury. This means that you can set out the saucer magnolia when it is about to bloom or even in full flower. Magnolias should always be moved without disturbing the earth around their roots so they are sold in containers or balled-and-burlaped. Any pruning should be done during or immediately after flowering.

Saucer (*M. soulangeana*) does well in Zones 5b to 9, inclusive. This is the deciduous tree that blooms very early in spring before its leaves have emerged. The flowers are spectacularly showy, about 6 in. across in cup shape with the inside of the petals creamy white and the outside purplish-pink. The plants begin to bloom when very young and shrublike. Eventually they become trees, 25 ft. or more high and at least that broad, so allow them space to grow. There are numerous named varieties. Alexander or 'Alexandrina' has flowers 7 in. across; *lennei* is dark rosy-purple and late-flowering.

Southern or Bull Bay (*M. grandiflora*) grows in Zones 7b to 10, inclusive. This is the evergreen with pyramidal shape, huge glossy leaves and large white, fragrant flowers 6 to 8 in. across. It eventually reaches 40 to 80 ft. high.

Usually the smaller the leaves, the smaller the tree will become, and the more possible it is to grow it in a confined space—as an espalier, for instance. This magnolia begins to bloom when about 15 years old. In its northern range, protect the leaves from winter wind and sunshine.

Star (*M. stellata*) is found in Zones 5b to 9, inclusive. A multibranched tall shrub or small tree, it grows slowly to a 15-ft. height. Its flowers are white, very fragrant, and appear extremely early in spring before the leaves emerge. They measure 3 in. across with numerous narrow petals. Blooming begins at an early age.

Sweet Bay (*M. virginiana*), in Zones 5b to 10, inclusive, is half-evergreen; deciduous in the North. It has 3-in. white, fragrant flowers among the leaves in early summer and also occasionally later. In the South it is a tall tree. It likes a moist site and generally does best in acid soil. The leaves are 3 to 5 in. long; white on their undersides.

Yulan (*M. denudata*), in Zones 5b to 10, inclusive, is a deciduous tree becoming 35 ft. high, with white, fragrant flowers, 6 in. across, appearing before leaves emerge in spring. It begins to bloom when about 7 years old. Allow 30 ft. of space.

MAYDAY-TREE or EUROPEAN BIRD CHERRY (*Prunus padus*). This deciduous tree grows 25 to 40 ft. high in Zones 2 to 8, inclusive, and is noted for leafing out exceptionally early in spring. Its white, fragrant flowers are small but carried profusely in slender clusters 3 to 6 in. long. There are several varieties.

MIMOSA, see SILK-TREE

MOCK-ORANGE, see ORANGE-JESSAMINE

MOUNTAIN-ASH, EUROPEAN (*Sorbus aucuparia*). This deciduous tree excels in cold climates, within Zones 3 to 8, inclusive. It grows 20 to 50 ft. high, in upright shape when young, but more spreading as it ages. Foliage is made up of small leaflets along a central stem. The spring flowers are small and white in clusters 3 to 5 in. across. In autumn comes the dazzling display of scarlet berries, and the leaves also take on a reddish hue. The tree likes sunshine. It is susceptible to borers.

ORANGE - JESSAMINE or MOCK - ORANGE (*Murraya paniculata*). This small, slow-growing, round-headed evergreen reaches a 10- to 25-ft. height in Zone 10. Its leaves are glossy and dark green. The ¾-in. bell-shaped flowers are white with a jasminelike fragrance. Bloom occurs several times a year.

ORCHID-TREE (*Bauhinia*). These are tropical small trees with profuse, orchidlike, 5-petal flowers. The leaves are 2-lobed and shed briefly in spring. The seeds are carried in long, flat pods. They are adaptable to sun or part shade, in well-drained soil.

B. binata is called Alibangbang in Hawaii. It grows to a 25-ft. height in weeping form, with white flowers having red stamens.

B. blakeana, called Hongkong Orchid-Tree in Florida, has exceptionally showy reddish-purple, fragrant flowers 5 to 6 in. across in late winter and early spring. It grows to 35 ft. high in a spreading shape.

PAGODA-TREE, JAPANESE (*Sophora japonica*). This round-headed deciduous tree grows 20 to 60 ft. high, with wide-spreading branches, in Zones 5b to 9, inclusive. It begins to bloom when about 20 years old, producing profuse white flowers in late summer. The ½-in. blooms, shaped like those of small sweet peas, are carried in showy, pyramidal clusters 12 to 15 in. long. These are followed by interesting long pods that are pinched-in between seeds, resembling a chain of beads.

PALO-VERDE, BLUE (*Cercidium torreyanum*). This small desert tree, spiny and often leafless, can be grown in Zones 7 to 10, inclusive. Its flowers are yellow and showy, ¾ in. across.

PALO-VERDE, MEXICAN, see JERUSALEM-THORN

PEACH, FLOWERING (*Prunus persica*). These trees grow where the fruiting type of peaches thrive, in Zones 6 to 10, inclusive, and are like them except that the blooms are larger and double, in white, pink or red. You can buy them in named varieties. For best flowers, the trees should be pruned annually. For how-to instructions, see the chapter on pruning.

PEAR, CALLERY (*Pyrus calleryana*). If you want a pear tree for ornament rather than fruit, this is it, in Zones 5 to 10a, inclusive. The leaves are glossy and deciduous; flowers are glistening white in early spring; autumn foliage color is purple-red. The fruits are tiny, round brown pears that the birds eat. The tree grows 25 to 30 ft. high. It is deep-rooted and resistant to pests, disease and drought.

'Bradford' is an outstanding selection.

PLUM, BLIREIANA (*Prunus blireiana*). In Zones 4 to 10a, inclusive, this small deciduous purple-leaved tree grows 10 to 25 ft. high with small pink flowers in early spring.

PLUMERIA or FRANGIPANI (*Plumeria acuminata* or *P. rubra acutifolia* hybrids). This small tropical tree, Zone 10, grows 15 to 20 ft. high, and is noted for its beautiful, exceedingly fragrant flowers, often used in leis. The blooms, white, pink, red or yellow, are funnel-form with 5 wide-spreading petals. The trees grow rapidly; branches are stiff and rather awkward-looking; leaves are long, broad, and are shed in winter.

POINCIANA, ROYAL or FLAMBOYANT (*Delonix regia*). In Zone 10 this deciduous tropical tree grows 25 to 40 ft. high, with a wide-spreading flat top. The foliage is ferny, and flowers are scarlet and orange in dazzling profusion. Individual blooms have 5 petals, one of which is white or yellow. They are borne in early spring or summer, sometimes beginning while the branches are leafless. Trees start to bloom at an early age. They like a fairly dry situation.

POMEGRANATE. See the chapter on shrubs.

REDBUD (*Cercis*). These small deciduous trees, rarely over 30 ft. high, have heart-shaped leaves. They begin to bloom when young, bearing numerous clusters of small magenta-pink pea-shaped blossoms before leaves appear in spring. The flowers are colorful and showy over an exceptionally long time. The foliage turns brilliant yellow in autumn. These trees will grow in full sun or part shade.

Eastern (*C. canadensis*), in Zones 5b to 9,

inclusive, is the native one seen through woodlands of the Northeast, Midwest and South in spring at flowering dogwood time. There is a white form, *alba*, commonly called whitebud.

Chinese (*C. chinensis*), in Zones 6b to 10a, inclusive, is similar, but does not stand as much cold.

SCHOLAR-TREE, see PAGODA-TREE

SERVICE-BERRY (*Amelanchier*). These small deciduous trees or large shrubs are found in Zones 3b to 9, inclusive. They have gray bark, and white flowers in showy clusters very early in spring. The fruits are berrylike, red ripening to black, and beloved by birds. The foliage turns yellow to orange in autumn.

Apple (*A. grandiflora*) reaches 15 to 25 ft. high, and is especially attractive grown with multiple trunks. Its flowers, 1¼ in. across, are larger than those of other service-berries.

SHOWER, see CASSIA

SILK TREE or MIMOSA (*Albizzia*). These are rapid-growing deciduous trees, 20 to 40 ft. high, with flat-topped form, and graceful ferny foliage that makes light shade. The flowers are pink, fluffy and fragrant throughout the summer. The tree can be grown with single or multiple trunks, and pruned high or low. It tolerates alkaline soil and irrigation. Attacks by mimosa webworm are a problem.

Common (*A. julibrissin*) may be grown in Zones 7 to 10, inclusive. Buy only wilt-resistant kinds.

Hardy (*A. julibrissin rosea*), for Zones 6 to 9, inclusive, is slightly smaller, with deeper pink blooms.

SILVER-BELL, CAROLINA (*Halesia carolina*). This deciduous tree growing 20 to 30 ft. high, in Zones 5 to 9a, inclusive, is native to the southeastern United States. In mid-spring its branches are hung with multitudes of ¾-in. bell-shaped white flowers. It will grow in sun or semishade, and likes rich, well-drained soil.

SNOWBELL, JAPANESE (*Styrax japonica*). In Zones 6 to 9a, inclusive, this flat-topped, slender deciduous tree or large shrub grows 15 to 30 ft. high. The flowers are bell-shaped, fragrant, white, ½ in. long, hanging in long-stalked clusters from the underside of leafy branches in June. The tree likes sun or high, filtered shade, slightly acid soil, and ample moisture.

SWEETSHADE (*Hymenosporum flavum*). Throughout Zones 9b to 10, inclusive, this slender, upright evergreen grows 20 to 40 ft. high. Its glossy leaves are carried like those of pittosporum—to which it is related. Tubular, fragrant yellow, flowers, 1½ in. across, appear in clusters in early summer.

TABEBUIA ARGENTIA. Known as Silver Trumpet-Tree and Tree-of-Gold, it is used in Zone 10. It grows 15 to 30 ft. high, with masses of gorgeous yellow trumpet-shaped blooms 2½ in. long in early spring while branches are briefly leafless. The foliage is silver-gray. The tree's trunk is irregular and picturesquely shaped. Branches may be brittle. It adapts to seaside conditions.

THEVETIA THEVETIOIDES. In Zones 9b and 10, this large shrub or small, round-headed tree grows to 25 ft. The flowers are gorgeous, wide-flaring trumpets in yellow, apricot or white.

TIPU-TREE (*Tipuana tipu*). This evergreen grows 30 to 60 ft. high in Zones 9 and 10. It has wide-spreading, pendulous branches forming an umbrella shape. The foliage is glossy, gray-green, composed of many small leaflets along a central stem. The flowers are golden yellow, butterfly-shaped in big showy clusters at the ends of branches in June and July. It tolerates heat and drought.

TREE-of-GOLD and TRUMPET-TREE, see TABEBUIA

YELLOW-BELLS or YELLOW-ELDER (*Stenolobium stans*). This quick-growing small evergreen tree or large shrub is used in Zones 9b and 10. It has big, trumpet-shaped, fragrant, yellow flowers in autumn, and also in spring. The foliage has numerous leaflets in feather form. The tree grows 10 to 15 ft. high and adapts to sun or shade.

8

Shrubs of All Sorts and Sizes

Shrubs are the major structural plants of your yard, and almost as permanent and dependable as its architecture. There are hundreds—evergreen and deciduous, short and tall, flowery or mostly foliage, sun-loving or shade-tolerating. Their uses are as varied as their appearance. Before you can make wise selections, you must decide where and how you are going to use each shrub, and the requirements it must meet. Then scan the available list to see what fills the bill for you and thrives in your region. Usually your choices boil down to only a handful of topnotch candidates.

The ideal shrubs look well the year around. Evergreens of course are superb, especially for entrance plantings and for areas that you see from your windows during winter. But deciduous shrubs are interesting also, even when leafless. Flowers may or may not be important. For example, with hedges and screen plantings, dense, healthy foliage is what you are after and blossoms are a secondary asset.

Take into consideration each shrub's eventual mature size and shape, so you will not have to keep pruning it to try to make it fit a smaller site. And plan spacing according to future needs. All bushes are deceptively small to begin with, unless you buy big, old specimens, so you can be fooled about how large they will become in a few years. The first season after planting they will grow very little, while roots become established. But within 3 to 5 years they will achieve full size. They grow best when uncrowded, so if you buy too many and cram them into a small space you waste money, and the plants do not do as well as if you had set out fewer. You can plant flowers to fill the empty areas between shrubs while they are small.

Best Time To Plant, in General

In the coldest climates, Zones 2 through 5, early spring is the ideal time. In mild climates fall and winter are the big planting seasons. In intermediate Zones 6 and 7, either fall or spring are satisfactory. Container-grown material can be set out any time during the growing season. If any important shrubs need to be planted at a special time, this will be mentioned where the shrub is discussed.

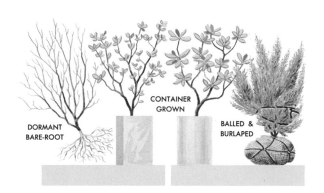

Pointers on Purchasing

To buy wisely, you should figure out what shrubs you want well ahead of planting time, while you can think unhurriedly. If you have made a planting plan for your yard, as suggested in the chapter on landscaping, you will know your needs precisely so you can concentrate on the matter of size and where to make your purchases.

The sources of plants can be either local garden-supply firms or reputable mail-order nurseries that publish catalogues. If you purchase locally, you can see the specimens and possibly buy in larger sizes than can be shipped by mail order. Moreover, you can take them home with you and plant at once. Ordering by mail, you can shop without leaving your house, and often have a wider selection of choice plants.

Prices vary according to the size of the plant, the way it is packaged or handled, and how difficult it is for nurserymen to propagate and grow. Some shrubs, especially dwarf evergreens, grow extremely slowly and may need 8 to 10 years of attentive care before they are of marketable size.

There are 3 ways of handling shrubs: a) "bare-root," having no soil around the roots; b) "container-grown," in pots or cans; and c) "balled-and-burlaped," dug with a ball of earth about the roots and enclosed in burlap.

Deciduous shrubs—those that lose their leaves for winter—are usually sold during their dormant season, with roots bare but protected in some way so that they do not dry out and die. Locally you may find them stored upright in bins of moist sawdust or similar material. Mail-order firms store them in a cold, dark, moist place prior to shipping, and mail them enclosed in moisture-holding polyethylene-coated paper or with some moist substance around their roots. Since it is difficult to move shrubs with bare roots after leaves have started to grow, garden centers pot them in containers for later-season sales. Container-grown plants are priced higher than bare-root ones.

Evergreens, both broadleaf and narrowleaf, are seldom sold bare-root, because they are always in leaf. They come either in containers or balled-and-burlaped. In shopping for them, especially if tempted by what seems to be a great bargain, make sure that the ball of earth has not become dry or broken. If the roots have been allowed to dry out, they will die, and so will the plant. This will not be obvious for weeks or even months, because the foliage of evergreens remains green long after the tree is lifeless—just as cut branches of evergreens do at Christmas time.

How To Plant

Before planting day, know where the shrub is to go, and plan its spacing in relation to other shrubs, the wall of your house, or whatever is nearby. Figure the spacing according to the expected mature size of the shrub. For example, a pfitzer juniper will grow at least 5 ft. across. Therefore a group or row of them should be set with plants 5 ft. apart; or if they are to be against a house wall, the centers of the plants should be at a distance from the building equal to ½ of their expected diameter—or 2½ ft. Roof overhangs must be taken into consideration, since little or no rain will get beneath them to provide water. Set shrubs so their centers are outside of the line of the eaves. Branches will extend back at least part way beneath the overhang.

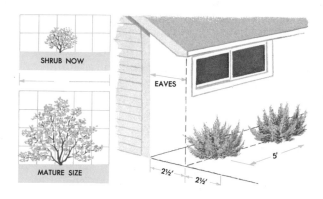

When the shrubs arrive, if you cannot plant at once, remember that you are dealing with living material and the key to future success is to keep the roots from drying. If the plants are in containers, or balled-and-burlaped, put them in a shady place out of the wind, and keep the roots watered, though not sopping wet. Bare-root material—if the delay is to be less than 24 hours—can be stored in a cool place with roots in a tub of water, or if it must wait several days, cover or wrap the roots in moist material such as earth, cloth, sphagnum moss, etc. If the shrub arrived by mail, and the wrapping is unbroken so no air is getting to the roots, it can be left packaged for a day or two if necessary, though having the roots in water for the 24 hours before planting is helpful.

Dig the holes larger and deeper than the size of the roots, for roots should not be crowded but allowed to spread out, and they need space in which to grow easily. Loosen the soil in the bottom of the hole, adding and mixing in either some of the best topsoil removed from the hole, or some garden loam brought from elsewhere in your yard.

Pruning at planting time is not necessary for plants that grow in containers, or balled-and-burlaped. But bare-root deciduous shrubs should have their tops reduced by about ⅓ to compensate for roots lost during the digging process. This can be done either before or after planting. First remove any weak or twiggy branches. Then shorten the remaining ones by about ⅓, cutting ¼ in. above a growth bud. This sounds severe, and you will hate to do it since you will be removing parts that make the bush look big. But pruned shrubs grow much faster and more vigorously than those left unpruned. Roots may need pruning too; you should remove any that are awkwardly longer than all others, and should trim any that are broken.

Set the bushes so the soil level comes where it did in the nursery. Those in containers should be removed gently so the soil remains intact about the roots. Balled-and-burlaped plants should be set in the hole with burlap intact; then, when the plant is properly positioned and the hole partially filled, loosen the burlap from around the top and push it down into the sides of the hole. The burlap will rot away soon and do no harm. Fill in around the roots with the best soil you have available. It is helpful to use ⅓ moist peat moss (moistened by putting it in a bucket, adding water and stirring until the moss has absorbed all it can take without being soggy). Firm the soil. Water thoroughly, making sure the shrub does not sink deep in its hole. Feeding is not necessary at this time.

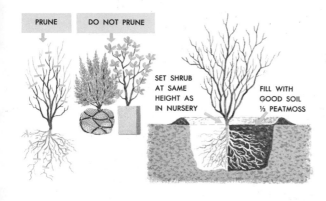

PRUNE DO NOT PRUNE

SET SHRUB AT SAME HEIGHT AS IN NURSERY

FILL WITH GOOD SOIL ½ PEATMOSS

Through the first 2 years, be sure the plant is watered deeply about once a week, if rains do not attend to it for you. When the shrubs have begun to grow well, they can have a light feeding. In future years feeding should be done, if needed, just before the main period of growth. For advice on pruning, see the chapter on that subject.

HEDGES

Many different kinds of shrubs can be used for hedges, depending upon the effect you are after. There are low hedges and tall, evergreen and deciduous, clipped and informally natural.

The main requirements for selecting shrubs are good-looking, dense, healthy foliage and, if they are to be pruned to a certain height or shape, a toleration of continual clipping.

The easiest hedges to maintain are those allowed to keep their normal shape. In other words, you should choose shrubs which, when mature, have the desired height, width, and appearance, with almost no pruning. Of course, they have a rather billowy look instead of being rigidly trim, but in many situations this is preferable, or at least desirably attractive.

Evergreens are excellent for hedging, since they remain beautiful even in winter. Either narrowleaf or broadleaf kinds can be used. Planting time is the same as for shrubs used for other purposes.

When shopping, remember that you do not need the biggest, most shapely, and thus the most expensive specimens. Since hedge plants are grown to become interlocking masses of foliage, you can start with small-size plants. Often in mail-order catalogues, and also in garden centers, you will find hedge plants marketed in units of 12, 25 or 50. The bigger their root systems, the better; and while husky small plants grow rapidly and vigorously, those slightly larger and bushier with more roots will give quicker results.

The number of plants to buy is figured on the basis of the size the shrubs attain when mature. But since your goal is not specimen bushes but dense, overlapping growth, multiply your count by 2. Plan to space the plants accordingly. Typical hedges, such as privet and barberry, are usually spaced 12 to 18 in. apart.

Before beginning to plant, put stakes at either end of the place where the hedge will be, and run a string between them to indicate the center line. Do not dig individual holes for the bushes unless they are types that will grow very large and therefore must be widely spaced. For small, bare-root deciduous shrubs, open a long trench with one side directly beneath the string marking the center line. Make the trench wider and deeper than the size of the root systems, and loosen the soil in the bottom. The plants can be lined up single file against the center-line side, or they can be placed in a staggered arrangement

OPPOSITE:
Aucuba

Rhododendron

Japanese Tree Lilac

Forsythia 'Lynwood Gold'

HANDSOME
BROAD-LEAVED SHRUBS

along both sides. They should be set the same depth as in the nursery.

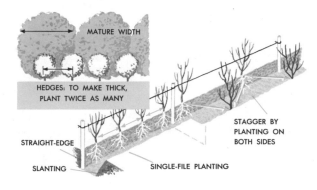

Whether you should prune at planting time depends upon whether your material is evergreen or deciduous. Evergreens from containers, or balled-and-burlaped, do not need pruning. Spring-set deciduous shrubs do, and fall-planted ones should be pruned early the following spring. This holds true even though the plants are several feet tall, because your goal is dense branching that begins near the ground. To produce such growth you must cut the bushes back to within 6 in. of the soil line! For full details and illustrations of how to develop a thick hedge, and how it should be pruned in future years, see the paragraphs on hedges in the chapter on pruning.

Feeding during future years should be done once or twice a year, especially just before the main spring growth. Water whenever rainfall is scant. Remember that these plants are growing in exceptionally crowded conditions and need all the encouragement you can give them.

Some Shrubs That Make Fine Hedges

De: Deciduous Ev: Evergreen S: Sun
PS: Part shade

Name	Zone	De.	Ev.	S.	PS.
			X	X	X
Abelia	6b-10		X	X	X
Arbor-Vitae					
American	3-8		X		X
Oriental	6-10		X		X
Barberry					
'Crimson Pygmy'	3-10	X		X	
Japanese	3-10	X		X	X
Mentor	4b-9	X	X	X	
Box, Common	6-9		X	X	X
Buckthorn					
Common	3-6	X		X	X
Glossy, Columnar	3-6	X		X	X
Italian	8-10		X	X	X
Cherry-Laurel	7b-10		X	X	X
Currant, Alpine	2-7	X			X
Euonymus					
Kiautschovica	6-10		X	X	X
Winged	3b-10	X		X	X
Forsythia	5b-8	X		X	
Hibiscus, Chinese	9-10		X	X	
Holly					
Chinese	7b-10		X	X	X
Japanese	6b-9		X	X	X
Yaupon	7b-10		X	X	X
Honeysuckle, most	3-8	X		X	X
Juniper, bushy and					
pyramidal types	4-10		X	X	X
Lilac	3b-8a	X		X	
Lime-Berry	10		X	X	
Myrtle, True	8b-10		X	X	
Nandina	7-10		X	X	X
Ninebark	2-8	X		X	X
Orange-Jessamine	10		X	X	X
Pea-Shrub	2b-9a	X		X	
Pernettya	8-10		X	X	
Photinia	7b-10		X	X	
Pittosporum	8-10		X	X	X
Plum-Yew	9-10		X	X	X
Podocarpus, Yew	8b-10		X	X	X
Privet					
Japanese	7b-10		X	X	X

NARROW-LEAVED EVERGREEN SHRUBS

These are the conifers, cone bearers, with narrow or needlelike foliage. They are discussed separately from broad-leaved evergreens because they look so different. They can be grown over most of the country, and most of them tolerate colder temperatures, more wind and drier air than do broad-leaved evergreens.

Since they come in both shrub and tree forms, be sure when shopping that if you want shrubs, you buy the varieties that stay low rather than grow up to be huge trees. You can get types that creep on the ground, or that make low, medium or tall bushes. Some demand a sunny site, while others tolerate shade.

Feed these like other shrubs. Watering is extra-important—especially prior to winter freeze-up in cold climates—since leaves continue to evaporate moisture at a time when it cannot be replenished.

Pruning methods vary. For instructions see that chapter.

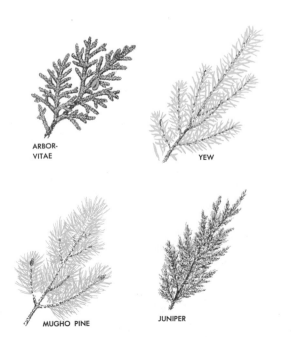

ARBOR-
VITAE

YEW

MUGHO PINE

JUNIPER

ARBOR-VITAE *(Thuja)*. These are shrubs and trees with fernlike foliage composed of flat, overlapping scales. Their cones are tiny, ½ in. to 1 in. long. The plants come in various shapes and heights; upright pyramidal forms are popular for hedges, screening and landscaping accents. They prefer cool climates, ample moisture, part shade, and dislike dust, smoke, summer heat, drying sun and winter wind.

American, or White Cedar *(Thuja occidentalis)* appears in Zones 3 to 8, inclusive. Shrub varieties include round 'Globe' and upright 'Pyramidal.'

Oriental *(T. orientalis)* is used in Zones 6 to 10, inclusive. It adapts to southern climates better than does American. Growth is more compact, and the fanlike foliage is carried in a neat, vertical arrangement. There are several low-growing varieties including *compacta* and its yellow-leaved forms.

FALSE-CYPRESS *(Chamaecyparis)*. These shrubs and trees come in varying forms, heights and types of foliage. Leaves of mature plants are usually scalelike, while juvenile foliage is needlelike and soft. In some varieties the juvenile type of foliage is permanent and these soft-needled forms are often called *Retinospora*. False-Cypress likes moist air and soil, and prefers acid conditions. It does not like hot, arid climates, drying wind, smoke or chemical fumes.

The following types are trees which have numerous dwarf or shrub forms, including some with yellow or blue-gray foliage.

Hinoki Cypress *(C. obtusa)* is grown in Zones 5 to 8, inclusive. Its leaves are in flat planes. The variety *nana* develops upright to a 3-ft. height.

Port Orford Cedar or Lawson Cypress *(C. lawsoniana)* is used in Zones 6b to 9, inclusive. 'Birds Nest' grows 3 to 4 ft. high and spreads to 8 ft. wide. 'Fletcheri' and 'Elwoodi' are conical, with blue-gray leaves.

Sawara Cypress *(C. pisifera)* appears in Zones 5 to 9, inclusive. It has a feathery foliage. Thread Cypress *(C. pisifera filifera)*, which has weeping branches, attains an 8-ft. height. Its dwarf form *nana* is moundlike, with a golden-leaved form, and grows 1½ to 3 ft. high.

Japanese podocarpus is a favorite shrub in mild climates. The little bushes edging the path in the background are dwarf box. Garden of the Bright Taylors, Ocala, Florida

POPULAR NARROW-LEAVED EVERGREEN SHRUBS

Dwarf mugho pines do not all grow at the same rate, or to the same height. They can be kept small by pruning the "candles" each spring.

These upright yews are quite old and if left alone would have become tall, wide-spreading trees. They have been pruned regularly to keep them dense and shapely within allowed space.

JUNIPER *(Juniperus)*. These come in many sizes, from prostrate creepers to trees. Their leaves are partly needlelike and partly scaly. The plants are rapid-growing, relatively inexpensive, very tough and durable. They like full sun, tolerate poor soil, and when established can withstand drought. They are among the hardiest evergreens and therefore especially appreciated in coldest winter climates. The following are among the most popular.

Common *(Juniperus communis)* is grown in Zones 2 to 9, inclusive, in various heights from low shrub to tree.

Creeping *(J. horizontalis)* excels in Zones 3 to 9, inclusive. It is a sprawler 1 to 1½ ft. high with long branches which gradually root where they touch ground. It spreads to cover 6 ft. or more. The varieties include 'Waukegan' *(J. horizontalis douglasi)*, which has a blue cast during the year and somewhat purplish tones in winter; 'Andorra' *(J. horizontalis plumosa)*, which is more compact in habit, turning bronze in fall; and 'Wilton.' For the quickest results buy well-started plants in containers or balled-and-burlaped. Plant 3 ft. apart, and prune them occasionally while young to make them more bushy. Prune also from time to time during their entire life to keep them where you want them; stop them from getting leggy, and let light into the lower branches, whose foliage dies and drops off if it is constantly shaded. (See the chapter on pruning.)

Japgarden *(J. procumbens)* is used in Zones 4 to 9, inclusive. Low-spreading, it grows about 2 ft. high, picturesquely shaped with bluish-green needles.

Meyer's *(J. squamata meyeri)* grows in Zones 5 to 9, inclusive. It has a picturesque shape with branches irregularly upright, and reaches a height of 6 to 8 ft. The foliage color is distinctively blue.

Pfitzer *(J. chinensis pfitzeriana)* is seen in Zones 4 to 10, inclusive. It is usually a big bush, becoming 5 ft. high and 6 to 12 ft. wide, though compact varieties are available. Branches arch in feathery plumes. Space the bushes 5 ft. apart.

Shore *(J. conferta)* thrives in Zones 5b to 10, inclusive. Mat-forming, it becomes 2 ft. high.

Tamarix *(J. sabina tamaricifolia)* grows in Zones 5 to 10, inclusive. It grows 3 ft. high with branches arching horizontally to make attractive mounds.

PINE *(Pinus)*. The Dwarf Mugho *(P. mugo mughus)* grows in Zones 3 to 6, inclusive. It is a low-growing dwarf with rounded shape, whose height varies. Cold-hardy, it likes sun and also tolerates wind. Though usually a compact pincushion-like shape at the time you buy it, the plant gradually grows. Some eventually become taller than head-high if not restrained by pruning a little each spring.

PLUM-YEW, JAPANESE *(Cephalotaxus harringtonia drupacea)*. This can be seen in Zones 9 and 10. It is an evergreen 12 to 24 in. high, looking like a dwarf podocarpus. Good for low hedges, it grows in sun or shade.

PODOCARPUS, YEW *(Podocarpus macrophylla)*. This slow-growing shrub or tree appears in Zones 8b to 10, inclusive. It has narrow leaves 3 to 4 in. long and can be sheared easily for hedges. It will grow in sun or shade, in various soils, and tolerates drought. Variety *maki* is an excellent type which grows up to 20 ft. tall.

YEW *(Taxus)*. These are the aristocrats among narrowleaf evergreens. Their leaves are dark green, 1 in. long, flat, and densely arranged on the stems. The plants will grow in sun or shade, and are ideal for the north side of a house. There are numerous varieties—low, spreading, upright or vase-shaped. Most of these can easily be controlled by pruning and, since they even tolerate shearing, are splendid for hedges. Most are slow-growing and thus fairly expensive. Because there are so many yews, it is wise to talk them over with your nurseryman, explaining what you are after so he can suggest which varieties best fit your need.

Fruits are red and berrylike, though they are modified cones. It is interesting to note that male and female flowers are usually borne on separate plants, so only female bushes produce fruit. The seed, foliage and wood of yew are poisonous if eaten in quantity, but the pulp of the fruit is edible.

English (*Taxus baccata*) grows in Zones 7 to 9, inclusive. Eventually it becomes a tree, if not pruned. A dwarf form is spreading English yew (*T. baccata repandens*), which usually reaches 4 ft.

Japanese (*T. cuspidata*) is used in Zones 5 to 8, inclusive. These slow-growing bushes or trees are the hardiest kind of yew. The most compact and low-growing forms are *T. cuspi-data densa* and *T. cuspidata nana*. These can be kept below 4 ft. Medium height varieties are *T. cuspidata densiformis* and *T. cuspidata thayerae*.

Taxus media lives in Zones 6b to 9a. These are hybrids of English and Japanese yew. There are upright forms such as 'Hicks' that are excellent for hedges, and broader pyramidal varieties such as 'Hatfield.'

THE BEST LOW-GROWING BROAD-LEAVED SHRUBS

NORTHEAST
Canby Pachistima
Cranberry Cotoneaster
Drooping Leucothoe
Dwarf Boxwood
Japanese Holly 'Helleri'
Mountain Andromeda
Rhododendron 'Boule de
   Neige'
Rose Daphne
Slender Deutzia
Warminster Broom

PLAINS AND INTERMOUNTAIN
Bluebeard
Chenault Coral-Berry
Cranberry Cotoneaster
Creeping Mahonia
Froebel Spirea
Hypericum kalmianum
Lead-Plant
Lodense Privet
Potentilla 'Gold Drop'
Yucca glauca

DEEP SOUTH
Coontie
Dwarf Firethorn
Dwarf Natal-Plum
Dwarf Yaupon
Glossy Abelia
Japanese Boxwood
Japanese Holly
Japanese Plum-Yew
Lime-Berry
Malpighia coccigera

MIDWEST
Alpine Currant
Clavey's Dwarf
   Honeysuckle
Cranberry Cotoneaster
Crimson Pigmy Barberry
Dwarf Japanese
   Flowering Quince
*Forsythia viridissima
   bronxensis*
Froebel Spirea
Kerria
Korean Boxwood
Western Ninebark

UPPER SOUTH
Dwarf Gardenia
Dwarf Japanese Quince
Dwarf Pomegranate
Floribunda Rose
*Hypericum patulum
   henryi*
Japanese Holly 'Helleri'
Korean Boxwood
Necklace Cotoneaster
Showy Jasmine
Yucca filamentosa

SOUTHWEST*
African Boxwood
Boxleaf Euonymus
Bush Morning-Glory
Compact Myrtle
Creeping Rosemary
Dwarf Gardenia
Dwarf Pomegranate
Japanese Boxwood
Santolina
Teucrium chamaedrys

* In the Southwest, Zones 5 and 6, use Plains and Intermountain list.

Pfitzer juniper has a plumy and billowy look though its small needle-like leaves are sharp. There are many other kinds of juniper, some almost prostrate and others tree-like.

PACIFIC NORTHWEST
Irwin Barberry
Japanese Holly 'Green
    Island'
Longleaf Mahonia
Nandina domestica
    'Dwarf'
Pernettya mucronata
Pink India-Hawthorn
Rhododendron 'Blue Tit'
Rhododendron 'Elizabeth'
Warty Barberry
Winter Daphne

NORTHERN CALIFORNIA
Abelia grandiflora
    'Prostrata'
Arctostaphylos 'Howard
    McMinn'
Compact Myrtle
India-Hawthorn
Japanese Holly, dwarf
    kinds
Rock-Rose 'Doris
    Hibberson'
Sarcococca humilis
Skimmia reevesiana
Spring Heath
Viburnum davidi

SOUTHERN
CALIFORNIA
Australian Bluebell
    Creeper
Camellia sasanqua
Dwarf Natal-Plum
Hebe menziesi
Hypericum moserianum
Myrtle 'Italica'
Nandina 'Compacta'
Sarcococca humilis
Star-Jasmine
White Rock-Rose

HAWAII
Akia Akia
Bush Thunbergia
*Chloranthus
    inconspicuus*
Crown-of-Thorns
Dwarf Pomegranate
Eugenia monticola
Malpighia coccigera
Mistletoe Fig
Shrimp-Plant
Ulei

ALASKA
American Green Alder
Bear-Berry
Bush Cinquefoil
Common Juniper
Creeping Juniper
Dwarf Arctic Birch
Dwarf Pea-Shrub
European Cotoneaster
Western Ninebark
Western Sand Cherry

THE BEST MEDIUM-HEIGHT BROAD-LEAVED SHRUBS

NORTHEAST
Chenault Viburnum
Convexleaf Japanese
    Holly
Dwarf Winged
    Euonymus
Japanese Andromeda
Knap Hill Hybrid
    Azaleas
Mountain-Laurel
Regel Privet
Spreading Cotoneaster
Torch Azalea
Wintergreen Barberry

MIDWEST
Dwarf Winged
    Euonymus
Father Hugo Rose
Forsythia intermedia vars.
Fragrant Sumac
Hills of Snow Hydrangea
Japanese Quince
    'Umbilicata'
Mentor Barberry
Regel Privet
Viburnum carlesi
Winter Honeysuckle

PLAINS AND
INTERMOUNTAIN
Austrian Copper Rose
Flowering Almond
French Hybrid Lilacs
Laland Pyracantha
Oregon-Grape
Peking Cotoneaster
Rose-of-Sharon
Sweet Mock-Orange
Tatarian Honeysuckle
Vanhoutte Spirea

UPPER SOUTH
Aucuba
Forsythia intermedia,
   various
Gardenia
Glossy Abelia
Hollies, low-growing
Japanese Quince
Judd Viburnum
Kurume Azaleas
Nandina domestica
Thunberg Spirea

DEEP SOUTH
Cleyera
Downy-Myrtle
Eurya
Indian Azalea
Ixora coccinea, hybrids
Japanese Pittosporum
Laurestinus Viburnum
Myrtle
Orange-Jessamine
Thyrallis

SOUTHWEST*
Burford Holly
Chinese Hibiscus
Euonymus japonicus
   grandiflora
Glossy Abelia
Japanese Camellia
Japanese Pittosporum
Myrtle
Nandina
Sandankwa Viburnum
Texas Ranger

PACIFIC NORTHWEST
Corsican Heath
Darwin Barberry
Drooping Leucothoe
Japanese Andromeda
Mexican-Orange
Nandina domestica
Osmanthus delavayi
Rhododendron 'Blue
   Diamond'
Rhododendron 'Jean Marie
   de Montague'
Skimmia japonica

NORTHERN CALIFORNIA
Ceanothus 'Julia Phelps'
Escallonia 'C. F. Ball'
Glossy Abelia
Mediterranean Heaths
Mexican-Orange
Nandina domestica
Osmanthus delavayi
Sarcococca ruscifolia
Strawberry-Tree
Viburnum burkwoodi

SOUTHERN CALIFORNIA
African Boxwood
Burford Holly
Cistus ladaniferus
Compact Strawberry-Tree
Glossy Abelia
India-Hawthorn, various
Mexican-Orange
Pittosporum tobira
   variegatum
Shiny Xylosma
Viburnum tinus
   compactum

HAWAII
Adenium obesum
Chinese Hibiscus
Eranthemum nervosum
Fijian-Daphne
Lime-Berry
Parsley Panax
Raphiolepis umbellata
   ovata
Thyrallis
Tiare Gardenia
Yesterday-Today-and-
   Tomorrow

ALASKA
Alpine Currant
Billard Spirea
Dwarf Illinois Ninebark
Greene Mountain-Ash
Littleleaf Pea-Shrub
Pacific Service-Berry
Peking Cotoneaster
Redleaf Rose
Red-Osier Dogwood
Rugosa Rose

*In the Southwest, Zones 5 and 6, use
Plains and Intermountain list.

THE BEST TALL BROAD-LEAVED SHRUBS

NORTHEAST
Columnar Buckthorn
Forsythia 'Spring Glory'
French Hybrid Lilacs
Japanese Holly
Laland Pyracantha
Maries Doublefile
  Viburnum
Redvein Enkianthus
*Rhododendron
  catawbiense* hybrids
Siebold Viburnum
Winged Euonymus

MIDWEST
American Cranberry-Bush
Autumn Elaeagnus
Columnar Buckthorn
Common Witch-Hazel
Cotoneaster multiflora
French Hybrid Lilac
Pagoda Dogwood
Panicled Dogwood
Wayfaring-Tree
Winged Euonymus

PLAINS & INTERMOUNTAIN
Amur Maple
Common Buckthorn
Fortune Fontanesia
Fountain Buddleia
Japanese Tree Lilac
Nanny-Berry
Pea-Shrub, Siberian
Redbud
Russian-Olive
Staghorn Sumac

UPPER SOUTH
Camellia japonica and
  sasanqua
Cleyera
Crape-Myrtle
Fortune's Osmanthus
Frazer Photinia
Hollies, tall kinds
Japanese Privet
Loquat
Pyracantha, various
Thorny Elaeagnus

DEEP SOUTH
Banana-Shrub
Camellia sasanqua
Chinese Holly
  (selections)
Chinese Photinia
Florida Anise-Tree
Japanese Camellia
Japanese Privet
Marlberry
Oleander, various
Sweet Viburnum

SOUTHWEST*
Chinese Photinia
Cocculus laurifolius
Japanese Privet
Oleander
Parney Cotoneaster
*Pyracantha crenato-
  serrata* or *P. fortuneana*
Red Bottle-Brush
Shiny Xylosma
Sour Orange
Thorny Elaeagnus

PACIFIC NORTHWEST
Abelia 'Edward Goucher'
Escallonia 'Appleblossom'
Ilex crenata 'Roundleaf'
Japanese Camellia
Oregon-Grape
Parney Cotoneaster
Pyracantha 'Rosedale'
Rhododendron augustini
Strawberry-Tree
Threespine Barberry

NORTHERN CALIFORNIA
Australian Tea-Tree
Common Cherry-Laurel
Italian Buckthorn
Laurestinus Viburnum
Osmanthus ilicifolius
Parney Cotoneaster
Pittosporum undulatum
Portugal-Laurel
Red Escallonia
Russian-Olive

SOUTHERN CALIFORNIA
Cocculus laurifolius
Cotoneaster lactea
Escallonia organensis
Fruitland Silverberry
Leptospermum scoparium
  hybrids
Japanese Privet
Oleander
Purple-leaved Dodonea
Rose Bottle-Brush
Sweet Hakea

*In the Southwest, Zones 5 and 6, use
Plains and Intermountain list.

HAWAII

Carissa grandiflora
Crape-Gardenia
Euphorbia leucocephala
Golden Dewdrop
Ixora macrothyrsa
Malpighia glabra
Nandina
Naupaka
Pittosporum tobira
Surinam-Cherry

ALASKA

American Cranberry-Bush
Arrow-Wood
Common Lilac
Late Lilac
Nanny-Berry
Siberian Pea-Shrub
Silverberry
Sitka Mountain-Ash
Tatarian Honeysuckle

❦ Outstanding Broad-leaved Shrubs

ABELIA. These semi-evergreen shrubs have small glossy leaves and little tubular flowers. They will grow in sun or part shade, and tolerate clipping. Flowers are borne on new wood. (For pruning instructions, see that chapter.)

Glossy (*A. grandiflora*), used in Zones 6b to 10, inclusive, grows 6 to 8 ft. high with pink or white flowers. Dwarf forms are 'Prostrata' and 'Sherwoodi' that are about 3 ft. high.

'Edward Goucher' is an excellent hybrid 5 ft. high with lavender flowers.

ALDER, AMERICAN GREEN (*Alnus crispa*). This Alaskan native likes a cool, moist site. It is usually 1 to 2 ft. high, and its leaves are oval, 2 in. long.

ALMOND, FLOWERING. Two deciduous shrubs carry this name. Both are very hardy [Zones 4b through 9], like sun, and bloom very early in spring before their foliage opens. One is *Prunus triloba*, which may be grown bushy or treelike, 3 to 8 ft. high, with pink flowers 1½ in. across. It is usually sold in its double form with blooms like little double roses. The other, called dwarf flowering almond (*Prunus glandulosa*), 2 to 5 ft. high, is a few days later in blooming. It has smaller single or double white or pink flowers in profusion.

ANDROMEDA (*Pieris*). These broad-leaved evergreen shrubs have glossy leaves and clusters of small white flowers resembling those of lily-of-the-valley. They grow best in moist climates, in either sun or shade.

Japanese (*P. japonica*), in Zones 6 to 9, inclusive, is 3 to 8 ft. high, with leaves 5 in. long. The flower clusters are drooping.

Mountain (*P. floribunda*), in Zones 5 to 9 inclusive, is lower-growing, 3 to 6 ft. high, with longer leaves. The flower clusters are held upright.

ANISE-TREE (*Illicium*). These are compact evergreen shrubs for mild-winter climates. They grow up to 10 ft. high, with aromatic leaves 6 in. long, and star-shaped flowers 1½ in. across in spring. They prefer part shade and slightly acid soil, and are easy to grow from seed.

Florida (*I. floridanum*) is native to Florida. Its flowers are dark red.

Japanese (*I. anisatum*) has greenish-yellow blooms.

ARCTOSTAPHYLOS, see MANZANITA

ARROW-WOOD, see VIBURNUM

AUCUBA (*Aucuba japonica*). This evergreen appears in Zones 7b to 10, inclusive, and is grown for its handsome foliage. Its leaves are thick and glossy, 7 in. long, oval, and coarsely toothed. The plants grow best in shade and burn in sun. They are not particular about soil but appreciate plentiful water. The small maroon flowers produce red berries; the sexes are on separate plants. (For data on pruning, see that chapter.)

Variety *variegata*, with leaves mottled in yellow, is called gold-dust tree.

AZALEA, see RHODODENDRON and AZALEA

BANANA-SHRUB (*Michelia fuscata*). This grows in Zones 8 to 10, inclusive. An evergreen, it grows 10 to 15 ft. high and is related to magnolias. It has flowers similarly shaped but only 1 to 1½ in. across, brownish-yellow, with the fragrance of ripe bananas. The leaves, 3 in. in length, are glossy and oblong. It prefers part shade.

BARBERRY (*Berberis*). These are deciduous and evergreen thorny shrubs grown primarily for their good-looking foliage; often as hedges. They prefer a sunny site but tolerate light shade.

Darwin (*B. darwini*) is used in Zones 8 and 9. An evergreen, it grows 3 to 10 ft. high, with hollylike leaves 1 in. long. Golden flowers in drooping clusters are followed by showy dark purple berries.

Irwin (*B. stenophylla* 'Irwin') appears from Zone 7 south. It is a low-growing evergreen, 18 in. high with an arching habit. The leaves are narrow, 1 in. long, spiny-tipped and white beneath.

Japanese (*B. thunbergi*) thrives in Zones 3 to 10, inclusive. This is the common deciduous shrub, growing 4 to 6 ft. high, with small leaves that turn scarlet in autumn; also thorns and bright red fruits through winter. Varieties include *atropurpurea* with purple-red leaves and a dwarf form 'Crimson Pygmy' which grows only 15 in. high and as broad.

Mentor or Greenleaf (*B. mentorensis*) is useful in Zones 4b through 9, tolerating cold, heat and drought. It reaches a height of 5 to 7 ft., with foliage that is semi-evergreen in cold climates, and evergreen in mild areas. Growth is upright and compact.

Threespine (*B. triacanthophora*) is grown in Zones 6 to 9, inclusive. It is an evergreen, 3 ft. high. Narrow bristle-edged leaves are blue-gray beneath. The fruit is blue-black.

Warty (*B. verruculosa*) appears in Zones 6 to 9, inclusive. It is an evergreen growing 1½ to 3 ft. high and wide. The glossy oval leaves, 1½ in. wide, are white beneath. It has blue-black berries.

Wintergreen (*B. julianae*) grows in Zones 5b to 10, inclusive. Its dense upright growth reaches 6 ft. It has spiny leaves 3 in. long, thorny branches and blue-black fruits.

BEAR-BERRY. See the chapter on groundcovers.

BIRCH, DWARF ARCTIC (*Betula nana*). This native of Alaska is a deciduous, graceful, many-branched shrub 1 to 3 ft. high. It prefers a moist site.

BLUEBEARD, BLUEMIST OR BLUE SPIREA (*Caryopteris clandonensis*). This lives in Zones 5 to 10, inclusive. It is a gray-foliaged deciduous shrub making a rounded mass 2 to 4 ft. high. The leaves are narrow, 2 in. long, and showy spikes of small blue flowers appear in late summer and autumn. Plants may be killed to the ground in cold winters but usually reappear and bloom in spring. They are sometimes grown as perennials. Provide them with sun and good drainage.

BLUEBELL CREEPER, AUSTRALIAN (*Sollya fusiformis*). This evergreen trailing shrub, or vine, is for mild-winter climates. It has glossy small leaves on slender twining stems. Its flowers are ½ in. bells, brilliant blue, carried in masses through summer. Grow this in sun or part shade, the latter preferred where summers are hot. Water amply.

BOTTLE-BRUSH. These are evergreen shrubs or small trees for Zones 8b through 10, bearing colorful spikes of tiny flowers whose protruding stamens give the effect of a bristly bottle-brush. They are not fussy about soil, and tolerate drought and seaside conditions.

Red or Lemon (*Callistemon citrinus* or *C. lanceolatus*) is a shrub or small tree, 10 to 25 ft. high, spreading 6 to 10 ft. The leaves are narrow, 2½ in. long. New growth is red; so are the flowers.

Rose or Pink (*Melaleuca nesophila*) is a shrub 8 ft. high with pink flowers.

BOX or BOXWOOD. This name applies to some unrelated but similar-looking, slow-growth evergreens used for their attractive foliage. They are listed here.

African (*Myrsine africana*), in Zones 8b to 10, inclusive, is 3 to 5 ft. high, with oval leaves ½ in. long on red stems. It will grow in sun or shade; flowers are inconspicuous.

Common (*Buxus sempervirens*), Zones 6 to 9, inclusive, may be shrubby or treelike, and may be clipped to control its shape. The leaves are smooth, ½ to 1½ in. long, with distinctive fragrance—and are poisonous if eaten. This box-wood prefers soil that has considerable humus and porosity, and does best on the East Coast and in the South. Within its northern range of hardiness it needs to be protected from strong, cold, drying winds and sunlight, especially in winter and after transplanting. The smallest variety, dwarf box (*B. sempervirens suffruti-cosa*), is called true edging box; it can be kept at a height of a few inches. (For instructions on pruning, see that chapter.)

Littleleaf (*Buxus microphylla*), in Zones 6 to 10, inclusive, resembles common box except the leaves are lighter green and its growth looser. It attains a 4-ft. height. Of its many varieties, best known are Japanese box (*B. microphylla japonica*) that grows 3 to 6 ft. high, and Korean box (*B. microphylla koreana*), 2 to 3 ft. high. The latter is the hardiest box, growing in Zones 5 through 8. It does best in shade.

Victorian-, see PITTOSPORUM

BROOM, WARMINSTER (*Cystisus praecox*). This grows in Zones 6 to 8, inclusive. It is a green-stemmed shrub, 3 to 6 ft. high, and has inconspicuous leaves. Its flowers are bright yellow, sweet-pea-shaped, fragrant, growing in profusion in early spring. It likes sun and thrives in poor, sandy soils.

BUCKTHORN (*Rhamnus*). These shrubs or small trees have inconspicuous flowers and small black fruits. They do well for hedges and screens, because they are durable, growing in sun or shade and almost any soil.

Common (*R. cathartica*) can be used in Zones 2 to 6, inclusive. It is deciduous and thorny, and grows 10 to 25 ft. high.

Glossy or Alder (*R. frangula*) has attractive, shiny deciduous leaves. It is thornless, with upright growth reaching 10 to 12 ft. or more if not trimmed. It tolerates cold into Zone 2. Nurseries list selections named 'Columnar' and 'Tall-hedge' that make excellent hedges or specimens in narrow spaces.

Italian (*R. alaternus*), Zones 8 and warmer, is an evergreen upright shrub or small tree, 10 to 20 ft. high. Its leaves are dark green above and paler below. There is a variegated form.

BUTTERFLY-BUSH or BUDDLEIA. These are deciduous shrubs with arching branches and blooms resembling those of lilacs. Not all bushes are hardy in severe winter climates, and many suffer winterkill to the ground but come up again and bloom on new growth. (For help on pruning, see that chapter.)

Orange-Eye (*Buddleia davidi*), in Zones 5b to 9, inclusive, grows about 8 ft. high and blooms in late summer. Varieties may be found with white, pink, red or purple flowers.

Fountain (*B. alternifolia*) thrives in Zones 5 to 9, inclusive. It grows 10 ft. high, with fragrant lavender flowers in spring.

CAMELLIA. These aristocratic broad-leaved evergreen shrubs and small trees are grown in Zones 7 through 10 for their gorgeous, long-lasting flowers. If you see them being grown by other people in your town, or in nearby parks, it is safe to assume that you also can grow them. There are many kinds. Blooms may be single or double, are usually 3 to 5 in. across, and may be white, pink, red or in combinations. These appear during the cold months—autumn, winter and early spring.

Planting time is during the dormant period—fall through winter. Since this is also the blossoming period, you can choose varieties you like in flower. Select a place to put them that is protected from wind and hot sun, preferably with high, filtered shade.

The plants must have acid soil. If your soil is alkaline, you can prepare a large hole by removing the earth and refilling beneath and around the plant with a mixture consisting of ½ previously moistened peat moss. The remainder of the mixture should be humus and topsoil. In highly alkaline soils, and especially if your water is alkaline, apply sulfur at the rate of 2 or 3 pounds per 100 sq. ft.

Camellias must have perfect drainage. Set the plants no lower than they were previously, and if your soil is clayey, or poorly drained, set them in a raised bed or "elevated hole" in a special mixture of porous soil. No fertilizer is needed at planting time, but in later years feed them a special azalea-camellia plant food before new growth starts in spring, and once or twice again during the summer. Water the fertilizer in. You can estimate about 2 cups for a 3-ft. plant, and 1 cup more for each additional foot of height.

Keep the soil constantly moist, and provide a summer mulch to keep roots cool. Spraying the foliage often with water during the summer is beneficial.

Remember, if you cut your camellia blooms with short stems and 3 or 4 leaves, you are following a safe rule for tip-pruning. However, on very young plants, take the blossom without any foliage. Let as many leaves as possible remain to nourish the plant and serve as the source of development of new bud-bearing shoots. Do not let seeds develop; remove fading flowers. (See chapter on pruning.)

C. reticulata has huge blooms 6 to 8 in. across on sparsely branched shrubs or small trees, which grow 15 ft. high or more. These like full sun.

C. sasanqua grows upright or arching; some varieties are practically vines. All are excellent for espaliering. They are grown more for garden attractiveness than for picking. They bloom early, September through January.

Japanese (*C. japonica*) is the most familiar kind and comes in a bewildering array of named varieties. Try to plant the early, midseason and late-blooming kinds.

CARISSA. This is used in Zones 9b and 10. The thorny, fast-growing evergreen shrubs have shiny leaves, and white flowers with jasmine-like fragrance. Their fruits, borne on new growth, are plum-shaped and used for jelly and pies. They grow in sun or part shade.

C. grandiflora or natal-plum grows 15 ft. high.

C. grandiflora 'Prostrata,' the dwarf natal-plum, has horizontal-type growth.

CEANOTHUS. These are California's wild lilacs, and are grown mostly on the Pacific Coast in Zones 8 through 10. They come in assorted sizes, from creepers to small trees. They bloom in the spring, are plumey, and bear white or blue blossoms. Nurseries carry many named varieties and hybrids.

Carmel Creeper (*C. griseus horizontalis*) is described in the chapter on groundcovers.

CHERRY, BARBADOS-, see MALPIGHIA

CHERRY, SURINAM-, see SURINAM-CHERRY

CHERRY, WESTERN SAND. See groundcover chapter.

CHERRY-LAUREL, COMMON or ENGLISH-LAUREL (*Prunus laurocerasus*). This thrives in Zones 7b to 10, inclusive. It is a fast-growing broad-leaved evergreen shrub or small tree growing 6 to 20 ft. high. The leaves are glossy, 3 to 6 in. long, and flowers are small, white, fragrant, in elongated clusters of 2- to 5-in. length, followed by purple-black fruits. It likes sun or part shade. Fruits and leaves should not be eaten.

CINQUEFOIL, see POTENTILLA

CLEYERA (*Cleyera japonica*). This shrub grows in Zones 7b to 10, inclusive. It is an evergreen growing to 10 ft. tall. Related to the camellia, it likes the same conditions, though its flowers are inconspicuous. Part shade is desirable.

COCCULUS LAURIFOLIUS. This evergreen is used in Zones 8b to 10, inclusive. It arches and spreads to a 20-ft. height, with glossy leaves 6 in. long. It will grow in shade.

COONTIE (*Zamia floridana*). This is a palmlike shrub with tufts of feather-shaped leaves 2 ft. high. It is native to Florida.

CORAL-BERRY, CHENAULT (*Symphoricarpos chenaulti*). This shrub appears in Zones 5b to 7, inclusive. It is deciduous, 3 ft. high, with fine-textured foliage, little pink flowers and decorative small red fruit dotted with white. It grows in sun or part shade.

COTONEASTER. These are shrubs grown for their attractive leaves and small fruits. They prefer sunny sites.

Cotoneaster multiflora, Zones 5 to 10, inclusive, is deciduous, growing 8 to 10 ft. high with arching branches. One of the showiest cotoneasters when in bloom, it carries ½-in. white flowers in profuse clusters in spring, followed by decorative red fruits, ⅜ in. across.

Cranberry (*C. apiculata*), Zones 5b to 9, inclusive, is semi-evergreen, growing about 3 ft. high with horizontal branching. The leaves are round, ¾ in. across; fruits are red.

European (*C. integerrima*) is hardy in Alaska. It is deciduous, grows 3 to 6 ft. high, and has red fruit.

Necklace (*C. conspicua decora*) is described in the groundcover chapter.

Parney (*C. parneyi*), Zones 7b to 10a, inclusive, is a vigorous and handsome broad-leaved evergreen with arching, rounded form, 6 ft. high and broad. It has red fruit. Sun or part shade is desirable.

Peking (*C. acutifolia*), Zones 3 to 9, inclusive, is deciduous, 8 ft. high, has glossy green leaves and conspicuous black fruit. It thrives in poor, dry soil.

Spreading (*C. divaricata*), Zones 5b to 9, inclusive, is deciduous, 3 to 6 ft. high, and has arching, spreading branches. Its leaves are ¾ in. long. The flowers are small and pink followed by red fruits.

CRAPE-MYRTLE

CRAPE-MYRTLE (*Lagerstroemia indica*) is used in Zones 7 to 9, inclusive. This deciduous shrub or small tree, which reaches 20 ft., is grown for its dazzling display of pink, red or white flowers through late summer. Individual blooms are 1½ in. wide with crinkled petals carried in clusters 4 to 9 in. long. In winter the trunk is handsome; shedding bark reveals pink underbark. You may grow it with one or more stems; size can be controlled by pruning. Since flowers are borne on new wood, prune it during winter or early spring. Crape-myrtle likes sun and warmth, tolerates various soils, and appreciates moisture and fertility if not overdone.

CROWN-OF-THORNS

CROWN-OF-THORNS (*Euphorbia mili* or *E. splendens*) is used in Zone 10. These are creeping plants with thorny dark stems, few or no leaves, and brilliant red small flowers in clusters. In cold climates they are grown as house plants. Its milky juice sometimes irritates skin.

CURRANT, ALPINE (*Ribes alpinum*), Zones 2 to 7, inclusive, is a deciduous shrub growing in moundlike form to 5 ft. high. Its leaves are small, lobed, tidy and dense. The plant makes good hedges, for it stands clipping well; also one of the most likely plants for heavy shade, and does best in cold climates.

DAPHNE. These shrubs are noted for their small, intensely fragrant flowers. Do not eat the berries or leaves, for those of several species are poisonous.

February (*Daphne mezereum*), Zones 5 to 8, inclusive, is deciduous, growing 3 to 4 ft. high. The blossoms are light purple and come early in the spring before foliage.

Rose (*D. cneorum*), Zones 5b to 8a, inclusive, is a low evergreen trailer, 1 ft. high and 3 ft. across with 1-in. leaves and pink flowers in late spring. It needs part shade and well-drained soil.

Winter (*D. odora*), Zones 7b to 10a, inclusive, is an evergreen that makes a dense mound 3 ft. high and is wider than tall. Fragrant flowers in pink, red or white—depending on variety—come in late winter or early spring. It needs fast-draining soil, especially in winter. Give part shade.

DEUTZIA, SLENDER (*Deutzia gracilis*). This deciduous shrub is used in Zones 5 to 8, inclusive. It stands 2 to 3 ft. high, with numerous small white or pink flowers in late spring. Sun or light shade is required.

DODONEA, PURPLE-LEAVED (*Dodonea viscosa* 'Purpurea'). This tropical shrub reaches 8 to 12 ft., with narrow leaves 3 to 4 in. long and inconspicuous flowers. It is tough and easy to grow, and is tolerant of smog and dry conditions.

DOGWOOD (*Cornus*). These are deciduous tall shrubs with many excellent qualities, though *not* the spectacular large blooms of the flowering dogwood tree, described in the chapter on trees.

Pagoda Dogwood (*C. alternifolia*) is grown primarily for its foliage and interesting, horizontal type of branching. It may be 8 to 25 ft. high. Flowers are small and creamy-white in 2½-in.

clusters; fruits are blue-black. Foliage turns red-purple in autumn.

Panicled Dogwood (*C. racemosa*) is a native shrub, 6 to 10 ft. high, with small white flowers in clusters and small white fruits that are liked by birds. It does well in shade or sun.

Red-Osier Dogwood (*C. stolonifera*) is used in Zones 3 to 8, inclusive. It is a native shrub, 6 ft. high with erect red branches, and spreads by underground stems. The flowers are white, in small clusters, followed by small bluish-white fruits. It does best in sun and moist soil. To assure red stems, see the chapter on pruning.

DOWNY-MYRTLE (*Rhodomyrtus tomentosa*). This tropical shrub is grown in Zone 10. It is 3 to 5 ft. high, with oval leaves 2 in. long. The flowers are pink, ¾ in. across, followed by edible purple berries. The plant adapts to various soils and likes ample moisture.

ELAEAGNUS. These are evergreens and deciduous shrubs and small trees with ornamental silvery or scurfy leaves and twigs. They have fragrant though inconspicuous flowers, and attractive berrylike fruit. They are hardy, wind-resistant and drought-tolerant.

Autumn Elaeagnus (*E. umbellata*) in Zone 4 and southward grows 10 to 18 ft. high. Its foliage has silvery undersides. The fruit is brown, turning red.

Fruitland Silverberry (*E. fruitlandi*) is similar to thorny elaeagnus described below, but its leaves and stems are more silvery when young.

Russian-Olive (*E. angustifolia*), Zones 3 to 9, inclusive, is a spiny, deciduous tree growing 10 to 20 ft. high, with slender silvery leaves 2 to 3 in. long, and silvery fruits shaped like small olives.

Silverberry (*E. commutata*), Zones 2b to 7, inclusive, is erect-growing, 8 to 12 ft. high. It spreads by stolons.

Thorny Elaeagnus (*E. pungens*), Zones 7 to 10, inclusive, is a spiny evergreen, 10 to 15 ft. high, with spreading shape. The foliage has a silvery underside, and the fruit is brown when young, red when ripe. There are varieties with yellow or white margins or markings.

ENKIANTHUS, REDVEIN (*Enkianthus campanulatus*). This deciduous shrub, 8 to 20 ft. high, is used in Zones 5 to 8, inclusive. Its flowers are bell-shaped, ½ in. long, in drooping clusters in spring, before leaves. They may be yellow, white or red, depending on variety. The foliage turns scarlet in autumn. You should provide acid soil and the same general conditions as for azaleas.

ERANTHEMUM NERVOSUM. This is a tropical sprawling shrub 2 to 6 ft. high, with rough leaves to 8 in. long, and brilliant true-blue flowers.

ESCALLONIA. These broad-leaved evergreens, Zones 8b to 10, inclusive, are for mild-winter climates. They bloom late summer and fall, like full sun where summers are cool, or part shade elsewhere. They tolerate wind and coastal conditions.

'Appleblossom' has arching branches 6 to 8 ft. high, and pinkish-white flowers.

'C. F. Ball' has bright red flowers on plants 3 to 4 ft. high.

Escallonia organensis is a dense grower, 12 to 15 ft. high and wide, with arching form and pink flowers.

Red Escallonia (*E. rubra*) is 10 to 15 ft. high with glossy rounded leaves and red flowers.

EUONYMUS. Of the many fine shrubs available, two are listed here.

Evergreen (*Euonymus japonicus*), Zones 7b to 10, inclusive, is a glossy-foliaged broad-leaved evergreen growing to a 10- or 12-ft. height. It can easily be kept lower by pruning, or be trained as a tree. There are many forms, including some with leaves edged in yellow or white. Its variety *microphyllus*, called boxleaf euonymus, has small leaves, grows only 1 to 2 ft. high, is compactly upright, and is often used for low hedges.

Winged (*E. alatus*) This deciduous shrub, Zones 3b to 10, inclusive, grows 6 to 10 ft. high, with distinctive corky ridges or "wings" along its branches. Its leaves turn an unusual shade of rose-pink in fall. The small purple fruits pop open to display seeds in a manner similar to bitter-sweet. Its lower growing form, called dwarf winged euonymus (*E. alatus compactus*), grows about 5 ft. high, and foliage turns bright red in the autumn. It thrives in sun or part shade.

EURYA (*Eurya japonica*). This evergreen shrub, Zones 8 to 10, inclusive, grows 4 to 5 ft. high, has glossy oval leaves and small white flowers. It likes the same conditions as camellia.

FIRETHORN, see PYRACANTHA

FONTANESIA, FORTUNE (*Fontanesia fortunei*) grows in Zones 5b to 7, inclusive. This is a deciduous upright shrub resembling privet, 6 to 12 ft. high. It has shiny leaves, 2 to 4 in. long; the flowers are small, white and in clusters. It is not particular about soil or site.

FORSYTHIA or GOLDEN BELL. These deciduous shrubs usually grow 4 to 9 ft. high with golden bell-shaped flowers in the spring before foliage develops. They like sunshine and are very easy to raise. Most shrubs bloom beautifully and regularly in Zones 5b through 8. In 5a and colder zones the shrubs grow well but flower buds tend to be injured by winter cold. There are numerous handsome species, varieties and hybrids. Pruning instructions, illustrated, are given in that chapter.

FUCHSIA. These tender shrubs have colorful bell-shaped or tubular flowers that hang on slender stems. Their colors may be red, purple, blue, white, or combinations. Popular hybrid kinds grow outdoors the year around in mild climates—especially Zones 9 and 10. Elsewhere they are summer bedding plants or pot plants. The hardiest kind is *F. magellanica*, Zones 7b through 10. They like moist air, moist rapid-draining soil containing a large amount of humus, and part shade. They excel along the Pacific Coast, especially in areas with cool summer temperatures, and fog to temper the sunlight. Because they are shallow-rooting, they appreciate frequent watering, especially if they are in containers. Mulches can help to keep their roots cool. If the weather is hot and windy,

sprinkle the foliage with water. Feed them a complete fertilizer in small weekly doses during the rapid-growth period. Pruning details are given in that chapter.

GARDENIA. These are warm-climate shrubs grown for their fragrant, white and waxy flowers, and their glossy foliage. Pruning instructions may be found in that chapter. If you wish to grow gardenias indoors, see the chapter on indoor gardening.

Gardenia or Cape-Jasmine (*Gardenia jasminoides*), Zones 8 to 10, inclusive, is an evergreen growing 2 to 5 ft. high, with leaves 3 to 4 in. long and double flowers. It likes full sun, acid soil, warm days and nights, and ample food and moisture. The dwarf form, with smaller blossoms, is *radicans*.

Tiare or Tahitian Gardenia (*G. taitensis*) is popular in Hawaii. It has single, pinwheel-shaped flowers often used in leis, and grows to a height of 6 ft.

GERMANDER, see TEUCRIUM

GOLDEN DEWDROP (*Duranta repens*) appears in Zones 9b and 10. This rapid-growing, tall, thorny shrub has oval leaves and clusters of light blue flowers in summer. Yellow berries hang on all winter. Its branches may be winter-killed, but the plant recovers quickly and blooms as usual.

GOLD-DUST TREE, see AUCUBA

GOLDEN BELL, see FORSYTHIA

GOLD-FLOWER, see HYPERICUM

GRAPE, OREGON-, see MAHONIA

HAKEA, SWEET (*Hakea suaveolens*) is found in Zones 9 and 10. This evergreen, growing 6 to 10 ft. high or more, has needlelike, stiff, spiny-tipped leaves 4 in. long. Its flowers are white, fragrant, and appear in fall and winter. It prefers light soils but also tolerates semidesert and seaside conditions.

HAWTHORN, INDIA-, see RAPHIOLEPIS

HAWTHORN, YEDDO-, see RAPHIOLEPIS

HEATH (*Erica*) and HEATHER (*Calluna*). These are similar low, spreading evergreens. Both have small bell-shaped flowers in pink, lavender or white, carried in spikes. Heaths have narrow leaves in whorls, while heathers have leaves that are scalelike and overlapping. Give them sun, and acid, rapid-draining soil that is primarily organic matter and sand. They are happy on a rocky site and grow primarily on the Pacific Coast and in the Northeast. (See also the chapter on pruning.)

Cornish Heath (*E. vagans*), in Zones 7 and 8, blooms in summer. (See also the groundcover chapter.)

Corsican Heath (*E. terminalis* or *E. stricta*) grows 5 ft. high or more. Its flowers are rosy-purple in late summer.

Scotch Heather (*C. vulgaris*), in Zones 5 to 8, inclusive, blooms mostly in summer.

Spring Heath (*E. carnea*), in Zones 6, 7 and 8, grows 6 to 15 in. high and 2 to 3 ft. broad, blooming from February to May, depending upon locality.

HIBISCUS. These shrubs vary in hardiness but have the same general type of flowers.

Chinese Hibiscus (*H. rosa-sinensis*), in Zones 9b and 10, is an evergreen which grows 8 to 10 ft. high in subtropical and tropical climates. Its spectacular blooms may be 6 in. across in pink, yellow, red, purple or combinations. There are single and double forms. In most varieties, individual blossoms last only one day but buds are continuously formed on new growth at the tips of the branches. These plants like sun, warmth in winter, ample water and fertilizer. They are easily propagated by softwood or hardwood cuttings. Pruning advice is given in that chapter. To grow hibiscus as a house plant, see the chapter on indoor gardening.

Hardy Giants or Rose Mallow (*H. moscheutos*). (See the chapter on perennials.)

Rose-of-Sharon (*H. syriacus*), Zones 5b to 10, inclusive, is upright, vertically branched and deciduous, growing 5 to 15 ft. high. Late-summer blossoms are 3 to 5 in. across, in white, red or violet. Some are double. Pruning advice is contained in that chapter.

HOLLY (*Ilex*). These broad-leaved evergreen and deciduous shrubs and trees can be grown in sun or part shade, like acid soil rich in humus, and do best along the East Coast, in the South, and on the Pacific Coast. They are desirable primarily for their handsome foliage but some have attractive berries—which are reported to be poisonous if eaten. Their flowers are inconspicuous and white; the sexes are on separate plants and only the females produce fruit—if there is a mate planted nearby. The following are among the best used as shrubs.

American (*Ilex opaca*), Zones 6 to 10, inclusive, is an evergreen tree sometimes used as a tall shrub. It has broad, glossy, spiny leaves and red fruit.

Chinese (*I. cornuta*), Zones 7b to 10, inclusive, is an evergreen which grows 10 to 20 ft. high, with large, glossy, spiny leaves 1½ to 5 in. long, and bright red berries ¾ in. across. Its variety 'Rotunda' or dwarf Chinese holly grows 4 ft. high. Variety 'Burfordi' has leaves that are practically spineless. It can be had in a dwarf form 4 to 6 ft. high.

Japanese (*I. crenata*), Zones 6b to 9, inclusive, is another evergreen, with small, glossy leaves 1 to 1½ in. long, and small, inconspicuous black berries. Because of their small leaves these shrubs are sometimes used as substitutes for box. They stand clipping well. Among low-growing kinds useful for plantings around the house and for hedges are 'Helleri' and 'Stokes,' which are less than 3 ft. tall, and 'Hetz,' 'Roundleaf' and 'Convexleaf' which may become 4 to 5 ft. high. 'Convexleaf' grows broader than high.

Yaupon (*I. vomitoria*), Zones 7b to 10, inclusive, is a large evergreen shrub or small tree native to the South. It has numerous slender branches, and small, smooth, oval leaves 1½ in. long. The fruits are scarlet. It is much used for hedges. Dwarf Yaupon (*I. vomitoria nana*) is only 3 or 4 ft. high.

HONEYSUCKLE (*Lonicera*). These may be found in both evergreen and deciduous forms. All are grown primarily for foliage, though most of them have attractive small flowers followed by colorful small fruits that attract birds. They are useful as hedges in natural or clipped forms. (See the pruning chapter.)

'Clavey's Dwarf,' Zones 3 to 8, inclusive, is deciduous and grows to 5 ft. high.

Tatarian (*L. tatarica*), Zones 2 to 8, inclusive, is deciduous, upright, vigorous, growing 8 to 10 ft. high. The flowers may be white or pink depending upon the variety. Fruits are profuse. It is excellent for tall screening.

Winter (*L. fragrantissima*), Zones 5b to 10, inclusive, is semi-evergreen with arching branches 8 to 10 ft. high, and fragrant white flowers in early spring followed by red fruits.

HYDRANGEA. These shrubs are grown for their showy blooms in large clusters in summer. Pruning instructions are given in that chapter.

French or Bigleaf (*H. macrophylla*) are found in Zones 7 to 10, inclusive. Their flowers are blue, pink or white in flat clusters on a deciduous shrub growing to 12 ft. high in mild climates. They like part shade and lots of water. Directions for growing them indoors, and how to change colors to pink or blue, will be found in the chapter on indoor plants.

Hills of Snow (*H. arborescens grandiflora*), Zones 4 to 10, inclusive, is a deciduous shrub, grows 3 to 4 ft. high, and has heart-shaped leaves 3 to 6 in. long. The flowers are white in showy ball-shaped clusters 4 to 6 in. across, and appear in early summer. It is excellent for shady sites and the north side of the house.

Peegee (*H. paniculata grandiflora*), Zones 4 to 10a, inclusive, is a deciduous shrub or small tree growing 8 to 25 ft. high with huge heads blooming in late summer. The clusters are 8 to 12 in. long, white at first and then turning rosy-pink as they age. Give it sun or part shade.

HYPERICUM or ST. JOHNSWORT. These low-growing evergreen or semi-evergreen shrubs have brilliant yellow flowers featuring fluffy stamens. They grow in sun or part shade, and tolerate sandy soil.

Hypericum calycinum. (See the chapter on groundcovers.)

H. kalmianum or Sunshine Shrub, Zones 5 to 8, inclusive, is an evergreen, 2 to 3 ft. high. Its leaves are 1 in. long and its flowers 1 in. across.

H. moserianum or Gold-Flower, Zones 7 to 10, inclusive, is a hybrid with bushy, arching form 2 ft. high. The flowers are 2½ in. across.

H. patulum henryi, Zones 7b through 10, is an evergreen, 2 to 4 ft. high with flowers 2 in. across. It includes varieties 'Hidcote' and 'Sungold.'

INDIA-HAWTHORN, see RAPHIOLEPIS

IXORA. These tropical shrubs have long glossy leaves and showy round flower heads composed of many small blossoms. They grow to varying heights and like acid soil. *I. coccinea* has brilliant red flowers and is often called flame-of-the-woods. Another handsome red-flowered kind with huge flower clusters is *I. macrothyrsa*.

JASMINE, CAPE-, see GARDENIA

JASMINE, SHOWY or FLORIDA (*Jasminum floridum*), Zones 7b to 10, inclusive, is a semi-evergreen with arching branches growing 3 to 4 ft. high. Its yellow fragrant flowers develop in large clusters. It likes full sun and good soil.

JESSAMINE, ORANGE-, see ORANGE-JESSAMINE

KERRIA (*Kerria japonica*), Zones 6 to 9, inclusive, is a deciduous shrub, 4 to 6 ft. high, with slender branches that remain green all winter. The flowers appearing in early spring are yellow, single or double. Twig tips frequently winterkill so a spring pruning to remove dead wood is normal. It likes light shade and multiplies by suckering.

KING'S-MANTLE, see THUNBERGIA

LEAD-PLANT (*Amorpha canescens*), Zones 3 to 6, inclusive, is a deciduous shrub 4 ft. high, grown for its gray foliage and 4-in. spikes of pea-shaped blue flowers. It does well in poor, dry soil.

LEUCOTHOE, DROOPING (*Leucothoe catesbaei*) is found in Zones 5 to 9, inclusive. It is an evergreen or semi-evergreen, with arching branches usually 3 to 4 ft. high. The leaves are lustrous, 7 in. long, turning bronzy-red in fall; flowers are waxy-white and small, hanging in clusters along the underside of stems. This shrub will grow in sun or shade, and needs acid soil with ample humus. It spreads by underground stems. Cutting old branches to the ground occasionally is beneficial.

LIGUSTRUM, see PRIVET

LILAC (*Syringa*). These are very hardy, deciduous shrubs with fragrant flowers. They like full sun, are not fussy about soil, but need cold winters to bloom. Pruning instructions with how-to drawings are given in that chapter.

Common Lilac (*Syringa vulgaris*), Zones 3b to 8a, inclusive, is the old-fashioned kind, a parent of hybrids.

French Hybrids are the wonderful named varieties that come in a wide range of colors. Outstanding ones include:

White: Singles, 'Vestale' and 'Mont Blanc'; doubles, 'Edith Cavell' and 'Ellen Willmott.'
Violet: Single, 'De Miribel'; double, 'Violetta.'
Blue: Singles, 'President Lincoln' and 'Firmament'; doubles, 'Olivier de Serres' and 'Ami Schott.'
Lilac: Single, 'Jacques Callot'; doubles, 'President Fallières' and 'Henri Martin.'
Pink: Singles, 'Lucie Baltet' and 'Macrostachya'; doubles, 'Katherine Havemeyer' and 'Mme. Antoine Buchner.'
Red-Purple: Singles, 'Maréchal Foch,' 'Capitaine Baltet'; doubles, 'Paul Thirion' and 'Mrs. Edward Harding.'
Purple: Singles, 'Monge' and 'Mrs. W. E. Marshall'; doubles, 'Adelaide Dunbar' and 'Paul Hariot.'
Japanese Tree Lilac (*S. amurensis japonica*), Zones 4b to 8, inclusive, is different-looking and is the latest blooming of the lilacs. It may be grown as a many-trunked big bush or as a small tree. The blossoms are white, in plumes 12 to 18 in. long in early summer, and slightly fragrant.

Korean Early Lilac (*S. oblata dilatata*), is used in Zones 4b to 8, inclusive. Its flowers are extra-early, large and fragrant, and appear before the foliage unfurls. Their color is pinkish-lavender. The leaves are large and glossy and color in the fall.

Late Lilac (*S. villosa*) can be seen in Zones 3b to 8, inclusive. Its season of bloom comes between French Hybrids and Japanese tree lilac, about iris time. The flowers are lavender-pink.

LIME-BERRY (*Triphasia trifolia*) is a thorny evergreen growing 3 to 10 ft. high in Zone 10. It may be easily sheared to use as a hedge. The leaves are 3-parted, 1½ in. long, and flowers 1 in. wide, fragrant, resembling orange blossoms. Its fruit is red; not tasty.

LONICERA, see HONEYSUCKLE

LOQUAT. See the chapter on fruit.

MAHONIA. These broad-leaved evergreen shrubs are native to the Northwest. Their foliage is composed of few to many hollylike leaflets. Their attractive yellow flowers are followed by colorful fruit, which should not be eaten. Here are some of the best.

Creeping Mahonia (*M. repens*). See the chapter on groundcovers.

Longleaf Mahonia (*M. nervosa*) is usually low-growing, to 2 ft. high. Its leaflets are narrow, and berries blue. This makes a good groundcover.

Oregon-Grape (*M. aquifolium*), Zones 5b to 9, inclusive, grows upright, 3 to 6 ft. high. It does best in shade or part shade, since the foliage may burn in winter in sun. It is tolerant of soils. The fruits are grapelike, dark blue. For pointers on pruning, see that chapter.

MALPIGHIA. These tropical shrubs or small trees have glossy leaves and cherrylike fruits.

M. coccigera, sometimes called holly malpighia or Singapore-holly, grows 1 to 3 ft. high with spiny hollylike leaves ¾ in. long and small pink flowers. It thrives in partial shade.

M. glabra, known in Hawaii as acerola and in southern states as Barbados-cherry, is 5 to 15 ft. high with leaves 1 to 3 in. long and pink flowers. Its fruit is prized for making jam.

MANZANITA (*Arctostaphylos*). These are broad-leaved evergreen shrubs with reddish bark, bell-shaped flowers and small fruits, native to the Pacific Coast. There are many named varieties.

MAPLE, AMUR (*Acer ginnala*). This appears in Zones 3 to 5, inclusive. It is a deciduous shrub or small tree, growing to 20 ft., which can be grown with single or multiple trunks, or as a hedge. The small-lobed leaves turn brilliant orange in the autumn.

MARLBERRY (*Ardisia paniculata*). This grows in Zone 10. It is a tall shrub native to southern Florida, with leaves 5 to 7 in. long; the flowers are white and fruits shiny black in clusters. It tolerates shade and seashore salt spray.

MEXICAN-ORANGE (*Choisya ternata*). This evergreen, 6 to 8 ft. high with shiny foliage composed of 3 leaflets, is used in Zones 8 to 10, inclusive. Its flowers, borne in spring and off and on during summer, are white, 1 in. wide, and fragrant. It likes sun where summers are cool; part shade elsewhere.

MOCK-ORANGE (*Philadelphus*). These deciduous shrubs, hardy in Zones 4b through 8, are grown primarily for their profusion of white, usually fragrant flowers in spring.

Sweet Mock-Orange (*Philadelphus coronarius*) is an old favorite, 8 to 10 ft. high, with fragrant flowers 1½ in. across.

MORNING-GLORY, BUSH (*Convolvulus cneorum*). This shrub grows in Zones 8, 9 and 10. It is an evergreen, 2 to 4 ft. high, with silvery gray leaves and light pink morning glory-type flowers all summer. It likes sun and perfect drainage.

MOUNTAIN-LAUREL (*Kalmia latifolia*). This broad-leaved evergreen, in Zones 5 to 9, inclusive, is native to the Eastern U.S.A., usually growing 4 to 8 ft. high. The showy spring flowers are pink and white in large clusters. The bush needs acid soil and ample moisture. It will grow in shade or sun. The leaves are poisonous if eaten.

MYRTLE, DOWNY-, see DOWNY-MYRTLE

MYRTLE, TRUE (*Myrtus communis*). This evergreen, Zones 8b to 10, inclusive, grows 3 to 6 ft. high and almost that wide. It has shiny, aromatic leaves 2 in. long. The flowers are white, ¾ in. across, followed by black berries. It adapts to varied soils and may be used as a hedge. It likes sun.

Compact or Dwarf Myrtle (*M. communis compacta*) is a slow-growing, compact form.

NANDINA or HEAVENLY BAMBOO (*Nandina domestica*). This evergreen or semi-evergreen with slender, feathery, divided leaves flourishes in Zones 7 to 10, inclusive. Its growth is pink when new in spring and turns brilliant red in fall—especially when planted in the sun. The flowers are small, grow in clusters, and are followed by shiny red berries. This shrub is good in sun or shade. Regular bushes can grow to 10 ft. high or be kept shorter. The low-growing varieties are 'Dwarf' and 'Compacta.'

NANNY-BERRY, see VIBURNUM

NAUPAKA (*Scaevola frutescens*). This tropical, tall shrub is especially useful in seacoast situations, since it tolerates salt spray. The leaves are oval and thick; flowers are small, white and fragrant, followed by little white berries.

NATAL-PLUM, see CARISSA

NINEBARK (*Physocarpus*). These are deciduous shrubs with leaves usually lobed in shape and turning an attractive color in the fall. Clusters of small, white spirealike flowers appear in the spring. They grow in sun or part shade.

Dwarf Illinois Ninebark (*P. intermedius*), Zones 2 to 8, inclusive, grows 5 ft. high.

Western or Mountain Ninebark (*P. monogynus*), Zones 2 to 8, inclusive, is usually 2 to 3 ft. high.

OLEANDER (*Nerium oleander*). This summer-flowering evergreen thrives in Zones 8b to 10, inclusive. It grows up to 20 ft. high as a many-stemmed shrub or single-trunk tree. The leaves are narrow, 5 to 8 in. long, and the flowers are single or double, white, pink, red or yellow. They like sun and tolerate heat and wind.

WARNING: *Leaves are poisonous if eaten, and contact with them causes skin irritation for some people.*

OLIVE, RUSSIAN-, see ELAEGNUS

ORANGE-JESSAMINE *(Murraya paniculata)*. This evergreen, 6 to 10 ft. high, with arching branches and many-parted leaves, is found in Zone 10. Its white ¾-in. blooms have a jasmine-like fragrance and occur chiefly in the late summer and autumn. Give it part shade and fast-draining soil.

ORANGE, MEXICAN-, see MEXICAN-ORANGE

ORANGE, MOCK-, see MOCK-ORANGE

ORANGE, SOUR or SEVILLE *(Citrus aurantium)*. This grows in Zones 8 to 10, inclusive. It is an evergreen spiny shrub or small tree with very fragrant flowers, and acid fruits 3½ in. in diameter that are excellent for marmalade.

OSMANTHUS. These slow-growing evergreens are used primarily for their foliage, which resembles that of holly. The flowers are inconspicuous but fragrant. They grow best in shade or part shade, and do not like alkaline soil. They can be clipped for a hedge.

Delavay *(Osmanthus delavayi* or *Siphonosmanthus delavayi)*, in Zones 7 to 10a, has arching branches 4 to 6 ft. high. The leaves are oval, 1 in. long.

Holly *(O. ilicifolius* or *O. heterophyllus ilicifolius)* grows 6 to 8 ft. high with leaves 2½ in. long. There is a variegated form.

PACHISTIMA, CANBY *(Pachistima canbyi)*. This dainty evergreen shrub, in Zones 5 to 8a, inclusive, grows only 1 ft. high with neat, narrow leaves ½ to 1 in. long. It thrives in sun or part shade and needs fast-draining soil. It is good for edgings, miniature hedges or ground-cover.

PANAX, PARSLEY *(Polyscias fruticosus* or *Nothopanax fruticosus)*. This aralialike tropical shrub is grown for its handsome large 3-parted leaves. It may reach 8 ft. high.

PEA-SHRUB *(Caragana)*. These are deciduous shrubs or small trees with yellow sweet pea-type blossoms and feathery compound leaves. They like sunshine and well-drained soils, are tolerant of alkali, and especially useful in harsh, cold climates. Hardy examples in Zones 2b through 9a follow.

Dwarf pea-shrub *(C. pygmaea)* grows 1 to 3 ft. high, with prostrate or pendulous branches.

Littleleaf pea-shrub *(C. microphylla)* grows 4 to 6 ft. high, spreading as wide as tall.

Siberian pea-shrub *(C. arborescens)* is an upright grower, 15 to 20 ft. high.

PERNETTYA, CHILEAN *(Pernettya mucronata)* lives in Zones 8, 9 and 10. It is an evergreen growing 1½ to 3 ft. high, with small lustrous leaves ¾ in. long and spiny-pointed. The flowers are small, white, bell-shaped and profuse in spring, followed by showy fleshy berries ½ in. across, white, red, pink or purple. It likes sun and sandy soil, and spreads by underground runners.

PHOTINIA. These shrubs have attractive foliage, white flowers and red berries.

Chinese *(P. serrulata)*, in Zones 7b to 10, inclusive, is evergreen, with glossy leaves 4 to 7 in. long that are copper-colored when young and in autumn. The flower clusters are 5 in. across. For the best leaf color, plant in sun and prune frequently.

'Frazer' is an outstanding hybrid.

PITTOSPORUM. These are broad-leaved evergreen trees and shrubs.

Japanese *(P. tobira)*, in Zones 8, 9, 10, grows 6 to 15 ft. high with 4-in.-long leaves that seem to be in whorls, and white flowers with fragrance similar to orange blossoms. They will grow in sun or shade, are not particular about soil, and tolerate seaside conditions. The variety *variegatum* has white-margined foliage.

Victorian-Box *(P. undulatum)*, Zones 8b to 10, inclusive, is a small tree, with relatively narrow leaves 4 to 6 in. long and white fragrant flowers.

POMEGRANATE *(Punica granatum)*. Deciduous shrubs and small leaves, Zones 7b to 10a, inclusive, have glossy leaves and attractive flowers and fruits. The edible kinds grow 8 to 12 ft. high. Dwarf pomegranate *(P. granatum nana)* is a compact shrub 2 to 3 ft. high, grown for its foliage and for flowers that are yellow or orange, single or double. The fruits of this dwarf plant are inedible.

PORTUGAL-LAUREL (*Prunus lusitanica*). This shrub, in Zones 7b to 10, inclusive, is similar to but slower growing than cherry-laurel. (See the latter entry in this list.)

POTENTILLA FRUTICOSA or BUSH CINQUE-FOIL. This many-branched shrub is used in Zones 2 to 6, inclusive. It is deciduous and grows from 1 to 4 ft. high. It has numerous yellow roselike 1-in. flowers all summer. It prefers sun and is soil-tolerant. Varieties include 'Gold Drop' and 'Katherine Dykes.'

PRIVET (*Ligustrum*). These deciduous and evergreen shrubs or small trees are grown mostly for their attractive leaves—as hedges. Their flowers are small, white and attractive. They grow in sun or part shade, and almost any soil, tolerating dust, wind, seaside conditions and frequent clipping. Their berries should not be eaten.

Japanese (*L. japonicum*), Zones 7b to 10, inclusive, is an evergreen, with glossy leaves 4 in. long, growing 8 to 12 ft. high. The flower clusters are 4 to 6 in. long.

Lodense (*L. vulgare lodense*), Zones 5 to 9, inclusive, is a low-growing, deciduous form of common privet.

Regel (*L. obtusifolium regelianum*), Zones 5 to 9, inclusive, is deciduous, 5 to 6 ft. high, with distinctive horizontal branching and a generally billowing effect. It is most attractive when allowed to grow in its natural shape.

PYRACANTHA or FIRETHORN (*Pyracantha*). These are evergreen shrubs with shiny small leaves, thorns, and clusters of small white flowers in spring, followed by brilliant red or orange berries. These persist into or through winter, to be eaten by the birds. The shrubs can be used as bushes, hedges or espaliers. For details of how and when to prune, see that chapter.

P. coccinea, Zones 5b to 10a, inclusive, is the hardiest. It includes varieties 'Lalandi,' 'Kasan' and selected dwarf forms. It is 5 to 6 ft. high as a bush, or climbs to 20 ft. when espaliered.

P. crenato-serrata or *P. fortuneana*, Zones 7b to 10, inclusive, is usually 6 to 10 ft. high.

'Rosedale,' Zones 7b to 10, inclusive, is an upright grower good for espaliers.

QUINCE, FLOWERING (*Chaenomeles*). These are deciduous shrubs with showy flowers in early spring, followed by applelike fragrant fruits which can be used for making jelly. Plant in the sun.

Japanese (*Chaenomeles lagenaria*), Zones 5 to 9a, inclusive, grows 8 to 12 ft. high, with suckering shoots that may be removed to start new plants. There are varieties with flowers that are white, pink or red. A good turkey-red one is 'umbilicata.' Since blooms appear on new growth, the bushes can be grown as a trimmed hedge and yet produce flowers. The main trimming should be done right after flowering season.

Dwarf Japanese (*Chaenomeles japonica*) grows 3 ft. high, but its variety *alpina* is only 1 ft. high. It is frequently called 'Japonica.' The orange-red flowers are about 1 in. wide.

RAPHIOLEPIS. These are broad-leaved shrubs for Zones 8 through 10, with white or pink flowers in showy clusters in spring. They are not fussy about soil.

India-Hawthorn (*R. indica*) grows about 5 ft. high and wide, with fragrant pink flowers.

Pink India-Hawthorn (*R. indica rosea*) has deeper pink blossoms.

Roundleaf Yeddo-Hawthorn (*R. umbellata ovata*) is a compact grower, 6 to 8 ft. high, with fragrant white flowers.

REDBUD. See FLOWERING TREES in the chapter on trees.

RHODODENDRONS AND AZALEAS. These are botanically one big group, but gardeners think of them as separate kinds of shrubs. The familiar kinds called azalea are deciduous or semi-evergreen, with relatively small leaves; those typically called rhododendron have larger broad evergreen leaves. This book discusses them with separate names.

Both rhododendron and azalea are easy to grow in the parts of the country where they are native or where the climate and soil suits them, but elsewhere they are a challenge or possibly cannot be grown.

They thrive in areas of acid soil (see map of acid-soil regions in the chapter on soils), with ample rainfall and humidity. Rhododendrons cannot tolerate hot summers, drying winds, or rapid changes of temperature; they like a partly shaded position but bloom best with some sunlight. Most azaleas need more sun than rhododendrons; deciduous kinds tolerate colder winters than evergreen kinds, and some do not demand acid soil.

Provide light, porous, acid soil—containing quantities of organic matter. If your soil is not like this, you can improve it by digging out half or all of it before planting, and replacing it with a mixture of moistened sphagnum peat moss. If it is necessary to make the soil more acid, add 2 or 3 lb. of sulfur per 100 sq. ft., preferably a month before planting. Drainage must be excellent; if your site is low or wet, raise the bed 10 or 12 in. or install drain tile. In heavy clay soil, do not dig a hole for your plant that may become a water-collecting well. Rather, loosen the top 6 in., add humus, and raise the level of the bed so excess water will drain away elsewhere.

Time and Method of Planting

Rhododendons should be planted in early spring, during blooming time, or in mild climates they can be set out in autumn. A good size for amateurs to buy is 12 to 15 in. without buds, or 15 to 18 in. with buds. These sizes transplant easily and will begin to bloom soon.

Deciduous azaleas should be moved when dormant, unless they are in containers. Evergreen types can be moved any time, even when in full bloom, but avoid doing it in late spring and summer when buds for the following year are being developed, lest you lose a season of flowers.

Follow the general instructions for planting all shrubs given at the beginning of this chapter. Set these plants at exactly the same level as in the nursery, making certain they will not sink too low as the soil settles.

Do not cover the top of roots with heavy soil, but use compost or other organic material. Pruning is not needed, unless to remove some broken branches.

General Care

The roots of these plants are fibrous, and right at the top of the ground, where they are in danger of drying or of being injured by cultivating. So it is important to keep the soil moist, and to protect roots by use of a thick but airy mulch. It is especially necessary to keep the soil moist during early summer when new stems, leaves and flower buds are forming.

Feed them in early spring, using a fertilizer recommended for azaleas and other acid-soil plants. If your soil needs additional acidifying, each year apply 1 tablespoon of sulfur to each 2-ft.-high plant.

Rhododendrons appreciate an overhead watering or misting during hot, drying days. Their withering blooms should be removed as they fade; do not let seeds develop.

Instructions on how and where to remove flower heads, and illustrated details on pruning, are given in the pruning chapter.

Do not eat the foliage. Leaves of all rhododendrons should be considered poisonous.

Kinds To Grow

Among rhododendrons there are types that are low-growing, and others that are tall. There are species and also gorgeous large-flowering hybrids in unusual colors. It is wise to see a large collection of plants in bloom before making up your mind which ones you want.

Azaleas come in hundreds of varieties. Some grow best in mild-winter climates, a few where winters are severe, and many in between. Most of them are hybrids, classified in groups according to their general parentage, with many varieties in each. If you are interested in yellow blooms, or shades of yellow, you will find them among the deciduous azaleas.

Evergreen or Semi-Evergreen Groups

Belgian Indian, Zones 9 through 10
Gable, Zones 6b through 10

Glenn Dale, Zones 7 through 10
Kurume, Zones 7 through 10
Southern Indian or Indica, Zones 8 through 10

Deciduous Groups

Exbury, Zones 5 through 7b
Ghent, Zones 5 through 8
Knap Hill, Zones 5 through 7b
Mollis, Zones 5 through 7b

Hardy and Durable
Species Tolerating Cold

Korean (*R. mucronulatum*), Zones 5 through 8
Pinkshell (*R. vaseyi*), Zones 5 through 9
Pinxter-Flower (*R. nudiflorum*), Zones 4b through 9
Royal (*R. schlippenbachi*), Zones 5 through 9

ROCK-ROSE (*Cistus*). These are low-growing evergreen shrubs for mild climates, Zones 8 through 10. They like sun, fast-draining soil and heat. They tolerate poor soil and seaside conditions, but they do not like acid soil, soggy conditions or cold. Their flowers resemble a single rose.

C. ladaniferus grows 3 to 4 ft. high and wide. Its leaves have white undersides. The flowers, in midsummer, are white with a crimson spot at petal bases.

'Doris Hibberson' grows 3 ft. high, is compact and has pink flowers.

White (*C. hybridus* or *C. corbariensis*) grows 18 to 30 in. high and 4 ft. wide, with gray downy foliage and branches. The flowers are white, 2 in. across.

ROSE (*Rosa*). Shrub types are treated just like ordinary shrubs; give them sunshine and good soil. Among the most useful and distinctive are those listed here.

Austrian Copper (*R. foetida bicolor*), Zones 5 to 8, inclusive, is deciduous, 9 ft. high. Its blooms are coppery color in June.

Father Hugo (*R. hugonis*), Zones 5 to 8, inclusive, is deciduous, growing 7 ft. high. The flowers that appear in June are single, and canary yellow, 2 in. across.

Floribunda. See the chapter on roses.

Redleaf (*R. rubrifolia*), Zones 2 to 8, inclusive, has purplish-red stems and foliage. Its flowers, deep red and single, 1½ in. across, appear in June.

Rugosa (*R. rugosa*), Zones 2 to 8, inclusive, are deciduous, 6 ft. high. Many varieties with single or double flowers, about 3 in. across, come in white, pink and purple. The flowers are followed by conspicuous red fruits 1 in. across. Their leaves are wrinkled and decorative. This is a very durable shrub.

ROSEMARY, CREEPING. See the groundcover chapter.

ROSE-OF-SHARON, see HIBISCUS

RUSSIAN-OLIVE, see ELAEAGNUS

ST. JOHNSWORT, see HYPERICUM

SANTOLINA or LAVENDER-COTTON. See the chapter on perennials.

SARCOCOCCA HOOKERIANA HUMILIS. See the chapter on groundcovers.

SARCOCOCCA RUSCIFOLIA. This low-growing evergreen is found in Zones 7 to 10a, inclusive. It becomes 3 to 5 ft. high and almost that wide. The leaves are rounded, 2 in. long. The flowers, borne in March, are small, white, fragrant, followed by berries that turn from red to black. It likes shade or part shade.

SHRIMP-PLANT (*Beloperone guttata*). This tropical sprawling shrub with intriguing blooms is illustrated in the chapter on indoor plants.

SILVERBERRY, see ELAEAGNUS

SKIMMIA. These are evergreens with glossy oval leaves 2 to 5 in. long. Their bushes make a compact rounded form. The flowers are small, white, fragrant, in clusters in spring, followed by hollylike winter fruits. They need acid or peaty soil, and are excellent in shade.

S. japonica grows 2 to 5 ft. high and wider. Male and female plants are needed to set fruit.

S. reevesiana is shorter and is self-fertile.

SPIREA. These are deciduous shrubs with small white or pink flowers showily grouped in some form of clusters. They are very hardy and nonfussy. They will grow in sun or part shade but flower best in sun.

Billard (*S. billardi*), Zones 2 to 8, inclusive, grows 4 to 6 ft. high. The flowers are fuzzy pink plumes.

Blue, see BLUEBEARD

Froebel (*S. bumalda froebeli*), Zones 5 to 9a, inclusive, grows 2 to 3½ ft. high and has rosy-pink flowers in flat clusters 4 to 6 in. across. 'Anthony Waterer' is similar.

Thunberg (*S. thunbergi*), Zones 5 to 10a, inclusive, is the earliest spirea to bloom, at the time of daffodils. Tiny white flowers cover the billowing fine-textured foliage. The plants are 3 to 5 ft. high, and their leaves color attractively in fall.

Vanhoutte (*S. vanhouttei*), Zones 4 to 10a, inclusive, has an arching form, 6 ft. high, completely covered with clusters of white flowers at the time of late tulips and early irises. It is one of the two spireas called "bridal wreath"—the other being *S. prunifolia plena*, which has tiny buttonlike double flowers.

STAR-JASMINE. See JASMINE in the vine chapter.

STRAWBERRY-TREE (*Arbutus unedo*) lives in Zones 8 to 10a, inclusive. It is an evergreen shrub or small tree native to the West Coast that grows 8 to 20 ft. high with basal suckers. The leaves are 3 in. long and red-stemmed. The flowers are small, white, in clusters, followed by strawberrylike warty red fruits ¾ in. across. This shrub prefers acid soil or you can incorporate considerable peat.

SUMAC (*Rhus*). These are deciduous shrubs and small trees. The ones listed below are durable natives, growing in sun or shade. Their leaves turn brilliant colors in fall; the seed heads are orange-red and showy. They spread by underground runners that can be a nuisance. In some areas they are considered weeds or annoying plants. The foliage of some undesirable species of *Rhus* causes painful skin irritation, including that of poison ivy (*R. radicans*), poison oak (*R. diversiloba*) and poison sumac (*R. vernix*).

Fragrant (*Rhus aromatica*), Zones 4 to 9, inclusive, grows 3 ft. high or more. The leaves are glossy, 3-parted, fragrant and dense.

Staghorn (*R. typhina*), Zones 3 to 9, inclusive, grows 10 ft. high or more. Its heavy, hairy branches, and large foliage with many leaflets along a central stem, make bold silhouettes.

SUNSHINE SHRUB, see HYPERICUM

SURINAM-CHERRY (*Eugenia uniflora*). This double-duty tall evergreen, in Zones 9b and 10, can serve as a hedge and also provide edible small red fruits that are excellent for making jelly. The flowers are white and fragrant. It will grow in sun or part shade, and tolerates clipping.

TEA-TREE, AUSTRALIAN (*Leptospermum laevigatum*). This tall evergreen shrub or small tree with shaggy bark and twisting habit of growth is useful in Zones 9 and 10. Its branches are slender and drooping, clothed in tiny gray leaves. It likes sun and sandy soil, and is a good choice for seaside sites.

TEUCRIUM or GERMANDER (*Teucrium*). These are small-leaved evergreens liking full sun and fast-draining soil. Their flowers are lavender spikes in summer. The shrub is good for hedges and can be clipped.

Bush (*T. fruticans*), Zones 8b to 10, inclusive, is gray-leaved and grows 4 to 5 ft. high.

T. chamaedrys, Zones 5b to 10, inclusive, grows 6 to 12 in. high. It is an excellent edging plant.

TEXAS RANGER or TEXAS SAGE (*Leucophyllum frutescens* or *L. texanum*). This thrives in Zones 8 to 10, inclusive. The leaves are 1 in. long, woolly white beneath, and the flowers bell-shaped, rose-purple, 1 in. across. The shrub is excellent in dry areas both inland and near the sea. It tolerates heat and can be clipped as a hedge.

THUNBERGIA, BUSH or KING'S-MANTLE (*Thunbergia erecta*). This is a slender-branched shrub, 3 to 5 ft. high, in Zones 9b and 10. It has trumpet-shaped flowers of rich purple with golden throats, borne throughout the growing season. It does well in part shade.

THYRALLIS (*Thyrallis glauca*). This low evergreen grows to a 5-ft. height in sun or shade in Zone 10. Its leaves are 2 in. long. The flowers are yellow, ¾ in. across, covering the shrub most of the growing season. It tolerates heat and drought.

ULEI or CHINESE BONE-BERRY (*Osteomeles schwerinae*). This evergreen growing to 10 ft. is for the mild climates of Hawaii, California and the South. Slender branches are covered with ferny leaves. Flowers are white, ½ in. across, in clusters carried on new growth.

VIBURNUM. This is a varied group of shrubs and small trees, some grown primarily for foliage and others for their flowers and berries.

American Cranberry-Bush (*V. trilobum*), Zones 2b to 8, inclusive, is deciduous, 8 to 12 ft. high, with lobed leaves 3 to 5 in. long. The flowers are showy, white, in clusters 4 in. wide. The fruits are scarlet, remaining most of the winter.

Arrow-Wood (*V. dentatum*), Zones 2 to 8, inclusive, is deciduous, 10 to 15 ft. high. It is grown for good, dense foliage and its fruits are black. The shrub is good in shade.

Burkwood (*V. burkwoodi*), Zones 5b to 8, inclusive, is semi-evergreen, 5 to 7 ft. high. Its flowers are outstanding, pale pink and intensely fragrant, borne in 3-in. clusters. They appear in early spring before new foliage emerges. The leaves color in fall.

Chenault (*V. chenaulti*) is similar to Burkwood.

Judd (*V. juddi*), Zones 5b to 9, inclusive, is similar to Burkwood.

Laurestinus (*V. tinus*), Zones 7b to 10a, inclusive, is a broad-leaved evergreen growing 10 ft. high and wide. It has glossy leaves 3 in. long and makes a dense natural hedge. The flowers are white to pink, fragrant, growing in 3-in. clusters through winter into spring. The fruits are black. The variety *compactum* is lower-growing.

Maries Doublefile (*V. tomentosum mariesi*), Zones 5b to 8, inclusive, is deciduous, grows to 9 ft., and is admired for the way its branches grow in horizontal formation. The flowers are showy, white in flat clusters, followed by red berries.

Nanny-Berry (*V. lentago*), Zones 2 to 8, inclusive, is a deciduous tall shrub or small tree with oval leaves, white flowers, black fruit. It is grown mostly for its foliage.

Sandankwa (*V. suspensum*), Zones 8b to 10a, inclusive, is evergreen, grows 4 to 10 ft. high, and has glossy oval leaves 4 in. long. The flowers are pink and fragrant, growing in small clusters.

Siebold (*V. sieboldi*), Zones 5b to 8b, inclusive, is a deciduous shrub or small tree. Its decorative deeply dented leaves 6 in. long turn red in autumn. The flowers are white, growing in flat clusters, and the berries turn from red to black. It is very ornamental.

Sweet (*V. odoratissimum*), Zones 8 to 10a, inclusive, is evergreen, 7 to 12 ft. high and wide, with glossy oval leaves 2 to 6 in. long. The flowers are white and fragrant, in 4-in. clusters; berries turn from red to black.

V. carlesi, Zones 5 to 9, inclusive, is similar to Burkwood, but is deciduous and slightly hardier.

V. davidi. See the groundcover chapter.

Wayfaring-Tree (*V. lantana*), Zones 3 to 8, inclusive, is a treelike deciduous shrub with coarse stems and rough oval leaves 3 to 5 in. long. The flowers are white in 4-in. clusters, followed by berries that turn from red to black. It tolerates dry soil.

WAYFARING-TREE, see VIBURNUM

WITCH-HAZEL (*Hamamelis*). These are native deciduous shrubs with attractive leaves that turn yellow in autumn, and yellow narrow-petaled flowers. They are excellent to grow in shade but thrive also in sun.

Common (*H. virginiana*), Zones 4 to 8, inclusive, grows up to 15 ft. high. It blooms in October or November after the leaves fall.

Vernal (*H. vernalis*), Zones 5 to 8, inclusive, grows 6 ft. high. It blooms in January or February.

XYLOSMA, SHINY (*Xylosma senticosum*). This evergreen, in Zones 8 to 10, inclusive, grows 4 to 6 ft. high with shiny oval leaves 2 in. long. The new growth is bronze. Its flowers are inconspicuous but fragrant. Plant this shrub in sun or shade. It tolerates desert heat.

YAUPON, see HOLLY

YESTERDAY-TODAY-AND-TOMORROW (*Brunfelsia latifolia*). This evergreen, in Zones 9b and 10, grows 3 to 4 ft. high, with fragrant flowers. The blooms open purple, become lavender the second day, and white the third. It will grow in sun or shade and is drought-resistant.

9

‚ÄñÁ‚Ä¢‚Ä¢ÁÇ‚Ä¢‚Ä¢ÁÇ‚Ä¢‚Ä¢ÁÇ‚Ä¢‚Ä¢ÁÇ‚Ä¢‚Ä¢ÁÇ‚Ä¢‚Ä¢ÁÇ‚Ä¢‚Ä¢ÁÇ‚Ä¢‚Ä¢ÁÇ

Roses Thrive on Loving Care

Roses are wonderful plants for beginners. They bloom gloriously their first year and are easy to grow if you follow a few simple instructions. They like to be humored and cared for attentively, which is fun, for you are having a part in the success of the lovely flowers.

They will want at least six hours of sunshine a day. In cool climates they need as much sun as they can get, while in hot regions they appreciate several hours of shade during midday or afternoon.

Put them where you can see them frequently, enjoy them intimately, and attend to them conveniently. They should be near your house, adjoining a doorway or patio, or highlighting a view from a window. Locate them as far as possible from big shrubs and trees whose roots, amazingly, extend farther than their branches and sap the soil of moisture and fertility. If your yard is new, and your trees and shrubs young and small, this is a wonderful time for you to grow roses. In windy areas (such as the Southwest) choose a sheltered location such as the protected side of a house or fence.

The time to plant depends upon your climate and convenience. In cold-winter areas [Zone 5 and north] early spring is recommended for setting out dormant bushes. In the mid part of the country [Zones 6 and 7] either early spring or late fall are fine, depending upon when you prefer to do it and whether plants can be obtained in the autumn before your ground freezes. In mild-winter climates [Zones 8, 9, 10] plant from late November into mid February. Container-grown roses, in any part of the country, can be set in the garden at any time during the growing season with almost no shock to the plant. They are the only ones that can be planted when in leaf.

❦ Tips on Buying

To shop wisely you should understand how rose plants are handled before you get them.

Bare-root plants are those which are dug in autumn after they have shed their leaves, become dormant, and been stored without soil under controlled conditions of cold temperatures and moist surroundings. They are ready to start a new cycle of growth in your garden. This is the kind most gardeners buy. These dormant rose bushes can be ordered by mail, and they will be shipped to you packed in material that will keep roots from drying, such as in polyethylene-coated paper. Or you can buy them from a local source that keeps them stored in a cool place with roots moist.

Prepackaged or boxed dormant plants look enticing and often are offered at amazing bargains. These may be excellent buys, or may be booby traps—depending upon the quality of the plants that were put into the packages, and how they have been handled. If the plants have been sitting in a warm store for an unknown length of time, look them over with a critical eye. If branches are drying out, or are shriveled (instead of being plumply green), or molding, or are developing pale, sickly-colored growth, they are no bargain!

Container-grown plants are the same dormant bushes described at the beginning of this section, but nurserymen have potted them and started them into growth. Results in your garden are quick. They are priced slightly higher than dormant bushes, since the plantsman had to give them more time and display space. If you are a beginner, there is lots of comfort and assurance in buying a plant that is obviously alive and maybe in bud or flower.

Top quality rose plants sell for about $1.50 to $3.50 each. Prices are highest on newly introduced and patented roses, including the All-America Rose Selections, and least on popular kinds that have been on the market

many years, or those whose patents have expired.

The best plants are #1 grade, according to national standard nursery ratings. With hybrid teas this means that plants have at least 3 big canes (stems); #1½ grade plants have only 2 big canes. You can imagine how scrawny lower grades are and why they cost less.

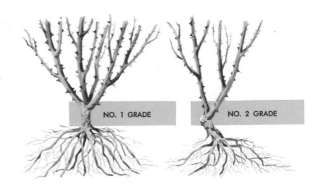

NO. 1 GRADE   NO. 2 GRADE

As for adaptability to climate, hardiness is not a matter of where the rose was propagated and raised, but depends primarily on each variety's inherited traits. No matter where you buy them, most roses will have been grown in one of the sections of the country especially adapted to large-scale production under ideal conditions.

✿ How To Plan and Prepare a Rose Garden

Grow roses in beds by themselves, rather than with other flowers in mixed borders. Then they are assured of good air circulation, and they are easy to get at for weeding, picking, spraying and dusting.

Type of soil is not important, as long as it drains well, has ample humus content and available · plant food. If other flowers and weeds grow well in your yard or your neighbor's, your soil will probably grow roses splendidly, too. If you are in doubt, or live in a region where soils are extremely acid or alkaline, see the chapter on soils.

The width of the bed should be as narrow as possible without crowding the bushes, and seldom more than 5 ft. This is to make it easy for you to reach in and care for the plants.

Spacing of plants varies with your climate. In cold-winter areas where tops are frozen back each year, hybrid teas, grandifloras and floribundas are spaced 18 in. to 2 ft. apart. In the South and West Coast where they grow bigger, allow each plant 3 ft.

Good preparation of beds pays off. Dig them at least 18 in. deep and work in organic matter (such as old rotted manure, moistened peat moss, or compost), allowing 5 or 6 bushels to 100 sq. ft. The level of the beds, in most parts of the country, should be a little below the surrounding ground to make watering easier—it will not run off. In irrigated country the level should be 4 in. below the normal surface. On the other hand, in rainy or poorly drained areas make the bed several inches higher, so water will not stand on it.

Edging plants around the bed are decorative, but do not use varieties that will spread over the entire ground, or whose roots will compete with those of the roses. One of the easiest and prettiest flowering edgings is sweet alyssum (annual) in white or lavender. Other good annuals for the purpose are blue lobelia, petunias or portulaca in a color that harmonizes with your roses, and pansies or violas. Tidy, permanent low-shrub edging hedges can be made of germander [Zones 6, 7, 8, 9 and 10a] and santolina [Zones 7b, 8, 9 and 10]. Do not use strawberries, lettuce, or other things you are going to eat, for the poison sprays you use on the roses will contaminate them.

✿ Types of Roses from Which You Can Choose

All roses are lovely, so how will you choose from among the hundreds available today? You will have to decide, first, why you wish to grow them. If you are after perfect blooms to pick for indoors, hybrid teas are probably your answer. If you are more interested in colorful garden effect, choose floribundas. For climbers, you will need to take your climate into consideration, especially if you live where winters are severe; this book will tell you which ones are best for various climate

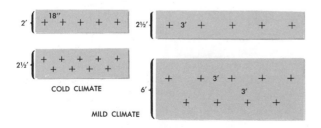

regions. Then there are durable shrub roses that are excellent for backgrounds, and for delightful flowers with no effort.

To get acquainted with varieties and their names, and to learn which ones appeal to you most, it is best to see them "in the flesh." Visit rose display gardens (often located in city parks). Attend rose shows; they are always open to the public, and varieties will be labeled. Get to know local rose hobbyists, for they will be happy to have you visit their gardens if they realize that you are interested. Send for catalogues of rose-specialist firms; some of them are free and others available for a small charge. For a list of some catalogue sources, see the back of this book.

GARDEN BUSH ROSES:
THE BIG THREE

FLORIBUNDA

HYBRID TEA

GRANDIFLORA

Hybrid teas: These are the ones like florists' roses, with lovely pointed buds and superlatively large flowers. They bloom almost continuously but put on their greatest show at the first of the season and during autumn.

Blooms are carried one to a stem, or only a few to a stem. Plants stand 3 to 6 ft. high, depending upon whether your climate has mild winters or severe ones that freeze the plants' tops annually. They can be grown anywhere, though in some parts of the Deep South they are treated as annuals, and in severely cold areas [Zone 5 and northward] they must have winter protection.

Floribundas: These have ancestors among the hybrid teas and among a group of bush roses sometimes called polyanthas. The latter (now generally classified and listed in catalogues with floribundas) have small blooms in large clusters and are very hardy. Floribundas combine the best traits of both sets of ancestors. Some have flowers and buds as perfectly formed as those of hybrid teas, though smaller and more numerous. They are marvelous for colorful mass plantings to front a rose bed, to use for cutting, and especially for corsage material. Some are tall (as 48-in. 'Else Poulsen') and others are short (as 18-in. 'Pinkie'). They tend to be hardier than hybrid teas but need winter protection in Zones 5 and north.

Grandifloras: These are usually descended from hybrid teas and floribundas. The flowers are large like hybrid teas, sometimes borne one to a stem, but more often several to a stem. They have great vigor and may grow extremely tall. In catalogues they are sometimes grouped with hybrid teas.

HOW TO PLANT

If they are dormant and "bare-root," plant immediately, should that be possible.

If you must postpone planting a few days, you can keep bushes in the package in which you received them. Put it in a cool (32° to 50°), dark place. Be sure the roots will be moist and the tops not exposed to drying. You may need to do some rewrapping, using damp cloths around the roots.

If there is to be a long delay, dig a shallow hole in your garden and bury the plants (after taking them from their package), covering them with 6 in. of moist soil.

Constantly be kind to roots. Before planting, soak them in a pail of water for an hour, or overnight. Continue to keep them in water, cover with something moist, or enclose in polyethylene, until you get them into the ground. Never let them dry!

COVER WITH SOIL

KEEP MOIST

A little pruning may be needed. Nurseries usually trim the plant's branches properly before selling them, but if they have not been shortened, cut them back to about 13-in.

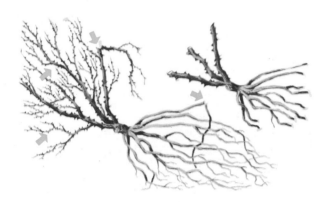

length. Cut off any small, weak twigs, broken roots and broken branches. Shorten any exceedingly long roots.

Dig holes 12 in. deep and 18 in. wide, even though the roots do not look as though they were going to need so much space. Make a mound of soil in the center of the bottom of the hole over which to spread the roots. Hold the bush so its point of graft (the knob where top and roots join) is at ground level if you live in a cold climate, or an inch above level in mild climates. The bushes will sink slightly as soil settles later. Fill in among the roots with fine, crumbly soil. If what you have dug from the hole does not look good enough, mix in 25% or 50% moist peat moss. When the hole is almost full, stand in it, and while holding the plant so it cannot sink below proper level, gently tramp on the soil to firm it.

Water—all the hole will take. When water has soaked away, finish filling the hole with loose soil.

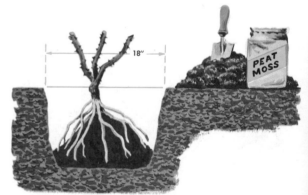

To help growth start, keep the branches from drying out before roots become established by covering the top of the stem with a mound of loose soil 8 to 9 in. high. As shoots emerge, level the soil gradually. In very dry, sunny climates, bush tops are sometimes en-

closed in polyethylene sacks, which are tied
about the neck of the plant, or sprayed with
a wiltproof solution available at garden supply stores. If sacks are used, slit them to let in
air as sprouts begin to show. Then in a few
days remove the covering.

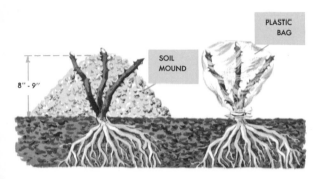

THROUGH-THE-YEAR CARE

If the plants are potted or come in containers, there is nothing to it! Dig a hole six
inches wider all around, and deeper than the
pot, and loosen the soil in the bottom with
your spade. Maneuver the rose into the hole
in such a way that the earth about its roots is
kept intact. (A good way to manage, if the pot
is of tar paper or similar material, is this: Cut
off the bottom part of the pot; place the plant
at proper depth; carefully slit the pot's side,
and gently remove the paper to keep the soil
ball as is.) The top of the pot's soil should be
even with the level of the ground. It will sink
a little, later. Fill the hole with earth, firm it
with your hands, and water generously. That
is all, except that you may wish to shade the
plant for the first few days if it has been sitting in a protected shelter such as a lath
house or greenhouse.

Pruning to prepare the plant for blooming is
the big early-season job with old bushes. If
possible, it should be done when plants are
dormant and before the new growth buds begin to swell. In the South and on the Pacific
Coast this will be during the winter. Where
winters are cold it will be March or April,
after you have removed whatever material
you used to protect the plants.

First take out all dead and diseased wood.
If the bush was frozen, it probably will be
black. Prune back as far as necessary to reach
live, healthy wood. Then remove all small
twiggy branches, and any that cross in the
middle of the bush. Cut them off smoothly
where they join the larger branch. You should
end with 3 to 5 sturdy canes. The final step
is to shorten these main structural branches.
In cold climates 12- to 18-in. height is desirable. In mild climates high pruning or 20
to 30 in. is the usual practice. Cut on a slant,
starting ½ in. above a plump bud that is
preferably on the outside of the branch. What

you have left may look to you like a plucked chicken, but it is good for the bush!

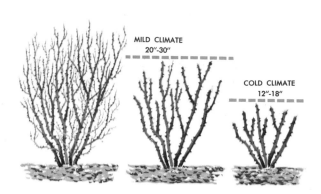

Roses need feeding. Use a "complete" plant food. There are some especially devised for roses, even though you can also use the same kind you buy for your other garden flowers. But do not use one recommended especially for lawns. Lawn fertilizers are high in nitrogen, to stimulate leaf growth rather than flowers. The fertilizer can be applied in dry powdered form, or in solution. Follow instructions on the package as to how, and how much, to use. Generally with a dry product this is about a handful, or ½ cup per plant. Scatter it on the ground around the plant, being careful not to let it touch the stems or leaves. If the soil is dry, water the feed in.

Foliar feeding (spraying onto leaves plant foods of specially prepared types) can be used in addition to ground feeding and can be included in pesticide sprays.

Newly planted roses are not fed until after their first crop of blooms.

Old bushes should have their first feeding early in the year, right after they have been pruned. Feed again after their first bloom period, to help the plant develop its next set of flower buds. Then feed after each big flurry of blooms as new growth begins to appear (you will find these bloom periods come in waves about a month apart). Then water, unless rain comes immediately.

In Zones 5, 6 and 7, stop feeding by August 1, so plants will not be in too succulent condition when frosts arrive. In the Deep South and mild-winter area of the Pacific Coast, feeding can continue any time that roses are growing and blooming vigorously—though you may wish to ease up during hottest summer.

Water is even more important than food to roses. Ideally, roses should get about an inch of rainfall a week, and soil at root depth should always be moist. So if rains do not come, or in arid parts of the country, or on very sandy soil, each plant will need an inch of irrigation water per week—or a bucketful. It is better to water deeply and thoroughly at relatively long intervals than to sprinkle a little every day or so. Put the water on the ground (or *in* it, with a deep-root waterer) rather than wetting the foliage, which tends to encourage various diseases. The best time of day is morning. In dry climates, winter watering may be needed. Always water after fertilizing.

Control of diseases and pests: Although roses have numerous pests, only a few are important enough to require chemical treatment. These can usually be controlled by a single combination spray or dust—preferably the former—applied more or less weekly from the time bushes come into full leaf until hard frost. Such sprays and dusts—containing approved fungicides, insecticides and a miticide—designed especially for use on roses, can be purchased at your garden supply dealer's under numerous brand names. For help on specific rose troubles, see chart in the chapter on plant diseases.

How to cut roses: Remove fading blossoms before petals start to fall. On hybrid teas, cut ¼ in. above the top five-parted leaf. A new bud-bearing shoot will arise from the axil of that leaf. On floribundas and other cluster-flowered roses, individual blooms may fade at different times and can be removed at the base of their short stems. But when the entire cluster has finished, cut the whole thing off as though it were one huge bloom. Cut above the next 5-parted leaf. A clever way to avoid periods of no bloom is to cut back half the branches when their flower buds are tiny. This will force them to make new growth and buds, so they will bloom on an alternating schedule with the other half of the branches!

Summer pruning influences flower production. Picking flowers is a form of pruning. It removes leaves which make food for the plant. Ordinarily, and especially the first year, cut blooms with the shortest possible stems and fewest leaves. Toward autumn, when the growing season is about over, you can pick with more abandon.

To induce large, long-stemmed flowers, you can make your cut near the base of sturdy canes, ¼ in. above a leaf. You will have show-size blossoms, but fewer of them, this way. Bear in mind that you will be sacrificing leaves and this is hard on the plant.

For whopper blooms: If there are little side buds in addition to the main bud on a stem, nip off the little ones as soon as you see them. All the strength will then go to the one flower.

To make "blind" shoots set buds: Occasionally you will notice new canes that have no buds in their tip. Treat them as though they had finished blooming. Cut back to a vigorous 5-parted leaf and a new bud-bearing shoot will arise there.

Mulching tip: A summer mulch lessens your work and is wonderful for the roses. (You can use peat moss, buckwheat hulls, ground up corn cobs or other loose material.) It serves as insulation, keeping roots cool and moist. It almost does away with cultivation and weeding. It gradually improves the soil by adding humus. Put on 1 or 2 in. in the spring, after getting out all weeds, loosening the soil surface, and applying the first feeding. (Later feedings can be watered through the mulch, or you can pull the mulch away from the plant while you feed.) Do not let any fertilizer touch the stems of the bushes; keep it 6 in. away. The mulch can stay in place permanently but you will keep adding to it. The best material depends upon what is easily available in your region. For choices, and their good and weak features, see chapter on soil.

Protect for winter in Zones 3, 4, 5 and 6: Your first step is to avoid having plants succulent when hard frosts come; do not feed them after August 1. In late autumn, preferably after light frosts but before the ground freezes, mound each bush with soil 10 in. high. If bushes are large, tie the tops together loosely first.

Soil should be brought in, not dug from between bushes (which would expose and damage roots and make holes in which water

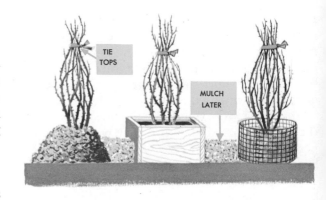

TIE TOPS

MULCH LATER

could stand). To hold soil in place, you can put small boards along the sides of the bushes, or make individual circles of large-mesh wire (10 in. high) or similar material that will let excess moisture drain away. Later, when the ground is frozen, a mulch of evergreen boughs, dead leaves, etc., can be added to insulate the roots. Putting it on too early makes a place for rodents to nest, and they will gnaw on your plants' stems. Avoid any form of winter protection that will keep stems warm, moist or wet, for it will cause winterkilling.

TREE ROSES ARE ASTONISHING

These are man-made combination roses. A bush variety of hybrid tea, floribunda or grandiflora is budded into the top of a tall cane of another rose plant (which has been previously grown especially to become the root system and trunk of a tree rose). The top develops just as it would if it were growing on its own roots, close to the ground. But the flowers look more elegantly handsome borne as a head-high bouquet.

Plant these like regular bush roses, but with extra care. Afterward, the branched top should be protected from drying while new growth buds are emerging (unless you live in a humid climate). One way to do this is to wrap the stems in burlap, which you can moisten occasionally. Another method is to place some damp sphagnum moss among the branches. Or slip a polyethylene sack over the top and tie it in place until growth starts, and then either slit the sack or loosen it for a few days before removing.

Because these plants are top-heavy, apt to sway and loosen the ground, give them a permanent supporting stake or metal pipe at the time you plant. The stake should preferably be on the sunny side of the stem, to shade it and lessen chances of sun scald. It should reach to the point where branching starts. Fasten securely, though loosely, at several places along the stem. Feeding, pruning and care are the same as for all garden bush roses.

They are easy to grow anywhere that hybrid teas do well, but bloom best in a mild climate. However, the problem of winter protection where temperatures go below 15° means a chore! The stems of the plants that are way up in the air are the most tender parts. You cannot mound them with soil, as would be desirable, so you improvise, beginning action after frost has made the leaves drop and has ripened the wood somewhat. In Zones 6 and 7, wrapping the top snuggly in several layers of paper and enclosing in a polyethylene sack, or wrapping the tree top to bottom in straw or evergreen boughs may do the trick. From Zone 5 northward, it is necessary to dig the entire plant, bury it 2 ft. deep, and mulch the spot; in spring dig it up and plant it as though it were new.

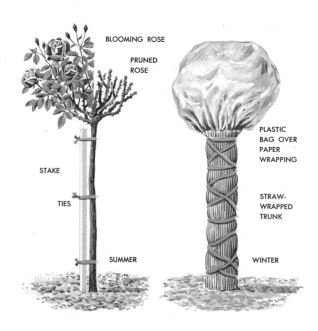

BLOOMING ROSE

PRUNED ROSE

STAKE

TIES

SUMMER

PLASTIC BAG OVER PAPER WRAPPING

STRAW-WRAPPED TRUNK

WINTER

MINIATURES ARE ADORABLE

Midget roses are tiny versions of normal-size bushes. They grow 6 to 12 in. high, with charming tiny buds and flowers that measure less than an inch across. They are every bit as hardy as large rose bushes, so can be used as edgings, in rockeries, window or planter boxes, or in special miniature gardens. Among the best are 'Baby Betsy McCall,' 'Baby Masquerade,' 'Pixie Rose,' 'Red Imp' and 'Sweet Fairy.'

Planting and care is exactly the same as for hybrid teas, floribundas, etc. They are often purchased in pots, but are also available in dormant bare-root condition. Space 10 to 12 in. apart.

They can be grown as house plants, too. For how-to, see the chapter on indoor gardening.

SHRUB ROSES FOR BACKGROUNDS

Think of these as you would any shrub that produces handsome flowers. They are mostly wild species and their hybrids, and very cold-hardy. Some bloom only once a year, but others are repeaters. Most make good 5- to 10-ft. background or screening material, and some are so lovely that you will want to give them show-off positions. Care for them like shrubs. Examples are 'Harison's yellow,' 'Father Hugo' rose and rugosa hybrids.

OLD-FASHIONED ROSES FOR NOSTALGIA

Here are the treasured roses of history and sentiment: cabbage and moss roses, China, French and damask, hybrid perpetuals, etc. They are a delight, though if your place is small, you may not have room to include them. Some are similar to hybrid teas, and others shrubby. Cabbage or hundred-leaved roses (*Rosa centifolia*), for example, are shrubs growing 5 to 6 ft. high, with fragrant double flowers about the size of small hybrid tea blooms. There are numerous varieties. Moss roses are a type of cabbage rose with a unique and charming mossy growth on buds and stems; some bloom only once a year while others are repeaters. (Portulaca, the small annual flower, is sometimes called moss rose incorrectly; its correct common name is rose-moss.) Most of the old-fashioned roses are very hardy.

HEDGES OF EVER-BLOOMING ROSES

Ideally, roses used as hedges should not need much care. They should be extra-hardy and healthy (not susceptible to diseases and pests). Preferably they should be inexpensive so you can afford a long row of them.

Among the best sold especially for the purpose are 'Robin Hood,' a cherry-red, hardy in below-zero weather; 'Red Glory,' and 'County Fair,' which is a pink single. The latter two are as hardy as floribundas. They all grow about 4 to 5 ft. tall in cold climates and taller where winters are mild.

Many floribundas can be used, such as 'Circus,' 'Fashion,' 'Frensham,' 'Spartan' and 'Summer Snow.' Where winter temperatures sink below zero, favorites for dependability are 'Betty Prior,' a tall pink single, and lower-growing 'Eutin' with huge clusters of small double red or double pink blooms.

Multiflora roses, though sometimes recommended for hedges, are not suitable for use in small home grounds. They can become 6 ft. high and as broad; are very thorny. They bloom only a few days once a year.

CLIMBING ROSES

Climbers like the same conditions, planting

and care as garden bush roses. They require good air circulation. So when they are grown on a house, wall or solid fence, they should be held several inches from it by some sort of trellis or other support. In hot climates this distance should be 8 to 12 in. If you are going to need to get behind the roses to paint the wall, the trellis should have a hook at the top so it is possible to fold it down.

They do not really climb. They have long, limber canes, which you can fasten to a supporting fence, post or trellis. Some kinds grow rampantly, some are more restrained and are called pillar types (to be tied to a pillar or post), and a few are trailers grown as groundcovers. If you are growing several along a fence or wall, they should be spaced 6 to 10 ft. apart.

Some climbers produce blooms the first year; others take a year or so to become established. In the first year encourage the plants to grow as many stems and leaves as possible, protect from diseases and pests, and water like other roses. After the first year, when the plants are established, training is in order.

There is a trick to getting the most bloom from climbers. In general, those fastened horizontally or in arching curves with the tips pointing down will bloom much more profusely than those that are growing upright. This applies even to pillar types that are ordinarily grown vertically on posts. With arching or fan-shaped training, the lower you can get the outer end of the curving canes, the more blooms you will have.

The reason for this seeming magic lies in the inner workings of the plant's system of growth and food supply. Ordinarily most blooms, and new extending growth on a cane, come at its upper and highest end. When a cane is placed in horizontal or arched position, upward growth is checked. The lower portion of the cane benefits from the food

formerly shunted to the tip. Flowering shoots emerge along the horizontal or curved portions since they are now in the top or high position.

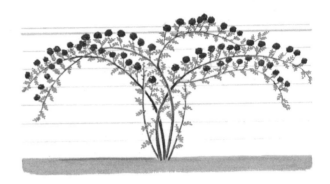

Feeding: In cold climates, once-blooming climbers such as ramblers and 'Paul's Scarlet' should be fed only once, in spring as growth starts. In warm climates they will appreciate additional feeding during or after bloom. Repeat bloomers, anywhere, should be fed during each peak of bloom, but in cold-winter areas do not feed after August 1. Give double the amount you feed bush roses, since climbers have twice as much top growth. In other words, if you are using a dry-type complete fertilizer, give each climber 2 handfuls.

Pruning: The main pruning should be done after the period of bloom. Most climbers flower on stems that emerge from canes that are at least a year old, so early spring pruning would cut away prospective bloom. The only pruning to do during the winter or in very early spring—at the time you prune bush roses—is the removal of dead or injured branches. As climbers grow old, you may possibly wish to remove one or two of the most ancient canes at their base. You will find details on how to prune various types of climbers later in this chapter.

This rose garden, outlined by a hedge of trimmed santolina, was designed to be seen from both street and patio. George Doolittle home, Albuquerque, New Mexico

It is pleasant to have roses adjacent to walks, where you can easily pause to admire them and sniff their fragrance. These are in the A. A. Plagman garden, Davenport, Iowa.

You, too, can have roses climbing over your doorway, if there is sunshine at least 6 hours a day. The evergreen shrub shown is yew, and the groundcover is pachysandra.

PLACES TO PUT ROSES

Winter protection: In the coldest parts of Zone 6, all of Zone 5 and northward, climbers are apt to be severely injured during winter. Those in protected urban places or against house walls will be safer than those out in the open on fences. The safest protection is to mound their bases first with 10 in. of soil. Then take the canes from their trellis and lay them on the ground; after the soil has frozen, cover them with earth or straw. Or cover them, in place on their support, with evergreen boughs or burlap. (If you are troubled with rabbits or mice, be warned that they love to eat rose stems.)

susceptible to mildew. Blooms are on canes produced the year before. Each year an entire new set of canes grows from the ground, and the ones that bloomed should be cut off at their base immediately after they have finished flowering. The best one is the red 'Chevy Chase.'

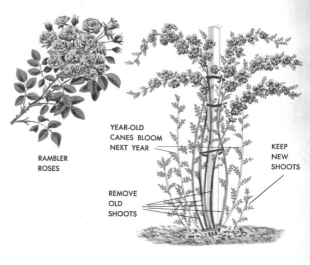

YEAR-OLD CANES BLOOM NEXT YEAR

KEEP NEW SHOOTS

RAMBLER ROSES

REMOVE OLD SHOOTS

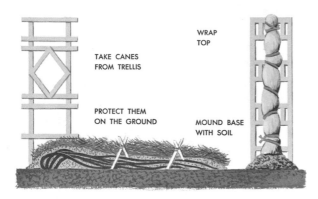

WRAP TOP

TAKE CANES FROM TRELLIS

PROTECT THEM ON THE GROUND

MOUND BASE WITH SOIL

KINDS OF CLIMBERS

There are several different types, varying in hardiness, in the way they grow and bloom, and the manner in which they should be pruned.

For cold-winter climates [Zones 4, 5, 6 and 7]: Ramblers have compact clusters of small flowers. They bloom once a year, in June, in most parts of the country. They are hardy to Zone 5 or perhaps Zone 4 (where, in worst winters, unprotected tops will be killed back and there will be no bloom that season). Some varieties have foliage very

Large-flowered climbers have loose clusters of blooms that are individually 2 in. or more across. Some bloom once a year. Others are repeaters and, in addition to the main season of bloom, have scattered flowers all summer and put on a good display in autumn. They bloom on new growth that arises from branches that are at least a year old. If winter kills the branches, you will have bloom only at the base (unkilled old wood) of the plant, and will need to wait for a big display until more growth develops and survives a winter. Prune when blooms begin to wither. Flowers should be cut off just below their necks or just above one of the top leaves. New buds will arise from growth buds in the axils of the nearest leaves.

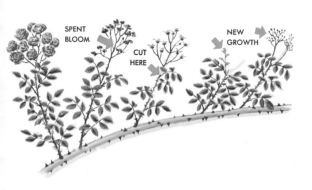

the base of these leaves. Examples are: climbing hybrid teas—red 'Etoile de Hollande' and 'Crimson Glory,' and pink 'Picture' and 'Parade'; climbing floribundas—pink 'Pinkie' and yellow 'Goldilocks.'

Noisettes, bourbons and climbing teas are additional favorites in Zones 8, 9, and 10, especially the South. They need little pruning, other than removing flowers. Among the favorites are: climbing China—red 'Louis Philippe'; noisette—yellows 'Lamarque' and 'Maréchal Niel'; bourbons—'White Banksia' and 'Yellow Banksia'; climbing tea—pink 'Gloire de Dijon.'

For milder climates [Zones 6, 7, 8, 9, and 10]: Climbing hybrid teas and climbing floribundas have flowers just like the bushes with the same names. They flower more or less continuously, developing buds on new shoots. They are excellent for the South and mild areas of the West Coast. Some varieties are hardy considerably farther north. To prune, cut off withering blooms, leaving 2 to 3 leaves on the remaining short stems. New stems carrying flower buds will arise from

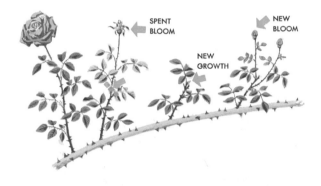

Trailing pink-flowered rose 'Max Graf' is an excellent groundcover.

10

Annuals for Quick Color

Annuals are quick and easy hurry-up flowers that bloom gloriously and for a long time the same season in which they are planted. You start them anew each year, for they complete their life cycle in one season, beginning from seed, reaching flowering stage, producing seed, and dying. They are such prolific bloomers, so colorful and inexpensive, that they are a joy for all gardeners, and especially new ones. An important thing to understand about these flowers is that their goal is seed production. If they succeed in ripening seeds, their reason for flowering is fulfilled and they will usually stop blooming. But if you keep the fading flowers picked off, so seeds cannot develop, the plants will continue budding until frost.

To succeed in growing annuals, give them as much sunshine as possible. Most will sulk, grow leggy, and not bloom if they are in shade. (For those that are satisfactory in shade, see Chapter 14.) They are not fussy about soil, and thrive in almost any that is deeply dug, especially if it has "complete" fertilizer mixed into it. If your soil is hard to dig, or if you have other reasons to doubt that it is good enough, see the soil chapter for advice. Do not think that you can scatter seed on hard, unprepared ground and get results. Annuals can be grown by themselves in borders or beds, mixed with perennials or shrubs, or used as edgings. They are also excellent in pots or planter boxes, window boxes, or pockets in paving. You can even make "instant" colorful rock gardens or mound gardens of annuals.

Some annuals have the delightfully helpful habit of self-sowing. That is, they shed their ripened seeds on the ground, where they germinate either later in the season or early the following spring.

A few of the plants grown as annuals in climates where winters are severe are really frost-tender perennials. These, in mild climates, live over winter or even year after year. Among them are wax begonia, coleus and Madagascar periwinkle.

❧ The Two Ways To Start Annuals

Buy already growing plants. This is the fast-result method and is sure and safe for beginners. Such plants (available at garden-supply dealers) come by the half-dozen, or dozen, in little boxes. Sometimes, though all in the same box, each plant will be in its own small pot made of peat or similar material that can be set directly in your garden. Large-sized plants are nearly always in individual pots. The younger and smaller the plants, and the larger the number you buy, the less they will cost.

Ideal-sized plants to purchase are in leafy rosette stage. They have not started to stretch up and make flower buds. They are just ready to do their major growing. When set into your garden they will expand vigorously, producing many side branches and thus much bloom. If you buy plants that are leggy, it is smart to nip their tops out as you set them. Cut them back to about 3 leaves. New branches will sprout from the dormant growth

buds at the base of those leaves and produce well-formed plants.

Before setting the plants in your garden, if they have been in a greenhouse or other protected place, accustom them to outdoor sun and wind gradually. This is called "hardening off." Put the boxes or pots outside in a spot out of wind and direct sun for a few days. Keep an eye on them to be sure they are able to take it.

When planting, choose a cloudy or rainy day if possible. Avoid a windy one. Evening is the best time. Have soil in your garden ready, loosened at least 8 in. deep, and moist. Water plants several hours before setting, so soil will cling to roots. If plants are growing several in a box, cut them apart like pieces of cake. If they are in individual peat pots, plant pot and all. If they are in clay pots, remove by turning the pot upside down and tapping its bottom. The big idea is not to disturb the roots, and to keep them enclosed in their soil.

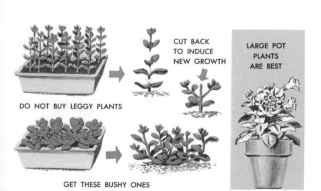

DO NOT BUY LEGGY PLANTS

CUT BACK TO INDUCE NEW GROWTH

GET THESE BUSHY ONES

LARGE POT PLANTS ARE BEST

STRIKE POT

CUT APART

BREAK OFF BOTTOM

Dig holes larger than necessary and soften the soil in the bottom. Place plants slightly below their previous soil level. Fill loose fine soil around them and firm it gently around the root area with your fingers. Water enough to soak below root depth. Provide shade for a day or so if weather is not coöperative. Single plants can be covered with inverted pots. A group of plants can be protected by an upside down large box. Rows of transplants can be shaded by a long board that is held above them on supporting bricks or pots.

PLANT DEEPER... FIRM SOIL... WATER... SHADE

Start plants from seed. This is exciting, and rewarding! You get lavish numbers of plants at minimum expense, for there are from 25 to 100 seeds in every packet. You have the fun of planting the seed, watching it "hatch," and mothering babies till they are mature. Then you get bushels of blooms.

Some annuals are so easy and quick to grow from seed that most gardeners plant them directly in the ground outdoors. They can be placed either in the location in which they are to bloom, or in a spot from which they can be transplanted later (dug with roots intact and moved). Seeds sown in the ground and not transplanted suffer no setback, and may bloom sooner than plants started earlier but transplanted.

Other annuals take such a long time to reach flowering stage that they would never make their deadline to bloom in summer unless given a headstart indoors, or with protection outdoors as in a cold frame. Either *you* start them, or you wait and buy started plants later from a dealer.

For complete instructions on how to grow annuals from seed, outdoors or inside, see Chapter 22 on starting plants.

❧ Time To Plant Outdoors

Much depends on your climate, and the conditions liked by the annuals you want to grow. Some prefer cool conditions; others want warmth. Many, bless them, are not particular.

The crucial date to know, if you live where winters have freezing temperatures, is that of the last frost in your area. This varies somewhat from year to year but not much. Most annual plants are not set outside in spring until after this date. Some seeds are planted outdoors before frost-free date, while others must not be planted until after that time or when the ground is really warm. This book will tell you which are which.

Locate yourself on this map. Memorize your date, and fit your planting plans around it. In areas where climate and altitude vary greatly within short distances, this map cannot give sufficient details, so consult local gardeners.

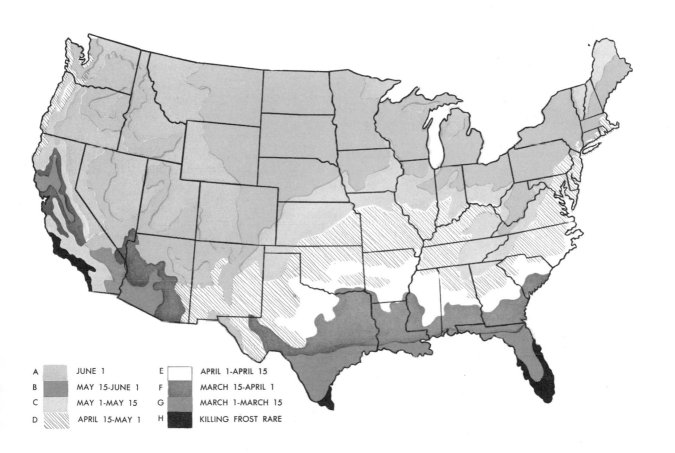

A	JUNE 1	E	APRIL 1-APRIL 15
B	MAY 15-JUNE 1	F	MARCH 15-APRIL 1
C	MAY 1-MAY 15	G	MARCH 1-MARCH 15
D	APRIL 15-MAY 1	H	KILLING FROST RARE

WHERE TO BUY PACKETS OF
FLOWER SEED

In spring you can scarcely enter a store that does not greet you with display racks of flower seeds. Besides garden centers and seed stores, you will also find them in hardware, grocery and drug stores.

Mail-order seed companies have attractively illustrated catalogues that are usually free for the asking. Just drop them a request by postal card. These catalogues describe and illustrate flowers so glowingly that they are often referred to as "wish books"—one can hardly choose from the many wonderful and exciting new varieties. Many also give directions for planting and other informative data. Some catalogues list flowers under their botanical names, while others use their common names, so if you do not find what you are looking for the first time, try again. To help you, we give both botanical and common names in our alphabetical list of annuals in this chapter.

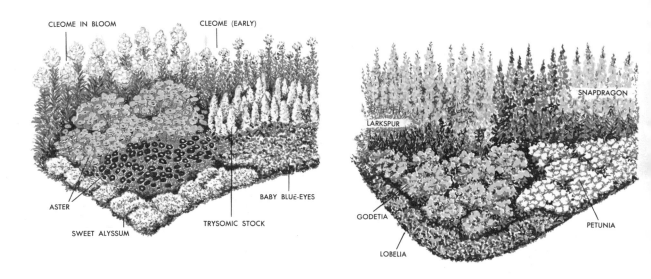

COOL SUMMER REGION

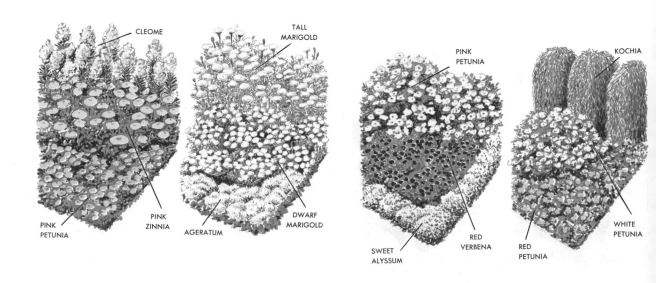

WARM SUMMER REGION

SUGGESTIONS FOR SELECTING VARIETIES

Give preference to varieties described as "improved" or "disease resistant," for though their seeds will cost a little more than the standard ones, you will have much better results. Plant breeders are continually striving for new or brighter colors, larger or better-shaped flowers, earlier bloom, disease immunity and drought , heat and rain-resistance.

For finest new varieties, you can depend upon the "All-America Selections." They are chosen after tests in trial grounds all over the country.

WHAT SEEDS TO SOW, WHEN

AND WHERE

Hardy types go outdoors early. These like cool weather and can stand some frost. Their seeds germinate best and plants grow best if you sow as early as you can work the soil— even if you must wear mittens to do it. In fact, these can be planted in late autumn in prepared ground to germinate at the first sign of spring. Or you can sow them during a thaw in winter, or on top of snow (if the soil has been made ready). They often self-sow.

Baby Blue-	Clarkia	Linaria
Eyes	Cornflower	Poppy
Calendula	Dianthus	Snapdragon
California-	Gilia	Stock
Poppy	Godetia	Sweet Alyssum
Candytuft	Larkspur	Sweet Pea

Easiest annuals are sown outside when ground is warm. These are ideal for beginners and a joy for everyone. Plant after soil and weather warm up in spring. They will come up and bloom in a relatively short time. If you are in a hurry, you can start them indoors a month before planting-out time.

Balsam	Four-o'clock	Nasturtium
Calliopsis	Gourd (vine)	Portulaca
Cleome	Marigold	Sunflower
Cosmos	Morning-Glory	Zinnia

Slow or tender annuals need a protected head-start. These are the ones most frequently sold as started plants. Seed must be sown 2 months before the time you want to set them in your garden. Try raising some this winter for fun and experience.

Ageratum	Nicotiana	Torenia
Browallia	Periwinkle	Verbena
Celosia	Petunia	Wax Begonia
Lobelia	Snapdragon	

Details on when to sow seed of each flower are given with the description of the plant in the alphabetical listing at the end of this chapter.

Some like cool weather. For winter (or spring) bloom in mild climates, start these cool-preferring kinds from seed or plants in autumn. In California start in late August in order to have blooms in January; or start in late fall for extra-early spring bloom. In the Deep South [Zones 9 and 10] start in October.

Baby Blue-	Forget-me-not	Petunia
Eyes	Godetia	Poppy
Calendula	Larkspur	Snapdragon
Candytuft	Linaria	Stock
Clarkia	Nemesia	Sweet Alyssum
Cornflower	Pansy	Sweet Pea
Dianthus		

Where summers are cool (at least at night), as in the northern states, mountain regions, cool coastal or lake areas, all flowers recommended above for winter bloom in mild climates will come out gorgeously during the summer. Start them in spring. Either buy plants after your frost-free date, or sow seed in the ground as early as it can be worked.

Additional annuals that appreciate cool

Alternate rows of purple and white sweet alyssum are planted in the paving cutouts of this California patio. A plant of New Zealand flax serves as accent. Creeping juniper is in the rear.

White petunias bloom all summer in the Hayward Gay garden in Cincinnati, Ohio. In spring, the area is filled with bulbs. The weathered wood "man" is an old root of a sycamore tree.

OPPOSITE:
It is simple to have quantities of glorious zinnias like these! They are among the easiest annuals to start from seed, and you sow them right in the garden where they are to bloom.

ATTRACTIVE WAYS
TO USE ANNUALS

summers and which can be planted after the frost-free date include:

Aster   Dahlia
Browallia   Lobelia

If your spring cool season is short, and summer warm, as in the corn and cotton belts, grow the cool-season plants as early as possible so they can bloom before temperatures sizzle. Otherwise, when hot days and nights come, they quickly burn out.

Some like warmth. If you have hot summer days and nights, these are for you! Most of them will continue to bloom in autumn.

Sow their seed outdoors (or set plants) after ground warms. You will not hurry things by starting sooner, for seeds will sulk, rot, and plants stand still. When conditions are right, they grow like mad.

In mild Zone 10 these annuals can be planted any time of year. By February you can plant in Zone 9. April is the month in Dallas and Ft. Worth. In Zone 5 wait until mid to late May.

A good rule of thumb for planting out-of-doors is the time when apple trees bloom.

Ageratum	Gaillardia	Salvia
Balsam	Marigold	Sunflower
Bells of	Morning-Glory	Sweet Alyssum
Ireland	Nicotiana	Torenia
Celosia	Petunia	Verbena
Cosmos	Phlox	Zinnia
Four-o'clock	Portulaca	

Some annuals make showier masses of color than others, and remain in bloom for a longer time. (See next page for border ideas.)

You will get better effects if you stick to one flower and one color for each row. Mixing colors gives a spotty effect; concentrating on one dramatizes your garden.

You can plant quantities of one flower (such as red petunias), or a row of low flow-

ers in front of a row of taller ones (lavender ageratum in front of yellow marigolds) or a 3-row combination from low to tall.

ANNUALS GOOD FOR PICKING

Annuals are wonderful for cutting. Whether you are planning on a special picking patch, or are going to pick flowers from your border, be sure to grow colors that will combine with the colors of the interior of your home and your decorating scheme. There is no sense growing pink flowers if your furnishings, dishes and tablecloth are in shades of yellow and orange, or vice versa.

When you know what you want, do not buy mixtures of colors, but packets containing the one color you are after. Then you will not waste space on useless things.

For Early or Cool Season

Babys-Breath (white, pink)
Calendula (yellow, orange)
Calliopsis (yellow, maroon)
Clarkia (pink, purple, white, red)
Cornflower (blue, pink, white)
Cynoglossum (blue)
Larkspur (blue, lavender, pink, white)
Nasturtium (yellow, red, pink)
Pansy (many colors)
Petunia (many colors)
Snapdragon (all colors but blue)
Stock (white, pink, lavender)
Sweet Pea (pastels, red, purple)

For Summer or Fall

Ageratum (lavender-blue)
Aster (white, rose, lavender)
Chrysanthemum (white, yellow)
Cosmos (white, pink, lavender, yellow)
Dahlia (all colors but blue)
Marigold (yellow, orange)
Petunia (many colors)
Salvia farinacea (blue)
Verbena (red, pink, lavender, white)
Zinnia (all colors but blue)

🍂 Help on Planning Borders of Annuals
CHOOSE HEIGHTS AND COLORS YOU NEED

	Ht.	Wh.	Red	Pink	Bl.	Lav.	Yel.	Or.
Tall								
Calliopsis	3′		X				X	
Cleome	3½′	X		X				
Corn, Striped	4′							
Cosmos	4′	X		X		X	X	X
Four-o'clock	3′	X	X	X		X	X	
Kochia	2½′							
Larkspur	3′	X		X	X	X		
Marigold	3′						X	X
Snapdragon	2½′	X	X	X		X	X	X
Sunflower	6′	X					X	
Medium								
Aster	2½′	X		X		X		
Babys-Breath	1½′	X		X				
Balsam	2′	X		X		X		
Browallia	2′	X			X			
Calendula	2′	X					X	X
Clarkia	2′	X	X	X		X		
Dahlia	1½′	X	X	X		X	X	X
Periwinkle	1½′	X		X				
Salvia	2′		X	X	X	X		
Stock	2′	X		X		X		
Low								
Ageratum	10″	X		X		X		
Candytuft	12″	X		X		X		
Linaria	15″		X	X		X		
Lobelia	5″	X	X		X		X	
Marigold	8″						X	X
Nasturtium	10″		X	X			X	X
Pansy	6″	X		X	X	X	X	X
Petunia	12″	X	X	X	X	X	X	X
Portulaca	6″	X	X	X			X	
Sweet Alyssum	5″	X		X		X		
Verbena	10″	X	X	X		X		
Zinnia	6″	X	X	X		X	X	X

Note: Heights given in chart above are average.
They will vary according to growing conditions.

🌿 Alphabetical List of the Most Popular Annuals, and Perennials Used As Annuals

AGERATUM or FLOSS FLOWER. One of the best blue-lavender flowers for low edging for summer gardens. Compact heads composed of many small, fluffy flowers on multi-branched plants 10 in. high. Because plants start from seed slowly, plan to buy plants or sow indoors 2 months before frost-free date. Seed germinates within 10 days. Transplant outdoors when weather has warmed. Give full sun in cool climates, and afternoon shade, if possible, in hot summers. An excellent dwarf variety is 'Blue Mink.'

ALYSSUM, see SWEET ALYSSUM

ASTER, CHINA or ANNUAL (Callistephus chinensis). A favorite for summer picking, as well as for growing in a border. It blooms best where nights are cool. Large 2- to 3-in. double or single flowers come in lavender, purple, pink and white on plants that grow 1 to 3 ft. tall, depending upon the variety. Wait until warm weather to place seeds or plants outdoors, but seeds can be started indoors 2 months before frost-free date. Seeds germinate in 8 days.

BABY BLUE-EYES (Nemophila). Dainty but profuse blue-and-white flowers and fine-cut foliage on semi-reclining plants 12 in. high. Begins to bloom in early spring on small plants, and continues over long period, especially in cool climates or part shade. Likes moist soil. Sow before frost-free date in spring, or in autumn, for seeds are hardy. Often self-sows.

BABYS-BREATH (Gypsophila elegans). Dainty little white or pink flowers on airy stems 1½ to 2 ft. high. Very quick from seed to bloom (6 weeks). Plant almost any time from early spring on. Stays in bloom only a short time so make several sowings. Can be planted late fall for early spring plants. Thin seedlings to 12-in. spacing. Good for picking. Likes lime.

BACHELORS-BUTTON, see CORNFLOWER

BALSAM (Impatiens balsamina), or GARDEN BALSAM. Has double flowers like little roses on bushy plants, a foot high in regular kinds or 8 in. in dwarf forms. Colors are pink, lavender, red, white. Easy to grow. Large seeds sprout in 5 days if planted in moist soil after ground is warm. Give full sun where summers are mild, or semishade in hot climates. Space tall kinds 12 in. apart, dwarfs 6 in.

BEGONIA, WAX (Begonia semperflorens). This is the profuse-flowering, low-growing, fibrous-rooted plant used for summer bedding in shady places or cool summer climates. They are tender perennials, 8 in. high with glossy, succulent foliage and stems; flowers in white, pink or red in single or double, and leaves either green or bronze. Put outdoors only after danger of frost is past. Seed is very tiny, and plants are slow to reach blooming size, so it is easiest to buy started plants. However, you can sow seed in a container in a warm place 2 months before frost-free date. It will germinate in 15 days. In the garden use in groups for mass effect, spacing plants only 6 in. apart. They like cool, humid temperatures and moist, rich soil.

BELLS OF IRELAND (Molucella laevis). An intriguing plant with what look like green bell-shaped blooms along its 2-ft. stems. (Actually the true flowers are tiny and white, in the center of the bells.) It is used in arrangements, both when fresh and when dried. Start from seeds sown outdoors after weather and soil are warm, or indoors in a warm place. Slow to germinate (25 days). Self-sows.

BROWALLIA. Small, petunia-type, lavender-blue flowers on sprawling branched plants that may be tall (2 ft.) or dwarf (9 in.). Good for summer blooms in sun or part shade. Sow seed indoors 8 weeks before frost-free date. It will germinate in 15 days. Space outdoors 6 in. apart.

CALENDULA (Calendula officinalis) or POT-MARIGOLD. Cool-season annual. 3- to 5-in. double or semidouble blooms in yellow, cream, glowing orange, carried singly on long stems on 1½- to 2-ft. high plants. Excellent for picking. For winter flowers in the South and mild

Western areas, start seeds or plants in late August. For cool-summer climates, start in early spring. Where summers are hot, start in summer for bloom during cool autumn. Seeds germinate in 7 to 10 days. Give 12-in. final spacing.

CALIFORNIA-POPPY *(Eschscholtzia californica)*. Cool-weather plant, easy to grow from seed sown in the actual place it will bloom in late fall or very early spring. Durable and stands drought and poor soil. Self-sows. Flowers are 2 to 3 in. across, in colors from cream and yellow through orange and red. Plants are 12 in. high, with silver-gray fine-cut foliage.

CALLIOPSIS *(Coreopsis tinctoria)*. Gay, extra-easy warm-weather annual. Glossy daisy-type flowers are in combinations of yellow, red and mahogany on wiry stems. There are tall kinds, 3 ft. high, and dwarfs, 1 ft. high, for edgings. Sow seeds where they are to bloom, in spring before or after frost-free date; they will be up in 8 days. Excellent for picking. Tall types bloom all summer if seeds are prevented. Dwarfs finish blooming quickly, but you can have them flowering over a long period by making several sowings at intervals of 2 or 3 weeks. Thin seedlings to stand 8 to 12 in. apart.

CANDYTUFT *(Iberis)*. Cool-weather, low-growing plants with blooms either in moundlike clusters (example: 'Magic Carpet,' 'Fairy') or hyacinth-like spikes (examples: 'Super Iceberg,' 'Empress'). The former come in charming pastel shades; the latter in glistening white. Both are good for picking. They grow quickly and easily from seed, so sow where they are to bloom. Sowing in autumn provides winter flowers in mild climates, or early spring bloom in cold-winter areas. Sowing in very early cool spring brings bloom in early summer.

CASTOR-BEAN *(Ricinus)*. Tropical-looking, large-leaved, tall (to 8 ft.) plant. Easy to grow from seed which should be planted in the ground after soil is warm. Will be up in 15 days. Excellent for quick screening. Perennial in frost-free climates.

WARNING: *These seeds are very poisonous. On the plant they are so attractively displayed that they are a temptation to children, so do not take any chances—remove developing flowerheads!*

CELOSIA OR COCKSCOMB. Warm-weather plants, handsome in borders or beds in the garden, and also can be cut and dried for winter arrangements. There are two basic types: the plume or feather, and the crested or cockscomb. Both come in tall or dwarf forms. Easy to grow from seed outdoors after ground is warm. Seeds are tiny and should be started in a row so you can supervise them. Germinate in 10 days. Later thin or transplant, spacing dwarfs 8 in. apart, tall plants 12 in. Or start indoors in containers 4 weeks before frost-free date. Outstanding varieties in plume type are 'Forest Fire,' tall, with red leaves as well as red flowers; and 'Dwarf Feather' in orange, gold or red, 10 in. high. In cockscomb type, red 'Toreador' is best known.

CLARKIA. Cultivated forms of a Western wild flower. Prefers cool weather, or at least cool nights. Blooms are 1 in. across—single or double in white, pink, red, purple, on slender stems 2 to 3 ft. high. Good for picking. Scatter seed outdoors on prepared soil either as early in the spring as you can work the ground, or in the fall.

CLEOME *(Cleome spinosa)* or SPIDER-FLOWER. Grows easily and well in all climates. Tall, airy-blossomed, warm-weather annual for back of the border. Comes in white, pink or lavender. Sow seeds ¼ in. deep outdoors after frost-free date, either in a row from which to transplant later or where they are to bloom. Space, finally, 2 ft. apart. Plants have single, trunklike stem; little foliage. They start to bloom when about 2 ft. high, and keep growing taller and blooming upward as lower blooms become seedpods. Reaches 4 ft. in height; keeps at it until frost. Self-sows.

COCKSCOMB, see CELOSIA

COLEUS. Foliage plant, whose gorgeously colored leaves are in combinations of gold, cream, green, salmon or wine-red. Flowers are inconspicuous. This is a tender perennial grown as an annual. You can select plants of the colors you like at your garden supply stores, or raise them from seed in warmth indoors. Seed germinates in 10 days. Plant outdoors after soil and weather are warm, spacing 12 in. apart. Sun or shade. Cuttings of leafy stems root easily in water. Good winter houseplant.

Aster, China or Annual

Baby Blue-Eyes

Balsam, Garden

Calendula

California-Poppy

Celosia

Clarkia

Cleome

Cornflower

Cosmos

Larkspur

Marigold

Nasturtium

Nemesia

Periwinkle, Madagascar

Petunia

Phlox, Annual

Pink, China

Poppy, Shirley

Portulaca

Snapdragon

Sweet Pea

Verbena

Viola

ANNUAL "PORTRAITS"

CORNFLOWER or BACHELORS-BUTTON (*Centaurea cyanus*). Famous as a blue lapel flower, but blossoms can also be white, pink or lavender. Plants are among the easiest to grow from seed outdoors. Plant any time in spring, before frost-free date or after. Or, in mild climates, plant in late summer or autumn for winter or very early spring flowers. Seeds are large, germinate in 10 days, and come into bloom about 8 weeks after sowing. Plants grow 2 ft. high. Good cut flower. Peters out in hot weather.

COSMOS (*Cosmos bipinnatus* and *sulphureus*). Daisylike flowers 4 to 6 in. across on tall, fernyfoliaged plants that bloom in summer and through fall. Some kinds grow only 2½ ft. high, others 6 ft. Flower colors are white, pink, lavender, yellow. Use at the back of borders. Sow seed in place any time during spring, or start plants indoors a month before frost-free date. Space plants 10 in. apart.

CYNOGLOSSUM or CHINESE FORGET-ME-NOT. Sprays of bright blue forget-me-not type flowers, on plants 15 in. to 2 ft. tall. Easy to grow from seed sown outdoors in early spring.

DAHLIA. All kinds *can* be started from seed and will bloom the first year. However, most tall, large-flowered, named kinds are started in spring from tubers (see Chapter 12).

Dwarf sorts used for bedding, such as 15-in. high Unwin Hybrids, are nearly always grown from seed. They are very easy. Start indoors in March to set outside after weather warms, or sow outdoors in the ground after soil is warm. They will come up in 5 days and reach blooming size in 4 months. They will do best where summers are cool. In warm-summer areas they will be disappointing until cool weather arrives toward autumn, then really go to town. 4-in. flowers may be single or double, in many colors. Excellent for cutting. Space 12 to 24 in. apart. They will produce tubers, which you can save for another year if you wish.

DIANTHUS, see PINK, CHINA

ESCHSCHOLTZIA, see CALIFORNIA-POPPY

FAREWELL-TO-SPRING, see GODETIA

FLOSS FLOWER, see AGERATUM

FLOWERING TOBACCO, see NICOTIANA

FORGET-ME-NOT (*Myosotis*). Dear little blue flowers on dwarf plants that love cool weather, moist soil and some shade. Annual or biennial kinds are grown the same way as pansies (which see), and used much the same way with spring bulbs as low edgings for winter and spring flowers. Pink and white varieties are available. Stems picked and placed in water usually develop roots.

FOUR-O'CLOCK (*Mirabilis jalapa*). A perennial in warm-winter areas; annual in cold climates; very easy to grow from seed. Bushy 2- to 4-ft. plants, covered with small fragrant flowers in gay colors, make quick temporary hedges for new homes. They like heat and are not fussy about soil; very easy to grow. Plant the large seeds outdoors in a sunny place, after the ground is warm. Sow sparsely in a row, and thin later, spacing 12 to 18 in. apart.

GAILLARDIA or BLANKET FLOWER. Comes in both perennial and annual kinds. Both have single and double varieties. Annual types are easy to grow from seed, planted outdoors after the ground is warm. Seed germinates in 7 to 10 days. Plants are 1½ ft. high and flower mostly in yellows and maroon.

GODETIA, SATIN FLOWER or FAREWELL-TO-SPRING. Cool-weather annual, 1 to 2½ ft. high with single or double flowers in white, pink, salmon. Excellent for picking. Sow seed where plants are to bloom, in prepared ground, either late fall or very early spring before frost-free date. Give full sun in cool climates, some shade in hot.

GYPSOPHILA, see BABYS-BREATH

KOCHIA (*Koh'kee-uh*) or SUMMER CYPRESS. Shrublike, green-foliaged annual 2½ to 3 ft. high, used as a quick temporary hedge or to look like shrubs. Leaves are narrow, dense, soft and billowy. This plant can be sheared like a real hedge. It grows in both warm and cool climates. Sow seeds where plants are to grow, early in spring. To permit plants to grow symmetrically, thin to 1½ ft. apart. Leaves turn bronzy-red in fall, which is why kochia is sometimes called burning bush.

LARKSPUR (*Delphinium ajacis*). 3- to 4-ft.-high spires of pink, white, blue, lavender florets above ferny foliage. Cool-season annual. For winter bloom in mild climates, sow seeds in prepared ground in late summer. Where winters are severe, sow in autumn, or very early spring—as soon as you can work soil. It often self-sows. Thin out seedlings ot 12 in. apart. Excellent as a cut flower.

LINARIA or TOADFLAX (*Linaria maroccana*). Looks like a miniature snapdragon. It is a cool-weather plant that flowers quickly from seed sown where it is to bloom, then is finished except where summers remain cool. Sow in fall or very early spring. Plants are 10 to 15 in. high, covered with flowers in pastel colors. Thin to stand 12 in. apart. 'Fairy Bouquet' (an All-America) is an excellent strain.

LOBELIA (*Lobelia erinus*). One of the most popular blue-flowering low annuals. Wonderful for edgings, containers, hanging baskets. Individual blooms are tiny but prolific. Likes cool summer weather, or part shade where summers are warm. Slow growth from seed, so buy plants after frost-free date or start seeds indoors in containers 2 months before that time. Space plants 8 in. apart. Varieties come in bright blue, dark blue, rose and white. Some are trailing types.

MARIGOLD (*Tagetes*). Are easily grown from seed; come up and grow so quickly (7 days) that they are usually started from seed planted in the ground outdoors. Wait until after frost-free date.

There are dozens of varieties, ranging from dwarf to tall, and small-flowered to large. They are mainly improvements or hybrids of the tall, large-flowered African marigold (*Tagetes erecta*), and the shorter, small-flowered French marigold (*Tagetes patula*). Some have strongly scented foliage, but new hybrid varieties are almost odorless. They are excellent for cutting.

Here are examples of some of the best: Dwarf, about 8 in. high, with small flowers—'Butterball', the 'Pigmies' and the 'Petites'; medium height, 12 to 15 in. high, with large yellow flowers—early-blooming 'Spungold' and later-blooming 'Cupid'; medium-height with small flowers—'Naughty Marietta', a yellow single snappily marked with maroon, and 'Red and Gold Hybrids'; tall, 2½ to 3 ft., and relatively late-blooming—'Crackerjack' and 'Climax' in yellow or orange, with magnificently large double flowers.

NASTURTIUM (*Tropaeolum majus*). Very easy to raise from large seeds planted ¾ in. deep in a sunny place, after the ground is warm. (They do not like to be transplanted.) They will be up within 10 days and bloom within 8 weeks. There are two main types—dwarf and climbing. The former, such as 'Gem' and 'Gleam,' grow about 10 in. high. Climbers may stretch up to 6 ft. Leaves are bright green and kidney-shaped. Flowers are fragrant and good for picking, in brilliant colors of yellow, scarlet, orange, rose. They bloom best in poor soil. Space seeds 6 in. apart.

NEMESIA (Nem-meesh'-ee-uh) (*Nemesia strumosa*). Low-growing (8-in.) plant covered with brilliant small flowers in many colors. Excels in cool weather. For winter bloom in mild climates plant seed outdoors in late summer. For early-summer bloom in other climates, start indoors a month before frost-free date, or sow outdoors when no more frosts are expected. Plant in full sun in cool climates; give part shade if heat is a problem.

NICOTIANA or FLOWERING TOBACCO (*Nicotiana alata*). 1½- to 3-ft. stalks carry slender, trumpet-shaped blossoms that are sweetly scented in the evening. White, also lavender, red and maroon. Stands heat. Where summers are long, sow tiny seeds where plants are to stand, scattering on top of prepared soil in spring after ground is warm. Where summers are cool or short, start indoors 2 months before frost-free date. Seeds germinate in 10 days. Flowers of older varieties open daily in the evening. Buy newer kinds that stay open all day, such as 'Daylight' and 'Sensation Hybrids.' Space plants 10 in. apart.

PANSY and VIOLA. Similar-looking except that viola blossoms tend to be smaller and without "faces." Both are short-lived perennials grown as cool-season annuals. The plants grow 6 in. high. To get bloom quickly, buy started plants. The best buys are compact young plants, just starting to branch. Plant in sun or semishade in rich, well-prepared soil. The more sun the more bloom until hot weather. Keep blooms (or developing seed) picked. Feed plentifully—every 3 weeks. Never let plants lack for water.

These are easy to grow from seed. The main problem is to start at the right time. Since they are cool-season plants desired for early spring flowers, they must be started the preceding August or September. This is true whether you live in mild climates or very cold ones. Sow either in a specially prepared small plot outdoors (preferably enclosed with protecting boards), or in a box or other container.

When seedlings have their second pair of true leaves, transplant to 6 in. apart. Tend carefully, and by mid-November you will have buds! Plants will bloom all winter in mild climates, if consistently picked. In cold climates they will remain evergreen but dormant through winter. In Zone 5 and north, mulch with straw or protect in improvised cold frame. The minute spring arrives they will begin to bloom.

You can also start them indoors in winter, to be transplanted to the garden in spring. Sowing seed outdoors in spring does not work well (except where summers are cool), for plants begin to bloom at exactly the hot season.

PERIWINKLE, MADAGASCAR (*Vinca rosea*). A heat-loving, tender perennial ordinarily grown as an annual. It is a favorite summer bedding plant in the South and other hot climates. Plants have handsome glossy leaves. They may be upright, bushy, and 1½ ft. high, or dwarfs that trail. Flowers are showy, 1½ in. wide, in snow-white, rose, pink, or white with red eye. They are slow to reach bloom size from seed so buy plants or start seed in warm place 2 months before frost-

free date. Space plants outdoors 12 in. apart. They stand wet or dry weather.

PETUNIA. Tender perennial used as an annual. It does well in all climates. You had better buy plants, unless you have had practice growing dust-fine seed, for seeds must be started in boxes or other special seedbed 2 months before transplanting to the garden. There are two main types of petunias. Each comes in double and single flowers, almost any color, and both hybrid and nonhybrid varieties.

Multifloras have compact plants covered with lavish numbers of fairly small blossoms 2½ to 3 in. across. They are marvelous for masses of color and have a fast comeback after a rain or bad weather. Examples of singles are 'Comanche' and 'Sugar Plum'; doubles are 'Cherry Tart' and 'Cardinal Riches.'

Grandifloras have big plants with greater spread, and large flowers 3 to 4 in. across, sometimes ruffled. Because individual blooms are so gorgeous, these plants are used not only for bedding but for close-up display in containers, hanging baskets, etc. Examples of singles are 'White Magic,' 'Calypso' and 'Maytime.' Doubles include 'Allegro' and 'Burpee Orchid.'

Planting time for winter bloom in mild climates is autumn. Elsewhere, set outside when apple trees and lilacs bloom. Space multifloras 18 in. apart; grandifloras 24 in. Use a complete plant food when you set them out, 3 weeks later, and as bloom starts.

PHLOX, ANNUAL (*Phlox drummondi*). 12-in. tall plants, with flat clusters of inch-wide blooms in vivid or pastel colors. It likes sun and blooms a long time if you keep old flowers removed. Good cut flower. Sow seed in the ground outdoors after frost-free date, or start earlier indoors.

PINK, CHINA (*Dianthus chinensis*). Annual pinks are easy and quick to grow from seed. They are very hardy, so seeds can be sown outdoors in the ground before frost-free date in spring, or in the fall—especially for winter bloom in mild climates. Plants stand about 10 to 12 in. high. The blooms are single or double, sometimes fringed, one or several to a stem in pink, red, white, or with combination markings. They are not fragrant. Space about 10 in. apart. If plants are cut back to 2 in. from the ground immediately after first flowering, they will re-bloom. If not allowed to ripen to seed, they will usually live over winter like perennials.

POPPY, SHIRLEY (*Papaver rhoeas*). Lovely, silken blooms in white, pink, scarlet, top slender stems 2 to 3 ft. high in early spring in mild-winter climates, early summer elsewhere. Likes cool weather. Seeds (very tiny) should be scat-tered where they are to bloom, on prepared ground, either in late fall, during the winter, or before frost-free date in spring. Difficult to transplant except when plants are less than an inch wide. Thin or space 8 in. apart.

PORTULACA or ROSE-MOSS. Trailing, ground-hugging, succulent-leaved plant that thrives in sunny, hot, dry places, and also where summers are cool. Its bright little poppylike flowers almost hide the foliage. The plants are yellow, white, scarlet, orange and rose in single or double forms. Where summers are hot and long, sow seed in the wanted location outdoors when ground is warm. In cool climates or where sum-mers are short, start indoors 8 weeks before frost-free date. Seeds come up within 10 days. Thin or space plants 4 in. apart.

SALVIA. Red-flowered kind called scarlet sage is almost blazingly vivid! It is seen most often as late summer and autumn flower because the plant develops slowly. Handsome when used with white flowers, such as spider-flower 'Helen Campbell,' or white petunias. Buy plants, or start indoors 2 months before frost-free date. Space 18 in. apart outdoors after ground warms. Tall kinds grow to 3-ft. height, and dwarfs, 1 ft. Pink and purple varieties are available.

Blue (*Salvia farinacea,* called mealycup sage) is perennial in mild climates but from Zone 6 north is usually treated as an annual. Two- to 3-ft. slender spires of blue or white extend above gray-green foliage in late summer and autumn. The flowers are excellent to dry for winter.

SATIN FLOWER, see GODETIA

SCARLET SAGE, see SALVIA

SNAPDRAGON (*Antirrhinum majus*). Tall spires carrying blossoms with "snapping jaws." Squeeze the blossom's throat between your fingers, and the jaws will pop open! A cool-loving, tender perennial, usually grown as an annual. Tall varieties grow 2 to 3 ft. high. Dwarf kinds are 6 to 12 in. You can have almost any color you wish but blue. Some have double blossoms.

Seed is easy to start, though it is so tiny it should be barely covered with soil. Plants take a long time to reach flowering size. For winter bloom in mild-winter climates, start in boxes or the garden about September 1. For early summer bloom in cold-winter climates, sow indoors 2 months before your frost-free date.

Grow where they have sun at least half the day. Space tall kinds 1½ ft. apart; dwarfs 8 in. When central spike finishes blooming, cut it back to the first pair of side branches. When entire first flush of bloom is over, prune plant to within 8 in. of ground, give a feeding, and new bud-carrying branches will start. Choose varieties labeled rust resistant.

STOCK (*Matthiola*). Has spires of fragrant, close-set blooms in pastel colors, loves cool weather, and is a favorite for spring cut flowers. There are tall kinds that grow 3 ft. high, and dwarfs only 12 to 15 in. tall. In mild-winter areas, sow seed outdoors in autumn for winter or early spring flowers. In warm-summer areas use only quick-maturing types, preferably 'Trysomic Seven Week's stock. Sow outdoors as early as you can work soil, and force early bloom by not thinning or feeding the plants.

SUMMER-CYPRESS, see KOCHIA

SUNFLOWER (*Helianthus*). Big blooms! Big plants! Likes heat and sunshine. Most familiar is the giant kind that grows 7 to 10 ft. tall, with an enormous daisylike yellow flower at its top. It produces the seed you feed to wild birds in winter and is very easy to grow.

Set outdoors after ground is warm, ½ in. deep, and 4 to 5 in. apart. Then get out of the way! Plants will be up in 5 days. Later thin, spac-ing 1 ft. apart. Watering and feeding plants every other week will make taller plants and bigger flowers.

Other sunflower types easy and fun to grow are ball-shaped 'Double Sungold,' 'Red and Gold,' whose flowers have alternating rings of maroon and red, and 'Italian White' with blooms like giant white daisies. The last two grow about 5 ft. high and are nice for picking.

SWEET ALYSSUM (*Lobularia maritima*). Prettiest, easiest, quickest low flower for edgings. It is so frost-hardy that you can sow in the spring as early as you can work the soil. The plant comes up in 5 days and blooms in 6 weeks. It blooms in winter in mild climates if seed is sowed in autumn. When plants begin to look tired, shear off the front half, and they will quickly send out new growth and bloom. Good to plant over beds of bulbs. Sow where it is to grow, and thin to space 2 in. apart. Or if you buy plants, space them 5 in. apart. Old-fashioned kinds grow 8 in. tall, but newer, improved varieties are more dwarf. Good ones are white 'Carpet of Snow,' purple 'Royal Carpet' and pink 'Rosie O'Day.'

SWEET PEA (*Lathyrus odoratus*). Fragrant, pea-shaped blooms in delicate colors on slender 6-ft. vines or on dwarf "bushes." Superb for cutting. It loves cool weather. Most varieties cannot tolerate heat, so if you live where springs are short and summer comes suddenly and thoroughly, choose sweet pea varieties called heat-resistant. (Examples: 'Cuthbertson's Floribundas' and 'Giant Heat-Resistant.') They will flower winters and early spring in mild climates if seed of "early-flowering" kinds is sown outdoors in August. For early spring bloom in Zones 7 to 10, plant in late autumn. In Zones 3 to 6 plant as early in spring as you can.

Select a sunny place and loosen the soil thoroughly 18 in. deep to provide a good root-run; work in humus and complete fertilizer at rate recommended on the package. Sow seeds 1 in. deep and 1 in. apart. Some people in dry climates place them in a shallow trench 1 in. deep that will catch water. Soak thoroughly after planting. When seedlings come up, thin and space 6 in. apart. Provide strings or fence for them to climb up. Do not let them lack moisture, and water deeply when you do. Applying a mulch keeps the soil desirably cooler. Pick flowers often so seed will not form.

TOADFLAX, see LINARIA

TORENIA (*Torenia*) or WISHBONE FLOWER. Delightful little bushy plant, a foot high, bearing purple blooms with yellow throats that from a distance remind one of pansy faces. It loves warmth, wants shade—except in cool-summer regions—and does well everywhere.

VERBENA, GARDEN HYBRIDS. Though perennial in mild climates, these are usually grown as annuals. Heat-loving, they form low, spreading, multibranched plants. Showy, flat flowerheads 2 to 3 in. across are so profusely borne that they hide the foliage. Their colors are white, pink, salmon, lavender or scarlet. They do nicely for front of borders, or to cover space where spring bulbs were.

It is wise to buy started plants, since verbenas are slow to grow from seed. Set in the ground, in full sun, after frost-free date. Space dwarf, erect kinds 8 in. apart; others 12 in.

To grow from seed, sow in the ground after soil is warm, or inside in containers 2 months before planting-out date.

VINCA, see PERIWINKLE, MADAGASCAR

WISHBONE FLOWER, see TORENIA

ZINNIA. So easy and quick to grow from seed there is no need to start it early indoors. It is warmth-loving, and tender to frost, so do not plant outdoors until soil and weather are warm. Then seeds come up in 3 days, bloom within 8 weeks, and flower continuously until frost in scarlet, orange, yellow, pink, or white. Giants grow 3 to 3½ ft. tall with double flowers 4 to 5 in. across. Some may have smoothly overlapping petals; others come in the dramatic cactus variety. Medium-height types grow 12 in. to 24 in. high with medium-sized flowers. They are listed as 'Cupid,' 'Lilliput,' and 'Cut-and-Come-Again' types. Dwarfs are only 6 in. high ('Thumbelina').

Plant all zinnia seeds 2 in. apart in a seed-bed row. Thin the plants so giants are 18 in. apart, medium types a foot apart, and dwarfs 6 in. Later transplant to their permanent place in the border.

11

Perennials and Biennials

Perennials are permanent—almost. They are plants that stay put year after year in your garden, survive tolerable neglect, and bloom reliably when you expect them to. Some may live longer than you! In cold climates most of them die to the ground each winter, after storing food in their roots, and start growth anew the following spring. In mild climates many are evergreen and their foliage looks attractive all year.

Some, including peony and tall bearded iris, thrive only where they get a good chilling and dormant period in winter. These grow superbly in northern states. Others, tender to frost, are the stand-bys of mild-winter climates. They include geranium (*Pelargonium*) and gerbera. Plants that behave as perennials in one region are often treated as annuals in another. Only a few unusually adaptable ones grow well in both cold and mild areas. Information on which perennials will grow where you live is included in the alphabetized descriptions of plants at the end of this chapter, in the sequence-of-bloom chart for your region in Chapter 25, and also in the general index. Bulbs are a special type of perennial and are discussed in a chapter of their own.

Use perennials as the backbone for the design of your garden. They will multiply and become increasingly handsome. They can serve as cornerstones around which you can develop an everblooming border, a series of bays among shrubs, a beauty spot adjoining your patio, a cutting garden, or just pleasant splashes of color anywhere.

These plants will bloom best in a sunny location. However, if you live where summers are extremely hot, they will prefer light shade in the middle of the day. A few adapt to conditions in a shady garden; these are discussed in the chapter Beauty in Shade. As to soil, the better it is, and the more care you take in preparing it, the more appreciation your plants will show. The old adage that a 10¢ plant in a dollar hole will do better than a dollar plant in a 10¢ hole, is true. And if you can prepare the equivalent of a "ten-dollar bed," with lots of humus and the proper amount of fertilizer worked into it, you will not regret the investment.

How To Get Starts

The quickest way to get blooming-size perennial plants is to buy them already started. Some are available at your local garden-supply sources in cans, flats, pots, or freshly dug from the ground. Others can be obtained from reliable mail-order nursery firms. These firms often ship the material dormant, enclosed in polyethylene bags, though some types of plants are mailed in pots.

Small young plants transplant most easily, cost least, and grow most vigorously. Unless you are in a terrific hurry for an immediate effect, they are the best buy. A few perennials mature almost as speedily as annuals, and bloom generously their first year—chrysanthemum and gloriosa daisy, for instance. Most of them develop more slowly, however, and seldom make much of a show before their second season.

Growing your plants from seed is the inexpensive way to achieve quantity in choice varieties that may not be found locally. It is the harder way but you will have more satisfaction. Details on how to do it appear in the chapter on starting plants, under the heading "Perennial Flowers from Seeds."

BUY PLANTS OR GROW FROM SEEDS

BY MAIL . . .

. . . . LOCAL NURSERIES

. . . FROM SEED

If your garden now includes perennials, they may produce volunteer seedlings. These volunteers appear in the garden where seeds have fallen on hospitable ground. They can be lifted with an adequate ball of earth around the roots and transplanted to a cold-frame or some other protected place in the garden. In the spring they can be transplanted to a permanent home of your selection. An exception to the list of perennials that may be propagated from seedlings is phlox, because the flowers of volunteers revert to an unattractive magenta color.

Planting and Transplanting Know-How

The best time to plant or transplant varies with different perennials. In general, do it in cold climates during early spring, or do it in the fall early enough so that roots have time to become established before the ground freezes. In mild climates, do it while plants are relatively dormant in late autumn, winter or early spring.

Be kind to plants while you are preparing to put them in your garden. Do not let roots dry. If the plants have arrived through the mail, examine their packing. Dormant plants, bare-root (without soil) enclosed in polyethylene bags, may look forlorn to you. But have faith that they are all right. This method of packing is an excellent one developed through modern research.

The plants are in good condition unless the bags are torn, which would let in air, or if they have become overheated, which could cause rot. Keep them in a cool place out of the sun. Potted plants that arrive by mail may need to have their soil watered. Leaves should be accustomed to light and sunshine gradually, for they have been in the dark for many days while traveling and might be injured if put instantly in outdoor sun and wind. Locally purchased potted plants that have been sitting in an outdoor sales yard are already conditioned to outdoor weather.

If plants are in clumps rather than single divisions, and if they are a type that can be separated easily, it is wise to pull them apart into several or many units before setting out. Each piece with a root and growth bud on top will become a complete new plant. Not only will you get several plants instead of one for your money, but the operation will be good for the plant. Dividing clumps keeps them from becoming crowded. Each segment has more room to develop and thus grows more vigorously. You can arrange the pieces in the garden in a group, giving the effect of an enlarged clump. Most perennials that grow in clumps do best when divided every few years.

When setting out plants, try to place them at the same depth—in relation to soil level—that they were before. Firm the soil around the roots but do not compact it. Water thoroughly. Then, if the plants are in leaf, shade them for a few days while they are getting adjusted.

PLANT SAME DEPTH—WATER WELL AND SHADE

Through-the-Year Care

In cold-winter climates it is wise to mulch newly set perennials the first winter, after the ground has frozen. The idea is to shade the soil and keep it from alternately freezing and thawing, which may heave the plants out of the ground. Wait to mulch until the ground freezes. Otherwise rodents may move into the snug quarters and eat the roots of your plants during the winter. A light mulch every winter is beneficial, though established plants are quite durable.

In the spring, clean off the mulch and old dead tops of plants. Pull weeds and cultivate close to the plants, but do not do general cultivating if there is a chance that desirable self-sown seedlings may be about to come up. Feed with a liquid plant food or by scattering dry fertilizer in a circle around the plant.

Watch for signs of insects. If you see some, get after them quickly before they multiply, so you won't be overrun.

Water thoroughly and deeply. The best time is morning, so that the plants will have time to dry off by night.

After each plant flowers, cut off the dead

blossoms before they develop seeds. If you wish some seeds to save and plant, cut off all of the stalks or seed heads except one or two.

BIENNIALS OPERATE ON A 2-YEAR PLAN

These plants look like perennials, and live through winters, but they have a shorter life span. Their first year from seed they produce foliage only. The next year they bloom gloriously, then usually die.

Some, like foxglove, self-sow abundantly if they are happy in your garden, and you always have some coming along. Others must be started anew from seed each year in early summer, or be purchased as started plants the year that you wish them to bloom.

But they are well worth the little extra effort. Most come into flower early in summer at a time when few perennials are in bloom, so they are showy when you need them most.

Favorites you should try are canterbury bell, hollyhock, foxglove and sweet william.

Biennials appear among perennials in the alphabetical list in the latter part of this chapter.

🍂 How To Plan for Continuous Bloom

This is an exciting goal, well worth whatever it takes to achieve! You will need to do much pleasant scheming, and manage cleverly, but you can do it. There are several ways to tackle the project. The most sensible is to consider your entire property as one big garden. Then try to have something in bloom, or interesting to look at, during every season of the year.

Isolated spots of beauty can take turns being the center of interest, for the entire yard does not need to be showing off at once. Perennials are just one of the many elements in the procession of blooms.

For instance, in very early spring you can have a doorstep corner devoted to early bulbs, such as crocus and daffodils. As they fade, a flowering tree can burst into bloom in the front entrance planting. Later, shrubs may take their turn.

Perennials can do a spring and summer stint along with some colorful annuals, and there are some gorgeous vines worth featuring. For fall there are shrubs and trees with brilliantly colored foliage. In winter, count on evergreens in important locations, and shrubs or trees with bright berries.

This system narrows down maintenance problems, for when one area of your yard has ceased being in the spotlight, it easily becomes part of the quiet background. It will look tidy without calling attention to itself. If it is not in full bloom, some other portion of the yard will be drawing admiration.

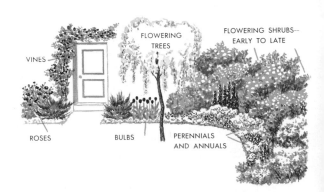

An ever-blooming border, like your grandmother's and the famous English gardens, is something else again. Traditionally this long strip measures about 6 ft. wide, with tall perennials planted at its back, low ones at its front, and medium-sized ones grouped between. Something is in bloom there throughout the growing season. The border is lovely to look at, and wonderfully handy for picking flowers. To be successful it needs careful planning because many perennials have relatively short periods of bloom. Some will be in flower for about 2 weeks, others for 3 weeks. So you must think ahead and plan a rotation of bloom.

It is smart to plan your border on paper before starting to plant. At least you should have a general idea of what you intend to do. Be sure to allow ample space. The area for the bed should be wide enough to accommodate several rows of plants, yet narrow enough for you to reach in from the paths to do cultivating and tending without stepping onto the soil. A width of 3 ft. is minimum, and will hold only 2 to 3 rows of mature plants, plus a row of edging plants. Five or 6 ft. is much better.

Plants can be arranged informally in interlocking groups or drifts, or they can be in rows. Those in rows are easiest to tend and keep track of, and if different plants are combined in them, the rows are not noticeable from a distance.

Begin to plan by deciding upon your key plants. These will provide your major bloom for each season and form the backbone of your planting, being showy, dependable and permanent. They should be spotted at regular intervals through the border, in much the same way that a design in a fabric or wallpaper repeats itself. Examples of key plants might be the following (listed in order of their season of bloom): moss-pink, iris, peony, day-lily, summer phlox and chrysanthemum.

Secondary or "filler flowers" are the next consideration. They are to bloom at the same time as the main ones, complement them and harmonize with their colors. They should be easy to grow—the sort that more or less take care of themselves and are almost as prolific

as weeds. They should give the border a feeling of bountiful bloom. Examples are wild sweet william, daisies, dames-rocket, coreopsis, double buttercup, sundrops, and perennial aster. The list varies depending upon your personal taste and where you live. Sometimes annuals will do the job for you, such as larkspur, poppy, baby blue-eyes, cleome.

Edging can be made from various kinds of low perennials, or perhaps a low annual such as sweet alyssum or dwarf marigold. With perennials, the main consideration is good foliage, for since the plant is permanent, it must look well when not in bloom. If the border is large, the edging can be a dwarf hedge made from a small evergreen shrub, or a trimmed evergreen vine.

Color combinations are important! Plan them as carefully as you plan the color schemes for the inside of your house. The same rules of color harmony will apply. If you are fond of pastel colors, stick to pink, blue, yellow and white. If you like warmer colors, feature red, orange, and yellow, with blue for contrast.

Annuals, or tender perennials tucked into the border, will help provide bloom in midsummer. Put them in wherever there might be a bare spot. While your border is young, it will need a great many annuals.

Do not worry if everything does not work out perfectly the first season, or the next, or the next. Part of the fun of gardening is changing things around. Most of the best gardens got that way because parts of them were forever on the move, in baskets or wheelbarrows.

HELP IN SELECTING PLANTS

To learn the sequence of bloom of important trees, shrubs and flowers in your region, see the chart of times-of-bloom in the section devoted to your region in the back of this book. Let it serve as your planting guide for seasonal interest.

As a quick survey of major perennials and biennials, study the following lists. Then, for more complete information on plants which interest you most, turn to the alphabetically arranged descriptions in this chapter.

🍂 Important Perennials and Biennials Grouped According to Height

B=Blue   O=Orange   R=Red   Y=Yellow
L=Lavender   P=Pink   W=White

Tall Plants for Back of the Border

Name	Height	Colors
Achillea 'Gold Plate'	4'	Y
Anchusa 'Dropmore'	3-5'	B
Artemisia 'Silver King'	3½'	W
Aster	2½-5'	W,P,L
Day-Lily	1½-6'	Y,O,R,P
Delphinium	3-7'	B,W,P,L
Foxglove	3-4'	L,W,P,Y
Globe Thistle	4-7'	B
Golden-Glow	5-7'	Y
Helenium	1½-5'	Y,O,R
Hibiscus	3-6'	P,W,R
Hollyhock	5-8'	W,P,R,Y
Iris, Louisiana	3-5'	W,B,L,R
Iris, Siberian	3-4'	W,L,B
Iris, Spuria	2-6'	W,Y,B
Iris, Tall Bearded	3-4'	W,P,B,L,Y
Jacobinia	4-8'	P,R,O
Lily (Bulb)	1½-6'	Y,P,W,R
Lupine	3-4'	B,W,L,P
Lythrum	3-4'	P
Phlox, Summer	3-5'	P,W,L,R
Poker-Plant	3-5'	R,W,Y
Sunflower	3-6'	Y

Medium Height Plants

Astilbe	½-2'	P,W,R
Babys-Breath	1½-3'	W,P
Balloon-Flower	2-3'	B,W,P
Bellflowers	½-3'	B,W,P,L
Bleeding-Heart	1-3'	P
Buttercup	2-3'	Y
Butterfly-Weed	2-3'	Y,O
Chrysanthemum	1-3'	Y,R,O,P,L
Coleus	2-3'	Y,R,O
Columbine	1-3'	Y,R,B,W
Coral Bells	1½-2½'	P,R,W
Coreopsis	1½-3'	Y
Daisies	½-3'	W,P
Dames-Rocket	3'	W,L
Day-Lily	1½-6'	Y,O,R,P
Feverfew	1-3'	W
Gas-Plant	1-3'	W,P
Geranium	1½-3'	R,W,P,O,L
Gerbera	1½'	W,O,P,Y
Impatiens	½-4'	R,P,W
Iris	3-5'	W,P,Y,R,L
Marguerites	1-3'	Y,B,W
Mist-Flower	1-2'	B
Monarda	2½-3'	R,P,L,W
Pentas	2-3'	B,P,W
Peony	2½-3'	P,W,R
Phlox, Summer	1-4'	P,W,L,R
Poppies	1½-4	R,O,P,L,W
Rudbeckia	2½-4	Y,O
Salvias	2-3'	B,L,W
Sedum, Showy	2'	P
Sundrop	1-2'	Y
Veronica	1-2½'	B,W,P

Plants for Front of the Border or Edgings

Alyssum Basket-of-Gold	6-12"	Y
Artemisia 'Silver Mound'	12"	
Begonia, Wax	6-8"	R,P,W
Bellflower, Carpathian	6-12"	B
Bellflower, Serbian	6-8"	B
Candytuft	8-12"	W
Daisy, English	6-8"	P,W
Forget-me-not	5-14"	B
Gazania	6-12"	O,Y
Iris, Dwarf Bearded	6-8"	Y,B,L,W
Lungwort	12"	B,P
Moss-Pink	6"	P,R,L,W
Nepeta	12-18"	L
Pink (Dianthus)	6-12"	P,R,W
Plumbago, Dwarf	9-12"	B

Primrose	4-16″	R,Y,P,B,L	Stokes Aster	12-18″	B,W
Rock-Cress	6-8″	W	Violets	6″	B,W
Santolina	12-24″	Y	Wild Sweet William	8-12″	L,W
Sedum	6-8″	Y,P,W	Woolly Yarrow	10″	Y
Snow-in-Summer	6-8″	W			

PRACTICAL PLANS FOR THREE PERENNIAL BORDERS

These are 10-ft. sections which repeat.

Yellow and Orange Emphasis in Gretchen Harshbarger's Border

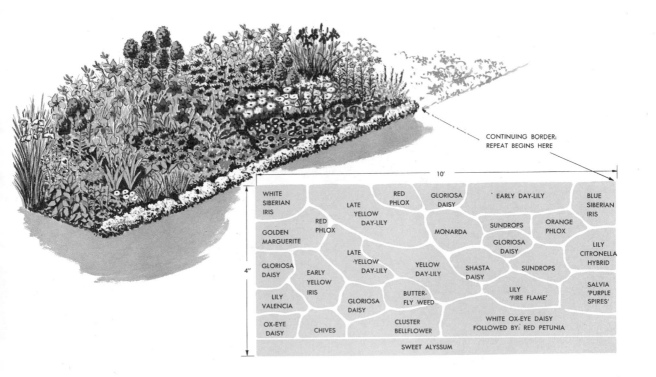

Warm, bright colors dominate the Harshbarger perennial border in Iowa. They are combined with, and accented by, blue, lavender and white flowers. None of these begins to bloom until iris time, for our earlier things, such as bulbs, are concentrated in another part of the yard. Iris season features tall bearded iris in early and late yellow varieties, underplanted with double yellow buttercups, and with a foreground of low-growing lavender-flowered chives and cluster bellflowers.

The chives are the same ones you use for seasoning, and are marvelous permanent garden plants, making handsome masses of round blooms and tidy clumps of foliage all season. They are grown from little bulbs (onions), and leaves should be trimmed back severely after blooming season.

Tall in the background at this time are large clumps of white Siberian iris. And mixed through the whole border are white ox-eye daisies which are pulled out after flowering. Day-lilies are the backbone of the border, and early mid-season varieties begin to bloom soon after irises quit. Others continue in sequence until autumn.

Planted among the day-lilies for the early part of summer are gloriosa daisies with tricolor blossoms in yellow, maroon and brown; golden marguerites, white Shasta daisies, vivid red mid-century lilies, and an underplanting of golden sundrops. Later in the season day-lilies are accented by orange and red phlox, red monarda, and a foreground of red petunias which have been set into gaps left by ox-eye daisies.

For autumn, tall red and yellow annuals (zinnias and marigolds) fill in among the resting perennials, and a new crop of gloriosa daisies (spring seedlings) come into full flower. Throughout the season, the edging of white sweet alyssum continues to bloom; to keep it looking good, either the front or rear half is sheared back occasionally.

A Pink, Lavender, Blue and White Border for Cold Climates

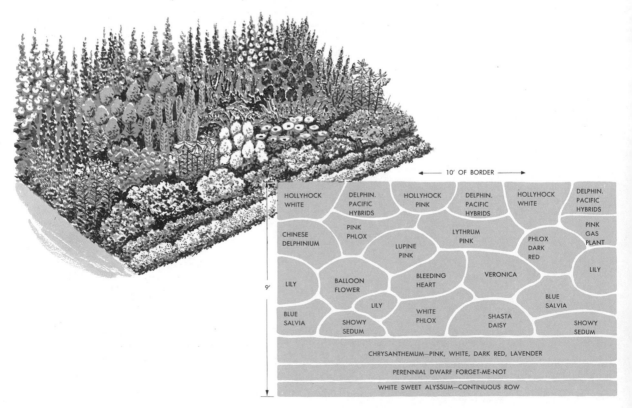

This border grows at the Frank Seiberling home in Iowa. It was planned by Nancy Seiberling, who explains the sequence of bloom this way: "My preference for pink, lavender, blue and white colors appears first in spring with the blooming of tulips. They are grouped in colonies of six of one color, and casually located over the entire border. Old-fashioned pink bleeding-heart and pink-and-white gasplants continue the display until lupines in blue, pink and white add to it.

"Later the spires of blue veronica, pink lythrum, and taller blue delphiniums and pink and white hollyhocks are accented by the simple whiteness of Shasta daisy. White trumpet lilies add elegance in midsummer and command attention as balloon-flower in shell-pink, blue and white, and phlox in pink,

red and white prepare to bloom. During the long phlox season the enchanting blues of *Salvia farinacea* and the darker salvia 'Purple Spires' provide accents.

"For autumn, there are pink-flowered showy sedums, and mounded masses of mixed chrysanthemums in the long foreground row. A few tall annuals are used in the border to give a sense of fullness of bloom. They include zinnias selected for compatible coloring, the very palest yellow marigolds, and the new All-America award-winning pink salvia 'Evening Glow.' Edging the front of the border is a row of perennial forget-me-nots, and a row of annual white sweet alyssum. The forget-me-nots, during summer, are gradually covered and hidden by the expanding chrysanthemum plants."

Border Planned for Regions with Mild Winters, Hot Summers

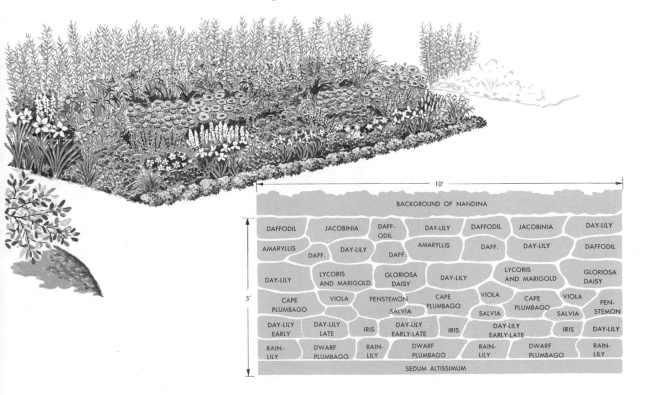

This yellow and blue border was designed by Margaret Kane of San Antonio, Texas, and is suited to sun or part shade. Plants are purposely crowded, so they will shade the soil and keep it cooler. The plan is basically rows of day-lilies interspersed with perennials and bulbs that will lengthen the bloom-season and lend diversity and color contrast.

Daffodils begin the flowering parade. They are located at the back of the border so their ripening foliage will be hidden. In the rear row are "yellow paper-whites" that begin to bloom in January. Alternating with them for later color are day-lilies 'Cosette' and 'Jewell Russell,' and tall *Jacobinia aurea* with long yellow flower spikes and large glossy leaves.

In the next to the back row are more daffodils in varieties especially recommended for the South: 'Carbineer,' 'Carlton,' and 'Fortune.' Between them are pale yellow day-lily 'Delta Girl' and amaryllis in salmon-orange colors. (A good hardy type of amaryllis suited to growing outside is Tunia's Australian Strain.)

In the third row from the back are the small-flowered day-lily 'Golden Chimes,' gloriosa daisies that flower from May through July, and clumps of red *Lycoris radiata* for October bloom. Since lycoris foliage dies down in May, and the space is vacant all summer, pale yellow marigolds (annuals) are started from seed in peat pots, and inserted to fill the gap.

Cape plumbago, with lovely blue blooms over an extremely long season, is the main plant in the next row. Mixed with it are Johnny-jump-ups which reseed themselves, white-flowered *Penstemon digitalis,* and blue *Salvia pratensis,* which self-sows.

Toward the front of the border are low-growing and early-flowering day-lilies 'Little Cherub' and 'Gold Dust.' The latter has a second crop of bloom in autumn. With them is iris 'Golden Cataract,' a low grower that flowers in both spring and autumn, and that withstands the watering necessary for the day-lilies.

For low foreground are clumps of bright yellow rain-lily alternating with blue-flowered dwarf plumbago. Gray-leaved *Sedum altissimum* is used for edging.

🍁 A Selection of the Most Useful Perennials and Biennials

ACHILLEA or YARROW. In this group are tall border plants and low ones for the rock garden. The flowers are mostly flat-topped heads carrying innumerable small blossoms. Most of them are yellow, but some are pink or white. The foliage is mostly ferny and aromatic. The plants like sun, and tolerate heat and dry soil. They are very cold-hardy.

'Gold Plate' and 'Coronation Gold' are spectacular tall border plants, blooming through summer. The former stands 4 ft. high with bloom heads 4 to 5 in. across; the latter is a little shorter with slightly smaller flowers: They form large clumps. Both are useful as cut flowers either fresh or dry. 'Moonshine' is a similar-looking plant, though only 1½ to 2 ft. high.

Woolly Yarrow (*A. tomentosa*) is a creeper with yellow flowers on stems 10 in. high.

Milfoil (*A. millefolium*) has pink or rosy-red flowers on stems 18 in. high.

ALYSSUM, BASKET-OF-GOLD (*A. saxatile*) In Zones 4 to 8, inclusive, this low growing plant attains a height of 4 to 12 in. and has gray leaves. In early spring, at tulip time, it is covered with myriads of tiny bright yellow flowers. You can buy plants or grow them easily from seed. They will be handsome placed at the front of your border, in a rockery, or in crevices in a stone wall. Space them 10 in. apart. Give them sun and fast-draining soil. Each year following bloom time, cut the stems back to within 4 in. of the ground. Compact new growth will develop. If you wish to save some seeds, you can let one flower cluster remain to ripen. There are several varieties, including one that is more compact, some with paler flowers, and a double.

A perennial border can look like this in late summer featuring summer phlox (background), white feverfew (foreground) and tall zinnias. The edging is composed of sweet alyssum and dwarf marigolds.

ANCHUSA or BUGLOSS. These look like giant forget-me-nots, with the same type of bright blue flowers.

Italian Bugloss (*Anchusa azurea* or *italica*) stands 3 to 5 ft. high, has coarse hairy stems, and is covered with bloom most of the summer. Its varieties include 'Dropmore,' 'Morning-Glory' and 'Loddon Royalist.' All do best in full sun but stand some shade. They must have well-drained soil.

Forget-me-not-Anchusa is *Brunnera*, described in the chapter on shade.

ARTEMISIA or WORMWOOD. These gray-leaved aromatic plants are grown for their foliage rather than their inconspicuous flowers. Sagebrush is a member of this group. So is the herb tarragon.

Artemisia albula 'Silver King' or ghost plant stands 3½ ft. tall. It is useful in the background of borders, can be picked for fresh or dried arrangements, and is sometimes naturalized as a groundcover for difficult spots in the West and Southwest.

'Silver Mound' (a variety of *A. schmidtiana*) is a low-growing novelty with fine-cut silky foliage only 12 in. high. It is excellent in rockeries, as an edging, or for pattern planting. It needs severe cutting back when the center of the plant falls open, spoiling the mound effect.

There are several other types.

ASTER, HARDY. These lovely flowers are one of the glories of early autumn. Selections or hybrids of wild types, they produce myriads of small daisy-type flowers in lavender, purple, pink or white. There are tall types growing 2½ to 5 ft. high, and neat little dwarfs only 1 ft. tall that are good for the front of borders. The tall ones are often called Michaelmas daisies. All are hardy, and will grow in sun or part shade. To get starts, buy plants of named varieties. You do not need many, for they increase rapidly and should be divided every year or so. Each division becomes a mature, full-flowering plant in one season.

ASTER, STOKES, see STOKES ASTER

ASTILBE. See the chapter on shade.

BABYS-BREATH (*Gypsophila*). This perennial grows in Zones 3 to 8a, inclusive. It produces clouds of tiny white or pink flowers in summer, which can be dried for winter arrangements. It likes a sunny site and resents acid soil. The familiar tall-growing sort is *G. paniculata*, 3 ft. high and at least that wide. Its form 'Bristol Fairy' has double blossoms. In setting out this plant, make sure the point where the top is grafted to the root is 1 in. below soil line. Creeping babys-breath (*G. repens*) grows only about 18 in. high, with trailing stems. It is good for a rockery.

BALLOON-FLOWER (*Platycodon grandiflorum*). In Zones 4 to 8, inclusive, this is one of the few blue perennials for late summer bloom. It has bell-shaped flowers 2 to 3 in. across, and puffy balloon shaped buds. Though blue is the usual color, there are pink and white varieties, and also doubles. The variety *mariesi* grows only 18 in. high as compared with the normal height of 2 to 3 ft. Since plants are slow to become established and make big clumps, it is wise to get your start by buying plants. However, it is easy to raise balloon-flower from seed.

Set out the thick fleshy roots with the crowns just below soil level. Shoots are slow to start growth in spring, so it is wise to mark the spot where the plants are. If your plants tend to be tall and loppy, stake them. Or, better, when they are half grown in late spring, cut them back halfway and they will become shorter and bushier. Balloon-flower likes full sun except in hot regions. Allow 14-in. spacing

BASKET-OF-GOLD, see ALYSSUM

BEE BALM, see MONARDA

BEGONIA, WAX. See the chapter on annuals.

BELLFLOWER (*Campanula*). If you love blue flowers, there are many bellflowers you should try. The following are among the most popular and useful.

Late spring produces a crescendo in perennial gardens. Oriental poppies are the foreground flower. Design by Mrs. H. I. Nichols

Day-lilies brighten this border through summer. They are interplanted with daffodils for early season color. Elizabeth Howerton, landscape architect

Canterbury Bells (*C. medium*) does well in Zones 4 to 9, inclusive. This one produces spectacularly showy large single or double flowers that are grouped in pyramid form on stems 2 to 3 ft. high. The colors are lavender, blue, pink or white, and the plants are biennial. To have blooms the first year you must buy started plants. Space them 10 to 12 in. apart. Seeds sown in summer will bloom the following spring.

Carpathian Harebell or Tussock Bellflower (*C. carpatica*) flourishes in Zones 3 to 8, inclusive. This is a dwarf 6 to 12 in. high, and a treasure for a rock garden or the front of your perennial border. The foliage appears in neat mounds; flowers are blue or white, cup-shaped in summer. Buy plants and space them 10 in. apart.

Clustered Bellflower (*C. glomerata*) and the variety *dahurica* or Danesblood Bellflower are hardy into Zone 4. They make dense clumps of purple-blue flowers 1 to 1½ ft. high at iris time. The blooms are carried in whorls up the stem, opening gradually. They will grow in sun or part shade, spreading pleasantly by underground runners. They are easy to divide, and plants or divisions should be spaced 10 in. apart. There is a dwarf form, *acaulis,* only a few inches high.

Peachleaf Bellflower (*C. persicifolia*) grows in Zones 3 to 8, inclusive. This one is tall—to 2½ ft.—and slender, with bells 1½ in. wide in blue or white, and double or single form. It is excellent for cutting. Start with plants, spaced 10 in. apart.

Serbian Bellflower (*C. poscharskyana*) is used in Zones 3 to 8, inclusive. A low grower, trailing or spreading, it produces small lavender star-shaped flowers in spring. It stands drought and is good on walls. Sun or shade is acceptable. Start with plants.

BERGAMOT, see MONARDA

BLEEDING-HEART. See the chapter on shade.

BRUNNERA. See the chapter on shade.

BUTTERCUP (*Ranunculus*). The one most seen in northern perennial gardens is the double

form of *R. acris.* It is a creeper with shiny 3-parted leaves, and small, bright yellow double flowers on stems 1 to 2 ft. high at iris time. Though handy as a "filler flower," it spreads rapidly by runner plants like those of strawberries, so must be kept under control. Since the roots are shallow it is fairly easy to weed out. It is rarely sold commercially so get starts from friends.

BUTTERFLY-WEED (*Asclepias tuberosa*). Here is a wild flower, useful in Zones 3b to 9, inclusive, whose sprays of brilliant and interesting small orange flowers can be a showpiece in your sunny summer garden, though you can grow it in dry, poor soil. It is especially attractive grouped with yellow day-lilies and gloriosa daisies. The leafy stems grow 2 to 3 ft. high, from a fleshy taproot. Set this out preferably in spring, placing the crown 2 in. below soil level. Then be patient, for plants are slow to become established. Be warned that butterfly-weed is slow to awaken each spring; mark the location so you will not forget and try to plant something else there. Propagate by root cuttings or seed.

CAMPANULA, see BELLFLOWER

CANDYTUFT, EVERGREEN (*Iberis sempervirens*). In Zones 5 to 8, inclusive, this is an excellent plant for edging borders, and for rockeries, for it looks well at all times of year. The plants are only 8 to 12 in. high, bushy, and clothed in short and narrow evergreen leaves. In spring, at tulip time, flat clusters of snowy white flowers cover the foliage. To get good-sized plants in a hurry, buy them already started. After that you may propagate them easily by making stem cuttings from the branches when you prune them back after each flowering season. To learn how to root cuttings, see the chapter on starting plants. Space plants 18 in. apart in sun or slight shade.

CANTERBURY BELLS, see BELLFLOWER

CATMINT, see NEPETA

CHRISTMAS-ROSE. See the chapter on shade.

CHRYSANTHEMUM. For fall color, nothing rates higher than mums. They are almost as easy to grow as annuals, and like annuals they become full-sized and bloom maturely the year that you plant them. They do well everywhere, North to South, though in coldest winter climates they may not be completely winter-hardy without protection.

You can grow bushy garden types informally to have masses of outdoor color plus armloads of flowers for picking. This is the usual, easy and simple way. Or, with special varieties, patience, skill and know-how, you can have the thrill of growing large specimen blooms similar to those the florists sell at football season. Any kind of mum can be grown in a pot and moved around where you need it.

The way to start is to buy young plants. These are rooted cuttings usually growing in small pots. They are available at local garden-supply sources but you can also get them by mail order through nursery firms and chrysanthemum specialists. Do not buy just any old variety! You will want your favorite colors for sure. Also the time of bloom is important.

If you live in the North where frosts come early, it is vital that you choose early-flowering varieties—the kinds that bloom before October 1. Otherwise your plants may not open their buds before being frozen. If you now have some old-fashioned late-blooming kinds, throw them out and get some of the fine new varieties that have been bred especially to bloom early. In mild climates, the time of bloom is not crucial.

The time to plant in mild-winter, hot-summer areas is early spring, so that the roots can become established while the soil is cool. Elsewhere, plant after danger of frost has passed. There is no great hurry; June is fine.

Give them a place in full sun if possible, or else where they can have sunshine at least half of each day. The soil should be deeply prepared, fertile, well-drained, and contain as much humus as possible. Well-rotted manure (not fresh), compost, or moistened peat moss are helpful additions.

Space the plants 2 ft. apart or more. Overcrowding will result in underdeveloped plants and may bring on leaf diseases. You will get more and better blooms with wide spacing. Water well at planting time and while roots take hold.

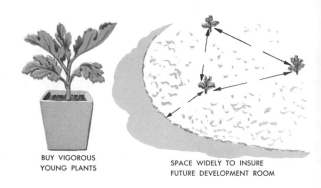

BUY VIGOROUS
YOUNG PLANTS

SPACE WIDELY TO INSURE
FUTURE DEVELOPMENT ROOM

The young plant must be pinched (pruned) to stimulate vigorous shoots, and to produce side branches and thus more flower buds. This is especially desirable for bushy border-type chrysanthemums. In the North do it once or twice before July 1, and then stop. In southern areas where bloom is not wanted until weather becomes cool, another pinch can be given a little later. Buds begin to form when days are shorter than nights, and reach flowering stage in 6 to 10 weeks. To have big flowers (but fewer of them), remove all buds except the end one on each branch.

Water generously and deeply. A mulch will help keep the soil cool. Feed about every 2 weeks. In sandy soil more feeding may be needed. If your area has lots of rain, or wind, plan to stake each plant inconspicuously.

To grow enormous flowers, like the florist's, you must first buy a large-flowered variety, usually from a chrysanthemum specialist. The young plants are pinched back soon after being set, to induce husky side branches. One of these is chosen to become the only stem. Its tip is pinched out just prior to July 1, and the best resulting side shoot should be saved and tied to a stake. All flower buds but one are removed (rolled out while tiny) so all the plant's strength goes into the one bud. Most large-flowered mums bloom late. In cold climates they will not open before frost unless potted and brought indoors. This is a challenge!

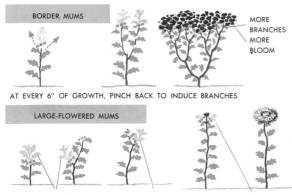

BORDER MUMS

MORE BRANCHES MORE BLOOM

AT EVERY 6" OF GROWTH, PINCH BACK TO INDUCE BRANCHES

LARGE-FLOWERED MUMS

PINCH BACK—REMOVE SIDE SHOOT—REMOVE SIDE BUDS

COLUMBINE (*Aquilegia*). Here is a very hardy flower, useful in Zones 3b to 9a, inclusive. It is 1 to 3 ft. high, depending upon the variety, and will grow in sun but prefers part shade. Blooms, which come in a rainbow of colors at iris time, are jaunty and graceful. They may be long- or short-spurred. These distinctive spurs are honey-holding extensions of the petals and sometimes as long as 1½ in. The leaves are attractive and 3-parted. Big plants that bloom prolifically may exhaust themselves and die if you allow them to set seed. So, immediately after flowering ends, cut plants to within 4 in. of the ground. New growth will arise. When setting out plants, the crown should be just at soil level. Columbines are easy to raise from seed, and you should get blooms the second season. Their roots are fleshy and difficult to divide.

CORAL BELLS (*Heuchera*). This plant thrives in Zones 5 to 8, inclusive. Its tiny red, pink or white bells dance at the top of slender stems 15 to 30 in. tall in early summer. Their effect is dainty, airy and charming. The foliage is as notable as the flowers, since it is low-growing and handsome all year. The leaves, heart-shaped and evergreen, come in compact clumps 6 to 8 in. high. Coral bells is a good edging plant if you remove the bloom stems as soon as flowering season ends. Grow it in sun or part shade. Buy plants and space them 12 in. apart. Propagate by division.

COREOPSIS (*C. grandiflora* and *C. lanceolata*). This does well in Zones 4 to 10, inclusive. Its brilliant yellow daisy-type flowers grow on slender, wiry stems 1½ to 3 ft. high in early summer. It likes sun; stands drought. You can use it as a good "filler flower" for borders, and the plant can be naturalized in sunny wild gardens. It is fine for picking. Start with plants or seeds. There are some dwarf forms.

DAISY, BLUE, see MARGUERITE

DAISY, ENGLISH (*Bellis perennis*). These spring-blooming, low-growing plants measure 6 to 8 in. high and thrive in Zones 5b to 10, inclusive. The flowers are mostly double, 2 in. across, in pink, red or white. They are grown much as pansies are, and like similar conditions. Hot summers and drought are bad for them, so in much of the country they are usually grown as biennials.

Seeds sown in late summer or autumn produce plants that will bloom in late winter in mild climates, or early spring elsewhere. These seeds germinate in about a week and begin to bloom in 6 months. For immediate effects buy plants. Space them 5 in. apart. After flowering they can be dug and the clumps divided. These are very pretty as border edgings grouped with spring bulb flowers, and also used in rockeries. Where contented they self-sow, may gradually revert to single-flowered forms, and also escape into your lawn.

DAISY, GLORIOSA, see RUDBECKIA

DAISY, MICHAELMAS, see ASTER, HARDY

DAISY, OX-EYE (*Chrysanthemum leucanthemum*). This is the wild white field daisy growing 1 to 3 ft. high. It self-sows weedily, but in new gardens is a good "filler flower," good for picking. It continues on and on if not allowed to set seed.

DAISY, PAINTED or PYRETHRUM (*Chrysanthemum coccineum*). In Zones 4 to 8, inclusive, this pink or rosy-red daisy-type flower blooms at iris time. Its foliage is ferny, and the 3- to 4-in.

blooms are carried on individual stems 15 to 24 in. high. These flowers are excellent for picking and like sun. You can buy plants or easily grow them from seed. Old clumps can be divided.

DAISY, PARIS, see MARGUERITE

DAISY, SHASTA (*Chrysanthemum maximum*). There are many varieties. The flowers may be single, double or fringed, 2 to 6 in. across, and 1½ to 3 ft. high. They are excellent both in the garden and for cutting. Bloom time is early summer. Generally the plants do best in Zones 6 through 8, though some varieties are quite permanent in Zone 5. They like rich soil and ample moisture during the summer, but cannot stand waterlogged ground in winter. Plants multiply rapidly and should be divided frequently to keep them vigorous. Space new plants or divisions 12 in. apart in sun or part shade. They are easy to grow from seed.

DAMES-ROCKET. See the chapter on shade.

DAY-LILY (*Hemerocallis*). Here is the top perennial for summer bloom, ridiculously easy to grow all over the United States, though some varieties grow best in cold-winter climates and others in mild. The flowers are large and lilylike, in yellow, orange, red, pink or combinations. Some have dashing eye-zones. They are borne profusely over an unusually long period. The foliage is ornamental all through the growing season, being slender and rising from the ground in graceful fountain form. Best of this flower's excellent features is the fact that it is loveliest during the hottest time of year when other garden flowers, and you, are wilting.

Bloom displays are not ruined by a day of scorching sun, beating rain, or wind, for each morning a completely new set of blossoms opens, fresh and unspoiled. Each remains open only one day, then withers and drops. But every scape (flowering stem) carries buds of various sizes that open in sequence over a period of 2 to 3 weeks. In addition, some plants send up a second and even third set of scapes, providing rebloom; this is most apt to happen in mild climates and where there is generous moisture. Because each stem carries so many buds, you

will probably not want to pick them and sacrifice so many days of potential bloom in the garden. However, you can pick individual blossoms daily, and use them with some sort of foliage in low bowls.

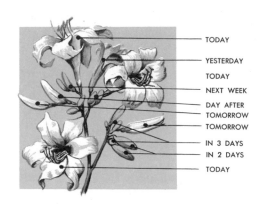

The heights of day-lilies vary from dwarfs only 18 in. high to back-of-the-border giants 6 ft. tall. Seasons of bloom differ, too. By choosing varieties carefully you can have flowers in the North from iris time until fall frost, and in mild climates from March until cold weather.

Set them out any time during the growing season, even when plants are in flower. However, in northern states it is wise to plant in spring, and never later than early September, so that the roots can become firmly established before winter. Mail-order firms specializing in day-lilies usually ship immediately after the blooming season. A commercial division consists of 1 or more fans of leaves with their attached roots. They can be shipped bare, or nearly so, for the thick roots hold reserve supplies of food and moisture.

Locate your treasures in sun or part shade. For extremely hot climates some shade is advised. Bloom is most profuse in sun. Trim the tops and roots to about 8 in. If there are any little side shoots with roots, they can be detached, planted separately, and will become big plants. Space varieties 2 to 3 ft. apart, realizing that the plants will multiply rapidly and become large clumps. Though day-lilies are not fussy about soil, they do best in well-prepared ground with ample humus. Set them out with the juncture of roots and leaves just at soil level. Firm soil about them and water well. The first year's blooms are rarely of normal size or height, but be patient. These are plants that increase in magnificence year after year.

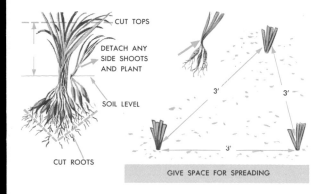

CUT TOPS

DETACH ANY SIDE SHOOTS AND PLANT

SOIL LEVEL

CUT ROOTS

GIVE SPACE FOR SPREADING

It is not essential to divide and transplant old clumps unless they are so crowded that they do not bloom well. However, to increase your stock, or share plants with friends, all you need do is dig rooted portions from your old clump. You can lift the entire mass in order to cut or pull it apart into divisions of one or several fans. But since newly planted divisions do not bloom well their first season, you may prefer to leave half of the parent clump undisturbed until the new divisions become established. When resetting portions of the same variety, group them together as enlarged clumps or drifts, to make large, superlative masses of color. Space such divisions 1 ft. apart, and they will soon intermingle.

PULL OR CUT APART

LIFT CLUMP—WASH SOIL FROM ROOTS

CUT BACK—REPLANT

In our yard we have a long day-lily border comprised of 4 varieties which bloom in sequence from May until late summer. Each variety is set in a continuous long row; plants were obtained by dividing huge old clumps. Set between these rows, to give color in early spring before the day-lilies get going, are rows of early and late daffodils interplanted with blue grape-hyacinths. As the daffodil foliage ripens and disappears, day-lily foliage fills in.

The best varieties for you depend upon your color preferences and whether you live where winters are very cold or very mild. If you live in the mid-section of the country you can grow any variety of day-lily superbly.

DELPHINIUM. Stately spires of lovely blue flowers (or lavender, white or pink) are this plant's gift to your garden. Its blooms may rise 5 to 7 ft. high and are ideal for the back of a border. The flowers open at the same time as roses, madonna lilies, early white summer phlox ('Miss Lingard') and Shasta daisies, and combine beautifully with them. The best-known kinds are the large-flowered hybrids such as the Pacific Hybrids and Wrexham strain, with single or double florets 1½ to 2 in. across. Because their glorious heads of bloom are so large and heavy, they should always be staked.

Other types of delphinium, though not so spectacular, can add the loved blue color to your garden. Especially useful are the graceful, open-branched delphiniums known as *bella-donna* and *bellamosum* (their correct botanical name is *Delphinium cheilanthum* var. *for-mosum*). They grow 3 to 4 ft. high. Similar, but growing only 1 to 2 ft. high, is Chinese delphinium (*D. chinense*) with blooms of light blue, dark blue or white. This one flowers the first year from seed, if started in early spring; it tends to be short-lived so new sowings should be made occasionally. Delphiniums may be grown from Zones 3b through 8, but are best where summers are cool.

For your first experience, buy plants that are at least a year old. Set them out in spring in cold-winter climates, and fall in mild-winter or hot-summer areas. Set them in a sunny place, unless you live in a very hot region and then some shade is helpful. Space them 2 ft. apart, and do not let the crown of the plant sink below soil level. Water well. As soon as the flowering season is completed, cut the stalk off just below the lowest bloom. New foliage will come up at the base of the plant and then the old stem can be removed. You are likely to have some repeat bloom in the fall. For winter it is wise to cover the crown with sand, and after cold weather arrives, mulch with light, airy material.

One of the many nice things about delphiniums is that they are easy to raise from seed. Nothing will give you a bigger thrill than growing your own plants and watching the astonishment of friends when they see the results. The trick for success is to use fresh seed and sow it as soon as possible after it ripens. That means July, August or, at latest, September. Buy seed of the finest varieties. To grow from seed, see the chapter on starting plants.

Seedling delphiniums will be husky little plants by autumn. They will be safest their first winter in a coldframe or its equivalent, and mulched so that they will not heave out of the ground. Move them to their permanent location in early spring and they will bloom that year.

Your plants will appreciate being fed in spring as they are starting growth. Scatter complete plant food in a circle around, but not touching, them.

Poisoning can occur from eating delphinium plants, including the annual type known as larkspur.

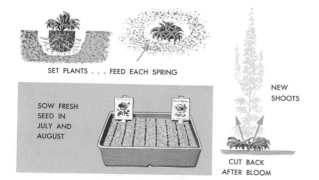

SET PLANTS . . . FEED EACH SPRING

SOW FRESH SEED IN JULY AND AUGUST

NEW SHOOTS

CUT BACK AFTER BLOOM

DIANTHUS, see PINK

FELICIA, see MARGUERITE, BLUE

FEVERFEW or MATRICARIA (*Chrysanthemum parthenium*). This has white or yellow single or double flowers on aromatic-leaved plants 1 to 3 ft. high, blooming in summer. Double forms are best; the single ones self-sow weedily. Feverfew provides good filler flowers in borders. The plant is not always reliably hardy in coldest climates, especially if soil is not well-drained. It can be treated as an annual since spring-sown seeds bloom by midsummer, and is good for cutting. Space plants 10 in. apart.

FORGET-ME-NOT. See the shade chapter.

FOXGLOVE. See the shade chapter.

GAS-PLANT (*Dictamnus*). This beautiful, unusual, and exceedingly long-lived perennial thrives in Zones 4 to 8, inclusive. Airy pink or white flowers are carried in 3-ft.-high terminal clusters at iris time, above a clump of leaves that remain attractive all year. The name gasplant comes from the fragrance of all parts of the plant, and from the fact that on a hot, still night, you can produce a burst of flame if a lighted match is held over the blooms. Because plants are slow to become large clumps, it is wise to buy them rather than raise them from seed. Allow 3-ft. spacing, and put them where they can remain forever, since they resent being moved.

GAZANIA. This is a low-growing tender perennial. Its brilliant daisylike flowers, measuring 1½ to 3 in. across in red, yellow, orange, brown and combinations, are borne on stems 6 to 12 in. high. Gazania is popular in California and other warm, dry climates where it blooms almost all year and is useful as a groundcover. In cold climates it may be grown as an annual. If you live where gazanias are commonly grown, you can buy them as started plants. Or, wherever you live, you can grow them from seed, starting preferably in early March. Space the plants 10 in. apart. They want sun and fast-draining soil. Blooms open in sunshine, and close at night, in shade, and on cloudy days. Propagate by dividing.

GERANIUMS. Two general types of plants bear this name. Least known are the true geraniums. *G. grandiflorum* with 1½-in. purple-blue flowers on a plant 18 in. high is hardy in northern gardens. So is *G. sanguineum* with rosy blooms ¾ in. across. Both will grow either in sun or part shade, spaced 1 ft. apart.

Pelargoniums are commonly called geraniums. They are the familiar tender perennials or shrubs grown in mild-winter climates as permanent garden plants, and in cold climates as house plants or summer bedding plants. They flourish especially in the fog belt of the Pacific Coast and like full sun except in very hot areas. Temperatures below 26° injure them. There are many varieties from which to choose, erect or trailing, large and dwarf, scented-foliage, etc. They are discussed in the chapter on indoor plants. For the method of starting them from cuttings, see the chapter on starting plants.

GERBERA (*G. jamesoni*) or TRANSVAAL DAISY. These gorgeous daisy-type flowers are hardy in mild climates, Zones 8 through 10. In Zone 8 they should be mulched for winter. They bloom almost continuously through the growing season, though tapering off in hottest weather. The flowers, 4 in. across on stems 18 in. high, come in exquisite shades of yellow, pink, cream, rose, orange and red. They last well in the garden or as cut flowers. Their foliage is gray-green, in a basal rosette. Plant them in sun or part shade, with rapid-draining soil. The crown, where roots and top meet, should be at soil level or slightly above. Purchase roots, or if you like to raise plants from seed, you can have gerberas in bloom within a year. Divide clumps every 3 or 4 years.

GHOST PLANT, see ARTEMISIA

GLOBE THISTLE (*Echinops ritro*). If you are looking for a tall, boldly decorative plant with blue flowers to bloom at day-lily time in midsummer, get globe thistle 'Taplow Blue.' It will grow 4 to 7 ft. high, depending upon your soil. The flowers are bristly spheres 3 in. across, misty blue in color. They can be dried for winter arrangements. Their foliage is spiny. The plants are very cold-hardy but not good in the Deep South. Allow them 3 ft. of space, and use in the back of the border.

GLORIOSA DAISY, see RUDBECKIA

GOLDEN GLOW, see RUDBECKIA

HAREBELL, CARPATHIAN, see BELLFLOWER

HELENIUM. This plant does well in Zones 4 to 8, inclusive. In late summer or autumn it is a showy sight. Hundreds of daisy-type flowers, about 2 in. across, in shades of yellow, red or bronze, cover bushy branches 1½ to 5 ft. high. Stalks arise from flat foliage rosettes. The plants multiply rapidly. You need only one of each variety to get starts, and soon you will have enough to share with friends. Helenium likes sun and ample moisture. Space it 2 ft. apart, near the back of your border, and plan to support the topheavy stalks with stakes. Divide the plants often and space divisions 12 in. apart in new groupings. Helenium blooms gloriously the first season. Do not eat any parts of this plant.

HEMEROCALLIS, see DAY-LILY

HIBISCUS or MALLOW, HARDY GIANTS (*Hibiscus moscheutos* hybrids). These are spectacular for late summer when few other perennials are blooming. The plants are large, 3 to 6 ft. tall, and shrublike, though they die in the ground in winters. They are hardy north into Zone 5. Their flowers resemble those of hollyhock but may be as large as dinner plates in pink, red or white. Each bloom remains open only one day, but there are quantities of buds to open successively. They grow best in sun, and with ample moisture. Allow plants at least 4 ft. of space. New shoots are slow to appear in spring. Hibiscus is easy to start from seed, which will produce blooming plants the second year. However, for the finest selected varieties buy plants of named kinds, such as 'Poinsettia,' red; 'The Clown,' white flushed with pink and having a crimson eye in its center; 'Radiant,' pink; and 'Snow White,' a low-grower 3½ ft. high with pure white blooms.

HOLLYHOCK *(Althaea rosea)*. This biennial, growing in Zones 3 to 9a, inclusive, sometimes lives several years. It self-sows, so that young plants are always coming along to replace those that die. The plants grow 5 to 8 ft. high, with single or double flowers 3 in. or more across in white, pink, red and yellow. Their bloom time is early summer. By purchasing plants you get quickest bloom, but hollyhocks are very easy to raise from seed. Plant them in full sun.

IMPATIENS. See the chapter on shade.

HOSTA, see PLANTAIN-LILY in the shade chapter.

IRIS. These are among the most popular, showy, easy and dependable perennials. No wonder they are a great hobby flower. Wherever you live, there are some types that will thrive for you. Though you will have no desire to eat the rootstocks, it is interesting to know that they can cause poisoning.

Tall bearded iris *(Iris germanica)* is the kind that is best known. It does well practically everywhere except in the Deep South, where conditions are too damp. The plants grow 3 to 4 ft. high, with blooms gorgeously large in colors of breathtaking loveliness. Their flowers are fragrant. The "beards" from which the group takes its name are decorative tufts of fuzzy hairs on the midrib of the lower petals or "falls." Their leaves are sword-shaped and arranged like an open fan. The roots, fleshy rhizomes that grow horizontally just below the surface of the ground, serve as food storage units and explain why these irises are so easy to transplant and grow; why they can be shipped "bare-root," or be dug and left lying in the air for several days without harm. Bearded irises are just plain durable.

There are hundreds of varieties, more being bred and introduced each year. Rare new ones demand high prices. But outstanding beauties that have been on the market a few years can be purchased for 75¢ to $3 each. They will multiply rapidly and bloom better each year.

Dwarf and Intermediate Bearded Irises are small duplicates of the big ones. Dwarfs grow only 6 to 8 in. tall, come in many colors, and bloom very early in spring. They are excellent for a rockery or front of your border. Intermediates are middle-size editions, taller and later blooming than the dwarfs, but shorter and earlier blooming than the tall. Together, the three types will give you a long season of spring bloom.

All these bearded irises are grown the same way. They like full sun but will grow and bloom with a half day of sunlight. In the South and Southwest they need part shade. They hate wet feet so be sure the soil is fast-draining; if it is not, it is a good idea to raise the bed a few inches above surrounding ground. Since irises like fertile soil, you will have best results if you prepare the place for them several weeks in advance, digging in additional humus and a complete chemical fertilizer at the rate of 1 oz. per sq. ft. Avoid fertilizers high in nitrogen.

The best time to plant or transplant in northern states is 2 weeks after the blooming ends, or as soon as you can obtain the plants. Dealers usually ship in July. In the South and Southwest, do the planting either soon after the blooming season, or wait until September or early October when the weather is cooler and the rains start. Bearded irises are transplanted in summer in accord with their life cycle. Immediately after flowering the plants take a little nap, dormant period, before bursting into new growth. Old feeding roots that have served their purpose drop off; new roots, leaves, and potential flowering parts develop during autumn. It is important that the rhizomes be in their new location before this activity starts, for the new roots will be the ones that anchor the plant for winter.

Place the rhizomes horizontally, with the end from which the leaves rise pointing in the direction that you wish the plant to grow. In planting iris, dig a hole 4 to 5″ in diameter and 3 or 4″ deep. In the middle of this hole, pile up a mound of well-worked soil reaching almost to the surface level, and place the rhizome firmly on this. Then spread out the roots fanwise into the deeper part of the hole, fill in with well-prepared soil, and tamp down firmly, leaving the rhizome barely beneath the surface level. This will discourage rotting at the base of the plant but give the roots the depth they need.

Different varieties, whether single plants or clumps, should be spaced 2 ft. apart. When planting several all-alike plants in one clump, arrange the rhizomes like the spokes of a wheel, with the leafy ends on the outside; space them 8 in. apart. Water plants well to get them started. For winter in cold climates, mulch lightly to prevent the plants from being heaved out of the ground by frost action.

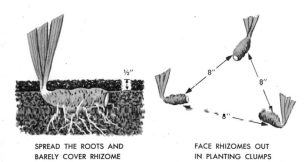

SPREAD THE ROOTS AND
BARELY COVER RHIZOME

FACE RHIZOMES OUT
IN PLANTING CLUMPS

Through-the-year care is simple. In early spring pull off and burn the old, dead iris leaves because they may harbor eggs of the iris borer. Scatter a handful of complete commercial plant food in a ring around each plant. To forstall possible trouble with borers, spray or dust the foliage weekly with DDT until bloom time. As each flower withers, nip it off, but be careful

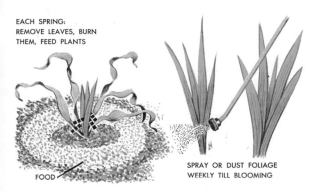

EACH SPRING:
REMOVE LEAVES, BURN
THEM, FEED PLANTS

FOOD

SPRAY OR DUST FOLIAGE
WEEKLY TILL BLOOMING

not to break off nearby flower buds. Do not let weeds or other plants shade or crowd iris plants. Sun and air must get into their hearts.

Large old clumps need to be lifted and divided when they do not bloom well or are crowded. The old parts should be cut off and burned. A rhizome that has bloomed will not bloom again; it is the newly developed side shoots that will carry the next season's bloom. If these new shoots are big and fat, they can be broken off and planted singly. Otherwise set them out as "doubles" attached to the old rhizome. Treat them just as though they were new plants.

Before you save, divide and replant an old clump of iris, ask yourself if you really want that variety or if you are being foolishly thrifty. Is it a kind that you chose, or was it here when you bought the house? If it is a color or type that you do not truly like, why not toss it out and give the space to a handsome new kind that you have been admiring?

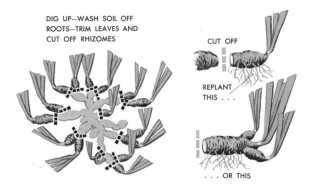

DIG UP—WASH SOIL OFF
ROOTS—TRIM LEAVES AND
CUT OFF RHIZOMES

CUT OFF

REPLANT
THIS . . .

. . . OR THIS

Crested Iris (*I. cristata*) is a dear little miniature iris that creeps along the surface of the ground. It is native to eastern woodlands and will grow in shade or part shade in garden or rockery if you live in Zones 5 through 8. The spring blooms are blue or white. Plant this one with the rhizomes barely covered by soil, 6 in. apart.

Japanese Iris (*I. kaempferi*) is exotic-looking with large, gracefully flaring flat flowers in iridescent colors of blue, white, pink, or blends.

The plants stand 3 to 3½ ft. high, and bloom long after tall bearded iris have finished—thus extending the iris season. They thrive both North and South, in Zones 4 through 9a, if given soil that is acid and humusy, a situation in sun or part shade, and generous amounts of water and food. In mild climates they can be planted in boglike conditions similar to the rice paddies of Japan where they are native. But in the North they must have good winter drainage.

Plant them in early spring in coldest climates, spring or fall elsewhere. Rhizomes should be about 2 in. below the soil, and plants 2 ft. apart. Do not expect good blooms until the plants are established. Water copiously in the spring before bloom time, and always in times of drought. Each spring, clear off and burn dead foliage and spray with DDT to avoid borers. They are easy to start from seed. Sow outdoors in the late fall; seeds will germinate in the spring, and if well tended may produce first blooms the next year.

Owing to their growth habits, all the irises are victims of the persistent inroads of tall, wiry weed grasses, which by midsummer give the plants an unsightly appearance. These grasses are difficult to pull out by the roots. The Japanese iris is particularly subject to these nuisances. One way to get rid of such weed grasses is to do so when the rhizomes are lifted to separate and replant. At that point it is easy to shake off the dirt and get rid of the roots of the weed grasses as you go along. Also, it is a good idea to separate Japanese iris about every two years and propagate more plants from the new vigorous growth.

Louisiana Irises are natives of boggy areas in the South and grow especially well in southern gardens, but adapt elsewhere if given suitable conditions. Some varieties are hardy in climates as cold as Zone 5. The plants grow 3 to 5 ft. high, with handsome blooms in varying sizes, shapes and colors. They like sun or part shade, a soil containing quantities of humus, and lots of moisture. They are especially attractive along the edge of a stream or decorating a patio pool.

In the South transplant from August to October. Set the tops of the rhizomes just below the soil surface. Keep them well watered until fall rains come. Blooms will come in late March through April and into May. During summer's heat the plants become dormant, and it is wise to shade the rhizomes from the sun with a mulch or an inch of soil.

Siberian Iris (I. sibirica) does well in both North and South. It thrives in average garden conditions, or in moist soil at the edge of a stream, pool or lake. Give it sun or a little shade. The plants grow 3 to 4 ft. high and flower at about the same time as tall bearded iris or slightly later. Though relatively small, the blooms are exquisitely formed and produced in quantity on slender stiff stems. They are showy and an ideal size for bouquets or corsages. The colors are white, purple, blue and raspberry.

Because the tall, slim leaves remain good-looking all season, clumps of Siberian iris are very useful in the perennial border. Plant in spring in cold-winter climates; spring or fall elsewhere. Always divide clumps into single divisions when setting out new plants or transplanting old ones. Space the divisions 5 in. apart in a clump arrangement, or space different varieties at least 2 ft. apart. They have dense, fibrous roots and should be set with the crown of the plant at soil level and roots spread vertically below. Leaves can be trimmed back to about a 6-in. height. Siberian irises resent transplanting and do not bloom well the first year, but multiply rapidly and soon become large clumps.

Spuria or Butterfly Iris (I. spuria) has magnificent blooms, resembling those of Dutch iris sold by florists as cut flowers. But spurias are hardy garden perennials. They grow 2 to 6 ft. high and are happy in a wide range of climates from the Pacific Coast, Southwest and Deep South, to Midwest and East. They probably do best in Zones 5b through 9a. They are not fussy about soil, or whether they are in full sun or a little shade, but do best in good soil with ample humus. Plant them where they are to remain, for they do not like being disturbed and may sulk a year after being transplanted.

Set them out with the tops of the rhizomes just below soil level; space the plants 2 ft. apart, or divisions 6 in. apart in a clump. Plant them in early spring in cold climates to give them a long season in which to become established; plant in fall in mild climates. The leaves can be cut back to 6 in. at planting time. Water generously while the plants get settled. Later, each spring, feed and water well until bloom time; let them become fairly dry during late summer. The flowers may be white, yellow, blue, purple, brown, or combinations. They follow tall bearded irises in season of bloom.

JACOBINIA. For mild-winter climates, Zones 9 and 10, use this tropical shrubby perennial. It grows 4 to 8 ft. high with large leaves and 10-in.-long, plumelike clusters of two-lipped tubular flowers that may be yellow, orange or pink depending upon species and variety. The tops may die off to the ground in winter, but they will sprout again in the spring. This plant is successful in sun or shade and needs plenty of water. It is very easy to propagate by stem cuttings taken after flowering. In cold-winter climates, grow jacobinia as a house plant.

LAVENDER-COTTON, see SANTOLINA

LEADWORT, see PLUMBAGO

LOOSESTRIFE, see LYTHRUM

LUPINE, PERENNIAL (*Lupinus*). These handsome spires of close-packed, pea-shaped flowers in blue, pink, purple or white grow on stalks 3 to 4 ft. high in Zones 3b to 8, inclusive. They do best in climates where summers are cool and moist, as in the Pacific Northwest, northern California and New England. Elsewhere they may be disappointing in their flower display and also short-lived. Set out plants in spring 18 in. apart, or sow seed outdoors in fall and it will germinate vigorously in early spring. These plants will grow in sun or part shade. Each year, as flowers fade, cut off the bloom stalks before they can start ripening seed. Do not remove any

more foliage than necessary. Foliage and seeds of some lupines are poisonous if eaten.

LUNGWORT. See PULMONARIA in the chapter on shade.

LYTHRUM or PURPLE LOOSESTRIFE. Here are spires of lovely pink flowers, on plants 3 to 4 ft. high, blooming a long time in midsummer. This is one of the finest pink perennials for borders, being hardy into cold Zone 3 and growing well in sun or shade, wet soil or dry, of almost any type. Buy plants of named varieties such as 'Morden Gleam' and 'Morden Rose.' Allow each plant 2½ ft. of space.

MALLOW, see HIBISCUS

MARGUERITE, BLUE or BLUE DAISY (*Felicia amelloides*). This is a tender perennial or sub-shrub, 1 to 3 ft. high, for mild-winter climates. The flowers are daisy type, blue, 1 in. across. It grows in sun or part shade. Clip off dead flowers and cut the entire plant back severely in late summer to induce new growth for fall flowers. It can be started from seed sown in spring; also self-sows.

MARGUERITE, GOLDEN (*Anthemis tinctoria*). This perennial has ferny foliage and yellow daisy-type blooms 1½ in. across on plants 2 to 2½ ft. high. It is very cold-hardy and blooms in early summer in northern gardens. Plant in the sun, allowing a 12-in. space. Propagate by division. It self-sows.

MARGUERITE or PARIS DAISY (*Chrysanthemum frutescens*). This plant, used in mild-winter climates, has white or pale yellow flowers 1½ to 2½ in. across on shrubby plants 3 ft. high. It blooms almost all year, likes sun, and is grown by florists for cut flowers. It propagates easily from stem cuttings.

MATRICARIA, see FEVERFEW

MIST-FLOWER (*Eupatorium coelestinum*). Often called hardy ageratum because it looks as though it should be one, this plant thrives in Zones 5b to 10, inclusive. Its small, fuzzy lavender-blue flowers are carried in clusters on stems 1 to 2 ft. high in late summer or autumn. Space plants 12 in. apart in sun or shade. They spread by underground runners and are apt to be slightly invasive. Mist-flower is a good "filler" for borders.

MONARDA, BEE BALM or BERGAMOT. This excels in Zones 4 to 9, inclusive. It produces showy flowers for late summer, with scarlet, pink, lavender or white flowers in shaggy heads on plants 2½ to 3 ft. high. The foliage has a pleasant, minty fragrance. These plants will grow in sun or part shade, dry or moist soil. Start by buying named varieties. Propagate by division and allow each plant 1½ ft. Good varieties are 'Cambridge Scarlet' and 'Croftway Pink.'

MOSS-PINK, see PHLOX

NEPETA or CATMINT (*N. mussini and N. faasseni*). These are low-spreading, aromatic, gray-leaved plants with small lavender flowers, useful in Zones 4 through 8. They like to grow in full sun, and tolerate drought, so they are lovely in rock walls as well as at the front of borders. The plants are 1 to 1½ ft. high, softly bushy or trailing. Shear them back after bloom. To start, get plants or divisions, and space them 14 in. apart. Propagate by dividing. Good named varieties include 'Blue Beauty' and 'Six Hills Giant.'

PENTAS (*P. lanceolata*). This perennial does well in frost-free climates, Zones 9 and 10, and elsewhere is grown as a house plant. It is a bushy plant 2 to 3 ft. high with clusters of small, star-shaped flowers nearly all year, in white, pink, red or lavender. It grows best in shade and makes a good cut flower. Propagate by stem cuttings rooted in water or soil.

PEONY (*Paeonia*). Gorgeous large and fragrant flowers for the garden and picking, handsome foliage all year, a rugged constitution and extremely long life are a few of the reasons why gardeners love peonies. They are very easy to grow in Zones 3b through 8, where they get their needed winter chilling. But in mild-winter climates they are disappointing. There are two main types. Best known are those that die back to the ground each winter (herbaceous). The other group are the shrublike tree peonies, with permanent woody branches. These formerly were rare and difficult to obtain, but now are more easily available.

Herbaceous Peonies (familiar garden kind) grow 2½ to 3 ft. high and wide. Their flowers are usually 5 to 8 in. across, though the early-blooming fern-leaf peony and a few other species or hybrids are smaller. They may be double or single, in red, pink or white. The singles, with attractive yellow stamens in their centers, and the Japanese type featuring tufts of yellow petaloids (stamens turned into petals) in their hearts, are particularly good for flower arrangements.

Peonies grow and bloom best in full sunshine, but will get along on 6 hours of sun a day. Give them space—at least 3 ft. apiece—and keep them away from the roots of trees and shrubs that would steal food and moisture. They are not fussy about soil, as long as it is not soggy. Plant where you wish them to remain permanently, for they do not like to be moved. The first year after transplanting they may not bloom, but each year after that you will have more and more flowers. You can figure that most varieties will bloom just a little later than tall bearded irises. However, there are early- and late-blooming peonies, so you can select different ones to stretch the season.

You can buy plants locally in pots, or packaged in dormant bare-root condition; or you can order by mail from nurseries. Firms specializing in peonies often have the largest selection of choice varieties, and it is fun to have outstanding ones that are different from the neighbors'. There are hundreds of varieties ranging in cost from about $1 for time-tested favorites to around $5 for newer kinds.

Typical commercial divisions of peonies are bare, woody roots from which foliaged tops and ends of roots have been trimmed. At their crowns are some dormant buds from which will rise next year's shoots. A good-sized division has 3 to 5 of these buds.

Dig a hole about 18 in. wide and deep, and loosen the soil in the bottom. If your soil is sticky clay, or very sandy, incorporate some humus such as moistened peat moss. Place your best soil in the bottom of the hole, adding some complete commercial fertilizer at the rate recommended on the package. This is where the new roots will develop. In placing the plant, the crucial factor is the depth of the growth buds. If you get them too deep, the plant will not bloom. In northern states, set them 2 in. deep; in central states, 1½ in.; and in the South, barely cover them. Allow for some settling of the loose soil. Firm the earth around the roots and water well. If your winters are severe, cover newly planted peonies with a mound of soil and remove it in spring.

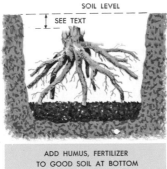

3 TO 5 EYES (BUDS)

SOIL LEVEL

SEE TEXT

TRIM BROKEN ROOTS

ADD HUMUS, FERTILIZER TO GOOD SOIL AT BOTTOM

Yearly care is minimal. Peonies appreciate an early spring feeding of a complete plant food scattered on the ground and watered in; also water during time of drought. A feeding after the period of flowering will help the plant build strength for the following year.

For the largest possible flowers, you can disbud. That is, leave only the main big bud at the tips of branches, and nip off all side buds while they are very tiny. In that way all energy goes to making one whopper flower. If you do not disbud, you will have more but smaller flowers, and they will give you a longer period of bloom since the small buds will not open until after the big ones have finished. Always remove withered flowers or seed heads. In picking flowers do not take many leaves. Never cut the plant to the ground until growth has stopped in autumn; this is because future flowers depend upon the food manufactured by the leaves.

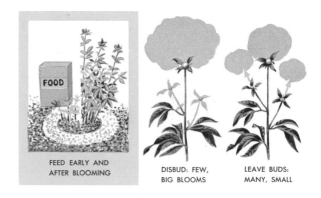

FEED EARLY AND AFTER BLOOMING

DISBUD: FEW, BIG BLOOMS

LEAVE BUDS: MANY, SMALL

Troubles? If your peonies do not bloom, they are probably planted too deep, or do not get enough sun. Ants crawling on buds do no direct harm though they sometimes spread disease and they are a nuisance on blooms you pick. You can get rid of them by scattering chlordane dust on the soil around the plant. For peony ailments, see the chapter on diseases.

Tree Peony. These are plants to treasure and to award a spot of honor in your garden, for they are among the loveliest and most aristocratic of garden flowers. You will find that they are priced rather like rare objects of art, too, and this is because they are difficult to propagate and slow to reach blooming size. But they are a long-time investment, for they will live indefinitely.

The plants are shrubby, with permanent woody branches. They lose their leaves in winter but do not die to the ground. Mature plants may be 2½ to 6 ft. high, and carry 20 to 100 blooms of exquisite form and translucent petals. The flowers may be single, double or semi-double. Colors include yellow and lavender, as well as pink, coral, red and white. They bloom earlier in spring than the more familiar herbaceous peonies.

Tree peonies grow well in Zones 5 through 8. They like rich fertile soil, deeply prepared. Plant them in early fall, allowing 4 ft. of space. Their setting depth is different from herbaceous peonies. Tree peonies should be placed so that the growth buds at the top of their roots are 6 to 8 in. below soil surface. During the first winter, protect with a mulch. They grow best if they are permanently mulched with 3 to 4 in. of sawdust or a similar material.

PHLOX. Summer perennial phlox (*P. paniculata*) is the long-lived favorite of summer gardens in Zones 4 through 9. The plants grow 3 to 5 ft. tall, carrying large clusters of inch-wide flowers at the top of their leafy stems. Their colors range from pink, red, white and lavender to orange and red. Though plants can be set out or transplanted almost any time during the growing season, the usual time in the North is spring. In mild climates, plant in autumn. Phlox likes full sun in northern states and where summers are cool, but if you live in a hot climate give them part shade. Space the plants 2 ft. apart, in rich, well-prepared soil, and give them plenty of water then and ever after.

Each year as they finish blooming, cut off the main cluster, and side shoots will develop and flower. Or, if you have only a few plants and plenty of time, remove individual flowers, and new buds will form where they were. Most important, do not let seeds form. This is not only to conserve the plant's strength but to prevent seeds falling onto the ground and sowing themselves. Such seedlings usually have poor color, yet are so vigorous that they crowd out their better-looking parents, and you may soon have a garden full of magenta-colored phlox instead of your good ones.

In autumn, cut the plants to the ground and burn their tops, as a form of disease prevention. Also keep your plants young, vigorous and uncrowded by dividing and resetting them about every 3 years; throw away the old woody centers at that time.

Propagation is easy by division or by root cuttings. For the latter, see the chapter on starting plants.

Moss-Pink (*Phlox subulata*) is the ground-hugging evergreen plant that covers itself in early spring with myriads of blooms, becoming a carpet of pink, crimson, blue or white. You have seen it in rockeries and in borders with spring bulb flowers. Individual plants make mounds 6 in. high and 1 to 2 ft. across. Foliage is neat, the short leaves being needlelike and a little prickly. The stems are reclining and root where they touch soil, which is why the plant makes an excellent groundcover.

It is fantastically easy to grow if you have a spot with sun and fast-draining soil, and if you will cut the plants back severely each year after they bloom. The cutting-back is important in order to induce compact new growth. Otherwise plants can become leggy and may also smother themselves; underportions may rot in hot, damp weather. To get a start, buy plants. You can set them out entire, or tear clumps into many segments, each having a few roots. Space plants 8 in. apart and shorten the leafy stems to 3 in. to encourage branching. Within a year even tiny single-stem plants will become nice-sized clumps.

Wild Sweet William (*Phlox divaricata*). From our woodlands comes this delightful 12-in. high, fragrant phlox. Its usual color is lavender, but sometimes you can find white or pink forms. Blooms appear in early spring, at the time of tulips and bleeding-heart, with which it looks lovely. During most of the year the plant makes a neat, inconspicuous ground-hugging mat. Only in spring do the stems rise to carry the blooms. These stems should be cut off later. Wild Sweet William will grow in sun or light shade. It is easy to propagate by dividing, and it also self-sows pleasantly. You will find it an excellent "filler flower" for spring and perennial borders.

PINK (*Dianthus*). These low-growing plants are excellent for sunny, well-drained sites at the front of borders or in rockeries. They like a neutral soil or one tending toward alkalinity. The flowers are predominately pink, white, red, or combinations. All pinks are easy to grow from seed.

Alyssum, Basket-of-Gold

Artemisia 'Silver Mound'

Aster, Hardy

Balloon-Flower

Cunterbury Bells

Bellflower, Clustered

Butterfly-Weed

Evergreen Candytuft

Chrysanthemum

Columbine

Day-Lily

Daisy, Shasta

Cottage or Grass Pink (D. plumarius), in Zones 4 to 8, inclusive, has intensely fragrant flowers 1 to 1½ in. across on stems 6 to 12 in. high. Its foliage is as attractive as the blooms, being slender and gray in mounds, and remaining good-looking all winter. Space plants 10 in. apart.

Hardy Carnation or Clove Pink (D. caryophyllus) includes greenhouse types. The hardy dwarf types, such as Chabaud's and Grenadins, survive winters in Zones 6 through 10, though they may need winter protection in their northern range. Space these 10 in. apart.

Sweet William (D. barbatus), for Zones 4 through 9, inclusive, has its showy, odorless blooms in clusters atop stems 1½ to 2 ft. high. The flowers may be single colors or calicolike mixtures. The plants are biennial; those started from seed one spring will bloom gloriously early the next summer. Then they usually become straggly, so it is best to keep new seedlings coming along for replacements. Space plants 6 in. apart.

PLANTAIN-LILY (Hosta). See the shade chapter.

PLUMBAGO, DWARF, or BLUE LEADWORT (Ceratostigma plumbaginoides, sometimes sold as Plumbago larpentae). These low, spreading plants have brilliant blue phloxlike flowers on stems 9 to 12 in. high in late summer and autumn. The foliage is semi-evergreen, turning bronze in late fall. They are suited for a rock garden, front of border, or as a groundcover. They like sun or part shade and will grow in Zones 6 through 9a, but need winter protection in the northern range and must have very well-drained soil to survive cold winters. Set the plants 1½ to 2 ft. apart. They spread by underground roots and are easily propagated by division.

POKER-PLANT or TORCH-PLANT (Kniphofia). Bloom stalks 3 to 5 ft. high rise above clumps of coarse, grassy foliage. The striking and exotic-looking flowers may be either in pastel colors, white, or vivid yellows and reds. The blossoms are tubular and clustered in poker-shape at the top of the stems. Set the plants, which have fleshy roots, in a sunny, well-drained site in spring, 18 in. apart. In the North buy new hardiest hybrids and plan to mulch for winter.

POPPY (Papaver). Two kinds are most popular.

Iceland Poppy (P. nudicaule) hails from arctic regions and does best when grown where summers are cool, or as a winter annual in warm-winter climates, or as an annual or biennial elsewhere. Dainty flowers 3 in. across, in colors predominately yellow, orange and white, are borne on wiry stems 1 to 1½ ft. high. In mild climates sow seed in autumn for flowers in late winter or early spring. In the North sow seeds in May or June. Transplant in early fall.

Oriental Poppy (P. orientale) is a flamboyant beauty putting on a dazzling show at iris time in spring. It can be grown in Zones 3 through 8. The flowers are whoppers 6 in. across in red, orange, pink, lavender, white, or two-tone. They may stand 2 to 4 ft. high. The plants like a situation in full sun, with exceedingly well-drained soil. These poppies have fleshy roots that cannot tolerate wet feet. Give them a place among other plants, for they will need to be hidden during late summer when their foliage matures and dies. It comes up anew in autumn and remains green through winter.

Set them out in August or September when the plants are dormant. At this stage roots can be shipped and handled bare—without foliage. Space them 1½ to 2 ft. apart, with the crown (juncture of roots and top) 2 in. below soil level. For the first winter, mound earth over the crown so water will not stand on it. Do not expect much of a flower the first season. Propagation of choice-named plants is by root cuttings. (See the chapter on starting plants.)

PRIMROSE. See the chapter on shade.

PULMONARIA. See the chapter on shade.

Delphinium

Gas-Plant

Globe Thistle

Helenium

Hibiscus, Hardy

Hollyhock

Iris, Tall Bearded

Lupine

Lythrum

Peony

Pentas

Phlox

PYRETHRUM, see DAISY, PAINTED

ROCK-CRESS *(Arabis)*. In Zones 5 to 8, inclusive, these low-growing, gray-leaved plants cover themselves with small white or pink flowers in very early spring. They bloom with daffodils and hyacinths. Rock-cress likes dry situations and does well in poor soil, in rockeries, and as an edging for borders. After flowering, shear off the clumps. These plants are propagated by division. The usual garden types are *A. alpina* and *A. caucasica*. Varieties with double flowers and variegated leaves are sometimes available.

RUDBECKIA. Here are excellent perennials that are improved forms of wild flowers.

Gloriosa Daisy *(Rudbeckia* Tetraploid Giant) has large 5- to 6-in. daisy-type flowers in yellow or yellow-banded-with-maroon, which are carried on 3 ft.-high plants. Blooms of some varieties are single, others double. The plants flower from seed as quickly as annuals, blooming fully in late summer from spring-sown seed. Stalks should be cut to the ground immediately after the bloom season, to encourage new basal growth, for the plants tend to be short-lived on the order of biennials. They self-sow generously, and it is easy to keep young plants coming along. Also save a little seed to sow each spring as security. Gloriosa daisies are excellent for picking, but use young blossoms rather than the largest with highest cones; the latter are past their prime and will not hold up. Get your start by sowing seeds.

Golden-Glow *(R. laciniata* var. *hortensia)* is an old-fashioned garden plant with quantities of double yellow flowers on stems 5 to 7 ft. tall. It is hardy in Zones 3 through 9. Though showy, it tends to spread in a rather weedy manner. Use at the back of the border and stake it. This plant is good for cutting. There are some low-growing forms sometimes available.

Rudbeckia 'Goldsturm' *(R. speciosa)* has golden yellow flowers 3 to 4 in. across, with dark eyes. The plants are 2½ ft. high, and long-lived. Blooms come in late summer when few other perennials are providing color. It is good for picking, and the foliage is handsome throughout the growing season. It multiplies fast and soon makes a big clump. Propagation may be done easily by dividing.

SALVIA. The following types are very useful.

Salvia farinacea has gray leaves and spires of blue flowers 2 to 3 ft. high. It is perennial in Zones 7 through 10 but annual elsewhere. It grows from seed.

Salvia pratensis is a perennial, 2 to 3 ft. high, with heart-shaped leaves. The flowers are usually blue-purple, but there are varieties with pink or blue blooms. It tends to self-sow.

Salvia superba is hardy and permanent in cold climates, making clumps 2½ ft. high, with numerous spikes of deep blue-purple flowers that continue all summer if old blooms are kept clipped off. Varieties 'Purple Spires' and 'Purple Glory' are excellent recent introductions. Buy plants and give them 18 in. of space in sun.

SANTOLINA or LAVENDER-COTTON *(S. chamaecyparissus)*. This aromatic silvery gray-leaved evergreen is a bushy plant that thrives in Zones 7b to 10, inclusive. It normally grows about 2 ft. high but can be clipped lower to form a dwarf hedge. Small yellow flowers appear in summer. Santolina likes sun and a light, rapid-draining soil. *S. virens* has green foliage.

SEDUM. Hardy examples of these succulent plants will grow from Zones 4 through 10. Many of them are low-growing, limber-stemmed trailers, with attractive evergreen leaves and gay seasonal flowers. They are decoratively useful in rockeries and walls, as groundcovers, and as edgings to borders. Others grow 2 to 3 ft. tall. They like sun but will tolerate some shade, and thrive in poor soil and dry conditions. Propagation is easy by division at any season, or you can root a piece of stem by sticking it into soil.

Low-growing varieties are innumerable! They may have foliage that is green, gray or reddish. Flower colors may be yellow, pink, white or rose. It is fun to see how many kinds you can collect. Any friend who has a plant will gladly give you a slip for a start. A quick-spreading kind, useful for fast-result groundcover, is *S. acre*. It has light green leaves and bright yellow flowers. Though invasive, it is easily weeded out.

Moss-Pink

Pink

Poker-Plant

Poppy, Oriental

Rock-Cress

*Rudbeckia,
Gloriosa Daisy*

Snow-in-Summer

Sunflower, Perennial

Sundrops

The best-known tall, hardy kind is showy sedum (*S. spectabile*). It grows 1½ to 2 ft. high, with gray-green leaves, and flat clusters of pale pink flowers in autumn. It dies to the ground in winter. There is a variety with yellow variegated leaves. Both make handsome specimen plants, are useful in a perennial border, or may be used as low herbaceous hedges or edgings.

SNOW-IN-SUMMER (*Cerastium tomentosum*). This ground-hugging, gray-leaved plant, with myriads of white flowers in early summer, is hardy north into Zone 4. It likes sun and tolerates drought so is excellent in a rockery, on a hot bank, or as a decorative groundcover. It should be cut back severely after blooming. Start with plants or divisions 18 in. apart. The plant multiplies rapidly and divides easily.

SPEEDWELL, see VERONICA

STOKES ASTER (*Stokesia laevis*) Excelling in Zones 5b to 10, inclusive. This is one of the most dependable summer-blooming perennials for the South. Its blue double daisy-type blooms 3 in. across are carried on stems 12 to 18 in. high. The plants grow in clumps. They like rapid-draining soil that is preferably fertile, and will adapt to either sun or part shade. Stokes aster is good for cutting, and handsome planted with day-lilies. Buy plants and space them 1 ft. apart. Propagate by division. It is sometimes available with flowers of white, pink or yellow.

SUNDROPS (*Oenothera tetragona* or *O. youngi*). These free-blooming flowers are good as fillers rather than specimen plants. In early summer they have clear lemon-yellow upfacing blooms 1½ in. across, clustered at the top of leafy stems 1 to 2 ft. high. They are showy, gay and simple to grow. Since they spread by runners, they could fill your garden, but are so shallow-rooted that they can be weeded out easily to the desired numbers after each blooming season. They are best in full sun. Set plants 10 in. apart.

SUNFLOWER, PERENNIAL (*Helianthus* and *Heliopsis*). These hardy kinds, thriving in Zones 5 to 10, inclusive, are a joy with their profuse,

relatively small golden blooms through the heat of summer. Some are tall; others only 3 ft. high. Some have single, daisy-type flowers, and others are roundly double or semidouble. They like sun, but will grow in part shade. While they tolerate drought and poor soil, they will be at their best when given good earth and ample moisture.

Heliopsis scabra incomparabilis, better known by such varieties as the double yellow 'Gold Greenheart' and 'Excelsa,' is one of the finest kinds for gardens. It grows in erect, bushy form, 3 to 4 ft. high, with flowers 3 in. across. It is good for picking. Buy plants and allow each a 1½ ft. space. Later you can propagate by division. Weed out self-grown seedlings. They tend to have flowers like their less attractive wild ancestors.

SWEET WILLIAM, see PINK

TORCH-PLANT, see POKER-PLANT

TRANSVAAL DAISY, see Gerbera

VERONICA or SPEEDWELL. These are superb garden plants, primarily blue-flowered though some varieties come in pink or white. Flowers are carried in gracefully slender, tapering spires. The plants may be ground-hugging trailers, or bushily branched and up to 2½ ft. high. Creepers are good in rockeries and walls. The taller kinds are splendid with other summer flowers.

Outstanding tall varieties include 'Blue Champion,' *V. longifolia subsessilis*, 'Minuet' (pink), 'Icicle,' 'Crater Lake Blue,' and 'Sunny Border Blue.' Slightly lower, and with distinctive silvery gray and velvety leaves is Woolly Speedwell (*V. incana*). It is a creeper, but bloom stems are 12 to 18 in. high. For a tiny, mat-forming kind, try *V. repens*. But beware of *V. filiformis* which may tempt you because it grows prolifically and has tiny forget-me-not-blue flowers; it is an invasive sort that is difficult to eradicate.

VIOLET. See the chapter on shade.

YARROW, see ACHILLEA

12

Bulbs and Their Beautiful Kin

(Including true bulbs, corms, tubers, etc.)

You can count on this group of plants for quick and almost certainly perfect results the first year! That is because most bulbs contain the equivalent of pre-packaged blooms! When you buy them, they are plump objects in dormant condition, usually dry, leafless and rootless. But they either contain a completely formed flower bud ready to emerge and put on a show, or they hold a reservoir of food that will get the plant off to a good start and maintain it until new roots and leaves are working. This is built-in insurance!

Some of the most gloriously beautiful bulb flowers are winter-hardy in severe climates, and can remain in the ground year after year. They like cold weather and must have a period of chilling annually or they will not do well. Others, native to mild or tropical climates, can be left in the ground all year in regions with mild-winter temperatures; while elsewhere these frost-tender bulbs are used for summer bloom, and then dug and stored in a warm place over winter. Wherever you live, there are bulbs that will do unusually well for you. You can obtain them locally at planting time, or order them by mail from seedsmen, nurserymen and bulb specialists.

Whether your bulbs perform well after their first year depends upon the care you give them while they are flowering and growing. To understand why, you must know about their cycle of growth. They bloom; their foliage produces food which is stored in the bulb; then they rest, dormant. In this cycle the most important phase, and the one during which you can do the most to help, is the one having to do with the growing of leaves. The more foliage a plant has, the more food is manufactured and stored in the bulb for next year's bloom. So, the time to feed bulbs, and to supply water, is while foliage is growing. Never cut off leaves until they have withered, or at least begun to turn yellow or brown.

All bulbs like soil that is deeply prepared (8 to 12 in.), moisture-retentive yet rapid-draining. This type of soil usually contains considerable organic material. If your soil is very heavy (clay) or very sandy, you can improve it by adding such organic amendments as moist peat moss, ground bark, sawdust, etc. Any of these should make up about ⅓ of the soil, by volume. You can spread it over the top of the ground 3 or 4 in. deep, and then spade it in. A "complete" commercial fertilizer should be applied at the same time, in amounts specified by the manufacturer, for the soil amendments mentioned above contain no nutrients.

🍁 Spring-Bloomers Are Planted in Autumn

These are the bulbs that glorify gardens early in the year. You plant them in the fall, when they are dormant but just ready to start root growth in cool, moist soil. Roots will develop rapidly. By late winter, leafy shoots will be poking through the soil, and flower buds will be waiting to open. Blooms will be glorious the first year. Thus, even if you are just beginning your garden, you can have a colorful show at once.

Here are some tips to help you spend your bulb money to best advantage, and plant the bulbs to get the best results. For earliest possible flowers, get some of the little early-blooming bulbs such as snowdrop, crocus, scilla and glory-of-the-snow. Plant them on the south side of your house, a south slope, or some other spot that is protected and warmed by the sun. Then the bulbs will be awakened early from their winter nap. Do not plant them on the north side of the house or on a north slope, where all growth is delayed.

You will get the showiest results if you plant bulbs in groups rather than stringing them out single-file. Use as many as possible of one color, and preferably all of one variety. A dozen 'Red Emperor' tulips will be a dazzling sight, while the same number of tulips in mixed colors of red, pink, white and yellow will give a motley and undistinguished effect.

Do not put bulbs here and there all over your yard but concentrate them in important places such as beside your door, beneath a small tree, in front of an evergreen shrub, or against a rock. Create pictures with them. Plan your color scheme before buying the bulbs, choosing colors that will look best with your house, or the setting in which you are going to use them.

Buy your bulbs as early in the fall as possible, while selection is good and quality high. If you have them on hand, you can take the first opportunity to plant the ones which need a long growing season, such as daffodils, grape-hyacinth, crocus, scilla and the other little bulbs.

Prepare the ground well. To remind yourself of the type of soil bulbs like best, and how to improve yours, reread the first paragraphs in this chapter. Make sure the soil is moist, though not soggy, at the time the bulbs are planted.

If you have been having drought, water the ground several days in advance of planting. Then dig down and make sure that the water has penetrated to a depth that will be below the bulbs, for without moisture the bulbs will not put out roots and grow. One way to moisten the soil deeply where clumps of bulbs are to be planted among other flowers or shrubs, is to dig the hole for the bulbs, then fill it with water and let the water seep away. Do not set the bulbs in the hole while it is muddy. Remember, it is the moisture beneath the bulbs, where the roots will be, that is important.

The best location for early-blooming bulbs has sunshine in the spring. It can be a spot beneath deciduous trees—those that are leafless in winter—since these trees will not leaf out and produce heavy shade until after the bulbs have grown their leaves and thus have stored away plenty of food for next year's bloom. For data on how to grow bulbs in pots for bloom indoors in winter, see the chapter on indoor gardening.

AMARYLLIS *(Hippeastrum).* Gorgeous large trumpet-shaped flowers, like lilies, in red, orange, pink, white, or striped, are borne on stalks 12 to 24 in. high, rising from big bulbs. Leaves are strap-shaped and usually evergreen. There are two main types. The bulbs of the Dutch hybrids, which have huge, broad-petaled flowers, may cost several dollars apiece. They are the aristocrats. The American hybrids are a little smaller and usually more trumpet-shaped.

In cold winter climates, amaryllis are usually grown as winter-flowering pot plants. They will take a good deal of care and attention throughout the year, but no plant is more rewarding if properly treated. For instructions on how to handle them, see the chapter on indoor plants.

In Zones 8b through 10 they can be grown as permanent outdoor garden plants. American hybrids are more reliable outdoors. Dutch hybrids vary in hardiness; some that perform well outdoors in Louisiana if given good drainage are: 'Bouquet,' 'Ludwig's Scarlet,' 'Roslyn' and 'Seventeen.' The time to plant is autumn. Prepare the ground deeply, working in compost or similar humus, and complete plant food. The depth to plant the bulb depends upon winter temperatures. Where freezing seldom occurs, Zones 9 and 10, place bulbs with necks above ground. Where the surface of the ground is apt to freeze, cover the bulb 2 in. deep and protect each winter with a mulch. Bulbs may be allowed to multiply in place for several years, or be dug, divided and replanted each fall.

Flowers are produced most profusely when amaryllis are planted in the sun, but they also thrive in part shade. They like a fertile, well-drained soil. Feed once a month all through summer, and water well to encourage leaves to grow.

ANEMONE *(Anemone).* The tuberous-rooted plants come in two quite different types. There are several cold-hardy ones, small and dainty, that are at home in northern woodsy gardens or rockeries. They have bright blue, pink or white flowers on stems 6 to 8 in. high. Examples are *Anemone apennina, A. blanda* and *A. nemorosa.* They do not do well in warm climates.

Better known, because of their large and flamboyantly brilliant flowers, are poppy anemone *(Anemone coronaria),* and scarlet anemone *(A. fulgens).* They are the ones seen in florists' shops as cut flowers during winter and spring, and in early spring gardens in mild climates, Zones 8, 9 and 10. They grow 6 to 18 in. high, with single or semidouble flowers 1½ to 3 in. across in vivid red, purple, blue or white. In cold-winter climates where these plants are not hardy, the tubers are sometimes planted in the outdoor garden in early spring. Whether they give good bloom depends upon how speedily summer and hot weather arrive.

All anemones like soil that is well-drained, deeply dug, and contains considerable organic material. A mixture of equal parts of garden soil, coarse sand, and moist peat moss is good.

Plant the small cold-climate anemones in autumn at the time you plant other small bulbs. Set them 1 in. deep, 6 to 8 in. apart, rounded side down. If the conditions in your garden suit them, they will live year after year and increase.

Large poppy-type anemones should be planted in November. Choose a location in full sun. Cover the tubers with 2 in. of soil (except where drainage is a problem, when they should be barely covered). Formerly it was recommended to soak them always before planting. In warm, dry climates, soaking for 1 hour may help them start growth. In humid climates this is not recommended or needed; they will swell and start by themselves. Too much moisture before growth starts can lead to rotting.

In climates ideal for their growth, large-flowered anemones live long, and multiply so fast that they must be lifted and divided frequently. However, in most areas they rarely do well a second year, and are usually treated as annuals.

POPPY TYPE ANEMONE

RANUNCULUS

BLUEBELL, ENGLISH and SPANISH, see SCILLA

CRINUM. These flourish in Zones 8, 9 and 10, and are favorites of the South, where they grow easily. The bulbs are enormous and the flowers are trumpet-shaped, fragrant, in white, pink or striped (called milk-and-wine-lilies). They are borne in clusters on stems that may be as tall as 4 ft. The leaves are strap-shaped, usually evergreen. The main blooming period is spring and summer, but they may bloom at other times. There are many types, some hardier than others. Their names are confused, so consult local dealers. Plant in fall or winter, when the plants are not in active growth. After being disturbed, they may not bloom for one or more years. Choose a place in part shade, where the bulbs can have rich, humusy soil. The depth for planting varies with your locality and the kind of crinum so, again, get local advice. Feed each spring. Water during summer. In cold areas, mulch deeply for winter. The bulbs should not be eaten.

CROCUS. In Zones 4 to 9, inclusive, these are among the earliest spring flowers, especially if planted on the south side of a house in a protected place. (There are also fall-blooming species of crocus.) The stemless blooms are white, yellow, blue, purple or striped, 2 to 5 in. high, among grasslike leaves. The corms should be planted as early as you can get them, 3 to 4 in. deep and 3 in. apart. They can be used beneath groundcovers such as vinca or ivy. It is also possible to naturalize them in grass, but if you do this remember that the grass must not be cut until after crocus foliage has ripened. Rodents consider crocus corms very good to eat, so if you are troubled that way, plant them in improvised baskets made of ¼-in. hardware cloth (wire).

CYCLAMEN, FLORISTS (*C. persicum*). This blooms in winter and early spring in mild climates, Zones 9b and 10. Plant it preferably during the dormant period, June to August, or buy sprouted bulbs from a nursery. Grow them in a shady place having rich, well-drained acid soil containing ample humus. The tuber should be placed with its upper half above the soil. For cyclamen care as a house plant, see the chapter on indoor gardening.

CYCLAMEN, HARDY KINDS. These are miniature plants, only a few inches high, that like the same conditions mentioned above for florists cyclamen. They should be planted with ½ in. of soil over their corms, spaced 6 to 12 in. apart. *C. coum,* Zones 7b to 9, inclusive, has crimson or white flowers in early spring. *C. europaeum,* Zones 6 to 9, inclusive, is crimson-flowered and blooms in autumn, as does pink- or white-flowered *C. neapolitanum,* Zones 7b to 9, inclusive.

DAFFODIL or NARCISSUS. These names are interchangeable. Both refer to the entire group of flowers that you may have heard called daffodil, jonquil or narcissus. Some have long trumpets, while others are small-cupped. Most are yellow, but there are also exquisite whites, and some near-pinks. Sometimes the blooms are in clusters, though usually they are carried one to a stem. A few varieties are double. The name jonquil refers to one special kind of daffodil with slender tubular leaves, and small, intensely fragrant flowers. Bulbs of daffodils are poisonous if eaten.

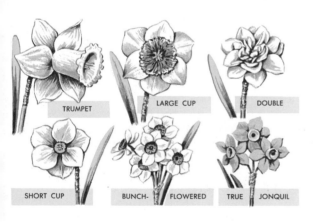

TRUMPET

LARGE CUP

DOUBLE

SHORT CUP

BUNCH- FLOWERED

TRUE JONQUIL

In Zones 4 through 8, if you can have only one kind of spring-flowering bulb in your garden, the daffodil should be your choice. They are early-flowering, beautiful, showy, long-lived and dependable. Bulbs increase rapidly and become large clumps that give more and more bloom each year. They are easy to grow.

However, it is well to lift the clumps every few years and separate them. Replant single specimens of the best bulbs, burn all culls, diseased or injured ones, and, if you want to take the trouble, plant the small immature bulbs in a nursery reserved for this purpose, for later use.

Plant as early as you can get the bulbs, September if possible. This is because daffodils begin to make their roots early. The soil must be moist. Otherwise the roots will not grow. If they do not become established before winter arrives, the bulbs may either die or send up strange, stunted shoots with blasted (dead) buds in spring. So, if your ground is dry, water before you plant.

Most of the varieties of daffodils that do well in the North, do poorly in warm-winter climates, especially the Deep South. In Zone 9, 'King Alfred' is the best bet in large-trumpet kinds. Some of the small-flowered jonquil and triandrus hybrids such as 'Silver Chimes,' 'Trevithian' and 'Stoke' will remain permanently in the garden. In Zones 9 and 10, some lovely bunch-flowered or tazetta types that are not hardy in cold areas will thrive. These include paper-white, 'Soleil d'Or' and Chinese sacred-lily (familiar in cold climates as the bulbs that are planted in pebbles for indoor bloom). They are planted from late September through October.

Daffodils grow best in sun, but thrive in the shade of deciduous trees that do not leaf out until after the bulbs' foliage has ripened.

You can use daffodils in clumps among shrubs, beneath groundcovers, naturalized in woodlands or grass, or as accents by your door or in the garden. They are also handsome and spectacular as borders that make ribbons of color in the springtime. However, if used this way, you must remember that their foliage will be unsightly for quite a while after the flowering period. To hide those ripening leaves, it is smart to place the row of daffodils behind a row of some plant that will come up and bloom later, serving as a screen. An excellent pairing is daffodils and early day-lilies. The latter begin to grow as daffodils quit. They can be interplanted as clumps or as rows.

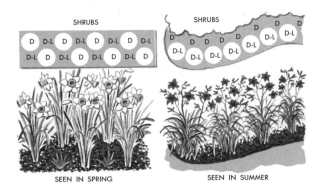

SHRUBS

SHRUBS

SEEN IN SPRING

SEEN IN SUMMER

There are hundreds of varieties of daffodils from which you can choose. Popular, time-tested ones cost less than rare new plants, so they are the ones to use in quantity. However, it is fun to try a few novelties each year.

Prices of any variety will vary, depending upon the size of the bulbs and the number of bloom stalks that they will produce. Single-nosed bulbs put up one flower stem; double-nosed, two.

Planting methods for clumps and rows are basically the same as for tulips (described in this chapter) except for depth. The base of daffodil bulbs should be 6 to 8 in. below the surface. It is wise to space them at least 8 in. apart. To naturalize daffodils in woods or grass, they should look as though growing wild, and be in all-alike "drifts" or "colonies." You can arrange the bulbs on top of the ground, and then dig individual holes. Or you can dig broad-bottomed trenches in informal shapes for planting a couple of dozen bulbs at one time.

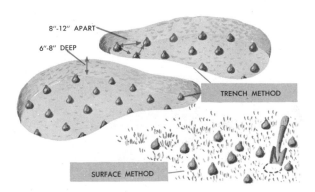

8"-12" APART

6"-8" DEEP

TRENCH METHOD

SURFACE METHOD

The general care of daffodils is simple. They must have ample water in autumn while roots are growing, and also in spring while flowers are developing and foliage growing. A feeding of complete plant food can be applied early in spring and watered in, but too much fertilizer is not good for bulbs. After flowers wither, pick them off at once so seed heads will not mature and take energy from the bulbs.

Dividing and transplanting clumps should take place when bulbs become so crowded that they do not bloom well. The ideal time to do this is after foliage has matured, turned yellow and died. But this is seldom the time you are thinking about doing it! I favor digging the clumps at the end of the blooming season while you are in the mood, can see the foliage, and also know where you want to plant the bulbs. Prepare the new location first. Then dig and pull the clumps apart, separating every bulb while retaining its foliage and roots. Plant these bulbs at least 8 in. apart. Water them. Do not worry if foliage lops on the ground and dies quickly; these bulbs would not have bloomed next year anyhow. But after a year or two of producing nothing but foliage they will become splendid blooming-size plants.

GLORY-OF-THE-SNOW (*Chionodoxa*). These clusters of small, brilliant blue, up-facing blooms with white centers on 5-in. stems do well in Zones 4 to 9, inclusive. They blossom very early and are lovely beneath bushes of forsythia or flowering almond. Plant these bulbs in quantity 3 in. deep and 3 in. apart in sun or part shade.

GRAPE-HYACINTH (*Muscari*). Adapted to zones 3 to 9, inclusive, these flowers resemble small upside-down bunches of grapes in blue or white. The plants stand 5 in. high. Their leaves are slender and grasslike, and come up in the fall soon after the bulbs are planted. They remain evergreen. Plant these bulbs 3 in. deep, 5 in. apart. They multiply rapidly. Blue grape-hyacinths are beautiful planted with yellow daffodils, or beneath pink bleeding-heart or a redbud tree. Plant them as early as possible.

HYACINTH, DUTCH or COMMON GARDEN

(*Hyacinthus orientalis* hybrids). These thrive in Zones 4b to 8, inclusive, and display spikes of densely clustered bell-shaped flowers in white, blue, purple and pink, 8 to 12 in. high. They bloom early and are fragrant, so should be placed near your door or a walk. Set the bulbs 6 to 8 in. apart, tops covered with 4 in. of soil. Since the blossoms are rather formal in shape, they are attractive in clumps to accent doorway plantings, or used in containers. They do not look well naturalized. Bulbs can be left in the ground or dug up after foliage has matured, and stored through summer. Bulbs should not be eaten.

IRIS, BULBOUS. The most popular and frequently grown examples of this type are listed here. Other irises may be found in the chapter on perennials.

English, Spanish and Dutch (hybrid) iris, for Zones 8, 9 and 10, are similar spring-blooming plants with orchidlike blooms in white, violet, yellow and blue on stems 1½ to 2 ft. high. They grow from true bulbs, and are the iris sold as cut flowers in florists' shops in winter and spring. English iris (*Iris xiphioides*) likes moist, acid soil, and cool temperatures. It is not suited to heat and drought. Spanish iris (*I. xiphium*) and Dutch iris require light soil, good drainage, full sun, and shelter from wind. They bloom in March and April in mild climates, May and June elsewhere. All should be planted 4 in. deep, spaced 4 in. apart. Mulch them over winter in climates where freezing occurs. For best results, dig up after foliage ripens, dry, and store the bulbs in a cool, dry place until time to plant in fall, though they may be left in the ground several years.

Iris reticulata, in Zones 5b to 8, inclusive, is a miniature, 6 to 8 in. high with lavender flowers marked with gold, and a fragrance like violets. It blooms in late winter in mild climates, March or April elsewhere, and is excellent in rock gardens. Plant this in sun in well-drained soil.

NARCISSUS, see DAFFODIL

RANUNCULUS (*R. asiaticus*). Useful in Zones 8, 9 and 10, these brilliant spring flowers are 1½ to 4 in. across in yellow, orange, red, pink, white, growing on stems 1½ to 2 ft. high. They are grown primarily in mild climates where they are planted in autumn. The tubers are hard and small, with fingerlike "claws" which should point downward when planted. Ranunculus resembles and is handled like poppy anemone. (See anemone for instructions.)

SCILLA. This is a large group of hardy and tender bulbs, including 3 favorites for spring gardens.

Siberian Squill (*Scilla sibirica*), in Zones 5 to 8, inclusive, is a tiny early bulb flower which makes a 5-in.-high carpet of brilliant blue nodding bells which in some areas appear when forsythia bushes and crocus are blooming. Plant these bulbs 3 in. deep, 3 in. apart. They self-sow and spread with pleasant rapidity. White and pink varieties are sometimes available. Plant in sun or part shade.

English Bluebell (*Scilla nonscripta*), in Zones 5 to 10, inclusive, is similar to Spanish bluebell, and grown like it.

Spanish Bluebell or Wood-Hyacinth (*Scilla hispanica*), in Zones 5 to 9, inclusive, resembles hyacinth, with loosely arranged florets on stems 12 to 18 in. high. It blooms relatively late in spring, at the time of darwin tulips and azaleas. It can be used in cultivated beds, or naturalized in part shade as in a woodland. The blooms may be pink, white or blue. Plant bulbs with their base 5 in. deep, 9 in. apart.

SQUILL, see SCILLA

SNOWDROP (*Galanthus*). Grown in Zones 5 to 9, inclusive, this is one of the earliest bulbs to bloom. It has small nodding bell-shaped white flowers tipped with green on 4-in. stems in late winter. These bulbs like moisture, so do well planted near the drip of an outdoor water faucet, or a downspout. They are not good in the South. Plant them early, 4 in. deep, 3 in. apart.

TULIPS. These are the most colorful spring-flowering bulbs. You can use them massed in beds, or in small groups to accent some important feature of your garden.

If you live in a climate with freezing weather, they will be no trick to grow, for normal winter temperatures give them the chilling they need. After they flower, they can be left in the ground to bloom again year after year, or they may be dug after the foliage ripens, stored dry for summer at 60 to 70°, and replanted in the autumn. In most home gardens, the bulbs are left in place, and annuals are planted among them to hide the ripening foliage and give summer bloom.

In warm-winter, hot-summer climates, tulips can be grown but they must be handled as annuals; the bulbs should be refrigerated for about 6 weeks at 40°, and then kept cool until planted after December 1. Garden stores handle bulbs that have been properly chilled. After bloom, the bulbs are dug up and discarded.

The best size of bulb to buy is at least 5 in. *around*. These are called "first" or "top" sizes. Any bulbs less than 3 in. around may not bloom the first season; sometimes these small ones are offered at prices that seem to be great bargains, but if you are after certain bloom, and large flowers, you will be disappointed in your purchase.

The time to plant can be any time after the ground becomes cool in autumn, and before it freezes. Usually this is October or November in the North; December in the South.

There are several methods of planting. An easy way to set out groups of bulbs that are to bloom as a clump, is to open a hole large enough to accommodate the entire number. Level the bottom of the hole and loosen the soil there so that roots can penetrate easily and good drainage is assured. Then arrange the bulbs, properly spaced, in the bottom of the hole. When tulips are to be planted in a large bed, you should spade the soil of the entire area to a depth of at least 10 in. Then, if the tulips are to be in rows, you can open deep furrows or trenches in which to place the bulbs. Or, after preparing the ground and smoothing the surface, space the bulbs on top of the ground as you wish, and then dig a separate hole for each one.

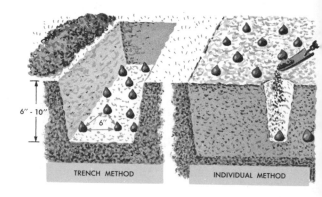

TRENCH METHOD   INDIVIDUAL METHOD

Place the pointed ends of the bulbs up. Space them about 6 in. apart. The base of the bulbs of standard kinds of tulips should be 6 to 10 in. below soil level. If your tulips are to be left in the ground permanently, rather than dug and replanted each fall, the deeper placement has advantages. At that depth, the bulbs remain blooming size for more years without multiplying into many smaller, nonblooming-size bulbs. Also the soil is cooler at the greater depth, protecting the developing flower buds from heat which could cause injury. Bulbs of species or botanical tulips are normally small, and should not be planted more than 6 in. deep.

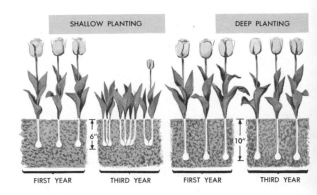

SHALLOW PLANTING   DEEP PLANTING

FIRST YEAR   THIRD YEAR   FIRST YEAR   THIRD YEAR

Crocus

Daffodil

Grape-Hyacinth

Hyacinth

Ranunculus

Siberian Squill

FAVORITE SPRING-BLOOMING BULBS

Snowdrop

Spanish Bluebell

Tulip

FAVORITE SPRING-BLOOMING BULBS

If you have many rodents around, such as mice or chipmunks, be warned that they love to eat tulip bulbs! They will find them whether they are in the ground or stored somewhere temporarily. For safety, you can plant the bulbs in ¼-in. wire mesh "baskets" that you improvise from hardware cloth; roots and moisture will be able to penetrate.

Spring care of tulips is important. They should be fed when they first come up in spring, because that is when leaves will be growing and storing nourishment for next year's flower bud. Use a complete plant food. If the season is dry, be sure to supply water as long as leaves continue to grow and are green. When flowers fade, snap off the developing seed pods that form where the flowers were.

If you need to move the bulbs, or to dig them up for summer storage, there are two possibilities. You can dig as soon as they have finished flowering, and transplant them with leaves and roots intact to a trench where they can live temporarily while they complete the ripening of their foliage. Or you can wait until after the leaves die. The latter method is the most difficult because it is not easy to locate the bulbs when the foliage has gone.

If some of your tulips come up with large leaves and no blooms the second year, it indicates that the large bulbs that you planted have multiplied or split into several small ones that are too small and crowded to bloom. They can be dug up, separated, and moved to a row where they can be cultivated. Eventually they will become big enough to flower. Basically this is the procedure outlined above for separating daffodils and growing baby bulbs for planting the next year. If tulips have good foliage, but flower buds are missing, it may mean that the bulbs were subjected to temperatures over 78° during their summer dormancy. This can happen whether bulbs are in the ground in the garden or in storage.

To have tulips in bloom over the longest possible period of time, plant some of each of the following types.

For extra-early color, treat yourself to some little species or botanical tulips. One of the earliest and greatest favorites is water-lily tulip (*T. kaufmanniana*). It grows only a few inches high, with wide-open flowers that are pale yellow on the inside and rosy-red on the outside. Another charmer is lady or candystick tulip (*T. clusiana*) with small pointed blooms, whose outer petals are marked with cherry-rose, on 12-in. stems. For an exceptionally long-lived darling, try *T. tarda*, sometimes called *T. dasystemon*. It has yellow and white wide-open flowers close to the ground and is delightful in a rockery, nestled against the trunk of a tree, or tucked into a spot near your door. It increases and stays with you. Get 'Red Emperor,' 'White Emperor' (also called 'Purissima') or 'Gold Emperor' (also known as 'Goldbeater') for bloom at daffodil time, several weeks before most tulips come out. A planting of any of these will stop traffic in front of your house!

Single-early and double-early tulips are classes with lovely large blooms on stems 12 to 15 in. high, which are somewhat shorter than those of later tulips. They come in white, pink, yellow, red and combinations.

Then comes the main season of bloom when the familiar tall darwins, lily-flowered, and cottage or May-flowering tulips fill everyone's gardens with beauty. There are marvelous varieties in any color your heart could wish. Parrot tulips, the shaggy ones, are "sports" of regular varieties.

Ending the parade are the double-late or peony-flowered tulips. There are many other tulips, but this will give you an idea of the basic groups and the time of their flowering.

WINTER ACONITE (*Eranthis hyemalis*). Useful in Zones 4 to 9, inclusive, these are yellow buttercup-like blooms 1½ in. across on stems 3 to 8 in. high above a ferny collar of leaves. Plant them as early as possible in autumn, 3 in. deep, 4 in. apart. They like moisture, part shade. The plants are poisonous if eaten.

WOOD-HYACINTH, see SCILLA

✿ Summer-flowering Bulbs Have Varying Schedules

These are the bulbs that bring beauty to your garden during hot weather. Many of them are treated in much the same manner as summer bedding plants. They are set out anew each spring, and, because they are tender to cold, they are dug up and stored in a frost-free place through winter—except in very mild climates. Others can stand freezing temperatures and are left in the ground permanently to serve as perennials. However, all are not hardy in the very coldest climates, so be sure to check the zones recommended for their use. Most of the hardy bulbs are planted in autumn.

ACHIMENES. This frost-tender relative of the African violet has trumpet-shaped flowers 1 to 3 in. across in pink, red, lavender and white. The plants are slender-stemmed, 8 to 18 in. high. They are natives of the tropics and like the same conditions of warmth, soil, moisture and light that African violets do. Use them in pots or hanging baskets on shady patios, or plant directly in the ground. They grow from small tubers. (Each scale, if detached, will serve as a root cutting and can develop into a plant!)

Purchase tubers in dormant condition in late winter or early spring. Plant them horizontally ½ in. deep in porous soil, preferably acid. Water only lightly until growth shows above ground. Then move them to a bright window, and later (when weather is warm), outdoors. Tubers are priced at about 25¢ to 35¢ each; they multiply fast naturally, and by cuttings of stems or leaves. To store over winter, let the tubers remain in their pots, dry, in a cool but frost-free place with temperature 45 to 50°. Start watering slightly in late winter.

TUBER

PLANT HORIZONTALLY

AGAPANTHUS, AFRICAN-LILY or LILY-OF-THE-NILE. This one thrives in Zones 9 and 10. Its handsome 2-in. blue or white tubular flowers are carried in large clusters on tall stems above strap-shaped leaves during summer and fall. The plants are tuberous-rooted and may be dwarfs 1 ft. high, or as tall as 5 ft. They like sun but need part shade in hottest climates. They are not fussy about soil. Feed and water them well during the growing season. They may die to the ground winters in Zone 9, where they should be mulched through the coldest months. In cold-winter climates grow agapanthus in containers outdoors for summer bloom, and let them rest over the winter indoors in a frost-free place.

AUTUMN-CROCUS *(Colchicum autumnale)*. Growing in Zones 4 to 8, inclusive, these plants have crocus-like flowers that appear unexpectedly, without leaves, in late summer. The large blooms, 4 in. across, may be white or lavender, depending upon the variety. Foliage, which is large and broad, 12 in. high, develops in spring and then dies. Because it is so big, you must bear its size in mind when deciding where to put the bulbs. Autumn-crocus will grow in sun or part shade, and thrives when naturalized in a woodland or shady garden. Do not eat it.

Plant the corms in late summer, with tips 3 to 4 in. below the surface. These corms will also bloom unplanted, without soil or water! You can lay them bare on a table, and they will go ahead and flower! It is fun to develop them this way in the house, to astonish family and friends, and then later plant them out-of-doors.

Autumn-Crocus

Caladium

Calla

Dahlia

Gladiolus

**FAVORITE
SUMMER-BLOOMING BULBS**

Madonna Lily

Tuberous Begonia

Ismene

Magic-Lily

FAVORITE SUMMER-BLOOMING BULBS

BEGONIA, HARDY (*B. evansiana*). This plant does well in Zones 6 to 10, inclusive. It has handsome leaves that are green above and red below, and produces showy spikes of flesh-pink flowers on red stems 1 to 2 ft. high. Plant the bulblike tubers during the spring, in humusy soil in shade. Leave them in the ground permanently except in cold climates where tubers are dug in the fall and replanted in spring.

BEGONIA, TUBEROUS (*B. tuberhybrida*). These elegant, colorful summer flowers are fine for planting in semishade, beneath high-branching trees, on the north or east side of a house, or under lath-houses. They come with double or single flowers, large blooms or small, plants of upright habit or trailing. You can grow them in pots or in the ground, and start them either from dormant tubers or young potted plants. They grow best where summer temperatures are relatively cool and the air moist. Protection from wind is important, since the plants are top-heavy and brittle-stemmed. Begonias need good air circulation, so some support, such as slender stakes, is indicated.

Tuberous begonias fail in the Deep South; they do not like the heat.

It is easy to start tubers, and you will be proud to raise your own plants. The time to begin in mild-winter climates is January or February; in the East and Midwest, late March and April. Use a shallow box. Put about 3 in. of slightly moist peat moss, sphagnum or vermiculite into it. Gently push the tubers down into this so tops are barely showing or slightly covered. (Tops are the hollowed-in side, usually with pink buds.) Put them in a warm place (65 to 75°), well lighted but out of sun. Keep them moist but not wet. When the plants have two leaves, or are 5 in. tall, they can be transplanted to individual pots, or, if weather is warm enough, outdoors into the garden. In Zone 10, set them outside in March or early April. Elsewhere wait until all danger of frost is past. Feed them when buds start to form. A house plant fertilizer will be excellent.

Proper soil in both pots or garden is vital! It should be loose, humusy, rich and rapid-draining, like the soil you use for African violets;

preferably at least ½ humus, such as moistened peat moss, sphagnum moss or compost. To increase speed of drainage, build outdoor beds a little higher than surrounding ground.

In planting, the upper roots should be 1 in. below the soil level. Turn your plants in the direction that the leaves are pointing; blossoms will face the same way. Through summer, keep the soil constantly moist but not soggy. Feed a complete fertilizer about once a month.

If flowers drop before opening well, it is probably because of overwatering, too much fertilizer, or hot weather.

To hold tubers over winter, bring potted plants indoors before hard frosts. There they can be allowed to complete blooming; then be gradually dried off and either left in their pots or removed. Dig up plants that are in the ground, with tops and roots intact and soil clinging to tubers. Dry them for about 2 weeks; then cut the tops back to 4 in. and allow tubers to continue to dry for several more weeks until stems pull off easily. Then clean off debris. Store the thoroughly dry tubers in dry peat moss or vermiculite, at 45 to 60°. They can be loose in a box.

TUBER

AT 2 LEAVES TRANSPLANT

START IN MOIST PEAT MOSS OR VERMICULITE

BLOOMS FACE SAME WAY AS THE LEAVES

CALADIUM. These glamorous summertime foliage plants have arrow-shaped leaves 6 in. to 2 ft. long, variously patterned with white, pink or red and occasionally producing small callalike white flowers. They grow from bulblike tubers, are tender to frost and like heat and warmth, so are not set outdoors in spring until weather and soil are warm.

Buy the tubers in late winter or early spring when they are in dry, dormant condition. The largest-sized ones will produce the most leaves and thus the most show, so are worth the slightly higher price. Do not be tempted to buy one each of every variety! Your plantings will be much more handsome if you use only one color or perhaps a group predominantly white to be planted against a group of pink.

In the North it is smart to give tubers a head start on growing by potting them indoors 1½ in. deep in slightly moist sphagnum moss or vermiculite. Roots develop in the tuber's top. It is difficult to know which side that is, unless you can find the scar left by an old stem; it is usually the knobby side. Fortunately caladiums will grow even if planted upside down. Keep them in temperature near 75 to 80°. Begin feeding when top growth emerges and keep it up every 3 weeks all summer. In mild climates an indoor start is not necessary. Wait to plant outside until soil is warm and daytime temperatures average 70° (about May 1 to 15 in mild climates; June 15 in the North). Otherwise tubers will rot.

Caladiums can be used in pots on a terrace or sunk in the ground, or can be planted directly in the garden, spaced 8 to 12 in. apart in a place appropriate for such a display of highly decorative leaves. They like moist, rich, well-aerated, quick-draining soil, and a location in semishade or where they can get early morning sun. Since they like the same conditions as azaleas, they are often grown in beds with them.

In autumn, before frost or when leaves begin to look tired, dig them up carefully (except in Zone 10, where they can be left in the ground all year). Without removing the leaves, put them in a cool place out of the sun to dry for about 3 weeks. Then remove roots and leaves, and store, loose, in dry peat moss or vermiculite, in a warm, dry place, 50 to 60°.

To propagate, large tubers can be cut into pieces, each with a bud. Let the sections dry in the air; then plant them similarly to seeds, in a box or pot of barely damp sphagnum or other sterile rooting medium. This should be done as the tubers start growth in spring.

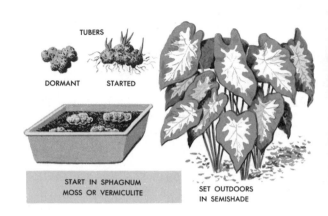

TUBERS

DORMANT   STARTED

START IN SPHAGNUM MOSS OR VERMICULITE

SET OUTDOORS IN SEMISHADE

CALLA. (*Zantedeschia*). In Zones 9 and 10 these lovely plants with lilylike white, yellow or pink flowers and arrow-shaped leaves are permanent outdoor garden plants. Though the tops may be injured at temperatures of 25° or lower, the plants will recover and produce flowers. They will grow in shade, on the north side of a house, or where they have morning sun. In cool coastal areas they can take full sun. They are handsome grown in containers and are excellent for cut flowers. The soil should be moist, well-drained, containing a large amount of humus. Plant in spring or fall. Place the rhizome horizontally, 3 in. deep in warmest climates or 6 in. where there may be frost, and 1 to 2 ft. apart. Feed plants every month of growth. They may become dormant in hot, dry weather.

Zantedeschia aethiopica is the common calla, with white flowers growing 3 ft. high. It blooms almost continuously in mild climates. The yellow or golden calla is Z. *elliottiana*. The pink or red calla is Z. *rehmanni*. The pink and yellow ones tolerate drier conditions than the white ones.

Callas may be grown in the North as winter-blooming house plants (by potting in the autumn), as exotic additions to a shady garden for summer, grown in the ground or in containers. For outdoor use start the rhizomes indoors in March or April, or plant directly outdoors after weather and soil become warm. Give them moist, humusy soil; feed and water well. After frost, dig and store them like tuberous begonias.

CYCLAMEN. The hardy, fall-blooming miniature kinds are grown like the similar winter or spring-blooming sorts. (See previous reference in this chapter.)

DAHLIA. These are superb, easy-to-grow flowers for late-summer garden color and picking. They are frost-tender, and in most parts of the country are started anew each spring. You can start them either by sowing seed (they are as easy to grow this way as zinnias) or by planting their tuberous roots. In either case, plants mature and produce a full crop of bloom the first season. Seed is the method used for dwarf bedding varieties, such as Unwin's Hybrids; choice named varieties are purchased as tubers since seedlings do not "come true" to their parents. For instructions on how to raise them from seed, see the alphabetical list in the chapter on annuals.

You can have blooms in almost any color you wish, except blue, and in any size from button-like miniatures to enormous specimens the size of dinner plates. Flowers may be single or double, neat pompon form or shaggily exotic. Plants grow in many sizes and you should purchase varieties according to the use you want to make of them. Some are dwarfs about 1½ ft. high, ideal for beds, window boxes and low flowering hedges. Taller sorts are better in background plantings, or grown in rows for hobby flowers and for picking.

Dahlias excel in climates where summers are cool or where the nights at least are cool. In such regions they should have full sun. Where summers are hot, buds may be damaged during the hottest weather, but the plants will come into their prime as temperatures grow cooler in late summer, and flowers will be marvelous through autumn until frost. In the hottest regions, dahlias will appreciate part shade.

They like a soil prepared at least 1 ft. deep, to which organic material such as compost, leaf mold or moist peat moss has been added. They must have good drainage.

To start them from tubers, do not put them outdoors until all danger of frost is past—the time that tender annuals and bedding plants are set out. There is no need to hurry, for dahlias do not grow well until the weather is warm. Space dwarfs 1 to 1½ ft. apart; big ones 3 to 4 ft. Plant tubers 6 in. deep on a cushion of well-pulverized soil or sand with the eye (growth bud) on the top side. For tall-growing varieties, drive a stout stake for each at planting time, so they will not be disturbed or injured by stakes being driven after sprouting. The tuber then should have its eye toward the stake, 3 or 4 in. from it. Water following planting. The ground may be leveled then, or the hole filled gradually as the sprout comes through.

To produce bushy plants, pinch back tops when plants are 12 to 18 in. high, or when they have at least 3 sets of leaves.

When plants begin to grow rapidly, they need lots of water, and monthly feeding with any complete plant food used according to manufacturer's instructions. Mulching the ground during summer helps keep the soil cool and moist. Grass clippings work well.

For giant blooms, you must start with a variety known to produce flowers at least 8 in. across. Then, as the plant grows, permit only 4 stalks to develop. Remove all flower buds except those on the tips of those branches, and 2 near the bottom of the stalks to bloom later.

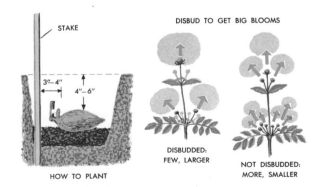

STAKE

3"–4" 4"–6"

HOW TO PLANT

DISBUD TO GET BIG BLOOMS

DISBUDDED: FEW, LARGER

NOT DISBUDDED: MORE, SMALLER

To keep tubers over winter in cold climates, they must be dug up and stored in a frost-free place. Dig them as soon as tops are killed by frost, handling the clumps carefully to avoid breaking necks of tubers, since it is on these necks that the vital growth buds are located. Keep clumps intact and remove soil by washing. Let them dry in a shady place for a week or more. They must be dry and cool before storing. Store in vermiculite, dry sand, dry sphagnum moss, or in a sealed polyethylene bag, at 35°. (If moisture collects in the polyethylene bag, open or slit it because moisture may cause rot.)

In spring, to replant, cut the clumps apart as the growth begins to sprout. Be sure that a piece of last year's stem with one eye remains on each tuber. Tubers without eyes will not grow and should be discarded. Each tuber, large or small, should produce a good new dahlia plant.

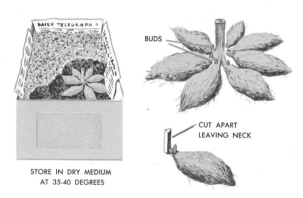

STORE IN DRY MEDIUM AT 35-40 DEGREES

BUDS

CUT APART LEAVING NECK

GLADIOLUS. To begin with, it is comforting to know that this name is both singular and plural, so you can use it to refer to one or many. Gladiolus are one of the easiest flowers to grow, quick and dependable everywhere. You can have blooms to enjoy, pick and share within 65 to 100 days after you plant. You can choose varieties that are big and tall, or you can have the new miniature or Tiny Tots that are the ideal size for bouquets for the dining table. All come in such a wide array of colors (everything but true blue) that you can have exactly the colors you love most, or that are most usable to combine with your home's décor.

The corms ("bulbs") can be planted outdoors any time after freezing weather is past and the ground workable. If you want blooms to continue for months, you can make a series of successive plantings; start some corms every 2 weeks through the period that allows enough time for flowers to develop before cold or hot weather, depending upon your climate.

In Zone 10, gladiolus may be grown all year, though in southern Florida they are rarely grown during midsummer heat. In mild-winter climates, the main plantings are made during late autumn or midwinter, in order to have bloom early in spring before hot weather.

Corms are sold by size. Blooming sizes are 1 in. or more in diameter (not circumference). Usually the larger they are, the bigger the resulting flower stalk will be. Those with high centers and a generally plump shape are better than large, flat, thin ones. For most garden purposes, corms 1 to 1½ in. are best. Tiny cormels need 1 to 3 years more growing before they become blooming size. Jumbos will give exhibition size blooms.

Since gladiolus are usually grown primarily for picking, they are easiest to care for when planted in rows. However, they are attractive used in a border with other flowers, especially if grouped in clumps of all-alike varieties such as groups of white, pink or yellow repeated at intervals.

The better you prepare your soil before planting, the better your plants will respond. Gladiolus like full sun (except in hottest climates) and fast-draining soil. Dig the ground at least 8 in. deep, incorporating a complete fertilizer at the rate of 3 to 4 lb. per 100 sq. ft. Rows should be 1½ to 2½ ft. apart. Make trenches 4 in. deep in average to heavy garden soils; 6 in. deep in sandy soil, if you plant blooming size corms, 1 in. to 1½ in. Large corms should go deeper; tiny cormels only 1 in. deep. The bottom of the furrow can be narrow if you wish to plant only one row of corms in it. But for the best use of your space, you can put two rows of corms in the one trench by making the opening 4 in. wide at its bottom. Corms should be placed with pointed side up; scar side down. Space them 4 to 6 in. apart.

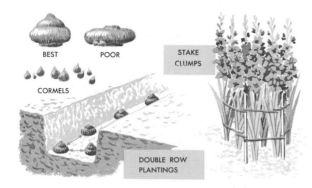

BEST POOR

CORMELS

STAKE CLUMPS

DOUBLE ROW PLANTINGS

For earliest blooms, choose early-flowering varieties, large-size corms, and set out early. As the plants come up, cultivate shallowly to keep weeds down. Water if needed. The worst pest, and one that is almost certain to be present, is thrips. Control measures must begin when foliage is 6 in. high. For instructions, see the chapter on plant diseases and pests.

When the plants are about 8 in. tall, hoe up the soil around their base, as props to keep them from falling over later from their own weight. To have superlative flowers, feed the plants when you can feel a bud between the leaves; use a complete fertilizer. Staking clumps keeps them in position. Rows can be staked by stretching strings along each side of the plants. For tricks about picking gladiolus, see the chapter on picking flowers.

In autumn, dig up and store corms. This is essential in cold climates. In mild areas, it is a matter of choice, though corms left in the ground are apt to rot, or if they endure, become too crowded to bloom well. Vigorous varieties tend to take over, while others decline and disappear so that you begin to think the varieties have changed.

Dig up when the foliage matures and turns

brown, or before hard freezing weather. Cut off the tops, rather than pull them off, just above the bulb. Dry in an airy, shaded place for 1 to 3 weeks. You will discover that your large corms are not the ones you planted, but new ones that have developed on top of the old ones, which are now withered and shrunken. Many small cormels, clustered at the base of the new corm, can be saved to plant and become big corms identical to the mother corm. (This is the main way that named varieties are propagated.) Remove old corms and roots. Dust the ones you are saving with DDT to control thrips during storage. Store loose in open trays or in paper sacks, open-mesh bags, etc., in a dark place at a temperature of 40 to 50°.

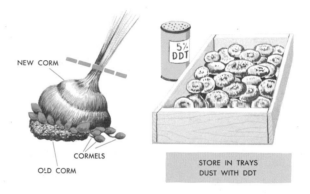

NEW CORM

5% DDT

CORMELS

OLD CORM

STORE IN TRAYS DUST WITH DDT

LILIES (*Lilium*). These are garden aristocrats, the royalty of summer-blooming flowers! Yet they can be grown just as easily as other perennials, if you select the ones suited to your climate and follow a few simple rules. You can choose varieties that are tall or short, with stately white trumpets, or with clusters of wide-open or recurving blooms in vivid red, sunny yellow, or apricot.

The new hybrid kinds are especially handsome and dependable. That is because breeders have intentionally crossed the hardiest and most beautiful lilies and then selected their most attractive offspring to propagate. All lilies grow from scaly bulbs. Each year a stalk arises carrying flowers at its tip. In autumn that stalk dies; the bulb remains in the ground permanently.

The majority of lilies grows best in Zones 4b through 8, where they get a chilling in winter.

In the Deep South, Easter lilies thrive and bloom gloriously. They can be left in the ground all year; however, where summer heat and wetness causes rotting of bulbs, it is wise to dig them up after flowering, and store them in dry peat or sand until planting time. Another lily that does well in mild climates is *Lilium formosanum* with white trumpets. Most others will bloom, but should be treated as annuals since they are short-lived or deteriorate rapidly.

Planting time is autumn, as early as you can get the bulbs, which is usually October or November. Lily bulbs should get into the ground immediately, for they are never completely dormant and ideally are sold with roots attached and plumply alive.

The best location is one in sun or light-shifting shade. The soil should be porous and rapid-draining, yet moisture-retentive. It should be dug deeply—at least 10 in. If it is heavy (clayey), loosen it by working in sand, moistened peat moss, compost, etc. The bulbs can be grown among other garden flowers or low shrubs.

In planting, cover large bulbs (those 3 in. or more in diameter) with 4 to 5 in. of soil; small ones with less. Roots will gradually pull the bulbs down to the depth they prefer. The reason most lilies like to be planted fairly deep has to do with their double root system. Attached to each bulb's base are permanent anchoring roots. In spring, the shoot that bears the leaves and flowers produces additional and important supplementary feeding roots along the underground portion of its stem.

An important exception to the rule of deep planting is the Madonna lily. Its bulb should be only 1 in. below soil, because it has roots only at its base. Plant as early as you can get the bulbs, in late summer. A rosette of leaves will arise at once and remain green over winter.

Space bulbs at least 10 in. apart. Holes for planting bulbs individually should be at least 12 in. across. Lilies look handsome planted in clumps of several of one sort. When setting

them this way you can open a large flat-bottomed hole large enough to hold 3 or more bulbs at proper spacing. Loosen the soil in the bottom of the hole before arranging the bulbs. For all planting, the ground should be moist so roots will begin to grow at once. Water them after planting. In cold climates, mulch the ground above the bulbs after freezing weather.

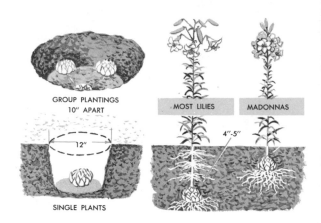

GROUP PLANTINGS 10" APART

SINGLE PLANTS

MOST LILIES

MADONNAS

4"-5"

12"

Shoots, carrying flower buds at their tips, emerge in early spring, often before the frost-free date. If a sudden cold snap is forecast, turn a box over your lilies, so the buds will not be ruined.

During the summer, cultivate shallowly since feeding roots are at the surface of the soil. A summer mulch of grass clippings, sawdust or ground bark is very beneficial; low groundcover plants can serve the same purpose. When blooming time is over, cut off the developing seed pods but do not cut off the stem or any of the leaves. The better the foliage grows, the more flowers you will have next year. Lilies like to be fed. Use a complete fertilizer in early spring and again in summer; be sure you water thoroughly afterward. Water, also, during any dry periods.

Propagating lilies is fun and simple to do. They can be raised from seed, but for beginners the following methods are easier.

The quickest way to get more lilies identical with the one you have is by using scales from the bulb. You can remove them on purpose, breaking off a few of the outer ones as close to the base of the bulb as possible, or you can use scales broken off accidentally as you are planting. They should be put in barely moist sphagnum moss or vermiculite, in a glass jar or polyethylene bag. But first dust the cut surfaces of the scales with a fungicide by shaking them in a paper sack with a pinch of Arasan. Keep the container in a temperature of 70°, out of sun. Bulbs may form in 5 weeks. When first leaves begin to show, plant them either in a box or in the garden, depending on the weather.

Some lilies produce little bulbs called bulbils on their stems. On tiger lily they are the small round black objects at the base of each leaf, and are ripe when they roll off easily. Plant them 1½ in. deep and they will bloom in 3 years.

Bulbs are also formed on the underground portion of lily stems. If you see small lily leaves (resembling fleshy-leaved grass) around your plant, they are rising from such baby bulbs. You can dig down with a trowel, locate and transplant them any time during the growing season. It is wise to put them in a row somewhere to cultivate for a year or two.

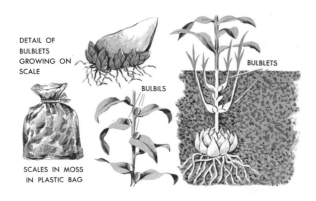

DETAIL OF BULBLETS GROWING ON SCALE

BULBILS

BULBLETS

SCALES IN MOSS IN PLASTIC BAG

These are some of the best lilies for beginners, listed in order of their time of bloom.

Coral Lily (*L. pumilum*) is early! It has small nodding recurved flowers in glowing scarlet on stems 1½ to 2 ft., and blooms at the time of the California-poppy.

Madonna Lily (*L. candidum*) is a favorite, producing lovely white fragrant, outfacing flowers on stalks 3 to 5 ft. high. It blooms at the same time as climbing roses and delphinium, an entrancing sight when planted in combination with them. It likes lime and must be planted only 1 in. below soil, preferably in August.

Mid-Century Hybrids are easiest, and best to grow among other flowers in a perennial border. They begin to bloom after spring flowers are gone and the early summer ones beginning. Their plants are 2 to 3 ft. high, with chalice-shaped blossoms in scarlet, yellow or apricot that may face upward or outward. They multiply rapidly, soon making big clumps.

Regal Lily (*L. regale*) is another popular fragrant one. It has stately trumpets, white on the inside and rosy-purple outside, on stems 4 to 6 ft. high.

Olympic Hybrids are similar to the regal lily, a little later and just as easy to grow. The flowers may be white or pink.

Aurelian Hybrids bloom at the peak of the day-lily season. They are tall plants 4 to 6 ft. high and carry fragrant white, pink or yellow blooms that may be trumpet-shaped or recurving and outfacing.

Speciosum or Showy Lily (*L. speciosum*) has recurving 4-in. white blooms spotted with crimson. There is also a white form. It is highly fragrant and lovely for corsages.

Tiger Lily (*L. tigrinum*) is an old-fashioned favorite with nodding, recurved blooms of orange-red spotted with black. There is also a double form of this hardy, durable plant.

LYCORIS, SPIDER-LILY or MAGIC-LILY. These are lovely amaryllis-like flowers in red, yellow or pink, that bloom as a surprise in late summer or early fall. They pop from the ground suddenly and unexpectedly on tall leafless stems, and are often in full bloom before you notice that they have started to come up. The foliage develops in early spring, and then dies and disappears. The leaves are strap-shaped, and look much like the foliage of daffodils, which is usually coming at the same time as lycoris leaves. The bulbs should not be eaten.

Magic-Lily or Hardy-Amaryllis (*Lycoris squa-migera*), in Zones 4b to 9, inclusive, has beautiful lavender-pink 3-in. blooms on 2-ft. stems, is winter-hardy in subzero climates, and is a vigorous, rapid-multiplying, dependable garden flower. It does not do well in the Deep South.

Golden Spider-Lily or Hurricane-Lily (*L. aurea*), in Zones 9 and 10, gets its common name from the fact that it blooms during hurricane season. It has 3-in. yellow flowers in August or September.

Red Spider-Lily or Short-Tube Lycoris (*L. radiata*), in Zones 7 to 10, inclusive, blooms several weeks later than the golden one, with scarlet flowers 1½ in. long.

Lycoris bulbs resemble those of amaryllis. They prefer a location in part shade in the South, sun or part shade in the North. Plant them in autumn. Bulbs of magic-lily should be planted with the base about 8 in. deep. Golden and red spider-lilies should be 4 in. deep (bulbs will be barely covered with soil). Space them 6 in. apart.

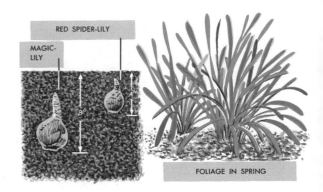

🍂 More Summer-blooming Cold-tender Bulbs

Name	Description	How to Grow and Store
Acidanthera	Resembles small gladiolus. Fragrant, nodding cream-colored blooms with dark blotch. Height 15 to 18″.	Plant corms 2″ deep, 4 to 6″ apart in sun. Long-lasting cut flower. In cold climates dig after first frost. Store dry, in peat, sand, or vermiculite at 50°.
Canna	Large, tropical-looking leaves on plants either dwarf (1½ to 2′) or tall (4 to 6′). Flowers red, yellow, pink.	Hardy Zones 8, 9, 10. Set roots (or plants started earlier indoors) in sunny spot in garden when ground warms in spring. Place horizontally, growth-tips just below soil. Space 1½ to 2′ apart. After frost in fall cut stalks; dig clumps intact. Dry and store upside down in peat or vermiculite at 50 to 60°.
Elephants-Ear (*Colocasia*)	Tropical plants with enormous heart-shaped leaves 2 to 4′ long. Grown for foliage.	Hardy Zones 9 and 10. Elsewhere start indoors in warmth; put outdoors in shade, with moist soil, when weather warms. Space 3 to 6′. Dig after frost. Store dry at 45 to 55°.

Name	Description	How to Grow and Store
Glory-Lily or Climbing-Lily (*Gloriosa*)	Brilliant, recurving 4″ flowers, red banded with yellow. Climbs to 6′ by tendrils on tips of leaves.	Hardy where ground does not freeze. Elsewhere, start in pots indoors, or outdoors when weather warms. Place V-shaped tubers 4″ deep, horizontally. For winter, dig and store like dahlia. All parts of the plant are poisonous if eaten.
Ismene or Basket-Flower (*Hymenocallis calathina*)	Resembles giant white daffodils on 2′ stems. Bulbs and leaves look like amaryllis.	Hardy Zones 9 and 10. Plant in spring, in part shade, bulb tips just below soil, 6 to 12″ apart. Will bloom within 6 weeks. Dig before frost; store dry, with roots intact, at 70°.
Summer-Hyacinth (*Galtonia*)	Loose clusters of small white bell-shaped blooms on stems 3′ high above strap-shaped leaves in late summer.	Plant in fall Zones 7 through 10 where it is hardy. Elsewhere plant in spring. Likes sun. Set bulbs 4 to 6″ deep, 8″ apart. In cold climates dig when foliage dies down or after first frost. Store dry at 55 to 60°.
Tigridia	Tuliplike blooms 4 to 6″ across in red, pink, yellow, white with dark markings; 12 to 30″ high. Foliage like gladiolus.	Winter-hardy in Zones 9 and 10. Plant after weather warms in spring, 3″ deep, sun or part shade. In cold climates, dig after leaves turn yellow or after first frost. Store corms, unseparated, and dry, in sand, peat or vermiculite.
Tuberose (*Polianthes tuberosa*)	Intensely fragrant tubular white blooms in spikes 2 to 3′ high. Foliage grasslike at plant's base.	Hardy Zone 10. In mild climates the tuberous roots can be planted January to March. In cold climates, plant after weather warms in midspring. Place in sun, 2″ deep, 8″ apart. When foliage dies, or before frost, dig and dry. Store warm.
Zephyr-Lily, Fairy-Lily or Rain-Lily (*Zephyranthes*)	Resembles big crocus in white, yellow, pink. Blooms shoot from ground suddenly after a rain, then vanish.	Hardy Zones 7b through 10, where time to plant is late summer or autumn. Elsewhere plant in spring, 2″ deep, 3″ apart in ground or containers. Prefer sun or some shade. Dig and store, dry, in vermiculite or dry soil. Do not eat bulbs.

13

A Fast First-Year Garden
and Gardens for Children

Y ou can have a yard bursting with bloom the very first summer! And you can give your place a landscaped look, even though the house is brand-new and the yard bare or the shrubs so young that they are small and inconspicuous. The way to accomplish this trick is to use mostly annual plants— those that grow from seed to maturity in one season. These come in several general types including flowering kinds, those that resemble shrubs enough to serve as their substitutes, and vines which can climb high and provide shade. There are also some remarkable long-lived plants (perennials) which grow to mature size and flower in their beginning year. All of these like to grow in sunshine, and thrive in the air and space of new properties. In fact, some of them will grow better for you now than after your permanent shrubs and trees become established.

If your yard happens to be an older one, it will take on new life if you give it a fast beauty treatment. Perk it up! If it has lots of sunshine, you have a wide choice of plants that will grow well. If trees shade the ground, you will need to be more thoughtful in your selection, and, in addition to reading this chapter, read the one entitled Beauty in Shade.

The more thinking you do before starting your hurry-up project, the more organized and therefore the more attractive your yard will be. Luckily the showiest effects are the simple ones. Plants of one kind and color, massed, are better-looking than mixed colors scattered about. So concentrate your flower groupings and colors. Use flowers in only one or two places, such as either side of your front door or along your driveway. For example, one of the most spectacular, satisfying, and easy plantings is a big mass of petunias, all of one color; red ones are most dazzling but pink ones are handsome also.

Your soil will influence the results you get. If grading operations have spread subsoil over the surface of your lot, you may need to incorporate some organic material and fertilizer in the beds that you prepare. This is one of the reasons why you should not tackle too much space the first year. The chapter on soils and fertilizers will give you a basic understanding of the sort of soil plants like, and how you can improve what you have.

Flowers You Can Have in a Hurry

Annuals and tender perennials: These were made to order for your purpose. Many of them are extremely easy to grow from seed planted outdoors where they are to bloom, and since seed is relatively inexpensive, you can have lavish numbers of plants for very little money. You can succeed, even if you are a beginner, by following the simple instructions given on each seed packet. See also our chapter on starting plants. Some kinds, however, are slow to reach blooming size, or have such tiny seeds that they are tricky to raise. It is better to purchase these as started plants. See the chapter on annuals for lists suggesting which kinds to grow from seed and which to buy as plants. There are also descriptions, information on how to grow each variety, and ideas for combinations that make attractive borders. Good annuals or tender perennials to use for a one-of-a-kind border in sun are petunia, cleome, phlox and zinnia. For shade, try wax begonia or impatiens.

Potted plants: Here is "instant" beauty. The plants can be geraniums, petunias, succulents, house plants or almost anything used with flair. The containers can be plain clay pots or something decorative that you dream up. Use them singly or in groups, in such places as by your front door or on your patio. For helpful hints on growing plants in containers, and some pictures, see the chapter on pots, window boxes and containers.

Roses: It seems almost too good to be true that hybrid teas, floribundas, grandifloras and the little miniature roses give a perfect display of flowers their first year. But they do! That is because the plants are 2 years old when you get them and full of stored food that will help them produce blooms. If you are starting your new garden in early spring, you can buy the roses as dormant bare-root bushes. If summer has begun, you can buy potted plants. Though they are in full leaf, and maybe have flowers, you can transplant them to your garden with almost no shock to them. For full details on roses, including instructions on planting, see the chapter on roses.

Perennials: Those that become full-sized blooming beauties their first year are mighty good investments. They give results almost as quickly as annuals, yet live over winter to repeat their flowering display year after year. You can use them as a beginning for your future perennial border. Showiest are aster, chrysanthemum and gloriosa daisy. All can be purchased as young plants or divisions in spring. They will bloom in late summer or autumn. Gloriosa daisies can also be raised easily from seed. For details on all, see the chapter on perennials.

Bulbs: Most kinds are ideal for providing quick, sure, and superb flowers, for the bud—or the makings of one—is already in the bulb when you buy it. If you are beginning your garden in spring, and your yard has sunshine, you can start the following bulbs outdoors in the spot where they are to grow: canna, dahlia, gladiolus. For a shady site, you can have caladium and tuberous begonia, and for speediest results you should buy them as started plants.

If you are beginning your garden in autumn, you can plant bulbs this fall that will bloom next spring, such as tulips and daffodils.

For information on how to grow all of these and others, see the chapter on bulbs.

Make-believe Shrubbery

This is where large-size annuals and tender perennials, growing from seed to full size in one season, come in handy. Of course they are not big at the beginning of the summer, but you cannot expect complete miracles.

Biggest of the group is castor-bean. Some varieties of it become 8 ft. high in one year. Leaves are enormous, often 3 ft. across. They may be green, bluish-gray or red. *As mentioned in the annuals chapter, its seeds are poisonous if eaten. Because they are attractive to children, you should remove them as they form.*

Another good pseudo-shrub is kochia or summer-cypress. It has feathery foliage, and grows in a rounded shape 2 to 3 ft. high which makes it excellent for temporary hedges or for backgrounds for flower borders.

Four-o'clock makes a bush 1½ to 2½ ft. high with pretty flowers. All three fake shrubs can be grown from seed started in the ground outdoors in spring after the ground is warm.

For tall plants to use in background situations, or for screening, you can use corn, sunflower, castor-bean and canna (bulb).

Something for Shade, and Privacy

Annual vines can give you a quick high cover or screen you from your neighbors. They can be started from seed outdoors where they are to grow, then trained on strings, rope, trellis, or a fence. Vigorous kinds with large leaves give speediest results. Pumpkin and gourd head the list, with morning-glory not far behind. To learn more about these, and others, see the chart on annual vines in the vine chapter.

🍁 Gardening for Children

Every child deserves to know the thrill of growing a plant from a seed, and of watching it develop to the stage of producing flowers or food. However, since children grow impatient with a long wait, it is wise to start them with plants that give quick and sure results. The more interesting and dramatic the outcome can be, the better.

Let them have their own patch of ground, and be sure that it is in a good location, with soil well prepared, so results will not be disappointing. Beginners should not have too large a space to maintain; it may overwhelm them as weeds begin to take over. Let each child choose what plants he or she wishes to grow—with some deft guidance on your part.

If vegetables seem in order, radishes are an excellent first choice, for they are planted early while enthusiasm is high, are easy, quick-maturing, and something that can be shared with friends or with parents and grandparents. Any of the child's favorite vegetables is an excellent selection.

In the flower line, the chapter on annuals lists those which are easiest to grow. They are the ones with which to start. But for special fun, here are some with which the entire family will enjoy experimenting.

Gourds: These are completely fascinating. The plant is a vine, rapid-growing and large-leaved, which you start from seed outdoors after the ground is warm in spring. Large yellow or white flowers are followed by fruits which may be small or large, in white, yellow, green or stripes. They come in assorted amusing shapes. They can be dried and used as bird houses or for winter ornament indoors. Try a package of mixed seed for some delightful surprises.

Peanuts: These grow in a surprising manner. Blossoms develop on above-ground stems, but then turn downward and bury themselves in the ground where they become nuts! Seed catalogues list them among vegetables.

Moonflower: A vine with large white flowers similar to those of morning-glory, but opening at dusk. They unfold slowly as you watch, and this show is so intriguing that it is worth inviting friends in to see. The plant is perennial in climates with little or no frost, but in cold climates is grown as a summer-blooming annual. Start from seed after the ground warms.

Pumpkins: Grow your own jack-o'-lantern material. The plants are large, big-leaved vines, similar to those of gourds. Start seed outdoors after the ground is warm in spring. Give them rich soil and lots of space.

Sensitive-Plant *(Mimosa pudica):* Fun to play with! If you touch one of its ferny leaves with your finger, it will fold up and droop. You can do it over and over. The plant is low-growing with ball-like clusters of airy pink flowers. You can pot some to keep as pets, or to give to visiting children.

Sunflower: Grow your own crop of seeds to feed the winter birds. Get the giant type sunflower that grows almost as tall as Jack's beanstalk and produces enormous flowers. For instructions see "sunflower" in the alphabetical list in the chapter on annuals.

Plants of colorful-leaved coleus can brighten a shaded corner during the summer season.

14

~~~~~~

Beauty in Shade

Gardening beneath trees, or on the north side of a house, is both rewarding and challenging. You can achieve effects, and grow plants, that will be the envy of all your friends who must garden in sunshine alone! Your garden can have special distinctive charms. It is possible to create an illusion of coolness and quietness, with emphasis on luxuriant green foliage. Or you can have bright splashes of color. But to get the special results that are possible, you will need to be very clever about solving the problems that are usually present in shady situations. These problems are the result of the factors that produce the shade. Adapt to your situation. Make the most of its good points, and moderate the bad ones. Concentrate on growing the plants that thrive in shade instead of attempting to grow those that do not like it! Then anticipate compliments.

Where summers are hot, many flowers that are supposed to be grown in full sunshine appreciate shade through the hottest part of the day, or light or filtered shade through most of it. You must learn some of these facts by experimenting and testing your conditions. However, bear in mind that plants grown under or near trees or big shrubs are competing with their neighbors for moisture and sustenance. In general, tree and shrub roots are the worst enemy of so-called shady gardens. Some trees are worse robbers than others, but probably the worst cannibals are the maples, which will impoverish the soil unmercifully. Where tree roots threaten to take over, one remedy—the hard one—is to dig the soil 8 to 12 inches deep and grub out all the tree roots —the tiny ones as well as the large—in the area where you wish to plant the more tender annuals and perennials. If you do this, the process will have to be repeated at least once a year, preferably twice. Otherwise the roots will be back as strong as ever. Nature is ruthless in its struggle for survival.

PROBLEMS OF SHADY SITES, AND SOLUTIONS

Poor Light: Most plants do not flower well without considerable sunshine. The general rule is that the more sunshine a plant has, the more flower buds it will develop. However, luckily, some plants will bloom in shady situations, especially if the shade is not too dense, or if it is missing at that crucial time of year when the plant does its major growing. The latter point is something worth remembering. You see, trees that shed their leaves in winter —deciduous types—do not put out new leaves in the spring until surprisingly late, long after many wild flowers and spring-flowering bulbs have finished their showy season and grown the leaves that will sustain them for the next year. By the time trees are in full leaf, and making dark summer shade, those spring flowers no longer need the sunshine!

The best kind of shade for gardens is high and airy, beneath high-branched trees rather than low and smothering shrubs with overhanging branches. Sunlight should filter through occasionally. You can let more sunshine come through your treetops by having the limbs of the trees thinned every few years. A professional tree surgeon can do this for you; it will be good for your trees and improve their appearance, too.

Dry Soil: This may be because of the trees, since their feeding roots extend from their trunks farther than their branches reach. It may be because the garden location is close to the side of your house, either under eaves or protected from rainfall by the wall of the house. In either case, it is a condition about which you can do something. You will need to increase the water-holding capacity of your

soil. Incorporate humus such as compost, moistened peat moss, vermiculite, etc. Also, be prepared to add moisture continually all summer. A mulch over the top of the ground —leaves, pine needles, or wood chips—will help retain the moisture.

Lack of Fertility: This is usually due to the trees and shrubs. Their roots take food, and will compete for it with any plants that you grow. Be prepared to feed plants that you grow in shade.

🍂 Plants That Will Succeed in Shade

Woodland Wild Flowers and Ferns

These are naturals for shade, for they grow in shade "back home." But your yard probably is not like a woodland, even though it is shaded, unless it is the genuine thing or unless you have carefully prepared your soil. For soil in a natural woodland is composed of native humus, which is the result of the decomposition of leaves, roots and sticks over many years. It is moisture-retentive and mulched on top with a layer of loose, undecayed vegetation. This is the type of soil that you should attempt to duplicate. Later, after you have established your wild flowers, do not go out each spring and neatly rake off all the dead leaves, so that the ground is bare! Let nature help you improve your soil and keep your plants happy by accumulating a natural mulch. Wild flowers will not have difficulty poking up from under leaves in the spring.

All wild flowers and ferns native to your area will grow for you, plus many from other parts of the country. While it is possible to collect plants from the woods, many are protected by law. Make certain that you are not taking such plants, and also that you are not trespassing. There are nurseries specializing in wild flowers, from which you can purchase sturdy plants, usually when they are in dormant condition. If you want them to look as though they had grown in your garden naturally, plant several of one kind together to form a colony or family. If they like you and the home you have provided, they will multiply.

Spring-flowering, Cold-hardy Bulbs

Daffodil, grape-hyacinth, snowdrop, glory-of-the-snow, Siberian squill, winter aconite and Spanish bluebell will flower early before deciduous trees are fully leafed out. Thus they will have sun during the crucial period when their foliage is growing and storing food for next year's bloom. By the time trees produce heavy shade in midsummer, the bulbs will have ripened their leaves and become dormant. They will no longer need sun.

The bulbs mentioned can be planted naturalistically and informally in drifts, if you have a patch of woodland, or in rows or clumps if your shady garden has a definite form. Even though they will grow in shade, the more sun they have early in the season, the better they will bloom. For best results, make certain that they have plenty of moisture in the autumn when they awaken from their dormant period and their roots begin to grow; also in spring while they are growing their leaves.

Daffodil varieties for naturalizing should be good old dependable kinds, rather than highly bred aristocrats; they will endure the problems of your shady area.

Tulips will bloom in shady gardens, at least their first year. But if you wish them to put on a glorious show each season, it will be wise to plant new bulbs each fall. For methods of planting bulbs, see that chapter.

Two of the most beautiful native American spring flowers are handled like bulbs, though they grow from thick rootstalks. They are bluebell (*Mertensia*) and trillium or wake-robin. The former, which is better known, has clusters of nodding pink-tinged blue bells on stems 6 to 24 in. high, depending upon the variety. They bloom about the same time as tulips. Trilliums have lilylike flowers composed of 3 petals. Colors are glistening white, pink, red or yellow. Some varieties are tiny miniatures only a few inches high, while others may be several times that height. Showiest is the great white trillium (*T. grandiflorum*) [Zones 3 through 8], 1½ ft. high, with flowers 3 in. across.

Both bluebell and trillium are purchased and planted when they are in dormant, leafless condition in autumn, just like bulbs. (If they are not available from a local source, you can get them through several mail-order nursery firms). They prefer moist, humusy-rich soil. Plant with the tops of the roots 1 in. below soil level, space 10 in. apart, and water if the soil is not already moist. Like daffodils, they will come up and bloom in spring, then ripen their foliage and disappear during summer. As with all bulbs, they need their leaves to make food to store for the next season, so if you pick the flowers with stems that include the leaves, you are either killing your plant, or at least setting it back woefully. Both these plants are long-lived perennials that will multiply and become large clumps, if you are kind to them.

House Plants on Vacation

Practically any plant that you grow indoors during the winter will be happy outdoors in summer in a shaded spot, out of the wind. Your large-leaved philodendrons can move to a sheltered corner of your patio. Coleus, wax begonias and impatiens can be propagated and used as colorful edgings along shaded paths. Ferns, African violets, gloxinias, azaleas, and almost anything else, can be left in their pots and sunk among groundcover plants on the north side of the house. Remember to keep all these treasures watered. For instructions on when and how to move them outdoors in summer and back inside in fall, see the chapter on indoor plants.

Annuals and Tender Perennials for Quick Color

Some of these are well-known bedding plants that are available at almost any store handling garden plants. They grow rapidly and give fast results. Others are easy to grow from seed. For additional information on most of them, see the alphabetical list in the chapter on annuals.

BEGONIA, WAX. This is low-growing, everblooming, in white, pink or red over glossy leaves that may be green or bronze. Use it in masses as borders or edgings.

COLEUS. This tender perennial is grown as a bedding plant for its colorful foliage.

FORGET-ME-NOT. The annual and biennial kinds bloom very early in spring. They like moisture.

IMPATIENS, PATIENCE or SULTANA (*Impatiens holsti and I. sultani*). This is a perennial when grown in frost-free climates; elsewhere, treat it as an annual. It makes a wonderful summer bedding plant for shade. The flowers are 1½ to 2 in. across in white, pink, orange or scarlet. The plants come in different heights. The tallest grow 2 to 4 ft.; dwarfs are only 8 in. They are easily grown from seed sown in warmth indoors, and will bloom in 3 months. You can buy started plants, if you prefer. Do not put them outside until ground and weather are warm. Stem cuttings root readily in water. To save plants over winter in cold climates, dig and pot and enjoy the flowers all winter; or take cuttings.

NICOTIANA or FLOWERING TOBACCO. This tall annual has white or colored tubular flowers. It adds fragrance, along with beauty, and tends to self-sow.

PANSY and VIOLA. Both appreciate the coolness of shade though they bloom best with some sunshine.

SALVIA. The red annual called scarlet sage puts on a vivid show in partial shade.

SWEET ALYSSUM. This dainty, low-edging annual comes in white, lavender or pink. It does surprisingly well in shade, though of course it blooms best with some sunshine.

TORENIA or WISHBONE FLOWER. This dainty little annual is 1 ft. high, bushy, carrying pretty light blue flowers marked with purple and with yellow throats. It prefers moist soil and is easy to grow from seed started indoors early or outside after weather and soil are warm. The seed germinates in 1 week; begins to flower in 3 months. Otherwise you can buy started plants.

Colorful Summer Bulb Plants

These include some of the showiest and most dramatically lovely flowers for shady gardens. Certain ones give you almost instant results! For full descriptions and instructions for growing them, see the alphabetical listing in the chapter on bulbs.

Cold-tender Types: In most parts of the country these are grown outdoors during the summer, and are stored over winter in dormant condition in a frost-free place.

ACHIMENES. These are dainty little floriferous plants for pots and hanging baskets.

BEGONIA, TUBEROUS-ROOTED. This gorgeous queen of shady gardens is known for its huge double or single flowers in fabulous colors.

CALADIUM. This fancy foliage plant has large arrow-shaped leaves which come in variations of green and white, or green with pink and red.

CALLA. These lilylike blooms appear in white, pink, yellow.

Hardy, Permanent Bulbs for Shade: Some of these are planted in autumn, others in spring, some at either time—depending upon when you can get the bulbs.

BEGONIA, HARDY (*Begonia evansiana*). This plant survives winters in Zones 6 through 10. Farther north its tubers are dug and stored over winter. It grows 1 to 2 ft. high and carries showers of flesh-pink flowers.

COLCHICUM or AUTUMN-CROCUS. This is a fall-flowering bulb that is often sold to bloom indoors. It will flower without soil or water, before it produces leaves or roots. But it is really an outdoor plant that is hardy in Zones 4 through 8. The foliage is poisonous if eaten.

CYCLAMEN. There are two distinct types: the large florist's plant, hardy only in mild winter Zones 9b and 10; and hardy miniature varieties that look at home in shady woodlands or rock gardens. They are *Cyclamen europaeum* [Zones 6, 7, 8 and 9], *C. coum* and *C. neapolitanum* [Zones 7b, 8 and 9].

LILIES. Most of the true lilies like to be grown where they have considerable sunshine, but the following adapt to part shade: tiger lily, regal lily, aurelian hybrids, olympic hybrids, *Lilium canadense*, *L. martagon album*, *L. michiganense* and *L. pardalinum*.

LYCORIS. These are the lilylike flowers that pop up without warning in late summer on tall stalks without leaves. Golden spider-lily or hurricane-lily is *Lycoris aurea* [Zones 8, 9 and 10]. Red spider-lily is *L. radiata* [Zones 7, 8, 9 and 10]. Magic-lily or hardy amaryllis, pink-flowered, is *L. squamigera* [Zones 4b through 9].

Perennials for Permanence

A gratifying number of perennials will bloom in shade. Those with good-looking or outstandingly handsome foliage should get special consideration; they are the ones to use along paths, or in positions that must look good all summer.

For frost-free areas, good perennials in shade include begonia, coleus, impatiens, shrimp-plant and strobilanthes.

For climates with cold winters, here are some of the most attractive and useful.

ASTILBE or FALSE-SPIREA. This has fern-like foliage and spikes of tiny fluffy flowers in white, pink, red or purple. It is found in Zones 4 through 9b, and the flowering heights vary from 6 in. to 2 ft. Moist, fertile soil is essential. Buy named varieties in order to get the colors you desire.

BLEEDING-HEART. This comes in two sizes in Zones 4 through 8. The old-fashioned kind (*Dicentra spectabilis*) grows 2 to 3 ft. high, with pink and white heart-shaped flowers on arching stems in late spring. After the plant blooms, the foliage dies and disappears until the following spring. Plant when dormant, preferably early spring. It likes a spot moist in summer but not soggy in winter.

Smaller fern-leaved types, 10 to 18 in. high, are native to both eastern and western United States. Some have pink flowers, and some white or cream. They flower almost all summer. There are several selected and hybrid named varieties such as 'Bountiful' with pink flowers, and 'Silver-smith' with white ones.

BRUNNERA or FORGET-ME-NOT-ANCHUSA. This grows in Zones 5 through 9. Its flowers resemble those of forget-me-not. The plants grow about a foot high, with large heart-shaped leaves. Sprays of small, dainty sky-blue blossoms appear in spring. When this plant takes a fancy to your shady garden, it will self-sow, and you will have an abundance of extras to share with friends. It is lovely planted with pink bleeding-heart.

CHRISTMAS-ROSE (*Helleborus niger*). This is not a rose but a beautiful white-flowered, winter-blooming relative of buttercups. It grows 12 to 15 in. high with evergreen leaves in Zones 4b through 10a. Moist but well-drained humus-rich soil, in a partly shaded place, suits its needs. Plant in spring, allowing at least 12 in. of space. It dislikes being moved, so try to find the proper location for it the first time! Roots and foliage are poisonous.

Helleborus orientalis is similar, with flowers in shades of purple, pink and green that open in the spring.

DAMES-ROCKET *(Hesperis matronalis)*. This has lavender or white fragrant phlox-type flowers on 3-ft. stems in late spring. It self-sows rapidly and will soon fill a woodland with blooms. It is easy to weed out if you think you are getting too many. A few plants are all that are needed to get a start, but you may sow seeds.

DAY-LILY *(Hemerocallis)*. This does well in part shade, especially in hot climates. Ordinarily it is considered a sun-preferring plant. (See the chapter on perennials for details on its culture.)

FORGET-ME-NOT *(Myosotis scorpioides)*. This is the perennial one, different from annual or biennial types that bloom in very early spring. It loves a moist site and some shade, and is found in Zones 4 through 9a. The sprawling stems grow 5 to 14 in. high, with delightful small blue flowers, which bloom almost continuously all summer. Stem cuttings root quickly in water.

FOXGLOVE *(Digitalis)*. These lovely, stately stalks, 3 to 4 ft. high, carry spires of tubular flowers in pink, purple, white and yellow. They appear in Zones 5 through 9. The finest foxgloves are the biennials, which must be started from seed anew each summer, unless they self-sow (which they usually do if they thrive in your garden). The first year a rosette of leaves forms. The second year the plants bloom and then die. In Zones 5 and 6, wintering these plants is sometimes a challenge, since the leaves are evergreen and, while needing protection, must not be smothered.

LUNGWORT *(Pulmonaria)*. This is a horrible name for a lovely plant. It is a relative of mertensia bluebell, and has similar bell-shaped flowers in spring at the time azaleas and tulips bloom. The flowers may be intense blue, or a combination of pink and blue. Foliage, in a moundlike clump, is about a foot high. My favorite is *Pulmonaria saccharata*. Its leaves are green, spotted with silvery white, and remain appealingly decorative all summer. It has flowers in pink and blue. Another good one is *P. angustifolia*, with green leaves and vivid blue blooms. All are vigorous-growing and easily divided. They prefer a moist situation but endure drought.

PLANTAIN-LILY *(Hosta)*. This is always at the top of my list. You may know it by its old name of funkia. I grow it primarily because of its dramatically lovely leaves, though it does have spikes of bell-shaped flowers. There are numerous species, with leaves ranging in width from a narrow 2 in. to a broad 12 in. Some leaves are plain green and lustrous, while others may be edged in white, splashed with white, or be of a unique silvery blue-gray color.

These plants are so handsome that one would be willing to work hard to keep them growing well, but they do not need pampering for they are as tough as they are beautiful. While they like rich soil and generous amounts of moisture, they will survive drought conditions. Plantain-lilies grow in fountain-form clumps, mutiplying and becoming larger masses year after year. They are very easy to divide and separate so that you can propagate one clump into many in a short time. Thus you can obtain enough plants to edge a path or to use as a groundcover. Leaves die to the ground each winter.

Among my favorites are short-cluster plantain-lily *(Hosta glauca*, often sold as *Hosta sieboldiana)*, which is the one with enormous blue-gray leaves; wavy-leaved plantain-lily *(H. undulata)* with variegated green and white leaves that make it pretty to use as an edging, and the blunt plantain-lily *(H. decorata)*, which has rounded leaves edged with white.

PRIMROSE *(Primula)*. These are among the most beloved and gay flowers of spring. Most of them prefer a climate cool and moist, like that of England. In the garden they want a spot shaded in summer, where ample water is available when needed. Use them in groups or for carpeting effects.

There are many kinds, but all produce low-growing rosettes or clumps of leaves from which the flowering stems arise. The blooms appear in a wide range of colors: white, pink, red, purple, yellow and blue. Among the favorite and easily grown cold-hardy kinds are the cowslip *(Primula veris)*, which has clusters of bright yellow flowers on stems 4 to 8 in. high; English primrose *(P. vulgaris* or *P. acaulis)*, low-growing with profuse flowers carried on individual stems;

PRECEDING PAGE:
Plantain-lilies beneath a winged euonymus shrub. The ones in the foreground with white-edged leaves are Hosta decorata. To their right is Hosta undulata.

Maidenhair-ferns with lacy leaves on wiry stems are in the foreground here. Behind them are bleeding-hearts, and in lower right-hand corner are some fuchsias.

Tuberous-rooted begonias in pots, and impatiens used as bedding plants along the walk below, add color to the shady entrance planting at the home of Mrs. William Teutsch, Corvallis, Oregon.

Yellow polyantha primroses used as a border-edging and a clump of daffodils, provide April color in this garden in Portland, Oregon. Primroses excel in cool, moist climates.

PLANTS THAT THRIVE IN SHADE

polyanthus primrose, bearing clusters of blossoms in many colors; and *P. japonica*, which is a tall late-flowering kind with flowers in whorls on 12-in. stems. For climates with hot summers but cold winters the most dependable and beautiful is Siebold primrose (*P. sieboldi*), which has 2-in. blossoms in pink, white or lavender on foot-high stems. It survives heat by going dormant, losing its leaves in summer.

You can get a start of hardy primroses by buying clumps or potted plants in bloom. When they are in flower, or immediately afterward, is the best time to transplant them. Space them 10 to 12 in. apart. Clumps can be pulled apart easily, to make numerous divisions. In early spring, dormant plants are available by mail order. It is also possible to start primroses from seed, though this takes a little skill because the seeds are tiny. Where winters are severe, plants should be mulched or otherwise protected, but do not smother their evergreen leaves.

Mild-climate primroses often grown in California gardens include *P. obconica*, a perennial usually grown as an annual, which has large, hairy basal leaves—to which many people with sensitive skins are allergic—and big pink or lavender blooms in clusters. Fairy primrose (*P. malacoides*) is an 8-to-12-in.-high annual with dainty pink, lavender or white blooms in tiers on slender stems. Both of these primroses are usually grown for winter or early spring flowers. Plants are usually available in early autumn or can be started from seed sown in late summer.

VIOLETS. Wild or tame, sweet-scented or just pretty, they are ideal for shady gardens. Wherever you live, there are many you can grow. All multiply rapidly, either by self-sowing or by being divided. The sooner you get a start of some, the better!

Groundcovers and Pebbles

Where nothing else will grow, groundcovers often will! They are not only attractive in themselves, but also keep down weeds, cover ugly bare soil, and lessen the amount of maintenance needed. One of the marvelous things about them is that they make difficult areas look gardened. You can let them take care of all your outlying shady areas, so that you can concentrate cultivated plants, and those needing most care, where they will show and count the most.

When your problem spot is so shady and dry that no plants can be grown directly in the ground successfully, as beneath overhanging eaves, some type of pebbles may solve your problem in an artistic manner. For ideas, see the chapter on rock gardens.

Some Good Groundcovers for Shade

Name	Zone	Name	Zone
Ajuga	5-9	Pachysandra	5-8
Babys-Tears	10	Peperomia	10
Bear-Berry	2b-9a	Sarcococca	6-9
Dichondra	9-10	Strawberry	3b-10
Epimedium	4-8	Vinca or Myrtle	5-10a
Goutweed	4-9	Violet	3-10
Hypericum	5b-10	Wandering	
Ivy, Algerian	8-10	Jew	10
Ivy, English	6-10	Wedelia	10
Lily-Turf	5b-10	Wintercreeper	5-9a
Pachistima	5-8a	Yellow-Root	4-9

For details on each, see the chapter on groundcovers.

Shrubs You Can Count On

Descriptions of most of the plants listed below are given in the chapter on shrubs.

Arbor-Vitae	Gardenia	Pieris
Azalea	Holly	Pittosporum
Barberry	Honeysuckle	Privet
Box	Hydrangea	Raphiolepis
Camellia	Hypericum	Rhododendron
Coral-Berry	Leucothoe	Salal
Currant	Mahonia	Skimmia
Daphne	Mountain-	Snowberry
Euonymus	Laurel	Sumac
Fatsia	Nandina	Sweet-Fern
Fothergilla	Osmanthus	Witch-Hazel
Fuchsia	Photinia	Yew

15

Rock Gardens and Casual Rocks

There are all sorts of fascinating ways to garden with rocks. Each is quite different and offers exciting possibilities for your creative skill. You can develop a naturalistic setting where stones look as though they had always been in your yard (maybe they have), and where the plants are the kind that grow normally in such situations. You can build a wall with soil pockets filled with flowers and succulents. A Japanese-type garden—or one that modifies and adapts Oriental ideas to the American way of life—is fun to construct and a delight to enjoy later. Pebbles, rock chips in different colors, aggregate, gravel, crushed brick, sand, and even coal, can be used as ground covers or in ornamental patterns. Some are used as surfacing for pavements. Specimen rocks can be so handsome that they are worthy of use as pieces of sculpture, or as the important background for a distinctive plant. Let your imagination have full sway. You will be surprised at what you can do.

Rocks make good homes for plants for reasons that you might not suspect. The soil beneath them, being shaded and being covered so that it is protected from the drying effect of air and sun, is more cool and moist than surrounding ground. Roots take advantage of this, though tops of plants may be in sunlight. Small pebbles or rock chips used in quantity as a mulch—several inches deep—serve the same soil-sheltering purpose as large rocks. Dark-colored rocks absorb and hold heat, while light-colored ones reflect it. The sunny side of boulders is warmer than their shady side. These facts can be useful when you plan your plantings. For instance, flowers that bloom very early in spring should be planted on the warm side of rocks so they will be awakened as early as possible. Evergreens injured by drying sunlight in winter should not be planted above white pebbles that reflect and intensify such light.

Plants usually considered as typical rock-garden subjects are those from mountain tops—true alpines—or those that are native to stony situations elsewhere. The high-altitude kind from above timberline are ground-hugging dwarfs that usually like cool temperatures and a ready supply of moisture (they are used to melting snow), and fast-draining soil. Rock inhabitants from lower elevations often have built-in, drought-defying, protective devices such as thick leaves that store water, or gray or hairy foliage that reflects or insulates against sun. To these true rock dwellers, gardeners tend to add all kinds of dwarf shrubs and low compact plants. In general, all of these plants are tolerant of various kinds of soil, though to keep them dwarf the ground should not be too fertile.

Because all kinds of rock gardens are very popular now, most garden centers are well stocked with assorted kinds of materials for them. These include lightweight rock and stone chips. Japanese garden accessories such as lanterns of metal, stone or concrete are also available. Rock for walls is usually obtained through a quarry. Smooth, water-worn pebbles can be found along the shore of oceans, certain lakes, and rivers, since it is the tumbling action of the water that wears them to such beautiful shapes. You will enjoy collecting such rocks and pebbles on trips, but you will find that they are surprisingly heavy; do not attempt to load too many into your car or you may break its springs!

Naturalistic Rock Gardens

These either utilize natural rocky sites or attempt to create a setting that *looks* as though it were naturally rocky. They can be as shady and woodsy as mountain glens, as sunny and dry as a desert outcropping, or anything in between. You can use plants native to your area, or others that like similar conditions and harmonize in appearance. A variation of this type of garden is a naturalistic arrangement of rocks with whatever plants appeal to you, even though the latter have a distinctly "cultivated" look.

If you are beginning from scratch, and must bring in or relocate rocks, here are a few pointers.

To look as though they had grown there, all rocks should be of the same kind, rather than a mixture that you have collected from your travels.

Look around at genuine rock outcroppings to see how you can arrange yours so they seem most normal. Usually rock formations are in relatively parallel layers or ledges. Duplicating this general pattern gives you a chance to stair-step yours, allowing space for soil pockets for plants.

The bottom row of rocks should not sit on top of the ground but be partially imbedded in it. Any single large boulder should be partly below ground.

Tip the rocks slightly, so water will run back into the soil where the roots of plants can use it.

Soil for plants should be placed behind and among rocks as you construct your garden, for it is difficult to insert it later. Most rock plants like fast-draining soil; be sure that yours is porous.

Rocks used individually should appear to be stable and not easily toppled. The long axis should be either upright or horizontal, not leaning at an angle that appears insecure.

If your ground is level, and you wish to create an effect of hills and valleys—or at least some variation in the appearance of the land, try this: Dig out soil from one area and pile it in another! Plant tall shrubs at the top—or just behind the top—of the "hill" area, to give it added height and camouflage the fact that it is a very small hill.

Plan some paths or other open areas where you can safely walk without stepping upon plants. The surfacing material should be harmonious with the setting.

which plants are to grow. For instance, you must be sure to leave pockets—spaces—of soil for the plants. Make certain the rocks tip backward enough so that water will run down to the plant's roots. The soil between rocks, and directly behind them, should be the kind that plants like—a good mixture being 2 parts good garden loam, 1 part peat moss or woodland leaf mold, and 1 part sharp sand. Since many of the plants that do well in rock gardens have long tap-roots, the special soil should extend 1½ to 2 ft. behind the wall. It should be firmed well, so that it will not sink away and leave roots exposed.

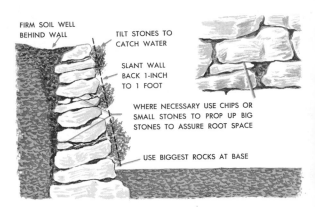

FIRM SOIL WELL BEHIND WALL

TILT STONES TO CATCH WATER

SLANT WALL BACK 1-INCH TO 1 FOOT

WHERE NECESSARY USE CHIPS OR SMALL STONES TO PROP UP BIG STONES TO ASSURE ROOT SPACE

USE BIGGEST ROCKS AT BASE

SIMULATE NATURAL ROCK PLACEMENT

TILT ROCKS TO ADMIT WATER

PARTLY BURY BOTTOM STONE

PLACE TALL SHRUBS BEHIND

DIG OUT SOIL: PILE UP, SET ROCKS IN IT

Planted Rock Walls

Retaining walls constructed without mortar can serve a double purpose. They can hold the slope and also become colorful vertical gardens.

To learn the vital basic principles of building a rock wall so that it will not collapse, see the section on hills in the chapter on landscaping. However, there are a few extra tricks you should know about preparing walls in

Planting is easiest to do while the wall is being constructed, for then it is simple to fit plants into the crevices, and roots into the soil between or behind rocks. The plant's crown—juncture of top and roots—should be even with the face of the wall. Cover roots firmly with earth and water them. Then add more soil so that the next rock will fit against that earth.

To get plants into a completed wall, you may need to remove some of the soil from the previously constructed pocket, or if the soil has dropped away you will need to add more. A long-handled spoon is a help for this. Poke soil in with a stick. After the plant is placed, fill in with moist soil. One way to do it is to make a ball of moist earth which can be squeezed into place. Water well, and plug the opening with a pad of moist sphagnum moss.

Any plants that are happy in their new site will self-sow, and their seeds will catch and grow in places where you would despair of inserting mature plants.

Among perennials that flower handsomely in sunny walls are alyssum basket-of-gold, Carpathian harebell, catmint, evergreen candytuft, Serbian bellflower, slow-growing low sedums and snow-in-summer. These are all described in the chapter on perennials.

Japanese-type Gardens

True Japanese gardens are designed according to principles quite different from those on which most American gardens are fashioned. Yet there is much that we can adapt from them to use in our way of life.

The people of Japan have deeply reverent love of nature. They study it, observe it, and like to enjoy quietly its every detail and aspect. Their gardens are planned to simulate nature in some perfect form and to provide a place for meditating about its beauty in quiet repose. These gardens are an extension of the house in a genuine indoor-outdoor relationship, so the family can intimately view the varying changes brought by weather and seasons. Instead of being centers for activity and an ever-changing display of blooms, they are a serene retreat from the workaday world.

In layout, the gardens strive for a feeling of spaciousness, privacy and changing vistas. Yet most of them are in extremely limited space, crowded by other houses. The solution has been to enclose them within fences and create landscapes-in-miniature, which are compact, executed in exquisite detail, and meticulously though inconspicuously maintained. Frequently some of the landscape elements are symbolic rather than real. The feeling of distance is implied by illusion.

Emphasis is on materials that do not change, such as rocks, evergreens and soil or pebbles. These give a sense of stability and permanence. All are used with tasteful restraint. Few colorful flowers are included. The trees and shrubs are carefully pruned each year so that they remain in their most ideal form and size, and they do not seem to vary over many years.

The best gardens are the simple ones, not the ornate ones filled with eye-catching gadgets. Accessories such as stone lanterns or hand-washing basins have religious meanings or are related in some way to the tea ceremony. Bridges are to aid you across water or allow you to view a stream or distant vista from the most advantageous site. Paths or stepping stones are laid to lead you around the garden slowly and appreciatively. They turn or in some way cause you to pause when there is something special to admire. They tempt you ahead by sights or sounds around a bend. You do not see all of the garden at once but are allowed to make a succession of pleasant discoveries.

Rocks are revered as sculptures executed by nature and are positioned so that their textures and silhouettes can be admired. Small stones are carefully grouped into arrangements that please the eye or serve as background or base for some larger boulder. They also cover bare earth.

Water is an important element in a Japanese garden, both for the sight of it and the sound. Even a trickle or a small waterfall can make pleasant music. If water is not available, it is simulated with "dry streams" made of pebbles graduated in size and arranged in flowing lines. Or coarse sand is raked to indicate ripples. Allowing your imagination to complete the picture is part of the enjoyment of these gardens.

While American gardens are often planned with symmetrical balance—exactly the same on both sides of a central axis—Japanese

OPPOSITE:

These mossy stones are grouped as a garden feature. Black-stem bamboo is the feathery shrub behind them, and creeping thyme carpets the space below. Lawrence Underhill, landscape architect

This small garden is in Honolulu, Hawaii. The stone lantern and well-placed rocks balance the strong design of the aggregate path. Takano Nakamura, landscape architect

Small carefully composed details, such as the arrangement of a hand-washing basin with pebbles, are typical of Japanese gardens. Arthur Erfeldt, landscape architect

JAPANESE-STYLE GARDENS

gardens are always asymmetrical. They have balance but it is not conspicuous. The design is carefully composed with various architectural and natural elements combining to make a work of art.

Ideas from Japanese-type gardens can easily be adapted to fit many situations. They are especially good with modern architecture, or homes where soil is rocky, sandy or dry. Only a little space is needed to create a charming spot. Let yours have the spirit of a Japanese garden, rather than be a copy of one.

For suggested books to read on Japanese gardening, see reference list' at the end of this book.

Practical Projects with Pebbles

Utilizing rocks or pebbles creatively does not mean that you must have an Oriental-type garden or duplicate Japanese methods. Your needs, way of life, garden, and even the rocks are different. Be inventive! Put the pebbles to the use for which you need them.

Pebbles, crushed rock, broken bricks, etc., make marvelous paths, especially if held in position by an edging of redwood boards, bricks or stones. Use types and colors that are in keeping with the architecture of your house and style of landscaping. The darker the pebbles, the less conspicuous and more natural-looking they will be. They can also be used for the surface of patios or for pockets within paved surfaces. You can even make small gardened units within paving pockets.

Do you have a problem area beneath wide overhanging eaves where rain does not fall and plants will not grow? This is an ideal place for some type of rocks. You can be totally utilitarian and merely make a wide band of gravel next to your house. It can be contained by a metal edging strip, masonry mowing strip, shrubs or groundcover plants. Or you can develop portions of the area that can be seen from windows, or that adjoin doors, as

rock and pebble gardens — artistically arranged. You can add living material to such areas by using drought-defying succulent plants, or potted plants that you can water. Or you might like a little pool or fountain that can serve as a birdbath.

Perhaps a tree in your yard can be the nucleus around which you can arrange one or two large stones and a foreground of pebbles.

A running brook or a waterfall is possible in this day of recirculating pumps. What fun one of these would be for the children, and what a delight for birds!

PLANTS FOR ROCK GARDENS

The best plants for you depend upon the type of rock garden that you are developing, and also upon your climate. But here are some general suggestions.

True alpine plants—those native to the tops of mountains—are not always easy to grow at low elevations, for they are used to cool temperatures, cool soil, a short growing season, snow or rain and very fast drainage. They are a challenge anywhere and often demand special preparation of the site and soil. If you would like to specialize in them, it would be wise to do some reading on them and their needs.

Most American gardeners are more interested in how a plant looks, behaves, and fits into their garden than in the place where it originated. So rock-garden plants are ordinarily any that do well among rocks, but especially low-growing creepers, dwarfs, miniatures, and those with interesting foliage, texture, shape, or showy flowers.

For shady rockeries, the list of possibilities is the same as for any shady garden, except that your preference will probably be for the smaller varieties of ferns, wild flowers, bulbs, etc., instead of the big ones. You will find help in the chapter on shady gardens.

PRECEDING PAGE:

The rocks in this New Jersey garden look so natural that one cannot tell whether they have been here for centuries or were brought from elsewhere and skillfully arranged.

Pebbles can make patterns in paving. Do units one at a time, since cement hardens quickly. The plants here are juniper and snow-in-summer. E. Hawkins garden, Englewood, Colorado

A groundcover of aggregate is used in the shaded entrance area at the Gerald Hillyard residence, Denver, Colorado. S. R. DeBoer architect; Lew Hammer, landscape construction

Terrazzo chips in red, gray and white fill and accent the interlocking curves of upright pieces of tile in the garden of William Scott, Fort Worth, Texas. The plants are lily-turf.

VARIED WAYS
TO USE ROCKS
AND PEBBLES

If your location is sunny, you can grow flowering plants that will cover the rocks with brilliant blooms, or you can use the stones as settings against which tiny jewel-like blossoms are displayed. For early spring try some of the little bulb flowers such as crocus, scilla, small species of tulips and miniature daffodils. Avoid the usual large varieties of tulips and daffodils which can be put in other places in your yard. Creeping or low-growing perennial plants with masses of blossoms include the dazzling pink, red and white varieties of moss-pink, sunshiny yellow alyssum basket-of-gold, white rock-cress, purple ajuga, white evergreen candytuft and rainbow-hued dwarf-bearded irises. For summer try dwarf kinds of pinks, yellow *Achillea tomentosa,* blue Carpathian harebell, Serbian bellflower, creeping veronicas, and white babys-breath. All of these are described—and many illustrated—in the chapter on perennials.

Dwarf or prostrate evergreens are always an asset, and usually the most important permanent plants in the garden. The amount of space that your rockery covers will determine how large and vigorous-growing your evergreens should be. Several popular kinds, such as the creeping junipers, are described in the chapters on shrubs and the one on groundcovers. True dwarfs are rare, slow-growing, expensive, and usually sold by specialists; you will be proud to own one.

Plants with gray foliage look distinctive and handsome in rocks. Some of the best perennial kinds include moundlike, lacy-leaved artemisia 'Silver Mound'; tufty blue fescue grass; furry lambs-ears (*Stachys lanata* or *S. olympica*); woolly thyme that forms a flat, fragrant carpet of tiny leaves; fluffily branched and lavender-flowered catmint; bushy santolina: flat-foliaged *Sedum sieboldi;* silvery-white-leaved *Veronica incana* that bears spikes of blue flowers, and quick-spreading, white-flowering snow-in-summer.

Succulents, including cacti, are made to order for sunny, fast-draining rocky situations. If your climate is mild, you have almost limitless choices. For cold-winter regions, there are very hardy kinds including sedums in many variations of foliage and flower color, and fascinating rosette-form hen-and-chickens or houseleek (*Sempervivum*) of different kinds, colors and traits. These are all easy to grow and fun to collect; when they multiply, you can exchange varieties with friends who have other kinds.

WARNING: *Do not introduce into your rock garden any of the invasive-type groundcover plants or you will fight them forever. While your garden is new, and you are striving for a planted effect, it is a temptation to use these rampant, fast-spreading things, but they will quickly crowd out choicer plants, and their roots penetrate deeply and widely. Be patient—the slower ones will be much nicer in the long run!*

For names of some firms specializing in rock plants and native plants, see list in the back of the book.

16

Containers, Pots, Planters
and Window Boxes

Container gardening is booming in popularity. The term *container* is a broad one, including everything from small clay pots to giant wooden or concrete boxes. The plants used in them can be anything from petunias to pine trees. Containers are extra special ornaments, calling atteniton to the spot where they are used, and also to themselves. In mild climates, shrubs, trees or vines in planter boxes can remain outdoors all year as permanent features. In cold climates, most potted plants must be brought inside for winter or— if they are expendable—allowed to freeze and then replaced the next season.

The advantage of having pots or other moderate-sized containers is that you can move them around wherever they are momentarily most effective or needed. You can switch them from indoors to out; from front door to back-yard patio. You can bring them into the limelight when they are looking their best, and banish them to the hinterlands when they go into a decline. If your garden is new and empty, you can dress it up instantly with some big pots full of geraniums, begonias or petunias. Your friends will be so impressed that they will not miss flowers you do not have. Fancy blooming plants are not essential. Foliage plants become glamorous when put into interesting containers or when used imaginatively. When shrubs or trees are pruned so that their stems make an interesting silhouette they suddenly become distinguished and choice. House plants can lead double lives, lending a tropical look to outdoor living areas during their summer vacation outside.

Planter boxes and window boxes are the equivalent of large, immovable containers. Their structure and design must harmonize with the architecture of your house and garden, since they are permanent, integral parts of it.

Whether growing plants in small containers or large ones, there are some general principles that are helpful to understand. To begin with, plants will dry out much faster than those growing directly in the garden. You will have to water them much more frequently—probably every day during hot and drying weather. Soil must be "special"; it must be porous and fast-draining, yet moisture-retentive. It is essential to provide a way for drainage of excess water from the container. Since plants will be crowded, they will need frequent feeding. Because they will be in conspicuous locations they will need to be continually groomed so they will look worthy of their important setting.

Basic Know-How for Plants Grown in Containers

Though there are some special things to learn about plants grown outdoors in pots or other containers, the fundamental principles covering potted plants, such as best types of pots, methods of potting, soil mixture, feeding, watering, etc., are the same as for indoor potted plants. That information is given in the introductory section of the chapter on indoor plants.

Kinds of Containers for Outdoor Use

Containers must be very strong and made of materials that stand continual moisture. They must have drainage outlets. The most attractive shapes are the simple ones without ornamentation. The most popular types are listed below but there are all sorts of other possibilities.

Unglazed clay pots: These are always good and easily available. They come in a wide range of sizes. You can buy them tall or low. Do not overlook the large flat ones sold as drip saucers for the others. These saucers are excellent for holding groups of small succulent plants. A big advantage of clay pots is that they are porous. Air can get to the roots. Also it is easy to water the plants in them thoroughly by dunking the entire unit.

One way to slow the speed of drying, and also insulate roots from the heat of outdoor air, is to place one pot inside another, leaving an inch of space between them which can be filled with sphagnum moss kept moist. Or set several small pots within one large one, perching them on inverted small flower pots and stuffing the space between the planted pots with sphagnum moss that should be kept moist. A third way to minimize evaporation is to group several pots close together on paving or soil.

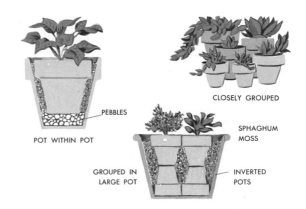

POT WITHIN POT — PEBBLES

CLOSELY GROUPED

GROUPED IN LARGE POT — INVERTED POTS

SPHAGHUM MOSS

Wooden boxes, tubs, barrel-halves, etc.: You can buy some of these at garden supply centers, or you can construct your own. If you build boxes, use a rot-resistant wood such as redwood or cedar. Boards should be 1 in. thick for strength and to provide desirable insulation for the roots. Fasten the parts of

OPPOSITE:
Evergreen Japanese andromeda in a red wood planter makes a handsome accent at the edge of a terrace in Portland, Oregon. Two lava rocks add weight at the shrub's base.

Small, all-alike containers can be grouped in many ways, and are easy to lift and move where needed. The ones shown are made of rough cedar and filled with white ruffled petunias.

A raised planter bed serving as a bench around a shade tree is filled with roses. As the tree grows, the plantings will change. Design by Thomas Church & Associates.

You can dress up a bare-looking patio in a hurry by adding gay flowers in containers. For this one, Japanese food-export tubs are planted with geraniums.

EXAMPLES OF EXCELLENT CONTAINERS

the box together with screws rather than nails, for the latter will be pushed out of place with the pressure of soil and water. Do not forget to provide drainage holes. Soil can be placed directly in the box, or you can use the box as a receptacle to hold plants in pots or cans.

If you are planning to move the containers here and there, plan their size accordingly, for when they are filled with soil they are astonishingly heavy. Sometimes it is wise to build a long box as several separate segments which can be used end to end or in other combinations.

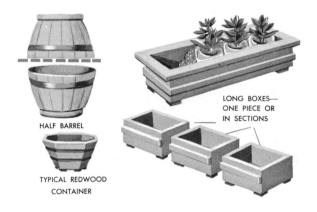

HALF BARREL

TYPICAL REDWOOD
CONTAINER

LONG BOXES—
ONE PIECE OR
IN SECTIONS

Tiles turned into containers: These have intriguing possibilities when used upright in various heights and sizes. They can stand on soil, or on "saucers" of flat pieces of wood. You can use ordinary round drain tiles or square chimney flue tiles. Both are available at lumber yards or stores dealing in builder's supplies. They can be cut to desired and assorted heights by using a hammer and chisel. First mark a line where you wish to cut all the way around the tile. Tap gently all around with a cold chisel, and make the final separating blows preferably with a brick set. The broken, rough edges can be smoothed with a brick set, or if the lower portion of the

container is to be imbedded in soil, the rough edge can be that hidden portion.

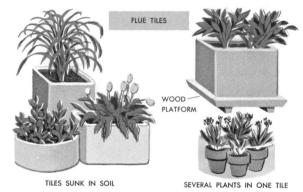

FLUE TILES

WOOD
PLATFORM

TILES SUNK IN SOIL

SEVERAL PLANTS IN ONE TILE

Feeding and Watering Techniques

Watering: As for indoor potted plants, the soil should be watered thoroughly and deeply, and then allowed to become fairly dry before being watered again. But outdoor plants dry more rapidly. You must watch them and learn their needs. On sunny, hot and windy days, they will need more water than during cool, moist weather.

When watering, soak the soil until it is evenly wet and excess water runs out of the bottom of the container. As soil dries it tends to pull away from the side of the container and leave a crack there. When you water, therefore, the moisture is apt to take the easy route and seep down around the outside of the soil, rather than in the center where the roots are. This is one of the big reasons for dunking pots when possible, or for watering them very slowly and over a considerable period of time. To remedy the crack, dig out a portion of the soil completely around the inside edge of the container, making a trench about 1 in. wide and as deep as the digging tool will reach. Mix a fresh batch of soil like that in the container, and pound it into the trench, using a potting stick or similar instrument. It must be tight. Then water the plant a couple of times and it is ready for a normal watering schedule.

Feeding: Because outdoor plants in containers need to be watered often, their food supplies are washed away and need frequent replenishing. Use a complete plant food, preferably one of the liquid or completely soluble kinds, following manufacturer's directions. Apply it about every three weeks, or even every week if you use it in much smaller amounts. Do not begin feeding newly set plants until they are established and growing vigorously.

How To Move Heavy Containers

To begin with, choose a time when the plant's soil is as dry as you dare to let it become—in order to reduce weight. Set it on a piece of canvas and pull it over the ground, or drag it on the broad, flat face of a shovel—a big snow shovel is excellent—with someone walking alongside to balance the pot and keep it in position.

Tip the container from side to side in a rocking movement as you maneuver it along the ground or floor in the desired direction. This will make it "walk," and less lifting will be necessary.

Use a wheelbarrow or coaster wagon.

Build or buy a sturdy dolly—a low platform on easy-swiveling castors. Garden stores sell such platforms in various sizes to set beneath individual pots.

Roll the container on a series of 3 rollers such as lengths of metal pipe. The container rolls on 2 of them, while you place the third in front as you gradually progress.

Borrow or rent a hand truck such as grocery stores use to move cases of cans, etc.

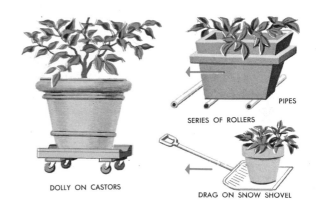

DOLLY ON CASTORS

SERIES OF ROLLERS

PIPES

DRAG ON SNOW SHOVEL

Hanging Baskets or Pots

Overhead hanging containers of trailing plants are very glamorous, and if you can grow them well you will win many compliments. But to succeed with them takes some doing, plus tender loving care. There are 3 primary problems. First, since they are up in the air, their soil dries with unusual speed. Second, because they are heavy, it is difficult to support them safely. And, finally, since they are high, they are a challenge to water. There is also the problem of dripping. But do not let this discourage you, for there are ways around all of the difficulties and the results are worth the effort!

The best baskets are wire frames manufactured for the purpose. Florists use them. You can buy them at garden supply stores—often already planted. The frame should be lined with sphagnum moss 1½ in. thick. This will keep soil from washing out and also serve as insulation. If you wish to use clay pots, they can be hung by fastening a circle of heavy wire or band of metal below the rim, and securing other wires to this for hanging.

The best plants to use are those that naturally droop or trail, such as trailing geraniums, cascade-type petunias, asparagus fern, *vinca major,* achimenes, fuchsia or wandering Jew. Hang the basket by some sort of strong hook arrangement, so that you can take it down for thorough watering either regularly or occasionally. That way it will be possible to dunk and soak the entire soil ball, and the after-dripping can be completed before you rehang the basket. Usually hanging containers need daily watering. You can do it in the evening. Feed every 2 or 3 weeks with a liquid fertilizer.

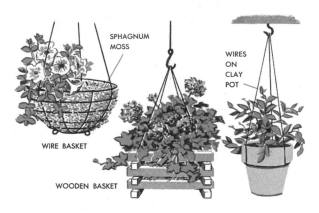

SPHAGNUM MOSS

WIRES ON CLAY POT

WIRE BASKET

WOODEN BASKET

Built-in Planters

Whether these are made of wood or masonry, they must be strong enough to contain heavy, moist earth and resist its pressures. As with all planters, they must also have outlets for excess water. Where freezing temperatures occur in winter, pressures are greatest, and extra precautions must be taken in the construction.

If your planter is beneath an overhanging roof, rain may never reach it, and all water may need to be applied artificially. This is a challenge for you and even more so for the plants. Only unusually tolerant plants will grow in such a location. Probably it will be wise for you to discuss your problem with your nurseryman and get his advice on plants that can take it. Maybe you will decide to use succulents combined with weathered wood or rocks. Or maybe you can devise some special method for irrigation.

Selection of plants will depend upon your climate, the location of the planter, and its size.

Window Boxes

These are practically permanent. Though each is designed to adorn a specific window, it also becomes part of the over-all look of a house. Therefore the boxes should be thought of as a part of your home's architecture. The plants in them become part of the landscaping. If there are several boxes on one side of the house, where they are all seen in the same view, they should be considered as a group rather than as separate small gardens, and be planted in a unified manner.

The size of the boxes is important for appearance, the health of the plants, and the ease of taking care of them. Most boxes are taken down from their perches for planting, so their weight is an important factor. The dimensions of each window makes a difference, of course, but in general the best measurements for window boxes are these. Length should be 3 to 4 ft., so that when filled with earth it will not be too heavy for 2 people to lift. Width should be a minimum of 10 in. at the top, to allow for 2 rows of plants—one upright and one trailing. Depth should be 8 in. for inside measurement.

The best material is wood, since metal tends to become too hot in the sun. Use cedar or redwood which are rot-resistant, 1 in. thick for strength and insulation. Or you can use one of the new pressed woods. Put the boxes together with screws rather than nails so they will not come apart.

To provide drainage in the bottom of the boxes, make ¾ in. holes 5 in. apart. Over the holes place broken bits of old flowerpots, etc., to assure fast drainage. Over this put your porous soil. Each year before planting, all old soil—or at least ⅓ of it—should be removed and new fresh soil added.

Some of the best flowers to use in sunny window boxes are ageratum, annual phlox, geranium, marigold, nasturtium, petunia, scarlet sage and sweet alyssum. For boxes in part shade or the north side of the house, try begonia, coleus, fuchsia, impatiens, lobelia, or torenia.

This summer, drive around town and notice which combinations of plants you admire that other people use. Jot them down to help you make decisions for another year.

An azalea in a handsome container is the spring accent for the moon gate that is built across the corner of the grape stake fence at the Bill Wheaton yard in Claremont, California. Various potted plants take turns here all year.

17

‍≀

How to Pick, Condition
and Preserve Flowers

Whether you grow flowers to bring indoors to decorate your home, or are primarily interested in having their beauty and color in your yard, there are some things you should know about how to pick them. If you want them for bouquets, you should know how and when to gather them. Cutting at the proper time of day and stage of development will make them last better in your arrangements. And since picking is a form of pruning, the manner and place where you make the cuts can be good or bad for the general well-being and future blooming of the plant. All flowers need care after cutting, but some flowers have very special requirements, which are simple when you know what they are.

This chapter will tell you when to cut flowers and how to improve their staying qualities; those best for drying and how to dry them; how to have blooms from shrubs weeks ahead of their regular bloom season by forcing branches indoors; also which foliage is desirable for cutting be serving for lasting beauty. It will also acquaint you with many idosyncrasies of your favorite flowers.

Importance of Time and Method for Cutting Flowers

The best time of day to pick most flowers is early in the morning or in the evening after the sun is down. Roses are an exception, explained in list of flowers in this chapter.

Carry a bucket of tepid water with you, so you can plunge stems into water immediately. Annuals, especially, need to get into water fast.

Select flowers that are in loose bud stage or that have recently opened, since their keeping qualities are best. However, zinnia, calendula, dahlia, marigold and China aster should be nearing their peak of beauty when picked, since their buds do not open well afterward. Avoid any blooms that are fully expanded or possibly past their prime.

Spiky blooms, composed of numerous individual flowers or florets, should be picked when ⅓ to ½ of the florets have opened. This group includes delphinium, larkspur, foxglove, snapdragon and branches of many trees and shrubs.

Flowers from vines will hold up better if, when picking them, you include a portion of the woody or older stem to which the bloom's stem is attached.

Make a slanting cut with a sharp knife or clipper, so there is a large area through which the stem can take up water.

The place where you cut the flower from the plant can determine how that plant grows, and the time and number of blooms.

With perennials, including bulbs, do not take away more leaves than necessary. The leaves are the plant's food factory. If you remove too many, you starve the plant and lessen the number and quality of blooms.

Annuals need to be picked, for they bloom best and longest when they are not allowed to mature seed. Many become leggy if not cut back occasionally to stimulate the growth of new side shoots. Picking serves as a beneficial method of pruning.

"Conditioning" Vital before Arranging

The process of preparing flowers to keep properly is called "conditioning" or "hardening." To assure that the flowers will hold up and not wilt, they must first be filled with moisture, and then provided with a continuing supply. The cut flowers should stand in water for several hours, or overnight, before you use them. The temperature of the water should be warm to begin with, and then cool, except for fleshy-stemmed flowers like tulips,

bleeding-heart and succulents, which should go immediately into cold water. Keep in a cool, dark place free from drafts. Cover lightly with paper or plastic to hold humidity.

Since flowers and foliage will continue to transpire—give off moisture—after they are cut, your major challenges in prolonging their lives are to help them take up water, and then keep them from losing it faster than they absorb it. There are several ways to do this—mostly prior to conditioning—and it pays to know as many tricks as possible.

Unneeded foliage should be removed from stems before they are conditioned. Take off all that is not essential for the arrangements that you are planning. Be especially careful to take off all foliage below water line, for otherwise it will decay and clog stems so that they cannot take up water. Branches of flowering shrubs should have at least half of their foliage removed.

Woody stems need special preparation. Branches of flowering trees and shrubs should have the lower 2 in. of stem pounded or slashed so they will take up maximum water. Even breaking the stem instead of cutting it will help.

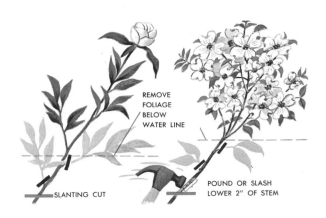

REMOVE
FOLIAGE
BELOW
WATER LINE

SLANTING CUT

POUND OR SLASH
LOWER 2" OF STEM

Stems that ooze a milky or colorless juice should have the cut end burned with a flame before conditioning. Such flowers include poppy, poinsettia, canterbury bell, balloon-flower and hollyhock. Char the stem end until bleeding stops. Stems will also ooze at places where leaves are removed, so sear these too. If you must shorten the stem later, for arranging, repeat the burning process. Another way to stop the flow of sap is to dip the lower inch of stem in boiling water for about 1 min.

Whichever method you use, be sure to protect the flower head from the flame or steam by cutting a hole in a piece of cardboard through which to put the stem; or wrap in a newspaper cone. After sealing the stems, put them in deep cold water to harden.

Some blossoms last but one day, whether they are in water or out of it. Examples are day-lily and Chinese hibiscus.

Double blossoms tend to last longer than single ones.

Loppy stems can be straightened during conditioning. Wrap them tightly in several thicknesses of newspaper, up to the flower heads, before putting them in water.

Stems that are unattractively straight can be bent and worked into artistic curves. For a deep curve, tie the tip and the end of the branch together and soak for an hour in cold water. Needle-leaved evergreens and pussy willow are especially adaptable. To curve spikes of delphinium, snapdragon, gladiolus or lupine, stand stems slantwise in a wide-mouth container during hardening.

SEAR ENDS AND WHERE LEAVES ARE REMOVED

CARDBOARD

PROTECT TOPS, AND DIP STEM ENDS IN BOILING WATER FOR 1 MINUTE . . .

WRAP IN NEWSPAPER—PLACE IN WATER

TIE INTO A CURVE—SUBMERGE IN WATER

Foliage is conditioned the same way as flowers. Exceptions are those plants that grow directly from the ground such as rhubarb, fern, plantain-lily and *Vinca minor*. They should be submerged in water for at least an hour.

Entire small flowering plants, such as pansy, lobelia and torenia, can be conditioned and used as decorations by themselves or in arrangements. Lift them, wash off the soil, and place the roots in water.

Ways To Make Flowers Last

Be sure your flower holders and containers are clean; wash in soapy water. Keep arrangements out of sun, drafts and heat. Put them in a cool place each night. Every day, make sure that water covers the base of the stems, for some flowers absorb a surprising amount. Recutting stems occasionally will help too.

Reviving Flowers That Become Limp

Sometimes after you have placed flowers in an arrangement, they "go down." It is often possible to remove and revive them, but you must not wait long before applying the emergency treatment.

General rule: Recut the stems, following the same techniques you used when first conditioning the flowers. For instance, if the stems are woody, pound or slit the lower 2 in. again. Then put stems first in water so warm that it is almost hot to the touch. Leave them until the water cools. Then place in deep cold water for at least an hour.

Lilac, pansy and violet take up moisture through their petals. If they are only slightly wilted, they will often revive if given a light spraying of cold water.

With hydrangea, the complete flower head should be submerged in cold water until it becomes crisp.

For roses, see the special list of flowers that follows in this chapter.

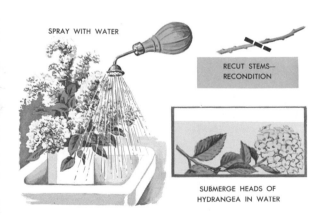

SPRAY WITH WATER

RECUT STEMS— RECONDITION

SUBMERGE HEADS OF HYDRANGEA IN WATER

Details on a Few Favorites

DAFFODILS. Because they bloom extra-early, they are especially appreciated as cut flowers.

They are excellent to use with spring-flowering branches since their own foliage should not be cut—it is needed to nourish the bulb that will produce next year's crop of bloom. Freshly opened flowers keep best. If you wish to hold them several days before using, cut buds that are about to open and store them in a refrigerator. Place cut stems in hot water for a minute to stop the flow of juice. After conditioning they need only the cut ends of their stems in water.

DAISY. These flowers are best used in informal arrangements since they turn their heads toward the light and you cannot depend on their staying in a certain position. If cut when they are newly opened and their centers tight, they are long-lasting indoors. In picking, cut above a side branch where another bud is forming. You will have a longer bloom season if they are not allowed to set seed.

GLADIOLUS. Cut the spikes on a slant when the first 1 to 3 florets are open. Let at least 4 leaves remain on the plant to mature the corm. Watch for possible second-bloom stems that may be developing on the stalk and cut above them; you may get another crop of smaller though equally lovely flowers. Buds that are not showing any color when cut probably will not open, so they can be removed to improve the appearance of the stalk. Blossoms will continue to open. As lower ones wilt, remove them; the stem can gradually be shortened. Gladiolus need only about an inch of water.

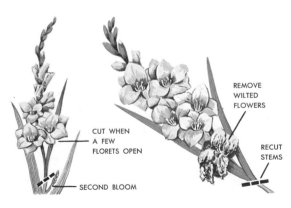

CUT WHEN A FEW FLORETS OPEN

REMOVE WILTED FLOWERS

RECUT STEMS

SECOND BLOOM

GOURDS (fruits, not the flowers). Harvest when the outer shell is hard, before the first severe frost. Light frost helps harden them. Cut with a short piece of stem attached—unless it drops off naturally. Be careful not to injure the outer covering. Leave gourds in a cool, airy, dry place until they are completely dry and their seeds rattle. If mold forms, keep it wiped off; it is caused by evaporation of moisture. Once dried, they will keep indefinitely.

LILACS. If you like lilacs picked with stems longer than 1 or 2 in., you will have some decisions to make about the importance of future blooms on your bush, because the shoots that will carry next year's flowers develop just at the base of the short stems that carry this year's flower heads. Cutting long stems removes most of next season's potential bloom. Turn to the chapter on pruning for illustrated instructions on where to pick.

Lilac blooms keep best if all foliage is removed except for 1 leaf cluster near the flower head. If you want more foliage, cut additional stems with leaves only. Since stems are woody, crush or slash the lower 2 in. before conditioning in water. To revive drooping blossoms in arrangements, spray them lightly, all over, with water.

PANSY. It is essential to keep these flowers picked so they will not go to seed. Cutting branch segments will not only give you longer stems to use in your arrangements but will stimulate development of new side branches. To revive wilting blossoms, spray them lightly with water, for they absorb moisture through their petals.

PEONY. The flowers should be picked when they are about half open. They will become surprisingly larger as they open in water. To hold for future use, cut the buds that are showing color and store them in the refrigerator. They can be kept two or three weeks. Do not cut longer stems than you need because you are also removing leaves that are needed to nurture the plant. There should be at least two pairs left on a stem. Peony foliage is excellent to use with other flowers throughout the season. If ants are

a problem, shake or brush them off before bringing flowers indoors.

PETUNIA. These are excellent material for informal arrangements. The flowers should be picked when freshly opened, though buds will continue to open indoors and will give you long-lasting beauty. Remove faded or dead flowers to keep your arrangement tidy. Make your cut just above a bud or branch. This is a way of pruning, and you can keep cutting a few at a time during the entire bloom season. If you are to be gone on vacation in late summer you can cut the entire plant back to about 8 in. When you return you will have a bushy new plant with a fresh crop of blooms for fall.

PICKING LONG STEMS FORCES BASAL GROWTH

DRASTIC CUT-BACK IN LATE SUMMER BRINGS NEW BLOOM

ROSE. The place where you make your cut has a great deal to do with the future health of your bush, and the number and quality of flowers that it may have. The fewer leaves you take, and thus the shorter the flower stem, the better for the bush. Usually people who love their roses cut the blooms with very short stems except for very special occasions or in autumn. The recommended place to cut is ¼ in. above one of the top 5-parted leaves. A follow-up bud-bearing shoot will develop at that spot.

For an illustration of where to make cuts so that the picking will serve as pruning, and for tips on how to grow occasional extra large or long-stemmed roses, turn to the chapter on roses and the paragraphs on round-the-year care of hybrid teas.

Rules for preliminary conditioning of cut rose blooms are the same as for other flowers, except that the preferred time for cutting them is midafternoon when the sun has been on them for a few hours. If they droop in arrangements, recut the end of the stems on a slant. Then make 2 vertical scrapes along the lower 1 to 2 in. of the stems, exposing the light green undersurface. Put stems in water so hot you can barely put your hand in it. Let stand until water cools, then place in cold water up to their necks for an hour.

To hold cut roses for future use—from a few days to 2 weeks—cut them in the best bud stage. Do not put them in water. Cover up each flower, complete with stem, with Saran Wrap. Be sure air does not get in. Keep them in the refrigerator until you are ready to use. Then treat the flowers as though they were the wilted blooms described above. (Many other flowers can be kept this way for later use. Experiment to discover which of your favorites can be counted upon, and how long they can be kept.)

WRAP IN SARAN

SCRAPE SIDE— PUT STEM IN HOT WATER

CUT AT SLANT

2"

SWEET PEA. The flowers must be picked to keep plants blooming. Cut when most of the flowers on the stem are open. Splurge once in a while and cut part of the graceful vine with tendrils to enhance your arrangements. Be care-ful not to get their petals wet.

ZINNIA. The best varieties to grow for picking are the cut-and-come-again and multi-branch types. The more you pick the better they bloom. Flowers should be fairly well opened but not past their prime. The buds are interesting to use, but do not count on them to open.

HOW TO FORCE BRANCHES OF SHRUBS AND TREES

To get an extra dividend from your flowering trees and shrubs, try forcing branches indoors; you can have flowers 2 to 6 weeks ahead of their outdoor bloom time! Interesting branches to force for foliage are Japanese maple and oak; also branches of trees that have an exciting array of catkins, such as beech, hazelnut, hickory and willow.

A mild day during a thaw, or just after a rain, is the best time to cut them. Learn to know the difference between leaf buds and flower buds so you will not be disappointed with your results. Flower buds must be plump or just starting to swell. The colors will not be as intense indoors, especially the pinks. For example, the bright orange-red of flowering quince will be a soft pink-peach.

Early blooming shrubs such as forsythia, azalea and witch-hazel can be cut for forcing as early as mid-January. Later-blooming ones, including the flowering trees, can be started in sequence of their outdoor bloom time.

Do not cut branches hit-or-miss. Bear in mind your plans for your tree or shrub, so you can do some needed pruning, thus shaping the plant, while you enjoy its branches. Also decide how many you can use, and how you will use them, in order to be selective in the size and shape you choose.

Cut branches at a slant, just above a node or back to the main branch. Pound or slit the lower 2 in. of stems and submerge entire branches in water for a couple of hours (a bathtub is a good place), or stand them in a deep container in the shower, spraying them with room-temperature water. Bring to a light window and enjoy watching them burst into flower. The time it will take depends on the kind of branch and stage of bud when cut. To speed up the process, or if your room is extra-dry, repeat the soaking or spraying from time to time.

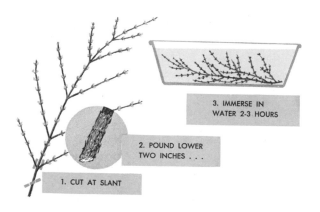

3. IMMERSE IN WATER 2-3 HOURS

2. POUND LOWER TWO INCHES . . .

1. CUT AT SLANT

HOW TO DRY FLOWERS FOR WINTER USE

The best conditions for picking flowers for drying are almost directly opposed to those ideal for keeping flowers fresh. Choose a bright sunny day, and pick when the sun is on them and all dew and moisture have dried off the petals. Strip off foliage immediately—leaves continue to give moisture to stems after cutting. Also, they do not dry attractively when attached to their stems. Some foliage, such as the rose, can be removed from stems and dried flat in sand, or pressed. Wire stems can be added to them later if needed.

Most flowers dry and hold color best if picked just before they are fully open.

Count on colors being darker after drying than they were originally. Yellow and orange dry most nearly true to color. Red roses become very dark. The orange-red varieties, such as 'Spartan,' dry a lovely red. Many pinks take on a lavender cast. Experimenting will help you in choosing what to dry. Colors hold best after drying if they are kept out of bright light. Dried flowers must be handled carefully to prevent them from shattering. Another problem is that petals tend to take up moisture from the air; this makes them shrivel and ruins their appearance. So be extra careful to store them in a dry place until you are ready to use them.

The two easiest methods of drying flowers are by hanging the stems with flower heads down, and by burying them in sand. The most satisfactory way to preserve foliage is with glycerin.

Drying Flowers by Hanging

Drying flowers by hanging is simple if you can provide proper conditions—a dry, dark, well-ventilated place. An attic is ideal, for you can drive nails into rafters for hanging, or string up lines far enough apart so flowers do not touch.

After stripping off foliage, tie the flowers in small bunches with Twist-ems (except large blooms, or clusters of blooms, which should be handled singly), and hang them with their heads down. Twist-ems or other covered wire make good fasteners because you can form loops to hang them from nails, or twist them over lines or coat hangers. Also, if stems loosen while drying they can be adjusted easily. Flowers will dry in 2 or 3 weeks. You can let them hang, or store them in boxes in a dry place until you are ready to use them.

Drying Flowers in Sand

The best kind of sand I have found for drying flowers is silica. It is white, fine as sugar, and can be used as is. It can be purchased in 50-lb. bags from your lumber dealer (enough for you and several friends). Another form of silica used in drying flowers is silica gel, which is more absorbent, and thus flowers dry faster. However, it is also considerably more expensive. It comes in 5-lb. cans and can be purchased at garden centers or flower-supply houses. If you use other sand, be sure that it is clean. Sift it with a fine-mesh strainer several times, because you will want it as fine as possible. To be certain that your sand is thoroughly dry before you use it, heat it in the oven, then let it cool. Repeat each time before you reuse it.

Choose a sturdy cardboard carton, or metal container such as a large baking pan, at least 3 in. deep. Fill the container ½ full of sand. Strip all foliage from stems and place the flowers face down in the sand so petals do not touch. Let the sand trickle through your hand over and around them, completely covering all parts of the flowers. Tie the stems in groups loosely, teepee style, to hold them in place.

A few flowers, including roses, dahlias and daffodils, dry best if they are placed face up with the base pushed gently into sand. First shorten their stems to ¼ in. and insert florists' wire through the stem into the base of the flower. Bend the wire stem horizontally, making the bend as close to the flower head as possible; keep the stem below the surface of the sand. Completely cover the flowers with sand.

Spiky flowers, such as larkspur and bells of Ireland, should be placed horizontally on a bed of sand. The entire stalk, and as long a stem as your box will accommodate, should be covered. In the latter two methods, where no stems protrude above the sand, use lids on containers for more effective drying. Set your containers in a cool, dry place. Check them after a week. Flowers vary in the length of time it takes them to dry. Experiment and keep records. Remember to keep them dry until you use them.

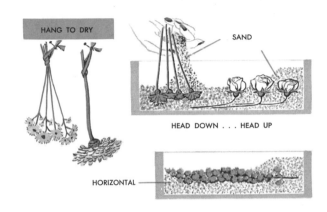

METHOD OF PRESERVING LEAVES WITH GLYCERIN

By far the most satisfactory way to preserve foliage is by the glycerin-and-water method. Leaves treated this way remain soft and pliable, with a rich satiny finish. Some change color, others only deepen—all are handsome. Magnolia leaves turn different shades of brown, depending upon the time of year you pick them and length of time they are left in the solution. Beech leaves, if processed while they are still green, will become a soft olive; treated after they turn gold in the fall, they will be a lovely russet. Pear leaves turn very dark brown, almost black. Most foliage that is bronzy-red naturally does not change color but takes on a little darker hue. Examples are forsythia, crab-apple, plum.

Glycerin-treated leaves last for years and years, so are a good investment of time and money. Since water does not harm them they can be used in fresh arrangements as well as dried ones. They can be cleaned with a damp cloth and should be stored in a box in a dry place when not in use.

The best time for processing leaves in glycerin is in late summer or early fall when the leaves are neither too young nor too old. Cut branches that have interesting lines, and with foliage in good condition. The maximum length of any branch should be 1½ to 2 ft., and you will want most of them shorter. (The length of the branch is important since the glycerin solution must travel from the cut end of the stem to the tip of the farthest leaf.)

Clean foliage thoroughly, and remove any unwanted or imperfect leaves. Pound with a hammer, or slit with a sharp knife, the lower 2 in. of stems. This will make them take up the solution more quickly.

Stand the branches in a glass jar, milk bottle or tall slender vase filled to a 5-in. level with a solution of ⅓ glycerin and ⅔ water. Do not crowd the branches. The preserving process will be speeded up if you wipe each leaf with a piece of cotton saturated in the solution. Repeat if the leaves begin to droop or dry.

Leave them in a well-ventilated room where you can watch them. Be sure the level of the solution remains above the crushed ends of the stems, and add more if necessary. You will be fascinated to observe the glycerin as it travels through the ribs to the tips and edges of the leaves, gradually changing their color. When the process is complete—from a few days to 2 weeks for most leaves—remove and hang them upside down for a day or two. Any solution left can be saved and reused.

Low-growing plants that absorb moisture through their leaves, such as galax, large or small-leaved ivy and *Vinca minor,* can be preserved by submerging in a solution of half-and-half glycerin and water. A Pyrex cake pan or casserole makes a good receptacle. The plants can be in layers but must be completely covered during the entire process. A weight on top will help to keep them in solution.

Individual leaves can be removed from branches (try beautiful fall-colored ones) and preserved in this manner. In fact, any leaf that will take up glycerin through its stem can be safely treated by submerging.

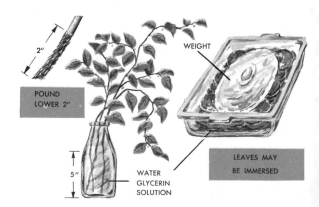

18

‚ÌÌ‚Ì·Ì‚ÌÌ

Vegetables and Herbs

The tastiest vegetables you will ever eat will be the ones you prepare fresh-picked from your garden. They will be superb and utterly unlike the tired, long-stored vegetables often found in markets. Those from your own garden can be harvested at their peak of perfection, and cooked while their flavor and vitamins are intact. Your family will dine like royalty.

While it is pleasant and interesting to grow some of your own food, I do not advocate trying to grow everything. Some crops take too much space for small yards, need special soils or climate, or are not worth the amount of time needed to grow them except for the fun and satisfaction of the experience. But you can grow some of the vegetables that your family likes most, including material for tasty salads and a few herbs to add unique flavors.

The chief requirement of a vegetable garden is a spot in full sunshine, away from roots of trees and shrubs, with relatively good soil. If your home is in a new subdivision, and minus big shade trees, this is your golden opportunity to have a vegetable garden. Also, if you have young children, this is the era when you will most appreciate bumper crops of homegrown food.

To obtain the best, most complete information on the vegetable varieties that will do best in your area, with details for growing them, get a bulletin on vegetable gardening from the office of your county agricultural extension agent. Usually these bulletins are free for the asking. Varieties suited to your state, soil and climate may be quite different from those recommended for other states. Why not have the best?

Do not attempt too big a plot the first year. Test your enthusiasm and skill on a modest-sized layout.

Preparing the Ground

If this is to be a new garden in a plot that is now in sod, it is wise to "skin off" the layer of grass and its roots before preparing the ground beneath it. This is important because grass has a remarkable ability to live, even when upside down, or torn apart and mixed deep in soil—it would keep coming up where you least wanted it. Put the removed sod on your compost pile where it can disintegrate and become excellent loam to return to your garden eventually. If your soil seems extremely sandy, or very hard and clayey, see the chapter on soils and fertilizers.

Spade the entire area, or rent a tiller to prepare the space easily. The ground should be turned over and loosened to a depth of 8 to 10 in. But before you do this, scatter complete commercial fertilizer over it at the rate of 3 lb. per 1,000 sq. ft. Use a fertilizer recommended for vegetables and general gardens—such as 4-10-6 or 4-16-4—rather than one recommended for lawns and therefore high in nitrogen. This should be incorporated thoroughly into the soil during its preparation. After the soil is prepared, rake the lumps out of the upper 2 in.

Buying Plants vs. Sowing Seeds

As you have undoubtedly noticed, many vegetable plants are sold in young sizes by garden supply stores at spring planting time. They are available either in pots or in little boxes. Some of these are plants that need such a long growing season that they might not mature their crop unless started early indoors or in a greenhouse. These include eggplant and pepper. Other types could be started from seed sown in the garden, but if you buy plants that are several weeks old you get a head start; these include cabbage, broccoli, cauliflower and tomato.

Among vegetables that are grown from seed planted directly in the garden—easy as can be—are beans, radishes, peas, lettuce, cucumbers, squash, melons, beets, chard, carrots, cabbage, broccoli, cauliflower and spinach.

Potatoes are grown from cut-up sections of potatoes that contain several "eyes" apiece. Sweet potatoes are grown from leafy-rooted sprouts that one buys by the bundle. Onions may be grown either from sets—which are tiny onions—or from seed.

Cool- and Warm-Season Crops Differ

Some vegetables grow best during the cool part of the year, and many of these can stand a little frost. This group includes lettuce, cabbage, cauliflower, broccoli, chard, carrots, beets, peas and radishes. They are grown as winter crops in mild-winter climates. If you live where winters are cold, start them in very early spring, or else in the late summer, so that they will reach maturity during cool autumn weather. If you are planting seed in the spring, get it into the ground before the frost-free date, while the ground is still cold and temperatures nippy.

There are other vegetables that will not succeed unless the weather is warm. These need warm soil in order for their seeds to germinate, and high temperatures to mature their fruits. They should not be set outdoors until all danger of frost is past and the earth is warm. This group includes beans, squash, cucumber, corn, eggplant, pepper, melons, tomato, sweet potato. Of these, beans and corn are started from seed sown directly in the garden.

Squash, cucumber and melons may be sown outdoors, or can be started inside early in individual containers. Tomatoes for early crops are started indoors or purchased. Eggplant and pepper must be given early starts in northern states because they need an unusually long time to grow to fruiting size.

As you can see, a vegetable garden can be a rotating affair, where one type of vegetable is grown during the cool time of the year, and an entirely different set during summer. In some cases early crops mature rapidly, and can be pulled to make room for their alternates. But in other instances, plants need their space over a period of many months. It pays to plan your schedule of planting carefully to make the best use of your area. Often you can intercrop—that is, start late plants between early-maturing kinds.

Use Safe Pest Controls

All-purpose sprays for the flower garden may not be safe on vegetables. Choose chemicals that do not leave a poisonous residue. For Mexican bean beetles, cucumber beetles, flea beetles, cabbage worms and other chewing insects, spray or dust with methoxychlor, rotenone or Sevin. For aphids, use malathion or nicotine sulfate. The latter is poisonous but quickly dissipated. Select varieties listed in catalogues as resistant to mosaic and other diseases disseminated by insects. To prevent tomato blight and other leaf diseases, use a fungicide—maneb or zineb—or use a general-purpose spray formulated especially for vegetables.

THE BEST VEGETABLES FOR SMALL SPACE

Your family's preferences and your climate must be taken into consideration. But if you are just beginning to grow vegetables, and want them on a modest scale, I think the following give the most reward for the space and effort.

BEANS, SNAP, BUSH and POLE types. These are a very easy warm-weather crop, raised from seed planted directly in the garden. In cold-winter climates, do not start them before danger of frost is past in the spring, and do not be in too big a hurry because seeds put in cold, wet ground tend to rot instead of germinate.

With bush types you can choose either green or yellow podded varieties. They will be ready to eat 50 to 60 days after sowing. ¼ lb. of seed will make a row 25 ft. long, and produce ½ bushel of beans. Plant them in a furrow 1 to 1½ in. deep, spaced 2 to 3 in. apart. If you make more than one row, leave 1½ ft. between them.

They appreciate a booster shot of plant food after they are about 5 in. high. Apply it as a side dressing—make shallow furrows along each side of the row of plants about 2 in. from the stems, and place the fertilizer there at the rate recommended on the package. In order to have beans over a long season, keep them closely picked. Also make more than one planting, with an interval of at least 2 weeks between sowings. The beans will taste best if you pick them when they are quite young, and certainly before they become tough and stringy.

Pole beans are grown like snap beans except that they need poles or a fence to climb, and take a longer time to begin to produce, but they do yield vast quantities.

LETTUCE. This is one of the easiest, most delectable, and usable foods you can grow. It is a cool-season crop, started from seed sown directly in the garden, and matures quickly. Loose-leaved types that do not make solid heads are the easiest to grow and are relatively tolerant of heat; you will be eating them a month after planting. Large-headed types are for very cool climates only.

In your garden you can grow succulent lettuces that are rarely available in markets because they do not ship well. Some of the best, most flavorsome varieties are Bibb, Matchless, Sweetheart, Ruby and Salad Bowl. Sow seed ¼ to ½ in. deep, spacing them about ½ in. apart. One packet will produce a surprising amount of lettuce.

When plants have their fourth leaves, the ones that make heads—small or large—can be thinned to a spacing of 6 to 15 in., depending upon their eventual size. The extra plants may be moved elsewhere. If you have loose-leaved lettuce, these plants can be thinned gradually by pulling leaves to eat. You can use the leaves by nipping some off here and there while others are left to nourish the plant, or you can cut off tops and new leaves will grow from the stumps to take their place. You may wish to make successive plantings of short rows.

When hot weather comes, lettuce becomes bitter, and shoots up to produce flowers and seeds.

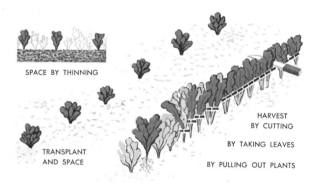

SPACE BY THINNING

TRANSPLANT AND SPACE

HARVEST BY CUTTING

BY TAKING LEAVES

BY PULLING OUT PLANTS

RADISH. This is a quick and easy cool-season crop. Early varieties mature in 20 to 30 days, and because they are at their prime only a short time, it is wise to make several plantings at 10-day intervals. Plant only a short row at a time. The seeds are small and round. Place them in a furrow about ½ in. deep, spaced roughly ½ in. apart. Later you can thin them to 1 in. apart so each has space to develop. They come up very fast and, since they also mature quickly, are often mixed with seed of slower-germinating vegetables to "mark the row" and then used before the later plants need the space.

TOMATO. Surely you have space in which to tuck in some tomato plants. If you do not have

enough room to let them sprawl normally on the ground, train them upright on a post, or tie them to a trellis like a climbing rose! This keeps the fruit off the ground and clean. Plants grown on the ground may spread to cover 4 sq. ft. apiece, but upright they will need only 1½ to 2 ft. They thrive on warmth and need a long growing season in which to mature—3½ to 4 months from the time seed is sown.

You can start the seed indoors while the weather is cold, in order to get a head start, but it is easier to buy started plants from a garden store when proper setting-out time arrives. Have at least 1 or 2 plants of an extra-early ripening variety. When transplanting, set the plants deeper than they were before, to encourage additional roots to form along the underground part of the stem. Feed about every 3 weeks, beginning 2 or 3 weeks after planting. Water generously. A mulch to cover the soil around the base of the plants will keep roots cool, and if any fruits rest on it they will be kept clean.

If you are growing the plants on stakes, begin tying them into position when they are 8 to 10 in. high. Keep at it, for they climb almost like vines to a height of 6 to 8 ft. Remove sucker shoots that develop in all crotches between leaf branches and the main stem. Left alone, these would become big branches and make the plant too heavy to stay in place on the stake.

Any green tomatoes remaining on the plants when frost threatens in autumn can be picked and brought indoors to ripen.

SECURE SHOOTS TO SUPPORTS

PINCH OUT THE SUCKER SHOOTS

SET PLANTS DEEPER

PRECEDING PAGE:
A wagon wheel herb garden is quaint and fun to have. The spokes serve as partitions to separate the various types of plants. This planting was designed by Mrs. Carolyn Wilkinson.

You do not need much space to grow the makings for salads. This compact planting contains onions and several types of lettuce. It was planned by Mrs. J. Mortimer Fox.

Beds of herbs can fit into the planned design of the landscaping of your yard. They are handiest near your kitchen door. Notice how the brick paths emphasize this terrace's pattern.

This is a fine example of a summer vegetable plot. Tomatoes are at left. Pole beans are starting to climb stakes in the foreground. Peppers, broccoli and cabbage are in other rows.

SAMPLE VEGETABLE
AND HERB GARDENS

❧ Notes on Other Popular Vegetables

Vegetable	Buy plants	Sow seed out-doors	Depth for seed	Grow in warm season	Grow in cool season	Spacing after thinning	Days from seed to harvest	Yield per 25 ft. of row
Asparagus (Perennial plant)	X				X	3'-4'	2 years	6 lb.
Beans, Lima		X	1"-2"	X		5"	120	½ bu.
Beans, Pole Lima		X	1"-2"	X		4"-6"	85-90	¾ bu.
Beets		X	1"		X	2"-3"	50-60	¼ bu.
Broccoli	X	X	½"		X	1½"-2"	60	25 lb.
Cabbage	X	X	½"		X	1½"-2"	65-120	14 heads
Cantaloupe		X	1"	X		3'	75-80	14 fruits
Carrots		X	½"		X	2"-3"	70-75	¼ bu.
Cauliflower	X	X	½"		X	18"	95	10 heads
Chard		X	1"		X	6"	75	10 lb.
Corn, Sweet		X	1"-2"	X		10"-12"	75-90	3 doz.
Cucumber		X	1"	X		3'	70	1 bu.
Onion	X	X	¾"		X	3"	100-125	¼ bu.
Peas		X	1"-2"		X	2"	65-75	2½ lb., shelled
Pepper	X			X		18"	115	1 bu.
Potato, Irish		*	3"-4"		X	1'	115	¾ bu.
Potato, Sweet	X			X		1'-1½'	140-150	½ bu.
Spinach		X	1"		X	3'	60-70	¾ bu.
Squash, Bush		X	1"	X		3'-4'	60-65	35 lb.
Turnip		X	1"		X	3"	60-80	½ bu.
Watermelon		X	1"	X		6'	100-130	15 fruits

* Use chunks of potatoes with 1 or more "eyes"

Herbs Grow Easily and Have Delightful Flavors

The usual pronunciation of the word herb—in America—is "erb," but when you are in England, sound the "h"! If you have always thought of herbs as grocery-store products sold as packaged powders, you are due for a new and exciting experience when you grow your own! They are attractive plants with fragrant and flavorsome leaves or seeds that can be used either fresh or dry to add distinction to your cooking. Some are perennials that live from year to year. Others are annuals started from seed each season. A few are biennials on a two-year life schedule. Most are grown primarily for their foliage, but a few have pretty flowers besides.

You will find them easy to grow in average garden conditions, and conversation pieces as well. When you have a plot of them by your back door or patio, you can dash out and snip a bit of this and that to add to your simmering stew or half-completed salad. Your cooking will achieve gourmet quality! Along with the pleasure of surprising your family and friends with your abilities, you will have fun growing the plants just to discover what they look like and how they taste when fresh.

It is not necessary to have an ornately designed, fancy herb garden. Yet it is well to arrange the plants in a pleasing way, since everyone will want to see them and will undoubtedly want to pick pieces to nibble. The plants can be in orderly rows, or scattered according to their needed space. They can grow directly in the soil or in containers. They can be in pots sunk to their rims among pebbles or in clay tiles up-ended to form planters. Edgings can be made of basil, parsley or thyme. Lettuce can be grown in rows that form patterns among the herbs. As you see, an herb garden can be whatever you wish to make of it. You can keep it simple or go all-out in having it decorative as well as useful.

Requirements for Outdoor Growing

Herbs will thrive in the same sort of situations, and by the same methods, that vegetables and most annual flowers like. They want lots of sunshine, moderately fertile soil and good drainage.

How to Harvest Leaves

The flavor is best and retained longest if the foliage is picked at the right time. To be saved for future use it should be properly cured and stored. Tender young leaves can be used fresh at any time. For drying, pick individual leaves, or stems carrying numerous leaves, just as the plants begin to flower. If the foliage is dirty or dusty, wash it in cold water before beginning the drying.

Drying should be rapid. A dark, well-ventilated place is best. Grandmother used to do it in a big attic. For outdoor drying, spread the leaves on cheesecloth spread over wire screens, and put them in a shady place out of the wind; bring them indoors at night or whenever conditions are moist. Oven-drying works, too. For this method, spread leaves or leafy stems on a baking sheet. The temperature should not be above 200°; the oven door should be left open.

To store, strip the dried leaves from the stems and put them in airtight, light-tight containers.

Tips on Growing Herbs Indoors in Winter

The ones that do best indoors are the perennials rather than the annuals, for the latter mature and die at the end of the growing season. You will have best luck with chive, mint, sage, sweet marjoram and thyme. Pot up young plants or divisions and help them grow vigorously. They must have a sunny window and frequent watering.

THE 10 MOST USEFUL AND

EASY-TO-GROW HERBS

Perennials

CHIVES. It is the leaves of these little onions that one dices to add to salads, sandwich spreads, etc. The plants and their round purple flower heads are pretty enough for any garden, and make attractive permanent edgings for herb gardens. They grow 8 to 12 in. high and like full sun. Plant the bulbs (onions) at any time, or you can start them from seed—though that gives much slower results. If any of your friends have chives, they will be happy to give you a start. Allow each onion 5 in. of space, for they will multiply rapidly. Cut the plants nearly to the ground each year after they flower, and new growth will come up immediately. Divide clumps every few years so they will not become overcrowded and do poorly.

MINT. Put some sort of barrier around this plant's roots, for it is an invasive spreader that will crowd out other plants. Set it inside a sunken tile or in a space enclosed by paving. There are numerous types of mint, but probably spearmint is the most popular. Its leaves are used to flavor cold drinks and to make mint sauce. To get your start, buy a plant. It will grow 1 to 2 ft. high in sun or part shade, and will

like moist soil. Leaves for drying should be cut before the flowering season.

PARSLEY. This handsome, dependable plant with curly, fringed foliage is a biennial usually treated as an annual, and does best during the cool season of the year. To speed the germination of seeds, soak them in water overnight before planting. Parsley likes full sun, is low-growing, only 6 to 8 in. tall, and makes an excellent garnish or edge for the herb garden as well as a garnish and flavoring for food. Leaves may be used fresh at any time or be dried in a very slow oven. You may dig and pot plants in autumn to bring indoors for use during the winter. Set the pot in a sunny window and give it good care.

SAGE. Plants are started from seed sown outdoors in spring in full sun. Each plant needs 18 in. of space. They grow 1½ to 2 ft. high, with woolly gray leaves that have a pebbled texture. It is these leaves that are used, fresh or dried, for seasoning meats and dressings. Pick them from the stem at any time to use fresh or dry. If you cut the plant back occasionally, new growth will develop.

THYME. Tiny aromatic leaves cover this creeping groundcover plant that is related to mints. It comes in many varieties and grows from 2 to 10 in. high. Get your start by buying plants, begging a division from a friend; or, if you are clever with seeds, you can start with them. Thymes like sun and very fast-draining soil. They tolerate drought. Each year, after the flowering season, cut the plants back severely— or do it in early spring.

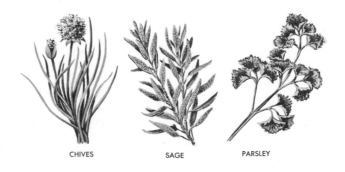

CHIVES   SAGE   PARSLEY

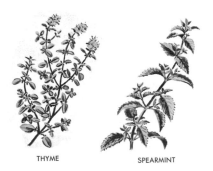

THYME   SPEARMINT

Annuals or Those Usually Handled as Annuals

BASIL. Start this plant from seed sown outdoors after danger of frost is over. You can choose varieties having either green or red-purple leaves. The latter are so handsome and decorative that they are used as foliage plants in flower beds. They grow up to 2 ft. high and should be thinned to be 6 in. apart. The scented foliage is used in cooking, and is especially delicious with tomato dishes. You can begin picking young leaves when the plants are 6 weeks old. Leaves to be dried should be picked before the plant's spikes of blooms appear.

DILL. These plants grow 2 to 3 ft. high, with bluish-green finely divided feathery leaves and flat clusters of small, yellowish flowers that develop into tasty seeds. Both leaves and seeds are used for flavoring pickles and other foods. The leaves have their best quality before the flowers open; seeds are harvested when ripe. The plants like to grow in full sun. Start them from seed in spring after danger of frost has past. Sow them where they are to grow, for seedlings are difficult to transplant. Thin the plants to a 10-in. spacing. The excess ones can be used or dried. Usually dill self-sows, so that if you grow it once you have it forever.

SUMMER SAVORY. You will enjoy using these leaves, fresh or dry, with meats, fish, soups or vegetables. The plant grows 12 to 18 in. high, with small, pungent foliage on wiry stems. There are tiny white or pink flowers. Grow it from seed started in early spring where it is to remain. Thin the seedlings to stand 6 to 12 in. apart. Harvest the leafy tops as the plants come into bud, and dry them hanging upside down.

SWEET MARJORAM. While this is a perennial, it tends to winterkill so is treated as an annual where winters have freezing temperatures. It is one of the most delightful fragrant and flavorsome herbs, very popular for adding to poultry stuffing and sauces for fish. The plant grows 8 to 12 in. high, with small velvety gray-green leaves. Each plant needs 8 in. of space. Start with seeds; these are very tiny and slow to germinate so are often started indoors. Soak them in water overnight before sowing. Outdoor planting should be done as soon as possible after the frost-free date in spring. Fresh leaves may be picked and used after the plants are growing well.

TARRAGON. Buy started plants. One or 2 are sufficient. They grow about 18 in. high and need 12 in. of space. Plants are multi-branched with narrow, twisted leaves that have a flavor similar to that of anise. Young leaves and tips of stems are used fresh in salads, or are used in vinegar or salad dressing in which they are steeped. Do not dry; the flavor is lost. Plants grow best in part shade but tolerate full sun.

DILL   TARRAGON

BASIL   SWEET MARJORAM   SUMMER SAVORY

19

~~~~~~

Fruits Suited to Small Space

Whether your yard is small or large, there are delicious fruits that you can grow. Nothing is more fabulously flavored than home-grown fruit, picked at its peak of correct ripeness. It is fit for kings or, more important, for your family and dearest friends. If your grounds are sunny, and your soil reasonably good, you have conditions that are right for raising fruit. Some varieties grow on trees, some on bushes or vines, and others on the ground. The trees are as beautiful when in flower as any trees you could plant for their flowers alone.

However, before you decide to turn your lot into a miniature fruit farm, you should consider seriously which fruits will fit your available space and prevailing soil without cramping your other outdoor activities, and which are worth the time, effort and cost of growing. All need attention if they are to produce well. Bush and tree varieties will need pruning. Most trees will not ripen fruit fit to eat unless sprayed many times a season. You will need to do this spraying, or hire someone to do it, which adds cost.

The kinds of fruits you can grow depend upon your climate and type of soil. Some, for instance, must undergo a period of chilling weather during winter. Others are injured by freezing. Among fruits suited to your general type of climate, certain varieties will do better in your specific locality than will others. To find out which ones these are, so that you can make wise choices and not have disappointments later, consult your county agricultural extension agent. He will probably have a printed bulletin to send to you, or can tell you how to get one. He can also tell you whether there are local firms that do custom spraying. Local nurseries are another source of advice.

Through such channels you should also check special soil requirements for fruit trees. The wise gardener will have a soil analysis made to determine basically whether his soil will welcome the type of fruit trees he intends to plant. After that, he should give his soil the treatment that analysis would indicate. Many plants and shrubs are fairly tolerant of any reasonably well-balanced soil but for best results on the larger fruit trees you should give them every possible attention so they can thrive and bear a good quality of fruit.

The time to buy and plant if you live in the North is very early spring; in Zones 6 through 8 you may plant either in early spring or autumn; in mild-winter climates, late fall or winter. Container-grown plants can be set out any time during the growing season.

FAMILIAR TREE FRUITS

In this group you will find the best-known large fruits. Trees in standard (normal) sizes generally become quite large when mature, and so must be allotted considerable space. They bear their crop by bushels. They can do double-duty by serving as shade trees, but this is not always as delightful as expected. If the fruit is sprayed regularly, many times a year, it will be excellent. But it can be a nuisance if it is unusable, and falls and rots on the ground! How much fruit do you really need? Trees that are dwarfs, or of small size normally, may be better for you than standard ones. With both standard and dwarf trees, it is wise to have more than one variety of each type of fruit, to assure cross-pollination of blossoms. However, peaches, apricots and sour cherries are generally self-fertile.

The following chart will give you an idea of which tree fruits can be grown in your hardiness zone. The space requirements given are for standard trees. The zones of satisfactory use apply to both standard and dwarf trees.

Fruit	Zones	Comments
Apple	4-8	Standard trees need 35′ space; bear first crop in 5 to 8 years.

Fruit	Zones	Comments
Apricot	5b-10	Allow 20′ space. Blooms early; may be caught by frost.
Avocado	9b-10	Evergreen, good as shade tree. Needs 30′ space.
Cherry		
Sour	4-7	Relatively small tree, needs 20′. Bears in 3 to 5 years.
Sweet	6-7	Big tree, give 35′ space.
Nanking	3-7	Very hardy. Big shrub or small tree; needs 10 .
Citrus	9-10	Evergreen. Orange and grapefruit need 25′ space. Kumquats are small, need 10′. Some lemon varieties are small.
Loquat	9-10	Decorative small evergreen; needs 15′ of space. Broad, long leaves; apricot-like fruit.
Mango	10	The "peach" of the tropics. Large tree; needs 35′ space.
Papaya	10	Tropical. Needs only 10′ space. Begins bearing within a year from seed.
Peach	5b-10	Relatively small tree; give 15′ space. Begins to bear in 3 to 4 years. Pink flowers.
Pear	5-8	Standard trees need 25′ space; start bearing in 3 to 6 years.
Plum	5b-10	Relatively small trees. Allow 20′ of space. Bear in 3 to 4 years.

For general instructions on how to plant standard fruit trees and care for them through the first years, see the chapter on trees.

Prune while the tree is young to develop strong basic scaffold branches, well spaced. Each year remove any dead, weak, or crossing branches, and shoots that arise from around the base of the trunk. After the tree begins to bear, some thinning of upper branches may be needed to let in sunlight and air to the center of the tree.

Peaches bear fruit on wood of the previous season's growth and require heavier pruning than other tree fruits to stimulate vigorous new wood. Pruning consists of thinning out shoots and cutting back to wood that is 2 or 3 years old.

Pear trees should not be pruned heavily, for they are susceptible to fire blight. Any blackened twigs—the sign of fire blight—should be removed by cutting back to healthy wood.

Dwarf trees have many advantages. They are not toys or oddities, but practical fruit-producers. They are as hardy as the same types in big-tree sizes, and as easy to grow. They take less space (only 10 ft.) so it is possible to have several in your yard. They bear sooner, often beginning the year after you plant them. Fruits are as big or bigger than those of the same variety on standard-size trees and often of higher quality. The trees are handier to spray, prune and pick, because they are at a height easier to reach. Of course you will not harvest as many bushels, but even that can be a blessing!

There are two main types of dwarfs. The first, of which there are very few, are naturally small-growing. Examples are 'Bonanza' dwarf peach and kumquat.

The second, and more common kind, are standard varieties that have been dwarfed by artificial techniques. Sometimes they are

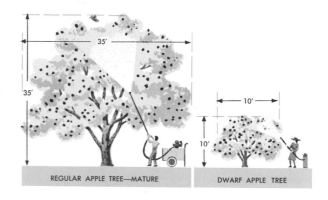

REGULAR APPLE TREE—MATURE   DWARF APPLE TREE

grafted onto a growth-inhibiting root system. Or else a short piece of stem of a dwarfing variety is grafted between the wanted top and the trunk of the seedling tree which is to provide the new tree's base and roots. In either case, the flow of food from the top of the tree (the food produced by the leaves) to the roots is restricted. The food accumulates in the upper part of the tree where it is utilized in producing more fruit. Because the roots receive little food, they do not grow as extensively as they would otherwise, and because they do not grow, the top of the tree is dwarfed.

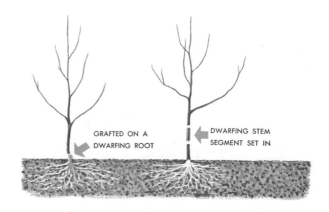

GRAFTED ON A DWARFING ROOT   DWARFING STEM SEGMENT SET IN

Locate the trees in full sun, and avoid windy places for dwarfed trees. Because of their small root systems and weak point of graft, they are easily blown over and broken. Space 10 ft. apart. Dig a hole wider and deeper than the roots. Set the plants at approximately the same level that they were in the nursery. The point of graft (which will be some sort of bulge or bump) should be above ground so roots will not develop above it and thus provide extra food for the plant and counteract the dwarfing action of the small root system. Place a supporting stake and tie the tree to it. Fill the hole with soil, adding moistened peat moss or other humus. Water well.

Through the first two years wrap the trunk with special tree-wrap paper, burlap or something similar. This will protect it from sunscald and rodents. For several years, until the trunk becomes old enough to be hard and rough, rabbits and mice will continue to gnaw on it during winter, especially in times of deep snow. So plan on wrapping it, or otherwise protect it with ¼ in. hardware cloth (wire). Mice can get through ½ in. holes.

Pruning at planting time, if it has not been done at the nursery, consists mainly of removing any broken or weak branches and any broken roots. Shorten side branches by about ⅓.

BLACKBERRIES AND DEWBERRIES
Including boysenberry and loganberry

These related bramble bushes bear similar, luscious fruits prolifically. Some of the plants are upright bushes while others have limber branches that trail. All but a few varieties are viciously thorny and, if uncontrolled, can escape and become a nuisance. All need annual pruning, and the digging out of "escapees."

Each year, immediately after harvest, all canes that fruited must be cut back to the ground. At that same time, young replacement canes that came up that spring either must be shortened (if they are to be self-supporting) or trained along a trellis or on wires stretched at the proper height for convenient picking.

Upright bush blackberries are hardiest (into Zone 4), and suited to growing in New England and the Middle West. They spread by suckering roots.

Trailing types (the dewberry group) include some with black fruits and others with red. They are adapted to the mild East Coast, South, and Pacific Coast.

Plant all kinds in early spring in the North; in fall or early winter in milder climates. Estimate that each bush will furnish 1½ qt. of fruit per year beginning about the third season. Give each a position in sun, with well-drained soil. Space 5 ft. apart in a row. In the

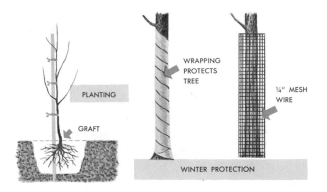

PLANTING
GRAFT
WRAPPING PROTECTS TREE
¼" MESH WIRE
WINTER PROTECTION

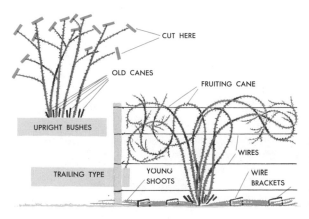

CUT HERE
OLD CANES
FRUITING CANE
UPRIGHT BUSHES
WIRES
TRAILING TYPE
YOUNG SHOOTS
WIRE BRACKETS

first year let the plants grow as they will, but begin training in the second spring.

BLUEBERRIES

The cultivated kinds are high-bush types, standing 3 to 5 ft. tall. To grow them successfully you must be able to provide acid soil that has high organic content (such as peat), maintain constant moderate moisture, along with good drainage, and protect the fruit from birds. The bird problem is serious. Blueberries thrive in Zones 5 through 10, though not all varieties are adapted to the same areas.

Choose a site in sun or part shade. If your soil is not the proper type, you may dig holes to a depth of 1½ to 2 ft., remove 2 or 3 bushels of soil and replace with moistened sphagnum peat moss alone (which is acid), or with a combination of such peat moss and sand or soil. Then, after the plant has been set, spread 1 lb. of sulfur over the soil, 3 ft. around the plant on all sides, and scratch it into the surface.

The best bushes to plant are 2-year-olds about 15 in. high that have been dug with a ball of earth about their roots or been grown in containers. Space them 4 ft. apart and set at the same depth they were in the nursery. You must have several different varieties in order to assure cross-pollination. This is an advantage, for you can choose kinds that ripen at slightly different times and thus prolong the season of picking. In estimating how many you need, count on about 6 plants per person, 2 each of 3 varieties. Mature bushes bear 8 to 10 qts. of berries each.

Because blueberry roots are near the soil's surface, do not cultivate them, but cover the soil with a 6-in. mulch. Use sawdust, wood chips, leaves or whatever is handy. Feed the plants every spring. Begin with about 1 oz. of complete commercial fertilizer (5-10-5) scattered over the ground. Gradually increase

the quantity each year as the plants grow, and level off as they reach maturity. Bushes should produce their first (small) crop the third year.

Pruning is not needed until the third year. From then on, in late fall or early spring, remove dead and broken branches, weak twigs and oldest stems which no longer produce vigorous shoots. Fruit is borne on year-old wood. Sometimes, to have fewer but larger berries, the fruiting shoots are shortened to 5 fruit buds during pruning.

A large tent-type netting is the surest device to protect the crop from birds. Sew it together firmly, leaving a way to open it for picking. This opening can be held closed with snap clothespins.

CURRANTS AND GOOSEBERRIES

These small fruits are used primarily for making jelly or preserves, and in the case of gooseberry, for pies. They are borne on permanent bushes, 3 to 5 ft. high, that are very easy to grow. They like cool, moist growing conditions, are hardy in extremely cold climates, and excel in northern states or where summers are cool. They are not for the South. You can grow them in a row, or tuck them among plantings of ornamental shrubs.

Plant in very early spring. Buy 1- or 2-year-old plants. Estimate one bush for each member of your family. Give good soil, sun or part shade (native gooseberries grow in woodlands), and space 5 to 6 ft. apart. Set plants slightly lower than they grew in the nursery, and shorten their tops by ⅓. Later care includes cultivating and watering during dry periods. Mulching with 3 to 6 in. of grass clippings, straw, wood chips, etc., will make for easy maintenance. Feed each spring with a complete fertilizer low in nitrogen, such as a 5-10-5 at the rate of 2 lb. per 100 sq. ft.

Heaviest crops of fruit are borne on branches that are 2 to 3 years old. Pruning, after bushes mature, should be done in very early spring while bushes are still dormant and buds have not begun to swell. Cut out several of the oldest branches (4 or more years old); leave 6 to 8 strong younger branches, including new ones—for renewal. Thin out small weak branches.

Planting restrictions: There are laws against planting currants and gooseberries in certain states or portions of states. This is to protect white pine trees, which are a major forest tree in many areas, from a serious disease called blister rust. This disease passes one stage of its existence on gooseberries or currants, before completing its life cycle and returning to the pine. Gooseberries and currants should not be grown within 900 ft. of a white pine tree.

FIGS

Figs are grown primarily in Zones 8 through 10 and in the tropics. However, if given a sheltered location and winter protection—such as an earth mound over the base of the plant—with the tops tied into a bundle and wrapped with burlap,—the hardiest varieties will live and bear in considerably colder areas. Even if the tops are frozen, growth will come from the roots and produce a crop.

On the Atlantic Coast, figs can be grown as far north as Washington, D. C. In the Pacific Northwest, they are marginal. In the tropics, some become huge trees, but most can be kept low if desired, by pruning.

They will grow in a variety of soils. However, in the South avoid sandy soil because of nematode troubles; choose heavy or clay soil. Shrubby and small-tree kinds need 10 to 20 ft. of space. They can be trained flat on a wall or fence, where their light-colored bark and decorative cut leaves make a handsome pattern. Keep them especially well watered the first year. After that they need little at-

tention. The only pruning needed is to remove dead wood and to keep the plant at the wanted size. Because plants are shallow rooted, it is not wise to cultivate them. Instead, cover the ground with a mulch.

Most figs bear two crops a season. The first comes on shoots that have lived over winter, and the second on new growth of the current season.

In cold climates, figs can be grown in a tub, wintered indoors in a cellar or similar place, and moved outside for summer and to produce fruit.

GRAPES

Grapes are woody vines and can do double duty in your yard as shade providers and fruit providers. Their leaves are large and handsome, and the vines durable, rapid-growing and long-lived. There are varieties suitable to both mild and cold climates. If you live where winters are cold, or in the Pacific Northwest, American bunch grapes will grow best. These, typified by 'Concord,' have been developed from the wild grape of the eastern states. If you live in California or the Southwest, you will be able to grow the more tender European or California varieties used for eating, for raisins and for wine. In the deep South, two sorts are popular. One is the native muscadine grape and its varieties, in which the fruits grow in clusters of only 1 to 3 berries, and the other is the American bunch grape. There are numerous varieties of all of these.

Get your start by buying plants. They should be vigorous 1- or 2-year-old size, with good root systems. Planting time in the North is very early spring; in moderate or mild climates, autumn or winter. Grapes need a sunny site with rapid-draining soil. Space them 10 ft. apart. Dig holes 12 in. across and deep. Prune before planting, cutting away all but the strongest cane (stem), and shortening that to leave only 2 buds (nodes). This will assure few but very vigorous new shoots. If the roots are longer than 6 in., trim them back to that length. Set the plants so that they are 2 in. lower than they were previously. Spread the roots and tamp the earth firmly around and over them; then water well.

During the first year, encourage as much growth as possible, so the leaves will manufacture food to enlarge the root system. The second spring you can start training your vine. If it is to cover an overhead arbor, choose several canes and encourage them upward; cut off all but your chosen shoots. Do no more heavy pruning until the vine covers the top of the arbor.

If you are growing the vines for fruit, they will need to be pruned annually and drastically after they are mature and have produced their first grapes. If left uncontrolled they will produce miles of vines and have insignificant small clusters of fruit.

For best fruit, grapes are usually trained on wires. The first step in training is to form the permanent framework of trunk and arms (side branches). Choose your best long cane and fasten it into a vertical position to become the trunk; cut off all others. When the trunk develops side-shoots, choose those at the proper heights to fasten horizontally along your supports, and cut off all others.

Prune each year, from then on, in winter or very early spring. It does not matter if the cane "bleeds."

The best clusters will be borne on shoots that arise this year from canes that developed *last* year from older wood. Thus it is the one-year-old canes (recognizable by their light-colored bark) that are the important ones to be saved. The most desirable ones are those about as big around as a lead pencil, with their point of origin near the main trunk. But you must not save the full length of them! Each mature vine is capable of ripening only a certain amount of quality fruit, so the one-year-old bearing canes must be shortened to control the number of prospective grape clusters. The general rule is to allow a combined length (counting all canes) of 30 growth buds or nodes per plant. Your goal in pruning is to cut away all of the vine *except* these chosen buds, and a few shoots to produce next year's bearing wood.

There are two basic methods for doing this. The first is used on cold-climate or bunch grapes (Concord type) and muscadines (Southern type). It is called the cane-renewal system and works this way: The vine is trained with a main trunk and 4 horizontal arms (2 each way). Each year you save 4 to 6 1-year canes that arise close to the trunk. Shorten each to 5 to 12 buds. Then, to produce the source of next year's bearing wood, select 4 additional 1-year-old canes near the trunk and cut them back to 2 nodes. *Cut off everything else! Be ruthless!*

The second method, used primarily on California or European grapes, is the spur system. With this, the trunk is first trained vertically. From it, arms may extend horizontally (cordon), upward in fan shape, or form a stubby top cluster. From the permanent arms arise the one-year canes, which each year are cut back drastically. They are shortened to 3- to 5-in. length, with 2 to 3 buds apiece, and a combined total of 30 to 40 buds. To have 40

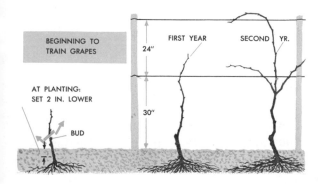

BEGINNING TO TRAIN GRAPES

FIRST YEAR   SECOND YR.

24"

AT PLANTING:
SET 2 IN. LOWER

30"

BUD

buds, you would leave 20 spurs. Each year, cut back the shoots that have borne fruit, to their bottom buds.

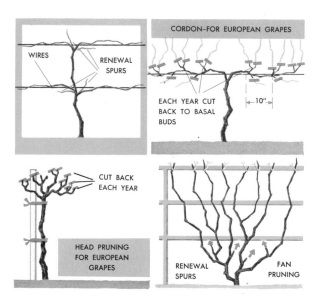

RASPBERRIES

When home-grown and picked fresh, these summer fruits are a taste treat worthy of gourmets. They are easy to grow if you live in the northern three-quarters of the United States, but are not adapted to the deep South or semidesert areas. The plants do not take much space, and need little care other than annual pruning and thinning. They are not fussy about soil as long as it is well drained. Fruits are borne at a height that makes picking them a comfortable process—no stooping.

The time to plant in the North is early spring; the plants will be dormant. In the South, autumn is preferred. You can estimate that each plant will provide 1 to 3 pints of fruit per season.

There are two main kinds of raspberries, red and black. (The purples are hybrids between the two.) They vary not only in color and flavor, but also in the way they grow and the manner of pruning. Both have perennial roots, but top growth operates on a 2-year schedule. Each year the canes that have produced fruit die. New ones arise to take their place. In the first season the shoots make foliage only; the second, they flower and fruit.

Red raspberries: (This group includes the yellow ones.) They grow stiffly erect. Canes are unbranched and prickly. They spread by underground runners or suckers, which can come up any place. Set new plants 3 ft. apart in a row, at the depth they grew before, and if they came with stems attached, cut those back to 6-in. height. New sucker plants will soon fill in the area around and between the original plants.

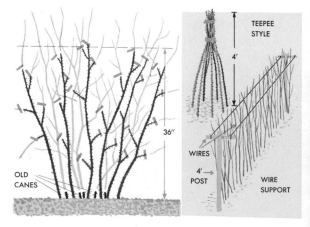

Spring-set raspberries will not bear fruit the first year (exception is "everbearers," see below). Early in the second spring, shorten canes by 1/3 their height, to stand about 3 ft. tall. The side branches that develop will bear fruit. After the fruit is harvested, canes that

Grapes are an excellent double-duty vine. The hardy, vigorous, large-leaved climber can shade your patio during summer while producing a crop of fruit that ripens in autumn.

One fruit tree, or several of them, can be part of your landscaping. Here full-size apple trees are the background for a garden. Dwarf trees would need less space.

To grow ever-bearing strawberries in a barrel, fill in soil by layers as plants are set. Provide a center column of sand to aid watering and drainage. Design: Mrs. Carolyn Wilkinson

Dwarf fruit trees are ornamental if grown as espaliers. They can be trained against a wall or be free-standing like this row. Mary Deputy Lamson, landscape architect

ATTRACTIVE WAYS TO GROW FRUIT

bore should be cut off at ground level so all the plant's strength will go into the canes which will produce the next season's crop; burn these old canes to prevent disease carry-over. At this time, also, thin the new sucker shoots so that they are spaced 8 to 10 in. apart in a row 1½ to 2 ft. wide. Dig out and destroy all excess plants to prevent a wild, unmanageable thicket. The plants can be supported by a pair of wires attached to cross-pieces on posts, or you may tie several together, "teepee" fashion, to support each other.

"Everbearer" types, such as 'Indian Summer,' produce a fall crop on canes that were new that year. Then they bear another crop the following spring. After that they can be removed.

Black raspberries: These grow as compact, nonsuckering plants. The canes are long and arch over until they touch ground, where they root and produce new plants. When setting dormant plants, place with the large-growth bud 2 in. below soil surface; if the plant is growing, plant at the same depth, but leave the hole partly open and fill in as the cane develops. Space 2 to 3 ft. apart in a row. Black raspberries can be trained and tied to wire trellises, similar to the method used with red raspberries. However, it is simpler to grow and prune them as individual bushes in a row.

The first year, when new shoots reach 2-ft. height, cut them back to 18 in. This will induce formation of side branches. In early spring, shorten these laterals to within 6 in. of the main stem. After harvesting the crop, remove canes that have borne, and burn them. Thin the new replacement shoots to the 4 or 5 best ones, and prune these back to 18-in. height.

Purple raspberries: Treat these the same as the black ones.

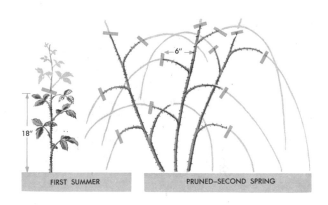

FIRST SUMMER PRUNED—SECOND SPRING

RHUBARB

While technically not a fruit, rhubarb serves the same purpose, besides being simple to grow and occupying little space. It is a hardy perennial that does best in cold climates where soil freezes several inches deep. It grows from a fleshy root. The part you eat (cooked as a sauce, in pies, or mixed with other fruits in jam) are the stalks of the big leaves. The leaves themselves are not edible, nor is the inch of stalk adjoining the leaf, for these contain an injurious acid. New varieties such as 'Valentine' have stalks red-colored all the way through, and are much sweeter than old kinds, thus needing less sweetening when cooked.

Allow 2 or 3 plants for each member of the family. Buy dormant roots in early spring. Plant in the sun, in deeply dug fertile soil, spaced 3 ft. apart. Top of the roots should be 2 in. below soil level. Cultivate, and water during drought. Do not pick the first season. After that pick (pull) stalks each spring, but stop before summer and feed the plant so it will grow large amounts of foliage that will produce food for next year's crop. Tops will die each winter. Apply a protective mulch 3 or 4 in. deep over the top.

Old clumps can be divided by digging the roots, cutting them into portions containing at least one growth bud apiece, and replanting at 3-ft. intervals.

STRAWBERRIES GIVE QUICK RESULTS

There are two main kinds of strawberries. The regular or June-bearers produce one big crop per year, over a period of about 2½ weeks. In mild climates they ripen in late winter or early spring; elsewhere in late spring or early summer. You can get early, main-season and late varieties to prolong the eating season. Everbearers stretch their bearing over many months, but produce most heavily in spring (at the same time as June-bearers) and in the fall. Best varieties of both types depend upon where you live, so rely on recommendations from your county agricultural extension office or state agricultural college. June-bearers are usually best if you wish to have quantities of berries at one time for freezing or jam-making.

To get a start, buy plants. They should be labeled "virus-free"; this is a form of health insurance. The best plants are young ones with vigorous roots that are white or straw-colored rather than black.

Planting time in cold-winter climates is as early in spring as you can prepare the soil, while temperatures are still cold. Dormant plants are available at this time, locally or by mail order, and will start growing quickly. Keep the roots cool and moist until they can be planted. Potted plants can be set at any time. You will get your first full crop from spring-set June-bearers a little more than a year after planting. The first crop from spring-set everbearers will be the autumn of the year in which they were planted.

In mild-winter areas, fall planting is recommended, and you will pick a crop the spring immediately following.

The number of plants you will need depends upon how many people are in your family. Figure on 20 to 30 plants per person, or estimate on the basis that each plant (whether June-bearer or everbearer) will produce a total of 1 pint of fruit per year.

Location of the bed should be in sun. The best soil is deep, sandy loam with considerable humus. It should drain well. If you live where irrigation by flooding is practiced, plan your bed accordingly, with plants set on ridges.

There are two general methods of arranging plants in beds. With the "matted row" system, plants are spaced 18 in. apart in rows. They develop baby plants at the tips of runners, and these young plants are allowed to fill the area between and around the mother plants. Together, they make a wide row. Preferably they are spaced 6 in. apart, and surplus runner plants are cut off as they develop. Five to 7 first-generation children should be enough for each mother plant. Such matted rows should be replanted every other year, or be renovated by spading under alternate strips of plants and letting new runner plants move into the spaded area.

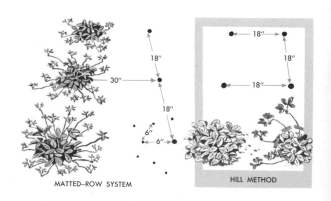

MATTED–ROW SYSTEM   HILL METHOD

The "hill" method, featuring individual plants, is usually preferred for everbearers. Space the plants 16 to 18 in. apart, either in rows or checker-board fashion in a bed. Never let any runners develop, but maintain the plant as a vigorous clump.

Planting in mounds made of stair-stepping circles of bands of metal is an interesting and attractive way to grow a few strawberries in a compact space. Everbearers are best adapted to this type of planting. Basic materials for constructing the mounds are available ready-to-assemble. Strawberries grown this way need attentive care if they are to live up to your expectations.

When setting plants, the area where roots and leaves meet (the crown of the plant) should be just at soil level.

First-year care is simple. With June-bearers, if spring-planted, remove all flower buds the first year, so the plant can use all of its energy for growing and making runner plants. With spring-set everbearers, keep spring blooms picked, but you may allow fall berries to ripen. Feed all newly set strawberries about a month after planting; water in the fertilizer. A summer mulch is beneficial the first year and all years. It can be sawdust, ground corncobs, grass clippings, etc., and should be applied after you have weeds under control by cultivating, have applied complete

fertilizer, and have watered deeply. For winter, in cold climates, a protective mulch of some loose material such as straw is advisable the first year and succeeding years.

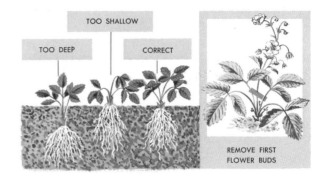

Annual care includes feeding both June-bearers and everbearers as they start growth in spring. Feed everbearers also immediately following their spring crop. Fertilizer can be applied through a mulch. Feeding in autumn will build strength for the following spring's fruit. If everbearers are to produce well in summer and autumn they must have an inch of water each week.

Whether your window is sunny or shady, delightful plants will thrive in it.

20

Indoor Gardening Brightens Winter

Nothing gives a room more of a loving finishing touch than a plant, or several plants. They are decorative—and alive! The key to growing handsome specimens is to choose types of plants adapted to the climate conditions of your room, or else change the conditions so that they are good for the plants! Most of us these days live in overheated houses with very dry air. Often we do not have sunny windows. Luckily there are some durable and handsome plants that tolerate such situations. This book will list them for you. Other plants, including most of the ones with showy flowers, have special requirements of light, temperature and humidity. These requirements are quite easy to provide when you know what they are; this book will give the information. In general, the aim is to provide conditions similar to those in the plant's native haunt—whether desert or rain forest. This challenges your skill. If you are a beginner, start with some of the easiest and most durable kinds. Then, as you gain confidence, try something special like a miniature rose, African violet or amaryllis. You will be an authority in no time!

When you shop for plants, choose healthy-looking specimens. Avoid any with yellow or wilted leaves. Those with flowers should be just coming into bloom, rather than at peak stage, so you will get full benefit of their show. If the weather is cold, protect the plant from temperature changes while you are getting it home. Have it wrapped in several layers of paper. A chilling may cause its leaves to drop. After getting the plant home, check to be sure there is a hole in the bottom of the container or through any outside wrappings, so excess water can escape. Water it well, and set in a light but not sunny place, out of the way of drafts or heat outlets, while it adjusts to its new home. Later move it to its permanent position.

WHICH PLANTS WILL GROW WHERE

These Are the Toughest
(Tolerate Poor Light; Dry Air)

Aspidistra	Philodendron
Chinese Evergreen	Rubber Plant
Dieffenbachia	Sansevieria
Fiddleleaf Fig	Schefflera
Monstera	Syngonium

For Bright Light; Little Sun
(North Window)

Airplane Plant	Kangaroo-Vine
Aluminum Plant	Monstera
Artillery Plant	Norfolk-Island Pine
Aspidistra	Palms
Babys-Tears	Panamigo
Bromeliads	Peperomias
Chinese Evergreen	Philodendron
Coleus	Piggy-Back Plant
Dieffenbachia	Rubber Plant
Dracaena	Sansevieria
English Ivy	Schefflera
Ferns	Screw-Pine
Fiddleleaf Fig	Syngonium
	Wandering Jew

For Part-time Sunshine
(East Window)

African Violet	Gloxinia
Airplane Plant	Kangaroo-Vine
Aluminum Plant	Monstera
Artillery Plant	Norfolk-Island Pine
Aspidistra	Palms
Begonia	Panamigo
Bromeliads	Peperomias
Chinese Evergreen	Philodendron
Coleus	Piggy-Back Plant
Dieffenbachia	Rubber Plant
Dracaena	Sansevieria
English Ivy	Schefflera
Episcia	Screw-Pine
Ferns	Syngonium
Fiddleleaf Fig	Wandering Jew
	Wax-Plant

Full Sun in Winter
(South Window)

Amaryllis	Hydrangea
Azalea	Kalanchoe
Bougainvillea	Lantana
Citrus Fruits	Rose
Gardenia	Shrimp-Plant
Geranium	Succulents
Hibiscus	Wax Begonia

These Want To Be Cool
(65° Daytime, 50° at Night)

Azalea	English Ivy
Bulbs, Spring	Hydrangea
Calceolaria	Jerusalem-Cherry
Cineraria	Primrose
Cyclamen	Rose

Some You Can Grow in Water
(They Appreciate Bright Light)

Blood-Leaf	Grape-Ivy
Chinese Evergreen	Philodendron
Coleus	Syngonium
English Ivy	Wandering Jew

WAYS TO KEEP HOUSE PLANTS HAPPY

Provide moist air: This will be good for your family's health, too! Ideal humidity for plants is 40 to 80%, similar to that in a greenhouse. But it is an almost impossible goal to reach in centrally heated homes, in climates where winters are severe. Even if you have an automatic humidifier connected to your furnace, your air is probably drier than you realize. At our house, we are grateful if we achieve 35%. Measuring gauges, somewhat similar to thermometers, can be purchased at hardware stores, drugstores and garden supply dealers.

FAVORITE GIFT PLANTS

Easter Lily

Azalea

Cyclamen

Hydrangea macrophylla

Calamondin Orange

Chrysanthemum

Gloxinia

Poinsettia

Kalanchoe blossfeldiana

Ways to increase humidity:

✸ Keep your teakettle simmering.

✸ Buy a portable electric humidifier, or a vaporizer such as used in sickrooms—preferably holding enough water to run many hours without refilling.

✸ Set your plants on saucers filled with pebbles kept moist.

✸ Place your potted plants over an improvised evaporating reservoir. Use any waterproof tray 1½ in. deep or more. Put in a layer of pebbles which you will keep partly covered with water. Lay a piece of heavy wire mesh across the top of the tray to support the pots and keep them from touching the water. Keeping the pots from touching the water avoids the possibility of getting the soil soggy. Also, there is less chance of the plants exchanging contagious troubles or nematodes by way of the water.

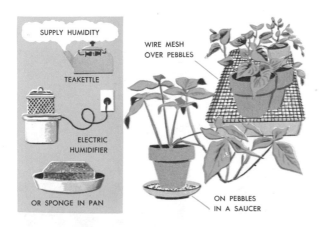

SUPPLY HUMIDITY

WIRE MESH OVER PEBBLES

TEAKETTLE

ELECTRIC HUMIDIFIER

OR SPONGE IN PAN

ON PEBBLES IN A SAUCER

Water plants well, and considerately: The preferred time of day is morning, and the main rule is to water thoroughly, soaking all the soil in the pot. Then wait to repeat until the soil on top is dry. You will find some plants must be watered more frequently than others. If you are too slow, they will tell you by wilting. Those that can wait the longest are generally the ones with thick, succulent or hairy leaves (cacti and succulents rot if given too much water). When the weather is sunny and the thermometer high, everything needs watering more often than in cloudy and rainy periods. At our house, in winter, most of the thin-leaved plants are watered twice a week. But toughies like philodendron, monstera and fiddleleaf fig are satisfied with a once-a-week drink.

Beware of overwatering. More house plants are killed by too much water than by too little. If soil is constantly wet there will be no room for air. Roots will suffocate and tops become limp.

The temperature of water should be the same as that of the room. Cold water chills and shocks plants. The easiest way to have it just right is to draw it the night before you plan to use it. In fact, it is smart to keep some on hand all the time. Do not keep it in a galvanized or brass container. Crocks, bowls or jars are fine.

Kinds of water to use: The best is rain or melted snow, warmed; distilled water (stirred to add air); defrost water from the refrigerator.

Next best is water from a well, city system or any that has not been treated with chemicals. If your water is chlorinated, it will be all right to use if you let it sit in an open nonmetal container for 24 hours.

Not good is chemically softened water with high sodium content. If you have your own water softening system, probably there is one faucet, or a place where one could be connected, ahead of the place where the water pipe enters the softener.

Methods of watering: The best way (especially for plants that seem to dry out rapidly) is to set the pot in a container of water that is at room temperature. Water should be ½ in. below pot's rim if you are using a porous pot (common clay pot). Let it sit for a couple of hours, or until the soil becomes moist on top. If you are using a nonporous pot, such as glazed pottery, water should be 1 in. over pot's rim. Let it sit for 15 minutes or until bubbles stop arising from the pot. In either case, you will want to set the pot where it can drain afterward.

If watering from the top, give enough to soak the entire root ball. Then let the pot drain. Do not let water remain in the saucer or container in which the pot sits; pour it out. Once a month, approximately, give an extra big watering from the top to flush out any accumulated harmful soil and fertilizer salts.

the side of the pot to use as a spout for pouring out excess water that accumulates.

When pots have no drainage hole, you must be unusually careful not to overwater and drown the roots. After each watering, turn the pot on its side and let the excess run out. It is smart, when potting in such containers, to put a layer of gravel in the bottom. Then, if possible, put a small pipe or tube in

Keep plants clean: Give a gentle shower bath occasionally to all plants. They love it! Not only does it put appreciated moisture directly on foliage, but it also cleanses leaves of dust and knocks off insects. Do it at least once a week. The easiest way is to take the plants to the sink, turn each pot on its side, and use the faucet spray attachment. Hit undersides as well as topsides of leaves. Water should be tepid (room temperature or slightly warmer). This is a fine time to do watering also.

To keep soil from falling out of pots when they are turned on their sides, use aluminum foil, polyethylene film, or several layers of newspaper. Cut a slit to the center so you can fit them around the plant's stem, and hold them over the top of the pot.

Let plants drain and dry out of the sun. This is especially important for plants with hairy leaves. If a day comes that is foggy or rainy with outdoor temperatures almost identical to indoors, set your plants outside to enjoy the moisture. But watch that temperature.

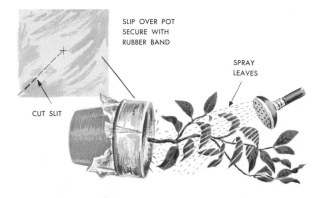

SLIP OVER POT
SECURE WITH
RUBBER BAND

SPRAY
LEAVES

CUT SLIT

Large, glossy-leaved plants like philodendron can be cleaned with a soft cloth or facial tissue. Special leaf polishes prepared for house plants are available if they appeal to you.

Hairy-leaved plants like African violet can be brushed. Use a soft brush.

Feed sensibly: "Complete" plant foods (fertilizers), packaged especially for use on house plants, are available almost everywhere that potted plants or garden supplies are sold. Some are liquid concentrates to be used diluted with water. Others are dry. Either form will do a good job for you if properly used. Because they vary in concentration of chemicals, it is vital that you read the manufacturer's directions carefully or you may injure your plants.

Do not overdo it! When a little is good, a bigger dose may make the plant sick. Regular small feedings are better than occasional big ones. A wise rule is to feed every other week.

Feed all plants that are growing actively. This includes bulb plants, like daffodils or amaryllis, that have finished flowering but are growing new leaves, since the leaves are producing food for next year's flower buds. When plants are resting, as during the short days of midwinter, feed less. On sickly plants, go easy! As with a sick person, the plant may or may not be needing a meal. To test the situation, water the plant, flushing the soil several times. Then give a small feeding. If the plant does not rally soon, it is sick for other reasons.

About special food for acid-preferring plants: Azalea, gardenia and hydrangea grow best in acid soil. They probably come to you potted in such earth. To keep the soil acid (especially important if you do not live in an acid-soil area), and to keep leaves from turning yellowish, there are several things you can do. The easiest are:

For feeding, use a plant food sold especially for use on azaleas, hollies or other acid-loving plants. This may be available only in an outdoor-type fertilizer, but it will work fine indoors. Follow instructions.

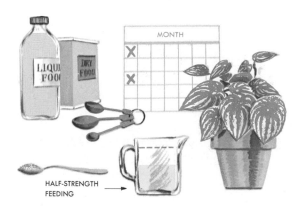

MONTH

HALF-STRENGTH
FEEDING

LIQUID
FOOD

DRY
FOOD

OUTDOOR
ACID
PLANT
FOOD

VINEGAR

HOUSE
PLANT
FOOD

Or use regular house-plant fertilizer. And then every time you water, add 1 level teaspoon natural (not synthetic) cider vinegar per quart of water. At least once a month use this vinegar water so copiously that it will flush through the soil and out the drainage hole.

When you repot, add sphagnum moss or sphagnum peat moss (which are acid) in amounts over half of the total volume of the soil. (Other peats are only slightly acid to alkaline.)

HOW TO GROW UNDER ARTIFICIAL LIGHT

Most house plants can live their whole lives from seed to flower and back to seed without a single ray of real sunshine! With electricity you can make lighted gardens out of dark corners, basements, closets, attics and hallways. There are even portable lighted carts and special table units to foster growth.

Types of lights: The most efficient units are 40-watt, 48-in. fluorescent tubes and their starters, installed in pairs or multiples as space indicates. A 40-watt setup will light an area 2 by 4 ft. For smaller areas there are 24-in., 20-watt tubes, or 36-in., 30-watters. Suspend lights horizontally over plants. Pulleys are fine where plants of varying heights are grown; otherwise chains can be used to hang the fixtures. A reflector, purchased or homemade from white-painted or foil-lined plywood, is necessary to force light down on the plants. If you contemplate basement or cabinet installations, paint the walls and cabinet insides white for better light diffusion.

A balanced blend of red and blue light rays is desirable. The new agricultural lamps (Gro-Lux, Plant-Gro and the like) have a high concentration of these rays. Plants grow well under them. These lamps emit a lavender-pink glow which gives plants an exotic look, intensifying the pink and red colors and deepening the greens. But you can grow plants to perfection with combinations such as these: One daylight tube for blue rays and one natural tube for red rays. Or one warm white tube and one daylight tube. Where heat is not a factor, scientists advocate the addition of 10% incandescent light to raise the concentration of red rays.

While incandescent lights give off more heat than fluorescents, a reading or desk lamp used over a plant for a few hours in the evening will helpfully increase the amount of light it receives per day.

Using lights and placing plants: Burn lights 12 to 16 hours daily for flowering plants like African violets, begonias, gloxinias and orchids; 4 to 10 hours for foliage plants. You can flick them on and off manually, or have a timer do it for you.

Light rays are strongest close to tubes. Place seedlings and sun-loving plants such as cacti, other succulents and geraniums about 4 in. from tubes. Cuttings root at 10 to 14 in. African violets will flower well when pot rims are 11 in. from tubes, although blue-flowered varieties can take more light than white or pink-flowered.

If leaves on short plants look long and willowy and blooms are few, boost them nearer lights by setting on inverted flowerpots. If foliage bleaches, burns or bunches, move plants farther from tubes or decrease hours of light.

You can start seeds of annuals and vegetables in any of the suggested light setups. Follow the basic instructions for starting seeds indoors in containers. (See Chapter 22.) Place about 4 in. beneath lights. Give 12 to 16 hours of light per day, and as they grow move farther from lights. Be sure to harden the seedlings properly before setting them in the outdoor garden by gradually accustoming them to outdoor air and light.

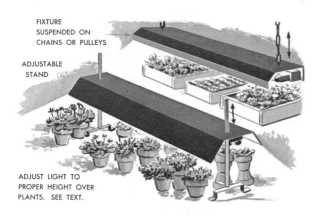

FIXTURE
SUSPENDED ON
CHAINS OR PULLEYS

ADJUSTABLE
STAND

ADJUST LIGHT TO
PROPER HEIGHT OVER
PLANTS. SEE TEXT.

POTS, POTTING AND SOIL

Merits of different kinds of pots: Ordinary clay pots are inexpensive and handy. Because they are porous, it is easy to water plants by placing the pot in a container of water and letting it soak and absorb. But the porosity also allows roots to dry out fairly quickly, so in a dry room clay pots should sit on damp pebbles or within some other container.

Glazed pottery and plastic pots are good in dry rooms, since they are nonporous and moisture cannot escape readily. If you use colored ones, and wish to show off your plants rather than the containers, have all the pots the same color. My favorite for the purpose is a soft dull green, but let the color scheme and décor of your room be your guide.

Metal containers of copper, zinc, brass, etc. can poison plants. If you want to use them,

cover interiors with 2 coats of **aquarium or swimming-pool paint**.

Containers with no drainage holes are attractive, but so difficult to water successfully that they are not recommended.

Jardinieres (large, usually ornamental containers without drainage holes) are handsome but plants should not be planted directly in them. Use them as outer protective enclosures for clay pots. Then they are marvelous, insulating roots from temperature extremes, and keeping moisture from evaporating. Since water may accumulate in the bottom and make plants sick, either put a layer of gravel or pebbles beneath the pot or invert a small clay pot under your plant. Filling the space between the pot and the jardiniere with sphagnum or peat moss which you can keep moist, will do pleasant things about increasing humidity.

I use baskets as jardinieres. They are good-looking, and serve some insulating purpose, but do not protect my carpet from water. So they will not leak when I water, I cover the inside bottom of the baskets with heavy aluminum foil.

CLAY POT

PLASTIC POT

GLAZED CERAMIC

USE
PEBBLES
IN BOTTOM
UNDER POT

JARDINIERES

FOIL "PAN"
IN BOTTOM

BASKET

The soil you use makes a difference: The ideal kind is loose and porous so that when you water, the moisture will get right to the roots. It should contain absorbent material to hold the moisture and plant food. It should be sturdy enough to hold your plants upright. It had better be pest-free or you may be in for trouble later. Fertility is relatively unimportant, since you will be feeding it regularly.

The easiest way to get an ideal kind is to buy it "ready-made." If you need only a little, you can purchase it in handy small packages at almost any store that carries house plant supplies. Greenhouses and garden centers will sometimes sell you some of the soil they prepare for their own use. It is wise to telephone and inquire about it first. Then, if the soil will be available, take a box or bucket with you in which to carry it home.

If you prefer to prepare your own soil, here is a basic recipe:

⅓ coarse sand
⅓ porous material such as moistened peat moss or sphagnum moss, vermiculite, perlite, etc. (available at garden stores).
⅓ garden loam
Mix together thoroughly

This is satisfactory for nearly all plants. For those that need something special, details will be given in the paragraphs where the plants are discussed.

Disinfecting your potting soil pays off. Sterilizing or pasteurizing rids the soil of pests that might cause you trouble. It assures a good start in life for young rooted cuttings, seedlings, divisions, etc. If you buy packaged soil at a store, it will already have been treated.

To pasteurize your homemade mix, get out your largest kettle that has a close-fitting lid. Put your soil in an uncovered gallon container, or in several one-pound coffee cans that can be stacked to allow good steam circulation. Set the containers on some pebbles inside the kettle. Put 2 in. of water in the bottom of the kettle. Cover and simmer for 1 hour. If you are not going to use the soil soon, dry it and store in a new plastic bag.

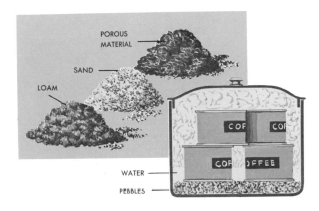

How to pot plants Proper pot size depends on the plants' root system. If it has outgrown its current pot, choose a new one only slightly larger—about ½ to 1 in. bigger all the way around. If the plant is a young one moving into its first individual container, choose one just a little bigger than its root system. Later, as it grows, transplant to others successively larger.

To determine whether a plant needs repotting (if you suspect its roots are crowded), take a look by removing the plant from the pot. This sounds difficult but it is not. Turn the pot upside down (using one hand to support the surface of the soil and the stem of the plant), and tap the rim of the pot on the edge of a table or something similar. If roots are using all the space, the plant will slip out neatly as a unit. If the mass seems to be all roots—very crowded—it is time to remove to a larger pot. If there is more soil than roots, put the plant back.

Another easy way to sterilize a small amount of soil is to bake it in an oven. Use shallow, uncovered pans. In order to know how long to continue the baking, place a small potato down in the soil. When the potato is "done," the soil will be, also. Let the material cool thoroughly before using it.

couple of days while they recuperate from the shock of the move.

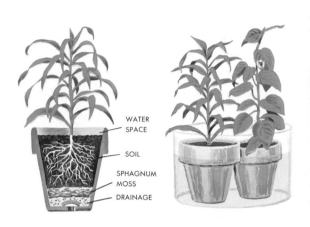

WATER SPACE

SOIL

SPHAGNUM MOSS

DRAINAGE

Before reusing old pots give them a good scrubbing, and boil them if they are made of material that can stand the heat. It pays to do a big batch of them at once and get the mess over with.

Make sure the drainage hole will function. Put a layer of gravel or pieces of broken pots over it so soil will not wash down and clog the hole. I usually add a little sphagnum moss over the top of the gravel, for insurance. If the pot has no drainage hole, put at least an inch of gravel or broken bits of pottery in the bottom.

Add the plant and soil. Hold the plant so soil level will be about ¾ in. below top of pot. Sift the soil around it, and firm it gently around the roots (or the ball of earth that surrounds the roots), using a stick or the handle of a knife. Aim to have the soil loose in the middle of the pot and on top to make it easy to get water to the roots.

Water at once, and thoroughly. I nearly always use clay pots, and when through potting set them in a container of room-temperature water that comes almost to their rim. It slowly soaks through the sides of the pots, completely wetting all soil and not puddling it on top.

Set plants out of the sun and wind for a

MOVING PLANTS OUTDOORS AND IN

Summering plants outside: This is like giving plants a delightful, health-building vacation. They will have fresh air, genuine daylight, and a chance to taste rain water. If they are located in a suitable "resort area" and have good accommodations and service, they will flourish and come home in the fall much better for the experience.

Make the shift to outdoors gradually, after danger of frost is past and temperatures are similar to what they have been indoors. Plants that have been inside for months are tender and not used to bona fide daylight and wind. You must toughen them up. Begin by opening your windows on pleasant days. Then, on cloudy, warm days without wind, set the plants outside for a few hours, in a protected place. Finally put them in their summer sites.

Plants that have been in sunny south windows indoors can take sun outside. But most house plants do best in a shaded spot such as the north side of the house. African violets, gloxinias, begonias, impatiens, coleus, etc., will love it there. They are easiest to care for (need least watering) when pots are sunk in the ground to their rims. You can prepare the ground by working quantities of moisture-retaining peat moss, sphagnum, vermiculite or perlite into it. Another place to put plants for easy care is on top of soil among ground-cover plants (such as ivy or pachysandra) that will shelter the pots.

If you plan to use some of your house plants for ornaments on your patio, put them in containers that will insulate roots from heat and drying. You can set their pots inside a redwood tub, or larger-sized clay pot, and fill the intervening space with peat moss or sphagnum moss to be kept moist.

Feed, water, and give baths (with your garden hose) as you do indoors.

will multiply like rabbits. It is easier to spray and cleanse them while they are outdoors than after you get them inside.

Some outdoor garden plants make good house plants. You can dig and pot chrysanthemums and marigolds in full bloom, water them well, set them in the shade for a few days, and they will complete their flowering happily indoors. Other flowers are best dug as small young plants that will come into bloom later. Hunt for immature plants of petunia, nicotiana, sweet alyssum. Pot them, and after they are acclimated to pot life, put them in a sunny window.

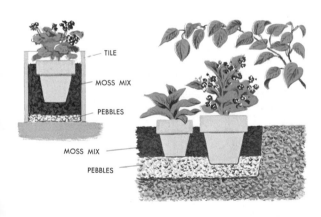

WHAT TO DO WHEN YOU GO ON

VACATION

Bringing plants indoors in autumn: Get this work done before frost time, while outdoor and indoor temperatures are similar, so plants will not be shocked. Some plants may have outgrown their pots and need to be moved to larger ones (see paragraph on potting). Give each plant a vigorous washing-off with the hose. It is also advisable to give a thorough spraying with a general purpose house-plant spray or one you use on roses. The point is that many insects may be hiding on your plants and when they get inside they

If it is winter:

Most plants can get along without watering for a week if you turn your thermostat down so the room is only 60 to 65°. Move the plants out of the sun. Group them together so that they will benefit from the moisture given off by each other's leaves. If possible, set them on a tray of moist pebbles. Water thoroughly just before you leave. Individual plants can be enclosed, pot and all, in a polyethylene sack and set in a cool, bright place out of the sun.

When you are to be gone longer than a week, and a friend is to come in and do the watering, put your plants all in one place so they will be easy to locate and tend. Set them on something waterproof (tray or sheet of plastic). Be sure the friend knows where to draw the water, and knows about having it room temperature.

If it is summer:

Put the plants outdoors, sinking the pots in the ground in shade, under shrubs or on the north side of the house. Be sure they are out of the wind. Water them and the surrounding soil thoroughly. Have a friend check on them once a week to add water when needed.

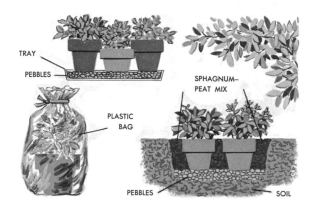

TRAY

PEBBLES

SPHAGNUM— PEAT MIX

PLASTIC BAG

PEBBLES   SOIL

PESTS AND HOW TO DEAL WITH THEM

Aphids or plant lice cluster at the growing tips of ivy, geranium, begonia, etc. You can suspect they are present if you find sticky droplets of honeydew that they secrete. Kill them with a house plant aerosol spray containing pyrethrum and rotenone (nontoxic and safe to use indoors).

Hold the can at least 18 in. from the plant, for if held closer, the propellent may burn its leaves. Keep mist away from aquariums, for the chemicals are deadly to fish. Dunking the top of the plant in a pail of room-temperature soapy water to wash the aphids off is another good treatment.

Mealybugs are covered with white powdery wax, and their eggs are a cottony mass. If you see only a few, you can pick them off with a cotton swab on a toothpick dipped in alcohol. Or use the house plant aerosol spray.

Whiteflies are most apt to be on coleus, fuchsia and geranium. Kill flying adults with house-plant spray. The young are green and scale-like; you will find them on the undersides of leaves. Honeydew is present, and sometimes a black mold. Treat by washing top of plant in a rotenone bath made by adding 4 level tablespoons of 4 or 5% rotenone powder to each gallon of water.

Scales are inconspicuous hard-shelled relatives of mealybugs that look like lumps on stems or leaves. The young ones crawl around, but old ones fasten to one spot. They secrete honeydew. Malathion sprays (use outdoors only) will kill crawlers. A brush and soapy water will dislodge most of the older ones. You will probably have to repeat the treatment.

Red spider mites, so tiny they are almost invisible, form webs on undersides of leaves and suck the plant's juices. Foliage turns yellow and falls. Mites increase when air is dry. Regular shower baths and moist air keep them in check. Or spray with Kelthane, which is reasonably safe.

Cyclamen mites, common on African violets, cause dwarfed, deformed center leaves and twisted stems. Spraying with Kelthane will help, but it is wiser to destroy affected plants and start new ones before mites crawl to other plants or before you spread them with your hands or clothing.

Earthworms that clog drainage holes in pots, and fungus, gnats, and springtails that develop in soils containing decaying plant material, can be controlled by watering the soil with chlordane, one-half tablespoonful of 50% wettable powder to 1 gallon of water.

For source of additional information on house plant pests, see list of bulletins.

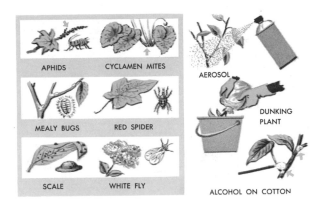

🍂 Plants You Will Especially Enjoy

GIFT PLANTS AND THEIR CARE

When a lovely plant arrives from the florist, there are several rules that you can follow to help it remain beautiful as long as possible. First, inspect the colored foil wrap around the pot, and make sure there is a drainage hole punched in its bottom so water will be able to escape. Then give a thorough watering—using water that is slightly warm—until the excess runs out of the hole. Set the plant in a place with bright daylight but where hot sun will not hit it. Avoid drafty places, or those near a hot-air register or radiator. Some plants have special requirements such as a cool temperature or an unusual need for water. You will find such details given where each plant is discussed. You will also find instructions on how to care for each plant so that it will bloom another year.

AZALEA. It likes a cool (60° if possible), light place, and acid soil kept constantly moist. For the way to maintain soil acidity, see instructions in the first part of this chapter. When the flowers finish, pick them off. Continue to water, and feed every other week. If you live in a mild climate you can move your plant into the garden permanently when spring comes. (See the chapter on shrubs for garden planting and care.)

Where winters are cold, the type of azaleas florists use probably will not prove hardy outdoors, but you can make them bloom again indoors year after year. Put the plant outdoors for the summer, preferably sinking the pot in the ground in semishade. Do not let it lack for water (it is a good idea to have it near the back door so you will not forget it). Feed it once a month, using the same plant food as indoors. By autumn, buds will have formed. They will be small but plump at the tips of branches. Bring the plant indoors to your coolest light location to rest. Do not feed it and give water sparingly. In January, start watering more. Give sunshine and begin feeding. Spray the leaves often with water.

BULBS, SPRING-FLOWERING: daffodil (*Narcissus*), tulip, hyacinth. Water thoroughly when top of soil feels dry; then wait until it feels dry again. These bulbs are all winter-hardy in coldest climates, and when spring comes can be planted outdoors to bloom there in future years. When they finish flowering indoors, cut off their bloom heads but not the foliage. Move the plants to full sunshine and feed and water to encourage leaf growth, which will provide food for the bulb.

When the leaves finally begin to turn yellow and die, reduce water and let the plant become dormant. Store completely dry. Any time before winter, move the bulbs from pot to garden. For instructions on how to plant, see the chapter on bulbs. They probably will not bloom well, if at all, the first year, but should recover by the second spring. You will have best success with daffodils. Paper-white narcissus grown in water are not worth saving. They are not hardy outdoors in the north and are not successful saved for more indoor bloom.

If you want to grow your own bulbs indoors, use top-size new bulbs, purchased early in the fall (not ones that bloomed indoors previously). Pot during October and November. Use garden soil combined with peat moss (moistened) or vermiculite. Space the bulbs ½ to 1 in. apart, with tops 1 in. below soil. Water thoroughly. The best varieties of tulips for forcing are those classed as "early flowering."

A crucial period follows. Bulbs must undergo 12 or more weeks of cold temperature, 40 to 50°. This breaks the bulbs' dormancy and gives them time to develop a good root system. During this time pots can be stored in a trench 1 ft. deep in the garden, or in a window well or similar protected place. Soil in pots must not dry out. Mulch to keep soil and surroundings cool and also to forestall freezing so you can get the pots out when you want them. After the chilling, bring

pots first to a cool dark place, and then to a cool sunny window.

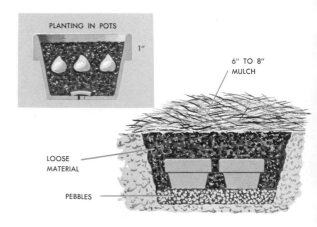

Some bulbs will grow in water. Hyacinths and paper-white narcissus can be set in pebbles, with water kept below the base of the bulbs. Put in a dark cool place until a mass of roots forms and shoots are 3 in. tall. Then bring to a cool bright window. Hyacinths tend to begin to bloom while short (whether growing in soil or water). To get a stalk to lengthen before flowering, make a cone from dark paper or cardboard to place over it; there should be a little hole in the top for light. Or use an inverted flowerpot to do the job:

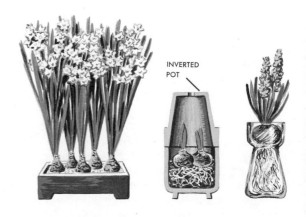

CHRYSANTHEMUMS. Their blooms will often last a month, if you keep plants out of the sun and watered. When flowering is completed, the plant can easily be saved to grow and bloom in your garden (or indoors) next autumn. Cut tops to within 2 in. of soil. Put the pot in a light window, with or without sun. Water often enough to keep the plant growing. New foliage will develop. In spring the plant may be removed from the pot, divided, and planted in a sunny place in your garden. (For how-to instructions, see the chapter on perennials.) Otherwise the plant can be left in its pot, and either sunk into the ground or placed on top of the ground. In either case, stems should be shortened to a height of 2 in. to induce branching. Feed and water through the summer. If buds do not show signs of opening before frost, your mum is probably a late-flowering kind so you should pot it and bring it indoors to a sunny window.

CITRUS: dwarf orange, lemon, tangerine. These are easy to grow and delightful to watch, with fragrant flowers and fascinating fruits borne more or less continuously. Place them in your sunniest window. Give ample humidity and shower baths for the foliage at least once a week. Water moderately, avoiding soggy soil. Feed once a month while the plant is growing actively; hold off during the dark days of early winter. To insure that fruits will set on blooms that open when the plant is indoors and there are no insects to help pollinate, it is wise to do some pollinating yourself. With a small water-color paintbrush, or a bit of cotton on a tooth-pick, brush some of the yellow pollen from the stamens of one flower upon the pistils of others.

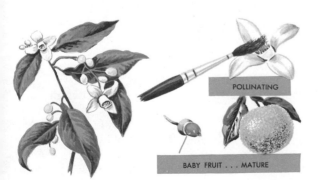

POLLINATING

BABY FRUIT . . . MATURE

For summer, set the pot in a sunny place outdoors, sunk in the ground; or set it within a larger container in order to keep the soil from drying too rapidly.

CYCLAMEN. This plant likes a cool room (50 to 60°) and morning sunshine. Soil should be constantly moist, but water must not stand on the plant's crown because it will cause rot. Saving the plant for another year is a challenge that is fun, even though the flowers you produce will not compare with florists' results. The trick is to nurse the corm (bulblike object from which the leaves arise) through a period of dormancy. When your plant finishes blooming and leaves begin to turn yellow, gradually reduce watering until soil is practically dry. Then set the plant in a cool place to rest. For summer, turn the pot on its side in a shady place outdoors where it may get a little rain or occasional light watering. If the corm has not rotted it will begin to send out tiny new leaves toward autumn. That is when to start watering slightly. Bring the plant indoors to a cool room with some sunshine and gradually increase watering. Feed every other week. Bathe leaves often under the faucet. Hope!

FRIENDSHIP PLANT, see PILEA

GLOXINIA (*Sinningia*). Its velvety trumpet-shaped flowers come in red, purple, pink and white. Some varieties are double. They grow from a plump tuber that resembles a tiny potato. Florists are most apt to have flowering plants in spring and summer. Give yours the same conditions African violets like: warmth (65 to 75°), high humidity, bright light with a little sunshine part of the day. Keep the soil moist but never soggy. Use water of room temperature—cold water on leaves may make marks on them. Feed every other week. When the flowers wither, pick them off at base of the stem. More buds and new leaves may develop, or the plant may drop its leaves and become dormant.

For summer you can set the pot outdoors, sunk in the ground in a shady spot. The plant may surprise you with blooms. Eventually, whatever you do, it will look "tired." This is normal, for gloxinias enjoy a period of dormancy. Ordinarily the rest period is autumn and winter. But whenever it comes, slow up on watering. Do not feed. Let the soil become practically dry, and leaves and stem drop off.

Over the winter, store the pot in a dry, warm (50 to 60°), dark place such as a closet shelf. Look at it occasionally to give a tiny bit of water if needed, and make sure the tuber has not started into growth. Toward spring small leaves will begin to show and you can bring the plant to light and begin watering again (just a little at first).

To start new plants, buy dormant tubers in late winter or early spring. Pot them with the top slightly above soil level. The top is usually slightly indented, with little leaves or lumps emerging from it. Use soil that is loose and rapid-draining. A pot that is 5 in. across is a good size. Water very little until growth starts. You can propagate by leaf cuttings during or just after flowering. Use a big leaf cut with a 1-in. long stem. Insert in moist sphagnum or similar rooting material. A little tuber will form at its base, and later a small plant will arise.

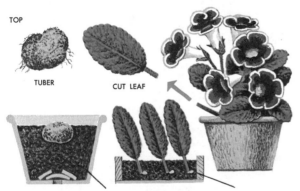

TOP

TUBER   CUT LEAF

PLANT IN LOOSE SOIL—INSERT LEAVES—TUBERS FORM

HYDRANGEA. The one you get from the florist (*Hydrangea macrophylla*) needs an amazing amount of water. Stand the pot in water (at room temperature) once a day and let it soak, then drain. If you live in Zones 7 to 10 inclusive, this hydrangea will be hardy outdoors. If you live farther north and want your plant to bloom next year, cut the stems back to 4-in. height after flowering stops. Repot in large container, adding new soil that is more than half sphagnum moss or sphagnum peat moss. This is done because hydrangeas prefer acid soil. Water and encourage growth.

For summer, sink the pot in a semishaded place in the garden; water and feed well. In the fall, leave it outdoors through the first cool weather but not hard frosts. The plant should begin to become dormant. Bring the pot indoors to cool storage (35 to 50°) and barely water at all; it will not bloom unless exposed to temperatures lower than 50° for 6 weeks. After New Year's Day, bring to a sunny, cool (60°) window, and gradually increase watering. When leaves are growing well, begin to feed every other week.

The flowers vary in their ability to turn blue or pink. In general, they will be blue if the soil was acid during the previous year's growing season and during the prebloom period while buds were expanding. They will be pink if the soil is neutral. Mixing 1 teaspoon superphosphate into the soil of the pot also promotes pinkness. (See data on feeding acid-soil plants in the early part of this chapter.)

JERUSALEM-CHERRY (*Solanum pseudo-capsicum*). The plant has decorative small round red fruits, which should not be eaten for they can cause poisoning. It likes humid air, moist soil and a little sunshine. In hot, dry air, the leaves turn yellow and drop. Spraying foliage with water frequently is a help. Plants can live to produce fruits another year if you prune them back severely in spring, and sink the pots in a sunny place outdoors through summer. Flowers will develop and fruits set by fall when you can bring them indoors. You can raise new plants from seeds removed from ripe "cherries" this spring. Sow them outdoors after the ground is warm.

Christmas Pepper (*Capsicum frutescens*) is similar to Jerusalem-Cherry but its fruits are more oblong in shape, and edible (though hot).

KALANCHOE (*Kalanchoe blossfeldiana*). This is a fleshy-leaved small compact plant with clusters of little scarlet flowers. Usually available around Christmas time, it prefers a relatively cool temperature. Outdoors for summer, though, it likes considerable sun. The plant can be propagated by inserting stems of leaves in moist sand.

LILY, EASTER. Keep in as cool a place as possible. Water whenever the top of the soil feels dry—probably every other day. When the plant stops flowering, cut off the withered blooms, but not any leaves, and you can make it flower again. Keep the plant growing lustily in a sunny window. Feed it every other week. If the foliage gradually dies, your plant is probably beginning its normal dormant period. Give less water, though the roots must never be completely dry. Set the plant in a cool place to rest.

When weather outdoors warms in spring, remove the lily from its pot (with soil intact) and plant it in a sunny place in the garden, 2 in. deeper than before. Cultivate, water and feed like other garden flowers. Blooms may appear in late summer! Easter lilies are hardy outdoors, Zones 7b to 10 inclusive. A few varieties such as 'Croft' and 'Estate' will survive winters in Zone 5b.

If you want your lily to bloom again indoors, dig the bulb (with roots attached) in fall after frost. Remove the old stem and soil. Store in the crisper drawer of your refrigerator, enclosed in a polyethylene sack along with some slightly damp sphagnum moss or vermiculite. The idea is to keep it cool but not frozen, at 35 to 40°. Remove and pot up (bulb and roots) right after Christmas, using a pot 6 to 8 in. across. Place the top of bulb 2 in. below soil. Put the pot in a cool (60°), sunny place, and water only slightly until leaves appear. Feed every other week.

POINSETTIA. These popular gift plants will remain handsome 6 weeks or more. However, they are sissies about drafts and chills. Sudden changes of temperature cause their leaves to turn yellow and drop. So place these plants away from doorways and frosty windows. They like a place with bright light or a few hours of sunshine, 60 to 70° temperature and high humidity. Soil should be constantly moist. Use water at room temperature.

Your poinsettia can bloom another year. When it has stopped flowering, and leaves begin to drop, gradually give less and less water until the soil is almost dry and the plant sheds all of its leaves. Then store the pot in a cool (55 to 65°) place, with or without light. Water only enough to keep stems from shriveling. When warm weather arrives outdoors, cut the stems back to a 4-in. height. Repot, using new potting soil. (Tops cut off can be rooted in moist soil to make new plants; use pieces 6 to 8 in. long. inserted 4 in. deep.) Sink pots in a sunny place outdoors. Water well all summer. Feed a complete fertilizer once a month. You can prune up to mid-July if you want to control the plant's height or induce branching so you will have more bloom.

In autumn, before night temperatures become chilly, bring plants indoors and gradually to a sunny window. Be careful about turning on lights at night! Poinsettias set their buds at the time of year when nights are longest. During October and early November, if they are kept in a room where lights are turned on after sunset, they will be thrown off schedule.

The sap can irritate skin or, if eaten, cause severe digestive distress.

STORE

4"

CUT BACK AND ROOT CUTTINGS

FAVORITES FOR FOLIAGE

AIRPLANE PLANT or SPIDER-PLANT *(Chlorophytum)*. Grasslike leaves, which are striped in some varieties and solid green in others, grow in fountain form from fleshy rhizomes. Small white flowers are borne at the end of slender stalks. Later small plantlets develop where the flowers were. They can be removed and potted. Large plants can be propagated by dividing. They will grow in moderate light or some sun.

ALUMINUM PLANT, see PILEA

ARTILLERY PLANT, see PILEA

BOWSTRING HEMP, see SANSEVIERIA

BROMELIADS. These plants belong to the pineapple family. Indeed the pineapple itself has the family's typical stiff rosette of decorative leaves. Some of this group are "air plants" that grow in tropical treetops. Others grow in soil. As house plants all can be grown in pots, in fast-draining material such as osmunda fiber, shredded bark, or a combination of peat moss and sand. They tolerate poor light and dry conditions, so they can flourish in living rooms. Though grown primarily as foliage plants, many have spectacularly colored flowers that last a long time on the plants. To bloom, they need bright light and a little sun. Leaves are "vase" shape. Bottoms of the "vases" hold water and should be kept filled. The soil should be on the dry side, especially in winter. Among the most popular bromeliads are cryptanthus, billbergia, vriesia.

CACTI, see SUCCULENTS

CHINESE EVERGREEN *(Aglaonema modestum).* This is one of the most foolproof indoor plants. It carries pointed broad leaves on thick stems, and can be kept low or grown to a 2-ft. height. It grows in either water or soil, and tolerates warm rooms and poor light. Once in a while it produces a flower resembling a small calla.

COLEUS. This plant has colorful foliage and develops to 3 ft. high. It grows either in water or soil, in any window with good light. Avoid soggy earth that may rot the base of the stems. Prune occasionally so the plant will become bushy. Pieces cut off can be rooted in water and later potted to move into your garden in summer. Blooms are inconspicuous, and not attractive. Cut them off to induce new leaf growth.

CRYPTANTHUS *(C. zonatus).* This is one of many interesting and ornamental bromeliads (members of the pineapple family) that are easy to grow as house plants. It is ground-hugging, with stiff, crinkly striped leaves forming rosettes to 12 in. across. Flowers are inconspicuous and hidden. For instructions, see BROMELIADS.

DIEFFENBACHIA or DUMB CANE. Dieffenbachia derives its common name from the fact that if a piece of the stem is put in your mouth, the juice will paralyze your tongue. The large leaves may be green, or combinations of green and white, according to variety. Keep out of the sun but give it bright light. The plant will gradually become taller, dropping its oldest lower leaves. If you want to shorten it, you can air-layer the top. (See chapter on starting and propagating plants.) Otherwise you can cut the plant into 3 or more parts, each of which can become a new plant. (a) Cut off a leafy top with 6 to 10 in. of stem; root it in water or moist sphagnum moss. (b) Cut remaining stem off near base of plant, leaving a stub 4 or more in. high, from which a new shoot can develop. (c) The removed portion of the stem can be cut into segments 3 or 4 in. long. These, when placed horizontally on moist sand or sphagnum moss and covered halfway, will develop roots and tops.

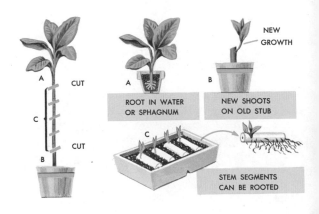

A CUT

C

B

ROOT IN WATER OR SPHAGNUM

A

NEW GROWTH

B NEW SHOOTS ON OLD STUB

C

STEM SEGMENTS CAN BE ROOTED

DRACAENA. Its leaves are usually narrow, plain green or striped, growing like those of corn. Sometimes they are in a tuft at the top of the stalk. An exception is *D. Godseffiana*, which has broader, more oval leaves, decorated with white spots. All dracaenas like bright light or a little sun, constant moisture but fast drainage, average house temperature. They propagate the same as dieffenbachia.

The Ti plant *(Cordyline terminalis)*, described later in this list, is often sold as a dracaena, and is grown like them.

FERNS. In general, they do not enjoy the conditions available in typical homes of today! Most of them need cool temperatures (55 to 65°) and very moist air, in addition to pleasantly soft light. However, a few beauties are quite tough and will be happy in a north or east window or any good light without hot sun. You should give them as moist air as possible, and give their leaves frequent shower baths. Among the best are hares-foot-fern, holly-fern, birds-nest-fern, and the small "table ferns" *(Pteris)*. The latter are commonly grown in dish gardens.

FIDDLELEAF FIG *(Ficus lyrata)*. Big shiny leathery leaves shaped like violins are carried on a woody trunk. The plant gradually becomes tall and treelike, but can be pruned to remain short. It is tough, and adapted to warm, dry air, dim light and occasional watering.

FRIENDSHIP PLANT, see PILEA

GRAPE-IVY *(Cissus rhombifolia)*. This vine with 3-parted leaves can be used to trail from basket or pot, or it will climb to the top of your window if you provide strings on which it can catch its tendrils. It prefers an east or north window, some sun, and average house temperatures. Cuttings will root in water.

IVY, GRAPE-, see GRAPE-IVY.

IVY, ENGLISH *(Hedera helix)*. This glossy-leaved vine comes in many varieties: large-leaved or small, curly, variegated, self-branching, etc. It will grow in water, or soil that is loose and rapid-draining. It prefers cool temperatures, a north or east window, or any light place out of hot sun.

Segments of the vine placed in water will develop roots.

IVY-ARUM, see POTHOS

IVY, DEVIL'S-, see POTHOS

MONSTERA or SWISS-CHEESE PLANT *(Monstera deliciosa)*. This vine is related to, and grown and propagated like, philodendron, which appears in this listing.

NORFOLK-ISLAND PINE *(Araucaria excelsa)*. This "Christmas tree"-shaped needle-leaved evergreen grows 2 to 4 ft. high as a house plant, though it becomes a tall tree in its homeland. It likes constantly moist soil, a window with some sun, and a cool temperature (50° to 70°).

PALMS. Place these out of sun but in bright light. They prefer a cool temperature (55° to 65°), but will stand average house heat. Do not let soil become completely dry but let the surface of the soil dry between thorough waterings. You can start date palms from seeds rescued from dried dates you eat. Tuck the pits into the pot of a plant whose soil you must keep moist. Be patient for you may have to wait several months for results.

PANAMIGO, see PILEA

PELLIONIA. These are creeping or trailing plants with thick leaves 1 to 2 in. long, interestingly netted or marked. At first glance you might think they were a type of wandering Jew. They grow in moderate light with the general care given all house plants. They are easily started from stem cuttings.

PEPEROMIA. These are easily grown, fleshy-leaved plants of many varieties. Some grow upright; others are trailers or creepers. Some have smooth green leaves (example, *P. obtusifolia*), others are variegated (example, *P. obtusifolia variegata*), striped (example, watermelon-begonia *P. sandersi argyreia*), or crinkled (example, *P. capreata*). They grow in average house temperatures, any light except hot sunshine, and prefer high humidity.

PIGGY-BACK PLANT *(Tolmiea menziesi)*. This is a conversation-piece plant because of the way it develops its babies. They materialize at the base of mature leaves, at the point where they fasten onto their leaf stalks. It is these little plants carried by their "mother leaves" that gives *Tolmiea* its common name. To propagate, pot up these leaves with plantlets attached, using a moist rooting medium; or start them in a jar of water, with the stem beneath water and the base of the leaf just touching it.

Piggy-back plant is native to the Pacific Coast, from Alaska to California, where it normally grows 1 to 2 ft. high. Indoors it will tolerate poor light and almost any temperature except very hot. It likes constant moisture and prefers high humidity.

PHILODENDRON. Some of these are vines; others are nonclimbing and called self-heading. Some have small leaves about 4 to 6 in. long; others have big ones 18 in. or more in length and dramatically decorative in shape. They tolerate dim light and casual attention to watering. However, for best growth give bright light but not hot sunshine, humid air, moist, rapid-draining soil, monthly feedings and occasional baths for foliage. Do not cut off dangling aerial roots of vines; they are helping to provide the plant with oxygen. The tips can be tucked into the soil of the pot.

To hold climbers upright, place a stake or piece of weathered wood in the pot. Otherwise, make a totem pole or moss stick. Fasten sphagnum moss to a tall stake by wrapping around it cord or fine wire, or make a tall tube of hardware cloth (wire) and fill it with sphagnum moss. Either way, keep the moss dampened and tuck into it the vine's aerial roots. Make the plant think it is back in the jungle climbing a rain-drenched tree. For a very tall vine, fasten a screw eye into the ceiling or high woodwork. Run a cord down from it to support the upper part of the vine.

To shorten a vine-type philodendron (large- or small-leaved) that has become too tall, or bare of leaves, conduct an operation. Prune it back to the height you desire, making the cut just above a spot where a leaf joins the main stem. New growth will soon develop from the base of that upper leaf. The removed top portion of the

plant can easily be rooted by placing the lower part of its stem in water. So can sections of the main stem if they are cut to include one or more healthy leaves, and enough stem so that 2 nodes can be covered by the water. This works with monstera also.

ROOT IN WATER

PILEA. Several familiar, relatively small and low-growing house plants are pileas. The most popular of these is aluminum plant (*Pilea cadierei*) with glossy green leaves marbled or "quilted" with silver. Artillery plant (*P. microphylla*) has fernlike foliage and small inconspicuous flowers that eject pollen in smokelike puffs. Panamigo or friendship plant (*P. involucrata*) has deeply veined copper-toned leaves and cream-colored lacy flowers. All these plants like bright light or a little sunshine, and moist soil.

POTHOS (*Scindapsus aureus*). This is also called IVY-ARUM and DEVIL'S-IVY. It resembles philodendron and is grown like it. The leaves, 6 to 18 in. long, are mottled and splashed with yellow. A favorite variety is 'Marble Queen.' It grows in subdued light, but the brighter the light the more attractive the color variations.

PRAYER-PLANT or RABBIT-TRACK PLANT (*Maranta leuconeura kerchoveana*). This has broad thin oval leaves 6 in. long with rows of decorative dark spots (like rabbit tracks) on either side of the midrib. At night the leaves turn upward like hands in prayer. It thrives in moderate light or part sun, and needs considerable moisture during spring and summer, but should be fairly dry during midwinter. Spray the leaves with water frequently. Propagate by division.

There are several other varieties of maranta with slightly different markings.

RUBBER-PLANT (*Ficus elastica*). This plant is one of the most foolproof, if not overwatered. It has handsome large thick leaves on a sturdy trunk. It likes bright light but little or no sun, and tolerates dim light, house heat, dry air. Wash the leaves occasionally or wipe dust from them with a soft cloth.

SANSEVIERIA, SNAKE-PLANT or BOW-STRING-HEMP. This has stiff upright leaves, is almost indestructible unless given too much water—especially during winter. It grows in cool or warm temperature, tolerates dim light, dry air, neglect and infrequent watering. Occasionally it produces a spike of small white flowers. There are tall (to 5 ft.) and dwarf (8 in.) forms. Propagate by cutting leaves into 3 in.-long sections and placing the lower half in damp sand.

SCHEFFLERA (*S. actinophylla*). This shrub has large leaves arranged like fingers or spokes of an umbrella. It is very durable, and tolerates poor light, house heat, casual care, but thrives on kindness. Water it thoroughly when the soil surface is dry.

SCREW-PINE (*Pandanus*). The plant has sword-shaped, narrow leaves with sharp edges, arranged spirally around a vertical stalk. Aerial roots prop the plants. It is easy and dependable if kept in bright light out of sun, and not overwatered. Water it only when the top of soil becomes dry. Propagate by removing sucker plants from base of stalk; pot in soil.

SEDUM. There are hundreds of varieties of these fleshy-leaved plants. Some are winter-hardy outdoor garden plants in subzero climates. Others, such as *Sedum pachyphyllum*, are susceptible to cold, so are handled as house plants except in mild climates. All are simple to grow, and they propagate easily from any piece of stem placed in soil. Sometimes their leaves serve as cuttings and produce roots and a plant. For indoor culture see succulents.

SNAKE-PLANT, see SANSEVIERIA

SPIDER-PLANT, see AIRPLANE PLANT

SUCCULENTS, including CACTI. These fleshy-leaved plants will adjust to drought conditions. They can get along fine in your house if given bright light or part-time sunshine. But be careful not to overwater them! They survive well with almost no watering during winter. Too much water causes them to melt into a rotten, squashy mess. Soil must be fast-draining, and should contain a large proportion of sand.

SWISS-CHEESE PLANT, see MONSTERA

SYNGONIUM or NEPHTHYTIS. Their leaves, on long stems, are usually arrowhead-shaped, though on some varieties (such as 'Trileaf Wonder') they are divided into 3 or more deep lobes or segments. Young plants are upright but gradually begin to trail or climb. They are very easy to grow, and durable—in water or soil, almost any place. When old vining stems lose leaves and become bare, rejuvenate the plant by pruning back nearly to its base where new growth will emerge. Use leafy ends of stems you cut off to start new plants; root them in water.

TI PLANT (pronounced "tea" like the beverage) (*Cordyline terminalis*). Narrow red or green leaves in a tuft on top of single stem. Similar to dracaena, grown like it, and often sold as a dracaena, described earlier in this list.

WANDERING JEW, see chapter on groundcovers.

WATERMELON-BEGONIA, see PEPEROMIA

FASCINATING FLOWERS

AFRICAN VIOLET (*Saintpaulia*). These plants make exceptionally fine pets because they like the same conditions as people! They prefer moderate temperatures (70° to 75° daytime and not lower than 60° at night). They enjoy bright light and moderate amounts of sunshine but can get burned in hot sunshine or in the glare reflected from snow. High humidity (40 to 60%) keeps them in their healthiest condition. While they are not very fussy about food and watering, they love to be pampered, and respond to loving care and humoring of their whims.

The best situation is an east window or a position beneath fluorescent lights. (For details of the latter, see the section on artificial light earlier in this chapter.) But every house is different. It pays to try your plants in what you assume will be the best place, and if it does not work, try another. If your plants bloom well in a spot that breaks the rules, do not worry! Keep them there! If the amount of light is not adequate, you may not get any flowers, and the leaves will have unusually long stems. If the light is too strong, the leaves will be squat and yellowish-looking, with edges curved downward. When the light is right, the foliage will form a beautiful, fairly flat rosette, and you will have flowers and flowers and flowers.

Feed every other week, using one of the many commercially available "complete" soluble houseplant fertilizers. Water it into the top of the soil when the soil is moist. Watering can be done from the top of the pot or by immersing the pot in water. But it is important that the water be as warm as the room's temperature. Repeat watering whenever soil surface is dry, but overwatering will cause foliage to become limp, and stems and crown to rot. Leaves are not harmed

by being wet, if the water is warm. In fact, it is good for them to be bathed occasionally, if you are sure to dry them out of sunshine.

Which varieties are best? There are hundreds from which to choose, and more being bred and introduced each year. Let your own preferences be your guide. Some varieties are remarkable for the size of their flowers (such as the types called Amazons, Du Ponts and Supremes). Others may be notable for being profuse, or fringed, or double. Double flowers, by the way, last longer on the plant, so give an impression of greater number; they need more feeding and watering than singles. Foliage of African violets is as interesting and as variable as the flowers.

GENEVA — DOUBLE — FRINGED — STAR — FANTASY
STANDARD — GIRL — SPOON — WAVED — HOLLY

Propagation is astonishingly easy, so you can soon share plants with your friends or exchange choice varieties. The simplest method is by leaf cuttings. They can be started either in water or in a soil-like rooting medium. Use leaves that are crisp, young and medium-sized. (Avoid large old leaves at the outer edge of the plant.) Cut them off with a sharp knife, at a slant, and let the cut dry in the air about half an hour.

To root in water, put a piece of foil over the top of a glass. Make a hole in its center and put the stem through it so that its bottom is under water. Place in a light but not sunny place with temperature about 75°. Roots should form in 2 to 4 weeks. Then leaves should be transplanted to a rooting medium (such as a mixture of vermiculite and chopped or sieved sphagnum moss, moist but not soggy), with the base of the stem ½ in. below soil. Small plants will develop at soil level, and can be separated and planted.

To propagate directly in a rooting medium, you can use a shallow pan or fix an "incubator" or "miniature greenhouse" that will help provide high humidity. For the latter you can use a large-mouthed jar, goldfish bowl, large casserole, etc. Lids should not be airtight but should allow some ventilation. Cut leaf with short (1 to 1½ in.) stem. Place end ½ in. below soil, propping the leaf if necessary with wooden toothpicks. A cluster of baby plants will form within 6 or 8 months. They can be separated when the leaves are 1½ to 2 in. tall, and transplanted to individual small pots or in rows in a larger container. Begin to feed them about a week after transplanting, and every other week thereafter.

You can easily identify your African violet cuttings by attaching names on sticky tape to the leaves as soon as you remove them from the plants.

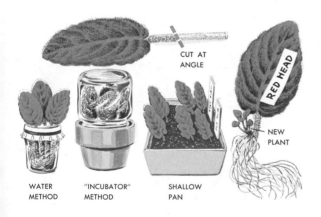

WATER METHOD "INCUBATOR" METHOD SHALLOW PAN CUT AT ANGLE RED HEAD NEW PLANT

African violets can also be grown from seed, either purchased or home-produced. To produce seeds, break open the two yellow pollen-holding anthers in the center of one of the blossoms, and dust the pollen on top of the pistil in the center of another flower. It will take 6 to 7 months for the seed pod to ripen. The seed is very tiny, but you can grow plants from it that will begin to bloom 6 to 9 months after sowing.

(To deal with fine seed, see the chapter on starting and propagating plants.)

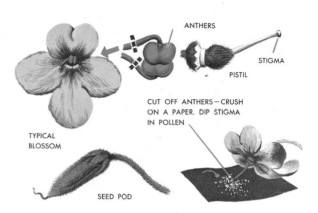

ANTHERS STIGMA PISTIL CUT OFF ANTHERS—CRUSH ON A PAPER. DIP STIGMA IN POLLEN TYPICAL BLOSSOM SEED POD

AMARYLLIS *(Hippeastrum)*. These gorgeous, lilylike flowers in red, pink, orange, white, or striped, are grown in outdoor gardens in Zones 9 and 10, but as potted plants in the North. Dormant bulbs should be purchased in midwinter. Plant them so the upper half is above soil. The best pot size is one that allows an inch of space between bulb and rim. After planting, water. Set the pot in moderate light and warmth while roots develop. Keep soil on the dry side until you see leaves or a bud emerging. Then bring to a sunny window. If the stalk leans toward the light, turn the pot around. Water more generously as growth develops. When flowering is finished, continue to water and feed every other week. Encourage leaves to grow! Next year's blooms depend on how much foliage (and therefore food) is produced this year. When summer comes, sink the pot to its top in a sunny place in the garden, out of wind. Water and feed all summer to keep the leaves growing. In autumn, withold water. Then lift the pot and store practically dry in a cool spot safe from freezing. Leaves may or may not die. In January, bring to light and warmth again. Repotting is not needed until roots crowd the pot, but each year some soil at the top of the pot can be removed and fresh soil added.

Dieffenbachia

Philodendron

Pothos

Rubber-Plant

Syngonium

FOLIAGE PLANTS THAT WILL GROW BIG

Schefflera

Monstera

Dracaena

Grape-Ivy

Airplane Plant

Aluminum Plant

Artillery Plant

Chinese Evergreen

Cryptanthus zonatus

Pellionia

Peperomia obtusifolia variegata

Piggy-back Plant

Prayer-Plant

Sedum pachyphyllum

Wandering Jew

Watermelon-Begonia

FOLIAGE PLANTS THAT WILL STAY SMALL

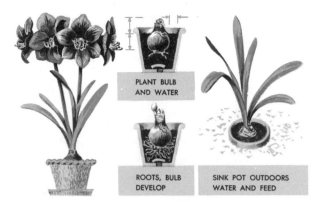

PLANT BULB
AND WATER

ROOTS, BULB
DEVELOP

SINK POT OUTDOORS
WATER AND FEED

BEGONIA. This tender perennial comes in many handsome varieties. Some are grown for their flowers, some for their decorative foliage, others for both. In general they like the temperature of your house, humidity above 30%, and considerable sunshine in winter (east window is ideal). Rapid-draining soil is essential, for the stems are so succulent that they will rot if plants are overwatered. During winter especially let the soil become practically dry between waterings.

The easiest begonias for winter flowers are the wax (*Begonia semperflorens*) with single or double blooms in many colors. They grow 8 to 12 in. high, have fibrous roots, and are easily propagated by stem cuttings rooted in water. In summer put them outdoors—in shade in hot climates, sun in cool climates.

Tuberous begonias that excel outdoors in summer want to rest, dormant, during winter. (For instructions, see the chapter on bulbs.)

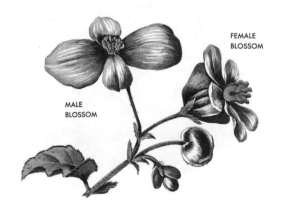

MALE
BLOSSOM

FEMALE
BLOSSOM

BOUGAINVILLEA. This tropical flowering vine or bush makes an excellent house plant. True blossoms are tiny and inconspicuous, but the petal-like bracts that enclose them are spectacularly showy in red, pink, purple or orange. The plant likes a sunny window, average house temperature, and thorough watering when top of soil becomes dry. Blooms develop at the tip of new growth during late winter. When flowering finishes, you can cut the side branches back to within 3 nodes of the main stem. This keeps the plant within bounds and makes it bushier. (10-in. pieces of branches cut off can be rooted in water if their lower portion is hard, mature wood.) New shoots will develop, which may carry another crop of flower buds. For summer move the pot outdoors to a spot getting sunshine most of the day. Water it as needed. Toward autumn, reduce watering and encourage the plant to become dormant. Let it drop its leaves and move to a frost-free but cool place, allowing the soil to remain almost dry. After Christmas, bring to your sunny window and start watering. Good varieties are 'Barbara Karst' red; 'Orange King' bronze-orange; 'Texas Dawn' pink; 'Temple Fire' dwarf red.

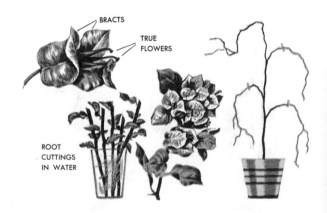

BRACTS

TRUE
FLOWERS

ROOT
CUTTINGS
IN WATER

GARDENIA. The best kind for house-plant use is the small-flowered *Gardenia veitchei*. Grow your own corsages! The fragrant waxy white flowers are borne on a glossy-leaved evergreen shrub. It likes a sunny window, humid air and acid soil. (For help on how to maintain acidity, see the earlier part of this chapter.) The plant needs lots of water, preferably given by setting pot in a larger container of water until soil is saturated; then wait to water again until the soil surface is dry. Wash or spray leaves with water once a week. The plant wants warmth during the day but at night the temperature should be near 60°, and if higher than 70°, buds may fail to open. The time to prune or cut back is after flowering in spring. For summer, sink the pot in a sunny or partially shaded spot in the garden. Continue to water and feed, and bring in before frost.

GERANIUM (*Pelargonium*). Indoors, during the winter, they like full sun, relatively cool temperature (70° to 75° in daytime, 55° to 60° at night) and soil kept barely moist. They bloom best on young growth, and in pots that are relatively small for the size of the plant. Feed once a month when the plants are growing vigorously and setting buds. Prune occasionally to make the plants bushy.

There are many kinds, upright growing and trailing, fancy-flowered and fancy-leaved, tall and miniature. Send for catalogues from houseplant specialists (some are listed in this book) and visit florists' greenhouses, and you will be agog at the tempting choices.

During the summer, plants can be placed outdoors, in or out of pots, with full sun except in hottest climates.

To carry geraniums over the winter, do not save the big old plants, but take 6 in.-long cuttings from their tops in summer or fall. Root them in a sterile rooting medium. Within 6 to 8 weeks roots will be developed enough for the cuttings to be potted in soil. These young plants should begin to flower in 2 to 4 additional months. (For details on softwood cuttings, see the chapter on starting plants.) If you are determined to save a big old plant in autumn, pot it, cut it back severely, and store in a cool, dimly lighted place. Water after you pot it, but after that the soil should remain almost dry. In late winter you can start the plant into growth and either produce blooms indoors or obtain cuttings from which to start plants for summer use.

If you like to grow plants from seed, gerani-ums are easy and fascinating. (Again, see the chapter on starting plants for the way to start seed in boxes.)

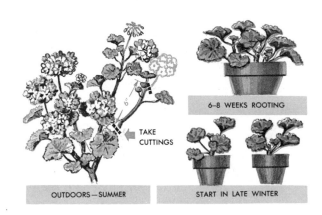

OUTDOORS—SUMMER TAKE CUTTINGS 6–8 WEEKS ROOTING START IN LATE WINTER

HIBISCUS, CHINESE (*Hibiscus rosa-sinensis*). This shrub has large tropical-looking flowers. It is an excellent indoor plant if you have a sunny window and considerable space. Since blooms develop at the tips of new growth, the plant can stand heavy pruning and thus be kept to a desired shape and size without sacrificing future blossoms. Flowers are exotically glamorous in red, pink, yellow, in single or double forms. Each bloom lasts one day and is so gorgeous that you will want to give a party in order to share its loveliness with friends. Buds are produced plentifully, though seldom do more than two flowers open on any one day. This plant needs lots of water and food. It can be set outside, in its pot, and prefers a semisunny place for summer. Prune it severely before moving it outdoors. Propagate by cuttings of semi-hardwood, in water or a rooting medium. Use your pruning clippings for this purpose.

IMPATIENS (*I. holsti* and *I. sultani*). This one is delightful, dependable, and everblooming! Bright blossoms 1 to 1½ in. across may be red, salmon, pink or white. The plants are succulent-stemmed, and may be fairly tall (to 3 ft.) or dwarf (1 ft.). Because of their constant bloom all year, indoors winter and outdoors summer, they have earned the name Busy Lizzie. Indoors for winter months they like a sunny window. When put outside for the warm months, they prefer shade. Cuttings root in water and will bloom there if in sunshine.

LANTANA. This shrubby evergreen perennial or shrub from the tropics is grown outdoors the year around in mild climates. Elsewhere it is used as an everblooming house plant in winter, and an outdoor bedding plant in summer. The round bloom heads, 2 in. across in yellow, white or lavender, are made up of many small tubular flowers. Some lantanas grow upright and may become 4 ft. tall. Others trail. Indoors they like a temperature of 65 to 75°, sunshine (if they are to bloom), good humidity, and frequent shower baths or mist sprayings for foliage. The soil should be moist, except during midwinter when plants tend to rest. This period is a good time to prune lantanas severely, so they will make bushy new growth. Outdoors they will thrive in sun or part shade. The leaves and fruit are poisonous if eaten.

ROSE, MINIATURE. These darlings bloom well indoors and later can be moved outside where they will be as hardy and permanent in your garden as floribundas and hybrid teas. If you obtain your tiny rose potted and in bud or flower (as they are often sold at flower shows) place it in a window that gets sunshine at least 3 hours a day. More is better. Cool temperature (65°) is preferred. Give as humid an atmosphere as you can and spray the foliage with water frequently.

The other way to start miniature roses is to buy dormant, bare-root plants during winter or early spring. Pot them at once. Place in a sunny window and treat as described above. They should bloom within 7 weeks following planting.

SHRIMP-PLANT *(Beloperone guttata)*. This conversation piece dangles flowers that resemble shrimp! The real flowers are small and white, peeping out from overlapping red bracts. This is an everblooming, durable and tolerant house plant, if given sun, a temperature of 65° to 75°, and watered only when the surface of the soil is dry. It appreciates humid air. In mild climates

[Zones 9 and 10] shrimp-plant is hardy outdoors and may become 5 ft. high. Indoors the average height is 1½ ft. It tends to become scrawny if not cut back occasionally, and will root easily from softwood cuttings. (See the chapter on starting plants.) In summer, set outdoors in sun or part shade.

WAX-PLANT *(Hoya carnosa)*. This vine has glossy thick leaves, and clusters of waxy white, star-shaped, fragrant blooms in spring and summer. It thrives in average house climate and likes sunshine. Without sun it will not bloom, though it will develop handsome dark leaves. An east window is preferred. Blooms arise year after year on the same permanent short stems or spurs, which should not be cut off. Cuttings root easily in water or moist sand, but often take 4 years to begin to bloom. For summer, place the plant in its pot in a shaded place outdoors. Mealybug is the worst pest; be on the lookout for it.

Miniature wax-plant *(Hoya bella)* is a dwarf, bushily erect, with pink flowers borne profusely.

21

~~~~~~

Soils and Plant Foods

by Dr. Robert Schery,
Director of The Lawn Institute

The soil in your yard is a mixture of many things inherited from its past. Included are bits of rock, living and dead plants and animals—mostly of microscopic size—air and water. What types these are, and their proportion in the general mixture, decides your soil's characteristics.

Good points and bad ones relate back to the soil's history. For instance: Did it originate as leafmold on a forest floor? Was it washed into your part of the country by a glacier? What type of rock was the "parent" that produced most of its mineral content? Has it been heavily cropped as farm land, or was it dug recently from a deeper layer during excavations for your house? Such things determine secondary characteristics too, such as whether worms and microörganisms are abundant, whether fertility has accumulated, and whether cultivation is easy.

No matter what sort of soil you have, there are a number of things that you can do to improve it for a particular purpose, or for future use. But because your soil is likely to be different from others, you must decide what to do about it on the basis of its own characteristics.

Importance of Soil

Soil plays a big part in the way plants grow because of its relationship to roots. Though plants obtain some of the raw material for their growth from the air, they depend on roots to gather most of the necessary moisture and fertility. This is where the soil comes in. Roots make use of it not only for anchoring plants and holding them in place, but also as a storehouse for food elements and water.

Since roots are alive and need oxygen, the

soil needs to be porous; air for roots to "breathe" is dragged into the pores of the soil behind water that drains through it.

Microscopic organisms in the soil perform useful duties, such as decomposing dead plants and thus unlocking nutrients for re-use, trapping nitrogen from the air and changing it into a form (nitrates) that plants can use, effecting transformations in the soil where many elements are temporarily "fixed" and then released later in different form. Conditions in the soil should encourage these workers.

Ideally, soil should be of crumbly and porous structure so that provisions for air and water are perfect. Its particles should be of a type able to absorb and hold vast fertility. It would be nice, too, if there were no weed seeds, insects or disease spores in it! How-ever, the only way to have all of this would be to gather special ingredients, and mix and sterilize them as a florist does his greenhouse potting soil. A more practical approach is this: if the soil in your yard is particularly poor in some respect, correct the major diffi-culty as best you can, concentrating your effort where it will do the most good.

What You Should Know about
Organic Materials

The term organic material refers to living organisms or their remains, as opposed to inorganic or nonliving rock and its decom-posed forms. Thus fallen leaves, twigs and stems, and corpses of animals are all organic. In speaking of the organic content of soils we assume that the material is at least partially decayed; the result of such decomposition is a black substance with a woodsy smell called humus.

Some gardeners practically worship or-ganic matter, while others may not appre-ciate it enough. A little in the soil is almost

essential for pleasant gardening; a lot is prob-ably a luxury, more important to you than to the soil.

In nature, soils range from the nearly or-ganicless desert soils and coastal sands, to the nearly all-organic mucks of low-lying areas. There is no set organic content that makes a garden soil good. The best prairie soils seldom have more than a few percent organic content, which is a clear indication that small quantities have great influence. It takes only a few percent of organic material to make any soil friable and more responsive. By and large, southern soils contain less or-ganic material than northern ones, because where temperatures are generally higher, all biological activity is speeded up, including decomposition.

Most of the humus in soils has accumu-lated through the ages from plants and ani-mals that have died. However, man adds organics when he spreads manure, compost, processed sewage, or agricultural residues, such as cottonseed meal, soybean meal, tank-age from slaughtering operations, etc. All of these materials return to the soil essentially the same elements that were extracted from it to make the plants or animals that fed upon them. As an additional good point, organics also provide food for the many microörgan-isms in soil that are on the whole beneficial to its structure and fertility.[1]

With so many seeming advantages, it is easy to overestimate the importance of or-ganic materials. The fact is, that crops can be grown year after year on the same soil with-out the addition of organic material. Of course, ample fertilizer is used. Some of the

[1]There is a school of gardeners that will use only organic materials and opposes the use of any chemi-cal fertilizer, claiming that the chemicals will sooner or later exhaust the soil, destroy its natural fertility and so weaken the soil that it becomes a ready host for plant diseases.—Editor.

most expensive, productive land in this country—the irrigated soils of California and Arizona—yields excellent harvests though the soil is almost devoid of organic content! So you *can* grow a lawn and garden on almost any soil. But you cannot necessarily make the soils easy and pleasant to dig into without plenty of organic material.

Differences between Topsoil and Subsoil

Topsoil is the surface portion of an undisturbed soil. It may be only an inch or so deep on thin mountainous land, or several feet deep in the prairies. It is usually a darker color than the deeper subsoil because of higher organic content. Because of this relative organic richness, it is generally easier to handle than subsoil. It cultivates better, is less sticky or likely to cake. But with these advantages come some disadvantages particularly the likelihood of weed seeds that accumulate in surface soil.

Subsoil is usually lighter in color, more sticky, less fertile and more difficult to handle. Typical are foundation diggings. Because such soil comes from greater depth, it usually contains no weed seeds. For lawnmaking this advantage may be big and even outweigh the disadvantages. Subsoils are fairly easy to improve.

HOW TO IMPROVE YOUR SOIL

If your soil is extremely light (sandy) you will probably want to mix in some fine-particle ingredients to make it less porous and more moisture-retentive. If your soil is very heavy (claylike) you will want to loosen it, making it more porous and better drained.

The ideal is, of course, somewhere between extreme lightness or heaviness. Such soils are called loams. Loam is a rather indefinite description as you can see, but implies enough large or coarse particles (like sand) so that porosity and drainage are good, and yet sufficient small particles (like clay or organic materials) to hold fertility, nutrients and moisture abundantly. Such a soil is almost automatically a good home for beneficial microörganisms.

What To Do If Soil Is Too Heavy

Clay soils are sticky-slippery when wet, and bake hard when dry. They hold water and fertility well. But the small clay particles pack so tightly together that they practically eliminate pore space. Roots can hardly penetrate, and water drains poorly. Such soils are difficult to cultivate except at a certain stage of moderate moistness which may occur only a few days out of a year! Usually they are so slow to dry out in spring that you cannot do early planting. Then in summer they may cake and crack unmercifully. While this may not be too bad under a lawn, it is bad in a garden.

For your garden soil, try mixing 1 in. of organic material into the top several inches of a cultivated bed, to loosen it and improve its structure. Or try adding one of the inorganic soil amendments described later in this chapter.

Drainage can be improved by loosening the soil through cultivation and by mixing in amendments. If the soil remains soggy much of the time, it may even be desirable to lay tile lines about 2 ft. beneath the surface, to carry off standing water to a drainage channel.

What To Do If Soil Is Too Sandy

Sandy soils suffer the opposite troubles from heavy ones. They tend to be so porous that water and nutrients flush through, and this means overly frequent watering and feeding. But they can be cultivated and trod upon at any time without fear of compacting them— a concern with clays. You can increase their ability to hold moisture and nutrients by adding clay-like minerals or organic materials. About 5% clay thoroughly rotary-tilled a few inches deep into sandy soil, or an inch of organic material similarly mixed in, should do the job.

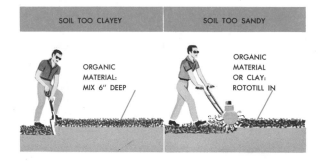

SOIL TOO CLAYEY	SOIL TOO SANDY
ORGANIC MATERIAL: MIX 6" DEEP	ORGANIC MATERIAL OR CLAY: ROTOTILL IN

Recommendations for Lawn Soil

While it is a pleasant advantage to have really good soil for the lawn, lawns can usually make out pretty well with whatever soil you happen to have. Growing grass of itself improves soil; the fine grass rootlets finger between soil particles, leaving beneficial organic remains, since about half the grass rootlets die each year and are replaced by new growth. Prairie soils became black and rich because they grew grass through the ages.

Lawn grass loves fertility, but you can furnish this with fertilizer. Roots penetrate deeper, and resist drought longer, if the soil is porous, and you can do something about this by cultivating the seedbed before planting, and by not squashing compactable soils with rolling or with heavy machinery.

If your soil is very sandy, you will have to fertilize and water more frequently than if the soil were heavier. But this is a lot easier than replacing the soil of your entire lawn.

If your lawn soil is sticky clay, it will hold fertilizer and water well, but you may have to soak such soils slowly, not run traffic over them repeatedly or try to cultivate them when wet. If a clay is so compact that it drains poorly and grass roots cannot grow deeply for lack of air, you may have to water more frequently to sustain the shallow-rooted turf. Such attentions are relatively simple, however, compared to the cost of bringing in or preparing a soil similar to that of a greenhouse potting mixture.

Facts on Acidity and Alkalinity

As if it is not enough to worry about the structure of a soil—and its fertility—there are other features, to be mentioned later, which have an influence on both of these qualities and upon the type of organisms that thrive in soil. Acidity-alkalinity, measured by pH readings, is an important one.

A pH of 7 is neutral, neither acid nor alkaline. A pH higher than 7—such as 8 or 9— means that the soil is strongly alkaline. A pH less than 7 marks the soil as acid, around 5 quite so. County agents or some commercial firms will make a pH reading for you, or a simple home soil test kit can be purchased in which you read the color of an indicator solution against a chart.

Most plants do well when the pH is between 6 and 7, just a shade on the acid side. If a soil shows an extreme pH, it is best that it be brought close to this desirable range— at least for most plants.

Liming is the usual way to correct acidity, or to make the soil "sweeter." The safest material to use for this is ground-up limestone rock, called agricultural lime. However, hydrated lime can be used. On a light soil, about 50 lb. of ground limestone per 1,000 sq. ft. should raise the pH about 1 unit, as from 5 to 6, but 75 to 100 lb. might be needed on a heavier soil for the same effect. It is best to take a pH test in order to determine whether liming is needed or not.

The other side of the coin is acidification of soils that are too alkaline. This is a problem only in the semi-arid plains country and in the western deserts, since most soils east of the Mississippi tend to be acid. About 40 lb. of agricultural sulfur per 1000 sq. ft. should reduce the pH nearly a point. Sometimes gypsum (calcium sulfate) serves better, if the soil lacks calcium.

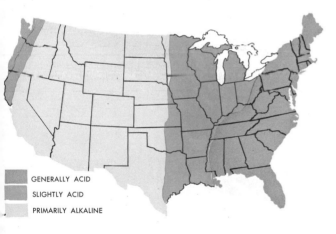

GENERALLY ACID
SLIGHTLY ACID
PRIMARILY ALKALINE

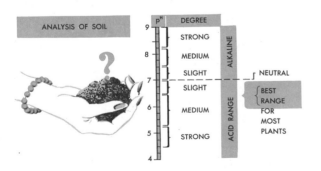

How You Can Produce Humus

An old-time method of increasing soil organic content was to grow ryegrass or soybeans, and then plow them under as green manure. Much the same effect can be obtained by mixing purchased organic materials—such as peat—into the soil. But avoid introducing weed seeds. This will be a hazard if you purchase manure from a local barnlot. There may be weed seed in old hay, or even in corncobs or piles of sawdust left to rot on abandoned land.

Such organics yield humus when they decompose, but they should be mostly decomposed when you use them. If organic materials high in carbohydrate (such as sawdust or corncobs) are mixed fresh into soil, a temporary imbalance of fertility results until decay has progressed. The little organisms which cause rotting compete with garden plants for nitrogen. If you are mixing incompletely decomposed organics into your soil, you should add at least 1 lb. of nitrogen to each 1000 sq. ft. or your plants may starve at the very time you think you are helping to nourish them.

Often organics are first put on as a mulch —that is, a surface layer. Some decomposition occurs during the season, and then the residues are mixed into the soil.

Many gardeners prefer to have a compost pile where they dump weeds, fallen autumn leaves, and grass clippings, and allow them to decompose into humus. Practically anything can be added, including garbage from the kitchen. Various techniques are used, but the main objective is to encourage the microörganisms to attack the organics. These little organisms need moisture and air in order to flourish. So a compost heap should be arranged to drain adequately, but it should be dished out at the top to trap rain rather than shed it. In some instances, purchased bacteria or earthworms are added, but usually nature supplies these adequately.

For quick composting, layers of rich soil are often interspersed between the organic material, possibly with lime and fertilizer added as well. Loosening or turning the compost pile aerates it and speeds the decomposition. A well-laid pile will function even in the depth of winter, for the internal activity releases heat.

The time it takes to produce humus, in favorable conditions, may be only a few weeks. But if you are not in a hurry, you can pile things up as they accumulate, and they will gradually rot to black humus in the oldest part of the pile.

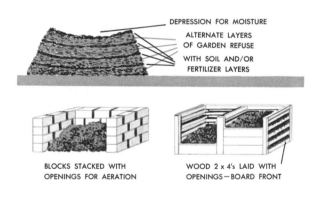

DEPRESSION FOR MOISTURE
ALTERNATE LAYERS OF GARDEN REFUSE WITH SOIL AND/OR FERTILIZER LAYERS

BLOCKS STACKED WITH OPENINGS FOR AERATION

WOOD 2 x 4's LAID WITH OPENINGS—BOARD FRONT

Inorganic Materials as Helpful Additions

It is not always economical or convenient to use organic materials to improve your soil, and there are other things that work well.

Sufficient sand or cinders mixed into clay make it more porous; or a little clay improves the retentiveness of sand.

Garden stores sell various products useful for loosening heavy soils. Among them are Vermiculite, which is made up of particles of puffed mica; calcined clays such as Tur-

face, which are special clays baked into bricks and then pulverized; and Perlite, which is pulverized volcanic stone.

These materials are often used in mixing greenhouse potting soils or for making golf greens. They may be helpful for limited portions of the garden, but treatment of extensive areas becomes rather expensive because you may need as much as 50% in poor-structured soil.

How Mulches Save You Work and Benefit Soil

Any material applied to the surface of the soil as a barrier, to retain moisture in the soil, prevent weed growth, etc., is a mulch. Plastics, roofing paper or insulation fiber will serve. However, natural organic materials are the things most often used; they decompose in time, contributing to soil improvement.

A good mulch should let rain seep through, but be tight and thick enough to smother sprouting weeds. Usually it is applied 2 to 4 in. thick in shrub, vegetable or flower beds, but only a fraction of an inch thick and very loosely on newly planted lawns. Organic mulches decay toward their bottom where they meet moist soil. This benefits the soil through the release of nutrients and materials that help make the soil surface crumbly. The mulch also helps by insulating the soil against extreme temperature changes and rapid drying.

One of the handiest sources of mulching material around the home is lawn clippings. Compost is excellent, if you have enough. Or you can purchase any number of materials at the garden store, including peat moss, ground-up corncobs, pulverized bark, and screened nut shells.

In some localities power companies chip up trimmings from street trees, which you can obtain free for the hauling. They make an acceptable mulch. Sawdust tends to pack a little tight, so rain and air cannot penetrate, but after it has partially decayed it is satisfactory. Hay, straw, tobacco stems or similar local materials are useful where their appearance is not considered unsightly.

Sometimes much of a plant's root system grows just under the mulch, as for example an azalea's. Then one has to be careful not to disrupt the mulch by too much cultivation. In the vegetable and flower garden, the mulch functions during the annual growth period; after that, it can be tilled into the soil.

🍁 Fertilizers, Commonly Called Plant Foods

Fertilizers add nutritious elements to the soil and, within limits, the richer the soil is in nutrients, the more a plant grows. Some of the elements are needed only in small amounts. Others, such as nitrogen, are required in considerable quantity. For the best plant growth, fertility should be "balanced." Too much fertilizer, or too much of any one element, can be as bad as no fertilizer at all.

Products used for fertilizing can be purchased wherever garden supplies are sold. Some are to be applied dry, others in solution. They are not poisonous and there is no harm in handling them. Instructions for their use are printed on the package containing them.

Content of Fertilizers

Every "complete" fertilizer, whether it comes in a big sack or small can, contains 3 major fertility elements. These are nitrogen, phosphorus and potassium—sometimes designated as N, P and K—and it is helpful to understand a little about them so that you can buy wisely. Stated very briefly, nitrogen encourages leaf growth, while phosphorus and potassium are helpful for flowering and fruiting.

Fertilizer bags tell the percentage of each of the 3 main nutrient ingredients. These are often mentioned as a series of 3 numbers such as 5-10-5. Each number stands for the percentage of one element, and they are always in the same sequence. The first always stands for nitrogen, the second for phosphorus, and the third for potassium. Thus a 5-10-5 fertilizer contains 5% nitrogen, 10% phosphorus and 5% potassium. The larger the numbers, and thus the greater the percentage, the more powerful the fertilizer is.

When you are shopping for a lawn fertilizer, you want one that makes leaves grow, so it should contain a high percentage of nitrogen—2 or 3 times as much as any other nutrient. Examples are 20-10-10 and 22-8-6. The same may be the case for vegetables in which leaves are the main crop, as spinach and lettuce.

For flower beds, you are after blooms rather than great amounts of foliage. So if you are buying a "complete" fertilizer to use on them, choose one in which phosphorus and potassium are equal to—or exceed—the nitrogen. Examples are 12-12-12 and 5-10-5.

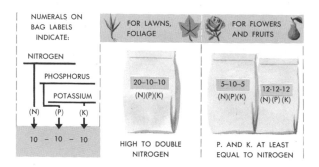

NUMERALS ON BAG LABELS INDICATE:

NITROGEN
PHOSPHORUS
POTASSIUM
(N)   (P)   (K)

10 – 10 – 10

FOR LAWNS, FOLIAGE

20–10–10
(N)(P)(K)

HIGH TO DOUBLE NITROGEN

FOR FLOWERS AND FRUITS

5–10–5
(N)(P)(K)

12-12-12
(N) (P) (K)

P. AND K. AT LEAST EQUAL TO NITROGEN

Secondary nutrients are needed for good plant growth, but in lesser proportion to the 3 listed above. Among these secondary ones are sulfur, calcium and magnesium. These are sufficient in most soils, and seldom are listed in ingredients in fertilizer, though they are there possibly as a result of manufacturing processes.

Finally, there is a group of minor elements required in only minute quantities. These are the so-called trace elements. Included are iron, zinc, copper, molybdenum, manganese and others. Lack of iron occasionally causes blanching (chlorosis) of lawn grasses where soils are very alkaline, as in the West, or with centipede-grass in the Southeast. Iron and other minor-element deficiency shows up more frequently in ornamental plants. Pin oaks often suffer iron chlorosis as do acid-loving azaleas and gardenias in alkaline soils.

Trace deficiency symptoms are difficult to diagnose exactly. Generally the first thing to do, if a minor-element deficiency is suspected, is to check the soil's pH. If it is either extremely acid or extremely alkaline, bring it toward the neutral condition or toward the condition preferred by the particular plant.

With azaleas and centipede-grass, for instance, you would increase acidity. Use methods described in the paragraphs on acid and alkaline soils earlier in this chapter. The trace elements may then become more "available" or soluble.

If the trace element is still lacking at a suitable pH, it may have to be added. To those soils that "tie up" or "fix" the trace elements, it may have to be added as the chelate, which is a chemical way of keeping it available; chelated compounds can be purchased at garden stores. Some "complete" fertilizers include trace elements; this is added insurance but perhaps unjustifiably costly since minor elements are usually adequate in most soils.

Merits of Organic and Chemical Fertilizers

Traditional organic fertilizers are derived from once-living tissue. Examples are processed sewage such as Milorganite, bone meal which is mainly phosphorus, tankage, fish scraps, cottonseed meal, corn gluten, soybean residues, etc. Several such ingredients may be mixed, and may be "souped up" with chemical concentrates. In general they are weak, of low analysis. The analysis may be something like 5-3-2 rather than 10-6-4 or better. As a result, organics are usually more expensive than inorganic fertilizers per unit of nutrient. But of course they have the advantage of organic materials—the ability to improve soil structure and release balanced nutrients slowly.

Inorganic or chemical fertilizers, in contrast, are a better bargain. But they are more hazardous in the sense that careless application may burn foliage. Granular, nondusty formulations are less likely to cause this difficulty, because the pellets roll easily off vegetation and onto the soil. Chemical fertilizers are quickly soluble, so their effect is immediate; grass may green within a day or two after fertilization. But by the same token, effects are not so long-lasting.

Much depends upon the kind of soil. Soluble fertilizers leach through sandy soils almost immediately and are spent quickly. On heavier soils the nutrients may be held by the clay, constituting a kind of "savings bank" upon which the plant roots can draw over a prolonged period. This is especially true when soil temperatures are cool—in the lower 50's.

Of recent years, man has somewhat bridged the gap between organic and inorganic fertilizers by synthesizing organic types, chemically speaking, from ingredients with inorganic qualities. For example, urea is combined with formaldehyde to make "ureaforms." These synthetic organics, often advertised as "slow release" or "nonburn" are mostly for special applications, or as one constituent in a blend. As with natural organics, the cost of such nutrients is high because of the extra processing. Likewise the nutrients are released by soil processes slowly and over a fairly prolonged period.

About Foliar Feeding

Most plants can absorb nutrients through the leaves or even the stems, in addition to the roots. Absorption may be less effective and costs are certainly greater than for fertilizers applied through soil. Also special precautions must be taken not to overdose so that foliage is burned.

This method stimulates a plant quickly, providing a sort of "shot in the arm" for languishing vegetation. Since these fertilizers are applied in solution, they are of course immediately absorbed. A chlorotic lawn sprayed with iron sulfate solution greens up within minutes. Roses sprayed with a soluble fertilizer may have darker green leaves within hours.

The analysis of a foliar fertilizer may run a bit higher in the scale than that of dry granular types. Even so, by the time the fertilizer is diluted for solution, total nutrient is not great. One of the biggest drawbacks to foliar feeding is that insufficient nutrients are applied to be enduring, or to justify the trouble.

To apply dissolved fertilizers, a sprinkling can or small hand sprayer can be used for individual plants or small beds. But when it comes to bigger gardens or lawns, you will probably want to use a siphon attachment on the garden hose. Inexpensive devices of this sort do a very nice job metering concentrated solution into the water stream. You regulate the outflow by covering a hole with the thumb (for suction); water alone issues when the thumb is removed.

By and large, foliar feeding is of limited practicality. It may lend itself to combination feeding-spraying for pests, or in weeding with 2, 4-D by the hose-siphon method.

22

~~~~~~

Starting and Propagating Plants

Planting a seed, transplanting volunteer seedlings, rooting a cutting, and dividing one plant into many, are great adventures! Once you have the knack, you may think propagating is the most fun of all the processes of gardening. Not only is it fascinating, but you get new plants for practically nothing, and in quantities. You can have masses of color, and armloads of flowers to pick, for a pittance of an investment. Using seeds, you can choose and raise flowers in varieties or colors not available locally. More important, you will have extra plants to share with others.

❧ Secrets of Starting Seeds Successfully

Seeds are alive but sleeping. Moisture and warmth will wake them up and start them growing. You can decide which seeds you will bring to life, and when you wish them to awaken. It is almost like magic.

Some seeds are so big and sturdy that they can be planted directly in the soil of the garden. Others are tiny, or have such exacting requirements of warmth and humidity that they need special soil, sterile conditions, and attentive care, as for incubator babies. Each seed packet carries instructions. If you are a beginner, stick to the easy ones the first year.

A good way to gain confidence in a hurry is to buy one of the small pre-planted seed boxes available at garden stores—marigolds are an ideal choice—and follow the directions. It is practically impossible to fail. Little plants will come up, bud and bloom in their little containers. You will see how easy it is. These boxes, by the way, are ideal for children and shut-ins.

HOW TO GROW ANNUAL FLOWERS
FROM SEEDS

Before reading the instructions below, refer to the chapter on annuals to learn which are usually sown directly in the garden, which should be started with more care and supervision, and the proper time to start each type of seed in your area.

Outdoor sowing in the garden: This is the simplest method, easy and sure with many favorite annuals. Choose a level spot that has sun most of the day. Spade it 8 in. deep. Soil should be moist at the time, but not sticky wet. If you are having a dry spell, water the area deeply several days before spading it; do this slowly so the moisture will be absorbed at least to the depth that you will dig; then wait to spade until the soil will crumble when dug—rather than come up in soggy chunks. If you believe that the soil lacks fertility, spread over it one of the "complete" dry garden fertilizers before spading (at the rate of 2 lbs. per 100 sq. ft.). If your soil seems cloddy, or too sticky, or too sandy, see the soils chapter for ways to improve it.

To make a suitable home for the baby plants and their delicate roots, spread 1 in. of moistened peat moss and sharp sand (not beach sand) over the surface of your garden plot, working it thoroughly into the top 2 in. of soil. Peat moss is available either in large bales (very economical since you will be wanting to use it many ways in your garden) or in small sacks.

Moist peat moss is important because if dry it will repel moisture instead of absorbing and holding it. Some peat moss is adequately moist when you buy it; not wet, but definitely not dry. To moisten dry peat moss, put it into a bucket, metal garden cart or wheelbarrow, and gradually add water as you stir. Later pour off the excess water by compress-ing and squeezing the peat moss. You may wish to let it soak overnight. After incorporating the peat moss and sand, rake the soil surface until it is both level and fine in texture.

Sow the seed in rows, rather than broadcasting it. Then, when your flower seeds, and millions of weed seeds, all come up at the same time, it will be obvious which are the flowers! Also it will be easier for you to cultivate and tend them. Rows should be 8 in. apart if this is merely a "nursery" from which you will later shift the plants to permanent places in the garden. But if the plants are to bloom in these rows, the rows must be spaced 10 to 18 in. apart.

To make straight rows, stretch a string between two stakes as a guide for making furrows with a stick or pointed hoe; or use a yardstick or lath turned on edge to make shallow indentations. The depth should be twice the thickness of the seeds. For instance, nasturtiums, being large, need a furrow ¼ in. deep. Poppies, being very tiny, go barely beneath the soil or are merely scratched into the surface. Sow seeds thinly, trying to visualize how crowded the plants will be if they all come up!

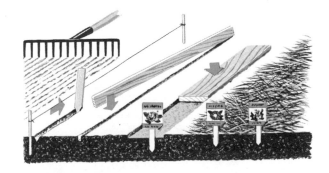

Cover the seed with fine soil, and firm it into contact with the seedbed by tamping it gently with a brick, a board, or your shoe. Put a label at the end of each row, for you will not remember what is where. Water with a gentle spray, and keep the soil moist until the seeds germinate. Covering the bed loosely with straw, dry grass clippings, or a layer of burlap, helps shade the soil and keep it moist. When sprouts appear, gradually remove any material used for shading.

The little plants will be surprisingly sturdy. However, their root systems will be near the surface of the soil where they will be susceptible to drying. Check on the situation frequently. Make sure that there is always adequate moisture so that the plants do not wilt —or die.

Thinning plants in the row is essential, if the remaining plants are to have space in which to develop properly. Information on proper spacing is given in the description of individual plants in the chapter on annuals, and is usually also given on seed packets. It varies according to the size each plant is expected to be at maturity.

The surplus plants can be transplanted to another place; or, if you have no use for them and no neighbor with whom to share them, nip them off at soil level without disturbing the roots of remaining plants. It is far better to thin plants than to get poor results by letting all grow.

Transplanting to permanent positions in the garden can be done any time after the plants have produced their second set of true leaves. Choose a day that is cloudy, rainy, or misty, and certainly not a hot, windy one. Have the soil at the new site dug at least 8 in. deep, and moistened to the same depth or more. If it is necessary to add water to the soil, do it a day in advance of your transplanting schedule. The seedlings should be watered thoroughly a day ahead of moving, and some plant food, at half its usual recommended strength, should be used in the water. Some gardeners use a hormone solution, available at garden supply stores, for this purpose. Such treatment insures the plant ample moisture and food to sustain it until its roots are operating normally in the new situation. Also, it helps soil cling to roots, and thus protects them.

Do not disturb seedlings' roots any more than you must. Take up surrounding soil with them. Do not let them become dry. If moist soil does not cling to the roots to protect them, carry the plants in a pan of water (roots in, tops out).

Set them out at the same depth they were before, using your fingers to firm the soil about their stems. Leave a slight depression to hold water, and then water each plant well. If needed, shade for a few days with a box, inverted flowerpot, or shingle stuck in the soil at an angle.

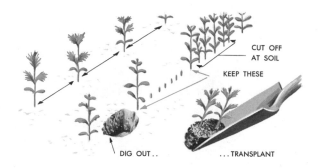

DIG OUT..   ...TRANSPLANT

CUT OFF AT SOIL

KEEP THESE

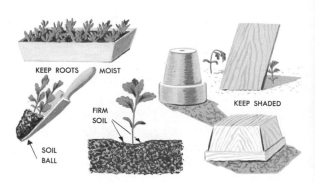

KEEP ROOTS   MOIST

SOIL BALL

FIRM SOIL

KEEP SHADED

Sowing in boxes or other containers, indoors or out: This is the best method for starting slow, small, choice or tender seeds. Warning: if sowing seeds during the winter to have plants ready to move to the outdoor garden in spring, do not start too soon! The average time needed from sowing to setting in the permanent place in the garden is 4 to 8 weeks. Plants grown indoors too long are apt to become crowded, weak and leggy.

Containers can be anything from the shallow wooden boxes the florists call flats, to small boxes manufactured and sold especially for planting seeds (one type is called Jiffy Flats), flowerpots, 1-lb coffee cans, or thoroughly washed milk cartons (close opened end of carton—staple it shut or use a paper clip; then cut out one side and you will have a horizontal "box"). The important thing is that they be clean and have holes in the bottom for drainage.

The planting medium is very important at least the top layer of it in which the seeds will lie. What you want is something that is sterile, moisture retentive, airy, and of fine texture suitable for tiny plants and roots. Luckily there are wonderful materials which can be purchased at garden supply stores. One of the best is sphagnum moss. It should be finely shredded or milled. You can purchase it that way or run the dry moss through a screen or sieve yourself (an old flour sieve propped over a large crock works well). It can be used alone or mixed with perlite and vermiculite, which are sterile, airy, lightweight popped minerals available at garden stores. None of these materials contains nutrients, but seeds need no food until they have germinated, for each has a built-in "lunch."

To prepare small containers, fill them to within ½ in. of the top with your sterile mixture (which previously has been thoroughly moistened and then squeezed to remove excess water). Press the material into place so the surface is level. Sow your seeds in rows 1 in. apart if your container is large enough. Then cover them with a layer of the dry sterile material to a depth amounting to twice the thickness of the seed. Sprinkle gently with a little water.

For larger containers, such as wooden flats, place a layer of coarse sphagnum moss in the bottom to cover drainage holes and keep the rooting medium from washing out. Add a layer of garden soil (preferably sterilized by baking or steaming) with some fine sphagnum mixed into it. Water well and let the container drain. Then add the important top layer, which is ½ to 1 in. of your sterile material, which has been previously moistened. This seedbed should be moist but not soggy when you sow the seed. Rows should be about 1 in. apart.

Place the planted containers, large or small, in semishade, where temperatures will be 68° to 75° during the day. Temperatures can be a little less at night. Whether outside or indoors, where air is dry, cover the tops of the containers with several layers of newspaper, a pane of glass, etc., or enclose in a polyethylene bag until seeds sprout. In an exceedingly humid atmosphere, such covering may not be needed. Watering probably will not be necessary until after the seeds sprout, but if you notice that the soil surface is becoming dry, moisten it with a gentle, fine spray.

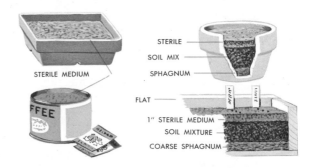

STERILE MEDIUM

STERILE
SOIL MIX
SPHAGNUM

FLAT

1" STERILE MEDIUM
SOIL MIXTURE
COARSE SPHAGNUM

When seedlings begin to come up, gradually give the container full sunshine and cooler temperatures. Keep the soil moist but never soggy. Until now the seedlings have not needed food. Begin, once a week, to use one of the soluble plant foods (such as Ra-pid-Gro, Hyponex or Plant Marvel) at half the strength recommended on the label.

First transplanting can begin whenever plants have their second set of true leaves. Move them to individual small peat pots, or put them in rows in larger boxes. Follow the same general instructions given for transplanting from outdoor seedbeds, except that spacing can be closer if plants are to be moved again later.

seeds in small containers. But these dust-fine seeds should be sown on top of the medium. This will make them unusually susceptible to drying, so they need humid air. They should be started in what amounts to a miniature warm greenhouse. This can be any container enclosed in a polyethylene bag, or having its top covered with plastic or a piece of glass; or you can use a goldfish bowl with a saucer as its lid, or a glass casserole dish. When drops of moisture accumulate on the under side of the lid, turn it over, or remove it a while to let air in.

African violets and gloxinias like a warmer than average temperature (75°), with bright light but no sun. You will get a thrill watching the little plants develop by observing them through a magnifying glass.

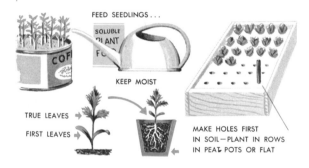

FEED SEEDLINGS . . .
SOLUBLE PLANT FOOD
KEEP MOIST
TRUE LEAVES →
FIRST LEAVES →
MAKE HOLES FIRST IN SOIL—PLANT IN ROWS IN PEAT POTS OR FLAT

SOW FINE SEEDS ON TOP OF MEDIUM
USE A COVERED CASSEROLE . . . OR ANY CONTAINER IN PLASTIC BAG

If and when plants are to be moved into the outdoor garden, "harden them off" first by gradually accustoming them to outdoor conditions. Set the container in a sheltered spot outside for a few hours at a time. They should be in shade, and out of the wind, while they acclimate.

HOW TO START VERY TINY SEEDS INDOORS

To start seeds such as African violet, wax begonia and gloxinia, use the same sterile planting medium described above for starting

PROBLEMS TO AVOID WITH INDOOR SEEDLINGS

Damping-off is the destruction of young seedlings, before or after they emerge from the soil, by fungi commonly present in soil. It can be prevented by starting seed in a sterile medium, or by treating the seed before planting with a fungicide protectant. Arasan may be used for most flower and vegetable seeds; Spergon for legumes; Orthocide 75 Seed Protectant; or Semesan. Tear off the corner of the seed packet and insert as much dust as will go on the tip of a penknife; fold the packet and shake very thoroughly.

Leggy, scrawny plants are the result of starting seeds too soon, growing them without enough sunshine, and in overcrowded conditions.

COLDFRAMES AND HOTBEDS

Coldframes and hotbeds are used for outdoor seed sowing and propagating. They are simple, rectangular frames, covered with glass sash or glass substitute, and serve as protective small greenhouses. Coldframes are heated only by the sun. Hotbeds are coldframes with additional heat supplied beneath the soil. Formerly hotbeds were warmed by putting a layer of fresh manure under the seedbed. Now modern, thermostatically controlled heating cables are available.

Frames can be as simple and temporary as a wooden box with its bottom knocked out; a sturdy structure made to order of rot-resistant lumber such as cypress or redwood; or purchased ready-made. Standard coldframe measurements are 3 x 6 ft., but if you have an old window frame to use as a top, build your frame to fit it. The back wall of the frame should be higher than the front, so water will run off, and also so more sunlight can get in. Locate it in a protected place out of the wind, such as against the wall of your house or garage. It should face south if possible.

Seeds can be planted directly in the soil, or grown in containers set on the ground; the latter is handier. They can be started in spring much earlier than they could be started in open ground outdoors. Young plants will be sturdier than those started indoors, because of more sunshine, cooler temperatures and fresh air. Daily attention is needed for watering, ventilating when temperatures rise, and possibly insulating with a blanket at night during cold spells.

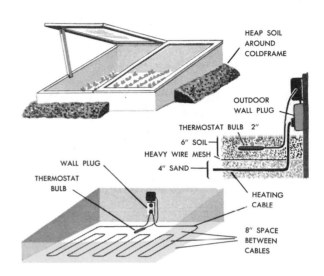

PERENNIAL FLOWERS FROM SEEDS

Growing perennials from seeds is an inexpensive way to produce them in quantity, and to get some not available otherwise. They are as easy to start as annuals, but slower to reach flowering size. Most begin to bloom their second year, though a few bloom their first season. Some that will give you special pleasure and satisfaction are columbine, delphinium, gloriosa daisy, hollyhock, lupine and pink.

Since seedlings will not be exactly like their parents, this is not the way to reproduce named varieties of iris, day-lilies, and phlox. To get exact duplicates of special named varieties, propagate them by vegetative (asexual) methods, such as cuttings, division or layering (see instructions in paragraphs that follow and data on each plant given in the chapter on perennials).

The time to plant can be spring or autumn. In cold-winter climates the autumn planting date is September, giving time for the plants to get a toe-hold before winter and a quick-start growing in spring. In mild-winter climates, fall sowing should wait until after hot weather.

Sowing can be either in portable boxes (for method see previous paragraphs on starting annual seed in boxes) or directly in the ground outdoors. If in the ground, it is wise to fix a special bed and enclose it protectively in a frame of boards. Prepare the soil carefully, as though it were to be in a small container, for these seeds are relatively small and need good care.

Cover with burlap, newspaper or anything that will conserve moisture until seeds sprout. But peek often, for babies need light and air as soon as they are up. Transplant to wider spacing in a "nursery" bed when the plants have their second set of true leaves. By autumn, some may produce buds and first blooms. Wait until spring to move them into the garden. In cold climates, the young plants should be mulched over winter or otherwise protected, as in a coldframe. Keep them from alternate freezing and thawing, which might heave them out of the soil.

Multiplying by Dividing

Separating one plant into several sections, each of which will become a replica of its parent, is the most popular means of propagating perennial flowers. It is practically sure-fire with those that grow in clumps, which can be torn apart so that a few roots adhere to each portion. These include daisy, moss-pink, primrose, day-lily, lily-of-the-valley and chrysanthemum. It is not practical with taprooted or single-crown perennials like oriental poppy, basket-of-gold alyssum, balloon-flower or columbine. If you are in doubt about a plant's rooting construction, poke around with your fingers and feel, or explore with your trowel. The best time to do the dividing is early spring before much growth starts, or after flowering finishes and plants are to be cut back, or in the fall.

Many bulbs, such as daffodil, grape-hyacinth, lily and chives, gradually become so crowded that they do not bloom well. They can be dug, pulled apart and reset at wider spacing. This should be done as their foliage begins to ripen and turn yellow, or any time during their dormant period.

There are two ways to accomplish the dividing. You can dig the entire plant, wash or shake soil from roots so you can see what you are doing, and operate with a knife or your fingers; or you can leave the plant in the ground, chop through it with a spade or trowel, and lift out one portion to reset or divide further.

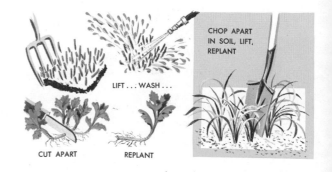

LIFT...WASH...

CHOP APART IN SOIL, LIFT, REPLANT

CUT APART   REPLANT

🍂 Cuttings of Many Types

A cutting is a piece of a plant which can be induced to develop roots and top, and eventually become a duplicate of the parent. You can grow new plants from stem cuttings (coleus, English ivy, geranium, forsythia, poinsettia), leaf cuttings (African violet, gloxinia, sansevieria, Rex begonia), or root cuttings (oriental poppy, perennial phlox).

The best materials in which to root cuttings are sterile, provide both air and constant moisture, and drain rapidly. Use coarse clean sand, coarse vermiculite and sphagnum moss.

Rooting in water: Some stem cuttings (often called "slips") will root in water! Nothing could be more simple. Lots of plants can be started this way. Among house plants try coleus, English ivy, impatiens, wax begonia, philodendron and wandering Jew. Outdoor plants include pussy willow and other willows, pachysandra, wintercreeper and forget-me-not. Use stems 6 or more inches long. Make your cut ¼ in. below a node or joint. Let foliage remain on the cutting, except that which would be below the water line and thus would rot.

Do not put cuttings in water at once, but let the cut end dry an hour or more. If leaves

PAPER OR FOIL HELD ON
GLASS WITH RUBBER BAND

tend to wilt during this time, place them between damp cloths. Use a container of dark glass, or one that is not transparent, so algae will not grow. The crucial period comes when young plants are removed from water and placed in soil; do it preferably when roots are about ½ in. long. Some leaves, complete with stems, can also be rooted in water. These include African violet and gloxinia.

Softwood stem cuttings: These cuttings are the same general type that, in some cases, root in water. The term softwood means that the stems are not hard, dry and mature like old branches of shrubs. Rather, they are soft and succulent like stems of most house plants, garden perennials, and youthful new growth at the tip of shrub branches.

Use one of the special sterile, moisture- and air-holding mediums for rooting described in the introductory paragraphs above. They aid good rooting and transplanting.

The preferred time to make softwood cuttings on outdoor plants is spring and early summer. House plants can be done any time.

The stem you select should be the end of a short, stocky shoot, young and brittle enough to snap off. It should have 3 to 5 eyes (nodes) and be 2 to 5 in. long. Make a slanting cut ¼ in. below a node. Remove any flowers, buds or seed heads, for they would be a drain on the cutting's vitality. Trim off lower leaves that would be below soil, but retain a minimum of 2 or 3 leaves to manufacture food for the cutting while it is making roots.

The larger the number of leaves that can be kept in good condition, the better the root development will be. However, large leaves tend to wilt; they can be trimmed to reduce their size. Let the cut end of the stem dry in the air an hour or so before inserting it in the rooting medium, but do not let the foliage wilt during that interval. Later the cut can be dusted with a rooting hormone powder.

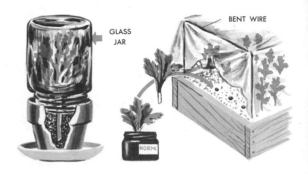

GLASS JAR   BENT WIRE

CUT BELOW LEAF NODE
REMOVE LOWER LEAVES

Insert the stem into the moistened rooting medium (which can be in a flowerpot, flat, etc., with drainage hole in its bottom). Two or 3 nodes should be below ground. Firm the rooting medium around the stem. Fix some method of keeping the humidity high. If you have only a few cuttings, you can invert glass tumblers or Mason jars over them; or put a polyethylene bag or canopy over your container. Place in a warm, light, but not sunny place. Soil must be kept moist but not wet. Transplant cuttings as soon as they are well-rooted. Among plants easily started from such cuttings are:

Begonia	Gardenia	Pink
Candytuft	Geranium	Poinsettia
Chrysanthemum	Impatiens	Sedum
Coleus	Lantana	Shrimp-Plant
Fuchsia	Periwinkle	Verbena

Semi-hardwood cuttings: As you would guess, these are partially matured wood, but not yet old and hard. Deciduous shrubs, and also evergreens of many kinds, are often propagated at this stage of growth, which is usually reached in midsummer. The best cuttings are those taken off current season's growth, pliable but brittle when bent.

Select, cut and insert these in special rooting medium, just the same as for softwood cuttings. House them in a humidity-holding outdoor frame or box with a translucent top to let in light. If you have a coldframe, use it. Sometimes you can be very successful with a nonfancy, casual type propagating nursery, where plants are started directly in the ground. Choose a spot behind protecting shrubs, out of wind and hot sun. The trick is to provide constantly moist soil and humidity. Mix moisture-holding peat moss or vermiculite with the soil. The most up-to-date method is the one using mist, described next. Some plants you can start from semi-hardwood cuttings include:

Abelia	Cotoneaster	Lavender
Arbor-Vitae	Forsythia	Lilac
Azalea	Fuchsia	Mahonia
Bitter-sweet	Heather	Pyracantha
Choisya	Hydrangea	Yew
	Jasmine	

ROOTING BED ON THE
NORTH SIDE OF HOUSE

ROOTING BOX, WITH
PLASTIC COVER IN
SHADED SPOT

Leaf cuttings: These are the most fun! Fleshy and succulent leaves are the ones most apt to root.

African violet, gloxinia and peperomia leaves will produce roots and young plants if their stems are inserted in a moist rooting medium.

For illustrations of how to start the first two of these plants, see the chapter on indoor plants.

Plump segments of subtropical sedums and echeverias will develop babies if their cut end is tucked into "soil" or even if they are laid on top of it.

Leaves of kalanchoes (*Bryophyllum* or airplant) will produce young at their tips, or around their edges—whether in soil or not! These are the ones that northerners often bring home with them from vacations in Florida, and pin to their curtains for watching.

Sansevieria or snake-plant foliage, cut into pieces 3 to 6 in. long and placed upright in a rooting medium, quickly produces new plants.

Rex begonia leaves (those with fancy colors) can be removed from the parent plant with a short piece of stem, and placed flat on damp sand. The stem is tucked into the sand. Cuts are made through the main veins of the leaves and it is at these points that baby plants develop.

Mist method: This is a relatively new technique used by nurserymen for both indoor and outdoor rooting of stem cuttings. Amateurs use it primarily outdoors, where cuttings begin to form roots quickly in full sun, in open air, under constant or intermittent artificial mist. Use a rapid-draining medium for rooting, in a frame with high enclosing sides (which can be of plastic film) that will keep the mist from blowing away. You can buy a special mist nozzle at garden supply stores. The spray of water should operate from early morning until about 5 o'clock in the evening, but allow time for leaves to dry before night. The mist keeps leaves cool and enveloped in moisture so that they do not wilt. Sunshine speeds growth, and roots develop surprisingly fast.

MIST
NOZZLE

ROOTING
MEDIUM

Root cuttings: Two popular hardy perennials are easy to propagate this way.

Oriental poppy has a thick, fleshy type of root. When the plant is dormant during summer, or as it begins to put out new leaves in late summer, dig the entire root or use your spade to remove some of the lower portions. Cut sections 2 or 3 in. long. Be careful to note which end is "up." Place vertically in the rooting medium, with the top barely beneath surface. Keep moist.

Perennial phlox has stringlike roots. Use the largest. Cut into 2- to 3-in. lengths and place horizontally 1 in. below the surface of the rooting medium. Start cuttings in spring.

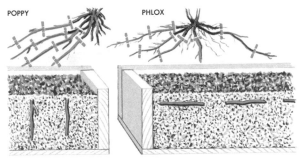

POPPY   PHLOX

❧ Layering in Soil and Air

By this propagation method, a stem or branch is rooted before being removed from the parent. The parent feeds the young developing plant until it has enough roots to be capable of "leaving home." You can multiply many herbaceous garden perennials this way, and also numerous shrubs. There are several methods. Basically all enclose a portion of the branch in a moist rooting medium, and induce roots to develop in the medium. The new plant is severed and transplanted at a time that will give it the best chance of getting adjusted before harsh weather arrives.

Simple layering: This technique is easiest and requires least attention. Bend a branch down to the ground and fasten it so that a portion is beneath soil. This section should have a wound (notch or small slit held open with a pebble) on its under side, to stimulate root development. Hold the branch down somehow with a peg or brick. The leafy end of the branch (5 to 10 in.) should be above ground, for it will be the top of the new plant. Spring is the best time for starting. Keep the soil moist. Perennials usually root in about 8 weeks. Shrubs may take years, but on rare varieties the wait is worth it. And, besides, it is an intriguing experiment.

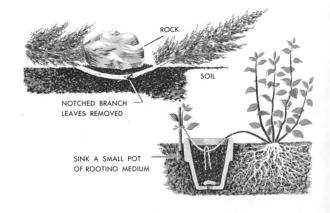

ROCK

SOIL

NOTCHED BRANCH
LEAVES REMOVED

SINK A SMALL POT
OF ROOTING MEDIUM

Plants you can increase this way include:

Azalea	Forsythia	Rhododendron
Candytuft	Hydrangea	Rosemary
Clematis	Junipers	Sarcococca
Cotoneaster	Peony	Wintercreeper
Daphne	Pinks	Yew

Air-layering: This works indoors or out.

For house plants: This method can be used on large foliage plants that become too tall and leggy. The idea is to produce a shorter plant from the top leafy portion by getting roots to form high on the stem, then cutting off the upper part and potting. The first step is to make a shallow cut ¾ of the way around the stem. It should be ½ in. wide and go through outer bark but not the center woody part. Dusting a rooting hormone onto the cut surface speeds rooting. Wrap the cut in damp sphagnum moss 1½ in. thick. Enclose in polyethylene film, fastened at the ends so the moss cannot dry. When the moss is full of a thick mass of roots (usually 7 to 10 weeks), cut just below the roots and pot the plant. Do not remove sphagnum. Keep in moist air and water well.

For outdoor shrubs and trees: The basic method described above works! But do not expect to be able to get a 6-ft. tree in one year. The most successful length of branch to use is less than 18 in. The best spot on the branch to make a rooting cut is at the base of last year's growth. The preferred time for starting the layering is at the first flush of growth in spring. The ticklish period comes when the new plant is cut from the parent and planted. It is wise to prune off ⅓ of the top at that time, to balance the small root system. In cold-winter climates, protect the plant the first winter with a mulch. Among woody plants successfully air-layered are flowering dogwood, forsythia, holly, rhododendron and rose.

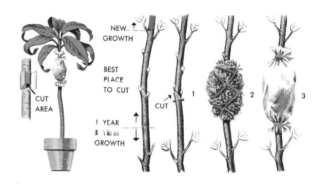

23

Pruning and Repairing

Pruning is one of the most exciting and creative experiences in the realm of gardening. You have powerful control over the manner in which your plants will develop, or how they will recover from wind or winter damage. And you work hand in hand with nature, making use of knowledge of how plants grow. Basic rules are so simple that you will soon feel as capable as an expert. By your choice of places to make cuts, you can stimulate emergence of new growth at positions where you desire it, and can make plants grow in the direction you wish. You can keep a shrub "in hand," make it become densely bushy or angularly picturesque, show its shape in decorative silhouette, frame your window, or adapt to vinelike pattern on a wall or trellis. You can control the number and size of flowers. You can repair damaged parts. And these are just a few of the challenging possibilities. Once you have gained confidence, you will want to prune everything! You will know the results you are after, and not want to trust anyone else to do the job. When you reach this exalted position, stop and remind yourself that though pruning is fun for you, it is a surgical operation for the plant. It is a procedure to be approached thoughtfully. There should be a reason for every cut.

HOW TO DETERMINE THE BEST TIME
TO PRUNE

In general, you should prune when plants are in their dormant or resting period, preceding a time of active growth during which the wound will heal rapidly. The usual time chosen is late winter or early spring. Then cuts have a long time in which to heal before the following winter. Another advantage of dormant-season pruning is that leaves are not present, or not fully grown; it is easier to see what you are doing.

Exceptions are plants that flower in spring from buds made the previous season. Winter pruning would destroy the current year's bloom. Such plants—the spring-flowering shrubs—should be pruned as soon after their blossom period as possible, in order to give them the maximum time to make new growth on which you will get next spring's flowers.

What To Prune in Late Winter or Early Spring

✻ Narrow-leaved evergreens (conifers) to improve their shape, keep them in bounds, induce bushy growth, or thin out unwanted branches. These include arbor-vitae, juniper, pine and yew. Details are given later in this chapter.

✻ Broad-leaved evergreens grown primarily for foliage rather than flowers, such as box, Japanese holly, euonymus, privet.

✻ Summer-flowering shrubs, vines, etc. You will not destroy the coming season's flower buds since they will develop on new growth made after you prune. Included are butterfly-bush, crape-myrtle, Hills of Snow hydrangea, hydrangea pee-gee, Chinese hibiscus, rose-of-sharon, lantana, oleander, trumpet-vine, bitter-sweet.

✻ Frost-injured plants in mild-winter climates. When danger of further freezing is past, cut away killed parts at your earliest convenience. There is no rush, for the frozen parts do no immediate harm to the remainder of the plant.

✻ Shrubs with colorful winter twigs. Shrub types of dogwood, having either red or yellow stems, have brightest coloring on young branches. If you are growing

them primarily for their winter effect, rather than summer screening, cut established bushes back severely each spring to promote the most new growth possible.

✻ Bush roses (hybrid teas, floribundas, grandifloras, miniatures) to repair winter damage, shape plants to induce flower-bearing shoots. This type of rose blooms on new growth.

✻ Climbing roses, which should have only winter-killed parts removed at this time, because in most types blooms develop on shoots arising from old wood. Any cane that has lived through the winter is a potential source of flowers, and therefore precious.

What To Prune after Flowering

✻ Shrubs or vines that have their flowers in spring, such as forsythia, flowering dogwood, crab-apple, rhododendron, azalea, lilac, wisteria.

✻ Climbing roses. For details see the chapter on roses.

TOOLS OF THE TRADE

You will not need a large arsenal of equipment. Essential is a really good pair of hand pruners, often called pruning snips. These come in a variety of models, sizes and qualities. Some will feel comfortable in your hand, and others will seem awkward, so it is wise to go to a store where you can hold and test several. Try them in an actual twig-cutting test, if possible. The better the quality, the more you will enjoy pruning. If the best seem an extravagance, tip someone off to get you a pair for Christmas, birthday or anniversary.

If you will be working with large old shrubs, or young trees, long-handled lopping shears are a boon. However, a small, curved-blade pruning saw does the same sorts of jobs and often demands less muscle power. Do not get a pruning saw with teeth on both top and bottom, for in tight situations you will do more damage than good.

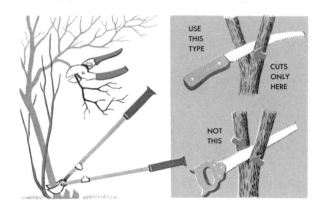

🌱 How To Go About It

UNDERSTAND A LITTLE ABOUT HOW PLANTS GROW

The way plants become taller and broader, lengthening and extending their branches, is by growth that takes place from buds located at the tips of shoots. After that growth is completed, the new portion hardens and remains in the same position permanently. It does not move farther up or outward. Only new growth at the tips continues to extend.

The circumference of branches and trunks increases each year, because a new layer of growth is added on the outside. The center part of the branch or trunk does not grow. On a tree, rose bush or woody shrub, you can scratch away some of the outer bark and find below it a thin green layer. This is the cambium, the precious part in which growth takes place. When a tree is cut down, you can see in its cross section the series of rings recording the amount of yearly growth.

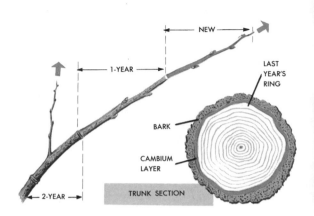

The location of a branch on a tree or shrub is permanent. However, each year as the tree grows higher, the stem or trunk, and the branches, become bigger around. You must look ahead and visualize how large those main branches may become, and provide space for them to develop without crowding.

Growth buds are the key to pruning. They are undeveloped branches. You will notice them on each stem or twig. In winter, on plants that shed their leaves, these buds are easy to see. During summer, or all year on plants with evergreen foliage, the buds will be inconspicuous in the axils of the leaves (the spot where the leaf stem joins the main stem). Each leaf indicates or marks the location of a growth bud. In some plants the buds are always arranged opposite one another along the stem—an example is lilac. In others they are always alternate, or somewhat spirally arranged—an example is spirea. These facts will play a part in the way you prune.

HOW GROWTH BUDS LOOK
IN WINTER AND SUMMER

Tip or terminal buds are the most important ones. They are at the top or end of each stem, and are larger than the lateral buds. They are the kings, the leaders, doing the most growing, extending the length of the branch in the direction that it is pointing. On branches with buds arranged opposite to one another, there will be a pair of terminal buds, and they will both be leaders and develop equally unless something happens to one of them.

If the end bud is removed, either by accident or by pruning, growth will stop at that point on the plant and the energy will be diverted to lower buds. The bud closest below the cut will take over the leader's job, and grow in the direction that it is pointing. If a pair of buds are in the leader position, and are removed, the pair of lateral buds immediately below the cut will grow, like twins,

unless one is removed. In both cases the remainder of the lower side buds will not be greatly affected and will generally remain small and secondary.

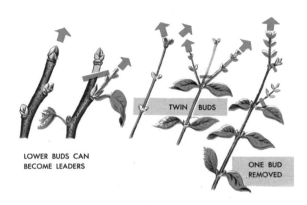

LOWER BUDS CAN
BECOME LEADERS

TWIN BUDS

ONE BUD
REMOVED

The amount of foliage that you remove from a plant makes a difference in your pruning results. Ordinarily, in established plants, the tops and root systems are approximately in balance. The leaves manufacture food necessary for the entire plant. They depend on roots for raw supplies. There are just enough leaves and roots to support each other.

Pruning upsets this balance in ways that you can turn to your advantage. If you take away only a moderate portion of the leaves, there will be a burst of new top growth. This is because the roots will continue to furnish to the fewer remaining buds the same amount of nutrients that they formerly divided among many more. (This is the principle you will use in rejuvenating old shrubs.)

However, if you take away too many leaves, especially on a young or unestablished plant, the roots will stop growing; the plant will be starved and dwarfed. If roots are reduced by pruning or injury, foliage will become less abundant. (This is the principle used in making a bonsai, whose tops and roots may be pruned.)

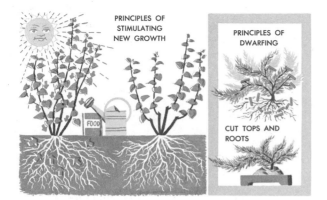

Whether you make your cuts high or low on a branch determines the general type of new growth that will result. Generally speaking, high pruning—far from food-supplying roots, and at the far end of old and inefficient food-conducting channels—produces numerous but small branches, and numerous but small flowers. Low pruning—at the base of a stem or branch, relatively close to food supplies—will give fewer new stems, but they will be larger and more vigorous, and flowers borne on them will be bigger. This is a basic principle you can follow on everything from house plants to roses, shrubs and trees. For instance, when a shrub is given a shearing across its top, the new growth emerges there, and is small and twiggy. The lower branches never fill out so the shrub always looks leggy and spindly.

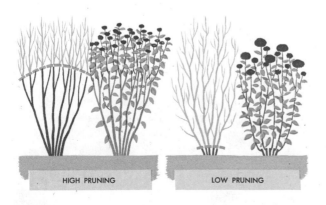

PROPER WAY TO MAKE CUTS

Cut just above a bud or branch. The place and method are important.

The cut should be made ¼ to ½ in. above the bud, and at a slight slant. Do not make it so slanting that it extends below the bud, exposing it to danger of drying and dying.

When shortening a branch, cut on a slant about ½ in. above a bud or side branch pointing in the direction you wish growth to develop. Usually one prunes above an outside-pointing branch, to avoid filling the center of the plant with a crowded mass of branches.

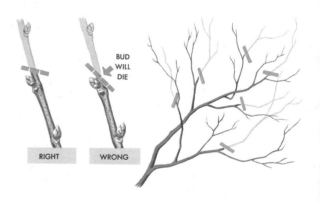

When removing branches or twigs, make the cut flush with the side of the larger branch or trunk to which it is attached. Avoid leaving stubs. Any portion of the stem left above the cut, if without growth buds, will die and gradually decay. It will be an eyesore, and also a channel through which disease organisms can enter the living portion of the stem.

To see an example of what happens when branches—or stubs of branches—die, look at the holes in trees where squirrels and woodpeckers build their nests. Usually these are spots where branches rotted back into the heart of the tree, leaving cavities.

All cuts should be made in such a manner that they heal rapidly. They should be made with a sharp tool, and have smooth edges. Rough edges and torn bark do not heal well; trim them.

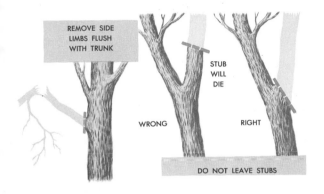

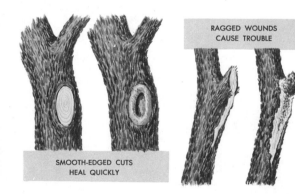

Use tree wound dressing on all cuts 1 in. or more across. This material can be purchased in cans, to be applied with a brush or cloth wrapped about the end of a stick. Or you can buy it in handy spray cans. When spraying be sure to hold the can at least 18 in. away from the plant because the propellent may burn plant tissues.

ELEMENTARY FIRST STEPS

If you have never done any pruning, and are about to take the plunge, here are instructions on how to begin. If you follow these simple steps you cannot fail or injure your plant, and you will do it a lot of good.

Remove any dead or injured branches. Make your pruning cut below the problem spot. It should be slanting, just above a bud or side branch that points outward rather than into the center of the plant.

Look for any branches that cross or rub against one another. Obviously both are trying to grow in the same space, and there is not room for both. Since they are going to become gradually larger rather than smaller, the problem will become worse. If they rub they will injure each other's bark.

Remove the less important of the branches. This means either the weaker, smaller one, or the one that is growing in the less desirable position or direction of growth in relation to the total structure of the plant. Cut it off flush with the branch or trunk from which it emerges. Make sure the cut and its edges are smooth. You may have to trim them with a knife. If the cut surface is an inch or more across, apply tree wound dressing.

Remove weak little insignificant branches that are doing no good. They keep air and light from important branches.

❧ How To Prune Shrubs

The manner in which you approach the pruning of a shrub, beyond the elementary first steps listed above, depends upon why you wish to prune each particular plant. It also depends on that shrub's manner of growing. Some shrubs develop so rapidly and exuberantly that you will need to prune them frequently in order to keep them within bounds. Others grow so slowly that they need almost no pruning, ever, except to remove dead wood or give the bush a little shaping. Some will bloom best if they are given an annual pruning.

Broad-leaved evergreen shrubs usually need less pruning than deciduous shrubs, and the slow growing ones can be greatly damaged by improper pruning. Broad-leaved evergreens that are rapid-growing can be pruned in the same manner as deciduous shrubs.

The time to prune varies according to your climate, the plant, and your goal. You will find general advice in the introductory paragraphs of this chapter. Specific data on the most popular shrubs is listed at the end of this section.

Best Shape for Shrubs

Generally, most shrubs look best, and are easiest to maintain, when they are allowed to develop in their distinctively natural form. Presumably each was chosen for its location because of its special appearance and shape, so those qualities should be preserved and enhanced. If the shrub insists upon being too tall, rangy, or the wrong shape, maybe you should consider replacing it with a different kind of shrub rather than trying to make your present one into something that it is not! Perhaps you have too many shrubs for the space.

Some cutting back may be necessary to keep any shrub looking tidy, within bounds, blooming the way it should, or constantly rejuvenated. It can be done in such a way that the natural form is not destroyed. It is a matter of removing branches by skillful selection rather than whacking off everything that extends beyond a certain point. This is where you, with your intimate knowledge of your plant, can do a better job than anyone that you might hire. Practice until you gain experience, then trust your knowledge and ability.

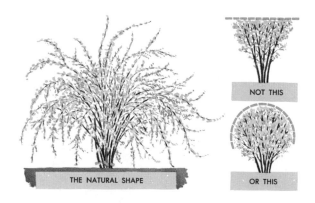

THE NATURAL SHAPE — NOT THIS — OR THIS

How To Cut Back with Subtle Skill

You can manage so cleverly that only you will know for sure that the bush has been trimmed! That is the mark of true success. First, follow the first steps described above. Then scout your plant from all sides and look into its middle. Decide how wide and tall you wish it to be when you finish your grooming. On each branch the lower portion is always the oldest. From it will arise branches growing in approximately the same direction as the parent branch. You can shorten each main branch by cutting back to a spot just above one of these lateral branches. How far back you go depends on how much cutting back you have in mind. It can be inches, or a number of feet. If you wish your bush to be more upright in shape, cut above a branch pointing up. If you wish a broader, more spreading shape, cut to an out-growing branch. The side branch itself can be shortened in turn, in the same manner, by removing some of its tip, back to the location of a side branch or bud. Sometimes big old useless branches should be removed at the soil line to make room for young replacement shoots.

This selective cutting-back procedure will stimulate new growth, since food will be channeled into the side branches that you chose to carry on the work of the shortened main branch.

How To Make Shrubs Bushier

The best time to make sure that a shrub will not become leggy is when it is young. Instead of letting it grow up and up—which is only temporarily a satisfying sight—prune it back ⅓ of its height at least once a year in the spring. Side branches will develop just below your cuts.

If old shrubs are bare at their bases, and you want branches to fill in, you will have to cut some of the branches back nearly to the ground. Or, if there are husky young shoots arising from the ground or a short distance up on the main branches, prune them back and make them branch.

Rejuvenation of Old Shrubs

For sudden and complete rejuvenation, saw off the whole shrub (with the exception of any young sprouts or sucker shoots arising from the ground) at soil level, in late winter or early spring. This may sound a bit drastic, but strong new shoots will soon appear, fed by the well-established root system. Select a few of these to become the framework of your new shrub. They should be spaced far enough apart so that they will not crowd one another. Cut off all others, so that all nourishment will be channeled into the few that you want. Feed and water the roots. To induce bushiness shorten several of the outer shoots by ⅓ their height the second spring.

For more gradual overhauling, remove only about ⅓ of the oldest wood, at ground level, each year, As new shoots develop and become a year old, remember to cut them back part of the way or they may grow very tall before producing branches. If you do not watch over the situation, you may be back to the same type of leggy shrub you were trying to avoid!

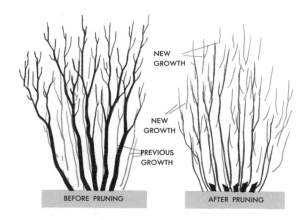

NEW GROWTH

NEW GROWTH

PREVIOUS GROWTH

BEFORE PRUNING

AFTER PRUNING

HEDGE-PRUNING ADVICE

There are two main types of hedges. Informal ones allow plants to grow to their normal height and develop their natural shape. They need very little maintenance after they are full grown. Formal hedges, on the other hand, are clipped to perfect shapes, and if they are to look attractive they must be trimmed frequently and meticulously.

The future good looks of all hedges depend upon their care and pruning when young. If they are rapid-growing plants they will tend to become tall, without lower branches, unless cut back frequently during their first couple of years. You cannot, in later years, go back and fill in missing lower branches. So you must be hard-hearted and prune early growth. This does not apply to slow-growing shrubs like box. Fast-growing shrubs, like privet, honeysuckle and barberry, should be cut back at planting time almost to the ground. Leave only 3 or 4 buds on each stem. Cut back again, about ⅓ of the height, each time the stems grow a foot. Continue the process for at least two years or until the hedge is the height and denseness that you wish.

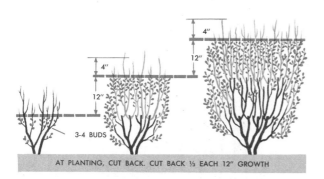

AT PLANTING, CUT BACK. CUT BACK ⅓ EACH 12" GROWTH

If you are dealing with a hedge that is to be clipped into a formal shape, guide its growth through early years' pruning so that it is wider at the base than at the top. This is done for two reasons. When the top is narrow, it does not shade the lower branches and keep vital sunshine from their foliage. Also, in cold climates, snow can slide off more easily, doing less damage.

The easiest and most pleasant way to trim a shaped hedge is with an electric hedge trimmer. Be sure the one you use has safety features. To cut a truly straight edge, do not trust your eye to guide you or you will have wobbly, wavy lines. Place stakes, with strings as markers.

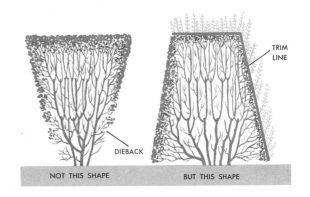

NOT THIS SHAPE   BUT THIS SHAPE

Time and frequency of pruning depend upon the kind of shrub you are using, and how the hedge is to be trained. A formally shaped, rapid-growing hedge, such as privet, needs several trimmings a year. Most other deciduous sorts need at least two. One of the trimmings can be made in late winter or early spring while the plants are still dormant, leafless, and easy to cut accurately. The other can be when the new growth is at its peak. Flowering hedges are not pruned until after the bloom.

Small-foliaged broad-leaved evergreens, such as dwarf hollies, are usually given their main pruning in the early spring, followed by a grooming later in the season.

Large broad-leaved evergreens, such as camellia and holly, need very little pruning, except for removing awkward branches. Always cut back to a small side branch that bears leaves, or to a group of buds.

For help with narrow-leaved evergreens, read the section immediately following.

Many deciduous hedges can be renovated with dramatic success. If you have inherited an old hedge, or let the one you started become run-down and bare at its base, you can make a new one out of it. The method is simple though drastic. (Better not tell anyone what you are going to do, or he might try to talk you out of it!) Cut it back to about 6 in. above the ground. Strong new shoots will burst from the base of the plants. Treat them like new shrubs, and cut them back 4 in. every time they lengthen by 12 in. Within 2 or 3 years you will have a hedge of which you can be proud.

❧ How To Prune Narrow-leaved Evergreens

As a group, narrow-leaved evergreens do not need or like as much pruning as deciduous shrubs and trees. A few tolerate frequent pruning or even shearing of their outer young branches. Others must be handled with discretion. Most do not produce new growth easily, or at all, if cut back to older, bare wood.

The best time to prune them is in the spring, just before they put out their new growth, or when the new growth is almost completed. You will be able to spot the new growth for it will be a much lighter and brighter green than the old foliage, and soft to your touch. Plants that grow rapidly can tolerate quite a bit of heading back. Slow-growers should have only slight touching-up.

A wise rule is never to shorten branches beyond the point where they carry green needles. Living leaves are a sign that there are active growth buds at their base available to develop into new shoots. If you prune below them, the branch will probably become a dead stub.

Winter pruning, in order to have evergreen branches to use for Christmas greenery, is all right if you have planned ahead and have specific branches in mind that would have to be removed anyway. It is not the best time from the point of view of the plant, since winter weather may delay the healing of the wound. And you certainly should not whack away at random with your thoughts on getting greenery rather than improving the plant.

ARBOR-VITAE. These tolerate considerable shearing of young growth. Any major pruning should be done before the start of spring growth, but shearing can be done any time during summer.

FIR, SPRUCE, DOUGLAS-FIR. These are conical-shaped, short-needled trees. They need almost no pruning, except to remove straggly growth or to encourage dense branching. To make them bushier, cut tips of branches back to a side branch that has needles.

If the tree has more than one leader, remove all but the best one. If the leader has become damaged, a side branch just below it should be selected to take the leader's place, and be staked or tied upright in the proper position.

shaping to be beautiful. If they become too big, it is possible to reduce their size by cutting out their tops and by shortening their side branches. But this can only be done if there are live leaves at the places on the branches where you plan to make the shortening cuts. Often in the heart of the tree, near the trunk, leaves are dead and the branches bare, and no new growth will come. You will be left with ugly bare stubs. You might be smarter to dig up unsightly old specimens, discard them, and get new plants that would be a proper size for the location.

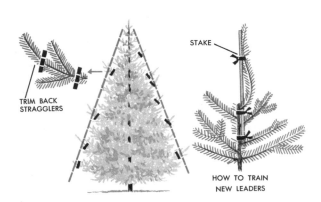

TRIM BACK STRAGGLERS

STAKE

HOW TO TRAIN NEW LEADERS

JUNIPERS (creeping, bush and tree). These evergreens have scalelike, prickly leaves. Young branches have innumerable growing points, so you can make pruning cuts almost anywhere on relatively new growth. You can even clip or shear outer tips. On growth several years old, cut back to a leafy side branch. Old bare wood will not produce new growth.

On creeping junipers used as groundcovers, it is smart to cut back or even remove long trailing branches that are covering, shading and killing the branches beneath them. If you do some selective cutting back each year, your plants will remain in healthier condition, with least dead wood. When deciding which branches to remove, try lifting various ones from their reclining position. See where they originate, how long they are, and what proportion of them is carrying leaves or is bare. Try to take out the oldest ones with the most dead foliage.

Pfitzers and other plumy shrub-type junipers have naturally beautiful shapes, so they should not be sheared unless you are using them in a formal-type hedge. However, these bushes sometimes get a wild look, with branches going hither and thither. To keep them under control, and also in youthful condition, shorten the longest branches occasionally, cutting them back to a side branch. Cutting back to vertical side branches will encourage erect growing.

Trees, growing vertically, need only moderate

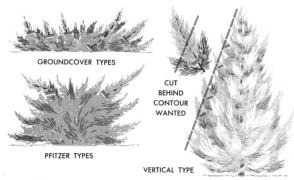

GROUNDCOVER TYPES

PFITZER TYPES

CUT BEHIND CONTOUR WANTED

VERTICAL TYPE

PINES (both shrub and tree kinds). These have a generally loose type of growth. New branches develop in whorls from "candles" carried at the tips of branches in spring. Any pruning or heading back should be done when these candles are expanding but have not reached full length. If you have a little cushionlike shrub, mugho pine, and want it to stay dwarf, you will need to prune it every year or it may become 4 to 10 ft. high. To restrain any pine's growth, or to make it more bushy, nip back each candle ⅓ to ½ of its length. You can do this with your fingers, pruning snips or knife. For more severe pruning, cut back to a side branch. To get an idea of how fast your pine is growing, note the distance between whorls of side branches attached to a main branch. The distance between whorls—which were formerly a bunch of candles—indicates one year of growth.

If your pine loses its leader, you can train a substitute in its place as described in the paragraph on pruning firs. If you wish your pine to become more spreading, or bushy (rather than growing taller and taller), you can remove its leader at whatever height you wish the vertical growth to stop and horizontal growth to be emphasized. By nipping out the tips of new growth, you can make the tree bushier, or by removing side branches you can thin the tree so that it displays its limbs in the oriental manner.

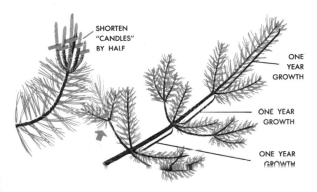

SHORTEN "CANDLES" BY HALF

ONE YEAR GROWTH

ONE YEAR GROWTH

ONE YEAR GROWTH

YEWS. These beautiful and expensive evergreens are very tolerant of pruning. They can be clipped or sheared if desired. Wherever they are cut, even on old wood that shows no sign of leaves or buds, they will send out new growth. Ordinarily one merely snips back the tips of new growth to control it and induce branching. Cut to any leaf or side branch. But if you have an old yew that has become too large or rangy, you can cut it back severely. Shorten the top, and head back side branches. Such a severely pruned specimen may look like a plucked chicken for one season, but it will quickly recover.

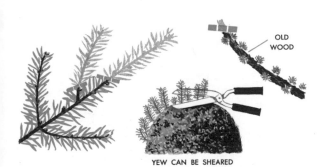

OLD WOOD

YEW CAN BE SHEARED

🍁 How To Prune Broad-leaved Trees

If your tree is newly planted, you will find instructions on how to prune it through its first year in the beginning of the chapter on trees. But if your tree has been planted several years, you will find instructions here. Do not attempt to work on large, mature trees. For them, call in a competent tree surgeon.

The main goal in pruning your tree is to guide its growth so that it will be well formed and future troubles will be avoided. You have no idea how much easier it is to prune a tree when it is young, and has slender easily cut branches, than when it is tall and the limbs are huge and heavy! Aim to develop the tree so that it has well-spaced branches, strongly crotched, that will not cross and rub each other in the future or become crowded as they grow bigger around. Branches should not be so numerous that light cannot filter down to lower leaves and also to the lawn below them. If wind is a problem in your area, a tree survives much better if the air can blow through it, rather than being stopped.

Another big reason for pruning trees is to correct or repair damage. This is partly a matter of removing broken or diseased limbs, and partly a matter of making the best of a bad situation when there is unexpected breakage after a wind or ice storm.

Guiding Growth of Young Trees

Selection and arrangement of permanent scaffold branches is your important job. Your young tree may have one or more leader branches and numerous side branches sticking out in different directions. If all are allowed to develop, there will be a thicket as each grows bigger around year by year.

Most shade trees should have only one main trunk (or, if you are purposely growing them in clump form, each of the several trunks arising from the ground should have only one leader). Thus, if yours now have more than one leader apiece, you should select the best one to remain and remove the others.

As to the side branches, the selection of permanent ones and removal of the extras must be a gradual process. You must not cut off too much any one year, because the loss of foliage will cause the tree to be starved. Choose branches to save on different sides of the tree, with considerable space between them to allow for future growth in circumference. One of the lowest should be on the south side of the tree, so there will be something to provide shade for the sunny side of the trunk and protect it from sunscald and similar weather injury. Young bark is tender and easily injured by hot sun, light reflected from snow, and the alternate warming and freezing of changeable winter temperatures. All of this is worst on the side of the trunk exposed to most sunshine.

The type of crotch from which branches spring is important. Save branches with wide-angled crotches rather than narrow ones, for they are much stronger and less apt to split in wind storms. Narrow crotches spell future trouble because even small splits invite entry of fungi or insects.

that growth does not get out of hand, or cluttery. Remove any sprouts that develop around the base of your tree. Also cut off water sprouts — big, vigorous, vertically growing shoots—that arise from branches. These soon crowd the tree. Try to keep branching open so sunlight can filter in, and foliage or top growth will not be so heavy that branches may break off in the wind.

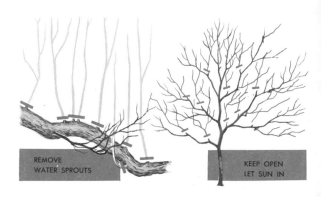

REMOVE WATER SPROUTS

KEEP OPEN LET SUN IN

First Aid to Injuries

Check over your trees following wind storms. Winter also brings damage. If a tree is girdled by rabbits or mice during the winter (a circle of bark chewed off all the way around), the tree will die within a year unless you do something about it. The top is already doomed, because the layer of bark in which the most vital transfers of food supplies take place has been destroyed. The way to save your tree is to saw it off cleanly, on a slight slant, just below the lowest part of the injury. Cover the surface with protective tree wound paint. New sprouts will arise, fed by the established root system. From these rapid-growing sprouts you can select one or more the next season to become permanent trunks. Cut off the rest. You will feel very clever, but remember from now on to wrap the trunks each winter to protect them from rodents.

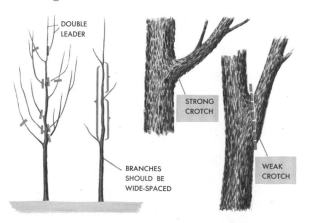

DOUBLE LEADER

STRONG CROTCH

WEAK CROTCH

BRANCHES SHOULD BE WIDE-SPACED

Pruning in Later Years

This is mostly a matter of watching to see

If a tree is blown over and broken, saw off the top just above a side branch. If there is no side branch, new sprouts will usually arise from the lower part of the trunk or from beneath the ground. The side branch or sprout will become the new leader; you may need to stake it into proper vertical position.

When crotches split, save the less-injured branch and cut the other off at a slant. Remove all of the ragged, injured wood so that only a smooth, easy-to-heal wound remains. You may need to reduce the branches on the upper part of the saved branch, so that it will not be top-heavy and in danger of breaking off.

CUT TRUNK BELOW GIRDLING DAMAGE

SAW OFF BROKEN TOP STAKE NEW LEADER

SPLIT CROTCH

How To Espalier Shrubs, Trees, Vines

Espaliering is the pruning and training of plants into flat form against walls, fences, trellises or wire frames. The possibilities for decorative effects are endless.

You can train and clip an evergreen vine into formal or informal patterns. You can fasten a flowering or fruiting shrub into a vine-like position and prune it so that its shape makes an ornamental silhouette. You can fashion dwarf fruit trees to combine beauty and bounty. The one thing essential for success is that you have an interest in plants, and a love of working with them and pruning

them. Plants trained to specific forms must be pruned at least once a year and often much more frequently if they are not going to get out of hand. This is what makes the espalier project one of the most exciting you will ever undertake, and the one for which you will receive the most awed compliments.

Plants best adapted to training are those that tolerate severe pruning, and that produce lots of side branches, even from old wood. Some frequently used include:

Vines: Evergreens—English ivy and wintercreeper. Deciduous—bitter-sweet.

Shrubs: Forsythia, camellia, flowering quince, ceanothus, escallonia, fuchsia, lantana, pyracantha, yew.

Trees: Dwarf fruits, fig, magnolia

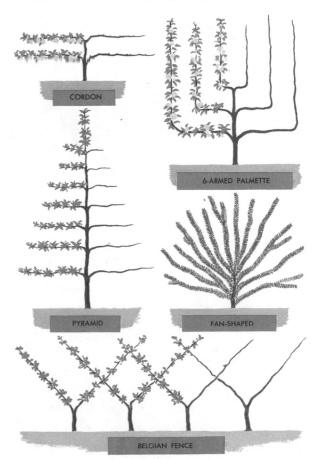

CORDON

6-ARMED PALMETTE

PYRAMID

FAN-SHAPED

BELGIAN FENCE

How to begin: Choose the location. East-facing walls or fences, or those in part shade, are better than those in full, hot sunshine. If possible, build a framework trellis of wood or wires that stands 4 to 8 in. away from the backing, so air can circulate behind the plant. Make the trellis large enough and strong enough for the eventual final size of your plant. If you are going to need to get behind the plant to paint, or if your espalier is to be a fruit tree that will need spraying, take this into consideration in your planning.

Use young plants. Sometimes nurseries and garden centers sell potted plants that have been started in their training—growing on little wooden trellises. This is a big help to you. Otherwise buy one- or two-year-old plants, either with side branches already formed in about the positions you desire, or with indications of prospects for side branching. Set them out the same way you would any shrub, preparing the ground deeply and well. But do not overdo feeding, for you do not want the plants to grow rampantly; the slower they grow, the better you can control them. If side branches are not already formed where you wish them, shorten the main trunk (leader) to the point where you wish branch-

es to develop. Later, when growth is higher, you can cut it back again if necessary. Fasten your chosen branches into position by bending them gently and tying them with some soft material, such as cloth, yarn or raffia. Avoid bare wire which might cut stems as they increase in girth, and which could also burn plant tissues when hot. If working on wooden frames, screw eyes are handy things to which to fasten side branches. Cut away all unneeded branches—making smooth cuts flush with the main stem.

Have fun! Be creative! Make your plant fit your spot, artistically.

🍂 Pruning Advice on Some Individual Shrubs and Trees

ABELIA. In mild climates prune in autumn; in cold climates prune in early spring. Thin old branches that have bloomed. To control size, shorten branches back to a young side branch. Old overgrown bushes can be cut back severely, even to the ground.

AUCUBA or GOLD-DUST TREE. In the spring remove wood that was damaged by winter. It can be cut back severely, if desired, to rejuvenate an old shrub. To shape and control, shorten the branches by cutting back to a side branch.

AZALEA, see RHODODENDRON

BOX. Slow growing, so prune only to maintain the shape you desire, and to remove frost-injured or dead wood. It tolerates clipping or shearing, which can be done any time from spring until early fall, but you should allow time for the new growth to harden before freezing weather is due.

BRIDAL WREATH, see SPIREA.

BUTTERFLY-BUSH (*Buddleia*). Blossoms develop on new growth of the current season. In mild climates, prune after flowering, cutting back the branches severely and removing a few of the oldest ones at soil line each year. In cold climates, tops usually are killed to the ground. During winter, or in early spring, cut them off

1. CUT BACK   2. TRAIN NEW SHOOTS   3. REMOVE SIDE SHOOTS   4. TRAIN SECOND CORDONS   5. TRAIN VERTICALS

TIES   CUT   CUT   CUT

at soil line. Strong new shoots, as tall as before, will spring up and bear flowers.

CAMELLIA. Most of these shrubs need little pruning except to maintain pleasing shapes, and to thin the branches enough so that light and air can get to all parts of the bush. Always, when shortening branches, cut back to a lateral. Time to prune is late in the blooming season, when the flush of new growth is about to take place. At this time wounds will heal most quickly. Also, since flower buds for next year have not started to develop, none will be lost.

Old plants needing rejuvenation can be cut back severely, and will sprout new growth, though they may look like skeletons temporarily.

CEANOTHUS or WILD LILAC. Prune immediately after flowering. Tip branches can be shortened, cutting just above a side branch, to induce bushiness.

DOGWOOD, FLOWERING. Needs little pruning except to select scaffold branches, and a little thinning and control-pruning. Wounds heal slowly. Prune after flowering period.

DOGWOOD, SHRUB TYPES. Those grown primarily for their colorful winter twigs should be pruned severely before spring growth each year. Young branches are the most highly colored. Other shrub dogwoods grown primarily for foliage should be pruned only to maintain the shape you desire. Do it in late winter.

FORSYTHIA. Only branches that are more than a year old carry blossom buds. Those that are 2 or 3 years old bloom best. Because forsythias bloom in early spring, from buds formed the season before, do not prune until immediately following the bloom season. Then, if your bush is 1 to 3 years old, do nothing but needed shaping. On older bushes, remove some of the very oldest, tired-looking branches at ground line each year. Shorten other old branches back to a young side branch. Do not remove vigorous young canes that have not flowered, for they are

preparing to produce for you. They are your future flowers.

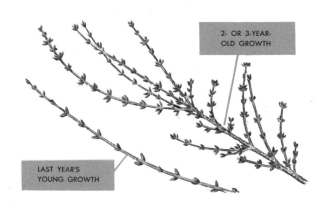

FUCHSIA. They can be trained in natural shape, tree form or espaliered. Varieties grow in different ways, so know the type of plant with which you are dealing. Fuchsias bloom on new growth, so each year they should be severely pruned to induce new shoots. The time to do it is after the last severe winter frost. Cut back all vigorous branches to 1 or 2 pairs of dormant buds. Weak branches should be removed entirely. Additional pruning to control the shape of plants can be done throughout the growing season. Pinch out tips to induce branching; do it as often as every other week until June. On trailing types, cut off branches that grow upright.

GARDENIA. Heading back vigorous top shoots prevents legginess. Occasional thinning-out may be a good idea. Pruning time is before spring growth starts. If you want your flowers to be the biggest possible, rather than most numerous, you can thin out the buds.

HIBISCUS, CHINESE. Flower buds are produced at the tips of new growth. Prune back severely before new growth starts in spring, taking off as much as one third of the length of branches. Cut back to vigorous side branches.

HONEY LOCUST. Sometimes, while young, these trees need considerable training and selective pruning in order to develop the proper form.

They tend to throw out branches like the legs of a spider. Staking the leader into erect position will help. If the leader is broken by wind or ice, cut it off at a slant just above the best nearby vigorous side branch, and stake that side branch into vertical position to become the new leader. Be sure to treat the wound with a tree wound paint, so that it will not dry out and split and damage the base of your new leader. If branches carry so much foliage that they are tossed about in every wind storm, and in danger of breaking, thin and shorten the growth on those branches.

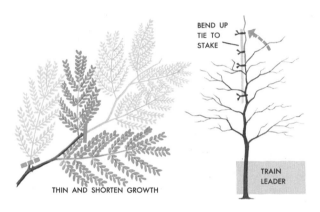

BEND UP
TIE TO
STAKE

TRAIN
LEADER

THIN AND SHORTEN GROWTH

HONEYSUCKLE, BUSH TYPES. When grown in their natural shape they need only occasional trimming, which can be done at any season. If the flower display is important to you, do your pruning after the bloom season. When grown as hedges, shearing can be done several times a season, but stop in time for wood to harden before winter if you live in a cold climate.

HYDRANGEAS. There are three main kinds of hydrangea grown in gardens, and they are pruned in slightly different ways.

Hills of Snow hydrangea is the very hardy white-flowered one that blooms in early summer on plants 3 to 4 ft. high. It will produce blooms on new growth whether you prune it or not. For largest flowers, cut the old woody stems to within 2 or 3 buds of the ground, in late winter or early spring. New stems will develop to the same height as the old ones, during summer, and produce bloom. For more numerous but smaller

flowers, do no pruning or merely remove part of the ends of the stems. Old flowers can be removed after they fade.

Hydrangea peegee carries its enormous heads of creamy white flowers tipped with pink in late summer. It may be bush form or tree form. It blooms on new growth produced during the current season. If you do not prune it, it will have many but relatively small flowers. If you prune (late winter or early spring), flowers will be larger. Cut back to a branch that did not flower the previous year. Branches on tree forms can be cut to leave only 2 or 3 buds on each main branch. Huge blooms will result.

French or house hydrangea is grown outdoors only in mild climates. It is pruned differently from the two hydrangeas mentioned above. Main flower buds develop from the top of shoots that grew the previous year. Thus, any pruning in late winter or early spring would destroy those major flower buds. Pruning should be done in summer, immediately after flowers fade. Cut each stem back to a sturdy side branch that has not flowered. If severe winter weather injures the main flower buds, some blooms may come later from lower side branches. Old, overgrown plants can be revitalized by cutting them back to the ground in late winter or spring, but the new growth that arises will not bloom that year.

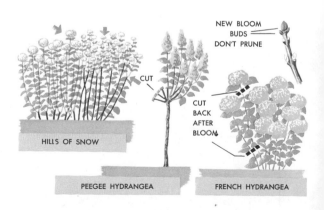

NEW BLOOM
BUDS
DON'T PRUNE

CUT

CUT
BACK
AFTER
BLOOM

HILLS OF SNOW

PEEGEE HYDRANGEA

FRENCH HYDRANGEA

LEUCOTHOE. Any desired pruning should be done after flowering. Branches that have flowered can be cut back to younger side branches.

Oldest branches can be cut back to the ground.

LILAC. The best and biggest blooms come on relatively young branches, so your goal should be to keep your bushes youthful. If you have a big old bush, tall, tired-looking, and surrounded by a thicket of sucker shoots, follow instructions given for renovating old shrubs, given earlier in this chapter.

Other than renovating, do not do any cutting in late winter or early spring, since flower buds develop in the season before they bloom and are carried over winter in dormant condition. Early pruning would destroy them. You can recognize the potential flower buds, for they are the fat ones at the tips of branches in winter. If the end buds are slim rather than plump, they probably contain only leaves.

Prune immediately after flowering. The places where you make your pruning cuts will influence the amount of bloom you will have in the future. The important thing to do each year is to remove withered flower heads so that they will not develop seeds. But be careful! This is the moment when you can destroy next year's flowers. Remove the old flower head with only the short stalk on which it is carried. If you pick it with a stem longer than just an inch or two, you will take with it the newly developing side shoots that will produce next year's flowers. Note: If you wish to pick lilac flowers for bouquets, and want them with long stems, take them from the top of the very oldest branches on your bushes—the branches that will be the first ones you remove when you prune to rejuvenate your bush.

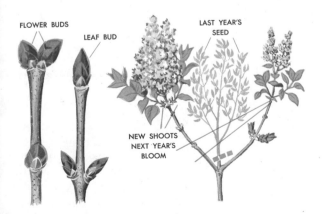

FLOWER BUDS

LEAF BUD

LAST YEAR'S SEED

NEW SHOOTS NEXT YEAR'S BLOOM

LILAC, WILD, see CEANOTHUS

LOCUST, HONEY, see HONEY LOCUST

MAGNOLIA. This needs little pruning other than guidance and selection of structural branches while young. Prune during or after flowering. On evergreen kinds, it is possible to remove branches to use for decorating purposes.

MAHONIA. In cold climates, pull off each spring old leaves that have been browned by freezing. Cut off any killed tips. If you live in a region where mahonias grow vigorously, they can stand severe pruning to control height.

MOCK-ORANGE (*Philadelphus*). Any pruning should be done after flowering, for flower buds are formed the season previous to blooming. Old bushes can be kept youthful by cutting back to a younger side branch those branches that have flowered. The oldest woody canes can be removed at soil line to allow space for new suckers. Thin suckers; they can be shortened to induce branching.

MOUNTAIN-LAUREL (*Kalmia*). Do any necessary pruning immediately after the period of bloom. Remove flower heads to prevent setting of seed.

NANDINA. This requires little pruning. If growth becomes crowded, some of the oldest canes can be removed at ground level in spring as growth starts.

OLEANDER. This can be trained as a shrub or small tree. Each year remove the old branches that have bloomed, and, if you wish to control the size of the plant, cut some of the remaining branches back to side branches. Sucker shoots around the base of the plant may be left, if you want a shrubby effect; thinned or dug out if you want to maintain a single-trunked tree. The time to prune is before spring growth starts.

PEACH, FLOWERING. The blooms come in early spring on growth that was new the previous season. Each year, immediately after flowering, shorten all year-old branches to about 6-in. length, to promote development of new flower-bearing wood for the next season. Exception: dwarf and weeping types should not be pruned as drastically as tree types.

PITTOSPORUM. This can be pruned as a shrub, hedge or small tree. Where winter weather is a problem, prune in early spring.

POINSETTIA. After freezing weather is past, cut back year-old branches, leaving only 2 buds on each spur. If, as summer advances, you think you would like the plants to be more compact and branched, shoot tips can be shortened. You will then have more blossoms, though they will be smaller.

PYRACANTHA. Can be grown as a bush, groundcover, hedge or vinelike espalier. Prune to control the shape you desire. For the largest crop of berries, prune immediately after the fruits fall. Take off the entire portion of the branch that bore fruit, cutting back to just above a side branch that has not yet flowered or fruited. If there are too many branches—a thicket—it will be wise to cut some of the oldest back all the way to the ground. Do not remove one-year-old branches unless you are willing to sacrifice their bloom and crop of berries.

RHODODENDRONS and AZALEAS. Do not prune during winter or in early spring because you will destroy flower buds. The buds are formed during the year preceding their blossoming, and held dormant through winter. They are the plump extra-large ones that you see at the ends of branches during winter months.

The correct time to prune is immediately after flowering. First step is to remove the flower head so the plant will not direct its energy into ripening seeds. The way to take it off is to cut or twist the base of the short stem supporting the cluster. Be very careful not to remove or injure the buds (or new shoots that develop from those buds) at the base of the spent flowers. These are the shoots that will produce next year's flowers.

As with other shrubs, pruning of rhododendrons and azaleas can make them more shapely or more densely bushy. Make cuts just above a group of leaves or side branch. The new shoots that result will usually produce only leaves the first year.

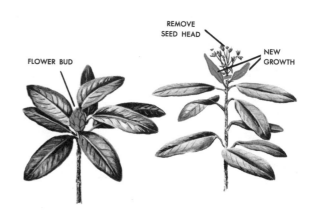

ROSE-OF-SHARON. Prune in early spring in cold climates, or autumn in mild ones. If you want the largest bush possible, trim lightly at the tips of branches. For largest flowers, cut back the one-year-old branches each year to two or three buds.

SPIREA. Spring-blooming kinds like bridal wreath should be pruned immediately after flowering. If your plants are old, and need revitalizing, cut some of the oldest branches at ground level. Shorten others to vigorous new side branches. Do not top by giving "butch haircuts."

Summer blooming sorts like *Spiraea bumalda* and 'Anthony Waterer' are pruned before their spring growth.

WEIGELA. Prune after flowering. Cut off all wood that has bloomed above a young side branch. If your bush is old, you can remove some of the oldest branches each year at ground level. Thin suckers.

WILLOWS. Pussy willows should be pruned severely during or just after flowering. Then they will produce many new shoots that will carry next year's blooms.

Weeping willows should be pruned during their youth to form a strong main trunk.

24

⁓⁓⁓⁓⁓⁓⁓⁓⁓⁓⁓⁓⁓⁓⁓⁓⁓⁓⁓⁓⁓⁓⁓⁓⁓⁓⁓⁓⁓⁓⁓⁓⁓⁓

Plant Diseases and Pests

by Cynthia Westcott
"The Plant Doctor"

When plants languish, the cause may be a physical condition, such as too much or too little water, fertilizer, soil acidity, or a biological organism, a specific pest. This chapter considers only the troubles caused by bacteria, fungi, viruses, nematodes, insects, mites and related animals.

Plant disease is an abnormal condition or process due to the continuing action of a fungus, bacterium or other irritant. The more or less transient action of an insect is usually termed injury. Most plant diseases must be *prevented* rather than cured. We use sanitary or cultural measures, or apply a protectant fungicide *before* symptoms appear. Most insects can be controlled by the application of an insecticide soon after first appearance.

The first principle in pest control is EXCLUSION, keeping diseased or insect-ridden plants out of the country, out of your state, out of your garden. This means conforming to all federal and state quarantines, not smuggling uninspected plant souvenirs from foreign countries, not transporting pest-ridden plants between states in your automobile, refusing to accept problem plants from your nurseryman, and buying plants certified free from certain viruses and nematodes.

ERADICATION means the removal of infested or infected plants or plant parts before the pest can spread to adjacent plants. Spring pruning and autumn cleanup campaigns are eradicant measures. So is the removal of an alternate host, such as getting rid of red-cedars to prevent cedar-apple rust on crab-apples. Some chemical sprays are eradicants but most chemicals strong enough to kill bacteria, fungi or other organisms inside a plant may injure the plant more than the pest.

PROTECTION, the most widely used method of control, means a fungicide applied to the susceptible plant part in advance of a fungus spore or bacterium, or an insecticide applied at the beginning of an insect infestation or in time to prevent egg laying.

IMMUNIZATION, the breeding or selection of resistant varieties, is the ideal but the most difficult type of control. As soon as a plant has been developed resistant to attacks by a fungus or an insect, the pest develops new forms to which the host plant is susceptible. It is a continuing race, with the pest usually several jumps ahead of man's efforts.

Most breeding for resistance has been done with vegetables. We have, listed in the seed catalogues, rust-resistant asparagus and pole beans, mosaic-resistant snap beans and cucumbers, wilt-resistant corn, peas and tomatoes, yellows-resistant cabbage. Work in flowers is mostly limited to wilt-resistant asters and rust-resistant snapdragon.

⚘ Plant Diseases

Plant diseases are caused by bacteria, fungi, viruses, and, rarely, by higher plants such as dodder and mistletoe. Diseases are usually named for their most prominent symptom, as blight, canker, leaf spot, but sometimes for the organism causing the disturbance, as powdery mildew, rust, smut.

Control depends on proper diagnosis, recognizing the type of disease and causative organism, and on knowing enough of the life history to choose the *right method* of attack and to apply it *at the right time*. Protective spraying is of no value whatever for a wilt disease where the invasion is systemic (inside the water-conducting system) but may be of great value for certain blights that externally resemble wilts.

The bacteria that cause plant disease are microscopic one-celled organisms that reproduce by simple cell division. They survive in soil or plant parts and may cause wilting, blights, rots, leaf spots, or galls.

Fungi have a more complex structure but they also lack the green chlorophyll found in higher plants. They must obtain their food *saprophytically* from dead plants or as parasites from living plants. Fungi possess a *my-celium*, which is a tangle of interwoven threads, and they are divided into three main groups according to the type of sexual reproductive structure arising from this *mycelium*.

A few fungi causing heart rots and other tree diseases belong to the *Basidiomycetes*, the mushroom group; a few, such as the downy mildews, belong to the *Phycomycetes*, the molds; but most of the fungi causing important diseases in home gardens belong to the *Ascomycetes*. These have their sexual spores formed in club-shaped sacs known as *asci*, which may line an open cup (*apothecium*) or a tiny spherical body (*perithecium*). *Apothecia* frequently arise from a hard knot of *mycelium* called a *sclerotium*. *Sclerotia* remain viable in soil or old plant parts for months or years. They are easily transported from nursery to garden, ready to produce azalea, camellia, peony and many other flower or leaf blights when weather conditions are right.

In addition to the sexual fruiting bodies, most fungi have an asexual or imperfect state where short-lived summer spores (*conidia*) are produced in chains, pustules, or minute structures similar to *perithecia*.

Occasionally we can prevent diseases by treating the soil with a chemical that will inhibit the production of fruiting bodies, but normally we must depend on a chemical spray applied to flower or leaf *in advance* of the arrival of the fungus spore. The chemical must be there in time to keep the spore from germinating and growing inside the tissue. That is why we spray *before rains* or else spray often enough to keep expanding plant surfaces protected at all times. To prevent azalea flower blight we start spraying as the bush comes into bloom and repeat two or three times a week until all flowers are out. To prevent a foliage disease such as rose blackspot, we start when the bush comes into full leaf and repeat more or less weekly until hard frost.

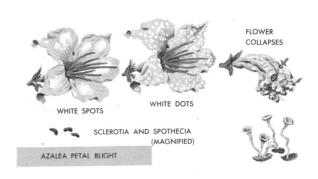

FLOWER COLLAPSES

WHITE SPOTS

WHITE DOTS

SCLEROTIA AND SPOTHECIA (MAGNIFIED)

AZALEA PETAL BLIGHT

Types of Disease

BLIGHTS are characterized by sudden death of shoots, foliage, flowers or whole plants.

Azalea Petal Blight (flower spot) is a devastating disease now present from New Jersey around the coast to California but more important in the southern fog belt. Very small, thin black *sclerotia* in or on moist ground send up minute *apothecia* from which *ascospores* are carried by air currents to petals above, producing large white spots that are wet to the touch. Secondary infection comes from *conidia* produced at base of petals and spread by wind, rain, insects to other flowers, bushes and gardens. Numerous small white spots over the petals show where each spore has landed and started to germinate. In moist weather, flowers reach the slimy limp stage in 24 hours and in 2 or 3 days *sclerotia* are forming in the petals. These resting bodies drop to the ground or remain for months in dried flowers hanging on bushes. They go to new locations with azaleas sold in containers. The only control, in areas where the disease is rampant, is to spray flowers with zineb every 2 or 3 days, starting as they show color.

Camellia Flower Blight is similar except that there is no secondary stage, no *conidia* to spread the disease from bush to bush during the season. Large compound *sclerotia*, formed in the center of blighted flowers rotting onto the soil, send up large cuplike *apothecia* for several springs, the spores being wind-borne a half-mile or more. Camellias bloom over such a long period it is impractical to spray the flowers or to pick up and burn all faded flowers. Spraying the ground with Terraclor just before *apothecia* are expected (January to March, depending on climate) often inhibits the development of *apothecia*. If you live in an area where these flower blights are not yet present it is folly to order azaleas or camellias from areas where these blights are known without having the plants bare-rooted, with all soil and all flower buds showing color removed.

Botrytis Blights are characterized by *conidia* forming a gray mold over infected tissue, by blackened buds or shoots of peonies, by spotted tulip flowers. Sanitation is the best control, removing fading tulips into a paper bag, cutting peony stalks (with possible *sclerotia*) at ground level in autumn. Zineb, ferbam or copper sprays are sometimes used in early spring.

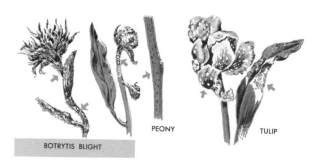

BOTRYTIS BLIGHT
PEONY
TULIP

Southern Blight (Crown Rot in the North) is another *sclerotial* disease, coming from mustard-seedlike bodies in the soil and white fungus threads spreading from plant to plant in moist weather. A hundred or more species of plants may rot down or topple over in warm, humid weather, with ajuga and delphinium particularly susceptible. Diseased plants and all surrounding soil should be removed immediately and the area treated with bichloride of mercury, 2 tablets to 1 quart of water (1-1000 dilution).

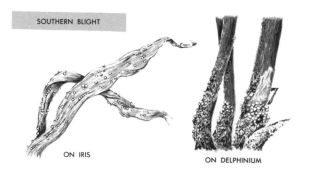

SOUTHERN BLIGHT
ON IRIS
ON DELPHINIUM

Fire Blight is a bacterial disease making twigs and branches of pears, apples, quinces, crab-apple, hawthorn and pyracantha appear as if burned by fire. The bacteria swarm down inside the tissues beyond the parts visibly blighted. Commercial growers often spray with streptomycin, an antibiotic. Home gardeners should prune out diseased branches, cutting 6 inches beyond visible blighted portions and disinfecting the pruning tool with denatured alcohol between cuts.

Cankers are localized lesions on woody stems, which are sometimes girdled and die back. In some cases the fungi enter through long stubs or jagged wounds left in pruning; in others, particularly if canes are kept too moist with a summer or winter mulch, fungi may enter through unbroken tissue. Use care in pruning; avoid excessive warmth and moisture around stems.

CANKERS
STEM CANKERS ON ROSES

Dodder is a seed plant parasitic on chrysanthemum, ivy and other garden, as well as field, plants. It is a leafless orange vine, feeding by suckers into stems of the host plant. Cut off all plant parts to which the dodder is attached before the clusters of small white flowers set seed.

DODDER

Galls are abnormal enlargements of plant tissue due to irritation by bacteria, fungi or insects. *Crown Gall* is a bacterial disease especially important on rose, raspberry and other brambles. The bacteria survive a year or two in the soil, entering plants through wounds made in cultivating or by nematodes.

The best control is exclusion, rejecting all plants showing the least symptom of galls. *Leaf Galls* of azalea and camellia are not serious. Removal of enlarged leaves is often sufficient control.

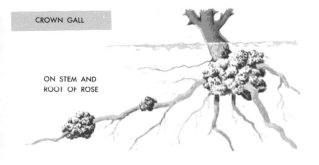

CROWN GALL

ON STEM AND ROOT OF ROSE

Leaf Spots are limited dead or dying areas in leaves. Many are more conspicuous than harmful but rose blackspot is most important, requiring protective spraying all season.

Powdery Mildew is a white, somewhat powdery coating on the surface of leaves, sometimes flowers and stems. It is made up of a tangle of *mycelium* with chains of spores. Plants may be deformed or dwarfed. Mildews are common on many annuals, perennials and shrubs, especially if these are grown in areas with little air circulation. Mildews are prevalent in late summer when cool nights follow warm days. The spores germinate in high humidity but not in actual drops of water. Heavy rains or spraying with the hose will partially control mildew. Acti-dione PM is a specific mildewcide.

Rots are a hard dry or a soft wet decay of plant tissue—in root, rhizome, bulb, stem, or fruit. *Brown Rot* attacks plums, cherries, peaches, producing gray spore cushions over the rotting fruit, which turns into hard, wrinkled "mummies." Cleaning up such infective material is as important as summer spraying with captan or sulfur. Tree rots are started by fungi entering through broken

limbs or long stubs. All final pruning cuts should be made flush with the trunk and shaped so they will quickly callus over.

Rusts are named for the rusty red spore pustules of the summer stage but they may have four spore forms. Some rusts produce two of these on one type of plant and the other two on an alternate host. Removal of one host breaks the life cycle. Sulfur or zineb sprays control some rusts.

Scab means an overgrowth of tissue in a limited area—a slightly raised or calloused leaf spot, stem or fruit lesion. *Apple scab*, our most important fruit disease, is controlled by an arduous spray schedule easier for the commercial grower than the backyard gardener. *Violet Scab*, also known as spot anthracnose, starts as small leaf spots and progresses to scabby symptoms. Remove and destroy infected stems and foliage.

Virus Diseases are due to complex protein molecules (too small to be seen except with an ultra-microscope) that act like living organisms. There is loss of color in definite patterns, such as mosaic (a yellow and green mottling), ring spot, streak, spotted wilt, or in a general yellowing. Most viruses are spread by insects — aphids, leafhoppers, thrips—but some only by propagation of infected plants. Immediately rogue (remove and destroy) infected plants; control insect vectors.

Wilts are systemic diseases with tissues becoming flaccid due to plugging of the vascular system or to a toxin introduced into it. In many cases the organism lives in the soil and enters the plant through root hairs or wounds. Spraying is useless; resistant varieties are the only hope. Where the fungus is spread by insects working in aerial plant parts, control lies in killing the vectors. A dormant spray of DDT or methoxychlor kills bark beetles spreading spores of Dutch elm disease.

🍂 Animal Pests

Insects differ from other animal pests by having 3 pairs of legs. They have 3 body parts—head, thorax and abdomen—covered with a protective shell. They breathe by means of spiracles (pores) along the body. Most insects have 2 pairs of wings in the adult stage. Their mouth parts are jaws adapted for chewing or beaks made for piercing plant cuticle and sucking out the sap. Most sucking insects have a gradual metamorphosis, young nymphs being similar to adults except for lack of wings. Most chewing insects have a complete metamorphosis, the larval stage of a caterpillar, grub or maggot being totally unlike the adult butterfly, moth, beetle, or fly.

Aphids, plant lice, are small, soft-bodied sucking insects of many colors—green, pink, lavender, gray, black, red, yellow, brown—clustered on succulent new shoots, or on buds, or inside curled leaves. Buds and flowers may be deformed. A black sooty mold may grow in the honeydew secreted by aphids on foliage. Aphids are usually found in wingless forms but when a population gets too thick on one plant, winged forms develop for migration to another, which may be an entirely different type of plant. Some aphids cause galls; others act as carriers of plant viruses.

Woolly aphids are covered with white, waxy threads, root aphids with a whitish powder. Ants foster root aphids for their honeydew.

Malathion and lindane sprays are commonly recommended for aphids, the latter being particularly good for woolly and gall aphids. A rotenone-pyrethrum aerosol bomb is good for spot treatment of a few aphids, indoors or out.

Beetles are chewing insects with a horny sheath covering membranous hind wings. The larval stage is a grub, often soft, dirty-white, with a brown head, somewhat hairy. Weevils are beetles with a snout and wing covers fastened down so they cannot fly. Many weevils feed at night, notching leaves in from the margin. Curculios are beetles or weevils with a long snout, often curved. Plum and apple curculios are responsible for wormy fruit.

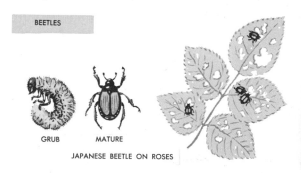

BEETLES

GRUB   MATURE

JAPANESE BEETLE ON ROSES

Borers are caterpillars, grubs, or sawfly larvae working in woody or herbaceous stems. Control depends on removal of infested wood

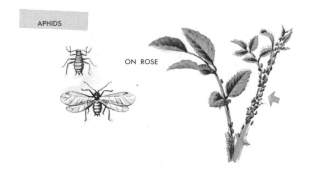

APHIDS

ON ROSE

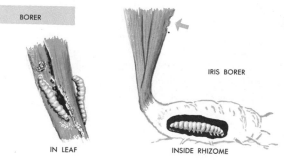

BORER

IRIS BORER

IN LEAF   INSIDE RHIZOME

and spraying to prevent egg laying by adult moth or beetle.

True *Bugs* are sucking insects with the upper half of the front pair of wings thickened and stiff, the lower half thin and membranous. The wings are folded flat over the back when at rest. There are many plant bugs, stink bugs and other bugs, but the most important in home gardens are the chinch bugs causing brown patches in lawns, and the various lace bugs that stipple foliage of azalea, rhododendron, hawthorn, pyracantha, andromeda and other ornamental shrubs. Most of these can be controlled with lindane, applied at the right time.

Caterpillars are wormlike larvae of moths and butterflies, smooth or hairy, ranging up to several inches long. They include: canker worms (inch or measuring worms); bagworms; cutworms (fat, greasy, living in soil); tent caterpillars, living in webs in branch crotches; hornworms; fall webworms, in webs over the ends of branches; gypsy moths defoliating hardwoods in New England, and many other voracious forms. Spraying with DDT or lead arsenate is the usual recommendation for control.

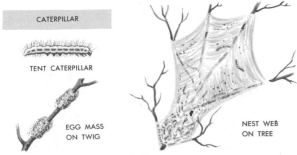

CATERPILLAR

TENT CATERPILLAR

EGG MASS ON TWIG

NEST WEB ON TREE

Leafhoppers are elongated, wedge-shaped, sucking insects with wings held in a rooflike position. They suck from underside of foliage, producing a stippled effect on the upper side. Sometimes there is burning and rolling of leaf margins. DDT or lindane is effective in control.

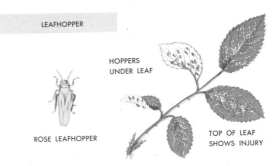

LEAFHOPPER

HOPPERS UNDER LEAF

ROSE LEAFHOPPER

TOP OF LEAF SHOWS INJURY

Leaf Miners feed between two leaf surfaces, making disfiguring blotches or serpentine markings. Different species require different chemicals for control, and timing of the spray is very important.

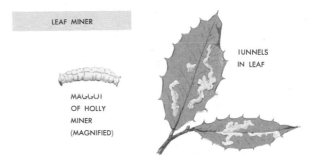

LEAF MINER

MAGGOT OF HOLLY MINER (MAGNIFIED)

TUNNELS IN LEAF

Mealybugs are small, sucking insects often found clustered at leaf axils of indoor plants, sometimes on yew and other outdoor shrubs. They have flat, oval bodies covered with white powdery wax that extends in short projections giving a crenulated effect. Eggs are formed in white, cottony sacs. Malathion is fairly effective in control. Summer oil sprays have been used. Mealybugs are illustrated in Chapter 20.

Millipedes are small, wiry, brownish "worms" with many legs, often found coiled like a watch spring. They are mostly secondary organisms working in decaying plant parts. Improve drainage; clean up refuse.

Mites are minute animals in the spider group, having 4 pairs of legs as adults. Spider mites (red spiders) turn leaves yellow or gray and make cobwebs on the under side. The cyclamen mite is too small to see with the naked eye, makes no webs, but seriously stunts delphinium and other plants, blackening the buds. DDT and other all-purpose insecticides often increase mites by killing their parasites. Spray with Aramite, Kelthane, or Tedion.

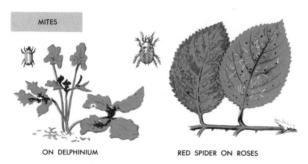

ON DELPHINIUM   RED SPIDER ON ROSES

Nematodes are microscopic wormlike animals living in moist soil or plant tissue. There are many parasitic forms, some causing knots in roots, some causing roots to slough off, some invading foliage or bulbs. Plants are stunted, generally unhealthy. Help from your local county agent is necessary for proper diagnosis. Nematocides safe around some living plants are Nemagon and V-C-13.

Sawflies are chewing insects related to bees but with larvae resembling caterpillars or slugs. Many species defoliate pine; the rose-slug skeletonizes rose foliage. DDT, lead arsenate and other pesticides readily control sawfly larvae if they are applied in time.

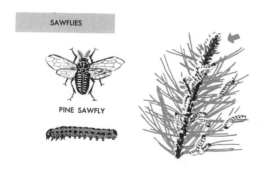

PINE SAWFLY

Scales are sucking insects closely related to mealybugs. Only the female causes plant injury. After a brief crawling period an armored scale sticks her beak into a plant cell and remains in that spot the rest of her life, covering herself with a hard shell. Soft scales have no separate shell and may move about very sluggishly. Standard control is a dormant oil spray applied before plants start growth in spring. This can be replaced by a malathion spray timed for crawling stages. A summer oil, such as Volck, or dimethoate (Cygon) may also be used.

FEMALE

MALE

EUONYMUS SCALE   MAGNOLIA SCALE

Slugs and *Snails* are related to oysters and clams. Both have soft, unsegmented bodies but the snail adds a shell. They eat large holes out of leaves or fruit near the ground, leaving a slimy trail. Baits containing metaldehyde are recommended for control, along with cleaning up their garden hiding places. For illustration, see Sawflies.

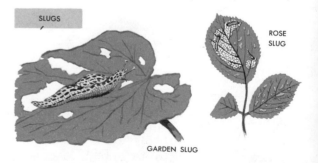

ROSE SLUG

GARDEN SLUG

Sowbugs have small gray, oval segmented bodies with 7 pairs of legs. They are often found rolled into a ball in decaying plant parts. They are mostly scavengers and special control measures are seldom necessary.

Spittlebugs are related to leafhoppers, which the adults resemble. The nymphs live inside frothy masses and may seriously injure pine and other shrubs. Spray with lindane or chlordane.

Thrips are tiny insects with bristly wings, rasping-sucking mouth parts. The flower thrips, causing rose and peony buds to ball, is hard to control. DDT takes care of thrips on gladiolus.

THRIPS

GLADIOLUS INJURY

Wasps are mostly very beneficial insects but two large forms may be garden pests. The cicada killer makes holes and earth mounds in lawns. The giant hornet tears bark from around branches of lilacs and other shrubs. Chlordane in the holes and a strong DDT spray over bark of shrubs may help.

WASPS

DIGGER WASP

VESPA HORNET

Whiteflies are minute sucking insects, snow-white, resembling moths as adults, flat scales as nymphs on underside of foliage. They secrete honeydew, fostering a copious growth of sooty mold. Malathion is fairly effective in control.

CHOOSING CHEMICAL PESTICIDES

There are hundreds of basic chemicals now sold under thousands of trade names and in thousands of combinations for garden pest control. Any one garden supply store can handle but a small fraction of these. Consequently, this list of chemicals includes only those likely to be widely available, reasonably safe to use without mask and protective clothing, and reasonably safe for plants if amounts directed on the package are not exceeded.

Acti-dione PM. An antibiotic, specific for powdery mildews.

Aramite. Excellent miticide for ornamentals, not for food crops. Use 1 tablespoon 15% wettable powder to 1 gallon of water.

Bordeaux Mixture. A copper-lime fungicide too conspicuous for wide use on ornamentals.

Captan. Safe organic fungicide and seed protectant, used for many fruit, vegetable and ornamental diseases. Usual dosage is 1½ to 2 tablespoons per gallon of water.

Chlordane. For ants, grubs, chinch bugs, grasshoppers and other pests. Use care in handling.

Copper. "Fixed" coppers may replace bordeaux mixture. Ammoniacal copper is used in some combination sprays.

Cygon. Trade name for dimethoate, a moderately safe phosphate spray for scales, whiteflies, mites, other pests.

DDT. For iris, lilac borers; boxwood, holly leaf miners; leafhoppers; gladiolus thrips; rose midges, sawfly larvae; beetle grubs and other pests. Use 2 tablespoons wettable powder to 1 gallon of water.

Dimite. Miticide, useful for cyclamen mite on delphinium. Dosage 1 teaspoon per gallon.

Ferbam (Fermate). Black iron fungicide for leaf spots, cedar-apple rust, some blights.

Karathane. For powdery mildew only; use ⅔ teaspoon powder per gallon of water.

Kelthane. Miticide safe for food crops and ornamentals; good for cyclamen mite; 1 to 2 tablespoons powder to 1 gallon of water.

Lead Arsenate. A stomach poison still useful for many caterpillars and beetles. Use 3 to 4 tablespoons per gallon of water.

Lime Sulfur. Safe fungicide, insecticide. Use at 1 to 9 dilution as a dormant spray for pine-needle, juniper, and rose scales.

Lindane. Good for lace bugs, birch leaf miner, woolly aphids, weevils, thrips. Use 1 tablespoon 25% wettable powder per gallon.

Malathion. A "safe" phosphate spray for mealybugs, whiteflies, scale crawlers, aphids. Dosage 1 to 2 teaspoons of emulsion or 3 to 4 tablespoons powder per gallon of water.

Maneb (Manzate, Dithane M-22). Fungicide for various blights and rose blackspot, especially useful in the South.

Methoxychlor. An analog of DDT, safer on food plants, less harmful to birds.

Mercuric Chloride. Highly poisonous disinfectant. Use 2 tablets to 1 quart of water for 1 to 1000 dilution.

Nemagon. Nematocide that can be used around some living plants. Insert 1 teaspoon of 10% granules in holes 6 inches deep, 1 foot apart.

Nicotine sulfate. Highly poisonous contact insecticide, usually sold as Black Leaf 40. For aphids use 1 to 1½ teaspoons with 1 ounce of soap to 1 gallon of water.

Oil Sprays. For a dormant spray use a miscible oil at 1 to 15 or 20 dilution on deciduous plants, 1 to 25 or 30 on evergreens. Summer oils, such as Volck, are used at 1 to 50 dilution. Do not apply oil when temperature is below 45°F. or above 85°F.

Phaltan. Trade name for folpet, an excellent fungicide for rose blackspot and other leaf spots, having some effect on powdery mildews. Use 1¼ tablespoons powder to 1 gallon of water. Can be combined with Isotox for all-purpose rose spray. Do not add any sticker-spreader.

Pyrethrum. Contact insecticide of low toxicity to man; included in many aerosol sprays.

Rotenone. Contact insecticide and stomach poison, safe for man, highly poisonous to fish. Do not use near garden pools.

Sevin. Trade name for carbaryl, broad-spectrum insecticide safe for the operator, toxic to bees and other beneficial insects. Highly effective against Japanese beetles and many other pests.

Sulfur. Our oldest fungicide and miticide. Effective for powdery mildew, rusts, some leaf spots but injurious at high temperatures. Used as a dust (25 to 90%) or as a spray (1 tablespoon wettable powder to 1 gallon of water).

Tedion. Trade name for tetradifon. Efficient miticide included in some combination sprays, such as Isotox.

Terraclor (PCNB). Soil fungicide for damping-off and various sclerotial diseases such as camellia flower blight, southern blight.

V-C 13 Nemacide. Can be used around some living plants to control nematodes.

Zineb (Dithane Z-78, Parzate). Fungicide effective for azalea petal blight, rose blackspot, some rusts. Use 1 tablespoon wettable powder per gallon of water.

Chemicals in Combination

Chemicals should not be applied to plants unnecessarily. To control lace bugs on rhododendron, for instance, one or two applications of a single chemical may be sufficient. But for efficient control of rose pests we need a combination spray or dust containing one or two insecticides, one or two fungicides and a miticide, and this is applied more or less weekly all season.

All garden supply stores have some combination pesticides and by reading labels you can find out if the ingredients are right for your particular combination of pests.

Applying Pesticides

Chemicals may be applied as dry dusts or as liquid sprays. Dusting is somewhat less efficient, may leave a more visible residue, but some find it easier. Some dusts are sold in small cartons designed to be used as dusters. These are most unsatisfactory. For best results use either a metal dust gun, with a plunger to push back and forth, or, preferably, a small rotary duster. This is made of light-weight aluminum and has an extension tube allowing the dust to adequately cover under surfaces of foliage.

Chemicals to be applied as sprays are sold either as wettable powders or as emulsions. The former are somewhat safer, the latter usually leave less visible residue. Sprayers vary from the small aerosol "bomb" and atomizer sprayer to large affairs with a motor. Compressed air sprayers, varying in capacity from 1½ to 4 gallons, are commonly used in home gardens. Very easy to operate, granted hose outlets and sufficient water pressure, is the hose-end sprayer with an extension tube.

Safety Rules

All chemical pesticides are poisons! Those mentioned in this chapter are reasonably safe to handle with the following precautions.

1. Read the entire label *before opening* the container, noting all warnings. Do not inhale the vapor of a concentrated chemical; if any is spilled on the skin wash it off immediately!

2. Always store in *original* container with label intact. It is not safe to share a pesticide with your neighbor.

3. Keep all pesticides out of reach of children and pets.

4. Never store pesticides in cabinets with food packages.

5. Destroy empty containers immediately. Bury or burn cartons, keeping away from smoke. Wash out glass and metal containers before putting in the trash can.

6. When operating, keep out of the spray drift. *Never smoke* while spraying. After spraying, wash hands and face before smoking or eating.

7. Cover bird baths, dog dishes, fish pools before spraying. Never leave a pail of prepared pesticide open to children, pets, or birds. Put baits for slugs under jar covers or boards.

8. Pour leftover spray into a gravel drive. Never leave puddles on an impervious surface to attract birds and dogs.

9. Do not increase the dosage over that recommended on the label. Do not spray to the point of run-off; don't drench the ground.

10. Do not plant mint, strawberries, tomatoes or other edibles near ornamentals that may be sprayed frequently with pesticides.

❧ A Chart for Pest Control

The following tabulation lists some of the more common insect pests and diseases of ornamental garden plants. It does not include house plant, fruit, vegetable, or lawn problems, which are treated under those subjects in this book. It includes some of the smaller trees that might be handled by a home gardener but not large shade trees requiring attention by an expert arborist.

HOST, PEST	DESCRIPTION	CONTROL
AGERATUM		
Greenhouse Leaf Tier	Leaves eaten, webbed, folded by pale green caterpillar.	Dust or spray with DDT or malathion.
Whiteflies	Leaves stippled white, often in late summer.	Spray with malathion or lindane.
AJUGA or BUGLE		
Crown Rot (Southern Blight)	Plants wilt, turn black; reddish-tan sclerotia on white threads.	Remove plants, surrounding soil. Treat area with Terraclor or mercuric chloride.
AMARYLLIS		
Convict Caterpillar	Dark larvae with cream bands, 2½ inches long, devour leaves.	Dust with DDT or lead arsenate.
Narcissus Bulb Fly	Hairy fly, like a bumblebee; large dirty-white maggot in rotting bulbs.	Dust bulbs before planting, and foliage after growth, with 5% chlordane.
Lesser Bulb Fly	Several yellowish maggots in decaying bulbs.	Plant only firm, healthy bulbs.
Bulb Mites	See Hyacinth.	Discard soft bulbs.
Leaf Scorch (Red Blotch)	Reddish spots on flowers, leaves, bulb scales; stalks deformed.	Avoid heavy watering; spray with zineb or ferbam.
ANDROMEDA (*Pieris*)		
Andromeda Lace Bug	Foliage grayish; dark nymphs, lace-winged adults feed from underside. Broods from April to November.	Spray with lindane, malathion or Sevin when bugs hatch; repeat for later broods.
Spider Mites (Red Spiders)	Yellowing leaves, sickly bushes.	Aramite, Kelthane, or Tedion.
ANEMONE, JAPANESE		
Blister Beetles	Long, slim black beetles feed on flowers, foliage.	DDT or malathion.

HOST, PEST	DESCRIPTION	CONTROL
ARBOR-VITAE		
Bagworms	Black and white caterpillars feed from spindle-shaped bags on twigs.	Cut off and burn bags. Spray in *late* spring with lead arsenate, Sevin or chlordane.
Spider Mites	Foliage dusty with fine webs; trees yellowish or brown.	Spray with Aramite, Kelthane or Tedion.
Root Weevils	Grubs feed on roots; adults notch leaves in from margin.	Spray soil, lower foliage with chlordane.
Arbor-vitae Aphid	Reddish brown lice with whitish bloom, on roots, stems, branches.	Spray with lindane or malathion.
Arbor-vitae Soft Scale	Large, brown, hemispherical shells on twigs.	Malathion or summer oil such as Volck.
Juniper Scale	See Juniper.	
Leaf Shedding	Inner leaves turn brown and drop in fall.	Natural old age; no control.
Winter Browning	Wind or sun evaporates water from leaves faster than replaced.	Windbreaks or spraying with Wilt-Pruf.
ASTER, CHINA		
Root Aphids	Plants yellow, wilting; gray powdery lice spread by ants.	Control ants with chlordane. Pour lindane spray into depression around stem.
Leafhoppers	Small, greenish-yellow hoppers sucking sap, transmitting yellows virus.	DDT or malathion spray.
Blister Beetles	Black, striped or margined beetles on flowers, foliage.	Spray or dust with DDT.
Tarnished Plant Bug	New growth blackened by small, mottled brown bug.	DDT spray or dust.
Aster Wilt	Plants wilt, die; soil fungus enters vascular system through roots.	Choose resistant varieties (marked WR in catalogues).
Aster Yellows	Stunted, yellowed plants with greenish flowers. Virus spread by leafhoppers.	Control leaf hoppers with DDT or grow plants under cloth frames.
ASTER, PERENNIAL		
Aster Aphids	Green lice clustering at tips of New England aster.	Spray with malathion or lindane.
Powdery Mildew	White coating in late summer.	Spray with Acti-dione PM.

HOST, PEST	DESCRIPTION	CONTROL
AZALEA		
Azalea Lace Bug	Coarse grayish stippling of leaves; rusty flecks, dark nymphs, lace-winged adults on underside. Usually 2 broods.	Spray with lindane or malathion; repeat for second brood.
Azalea Bark Scale	White fluffs like mealybugs on stems, followed by sooty mold.	Spray with malathion or a summer oil (Volck).
Peony Scale	White circles on twigs, where small brown shells rub off. Serious in the South.	Volck spray before growth starts or malathion later.
Southern Red Mite	Leaves turn yellow and drop.	Spray with Aramite, Kelthane or Cygon.
Azalea Leaf Miner	Small caterpillar rolls leaves.	Malathion or lindane.
Azalea Caterpillar	Striped larvae feeding in groups.	Lead arsenate or DDT.
Azalea Stem Borer	Yellow caterpillar in twigs.	DDT or malathion. Cut and burn infested twigs.
Azalea Whitefly	Pale green ovals on underside of leaves of hairy white varieties.	Spray with malathion.
Azalea Flower Spot, Petal Blight	Flowers spotted, then wilt to brown slimy mush; black sclerotia in petals. Very common in the South.	Spray 2 or 3 times a week during bloom with zineb. Do not accept azaleas from the South unless bare-rooted, flowers removed.
Azalea Leaf Gall	Leaf enlarged into thick gall, first white, then brown.	Cut off as noticed.
BARBERRY		
Barberry Aphid	Small yellow lice on shoots.	Malathion or lindane.
Barberry Scale	Convex, reddish scale on twigs.	Dormant oil or malathion.
Barberry Webworm	Leaves, twigs, webbed together.	Lead arsenate or DDT.
Wheat Rust	Common barberry, alternate host, is prohibited in many states.	Use resistant Japanese varieties.
BIRCH		
Birch Leaf Miner	Large brown blotches on leaves; tree appears blighted by disease.	Lindane or malathion in May; repeat in 6 weeks.
Bronze Birch Borer	Trees die back from the top.	Spray bark with DDT.
Cankerworms	Inchworms eat holes in foliage.	Lead arsenate or DDT.
Birch Aphids	Dense clusters of greenish lice.	Spray with malathion.
BOX-ELDER		
Boxelder Bug	Red and black bugs on flowers, fruit, foliage, and in houses.	Spray with lindane or chlordane. Remove pistillate box-elders.

HOST, PEST	DESCRIPTION	CONTROL
BOXWOOD		
Boxwood Leaf Miner	Yellow maggots in blistered leaves; orange flies emerge in May (April in South)	Spray with DDT just before emergence or spray in July with lindane or Cygon.
Boxwood Mite	Foliage gray or yellow with minute scratches.	Aramite or Kelthane.
Oystershell and other scales	Dark brown, oyster-shaped shells.	Malathion for crawlers.
Volutella Blight, Nectria Canker	Branches dying, tips tan; salmon pustules on stems, leaves.	Clean out bushes annually. Spray with 1-50 lime sulfur.
Boxwood Psyllid	Terminal leaves cupped.	Lindane or malathion.
Meadow Nematodes	Bushes stunted, roots sloughed off; witches' broom of new roots.	Treat soil with Nemagon as directed.
Wind Burn, Sunscald, Freezing Injury	Tops bleached in spring sun, wind; stems split by frost.	Use a windbreak and mulch. Spray with Wiltpruf.
CALENDULA		
Green Peach, Bean Aphids	Black or green lice common on buds and flowers.	Lindane, malathion, nicotine, or rotenone.
Cabbage Looper	Green caterpillar with white stripes.	Malathion or lead arsenate.
CAMELLIA		
Tea Scale	White filaments with dark oyster shells; leaves mottled yellow.	Spray with Cygon soon after bloom is over.
Peony Scale	See Azalea.	
Fuller Rose Beetle	Notches eaten from leaf margins at night by gray-brown weevil.	Dust stems with chlordane, lindane, or malathion.
Rhabdopterus Beetles	Small, shiny black beetles feed on buds, causing irregular holes in foliage.	Spray with methoxychlor (DDT may injure Camellias)
Camellia Flower Blight	Flowers turn brown and drop; large black sclerotium formed in center.	Treat soil with Terraclor just before blooming; clean up all drops. Buy bare-rooted, all color buds removed.
Dieback	Tips die back, leaves brown; cankers form on wood.	Cut out diseased portions. Use a copper spray.
Leaf Gall	Leaves greatly swollen.	Cut off and burn.
Leaf Spot (nonparasitic)	Silvery or brown spots from sun or wind; secondary fungi.	Provide light shade, as under tall pines.
Variegation	Mottled foliage and flowers, due to a virus or physiological condition.	No control. Some are fostered as desirable novelties.

HOST, PEST	DESCRIPTION	CONTROL
CANNA		
Japanese Beetle	Metallic green and copper, on flowers, foliage.	Spray or dust with Sevin or DDT.
Canna Leaf Rollers	Large green and small yellowish caterpillars roll and tie leaves.	Apply lead arsenate or DDT early in season.
Canna Bud Rot	Yellow to brown leaf spots; gummy stalks; decayed flowers.	Discard diseased plants.
CHERRY, FLOWERING		
Tent Caterpillars	Hairy caterpillars in large nests at tree crotches; eggs in varnished bands around twigs.	Cut out egg masses in winter. Wipe out nests or squirt in DDT.
Cankerworms	Inchworms. See Birch.	
CHRYSANTHEMUM		
Leaf Nematode	Brown wedges in leaves between veins; progressive dying and drying up the stem, from nematodes moving up in water film.	Start plants from tip cuttings; do not make crown divisions. Avoid overhead watering; use a mulch.
Chrysanthemum Aphid	Large, dark lice on terminal shoots. Growth is stunted.	Spray with lindane, malathion or pyrethrum.
Four-lined Plant Bug	Red nymphs, green adults with 4 black stripes make tan depressed circles in foliage.	Dust with DDT or rotenone, or spray with malathion.
Chrysanthemum Gall Midge	Small, conical galls in buds, stems, leaves.	Spray with lindane, in evening; repeat in 5 days.
Chrysanthemum Lace Bug	Foliage bleached; brown specks on underside.	Lindane or malathion.
Spittlebugs	White frothy masses enclose greenish nymphs.	Dust with DDT, methoxychlor, or lindane.
Leaf Spots	Small, dark spots, starting on lower leaves which dry up the stem.	Spray with ferbam, captan, or zineb.
Dodder	Orange tendrils and small white flowers of a parasitic vine.	Remove and burn all infested plant parts.
Powdery Mildew	White coating on foliage.	Acti-dione PM spray.
Rust	Reddish pustules on backs of leaves.	Zineb or sulfur.
Verticillium wilt	One-sided wilting, dying; black streaks in cut stems.	Remove infected plants.

HOST, PEST	DESCRIPTION	CONTROL
CLEMATIS		
Blister Beetles	Slim, black beetles devour flowers, foliage.	Spray or dust with DDT.
Clematis Borer	Dull white larvae hollow out stems and roots; vines are stunted, branches die.	DDT spray or dust in early spring; dig out larvae in crown.
Root-knot Nematodes	Knots on roots; plants stunted, wilted, may die.	Treat soil with a nematocide before planting.
Leaf Spots, Stem Rot	Stems girdled near ground, upper portion dying back. Tan or gray spots on leaves.	Spray with sulfur, captan, zineb or ferbam.
COLUMBINE		
Columbine Borer	Salmon caterpillar, to 1½ inches, works in fleshy roots.	Dust with DDT weekly in spring; scrape away soil to remove eggs.
Columbine Leaf Miner	White, serpentine tunnels in leaves, with black specks.	Spray with lindane, or malathion; pick off leaves.
COSMOS		
Corn and Stalk Borers	See Dahlia.	
Spotted Cucumber Beetle	Flowers eaten by small, greenish beetles with 12 black spots.	Malathion, DDT or methoxychlor.
Japanese Beetle	Also feeds on flowers.	Malathion, DDT or methoxychlor.
CRAB-APPLE, FLOWERING		
Tent Caterpillars and Cankerworms	See Cherry, Flowering.	
Fire Blight	Branches die back, foliage appears scorched. Bacteria inside stems.	Prune out six inches below blight; disinfect shears.
Cedar-apple Rust	Orange spots on leaves, fruit; branches die. Red-cedar is alternate host.	Eliminate red-cedars or remove galls before spore horns form. Replace native with Asiatic crabs.
CRAPE-MYRTLE		
Crapemyrtle Aphid	Shoots infested in early spring. Sooty mold grows in honeydew.	Spray with malathion or lindane.
Powdery Mildew	White growth on young foliage, which is thickened, does not develop.	Dormant lime sulfur before buds break or Actidione PM later.

HOST, PEST	DESCRIPTION	CONTROL
DAFFODIL (*Narcissus*)		
Narcissus Bulb Fly	Bumblebee-like fly lays eggs on leaves near ground; fat yellow maggot tunnels in rotting bulbs.	Dust trench and bulbs with 5% chlordane before planting. Sprinkle naphthalene flakes on ground around plants.
Bulb Nematode	Dark rings in bulbs; growth abnormal; lumps in leaves.	Discard infested bulbs, sickly plants.
Basal Rot	Chocolate-brown rot at base of bulb scales.	Discard bulbs with rot.
Smoulder	Plants stunted or missing; masses of black sclerotia on bulbs.	Inspect bulbs before planting in new location.
Leaf Scorch	Red, yellow or brown spots near tip of leaves.	Spray or dust with maneb or zineb.
Mosaic, Streak	Mottling and streaking due to a virus.	Rogue diseased plants.
DAHLIA		
European Corn Borer	Flesh-colored caterpillars tunnel in stems, which break over.	Destroy old stalks and weeds in autumn. Dust or spray stems with DDT.
Stalk Borer	Brown, white-striped larvae in stalks.	Destroy old stalks and weeds in autumn. Dust or spray stems with DDT.
Beetles	See Cosmos.	
Potato Leafhopper	Leaf margins are brown, curled; plants are stunted.	DDT spray or dust.
Tarnished Plant Bug	Tips wilt, turn black, buds are deformed.	DDT or malathion.
Powdery Mildew	White coating on foliage in late summer.	Acti-dione PM spray or can safely ignore.
Dahlia Mosaic, Stunt	Mottled foliage, margins uprolled; plants stunted. Virus transmitted by aphids.	Rogue infected plants. Control aphid vectors.
Dahlia Ring Spot	Virus, spread by thrips, causing rings or zig-zags in leaves.	Rogue plants; use DDT to reduce thrips.
DELPHINIUM		
Cyclamen Mite	Leaves deformed, buds black, plants stunted. Mites spread in handling, cultivating.	Remove deformed plants. Spray early with Kelthane or Dimite.
Broad Mite	Leaves appear glassy.	Spray with Dimite.
Crown Rot	Plants rot at crown. White fungus mycelium with reddish tan sclerotia spreads out into soil.	Remove plant and surrounding soil immediately. Treat area with Terraclor or mercuric chloride.

HOST, PEST	DESCRIPTION	CONTROL
DELPHINIUM (cont'd)		
Black Spot	Bacteria cause black, tarry spots on leaves.	Remove infected foliage. Spraying is seldom necessary.
DOGWOOD		
Dogwood Borer	White caterpillar, larva of a clearwing moth, works in cambium; kills branches and young trees.	Wrap newly planted trees. Spray trunks of others with DDT. Squirt borer paste into holes.
Dogwood Twig Borer	Yellow grub, larva of a long-horned beetle, girdles twigs, which die.	Prune out and destroy infested twigs.
Crown (Bleeding) Canker	Trunk girdled at base from fungus entering through wounds. Tree may die.	Use guard around trunk to prevent mower and other injuries.
Botrytis Blight	Gray mold on blossoms rotting down onto leaves in wet weather.	Spray with zineb or captan.
Leaf, Flower Spots	Brown, tan or gray spots with purple margins on leaves, flowers.	Spray with maneb or captan, starting at bud break.
EUONYMUS		
Euonymus Scale	Thin white males, brown oyster-shaped females encrust stems. Yellow crawlers in late spring, summer.	Dormant oil spray before growth starts plus malathion for crawlers in May, June, August.
Bean Aphid	Black lice on new growth.	Spray with malathion.
Powdery Mildew	White, felty coating on leaves. Common in the South, Southwest.	Syringe off with water; dust with sulfur or spray with Acti-dione PM.
Crown Gall	Large, irregular galls along vines, usually not at crown.	No control except purchase of healthy plants.
FIR		
Balsam Twig Aphid	White, cottony, on young shoots; twigs roughened, tips curled.	Spray with lindane in late spring.
Bagworms	See Arbor-vitae.	
Spruce Spider Mite	See Spruce.	
Tip Blight	New tips yellowed, curled; twigs may die.	Spray with bordeaux mixture, starting at bud break.
FORGET-ME-NOT		
Potato Flea Beetle	Minute, black beetle eats tiny round holes in leaves.	Spray or dust with DDT or methoxychlor.
FOXGLOVE		
Foxglove Aphid	Green lice causing leaf yellowing, curling, distortion.	Spray or dust with malathion.

HOST, PEST	DESCRIPTION	CONTROL
FOXGLOVE (cont'd)		
Red Spiders	Leaves grayish or yellowish.	Aramite or Kelthane.
Onion Thrips	Leaves rusty or silvery with black specks.	DDT or malathion dust or spray.
FUCHSIA		
Whiteflies	Leaves mottled, stippled or yellow, with honeydew and black sooty mold.	Spray with malathion.
Mealybugs	White ovals at leaf axils.	Spray with malathion.
False Spider Mites	Minute red mites cause rusty areas on leaves, which may drop.	Spray with Kelthane.
GARDENIA		
Whiteflies	Very common in the South; foliage covered with sooty mold in honeydew.	Spray with malathion or Cygon.
Mealybugs	See Fuchsia.	
Brown Soft Scale	Green to brown flat scale with copious honeydew.	Spray with malathion.
Stem Canker	Sunken brown areas at base of stem.	Destroy infected plants.
GERANIUM		
Whiteflies, Mealybugs	See Fuchsia.	
Botrytis Blight	Gray mold on fading flowers and foliage when plants too moist.	Spray with zineb. Remove diseased parts. Increase air circulation.
Cutting Rot, Blackleg	Black rot at base of stem.	Start cuttings in vermiculite or sterilized sand.
Oedema	Swellings on leaves, corky ridges on petioles from overwatering.	Withhold water in cloudy, humid weather.
GLADIOLUS		
Gladiolus Thrips	Minute, slender, yellowish. Leaves silvered, flowers streaked, deformed.	Dust with DDT, starting when foliage is 6 in. high. Dust corms with DDT after harvest.
GOLDEN-GLOW		
Goldenglow Aphid	Large red aphid covering upper portion of stems.	Spray with malathion or lindane.
Powdery Mildew	White coating.	Acti-dione PM or sulfur.
HAWTHORN		
Hawthorn Aphid	Young leaves curl tightly around greenish lice.	Spray early with malathion.
Rosy Apple Aphid	Leaves curled around pink lice covered with white wool.	Spray with malathion.

HOST, PEST	DESCRIPTION	CONTROL
HAWTHORN (cont'd)		
Woolly Hawthorn Aphid	White cottony masses on trunk and branches.	Spray with lindane.
Hawthorn Lace Bug	Leaves stippled white, brown flecks on underside.	Spray with lindane.
Tent Caterpillars	See Cherry, Flowering.	
Fire Blight	See Crab-apple.	
Hawthorn Leaf Blight	Small dark spots on leaves; defoliation in late summer.	Spray with ferbam or bordeaux as leaves expand; repeat in 10 days.
Quince, Hawthorn, Cedar-apple Rusts	Orange spots on leaves, fruit with white papery projections.	Eliminate red-cedars or spray with ferbam-sulfur.
HEMLOCK		
Spruce Spider Mite	Needles nearly white. See Spruce.	Spray with Aramite or Kelthane.
Root Weevils	Grubs on roots may kill trees. Adults notch needles at night.	Spray in June with chlordane or lindane.
Bagworms	See Arbor-vitae.	
Hemlock Looper	Yellow, black-dotted caterpillar; may defoliate.	Lead arsenate or malathion.
Hemlock Borer	White grub makes shallow galleries in bark.	Cut out infested wood.
Hemlock Scales	Gray, circular, on needles; waxy on twigs.	DDT with malathion; repeat as necessary.
HOLLY		
Leaf Miners	Blotch, sometimes serpentine, mines in American holly. Small black flies in late May.	Spray with DDT when 2 to 4 new leaves open; repeat in 2 weeks.
Southern Red Mite	Foliage looks as if dusted with red pepper.	Spray with Aramite or Kelthane.
Tea Scale	Common on Burford holly in South.	Summer oil spray.
Leaf Spots	Dark, purplish spots may be due to fungi, weather, or spine pricks.	No practical control.
HOLLYHOCK		
Garden Slugs	Small or large, soft, gray, brown or mottled, eating large holes, leaving a slimy trail.	Use a metaldehyde bait or spray foliage with chlordane or lead arsenate.
Japanese Beetles	Common on flowers, foliage.	Try Sevin.
Spider Mites	Leaves yellow, cobwebs on underside.	Aramite or Kelthane spray or sulfur dust.
Hollyhock Rust	Reddish pustules on underside of leaves and stems; yellow spots on upper leaf surface.	Spray with zineb; pick off rusted leaves; cut down stalks in autumn.

HOST, PEST	DESCRIPTION	CONTROL
HONEY LOCUST		
Mimosa Webworm	Serious pest. See Mimosa.	
Honeylocust Mite	Trees yellow, often defoliated.	Spray with Kelthane.
Honeylocust Pod Gall Midge	Leaflets completely galled and shed prematurely; many broods.	Spray with lindane.
HONEYSUCKLE		
Honeysuckle Aphid	Green aphids thick on new shoots.	Spray with malathion.
Honeysuckle Sawfly	Defoliation by gray-green larvae with black spots.	DDT, malathion, or lead arsenate.
HYACINTH		
Bulb Mites	Minute white mites in rotting bulbs.	Discard soft bulbs.
Bulb Nematode	Dark rings in bulb. See Narcissus.	
Soft Rot	Vile bacterial rot, often after mites.	Discard bulbs.
HYDRANGEA		
Lily and Melon Aphids	Yellow, green or black lice on shoots.	Spray with malathion.
Hydrangea Leaf Tier	Terminal leaves tied around flower buds.	DDT very early.
IRIS		
Iris Borer	Leaves ragged, water-soaked. Large flesh-colored larva hollows out rhizome.	Spray or dust with DDT, starting early spring. Clean up after frost.
Iris Leaf Spot	Oval brown spots with reddish borders on upper portion of leaves.	Spray with zineb. Clean up in autumn.
Soft Rot	Rot with yellow ooze, evil odor, often after borers.	Prevent borers. After division soak in mercuric chloride. Dry in sun.
Crown Rot	In crowded plantings. See Delphinium.	
IVY, BOSTON		
Japanese Beetles	Leaves eaten in lacy pattern.	DDT.
Virginia Creeper Leafhopper	Leaves whitened.	Spray with DDT.
Leaf Spot	Irregular brown spots, especially on new leaves in wet seasons.	Spray with ferbam-sulfur or copper, starting when leaves expand.
IVY, ENGLISH		
Bean, Ivy Aphids	Purple, brown or black lice thick on new growth.	Spray with malathion. Use an aerosol indoors.
Spider Mites	Leaves gray, mealy or webby.	Aramite or Kelthane.

HOST, PEST	DESCRIPTION	CONTROL
IVY, ENGLISH (cont'd)		
Scale Insects	Various species; important indoors	Weekly bath; malathion spray.
Dodder	Common on outdoor ivy.	See Chrysanthemum.
JAPANESE QUINCE		
Melon Aphid	Green, brown or black lice inside curled leaves.	Spray with malathion.
Japanese Beetle	Leaves skeletonized.	Sevin or DDT.
Hawthorn Lace Bug	See Hawthorn.	
San Jose Scale	Small, round, dirty gray shell with a nipple in center.	Dormant oil spray or malathion for crawlers.
Fire Blight	See Crab-apple.	
JUNIPER (including Red-cedar)		
Juniper Scale	Very small, round, dirty white on needles; shrubs yellow or gray.	Dormant 1 to 9 lime sulfur; malathion for crawlers.
Spruce Spider Mite	Shrubs grayish with webs.	Aramite or Kelthane
Bagworms	See Arbor-vitae.	
Juniper Webworm	Needles webbed by reddish-brown caterpillars.	Spray with DDT but add a miticide.
Cedar-apple Rusts	Brown galls put out orange horns in spring; spores infect Crab-apple, Hawthorn.	Cut off galls in winter.
Nursery Blight	Branches of seedlings and young ornamental trees die back.	Remove infected plants or parts; avoid wounds.
LARCH		
Bagworms	Often defoliate.	See Arbor-vitae.
Larch Sawfly	Olive-green larvae with black heads, tubercles, defoliate trees.	Spray with lead arsenate or DDT.
Woolly Larch Aphid	White woolly masses on needles.	Spray with lindane.
LARKSPUR, ANNUAL		
Delphinium Aphid	Red lice thick between flowerets.	Spray with malathion.
Cyclamen Mite	Buds black, plant deformed.	See Delphinium.
Crown Rot	See Delphinium.	
LILAC		
Oystershell Scale	Small, oyster-shaped, gray to brown shells on bark; common.	Dormant oil or lime sulfur; and malathion for crawlers.

HOST, PEST	DESCRIPTION	CONTROL
LILAC (cont'd)		
San Jose Scale	See Japanese Quince.	Dormant oil or lime sulfur; and malathion for crawlers.
Lilac Borer	Sawdust from holes in trunk; limbs dying. White caterpillar.	Spray or paint bark with DDT in late spring.
Giant Hornet	Very large wasp, banded with yellow, girdles limbs, which die.	Spray or paint bark with DDT in late summer.
Lilac Leaf Miner	Small yellow caterpillars mine, roll, skeletonize leaves.	Lead arsenate before leaves are mined, malathion later.
Powdery Mildew	White coating on foliage, common but not very injurious.	Spray with Acti-dione PM or ignore.
Lilac Blights	Leaves spotted, shoots, blossoms dying in wet weather.	Prevent crowding; prune for air circulation.
LILY		
Lily Aphids	Yellow and black lice infest buds, underside of leaves; transmit mosaic.	Spray with malathion.
Botrytis Blight	Oval, tan spots on leaves, which turn black, die up the stem in wet weather; gray mold.	Spray with bordeaux or other copper at 7 to 10-day intervals.
Mosaic and other Virus diseases	Leaves mottled light and dark green, plants stunted; spread by aphids.	Buy virus-free bulbs. Rogue diseased plants. Control aphids.
LUPINE		
Lupine Aphid	Large, green, covered with white powder, dense on flower stems.	Spray with malathion.
MAGNOLIA		
Magnolia, Tulip-tree Scales	Large, convex, brown, soft, on bark; copious honeydew with sooty mold.	Spray with malathion for crawlers in August.
MARIGOLD		
Japanese Beetles	Serious on African marigolds but not on French.	Spray with Sevin or DDT.
Botrytis Blight	Gray mold on fading flowers in wet weather.	Keep old flowers cut off.
MIMOSA or SILK-TREE		
Mimosa Webworm	Dark brown caterpillars, ½ inch, web and skeletonize foliage. Tree appears scorched. Two broods.	Spray with lead arsenate or DDT, June and August.
Mimosa Wilt	A killing disease from a soil fungus; very serious in South.	Use resistant varieties 'Tryon' or 'Charlotte.'

HOST, PEST	DESCRIPTION	CONTROL
MONKSHOOD		
Cyclamen Mite	Flowers deformed. See Delphinium.	
Crown Rot	See Delphinium.	
Verticillium Wilt	Stalks die one by one; vessels are black in cut stem.	No control. Remove infected plants.
MORNING-GLORY		
Morning-glory Leaf Miner	Serpentine mines in leaves.	Lindane or malathion.
Tortoise Beetles	Gold, or mottled, tortoise-shaped beetles eat foliage.	DDT, malathion, or lead arsenate.
MOUNTAIN-ASH		
Japanese Beetles	Skeletonize leaves.	Sevin, DDT, or lead arsenate.
Mountain-ash Sawfly	Green larvae with black dots ravage upper foliage in June.	DDT, lead arsenate, or malathion.
San Jose Scale	See Japanese Quince.	
Apple Tree Borer	Yellow larva in trunk; frass on bark, young trees killed.	Spray trunk with DDT in mid-May; repeat twice.
Fire Blight	See Crab-apple	
MOUNTAIN-LAUREL		
Rhododendron Lace Bug	Leaves stippled gray.	See Rhododendron.
Azalea, Rhododendron Borers	See Rhododendron.	
Mulberry Whitefly	Tiny, round, scale-like; jet black with white fringe.	Spray with malathion.
Leaf Spots, Blight	Gray or brown spots of blotches on leaves, especially in the shade.	Zineb or ferbam spray when buds break; repeat in 14 and 28 days.
NASTURTIUM		
Bean Aphid	Black lice densely congregated on stems, underside of leaves.	Hard to control. Spray with malathion or lindane.
OLEANDER		
Bean, Green Peach Aphids	Black or green lice on new growth.	Spray with malathion or nicotine sulfate.
Oleander Aphid	Yellow and black lice.	Spray with malathion or nicotine sulfate.
Oleander Scale	Pale yellow, circular, flat, on stems, leaves.	White-oil spray (Volck) in winter; malathion in summer.

HOST, PEST	DESCRIPTION	CONTROL
PACHYSANDRA		
Euonymus, Oystershell scales	Both common on this host.	See Euonymus, Lilac.
Leaf Blight	Large brown areas in leaves; pink spore pustules on stems; common after injury, as near a path.	Avoid excess moisture; remove leaves fallen down from trees. Spray with ferbam or bordeaux.
PALMS		
Scale Insects (many species)	Flat or convex, round or long, brown, white or purple, on leaves, stems; plants weakened.	Keep foliage washed off. Spray with Volck or malathion.
Palm Leaf Skeletonizer	Caterpillars feed under webs on leaves which turn brown and die.	Spray with DDT, lindane or chlordane every 2 months.
PANSY		
Garden Slugs	Large holes in leaves	See Hollyhock.
Botrytis Blight	Gray mold on plants too crowded and moist.	Remove diseased plants; reduce watering.
Violet Scab	See Violet.	
Anthracnose	Brown spots with black margins on leaves; flowers abnormal.	Spray with maneb or zineb.
PEONY		
Rose Chafer	Tan, long-legged beetles feed on blossoms.	Spray or dust with DDT or malathion.
Flower Thrips	Flowers ball or have brown edges to petals.	Difficult; try malathion or lindane.
Botrytis Blight	Common, serious. Young shoots rot, buds turn black, flowers blast. Minute black sclerotia on stems.	Cut stalks at ground level in fall; burn. Spray with zineb or ferbam in spring.
PETUNIA		
Potato Flea Beetle	Leaves riddled with tiny shot-holes.	See Forget-me-not.
Colorado Potato Beetle	Large holes in leaves.	Dust with DDT.
Tobacco Mosaic	Foliage mottled, leaves crinkled; virus spread by contact.	Do not smoke while handling seedlings. Rogue diseased plants.

HOST, PEST	DESCRIPTION	CONTROL
PHLOX		
Red Spiders	Leaves yellow, webby underneath.	Kelthane, Aramite, or Tedion spray.
Phlox Plant Bug	Orange and black bug makes pale spots in leaves.	Spray with malathion.
Stem Nematode	Plants stunted, stems swollen or cracked, leaves deformed, no flowers.	Remove infested plants. Treat soil with Nemagon.
Powdery Mildew	White, felty coating on leaves, stems, with numerous black dots.	Spray with Acti-dione PM or dust with sulfur.
PINE		
European Pine Sawfly	Gangs of green, light-striped larvae devour all mature needles.	Spray with DDT or lead arsenate in May.
Red-headed Pine Sawfly	Yellow larvae with black spots, red heads, feed in summer.	Spray with DDT or lead arsenate when noticed.
European Pine-shoot Moth	Crooked, tan tip, with pitch; brown caterpillar inside. Common on mugho and red pines.	Break infested tips into paper bag before moths emerge in June.
Nantucket Pine Moth	Larvae mine in buds and web needles.	Remove infested tips in winter; DDT in April.
Pine Bark Beetles	Small brown or black beetles make galleries under bark.	Keep vigorous with food, water; spray bark with DDT.
Pine Needle Scale	White, pear-shaped shells on needles; branches turn yellow.	Dormant lime-sulfur spray; malathion for crawlers.
Pine Bark Aphid	White fluffs on trunk, branches.	Spray with lindane.
Pine Webworms	Needles webbed near tips of branches by brown caterpillars.	DDT or malathion.
White-pine Weevil	Leader of white pine turns brown from grubs boring into base.	Cut off terminal below infested portion. Spray with DDT as buds swell.
Spittlebugs	Nymphs under frothy spittle; Scotch pine may be killed, others injured.	Spray with lindane, chlordane, or malathion.
White-pine Blister Rust	Swollen white blisters filled with orange spores on trunks; needles turn brown.	Remove alternate hosts— black currant for 1 mile, red currant and gooseberry for 300 yards. Paint cankers with Acti-dione BR.
PITTOSPORUM		
Aphids	Black lice on young shoots.	Spray with malathion.
Cottony-cushion Scale	Fluted white sacs on twigs, leaves; honeydew followed by sooty mold.	Spray with malathion or encourage lady beetles.

HOST, PEST	DESCRIPTION	CONTROL
POINSETTIA		
Oleander, Brown Soft, Cottony-cushion Scales	Yellow or brown flat scales or white cottony sacs.	Spray with malathion.
POPPY		
Bean, Peach, Melon Aphids	Black or green lice clustering on leaves, buds.	Spray with malathion.
Bacterial Blight	Black spots, gummy exudate, on leaves, flowers.	Destroy plants. Reseed in new location.
PRIMROSE		
Red Spiders	Leaves turn yellow with mealy webs; die down in midsummer.	Spray with Aramite or Kelthane; syringe with water.
Garden Slugs	Holes in leaves.	See Hollyhock.
Black Vine Weevil	Roots eaten by legless grubs.	Treat soil with lindane or chlordane.
Botrytis Blight	Gray mold on leaves, flowers, in moist weather.	Remove fading flowers. Spray with zineb or captan.
PRIVET (*Ligustrum*)		
Whiteflies	Very common in the South, with much sooty mold in honeydew.	Spray with malathion.
Privet Thrips	Hedges turn gray and dusty. Common in the North.	Spray with lindane or malathion.
Privet Mite	Foliage bronzed by red mites.	Spray with Kelthane.
White Peach Scale	Grayish scales at base of branches, which die.	Dormant oil spray.
Anthracnose, Dieback	Twigs of main stems die back with cankers at the base.	Cut out infected portions. California privet is somewhat resistant.
PYRACANTHA		
Hawthorn Lace Bug	Very common in South. Foliage gray.	Spray with lindane.
Pyracantha Webworm	Leaves, shoots webbed together.	DDT or lead arsenate.
Fire Blight	Branches die back.	See Crab-apple.
Pyracantha Scab	Black scabs on leaves, fruit; very disfiguring.	Spray with ferbam or zineb.
RHODODENDRON		
Rhododendron Lace Bug	Foliage in sun stippled yellow. Dark nymphs, lacy adults, brown flecks on under surface.	Spray with lindane, or DDT plus malathion.
Rhododendron Borer	Sawdust from holes in trunk, branches die.	Spray or paint trunks with DDT.

HOST, PEST	DESCRIPTION	CONTROL
RHODODENDRON (cont'd)		
Azalea Bark Scale	See Azalea.	
Black Vine Weevil	Leaves notched in from margins.	Chlordane or lindane in June.
Dieback, Wilt	Soil fungus rots roots and crown; twigs die back.	Avoid deep, moist mulch too close to stems.
Sunburn, Wind Burn	Brown areas or silvery spots in leaves.	Provide winter windbreak or spray with Wilt-Pruf.
ROSE		
Rose Scale	Round, dirty white scales on canes.	Dormant lime-sulfur spray.
Potato, Rose Aphids	Green or pink lice on buds, new shoots; flowers may be deformed.	Malathion, pyrethrum-rotenone or lindane in any combination spray.
Rose Leafhopper	Leaves stippled white in early spring, again in fall.	Spray as for aphids in spring; add DDT for fall brood.
Rose-slugs	Small, sluglike, green sawfly larvae skeletonize leaves.	Lead arsenate, methoxychlor, or DDT applied early.
Rose Chafer	Tan, long-legged beetle on early flowers.	Spray with DDT.
Japanese Beetles	Metallic green and copper, devouring flowers, foliage in summer.	Weekly combination spray with Sevin, DDT, lead arsenate or methoxychlor.
Spotted Cucumber Beetle	On flowers in late summer.	Weekly combination spray with Sevin, DDT, lead arsenate or methoxychlor.
Rose Leaf Beetle	Small, shiny green to blue beetle on buds, flowers, foliage.	Weekly combination spray with Sevin, DDT, lead arsenate or methoxychlor.
Rose Curculio	Red and black snout beetle drills holes in buds.	Spray or dust with DDT.
Flower Thrips	Minute, slender, inside petals; buds ball, turn brown. Thrips come to roses daily from grass and tree flowers. Control is difficult.	Cut off and burn infested buds. Lindane or malathion.
Rose Midge	Young buds turn black; all bloom ceases.	Spray bushes and soil with DDT.
Leaf-cutter Bee	Ovals and circles cut from leaf margins for nests.	No practical control.
Pith Borers	Small bees and sawflies tunnel in pith; yellow maggots.	Cut below infested portions.

HOST, PEST	DESCRIPTION	CONTROL
ROSE (cont'd)		
Rose Stem Girdler	Spiral mines around canes, which split.	Cut out swollen canes in spring.
Raspberry Cane Borer	Double row of punctures around cane; tip dies.	Cut out wilting shoots.
Red Spiders	Leaves yellow or gray, webby; bushes may defoliate.	Include Aramite, Kelthane or Tedion in combination spray.
Blackspot	Black spots with fringed margins over leaves which may turn yellow and drop. Spores splashed by rain or overhead watering.	Spray weekly with Phaltan, maneb, copper, or captan. Do not wet foliage late in day.
Powdery Mildew	White coating, curled leaves, deformed buds; prevalent in late summer.	Spray with Acti-dione PM, Karathane, copper, Phaltan or sulfur.
Rose Rust	Orange pustules on underside of leaves, black pustules in winter.	Spray with zineb.
Spot Anthracnose	Light spots with reddish borders on leaves, canes.	Spray as for blackspot.
Cercospora Leaf Spot	Tan spots with purplish borders, common in South.	Spray with maneb.
Brown Canker	Small white cane spots, with reddish margins grow together to large cankers.	Cut out diseased canes. Avoid a moist winter mulch.
Common Canker	Smutty areas near wounds, frost cracks or pruning stubs.	Cut canes just above a bud or leaf. Avoid wounds.
Crown Gall	Large, rough, irregular gall at crown or smaller galls on roots, from bacteria in soil.	Never plant a bush with a gall. If roses die with crown gall, change soil or wait 2 years to replant.
ROSE-OF-SHARON		
Cowpea Aphid	Dark, numerous, at tips of branches.	Spray with malathion.
Japanese Beetles	On flowers, foliage.	Spray with Sevin.
SNAPDRAGON		
Cyclamen Mite	Leaves thick, curled, buds deformed.	Remove plants; spray others with Kelthane.
Snapdragon Rust	Brown pustules on underside of leaves yellow areas above.	Order resistant varieties or spray with zineb.
SNOWBALL (*Viburnum*)		
Snowball Aphid	Black lice inside tightly curled new leaves; general on common snowball.	Substitute Japanese varieties or spray with malathion as buds break.

HOST, PEST	DESCRIPTION	CONTROL
SPIREA		
Spirea Aphid	Green lice dense on new tips.	Malathion or lindane.
SPRUCE		
Eastern Spruce Gall Aphid	Pineapple-shaped galls at base of Norway spruce twigs open to release aphids in midsummer.	Spray with lindane in April and/or late summer.
Cooley Spruce Gall Aphid	Elongated galls at tips of blue spruce. Douglas-fir is alternate host.	Cut off galls before opening. Spray with lindane or malathion.
Spruce Spider Mite	Needles gray, cobwebby; trees unhealthy.	Spray with Kelthane or Aramite.
Bagworms	See Arbor-vitae.	
Spruce Budworm	Terminals killed by reddish-brown caterpillars. Needles webbed, buds eaten.	Lead arsenate or DDT as growth begins.
Spruce Canker	Lower branches dying, often oozing pitch.	Avoid wounds. Remove diseased branches but not when wet.
TULIP		
Tulip Bulb Aphid	Powdery white or grayish aphids common on stored bulbs.	Dust with lindane before storing.
Green Peach, other Aphids	Transmit virus diseases.	Malathion or lindane.
Botrytis Blight, Fire	Plants stunted, leaves blotched, buds blasted, flowers spotted; gray mold and general blighting.	Plant new bulbs in new location. Spray with ferbam or zineb. Remove fading flowers.
Cucumber Mosaic, Lily Viruses	Foliage streaked or mottled, flowers broken in color.	Do not grow near cucumber, gladiolus, lilies.
VIOLET		
Garden Slugs	See Hollyhock.	
Red Spiders	See Primrose.	
Violet Scab	Red spots with white centers progress to raised tan scabs on leaves, stems.	Remove and burn infected foliage. Spray with maneb or zineb.
VIRGINIA CREEPER		
Virginia Creeper Leafhopper	Foliage stippled white in late summer, autumn.	Spray with DDT.
Japanese Beetles	Lacelike holes in foliage.	Sevin or DDT.
Eight-spotted Forester	Foliage eaten by white caterpillars with orange bands, black spots.	DDT or lead arsenate.

HOST, PEST	DESCRIPTION	CONTROL
WILLOW		
Oystershell, other Scales	Common on pussy willow.	See Lilac.
Aphids	Black lice prevalent on weeping willow.	Malathion or lindane.
Willow Leaf Beetle	Blue-black sluglike larvae skeletonize, small metallic blue beetles eat holes.	Lead arsenate or DDT.
Poplar and Willow Borer	Trunks girdled, branches knotted by small grubs.	Spray trunk, branches with DDT.
YEW *(Taxus)*		
Taxus Root Weevils	New shrubs may die from grubs imported in soil from nursery. Adult weevils notch foliage.	Spray soil and lower foliage when adults appear (usually June).
Taxus Mealybug	White, cottony bugs covering interior of bush.	Spray with malathion very thoroughly.
Cottony Taxus Scale	Small, brown, with white, fluted egg mass.	Dormant oil and/or malathion for crawlers.
ZINNIA		
Japanese Beetle	Feed on flowers, foliage.	Sevin or DDT.
Powdery Mildew	White coating in late summer.	Acti-dione PM spray.

25

Gardening in Your Own Region

In the previous chapters of this book you have been given the basic principles of gardening—what, where and how to plant, and other necessary information on how to beautify your grounds. Yet within the broad expanse of our 50 states, we naturally have great extremes of climate, altitude, sequence of seasons and other controlling factors. Primarily, of course, one must reckon with the frost and frost-free zones, which have been noted throughout the text. But that is not all. Rainfall, soil conditions and general climate differ widely in these areas. This chapter aims to tell you how to apply to your own region the principles set forth in the earlier chapters.

The information has been prepared by experts in each area. Every one of them has had years of practical experience, loves plants, and has worked with and advised beginning gardeners. If some suggestions differ slightly from the general advice given in the main body of the book, it is because there are many ways to garden successfully!

Charts or tables of what-blooms-when have been added to help you plan for all-season garden beauty. They are in condensed form, to serve as the simple framework upon which you can elaborate.

This chapter, therefore, in separate sequences deals with the special conditions in The Northeast and Midwest in one section; The Upper South and The Deep South in the next; The West, which is defined as the Intermountain and Plains region and The Southwest; and finally, the region generally called The Pacific Coast, which is divided into The Northwest, Northern California and Southern California. If you live in any one of these various regions, the information and tables will be invaluable to you.

Regional Calendar of
What To Do Month-by-Month

🍁 The North

The Northeast—by Dorothy Ebel Hansell, former Editor, *The Garden Journal*, New York Botanical Garden, New York City

The Midwest—by Eleanor B. McClure, Editor, *The National Gardener*, Horticultural Writer, *Missouri Botanical Garden Bulletin*

JANUARY

Northeast

Use your discarded Christmas tree, and others, to protect choice plants from winter weather. You can buy Christmas trees for practically nothing after the holidays. Alternate freezing and thawing can heave plants out of the ground, especially those which have shallow roots. This can cause considerable injury or loss. Boughs of spruce, pine, hemlock and cedar provide good protection for perennials and low evergreens. But wait to apply the covering until you are sure that the ground is really frozen. The date varies from one area to another, and also from one winter to another. Some years the ground is frozen hard by mid-December, and other years not until late January.

Sun and strong winds may cause damage toward the end of the month—and into February and March. It is a good plan to protect recently planted evergreens with a burlap screen. Or you can use old Christmas trees to provide the screening; place them around and among the evergreens. Also it is well to wrap the trunks of newly planted young trees with burlap to prevent their bark from cracking.

Remove snow from evergreens, shaking the branches gently or tapping them lightly with a bamboo lawn rake or a house broom. But do not attempt to remove ice if it forms— let it melt.

Attract birds to your garden by keeping

feeders well supplied with mixed bird seed and by hanging suet racks. Providing food is most important when the ground is covered with snow.

House plants should be given a little extra care. The furnace runs to keep you warm and comfortable, but the temperature of 70 to 72° and the dry air are not kind to most plants. (For ways to increase humidity, and to water plants correctly, see the chapter on indoor gardening.) Spraying leaves with room-temperature, clear water once or even twice a day helps your plants endure the winter discomfort. Occasionally stand the pots in a sink or bathtub overnight, in 2 or 3 in. of water. In this way they will get a thorough watering and the surface of the soil will not pack, as happens when potted plants are watered too frequently from the top.

You can get a foretaste of spring by forcing branches of fruit trees and flowering shrubs—crab-apple, spirea, forsythia and pussy willow. (See the chapter on how to pick flowers.) Forsythia takes about 4 weeks to be forced into bloom if you start it in late January.

On long winter evenings, pursue the pleasant pastime of "fireside gardening" by browsing through catalogues of seedsmen, nurserymen and plant specialists and by reading good books and periodicals on gardening and landscaping. If this is your first year of gardening, you had better select the well-known varieties of plants, which can be counted on to perform satisfactorily, for the major part of your seed and plant orders.

Midwest

This is the season for fireside gardening—reading books, thumbing through garden catalogues, and making plans for the coming year. Seed and plant orders should be sent

away soon. List these in a garden record book. As the season progresses, add planting dates, time of bloom or harvest, and a record of performance.

A second important step: Prepare a good over-all plan of the entire home property, showing buildings, walks, drives and existing plantings. Then review the whole planting with a critical eye, remembering that it is easier to do this now, while trees and shrubs are bare of foliage. Check to see whether each tree, shrub and evergreen contributes to the total effect or at least performs some function. Perhaps some should be moved, or even discarded. Others may need pruning or shaping. Finally, study the over-all plan, and sketch in any new plantings needed to enhance the garden picture. This could well be a long-range program, divided into projects for different years. Decide on the project to complete this coming year.

It is wise to check plantings and see that everything has adequate protection, for major damage can and often does occur in January. Discarded Christmas trees can be made to serve a useful purpose, as suggested previously for the Northeast; also they may be used for the protection of evergreens in foundation planting and elsewhere.

Snow from walks and drives should never be shoveled onto nearby plants. Instead of using salt on paved areas, try a sprinkling of chemical fertilizer, or use sand or wood ashes —materials that are not injurious to plants.

Evergreens and trees that have been damaged by ice may need first-aid treatment. First prune off broken branches. Then, if it is necessary, use a splint or brace to straighten the top of an upright yew or juniper. Taller trees can be pulled erect with guy wires attached to the house or to stakes in the ground. Thread the wire through a piece of old garden hose at the point where there is pressure on the trunk of the tree.

FEBRUARY

Northeast

If you did not take care of your tools properly when you put them away in the fall, better do so now. Rubbing linseed oil or furniture wax over wooden handles gives them a protective coating; they are less likely to become rough and splintery.

Continue to force branches of flowering trees and shrubs for a touch of spring indoors.

Examine your winter protective covering. It should not be removed, but see that it is not packed down and preventing air circulation. If it is quite solidly packed, lift it up a little and then let it fall back lightly.

If any perennials have been heaved out of the ground by frost action, push them gently but firmly back into the soil, adding more soil if necessary to cover their roots fully.

Unless your spring-flowering trees and shrubs were neglected last year—not pruned and therefore overgrown—they should not be pruned at this time. Wait until they have finished flowering. However, if their branches are tangled and criss-crossed, you should prune them, sacrificing some of this spring's floral display to restore their well-being.

Trees and shrubs which flower late in summer may be pruned on a balmy springlike day this month or early next month. Cutting out the older wood will make room for the new stems to develop and grow lustily.

House plants are entitled to the same attention this month that they received last month. Continue to water and feed them regularly, syringe to remove dust from their foliage (you can use a damp cloth to wipe the dust from large leaves), and pick off dead leaves. The last of February, cut the geraniums back to 6 or 8 in. New side shoots will start.

If you are interested in growing annual flowers from seed, you should now sow petunia, snapdragon and verbena indoors. They require a longer period in which to germinate and grow to outdoor-planting size than do other annuals.

Midwest

During warmish days in late winter many deciduous trees and shrubs can be pruned. The most drastic cutting and shaping should be done while the plants are dormant, since summer pruning tends to inhibit growth.

Young shade trees are best shaped while they are in the young, formative stage. Lower branches can be removed to provide more head room. A weak crotch (where 2 branches make a sharp, narrow V) can be corrected by cutting off one branch. The bark will quickly cover these small wounds and the tree can develop the desired symmetrical shape.

Large trees that might be a hazard during a storm need a health check. Dead branches should be removed, and weak crotches cabled or braced (best done by a professional). Suckers and water sprouts (long, twigless whips) should be cut from the trunk and main branches of larger flowering trees. In the lower Midwest (Zone 6) it is time to prune fruit trees, grapevines and other small fruits.

While spring-flowering shrubs are usually pruned after their flowering season, this is a good time to trim tired shrubbery and neglected climbing roses. Now, while there is no foliage, it is easier to see the architecture of the plant and to untangle the branches. Dead branches (which will look brown beneath the bark) should be cut off, along with about ⅓ of the largest remaining ones. If possible, avoid cutting back branch tips that are scheduled to bloom in the spring.

Summer-flowering shrubs (abelia, caryopteris, crape-myrtle and chaste-tree) can be cut back severely. Branches of rose-of-sharon, hardy hydrangeas and hypericum can be shortened by about ⅓.

In Zone 6, indoor seed sowing may begin this month, starting with slow-growing annuals such as petunias and snapdragons; biennials like Canterbury bells and foxglove; and such perennials as bellflowers, columbines, coreopsis, delphiniums, pinks, lupines, Shasta daisies, hardy alyssum, evergreen candytuft and rock garden plants.

MARCH

Northeast

Toward the end of this month, or a little earlier, if you are really sure the frost is gone from the ground, you can become active outdoors in the garden. March is unpredictable, so it pays to be a little cautious.

Remove protective covering gradually from shrubs and perennials, preferably on an overcast or cloudy day.

Before you start digging soil, be sure that it is dry enough; it should crumble when you squeeze some lightly in your hand. If it becomes lumpy when you do so, it is not yet in working condition.

Get all spring pruning completed this month, including roses. Some rosarians have a saying, "When forsythias bloom, roses are pruned."

This is a good time to shear a hedge into shape. Doing it early means that the cut ends will be concealed by new growth before too long.

Lawn care is a "must." Fertilizer should be applied before the grass begins to grow. If there are poor spots, reseed them after loosening the soil, liming and fertilizing.

Pre-emergence crabgrass killers or herbicides (obtainable as brand-name dusts and sprays) can be applied in March and again in April as may be necessary. They will help to control crabgrass in your lawn, even if weeds run rampant in your neighbor's.

When perennials have grown 2 to 3 in. above ground, about the last of March, it is time to give them some fertilizer. Spread this over the soil, then cultivate it in carefully so as not to disturb near-the-surface roots.

If any perennials have become too large, you should lift, divide and replant them. Select young, healthy divisions, discarding the older, inner parts of the clumps. Peonies, however, should not be divided or transplanted so long as they flower freely; they resent disturbance.

Pansies can be set out as soon as the ground is workable. They will give more bloom over a longer period if you pick the flowers regularly.

Sow seeds of gaillardia, salvia, marigold and zinnia indoors, and also seeds of petunia, snapdragon, stock and verbena if you did not get these sown in February.

Start tuberous-rooted begonias and caladiums indoors.

Do not neglect dormant spraying—with a miscible oil preparation or one of the new all-purpose sprays—on fruit trees, flowering cherry, crab-apple, hawthorn, mountain-ash, lilac and other shrubs. This should be done before leaf buds open.

House plants need repotting at this time if they appear to be pot-bound; that is, if their roots are crowded and filling the pot. On plants which do not need to be repotted, remove some of the surface soil, being careful not to damage the root system, and replace it with fresh potting mixture.

When side shoots appear on the geraniums which were cut back last month, repot them in larger pots.

You can now sow radish and lettuce seeds and plant onion sets outdoors.

Midwest

In the lower Midwest, lawn work can be

started as soon as the ground firms enough to make a good walking surface. Dead grass should be raked out or removed with a vertical cut mower. Then feed the lawn.

Crabgrass-control chemicals can be applied at the same time, but be sure to follow the manufacturer's directions! Since controls inhibit sprouting of bluegrass seed, major seeding should be deferred until fall. Worn spots can be reseeded, but crabgrass controls should not be applied to those areas.

The litter of twigs, leaves and grass raked from the lawn can be spread as a mulch beneath evergreens and shrubs, or it may be added to the compost pile. Groundcovers should be raked to remove litter. Vines of euonymus and ivy should be clipped to produce low, dense branching.

When euonymus buds begin to swell (about a week or so before they leaf out) it is time to spray with winter oil, which controls the pesky euonymus scale. At the same time spray pachysandra and shrub roses and add lime sulfur for a dormant spray on fruit trees. The oil spray is best applied on a sunny day when the temperature is between 45 and 60°.

It is wise to check plants of columbine, day-lily, iris and other perennials which may have been partly heaved out of the ground. Instead of trying to reset them, just cover the exposed roots (but not the crown of the plants) with rich, leafy compost or a very light soil mix. Protected this way, the roots will anchor themselves again, pulling the plants to the proper level.

Remove winter protection this month. Do the job in easy stages for any new shoots that have grown beneath the cover will be vulnerable to sun, wind and sudden freezes.

Soon after new growth starts on roses and perennials, a fungicide-insecticide can be sprayed on their canes or crowns and the soil surrounding them.

Most plants appreciate a good meal at this season, since roots have been hard at work long before the new leaves appear. Use a balanced fertilizer applied at the rate of 4 lb. per 100 sq. ft. for flower beds, shrubbery borders, trees and evergreens. Acid-loving plants, such as azaleas and rhododendrons, should have a special camellia-azalea fertilizer, or a 50-50 mix of powdered sulfur and iron sulfate.

Plant bare-root trees, shrubs and roses as soon as possible, before new growth starts. Balled or canned evergreens are best planted early, too.

New flower beds and vegetable gardens should be dug as soon as the soil is workable. Manure or compost should be spaded under, along with balanced chemical fertilizer and superphosphate (1 lb. per 100 sq. ft.). By mid-March it is often possible to plant cornflower, larkspur and poppy right in the bed where they are to bloom. Leaf lettuce, spinach, carrots, peas, Irish potatoes, onion sets, radishes, kale and greens can go into the vegetable garden. Start these vegetables indoors: tomato, leaf lettuce and eggplant. These flowers also should be started inside: ageratum, alyssum, nicotiana, salvia, aster, calendula, cockscomb, pink, annual phlox and scabiosa.

In the upper Midwest: Although March often brings a few very warm days, do not rush to uncover bulb and perennial beds. Just loosen the mulch a little. Fruit trees, grape vines, deciduous trees and shrubs can be pruned (see February). It may be possible to feed or renovate the lawn this month, but extensive repair work should wait until soil is workable in April. To control cankerworm, spray the trunks of shade trees with either DDT or lead arsenate. Use a follow-up spray 10 days later.

In the far North: Even though it may be wintry, seeds of hardy annuals and perennials can be planted indoors about March 15. This is also a good time to take geranium slips and start tuberous begonias.

APRIL

Northeast

You can still plant dormant rose bushes and have them come into bloom this season. Later plantings should be done with container-grown plants. Container-grown roses, and flowering shrubs also, can be planted even when they are blooming. Give established roses a liberal feeding.

If, for appearance's sake, you cleared away leaves from rhododendrons, azaleas, mountain-laurel and andromeda (*Pieris*), spread a mulch of peat moss, oak leafmold or wood chips around them to keep their roots cool. Mulching also reduces weeding and can be used, not only among broad-leaved evergreens but also among other evergreen and deciduous shrubs.

Examine beds and borders which contain perennials. Chrysanthemums, hardy asters, phlox and others which flower late in summer or early fall may need to be divided. Pull apart the crowns, roots or tubers, discarding the inner worn-out portions and replanting the outer. Spring-flowering perennials can be transplanted now. But move the whole clump —do not divide until after they have flowered. Fertilizer can be spread and lightly cultivated in the soil around perennials.

In the vegetable plot, successive sowings of radishes, onions, lettuce and Swiss chard can be made. Carrots, kohlrabi and spinach are sown the latter part of the month. The last week of April, set out plants of broccoli, Brussels sprouts, cabbage and lettuce, which you may have started indoors or purchased from local suppliers.

You can put in a row of small divisions of chrysanthemums in the vegetable garden. These will grow into nice-sized clumps if you pinch them back several times, and can be used in early fall to set into vacant places in flower borders or among shrubs.

Prune forsythia and any other shrubs which have finished flowering. (See the chapter on pruning.)

Do not destroy the leaves of crocus, daffodils, tulips or other spring-flowering bulbs by taking too many when you pick the flowers, or by cutting them down with shears or lawn mower. Let the leaves turn brown and begin to wither before you remove them; they are making food for the bulbs.

Gladiolus corms may be planted in a sunny place, beginning the middle of the month. If planted deeply, 4 to 5 in., the flower stalks are more likely to remain erect without staking. Continuing to plant them at 2-week intervals until the middle of June will furnish a succession of gay blossoms for flower arrangements.

Seeds of the following annuals may be sown outdoors where they are to flower: sweet alyssum, candytuft, cornflower, gaillardia, California-poppy, love-in-a-mist, phlox. Unless you are raising them just for cutting, do not sow them in a straight row; they look much better in groups. Thin the seedlings to stand 4 to 6 in. apart so they will have room to make shapely plants.

Evergreens should be planted near the end of April, but can also be planted in May.

Move the tuberous-rooted begonias and caladiums, which you started last month, to a porch or coldframe so that they will harden off and be ready to move into the garden in late May.

Midwest

In the lower Midwest this is the big spring planting season. Bare-root trees, shrubs and roses should go into the ground by April 15. Even balled evergreens and trees are best planted early so that they can be established before hot weather.

Lift and divide chrysanthemums, hardy asters and Shasta daisies, discarding the hard, woody centers and replanting only strong, young shoots. Most spring-flowering perennials can be moved, if need be, although care should be taken to lift them with a generous ball of earth. Areas to be replanted may be renovated first, by digging in an inch or so of compost, rotted manure or peat moss, along with an application of chemical fertilizer and either superphosphate or bone meal.

When leaf buds begin to break on roses, it is time to do their spring pruning. Many evergreens too should be pruned at this time, just as new growth starts. Remove dead branches from hollies and prune tip branches to encourage new growth. Shape or shear yews and junipers.

Feed both old and new plants of roses and perennials with balanced chemical fertilizer. For rapid, sturdy growth, leaves and roots alike can be fed with a liquid fertilizer every week or 10 days. An all-purpose spray or dust should be used about twice a month, beginning when new growth starts. Irises should be sprayed with DDT to control the iris borer.

If the vegetable garden was started in March, second plantings can now be made of lettuce, spinach, carrots, greens and radishes. Asparagus, rhubarb and strawberries can be planted in early April. After the middle of the month, first plantings of green beans, sweet corn, lima beans and okra can be made. For early crops of tomatoes and cucumbers, try planting a few under paper or plastic plant protectors.

Seeds of cosmos, marigolds, zinnias and sweet alyssum may be started indoors. Cold-tolerant annuals and perennials that have been growing inside can be hardened off and moved into the garden later in the month. Starting in late April, make plantings of gladiolus at 2-week intervals. Cannas and dahlias can also be planted.

In the upper Midwest, gardening really gets under way this month, for with the exception of the far north, the frost usually goes out of the ground in early April. Lawn work can be completed as soon as possible, and deciduous plants should receive dormant sprays (see March).

After flower beds have been cleaned up, roses, perennials, trees, shrubs and evergreens may be fed with both chemical and organic fertilizers. When the soil is dry enough for digging (late April or early May in most areas), new beds can be prepared and old ones reconditioned. Bare-root roses, shrubs and trees can be planted or transplanted. After new leaves appear it is best to buy balled or container-grown stock rather than bare-root.

Mid-April is a good time for indoor seeding of such tender annuals as zinnias and marigolds, and vegetables like tomatoes and eggplants. Cannas and ismene can be started indoors.

MAY

Northeast

May is one of the most enchanting months of the garden year in the northeastern section of this country. Dogwoods, magnolias, azaleas and lilacs bear their floral displays. Tulips, moss-pink, wild sweet william, forget-me-nots, pansies, primroses, rock-cress and evergreen candytuft bring color to beds and borders, wall gardens and rock gardens.

This is the month to visit gardens—those of your friends, arboretums, botanical gardens, public parks and nurseries. You need to see what is being grown, to become acquainted with unfamiliar plants and to compare notes with other gardeners.

Keep a notebook to record plants or different plant combinations you want to try; garden gadgets or equipment you should acquire; new methods of insect, disease and weed control; the planting and blooming dates in your garden; the dates on which you sprayed or dusted for certain insect pests and diseases. All this will be helpful information for the years ahead.

Peonies should be watered thoroughly. They need plenty of moisture to produce flower buds. Also give them an application of a quick-acting fertilizer. Pinch off the side buds while they are still small, leaving the terminal flower bud on each stalk to develop into a good-sized bloom.

Remove withered flower clusters on lilacs, mountain-laurel and rhododendrons. This practice results in better flower production the following year. For details, see the chapter on pruning.

Seeds of the following annuals may be sown outdoors the middle of this month: balsam, calendula, coreopsis, marigold, nasturtium, nicotiana and zinnia. Toward the end of the month you will be able to purchase annuals in a wide variety by the dozen or by a whole flat at garden centers and nurseries. The plants set out then will bear flowers earlier than plants from seeds you sow outdoors now.

Thin your seedling annual flowers and vegetables before they crowd one another. The plants remaining in the rows will grow bigger and better.

If you have only a small vegetable garden, grow pole beans instead of bush varieties. They take up a little more space but yield more bountifully over a longer period. And they are easier to pick—no stooping.

Tuberous-rooted begonias and caladiums can be moved from porch or coldframe to the partially shaded position you have already chosen for them, when weather is settled.

Some years, a dry spell occurs in May, so do not neglect to water newly planted trees, shrubs and evergreens. A mulch of peat moss, leafmold or wood chips helps to keep the soil moist and weeds from growing.

House plants will benefit by being moved outdoors for the summer. Do it near the end of the month. African violets and their relatives, the episcias, may be moved to a porch which is covered and shaded, or kept indoors in a window that does not receive the sun's direct rays.

You can set out tomato plants the third week in May, but do not be in too great a rush. Plants can suffer a setback in unexpected cold weather, even from soil which has not really warmed up.

Dahlia tubers may be planted the third week of May.

Sow seeds of columbine, pink, forget-me-not, foxglove, hollyhock, pansy and other biennials, and short-lived perennials outdoors about the end of the month. Thin out the seedlings when the second pair of leaves have developed. Then transplant them to a section of the garden where they can grow until you are ready to place them in their permanent quarters early in the fall or next spring.

Midwest

In central and northern areas this is the busiest gardening month. The first task is to finish soil preparation so planting can be done as soon as weather permits. Bare-root roses, shrubs and trees should go into the ground in early May. Evergreens are also best moved before the new growth starts, but the planting season for balled and potted stock can continue many weeks.

Chrysanthemum, Shasta daisy, phlox and day-lily can be divided. New perennials can be planted. Seedling perennials and hardy annuals that were started in the house can be moved to the garden. Seeds of cold-tolerant annuals like candytuft, cornflower, larkspur and lobelia may be sowed outdoors. Early crops of lettuce, spinach, carrots, beets and radishes can go into the vegetable garden. Except for the far north, the first plantings of green beans, lima beans and sweet corn may be made in late May; and tomato and pepper plants can go into the garden.

The time to set most tender bedding plants and annuals outdoors is after the middle of May in the central Midwest, but it would be better to wait until after June 1 in the northern area.

Most plantings will respond at this season to a generous feeding program of balanced chemical fertilizers supplemented with helpings of compost or manure. It is also time to start the systematic spray or dust program on roses and perennials to control pests and disease. To control scale on pines and spruces, use a malathion spray when lilacs are in bloom, and spray again 10 days later. Apples, crab-apples, dogwoods and mountain-ash need 2 applications, the first of which may be timed with apple-petal fall.

Yews, junipers and other small evergreens should be sheared or trimmed this month. To promote dense growth, tip branches of hemlocks can be sheared. "Candles" of young pines can be shortened.

In the lower Midwest, gardeners are enjoying the show of iris, peony, poppy and a host of other perennials, along with the first bloom of roses. After May 1, the weather is usually settled enough to plant bedding plants in the garden. These, and other garden flowers, can be encouraged with 2 or 3 foliar feedings this month, and by deep irrigation amounting to at least 1 in. of water applied once a week during hot summer weather.

Buxom peonies usually need support this month, and so do skyscrapers like delphinium and hollyhocks. Pinch the tips out of chrysanthemums to encourage branching, and also annuals such as petunia, marigold and snapdragon. Clip off dead blooms and seed pods from perennials to produce bloom on side shoots. Cut back foliage of early low-growing flowers, such as pinks, evergreen candytuft and moss-pink, so that they will form tidy mats of green.

Do not allow tulips and daffodils to go to seed. Conceal their ripening foliage with fast-growing annuals, such as zinnia, marigold, aster or snapdragon for back of the bed, and an edging of sweet alyssum, ageratum, pygmy marigolds or dwarf zinnias. These shallow-rooted plants will not interfere with the bulbs but will provide needed shade.

Tender vegetables can be planted by May 15. For tomatoes and cucumbers, make "bushel-basket" holes and fill them with compost or well-rotted manure, topped with two or three inches of good soil. If the ground is dry, soak seeds of pole beans, lima beans and corn for a few hours and plant in furrows that have been thoroughly moistened.

Seeds of sweet alyssum, marigold and zinnia may be planted for use as late summer fill-ins.

To protect American holly from leaf miner and foliage diseases, use a combination spray of malathion or DDT and zineb, and repeat 10 days later. To catch the euonymus scale in the crawler stage, sprays of malathion should be repeated at weekly intervals for 3 or 4 weeks, starting in late May.

For lawns, plugs of Meyer zoysia may be started in sunny areas. But avoid bermudagrass like the plague!

JUNE

Northeast

This is the month of roses, if you have carefully pruned, cultivated, watered, fed, mulched, and sprayed or dusted! This attention must continue to assure healthy plants for next year.

Low-growing perennials that have finished their flowering should be cut back severely to induce new, compact growth. These include basket-of-gold alyssum, rock-cress, aubrieta, evergreen candytuft and moss-pink. You can use some of the young growth that you remove as cuttings.

Cuttings from house plants, perennials and shrubs can be started in a shaded coldframe or a lightly shaded and protected outdoor location.

As flowers on iris wither, remove them so that seed pods will not form.

Tulip bulbs planted in the fall may be left where they are or they may be dug after their leaves have turned yellow, then dried and stored in a cool, airy place until fall. Older bulbs—those 2 or 3 years old—should be dug, since they have deteriorated and their blooms in future years will be smaller and disappointing. You can plant their small offsets in rows in the vegetable garden and let them gradually grow into a larger size to replant in beds or borders. Most home gardeners, however, do better by buying new tulip bulbs every 2 or—at the latest—3 years.

If you must move tulips before the leaves have turned yellow, in order to set other plants in that space, lift the tulips complete with leaves, bulbs and all—very, very carefully. Replant them in a shady place. Water them well and allow the leaves to die down naturally before you dig and dry the bulbs for storage until fall.

Small spring-flowering bulbs, like glory-of-the-snow, crocus, grape-hyacinth, scilla and snowdrop, are left where they grow. They are not dug and replanted unless they become depleted or are lost to rodents. These small bulbs multiply well.

Watering is one of the most important tasks in June. Lawn, shrubs, perennials, annuals and vegetables all need adequate supplies. Do the job thoroughly, so that water goes down well into the soil—at least an inch —not just into the surface. No benefit is gained by surface sprinkling. Letting the sprinkler run a few minutes here and there, or playing the hose lightly as you move from spot to spot, does more harm than good.

Bedding plants, among them fuchsia, geranium, heliotrope and lantana, are set out this month. Timing varies from the last week in May through the first 10 days of June.

Gladiolus corms and dahlia tubers can be planted until the middle of June.

Annuals that can be started from seed early this month to produce late-season bloom include cosmos, marigold, moss-pink and zinnia.

Chrysanthemum plants need to be pinched back this month, removing about 3 in. of the growth made since they were set out.

Cultivating between rows of vegetables every week or 10 days is just as important as cultivating among flowers.

House plants summering outdoors should be sprayed with water weekly. Hit the underside of leaves as well as their top surface.

Midwest

In northern areas, this is the month of fabulous blooms. Tulips, moss-pink and early perennials are quickly followed by iris, columbines, poppies, peonies and roses, against a backdrop of flowering shrubs—lilacs, spirea and mock-orange. Window boxes have been filled, and most annuals and bedding plants set out, in early June. Potted roses may be planted this month, and annuals and perennials planted in bare spots in the perennial border. A little later, annuals may also be planted to hide the ripening foliage of bulbs.

Early June is a good time to move house plants to summer quarters where they can have some shade and be protected from wind.

Gladiolus can be planted at 2-week intervals to provide continuous bloom. Tomatoes can be set out in the far North. Successive crops of corn, green beans and limas can be planted.

Throughout the Midwest, June is a month for tidying up the garden and getting plants into readiness for the coming heat waves and drought. First, prune spring-flowering shrubs soon after they have finished blooming (by mid-June in the South, possibly mid-July in the North). Cut out dead and tired branches and shorten top growth to give a natural, shapely look.

Pinch chrysanthemums and keep annuals and perennials from going to seed. Continue the regular spray or dust program for roses and perennials. On gladiolus, use DDT to ward off thrips.

Mulches applied now help both garden and gardener through the difficult summer months. The ground should be moist when the mulch is put on. It should also be lightly cultivated first, though you must avoid damaging the plant's surface roots. To make up for possible nitrogen loss after the mulch is applied, spread a balanced chemical fertilizer on the soil around each plant, taking care to use a special azalea-camellia formula for acid-lovers such as azalea. A very light sprinkling of fertilizer may also be used on top of the mulch—or mix in 1 lb. of ammonium nitrate to 2 bu. of mulch.

In the southern Midwest, drought often starts in June, so be vigilant and start watering before the plants really suffer. Add at least 1 in. of water at one time (set a coffee can beneath the sprayer to serve as a gauge). It is best to water early in the day, for moisture toward evening encourages blackspot and other leaf diseases, which flourish in warm, damp, dark conditions. If necessary to water later, let the hose run all night, so that plants are kept cool as well as moist. Contrary to general belief, it is perfectly safe to water in full sunlight, provided the hose is left in one place for several hours, until soil and plants are thoroughly saturated.

Daffodils and other spring bulbs can be divided this month, and it is easier to replant at once than to store them over the summer. Except for a precious variety, save only the larger bulbs and discard the smaller ones. There is not much use in bothering with tulips, for they tend to peter out in a few years.

By late June, tips of broad-leaved evergreens, azaleas and *Pieris japonica* will have matured. These plants can be pruned and the clippings treated with rooting powder to make softwood cuttings. Cuttings may also be taken from hardy carnations, moss-pink, rock-cress and various varieties of evergreen candytuft that cannot be grown from seed. Yews and boxwoods can also be rooted now, but their cuttings should be treated with Hormodin No. 3. For instructions on growing plants from cuttings, see the chapter on starting plants.

This is the time to watch all plantings with an eagle eye. A drooping plant may be showing a need for water. Leaf discoloration may be the first sign of insect infestation or foliage diseases. Carry a paper bag with you so that you can collect and burn the first pest-infected leaves.

JULY

Northeast

Watering becomes an all-important garden chore, for July is a hot and all too often dry month. A thorough soaking once a week does the job much better than 2 or 3 light sprinklings.

Plastic soil soakers, perforated on one side, are good aids. They can be laid between rows of plants and among shrubs, with the perforated side down, thus watering soil without wetting foliage.

Do not cultivate the soil around shallow-rooted plants like azalea, rhododendron and blueberry. These plants are happiest when furnished with a mulch of oak leafmold, peat moss or wood chips.

Annuals making a show with their abundant blooms this month include pinks, nicotiana, calendula, snapdragon, stock, nasturtium, petunia, marigold, verbena and zinnia.

To keep annuals and perennials flowering freely over a long season, remove the flowers as they fade. Letting them go to seed reduces flower production.

Blooms on bush roses should be removed as they pass their prime. Giving the plants a little fertilizer at the same time will be beneficial. Climbers should be pruned when they finish flowering. For detailed instructions, see the chapter on roses. Dust or spray all roses regularly, but not when the temperature soars to the high 90's.

If a mature wisteria failed to bloom well, give it a good trimming, shortening the new shoots of the present season back to 3 or 4 nodes.

Feed peonies a 5-10-5 fertilizer after they flower, to boost their next year's bloom.

If bearded irises need dividing, do the job after they finish flowering. (See the chapter on perennials.)

Evergreen hedges, such as yew, arborvitae and hemlock, will need shearing this month if they are trained in a formal shape. Deciduous hedges also will likely need a clipping.

Water all evergreens thoroughly. Spray their foliage with water, too. This is one group of plants which can be watered late in the day to their advantage rather than detriment.

Cut back pansies and violas severely to encourage further flower production.

Seedlings of perennials and biennials are ready to be transplanted when they have developed 4 leaves and can be handled without difficulty. Do this task preferably on a cloudy day. If this is not possible, then keep the newly moved plants shaded. Water them thoroughly, and sprinkle lightly twice daily until they have recuperated from the shock.

Gladiolus need to be watered well as they come into flower.

Chrysanthemums should not be pinched back after mid-July. Giving them some 5-10-5 fertilizer or pulverized cow or sheep manure, and watering it well into the soil, will help them furnish a good fall show in your garden.

Crabgrass can be a problem this month. You should go after it with a specific crabgrass killer or weed by hand—and do so before it has a chance to go to seed.

You can still sow and plant for late crops in the vegetable garden. Bush beans take 55 to 60 days to mature, and sweet corn from 80 to 90 days, depending on the particular variety. A sowing of Chinese cabbage will give you a pleasing substitute for lettuce, which does not do well in northeastern summers.

Midwest

Garden chores can be held to a minimum during July heat waves. See that all new plantings have at least 1 in. of water each week, and do not neglect established gardens either.

Roses in northern-Midwest gardens should be fed at the end of the first bloom in early July. In the lower parts of the area a light mid-July feeding is in order—the last of the season—to give the plants a chance to harden off tissues in preparation for frost. Shrubs, trees and evergreens may be fed at that time. Supplimentary foliage fertilizers may also be used and continued into August. Although they take effect quickly, they feed for a very short time and thus do not encourage the late, soft growth that is vulnerable to freezes. Even shrubs and trees will benefit from a foliar spray, but they should have double-strength solutions.

Delphinium stalks should be cut back to produce new side shoots. Chrysanthemums should have their final pinching this month. Continue regular spraying and dusting for susceptible roses and perennials. Watch for signs of spider mites on both deciduous plants and evergreens as evidenced by grayish or yellowish mottling of upper leaf surfaces (although the pests are underneath). Spray with an insecticide containing malathion, or use Aramite.

In the upper Midwest, you may divide and transplant daffodils and other spring-flowering bulbs (See June).

In southern areas, it is time to plant cucumbers, pole beans and early-maturing corn for fall crops. To get them up quickly, drench the furrow with fertilizer solution and soak the seeds for a few hours before planting. Cover with an airy mix of compost, soil and perlite, and add pieces of brush to provide light shade.

AUGUST

Northeast

Maintenance of a garden is not as stimulating as getting things started in spring! However, the general appearance of your home grounds and the health of your plants demand that these less exciting tasks be carried out. Mow the lawn and water it deeply about once a week. Spray and dust to control insect pests and diseases. Pick off faded flowers so they will not go to seed. Trim back any annuals which have become "leggy" or invasive. Thin out plants in the rockery or wall if they have spread to occupy too much space.

A very pleasant job is that of making up your bulb order for fall planting. The list must be sent to your supplier without delay, for daffodils should be planted in late September or early October. Small bulbs such as glory-of-the-snow, crocus, grape-hyacinth, scilla and snowdrop can go into the ground when you plant the daffodils. Tulips do better if planted in late October, early November, or even early December.

Phlox needs ample water and some plant food while it is in flower. Remove blossoms as they fade. Otherwise you may find magenta or other undesirable colors showing up in your border, marring your color scheme.

Roses should not have any plant food from now on—it would encourage new growth which might not harden off before freezing weather.

Dormant roots of Virginia bluebell can be planted this month or even early in September. This flower's pink buds and clear blue flowers are charming when blooming among daffodils.

Orders for peonies should be placed now, so they will be delivered in time for planting early in September.

Dahlias should be fed and watered weekly. Keep the soil mounded and mulched around them.

Seeds of pansy, viola, primrose, columbine, hardy pink and other perennials may be sown in the coldframe. If this is your first year of gardening, you may not have a coldframe. It might be wise to consider acquiring one, either by purchase or by making it in winter when outdoor activity has abated.

It is time to plant evergreens. For instructions, see the the chapter on shrubs. If you move some from one position to another on your property, lift them with a large ball of roots and soil. Be sure to water them repeatedly all fall, for they should not face the rigors of winter dryness.

Your order for lilies should be placed now. You will receive most of the bulbs in time for fall planting—which is preferable to spring planting.

You can take cuttings of ageratum, coleus, fuchsia, geranium, lantana, sage, santolina and thyme, and start them under inverted Mason jars in the garden or in a coldframe. When they are of a size to be handled easily, pot them for wintering in a cool basement or porch for next year's planting out. Coleus, fuchsia, geranium and lantana will also make nice small house plants for a sunny window.

Removing some of the leaves around tomato fruits will help them to ripen—but do not expose them too much too soon.

Midwest

Northern gardens are bright with blooms of gay annuals and hardy phlox this month. Do not allow the phlox to set seeds. As elsewhere, self-sown seedling plants produce ugly magenta-colored flowers. Pinch excess buds from dahlias and chrysanthemums. Give extra food to gladiolus as their flower buds swell.

In all parts of the Midwest, late summer or early fall is a favorable time for moving or dividing many perennials. Crowded clumps of iris and day-lily may be dug and divided, along with such spring bloomers as columbines, Virginia bluebells, bleeding-heart and lily-of-the-valley. Peony, oriental poppy and bearded iris can be ordered now for fall delivery.

To combat red spider mites, use 2 malathion sprays, spaced about 3 days apart. Malathion can be used on euonymus, too, to catch scale insects which may be in the crawler stage. Spray the new growth of American hollies with a zinc spray, such as zineb.

Among perennials which may be started from seed in August are delphinium, primrose, pansy, columbine, coreopsis and Shasta daisy. Plant in a special bed where they can be kept shaded and watered.

In southern areas, watering is often the most important task in August. Take care of the new plantings first, and then old-timers. Skip the lawn, for when bluegrass goes dormant, watering merely encourages crabgrass. During prolonged drought, lawn areas may be given a good soaking (at least 12 in. deep) once or twice a month.

In mid-August, fall crops of spinach, carrot, beet and leaf lettuce can be planted. Turnips can be broadcast to provide succulent greens and crisp roots.

SEPTEMBER

Northeast

Cooler evenings should revive your gardening enthusiasm. This is the time to make new lawns or remake old ones. Established lawns should be fertilized, watered, and grass seed planted over any poor spots. Lower the setting of the blades on your mower to 1½ in. from now until grass stops growing.

Plant bulbs of daffodils as soon as you receive them. Mix bonemeal well into the soil at the bottom of holes. The small miscellaneous bulbs may be planted either at the same time as the daffodils or later in the month.

You can put several bulbs of paper-white narcissus or the yellow 'Soleil d'Or' in a bowl filled with pebbles and water, for indoor flowering. Growth will start a few weeks after the bulbs have been planted.

Roses should have no more cultivating or feeding this season. Water them only if there is an unexpected dry spell. But continue to be on the alert for blackspot and mildew, spraying or dusting, and removing any infected leaves, stems and old blooms. Destroy the infected material—do not put it on the compost pile.

If the grouping of plants in your perennial border did not please you, you can shift them around now. Divide any which have grown too large. Before you do the actual work, take time to sketch a plan showing where you want the plants to go according to height, flowering period and color.

New perennials should be ordered without delay, so that you will receive the plants in time for planting the latter part of this month or early in October.

Plant Madonna and other lilies as soon as you get them. Be sure to plant them at the proper depth. Madonna lilies must be only 1 to 2 in. below the surface, while the others are covered with 4 to 5 in. of earth.

Chrysanthemums that you have been growing in a row in the vegetable or cutting garden can now be moved into the perennial border for autumn display. It is wise to do this before buds begin to open. Do the transplanting preferably on a cloudy day. Water the plants promptly and thoroughly. They can be held erect by using peony supports—double hoops of wire—or you can tie the plants to stakes with Twist-ems.

Lily-of-the-valley (poisonous) can be transplanted this month. Separate the crowns and plant them about 3 in. apart each way. Such dividing needs to be done only every 3 or 4 years if the plants are healthy and flowering well. Dig gladiolus corms when the foliage turns yellow. Lay them in the sun to "cure" before storing in a cool, dry basement.

Lift caladium, dahlia and tuberous begonia after the first frost; dry and store them in a cool place for winter. Dahlias should be dug and not pulled; pulling is likely to break the necks of the tubers and then they will not grow. In fact, it is not a good idea to pull up any plant.

All house plants that you kept outside during the summer should be moved into the house. Repot those that have outgrown their pots and give all an application of fertilizer.

Midwest

Early fall is an important planting season in all parts of the Midwest. Although the actual timing will vary with the season and the availability of nursery stock, early planting is best for everything from bulbs to evergreens. Plants should have time to put down roots before the first deep freeze.

In the central and northern areas of the

Midwest, it is important to plant evergreens as soon as they are available, for the plants are closest to dormancy in early September. Early fall planting is recommended for balled shrubs and trees, too, for freezes often come early. It is better to wait until spring for bare-root roses, and for such shrubs and trees as weigela, euonymus, barberry, Russian-olive and fruit trees.

Throughout the Midwest, Labor Day marks a favorable time to start new lawns, or to renovate old ones. In the southern areas it will be necessary to thin out those dense mats of crabgrass with a rake, or better still, a contour mower that chops through the weeds without damaging bluegrass. Lawns should be fed with a balanced chemical fertilizer and reseeded with a good quality bluegrass. Newly seeded areas should be kept moist for the first few weeks, but all lawns will benefit if they have abundant moisture during this important growing season.

Old perennial flower beds can be rejuvenated now and new ones made at this time, for the ground is usually in fine, workable condition. Early planting of young seedlings or divisions is desirable, to give them time to grow and develop into blooming-size perennials next year. This is a good time to add some of the new hybrid irises, day-lilies or peonies. A few balled or potted chrysanthemums can be planted for immediate color, since they move easily when they are in flower.

Give a final feeding to chrysanthemums, hardy asters and dahlias as their flower buds form. These flowers should also have ample moisture. But do not give too much water to roses, azaleas and other woody plants that must harden their stems and branches in preparation for frost.

House plants should be brought inside before the nights get too cold. It is best to repot them and clean them up a week or two before they are to be moved.

Gladiolus should stay in the ground until the foliage turns yellow. Do not let the cold nip tuberous begonias or amaryllis, but cannas and dahlias can remain until their foliage is cut by heavy frost.

For an extensive bulb planting, make a bed at least 12 in. deep. Extra soil is needed over the bulbs in the north as a protection against extremely low temperatures. In southern areas, deep planting tends to keep the bulbs from splitting up or dividing, so that tulips may not peter out, and daffodils may be grown for several years before they must be lifted and replanted. Small bulbs like crocus, snowdrop, grape-hyacinth and scilla can also be planted a little deeper in a good bed. September is the best time to plant small bulbs and also daffodils. But wait for October to plant tulips and hyacinths.

OCTOBER

Northeast

Chrysanthemums are the pride of October, though several fine varieties come into flower the latter part of September. You have a wide choice of type — pompon, single, spider, show, etc. There are two groups generally considered: the tall-growing, which bears exhibition-type blossoms; and the low-growing, which carries sprays. Sometime this month you should visit chrysanthemum shows in your locality, so that you will be able to make an intelligent selection from the many varieties available.

When frost puts an end to chrysanthemum bloom, cut the plants to within 4 in. of the ground. If they have been growing in well-drained soil, they can remain there for the winter. If the soil is inclined to be wet and heavy, plants should be lifted and carried over winter in a coldframe.

Roses should be ordered now for planting later this month or early in November. Fall planting of dormant shrubs is recommended for the northeastern area, except in the extreme northerly sections where zero or sub-zero temperatures may occur. When the dormant plants arrive, they should be soaked in water for an hour and then immediately planted. If their permanent site is not ready, you should "heel in" the plants temporarily in a trench.

Plant tulip bulbs the latter part of October. Where moles, field mice or chipmunks are a nuisance, it may be worth the effort to plant the bulbs in wire cages.

When you rake leaves, save, do not burn them. Add them to the grass clippings and refuse from the vegetable and flower borders —disease-free, of course—that you have been collecting all season for the compost pile.

October is an excellent time of year for planting most deciduous trees and shrubs. They have a period to get established before really cold weather sets in, and you have more opportunity for such work than you do in the spring rush.

If you have a coldframe, you can pot bulbs of crocus, daffodil, hyacinth and tulip and keep them in the frames for 6 or 8 weeks while they are making good roots. Then take them into the house to bloom, shading them from direct sunlight at first and gradually giving them full light.

You can make a sowing of seeds of the Swiss giant pansies where they are to flower — in well-drained soil — and cover them lightly with straw or salt hay after the first hard frost. You will have nice flowers early next spring.

Hill up the soil around the base of rose bushes just before the ground freezes hard. It is better to bring in soil than to take it from among rose bushes, for in so doing their roots might be exposed—and that must be avoided.

It is clean-up time. Nothing should be left in flower beds, shrub borders or vegetable gardens which might harbor insects, disease or rodents. Any insect-infested or diseased plant material should be burned. Put all else on the compost pile. Paths and driveway should be raked free of leaves as well as the lawn. Garden furniture and garden equipment should be moved indoors, fences mended and painted, and any construction work such as new paths, rock wall, terrace or coldframe started.

Midwest

In the upper Midwest, balled shrubs and trees may be planted this month, but be sure that each plant is watered well and protected with a heavy mulch of oak leaves, manure, ground corncobs or marsh hay. Plants set out last spring should also have a heavy mulch. Tulips planted this month will need protection, too. Toward the end of October, rose bushes should be loosely tied (to prevent whipping in the wind). Both bush roses and climbers should have earth mounded around their base. (See the chapter on roses.)

In southern areas of the Midwest, October is a busy planting season. Since changing leaf color in mid-month usually marks the beginning of dormancy, most deciduous shrubs and trees can safely be moved at this time. Larger trees and evergreens can be transplanted during favorable periods of winter weather as long as the ground surface is firm and the frost has not penetrated too deep. Azaleas, American holly, *Pieris japonica* and other broad-leaved evergreens can be planted in October, but should go into the ground as soon as possible to reduce the hazards of winter burn. Spring is a more favorable planting season for the oriental hollies and for Southern magnolia. Some gardeners also prefer spring planting for deciduous magnolias, dogwoods, sweet-gums and birches.

Spring-flowering bulbs may be planted this month, and even into November if the weather holds. This is the last chance to set out peonies, iris, day-lilies and other perennials, but they must be protected with 2 to 4 in. of organic mulch.

Although frost dates vary in the Midwest, flowers and vegetables can often be protected from the first severe frost to provide 2 or 3 more weeks of enjoyment. When a freeze is forecast it may be wise to capture some of the day's warmth by covering plants in late afternoon with newspapers, corrugated boxes, baskets or even old quilts.

Green tomatoes will ripen fairly well when individually wrapped in pieces of newspaper and stored in a dark place.

Plants of calendula, impatiens and other annuals can be potted and grown on a sunny window sill.

Water all permanent plantings during periods of drought, for they need abundant moisture as winter approaches.

Roses should be sprayed or dusted as long as they are in active growth. Although fall planting of roses is not recommended for this area, beds may be prepared now for early spring. Dig in manure, leaves, grass clippings or peat moss, along with chemical fertilizer and superphosphate, leaving the soil rough over the winter.

Preparations for next year's vegetable garden are properly started in the fall, to insure an early spring start. Dig in leaves and garden remnants which can be composted right in the soil, along with animal manures, etc. Balanced chemical fertilizer should be added. Leave the ground rough over the winter, but select one well-drained area and rake and level it so that it is about 6 in. above the rest of the garden. Cover it with a thick layer of leaves and brush and it will be ready for that earliest sowing of lettuce, spinach and onions.

Among hardy annuals that can be planted at this season in the beds where they are to flower next spring are cornflower, larkspur, poppy, cosmos and calendula. In the cold-frame or a protected seedbed, try sweet william, pink, pansy, snapdragon and English daisy.

NOVEMBER

Northeast

The early days of this month permit doing some of the tasks either left undone or unfinished last month. Tulip bulbs can still be planted. So can certain lilies, roses and deciduous trees and shrubs. The removal of debris continues so that the garden is left in a tidy condition when outdoor activity ceases. This includes taking leaves out of gutters and drain pipes; water falling heavily from clogged gutters can play havoc with foundation plantings beneath them.

Later this month you may find time to oil or grease tools before putting them in their winter quarters. And do try to send the lawn mower and other power equipment for repair—if that is called for—or for sharpening. In the spring the shop has usually more work than it can handle.

If you label bulbs and late-starting perennials with clearly seen markers, you will not be so likely to disturb them when you work around them early next spring. And labeling is a good habit to acquire so you will know just what plants you have and where. It is not easy to recall every variety from memory.

Young perennials raised from seed during the summer should be moved to the cold-frame for winter. If you do not have a cold-frame, cover them with straw or salt hay when the ground is frozen. Better still, make a temporary coldframe over them by enclosing them within boards and laying sash on the boards. Remember to ventilate during warm spells by lifting the covering.

Along with other equipment, store tomato and bean poles under cover. They only deteriorate if left outdoors. Also coil the garden hose carefully and hang it on a wheel in a safe place, and shut off any outdoor faucets.

Have you a corner in the garage or basement for a box of good soil? It will come in handy for potting house plants during winter and for seed-sowing indoors very early next spring. You will also find a supply of peat moss, sand and vermiculite useful.

Be sure there are no dead or diseased leaves around the rose bushes. Clear them all away before hilling soil around the base of the bushes. Also check to see that climbers are securely fastened to the fence, house or trellis before winter winds blow.

Fall spading of the salad or vegetable garden is another task which can be undertaken to good advantage, leaving the soil rough and lumpy and adding material from the compost pile which may not be fully broken down. It will decompose through the winter and can be incorporated in the soil when the garden is prepared for spring planting.

Your house plants are again on normal schedule. Water them sufficiently to prevent them from wilting but not so much nor so frequently that the soil becomes soggy and causes root rot. Water them during the day—

morning or early afternoon; the leaves should not be wet as night approaches. If weather is at all dull, feed only lightly, if at all.

Midwest

Late plantings of bulbs, shrubs, trees and evergreens can be made in most areas this month, provided beds are covered with at least 12 in. of leaves, marsh hay or other mulching material. The most important task, however, is to complete the garden clean-up and see that all plants are prepared for winter.

First, be sure that all parts of the garden are amply supplied with water. Then, as leaves, brush and dry grass are raked from the lawn, this airy mix can be spread beneath trees and evergreens and in shrubbery borders. If oak leaves predominate, the mulch can be 12 in. deep. Leaves that mat down, such as maple, should be in thin layers 4 in. deep, with bits of brush between them. For a neat and tidy look, beds can be edged with a sharp spade, and the earth thus removed can be scattered on top of the leaves. Beds may also be dressed with a light layer of peat or rotted sawdust.

A winter mulch is especially helpful to all new plantings and to both conifers and broad-leaved evergreens. "Winter-burn" damage to evergreen leaves is actually a drying that occurs when roots imprisoned in frozen soil are unable to replace moisture lost through the foliage during periods of warm winter weather. Since mulches prevent the "deep freeze," at least part of the root system has access to moisture. Fluctuations in the temperature of the surface soil are also reduced, thus preventing the alternate freezes and thaws that cause plants to heave from the ground.

Before applying mulch to flower beds, remove dead annuals, and cut off tops of perennials close to the ground—lest they provide winter quarters for insect pests. Check perennial beds to see that all plants have good drainage. If necessary, make small ditches to carry water away. When mulching, do not cover the crowns of evergreen perennials like Madonna lily, foxglove and oriental poppy. Soggy mulch can cause crown rot infection in delphinium, columbine and Shasta daisy.

Chrysanthemums can endure cold, but not poor drainage. Plants can be lifted and clumped close together in a coldframe or a simple box frame made of 4 boards. A light covering of corn stalks or evergreen boughs can be added with burlap on top for extra shading.

Tulips, daffodils and other spring bulbs may be planted in pots now for indoor bloom. For the right method, see the chapter on indoor plants, under spring-flowering bulbs.

DECEMBER

Northeast

Outdoor gardening is at a standstill, save for completing the tasks indicated for November and applying winter protection with the ground hard-frozen. Caution: Be sure that it *is* hard-frozen. In some northeastern sections, the ground has remained soft until early January. Remember, you are providing protection, not to keep plants warm, but to keep the frost in the ground. This prevents alternate freezing and thawing of soil, which damages roots. Whatever protection you provide, such as salt hay, straw, leaves and evergreen boughs, it should be placed lightly so as not to mat and shut out air. (See also suggestions for January.)

A mulch of oak leaves (you can buy oak leafmold if there are no oak trees on your property) is beneficial to rhododendrons, azaleas, mountain-laurel, andromeda, leucothoe, etc. And while the ground remains open and soft, these plants can be watered in the early part of the day. If evergreens are growing in planters along entrance steps or terrace, they, too, should be well-watered and mulched.

Coldframes should be ventilated when the weather continues relatively mild. When cold sets in and the ground is frozen, the frame is closed and covered with straw mats for the rest of the winter.

Check the condition of the bulbs of tulip, hyacinth, daffodil or crocus which you potted in late October or early November and placed in a coldframe or basement. If they are making good roots, they are ready to be moved into your home for further growth and flowering.

You may start potting amaryllis the last week in December. Place 1 bulb to a 6 in. pot in a fairly rich soil mixture of fibrous loam, leafmold, some coarse sand and bonemeal. By potting bulbs successively through March, you can enjoy an extended flowering period.

Geraniums will bloom better during the winter if they are placed in a window where they receive sunlight the better part of the day, and in a room where the temperature remains between 70 and 72°.

Dust and grime are removed from the leaves of house plants by a gentle syringe or soft sponge. Even the leaves of such plants as African violets and episcias are benefited by being wiped, very gently, with a damp sponge now and then. Removing dust and grit enables the leaves to breathe better.

Feeding stations and racks for the birds need to be well supplied with seeds, suet, bread spread with peanut butter, etc. This is especially important when snow mantles the earth. Everything should be done to invite birds to your garden. They are among a gardener's best friends.

THE NORTH

*Tulips and blossoming trees are symbols of springtime
in the North. Agnes Selkirk Clark, landscape architect*

Midwest

In this closing month of the year, first of all see that the garden is prepared for the winter. If this work was hampered by an early snowfall in November, it can be done now. Mulches have to take over when the insulating snow blanket goes. Check again to be sure that the soil is moist. During unseasonably warm spells, the leaves and needles of evergreens may be refreshed by a misty spray from the hose.

The trunks of young flowering and fruit trees should be protected from rabbits and mice with a wrapping of burlap or foil. The trick is to make these barriers high enough to protect the trees from rabbits standing on their hind legs on a snowdrift.

With the approach of the holiday season, eye your evergreens for trimmings that will make decorative Christmas greens. Mugho pine has nice curving branch tips that are so fine for decorations that every home planting should contain one. Gardeners in Zone 6 can enjoy American and Chinese hollies, boxwoods, and Oregon-grape. Nandina berries are often decorative at this season.

If you need a large evergreen, you might select a living Christmas tree, preferably a spruce, fir or pine. The nurseryman will usually keep the tree until the proper time, but it is necessary to dig the planting hole in early December, before the ground has frozen deep. Soil removed can be stored in the basement or a warm garage so that it will be ready for the planting. When the tree is kept in a large tub it may be watered from time to time, and kept indoors for 10 days or 2 weeks.

Right after the holidays, collect surplus and discarded Christmas trees in the neighborhood, since they can be added to mulches and give increased protection. The greens are ever so effective, and unlike other types of winter protection, they look well too.

Now that the year is over, evaluate your garden year. Go over your garden records, noting successes and failures. Make plans for desirable changes or additions. As every veteran gardener knows, the most beautiful plants of all invariably grow "in next year's garden."

COMBINED NORTHEAST AND MIDWEST SEQUENCE OF BLOOM

Listed in approximate order of flowering in normal or average seasons.

(For descriptions, including hardiness, see appropriate chapters.)

Early Spring

Bulbs: Snowdrop, crocus, Siberian squill, glory-of-the-snow, hyacinth, species tulips, daffodil, grape-hyacinth, Virginia bluebell, tulip

Annuals: Pansy, viola, forget-me-not, English daisy

Perennials: Dwarf bearded iris, wild sweet william, primrose, rock-cress, basket-of-gold alyssum, evergreen candytuft, moss-pink, brunnera, bleeding-heart, lily-of-the-valley

Shrubs: Flowering quince, forsythia, *Viburnum carlesi*, Nanking cherry, flowering almond, thunberg spirea, lilac, azalea, andromeda, rhododendron, vanhoutte spirea, bush honeysuckle

Trees: Star magnolia, saucer magnolia, blireiana plum, flowering peach, redbud, serviceberry, crab-apple, flowering dogwood, silver-bell

Late Spring to Early Summer

Bulbs: Chives

Annuals: California-poppy, poppy, larkspur, candytuft, sweet alyssum

Perennials: Columbine, bearded iris, dames-rocket, clustered bellflower, Siberian iris, tree peony, herbaceous peony, spuria iris, oriental poppy, early day-lilies, coreopsis, delphinium, pinks, canterbury bells, astilbe, coral bells

Shrubs: Roses, mock-orange, weigela, late lilac. Northeast only: Mountain-laurel, leucothoe

Trees: Flowering cherry 'Kwanzan,' Washington hawthorn, Japanese tree lilac, golden-chain, mountain-ash, Chinese dogwood

Early Summer to Midsummer

Bulbs: Madonna lily, Mid-Century Hybrid lilies, regal lily, Olympic Hybrid lilies

Annuals: Stock, pink, phlox, sweet alyssum, nicotiana, calendula, snapdragon, petunia, zinnia, nasturtium

Perennials: Shasta daisy, golden marguerite, phlox 'Miss Lingard,' Japanese iris, large-flowered clematis (vine), monarda, hollyhock, gloriosa daisy, butterfly-weed, lythrum, globe thistle, day-lily, balloon-flower, phlox, veronica

Shrubs: Hydrangea hills of snow, butterfly-bush, chaste-tree

Trees: Goldenrain-tree, silk-tree or mimosa, pagoda-tree, sour-wood

Late Summer and Fall

Bulbs: Tuberous begonia, caladium, gladiolus, dahlia, canna, Aurelian Hybrid lilies, magic-lily, *Lilium speciosum* and hybrids

Annuals: Ageratum, aster, cleome, sweet alyssum, lobelia, petunia, marigold, salvia, verbena, zinnia

Perennials: Late day-lilies, phlox, rudbeckia 'Goldsturm,' helenium, super-giant hibiscus, hardy aster, chrysanthemum

Shrubs: Roses, bluemist or blue spirea, crape-myrtle, peegee hydrangea, rose-of-sharon

Regional Calendar of What To Do
Month-by-Month

🍁 The South

The Upper South—by Dr. Fred Galle, Director of Horticulture, Callaway Gardens, Pine Mountain, Georgia

The Deep South—by John V. Watkins, Professor Emeritus, University of Florida, Gainesville

JANUARY

Upper South

January is often considered the dormant garden season, yet this can be the real beginning. Look over your plans for the coming year. Outline projects you would like to do. Go through the seed catalogues and booklets that are available at this season to aid you in planning your garden.

Considerable pruning can be done during the winter. Muscadine and bunch grapes can be trimmed this month. Cut their long canes back to short spurs. The grape flowers and fruit will develop on new shoots produced in spring from these spurs.

Deciduous shrubs that do not flower until summer, such as crape-myrtle and hydrangea, can also be pruned now. However, shrubs that bear their flowers in spring, such as forsythia, spirea and jasmine, should not be pruned until after they have blossomed. Red- or yellow-stemmed shrub dogwoods, grown for their colorful winter twigs, may be cut back either in late winter or early spring. Broad-leaved evergreens are best pruned later in the season. For roses, wait until early March.

Bulbs of daffodil and Dutch iris can still be planted at this late season and often are available at a very reasonable price.

Care of house plants during the winter months is important. (See the chapter on indoor gardening for this.)

January is an excellent time to plant new trees and shrubs. Before purchasing the plants, plan where you are going to put them, and prepare the holes and soil.

Choose some fragrant flowering shrubs to add interest and spice to your garden. There are many from which to choose. Those that flower in winter are especially appreciated. The flowering period of the delightfully fragrant winter honeysuckle comes in late winter; it is a southern favorite and excellent for background or shrubbery border.

Winter daphne, an evergreen shrub for Zones 7b and 8, is the most fragrant of all daphnes. Its clusters of small pink flowers appear in later winter or early spring. There is an excellent form with variegated foliage. Grow winter daphne in shade; mulch and water it during periods of drought.

Deep South

This is an important month for planting. Deciduous trees, shrubs and vines are dormant, and can be moved in bare-root condition. Usually garden centers offer varieties that are best for your locality, but check the list of recommended plants for your region given in the appropriate chapters of this book.

After planting trees, wrap the trunks with burlap, paper or Spanish-moss as protection against drying, sunscald and borers. Yellow pines, native evergreens, can be obtained and planted this month.

Sow seeds of the following annual flowers that like cool weather: calendula, California-poppy, candytuft, carnation, chrysanthemum, clarkia, cornflower, dimorphotheca, gaillardia, godetia, babys-breath, larkspur, lobelia, nicotiana, pansy, petunia, phlox, pink, poppy, sweet alyssum, sweet pea, verbena.

Bulbs and roots that can be ordered for planting now or later include agapanthus, alstroemeria, amaryllis, crinum, freesia, gladiolus, gloriosa, hyacinth, ranunculus and tuberose.

Prune frost-injured shrubs, especially poinsettias. If you have not done so, prune back your crape-myrtle after leaves fall. Roses should be pruned after severe cold checks their growth.

Azaleas are beginning to flower in the southern areas. Petal blight, which is a very troublesome disease, can be controlled by spraying every 3 days with Acti-dione or other fungicide under high pressure. This routine must be begun when buds first show color, and followed exactly. Daffodils should be fertilized after they finish blooming to assure flowers for next year.

Camellias may be grafted this month while the root stocks and twigs to be used as scions are completely dormant. If possible, watch an advanced camellia hobbyist in your community perform the work. Do-it-yourselfers are inordinately proud of specimens in their yards that they have grafted themselves when they have been able to acquire scions of rare varieties. The procedure is not as difficult as it appears.

All plants should be fertilized. Use a complete fertilizer with a formula approximating 6-6-6, and distribute it at the rate of about 5 lbs. per 100 sq. ft. Wash it in with the hose. Plants growing in the lawn will need to have their fertilizer placed in holes a foot or so below the surface.

Plant gladiolus corms the last week in January if you wish to have them bloom for Mother's Day and ahead of the hot weather. Ivies, excellent groundcovers for deep shade, can be set out in new areas now.

Kumquat, a hardy miniature citrus, has bright-colored fruits that provide winter color in the garden, as well as furnishing the makings for marmalade. Buy a tree budded upon a root stock of *Poncirus trifoliata*, hardiest of the citrus stocks.

Magnolias of the deciduous, oriental types such as the saucer magnolia are starting to open their flowers now. If you would like to have one, visit garden centers to choose the

color and blossom form that you most admire. This is planting time.

Flowering quince hybrids bloom toward
the end of January in Zone 9. Surely there
will be room for one in your shrubbery bay?
If you live in southern Florida, where quinces
do not thrive, substitute an hibiscus or gardenia.

FEBRUARY

Upper South

If your lawn was reseeded to ryegrass last
fall, it will require a light feeding now. Use
a complete fertilizer such as 10-6-4 at the
rate of 5 lb. per 1000 sq. ft., or an application of straight nitrogen, such as ammonium
nitrate, at the rate of 1 to 3 lb. per 1000 sq.
ft. This will be adequate to keep green color
throughout the winter months.

Many of our broad-leaved evergreens, such
as hollies and camellias, are susceptible to
scale insects. Spray these plants with dormant oil sprays in the latter part of this
month when the temperatures are above 40°
and no drop below freezing is expected within 48 hours. Be sure to cover the underside
of the leaves thoroughly where the scale insects congregate.

Grafting of camellias is done late in February and early in March.

The latter is the time for pruning rose
bushes, cutting them back to 12 in. Some
varieties are more vigorous than others and
they may be pruned back more than half
their height, depending on the type of plant
you wish to have during the next growing
season.

Planting season continues. If you have
space to plant a new tree, check over the list
of those recommended for the Upper South
in the chapter on trees. Small flowering types
are excellent for use on small lots and for
one-story houses.

Flowering cherries and flowering crab-
apples can be purchased bare-root, and many
will also be available as canned specimens.
Flowering cherries that are most satisfactory
in the Upper South are sargent, yoshino,
higan and *Prunus serrulata* varieties. Outstanding and dependable crab-apples for this
region are 'Dorothea,' Japanese flowering and
tea crab. Numerous other varieties are available including purple-leaved forms, dwarf,
and even weeping types.

Flowering peaches are fast-growing and
have handsome flowers in white, pink or red,
but they are subject to many diseases and
insect pests including peach tree borers.

The best time to plant magnolias is now—
spring. While deciduous types can be planted
bare-root, they—and also evergreen magnolias—are best moved when balled and burlaped. All are wonderful for their large flowers. Some deciduous magnolias bloom in early
spring before their leaves appear, while the
evergreen sweet bay and southern magnolia
flower in late spring and summer. One of the
earliest is Yulan magnolia with large white
fragrant blooms. Star magnolia is another
extra-early specimen with double white, fragrant blossoms; it is available in pink varieties 'Rosea' and 'Rubra.'

If you would like a saucer magnolia different from the usual kind, see if you can
locate these varieties: 'Amabilis' with white
flowers; 'Alexandrina,' rose-purple outside
and white inside; 'Grace McDade' with large
white flowers, pink at the base on the outside;
or 'Lennei' that is dark purple and late-flowering. All begin to bloom when young.

Deep South

This is the last month for planting bare-root nursery stock. However, plants that are balled and burlaped, or those grown in cans can be set out at any time of year.

Azaleas reach their peak of perfection this month. Continue to spray every 3 days, regularly, to control petal blight. Buy and set out new azaleas while they are in bloom. You can also move plants about in your yard at this time, if you would like to improve their color combinations.

Camellias are still in full bloom, so travel to find new kinds to add to your collections. If you did not try grafting last month, there is yet time to do this work provided you live in the cooler sections of Zone 9.

Feed trees and shrubs, using a fertilizer high in nitrogen. Always water well after fertilizing.

The way you water plants may mean success or failure. Some years the months of February, March and April are very dry. Run your hose so it distributes about 1 in. of water each rainless week. However, remember that water leaches out fertilizer, so do not water more than needed.

Bulbs that can be ordered now for planting, either immediately or later, include aga-panthus, alstroemeria, amaryllis, calla, crinum, dahlia, freesia, gladiolus, gloriosa, haemanthus, montbretia, tuberose, watsonia and zephyranthes.

Prune and destroy those monstrous, distorted yellow-green growths that come out on azalea and camellia foliage. Those are leaf galls that result from fungus infections. Later in the season you will not find these abnormal growths.

Start spraying roses regularly as their new leaves begin to emerge.

Seeds of the following annuals may be sown: ageratum, babys-breath, China aster, celosia, chrysanthemum, cosmos, dimorphotheca, gaillardia, marigold, nasturtium, phlox, pink, poppy, sweet alyssum and verbena.

Feed and mow winter-annual grass frequently to keep it looking attractive.

Young annual flowering plants should receive frequent, light fertilization, rather than a single, heavy application.

Dogwoods, glory of winter landscapes, are coming into bloom now. If you live in the northern part of Zone 9, you will want to plant a pink-flowering one. In southern Florida, you will have to substitute a tropical flowering tree, such as an orchid-tree.

MARCH

Upper South

Spring-flowering bulbs can be fed as they begin to come through the ground. Use a fertilizer with a formula such as 8-8-8. Be careful not to walk over these young shoots, for they are easily broken off. If mulch over them is heavy, it should be thinned to help them come through. When the bulbs have finished flowering, do not cut off their leaves, for these are necessary for the process of forming new bulbs to bloom next year. If the tops look unsightly, you can bend them down out of the way to permit setting out of other plants later in spring.

Many annuals and vegetables can be started from seed now, either in containers in the house or in coldframes outside. They will be ready to transplant into the garden in April. Seed of early vegetables such as 'Bibb' lettuce can be sowed outdoors. Be sure you have plenty of seed of annual flowers on hand

—especially marigolds and zinnias. Many annual plants will be available from garden centers later, and you can set them out as started plants rather than waiting for your own seedlings.

Pre-emergence crabgrass killers can be applied to your lawn in March. There are numerous such materials available at garden stores. Before applying them, rake and clean off your grass if it is covered with pine straw and leaves.

Begin preparing your flower bed areas, digging in additional organic matter such as peat, compost or sawdust to be ready to plant next month.

Winter often damages many shrubs, so that they must be pruned. I advise waiting to do this until very early spring, to see what plants may do in the way of putting out new growth. If the damage is severe, you may cut them off completely—to the ground. If damage is light, only slight pruning may be needed.

Established lawns of zoysia should be cut very low in the early spring to remove old brown tops. Verticut mowers can often be rented, and they aid in removing thatch.

Dahlia roots that were left in the ground over winter should be dug this month for dividing.

Chrysanthemums should be divided in early spring. The new shoots should be saved and replanted, and the old parts destroyed.

The first plantings of gladiolus should be made in late March. Plant some every 2 weeks until late June to have a succession of flowers all summer.

Toward the end of the month, set out cannas, tuberose, ismene, amaryllis, ginger-lily, sprekelia and other summer-flowering bulbs.

Flowering quince is a very colorful shrub for early spring, and can be planted now. There are many varieties available with single or semidouble flowers from dark red to pink or white. Highly recommended varieties include 'Nivalis,' white; 'Juliet' and 'Margaret Adams,' coral pink; 'Phyllis Moore,' semidouble geranium-like pink; 'Pink Lady,' clear pink; 'Texas Scarlet,' low grower, watermelon red; 'Simmon,' semidouble, low, deep red; 'Stanford Red,' vigorous, tomato red; 'Crimson Red,' crimson, late-flowering; 'Toyonishiki,' pink and white.

Deep South

Azaleas continue to be beautiful in cooler parts of Zone 9 during March. Petal blight cannot be controlled after flowers wilt; you must begin the routine of spraying at the time that buds first show color.

Any azalea bushes that have become too large can be pruned as drastically as necessary right after they finish flowering. If you would like to rearrange your azalea planting, it is not too late to do it just as they complete blooming.

Even though there are balmy days, we may have frost. Old-timers hold that there will be no frost after pecan leaves reach the size of a mouse's ear.

If you have not gotten around to fertilizing all of your plants yet this year, get the job done without delay.

Prepare beds for summer-blooming bulbs and other flowers.

If you live in Zone 10, start seeds of heat-tolerant annual flowers for summertime cutting. These include ageratum, sweet alyssum, balsam, celosia, chrysanthemum, cosmos, dahlia, gaillardia, globe-amaranth, marigold, morning-glory, nasturtium, phlox, rose-moss, salvia, sunflower, tithonia, torenia, verbena and zinnia. Insects and mites increase alarmingly this month, so pest control must begin in earnest.

Low rainfall and high winds are typical of March, and can be damaging to plants. Water your garden every week that there is no rain, running the sprinklers long enough to distribute an inch of water.

Daffodils of all types should be fertilized after they complete flowering, to assure strong flower spikes for next year.

This is a good month to increase plants by cuttings. (See the chapter on starting plants.)

The following bulbs and roots can be planted at once: caladium, calla, dahlia, eucharis, haemanthus, gloriosa, montbretia, tuberose and zephyr-lily.

Spring-flowering trees and shrubs should be pruned or cut back as soon as flowers fade. (See the chapter on pruning.)

Roses are blooming now. Continue to dust or spray regularly to protect them from diseases and pests.

While it is too late to plant trees and shrubs in bare-root condition, you can continue to set out plants that have been grown in cans. Your garden-center manager will zip down the sides of the cans with his special shears. Then you can bend back the sides and set the plants into their permanent positions with no disturbance to their root systems.

Thrips, tiny flying insects, are troublesome to all flowers, including roses. A malathion spray, put out every 3 days, may help in reducing their numbers in your garden. However, thrips fly in such hordes that control is impossible.

Continue to water, fertilize and mow your winter-annual grass for a while longer this spring.

Zephyr-lilies are in full bloom in some sections now. You can still buy dormant bulbs, and can also transplant flowering plants without loss.

APRIL

Upper South

April is a busy season with the general clean-up and applying of fertilizer to lawns and shrubs. On lawns, use a 10-6-4 fertilizer at the rate of 20 to 30 lb. per 1000 sq. ft. The same type of fertilizer can also be used on the trees and shrubs.

If your lawn had ryegrass during the winter, begin cutting the rye frequently and closer, to encourage the bermudagrass to come forth later in the month.

The seeding of new lawns, using bermudagrass or centipedegrass should be done in mid to late April, when temperatures are over 60° at night. Sow at the rate of 3 to 5 lb. of seed per 1000 sq. ft.

New lawns can also be started by sprigging or sodding with bermudagrass or zoysia. 'Tifgreen' bermuda is a fine-bladed grass, best used in open or only lightly shaded areas.

'Emerald' zoysia is best for shady areas. ¾-in. squares of zoysia set on 12-in. centers will generally give complete coverage by late summer. Bermuda plugs will give faster coverage. Weeds should be kept under control in newly sprigged or plugged areas. A light covering of sawdust will help keep soil moist and cool.

The use of the new urea formaldehyde forms of nitrogen for lawns has proven to be very satisfactory. Materials such as Uramite are recommended, applied at the rate of approximately 15 to 20 lb. per 1000 sq. ft. Normally one application, applied in early spring, will be sufficient until late summer when another will need to be applied.

Spring-flowering shrubs, such as spirea, jasmine and forsythia, should be pruned after they finish flowering, so that they can develop new wood and new flower buds for next year.

Numerous annual plants can be set in the

garden in late April, after late frosts have passed. Marigolds are one of the finest annuals, since they flower throughout the entire summer and fall. Zinnias are excellent for spring and summer, but by fall they are troubled with mildew unless sprayed frequently.

Vegetables, including tomatoes, may be planted outdoors around April 15 to 20.

It is also time to plant caladiums outdoors.

Azaleas are at their prime in April, and can be selected at garden centers—and planted—while in flower. There are thousands of named varieties. In the Upper South the Kurume azaleas are the predominate group. In lower sections of Zone 8, many Indica azaleas are found, but these are less hardy than the Kurumes. Glenn Dale azaleas are also coming into prominence. They are large-flowering types, with hardiness similar to the Kurumes, and are adapted over the entire area. Among them are early varieties, some midseason, and some so late that they will be blooming in May and June. Macrantha azaleas also flower in late May and early June. So, with proper selection of varieties one can have azaleas flowering from early April into early June.

Midseason and late-flowering azaleas should be planted in partial shade, avoiding afternoon sun, for hot summer temperatures play havoc with these large flowers.

The time to feed azaleas is when they are in flower or just afterward, using a special azalea-camellia fertilizer. Lace bug and red spider become problems on azaleas in late April, and spraying will be necessary. Petal blight might also be noticed on blooms; it is characterized by small brown blotches. It is necessary to spray while plants are in bloom for control.

Avoid buying collected native plants of rhododendron or azalea unless they have been nursery-grown for several seasons to develop a new root system.

Deep South

New leaves on camellias must be protected against tea scale by a white summer oil spray. This should be done as soon as the young leaves are firm. The tea scale will occur in April in part of our region, and May in cooler areas.

Earliest blooming varieties of day-lilies will come into flower in Zone 9 late this month. Plan to visit nurseries, or the gardens of hobbyists, to see new varieties that you might like to add to your garden. Day-lilies can be moved when in bloom.

Your worries about frost are almost over. Frost rarely occurs in Zone 9 after April 21, and never in Zone 10 after that date.

Fire blight disease may appear in pyracantha, loquat, pears and related trees and shrubs. The branches will blacken and die back in alarming fashion. The only control is to cut off the affected branches well below the diseased area, sterilizing your cutting tool between cuts so that you will not spread the trouble.

Gardenia leaves will be visited by myriads of white flies which cause unsightly, despised sooty-mold fungus. Spray with white summer oil plus malathion as soon as foliage has expanded and is partly hardened.

The annual flowers that have been blooming during the cool season of the year will begin their decline late this month in Zone 10 and much of Zone 9. This is the time to replace them with heat-tolerant summer-flowering annuals.

You can sow seeds of these annual flowers: ageratum, balsam, celosia, cosmos, dahlia, gaillardia, globe-amaranth, marigold, morning-glory, rose-moss, salvia, sunflower, sweet alyssum, tithonia, torenia and zinnia.

Italian rye and other winter grasses are making their last stand now. Feeding them, watering and mowing will help them carry on a little longer.

Maintain a program of pest control. If you find this an unpleasant task, you can contract with pest control firms to do the necessary spraying at the proper time.

Jasmines should be cut back after they bloom, and the tips of branches pruned all summer to keep them within reasonable bounds.

Bulbs to order or buy for immediate planting include caladium, eucharis, gloriosa, haemanthus and lycoris.

This is the month when wisterias bloom. They make gorgeous shows in the tops of southern pines, but some gardeners dislike them there and prefer them grown as little flowering trees. For instructions on how to grow and prune both vine and tree types, see the chapter on vines.

Jerusalem-thorn tree makes a great show during April and May. You can plant one now, if you purchase it growing in a can.

Though this is not the season to do major pruning on shrubs, do cut back vigorous shoots that spoil the contours of your shrubs, including hedges.

Keep up your campaign of keeping pests and diseases from your roses. Sprays or dusts must be on the foliage continually.

MAY

Upper South

May is frequently a dry month and watering will be needed. Any period in which we do not receive an inch of rain during a week may be considered a drought, and additional water is necessary. Water heavily rather than giving frequent light sprinkles.

Roses are in full flower. Spraying for control of insects and diseases should begin. Use a combination insecticide and fungicide weekly as a spray or dust.

Lawns should be mowed frequently. Cut bermuda and centipede once a week, zoysia every other week. The mower blades should be set so that they are at least 1½ in. high. If the lawn is allowed to get too high between mowings, it is necessary to remove the clippings.

Many broad-leaved weeds are a problem this month, and it may be necessary to apply post-emergence weed killers. Apply these directly to the weeds, but keep in mind that the most common material used on broad-leaved weeds is 2,4-D, and it is hazardous to use promiscuously in the garden area. Once a sprayer has been used for this material, it should not be used for other materials, such as insecticides and fungicides, since 2,4-D cannot be washed out adequately.

To control bermudagrass along walks and flower beds, Dalapon can be applied either as a spray or in a waxed bar, such as one can buy at garden stores; it kills off the runners. Another remedy is to put an edging of metal or brick around beds to a depth of 6 in. Bermuda runners will go 6 in. deep or more and then sprout up in the bed.

Camellias and gardenias are often troubled with scale in May, and can be sprayed with malathion or any of the scalicides.

Gardenias may have sooty mold. Block this by controlling the insects commonly found along with the mold, for the mold feeds on the sweet, honeylike secretions of the insects.

Annuals can still be planted. Also, successive plantings of vegetables can be made. Tomato plants should be pruned and staked, and a regular spray program applied.

Many of the spider-lily (*Lycoris*) bulbs are available at this season and can be planted in the garden. They flower in late summer and fall, but do not expect bloom the first year. It may take 2 or 3 years for bulbs to become sufficiently established to bloom. The red spider-lily is the most common and hardiest.

House plants can be moved outdoors to their summer location in late April or early May. Plan to bring them back inside about mid-October, before the first frost.

Deep South

Gardening activities reach their peak during May in the Deep South. It is the finest month of the year in many areas, and the last one before heat and humidity make gardening more of an imposed task than a pleasure.

Window boxes that contained winter-blooming flowers will have to be changed over to heat-resisting plants now. One of the best heat-tolerant flowers for Zones 9 and 10 is Madagascar periwinkle *(Vinca rosea)*. It may be annual or perennial, depending upon the severity of winter.

Fancy-leaved caladiums in gallon cans are for sale in your supermarket and at your garden center. Select them in leaf colors that best fill your needs.

Sow seeds of these annual flowers: balsam, celosia, cosmos, cypress-vine, dahlia, gaillardia, globe-amaranth, marigold, morning-glory, rose-moss, salvia, sunflower, tithonia, torenia and zinnia.

Prune poinsettias to make them branch. Do not prune azaleas, hydrangeas or camellias at this time, lest you destroy next year's flower buds which are being formed in May. Continue to clip and trim the soft new growth on your hedges as it appears.

If your lawn is St. Augustine grass, you may notice the first telltale brown spots that indicate the presence of chinch bugs. If chemical control of them seems to be too big a job for you, contract with a reliable pest control firm. Your county agricultural agent or Chamber of Commerce secretary can give you names of dependable organizations that do such work. Camellia foliage should be sprayed with white summer oil to kill tea scale insects. Leaves on your azaleas may be eaten late this month by caterpillars. Be ready to spray.

Watch day-lily flower stalks, hopefully, for signs of little plantlets called "proliferations" which sometimes develop on them. If these are cut out carefully and placed in moist sand or even in a fruit jar containing water, they will develop roots and can be planted. They will become plants identical to their parent variety.

Unused garden plots should be sown to crotalaria or cow peas to discourage nutgrass and weeds and to reduce oxidation of organic matter. In the autumn this material should be roto-tilled into the earth as green manure.

This is a good month to propagate many plants by cuttings. For instructions, see the chapter on starting plants. Azalea branch tips will be perfect to take as cuttings when the tiny bristles turn from yellow to reddish in color. This mark of maturity will occur in all of Zone 10 and much of Zone 9 during May and June. Camellia twigs should also root well during this period.

The only kinds of plants that can be transplanted safely from now until next winter are those growing in cans or other containers.

JUNE

Upper South

Propagation of many shrubs can be done at this season. Azaleas, particularly, can be propagated by cuttings after growth has hardened sufficiently. Follow directions given in the chapter on starting plants.

Chrysanthemum plants, in bloom, can be bought at many garden centers during spring. When through flowering, these can be cut back severely, and will then develop into good flowering plants in the fall. During the time that they are growing new tops, the plants should be pinched back every 2 or 3 weeks through summer—until late August or early September. Many of the removed tips of branches can be rooted to start new plants.

Foliage of daffodils has matured and turned brown, so it should be cut off and destroyed.

Bulbs of daffodils and Dutch iris can be divided and transplanted this month, especially if you have some in such large clumps that they are crowded and not producing many flowers. The young bulbs should be separated and replanted so that each has enough space to develop.

Fix supports for tall plants, such as lilies and dahlias. Use small stakes of bamboo or iron. Plastic ties are ideal to use for fastening plants to the supports.

Chinch bug is a common pest on many lawns of St. Augustine grass and will be a problem all summer unless given adequate control. Large brown patches will develop through the grass. The chinch bug is a very small brown insect, working at the soil's surface. If you wet the ground prior to applying a spray, the insects will come to the top of the grass and come in contact with the material. If a dry product is used, the lawn should be watered thoroughly after the application. DDT, chlordane and other chemicals are recommended for chinch bug control.

Army and sod webworms are common on bermudagrass now and through all of summer. Applications of DDT and Sevin are effective.

Annual plants can still be added to the garden. Old blooms of petunias should be pinched off without allowing them to go to seed, to give a longer season of bloom.

Mulching of plants through summer is important to conserve soil moisture. Pine straw is an excellent mulch for this section. Pine bark, which is becoming readily available, along with sawdust, is also good. If you use sawdust, be sure to add nitrogen fertilizer to it. Peat moss is often used, and also well-rotted leaves.

Hedges should be trimmed after new growth develops. Do not shear drastically, but just enough to maintain the form. It may be necessary to shear again later in the summer.

While it is possible to set out container-grown shrubs and trees during summer, such new plantings require much more care and maintenance than those planted in late fall, winter or very early spring. They need extra watering and mulching especially.

Deep South

If your azaleas have sent out shoots that are too vigorous and ungainly, you can prune them now, to make them more compact and shapely. Reach deep within such plants and use sharp pruning shears to clip out the straggler branches. New growth will develop from low on these cut branches.

Hedges or edgings of box, box-thorn, limeberry or holly malpighia must be clipped often to keep your garden neat. The tips trimmed away make excellent cuttings to be rooted.

Crape-myrtles, the most colorful landscape plants of early summer, must have their fruit clusters removed when blossoms fade. Specimens growing in shaded, windless positions must have their foliage protected against powdery mildew by frequent applications of Acti-dione PM, Karathane or sulfur dust.

Deciduous trees transplanted bare-root last winter have low resistance. Be sure they have enough water, and keep their trunk wrappings in place for at least a year.

Easter lily plants should be fertilized lightly so that good bulbs will be ready for next year. Plants with flecked, malformed leaves are infected with virus disease and must be destroyed. Otherwise all of your lilies can become virus-infected.

If you would like to have some fragrant flowers near your lanai or screened porch, plant some night-blooming nicotiana nearby. Gardenias are too intensely fragrant for many persons.

Foliage of bulbs that bloomed during cool weather has matured and is turning brown. Dig gladiolus for indoor storage, but leave daffodils and Easter lilies if your soil is well drained. While this is not the time to order bulbs, by all means accept gifts from neighbors who offer divisions from old matted clumps that they are dividing.

Add more mulch on top of any that has become thin through decomposition. Mulching is one of the most important gardening practices in the Lower South.

Poinsettias grow rapidly and must have their tops pruned out now to assure compact, well-branched plants.

Rose foliage must be continuously sprayed for leaf-spotting diseases. This is a never-ending garden chore.

It is time to sow seeds of these annuals: balsam, cosmos, gaillardia, morning-glory, rose-moss, torenia and zinnia. These are all heat-resistant and will bear late summer blooms. Started plants of some are available at garden stores.

Palms can be transplanted now when rains start, provided you will be home all summer so that you can run the hose over the root zones during dry times. They transplant most easily when temperatures and humidity are high, and natural rainfall creates an environment that makes for rapid root growth.

Tree forms of wisteria need constant pruning at this season to keep the fast-growing tops in check. In Zone 10 you can plant queens wreath—a tropical evergreen vine.

JULY

Upper South

Day-lilies and tall bearded irises can be transplanted and divided this month. For instructions of exactly how to do it, see the chapter on perennials.

Crape-myrtles are common summer-flowering shrubs all through the Upper South. They are often subject to mildew during July and later in the summer. Various fungicides are recommended for control. Crape-myrtles planted in open areas are less apt to be troubled with mildew than those in shady locations. Dwarf crape-myrtles are becoming popular and are excellent permanent shrubs growing only 2 to 3 ft. high. 'Near East' is a very light shell-pink that blends well with the common pink crape-myrtle and also with 'Watermelon Red.'

Vegetables for autumn use can be started in July. Sow seeds of tomato, broccoli, cauliflower and lettuce, to set in position in the garden in August. Tip shoots of tomatoes can be rooted.

Several flowering plants that produce their blooms in early spring can be started from seed now. These include pansy, wallflower and English daisy.

Shrubs should receive their last fertilization this month, making sure that it is watered into the soil thoroughly. Lawns can be fertilized later in the summer; so can annual plants and chrysanthemums.

Roses can be given their last feeding in August in this area, and still harden off before severe freezing weather.

If you remove old withering flower heads of crape-myrtle and chaste-tree, they will often give repeat-flowering.

Use post-emergence weed-killer materials on your lawn for control of crabgrass and dallisgrass in bermuda and zoysia lawns. Do not use them on St. Augustine or centipedegrass.

Deep South

Lawns require their greatest maintenance just now. All kinds should be fertilized, watered during dry periods between rains, and mowed endlessly. If you have St. Augustine grass, it should be sprayed for chinch bugs. Yellow spots in centipedegrass indicate the need for iron there. Sprinkle such spots with a suspension of ferrous sulfate or iron chelate. Your garden-center manager will tell you how much to use.

Divide and transplant matted clumps of day-lilies and other perennials that have finished blooming.

You can sow seeds of these annual flowers to provide bloom in late summer and autumn: cosmos, gaillardia, rose-moss and zinnia.

Cypress-vine is the dainty, ferny-leaved annual vine with red flowers that thrives during midsummer. If you did not sow seeds, you can probably find small seedlings in places where vines grew last year. Usually these vines self-sow, and once you grow them, you do not need to replant them each year.

Azaleas should not be pruned any more this summer. The only pruning to do now is hedge-clipping, and shortening new growth on poinsettias.

Container-grown plants can be purchased and planted at any time.

If torrential rains occur, as expected at this times of year, apply nitrogen fertilizer to plants whose leaves have become yellowish.

Old hibiscus plants—in Zone 10—will develop colonies of snow scale low down on mature wood. Mop these with a cloth moistened with white summer oil emulsion mixed according to directions printed on the label.

There are several other diseases and pests for which you must be alert and take action. For example: Azaleas should be sprayed if caterpillars appear. Camellia foliage should be protected against tea scale. The many kinds of euonymus are very subject to euonymus scale so must be sprayed periodically. Holly leaves must be protected all summer long against attack by spittlebugs. Rose foliage must always have a coating of fungicide. Zinnias very often develop powdery mildew at this season when rains are heaviest. To learn more about these troubles and how to handle them, see the chapter on plant diseases and pests.

AUGUST

Upper South

August is generally another dry month, so watering may be necessary.

If you are interested in buying irises or day-lilies, this is the time to order them. They can be planted in September. Both of these perennials are available in many excellent varieties. Some of the newer ones are extremely expensive, but many beauties are available in the reasonable price range. Consider some of the repeat-flowering day-lilies which bloom in May and June, and then again in August and September. You may hear reference made to "evergreen foliage" types, but most people do not feel that this feature is of great importance. You will find names of mail-order firms that specialize in irises and day-lilies in the back of this book.

Ants are a problem in late summer—particularly fire ants. Use poison bait (Mirex) or chlordane.

Chrysanthemum plants should be given one last pinching in late August.

Humid weather encourages blackspot on roses, and mildew on crape-myrtles, so keep up with weekly spraying.

Many perennial plants, such as gaillardia and foxglove, can be started from seed in late August and early September. They will be large plants by next season.

Lace bug, common on azaleas, may need a second spraying at this season; use malathion.

If you sowed seed of tomato, broccoli, cauliflower etc. last month, the young plants should be ready to transplant to wider spacing in your vegetable plot.

Make repeat sowings of seed of vegetables that will grow well during fall's cooler weather. These include radish, lettuce, and the various relatives of cabbage.

Fertilize roses for the last time this month.

Deep South

August is the month of doldrums in southern gardens. High temperatures, high humidity, heavy rainfall, and sometimes high numbers of chiggers and insects, make gardening less than pleasant. It is primarily a month for maintenance chores.

Compost should be prepared. It is invaluable to gardeners everywhere, but in the Deep South this decomposed organic material has blue-chip rating because it improves coarse, open, sandy soil, as well as stiff, heavy clay. Excellent humus may be made in less than 2 years. The best site for a compost pile is in the shade. You can use many ingredients such as leaves, sawdust, plant remains from garden and kitchen, peat, sludge and manure. Instructions for how to do it, and an illustration, are given in the chapter on soils and plant foods.

Do not neglect your lawn. Chinch bug control in St. Augustine grass, armyworm and sod webworm elimination in other species, and endless mowing must be faced.

Native iris and spider-lilies can be moved in from the wild now, if you receive permission from the landowner.

This is not the time of year to buy or order bulbs or roots. However, if friends or neighbors are dividing husky perennials, by all means accept their offerings.

Continue to clip your hedge; this chore cannot be discontinued for another month. Do not prune other shrubs except to remove vigorous shoots that have grown out and spoiled the shape.

Hurricane season is just around the corner. Do not set out any new shrubs or trees. Brace and guy palms and other trees that have been set within the year. You should use unusually heavy stakes and braces, for 100-mile-per-hour winds are devastating. These Atlantic-bred blasts cannot be forecast far in advance, are to be expected, and can never be ignored in Zones 9 and 10.

If you admire yellow flowers, there are many of that color in autumn. Some you will enjoy are cassia, crotalaria, marigold, sunflower and yellow-elder.

The only seeds that should be sown this month are those of tropical fruits. These should be sown as soon as you eat the fruit.

Your roses will continue to bloom heavily if leaf spot control and fertilization have been carried out on schedule. There is no vacation for rosarians.

SEPTEMBER

Upper South

Chrysanthemums will be coming into bud and flowering later in September. If the plants are tall, they may need to be staked so that they will not fall over during rains. Dahlia stakes should now be reinforced to sustain the weight of luxuriant growth.

Pansies and other winter annuals can be set out this month. Water them well to help them become established.

Bermuda lawns are often overseeded with ryegrass late this month or early in October. Prior to this, cut the bermuda short—to less than ½ in. Then broadcast ryegrass seed over the lawn area at the rate of 3 to 5 lb. per 1000 sq. ft. Water it in well. It is not necessary to apply top dressing unless there are low areas which you wish to raise. You do not need to apply fertilizer at the time of seeding, due to the large ryegrass seed which has sufficient food storage in it. Fertilize lightly after the young grass is up, approximately 2 to 3 weeks after seeding. Ryegrass should be mowed frequently, starting when it is 1½ in. high and continuing throughout the winter months as needed. Ryegrass is difficult to establish on zoysia lawns and should be used only on bermudagrass.

Plant new irises and day-lilies, or transplant old clumps that have become too crowded. For instructions, see the chapter on perennials.

Root some cuttings of coleus and other annuals that you wish to winter-over in the house.

Plant late crops of turnip greens and spinach.

Tent caterpillars are common in the fall. Use DDT or other insecticides, with sufficient pressure to get inside the tent. Burning of tents is dangerous and may injure the tree or shrub. Armyworms can be controlled with Sevin or DDT.

Cuttings of many hollies and other broadleaved evergreen plants can be taken now and rooted in a coldframe over winter.

Deep South

This month begins the garden year, if you are just back from your vacation. You can sow seeds of these annual flowers that will give you bloom during the cold months: African daisy, babys-breath, browallia, calendula, California-poppy, carnation, clarkia, cleome, gaillardia, lobelia, lupine, mignonette, nasturtium, nicotiana, nierembergia, petunia, phlox, pink, stock, sweet alyssum, verbena, viola and wax begonia.

Beds for annual flowering plants and bulbs must be prepared by incorporating organic material, such as peat and compost. You can hire this tough job done with a roto-tiller.

Bulbs and roots to order for immediate planting include daffodils and ranunculus. At the same time you can order refrigerated bulbs of tulip and hyacinth for later delivery; they should not be planted until November.

Daffodils of the tazetta type (Zone 10) and trumpet types (Zone 9) should be planted in enriched beds. If you have old plantings of daffodils, and did not lift them last spring, be sure to fertilize their bed now.

Lycoris bulbs will send up flowers in September. Both the golden and red types produce their slender stalks without any foliage —the leaves are produced in spring. Since it is easy to forget where the bulbs are planted, you should indicate their position with small but sturdy wire or plastic markers. Then you will not be in danger of cutting through the stalks with a hoe.

Do no transplanting or planting until winter, but be prepared to repair, straighten or brace any trees that have been damaged by wind.

If you wish your camellia flowers to be as large as possible, disbud them now. With your thumb and forefinger, roll out all of the buds in each cluster except the largest one. Then this single terminal bud will receive all of the food manufactured by that shoot.

Divide crowded perennials if you did not get this done earlier.

Easter lilies should be dug and reset in enriched beds, or they can be stored in dry sand for a while if need be.

Fertilize chrysanthemums and other fall-blooming flowers.

Hybrid mallows, with their spectacular dinner-plate-size blossoms, are blooming now. Take notes on the varieties you would like to add to your garden in spring.

Insects and disease will continue to plague you and your garden during this hot autumn month. Azalea foliage may be eaten by caterpillars. If rains stop, mites will become numerous; you should wash them from the leaves with a strong spray of water from your garden hose, or kill them with Aramite or Kelthane. Grass will be attacked by armyworm and sod webworm. Rose foliage should be covered continuously with a fungicide.

Final pruning chores for the year are to head-in poinsettias and give hedges a clipping—probably during the Labor Day weekend. Then oil your pruning shears and put them away for the winter.

OCTOBER

Upper South

The leaves are beginning to fall and should be collected from the lawn and put onto a compost pile rather than burned. Large bins can be made of chicken wire, or you can make more permanent structures of masonry block or brick in which to store composting materials. Common garden fertilizers are excellent to add to the leaves, etc., to use as an aid in rotting them for use in your soil later. For an illustration of how to make a compost pile, see the chapter on soils and plant foods.

Bring in many of the house plants that you have had outside during the summer. Also take cuttings of any annuals, such as coleus, that you may wish to keep through winter.

October is frequently a dry period in the South, and water is needed at this time, although many plants are beginning to go into dormancy. Plants that are well watered in the fall will go through winter with less winter damage than plants that are dry. However, do not water so frequently that you force new growth to develop during a prolonged warm period. Such succulent new shoots are easily damaged by freezing weather. Autumn watering is especially important for camellias and other broad-leaved evergreens.

Camellia sasanqua and its many varieties bloom in October. These plants, and *Camellia japonica* which blooms in late winter, are generally planted in late fall and early winter. Plants will be available as canned specimens.

Watch both types of camellias now for signs of scale. A dormant oil spray can be applied on a day when the temperature remains over 40° and under 85°.

This is the time to place orders for daffodils and other bulbs to be planted in the garden later this month and in November. Tulips are normally not too satisfactory in the South, particularly in Zone 8 and farther south; they can only be considered as annuals and not as permanent bulbs. However, they are satisfactory in most of Zone 7. They should be planted deep—usually 8 to 10 in. down. Some of the species tulips flower a second year, but they are not as good the second year as they were the first.

Hyacinths and crocus are excellent plants for the Upper South. In areas where rabbits are abundant, crocus may not be satisfactory since the rabbits will keep their foliage and flower buds cut off. They will not touch daffodils or hyacinths.

Deep South

Annual flowering plants are in the garden spotlight this month. Now is the time to start seeds of those that like coolness; they will brighten your garden through winter and spring. They are especially useful planted in bays in shrubbery borders, and in the service area to furnish flowers for cutting.

You may find self-sown seedling plants in spots where African daisy, petunia, larkspur and other annuals have grown. These plantlets can be moved to sites where you would like them to bloom.

Seeds to sow at this time include babysbreath, browallia, calendula, California-poppy, calliopsis, candytuft, carnation, clarkia, cleome, cornflower, delphinium, gaillardia, English daisy, godetia, hollyhock, larkspur, lobelia, lupine, mignonette, nasturtium, nicotiana, nierembergia, petunia, phlox, pink, poppy, snapdragon, stock, sweet pea, sweet alyssum, verbena, viola and wax begonia.

The only seeds worth sowing are the very best. New hybrid strains produce fabulous flowers for cutting and for exhibiting in the spring flower shows. Seeds saved from hybrids do not "come true." Likewise, self-sown seedlings from hybrids are worthless.

Proper sowing is as important as starting with good seed. For details on how to do it, see the chapter on starting plants.

Be sure that you thin seedlings ruthlessly as they grow. Otherwise they will become leggy from being too close together. Another thing that causes legginess is shade, so keep the seed flats in sun.

As young annuals develop, pinch out their terminal shoots so that they will send out low branches. Many gardeners also nip out the first flower buds, for the good of the plant.

Winter lawns of frost-resistant annual grasses should be started during the first cool spell.

Bulbs and roots to order in October for immediate and later planting include amaryllis, freesia, Dutch and native iris, Easter lily, lycoris, daffodil, ranunculus and sprekelia.

This is the time to order roses from nurseries that specialize in canned plants whose tops are grafted onto roots of *Rosa fortuneana*. Roses grafted onto this stock are the only kind unreservedly recommended for the Deep South. Grow some of these beside the usual shipped-in bushes and note the difference.

Transplanting season starts in earnest late this month. You can move things about in your yard, or add new specimens from your nursery.

Yellow flowers crown the tops of golden-rain-trees in October. These easy-to-grow deciduous trees are among the most popular in the Deep South.

Zebra plant and other plants related to *Calathea* will lose their leaves because of shortening days and cool nights. Where soil freezes, calatheas should be wintered indoors. However, in Zone 10 these tropical exotics are left in the earth the year around.

NOVEMBER

Upper South

Plant the daffodils and other spring-flowering bulbs that you ordered last month, getting them into well-prepared soil.

Collect materials for making dried arrangements for winter decoration. Pine cones should be gathered while they are still fresh and clean, and stored for later use.

Garden tools, lawn mowers, etc., which are not being used at this season, should be brought in and stored. Wipe them with oil to prevent rust during winter months. It is also advisable to have mowers overhauled now, when service shops are not so busy as they are during the spring rush.

Late fall is a good time to choose and plant camellias and many other beautiful broad-leaved shrubs which we are fortunate to be able to grow in the Upper South.

Among the broad-leaved evergreens that are especially attractive through autumn and winter—many producing fruits which attract birds—consider the following.

Osmanthus blooms in autumn—infrequently throughout winter—and has a delightful fragrance. In the cooler areas, rely on holly osmanthus, while in milder areas both Fortune's osmanthus and tea-olive can be grown.

Aucubas are excellent in this section. They should be used in moderate to heavily shaded spots since their foliage will not stand sun. They are fruiting shrubs, provided you have both male and female plants in the garden, for only the female plants produce the large cherrylike red berries.

Nandinas are splendid for foundation plantings. In addition to the familiar red-fruited form, there is a white-fruited one, and some dwarf forms.

Pyracanthas should be in full fruit at this season. There are numerous good red-fruiting varieties available throughout this area, in addition to orange-fruited and yellow-fruited ones.

Deep South

Annuals dominate your activities again this month. The most important task is to transplant seedlings that have become large enough. (See the chapter on starting plants.) Choose a cloudy afternoon for the job. Distribute cutworm bait down each side of each row for a week or so. This poison, for sale at garden stores, is essential for success.

Pyracantha fruits reach perfection during cool autumn weather. If you wish to buy a new plant, choose a small one in a gallon can, because pyracanthas are difficult to transplant in large sizes.

Hollies, too, are at their loveliest. Best buys are small berried specimens in gallon cans, much preferred to wild trees whose fruiting habits are not known. Yaupon, outstanding fruiting native holly, can be bought in gallon cans. Its popular dwarf form 'Nana' does not fruit heavily, if at all. Unisexual plants such as holly, Brazilian pepper-tree, etc., have fruits only on female individuals. Males supply pollen but never fruit. That is why it is wise to be on the safe side and buy new plants as canned specimens which are in fruit.

Violets should be lifted, divided and set into rich soil. Pinch off and destroy all leaves that show signs of disease.

Wooden-roses, used for dried arrangements, mature only in southern Florida—the warmest parts of Zone 10—and are not successful in Zone 9.

Poinsettias are showing color. Each year we hope some may escape frost until after Christmas. When frost is forecast, cut some stems and plunge the ends at once in boiling water. Do not break off leaves after this or the colorful bracts will surely wilt.

Tulip planting time has arrived. Preliminary cold storage is essential for success.

You can sow seeds of the same annual flowers listed for sowing in October.

Bulbs which can be planted include alstroemeria, amaryllis, freesia, hyacinth, Dutch and native iris, Easter lily, daffodil, ranunculus and tulip.

November is frost time in many parts of Zone 9. Tender shrubs can be protected by pulling mulch over them. Young annuals can be protected by mounds of Spanish-moss.

Mist-flower, sometimes called hardy ageratum because it resembles that excellent little annual, is at its showy best now.

Goldenrain-tree, which was covered with yellow blossoms last month, is now decked in bright pink fruits. You can usually find volunteer seedlings under old trees and these can be transplanted.

Ivies in scores of leaf forms are offered in chain stores at this season.

Oaks may be transplanted, bare-root, in November. By all standards, live oak is the finest shade tree for this area.

Mallows die to earth during winter months. Cut off dead tops at the soil line. New shoots will appear next spring on schedule.

DECEMBER

Upper South

This is an excellent month to plant trees and shrubs. However, we in this area can plant through the entire winter, except when the soil is too wet. Planting season continues until March and early April.

Roses planted in December do far better than those set out during the spring months. They should be set with the crowns at soil level. Do not mound soil around the bush after it is planted, as is recommended for the North, but do provide a heavy mulch.

Pots of flowering plants received as Christmas gifts will need special care. You will find instructions in the chapter on indoor plants. Poinsettias are not hardy outdoors in the Upper South, so when your plant is through blooming and drops its leaves, it should be stored, almost dry, in a cool section of the house. When spring comes it can be grown in the garden—if you wish—until next fall.

Many azaleas sold by florists at Christmas time are varieties that are hardy outdoors in the Upper South. They can be kept in the house until planting time in spring. However, many of the double azaleas and Belgian hybrids are not hardy here and should be considered strictly as house plants. These can be set outdoors for the summer and brought indoors for winter.

You will often find hollies featured by garden centers at Christmas time. This is an excellent season of year to choose and plant them. However, it pays to learn a little about the different types first, for they vary considerably in their eventual height, spread, shape and general manner of growth. Some are shrubs and others trees. Some have showy fruits while others are grown mainly for their foliage.

You cannot guess future appearance from looking at the beautiful canned specimens in the shops. It is wise to visit old established plantings and arboretums in your locality to see how various kinds look when full grown. For example, a common fault of Burford holly is that it does not remain low enough to be a good foundation-planting shrub. You will know why when you see mature plants 20 to 30 ft. high! Burford is better used for backgrounds, screen plantings, or as a specimen. However a dwarf form is becoming available in nurseries and it will be more suitable for low plantings.

American hollies become large trees. Since there are numerous named varieties, it is advisable to see as many of them as possible and get recommendations from your local nurseryman. Some commonly available in the Southeast are 'Croonenburg,' 'Taber No. 3,' 'Howard,' 'Hume No. 2,' and 'East Palatka.' One that is receiving considerable interest, since it sets fruit without having male plants available for pollination, is 'Pearl LeClare.'

Here is a tip for placing a holly that you wish to admire when looking out of a window. Locate it so that the sun will shine on the berries, for when sunlight is on the back of a holly, you will hardly notice the fruit.

Pines are of special interest in winter and can be planted now. Natives such as loblolly and shortleaf are difficult to transplant as big trees, but young ones obtained as nursery-grown canned specimens grow very rapidly if given sufficient water and fertilizer each year. These canned plants do better than those collected from the wild, or sold with balled roots. White pines, familiar in northern states, can be used here if given good soil and ample water during dry summer periods.

Deep South

December is a month of very little garden activity since all thoughts and plans are for the holidays. However, certain plants require continued care, and some need to be covered on cold nights.

Azaleas are shallow-rooted and cannot tolerate drought. Do not neglect them during dry times in winter. Soil around them must never become powder-dry, for roots are functioning even when temperatures are low, and water absorption goes on day and night.

Winter lawns of annual grasses need attention. For their best appearance, mow, water and fertilize them with nitrogen at half-strength.

On all annual plants that are flowering, cut off blooms as they fade, so the plants will continue to produce buds and thus have a longer season of color.

Crape-myrtles should be pruned severely when the leaves fall. You can use 10-in. pieces of pencil-sized branches as hardwood cuttings.

Holiday festivities require lots of cut material. If you do not have what you need this year, make notes to add hollies, cedars, Brazilian-pepper trees, pyracanthas and so forth during the present transplanting season. Then you will have your own shrubs and trees from which to cut foliage and berries in the future.

Though Christmas trees are traditionally conifers, there is no reason why palms, citrus, hibiscus and other tropical exotics can not be dramatized for Christmas celebration in the Deep South. Kumquat or calamondin trees in full fruit are possibilities, as are cacti and yucca. Norfolk-Island Pine and the monkey-puzzle have great appeal.

Started plants of all kinds of cool season annuals are ready for purchase at garden centers—if you were not able to sow seeds last fall.

All kinds of shrubs and trees can be set out now.

Camellias are coming into their own. Early varieties are opening their flowers.

THE SOUTH

*Southern gardens with pleasing structural form
are attractive in all seasons.*

UPPER SOUTH SEQUENCE OF BLOOM

BULBS   J F M A M J J A S O N D

Crocus
Narcissus
Hyacinth
Tulip
Dutch Iris
Anemone
Gladiolus
Dahlia (tubers)
Spider-Lilies

TREES   J F M A M J J A S O N D

Service-Berry
Silver-Bell
Saucer Magnolia
Flowering Peach
Flowering Cherry
Crab Apple
Flowering Dogwood
Redbud
Fringe-Tree
Tree Lilac
Silk-Tree or Mimosa
Southern Magnolia
Sour-Wood

SHRUBS   J F M A M J J A S O N D

Holly (fruits)
Nandina (fruits)
Camellias, various
Japanese Quince
Winter Daphne
Winter Jasmine
Burkwood Viburnum
Winter Honeysuckle
Thunberg Spirea
Forsythia
Andromeda
Azaleas, various
Common Lilac
Broom
Mock-Orange
Rhododendron
Weigela

SHRUBS (cont'd)   J F M A M J J A S O N D

Rose
Abelia
Gardenia
Mountain-Laurel
Hydrangea Hills of
    Snow
Crape-Myrtle
Chaste-Tree
Rose-of-Sharon
Peegee Hydrangea
Elaeagnus
Osmanthus
Pyracantha (fruits)

ANNUALS   J F M A M J J A S O N D

Pansy
English Daisy
Wallflower
Petunia
Marigold
Zinnia
Ageratum
Rose-Moss
Cleome
Dahlia (bedding)
Salvia

PERENNIALS   J F M A M J J A S O N D

Evergreen Candytuft
Violet
Wisteria
Primrose
Bluebells
Iris, various
Peony
Coral Bells
Butterfly-Weed
Day-Lily
Pinks
Sunflower
Balloon-Flower
Yarrows
Poker-Plant
Shasta Daisy
Chrysanthemum

DEEP SOUTH SEQUENCE OF BLOOM

GARDEN FLOWERS   J F M A M J J A S O N D

Calendula
Pansy
Linaria
Gladiolus
Sweet Pea
Amaryllis
Carnation
Hollyhock
Larkspur
Iris
Nasturtium
Petunia
Day-Lily
Torenia
Marigold
Zinnia
Four-O'Clock
Mallow
Chrysanthemum
Daffodil

SHRUBS   J F M A M J J A S O N D

Camellia japonica
Poinsettia
Flowering Quince
Oriental Magnolia
Azalea
Spirea
Allamanda
Hibiscus
Ixora
Rose
Bottle-Brush
Lantana
Thryallis
Oleander
Hydrangea
Rose-of-Sharon
Camellia sasanqua
Ardisia
Nandina
Pyracantha

TREES   J F M A M J J A S O N D

Redbud
Red Maple
Dogwood
Citrus
Jacaranda
Fringe-Tree
Southern Magnolia
Silk-Tree or Mimosa
Jerusalem-Thorn
Crape-Myrtle
Chaste-Tree
Cassia
Royal Poinciana
Geiger-Tree
Queen Palm
African Tulip-Tree
Orchid-Tree
Brazilian Pepper-Tree
Manila Palm
Holly

VINES   J F M A M J J A S O N D

Bougainvillea
Carolina Yellow
   Jessamine
Wisteria
Climbing-Lily
Allamanda
Cats-Claw
Confederate-Jasmine
Queens Wreath
Honeysuckle
Painted
   Trumpet-Vine
Chalice-Vine
Jasmines
Cape-Honeysuckle
Pandorea
Rangoon-Creeper
Mexican Flame-Vine
Combretum
Coral-Vine
Flame-Vine
Woolly Congea

Regional Calendar of
What To Do Month-by-Month
🍁 The West

Intermountain and Plains—by George Kelly, Garden Writer and Nurseryman, Littleton, Colorado

The Southwest—by John M. Harlow, Nurseryman and Landscape Contractor, Tucson, Arizona

JANUARY

Intermountain, Plains, and Southwest Zones 5 and 6

This month may bring our coldest weather, as well as the start of a new year. While you cannot do much outdoor work, you can make good use of indoor time to review the successes and failures of the past season, and make plans for a bigger and better garden in the year ahead.

If you want to buy plants for new areas in your yard, or for remodeling old parts of the garden, you should think carefully about the best ones to select. Be sure that each will fill the specifications for which you want it. It should grow to the right shape and size, and be able to thrive in the location where it is planted.

If you do not know much about shrubs and other plants, now is the time to study them. Also, locate some nurseryman who knows plants and how to care for them.

January is an excellent time to observe how plants with winter beauty can add interest to your landscaping. There are evergreens such as pines, spruces, firs and junipers. Many shrubs have bright berries, including Japanese barberry and several kinds of cotoneaster. Some deciduous trees and shrubs have colorful twigs. These include red-stemmed dogwoods and golden weeping willows.

If you kept a garden notebook or diary last year, now is the time to look it over, see what you jotted down during the season, and act on ideas that were good at that time.

On the other hand, if you have never kept a combination garden scrap-and-notebook, this is the month to start one. Keep a record of your garden, the plants you buy, dates of bloom, kinds of sprays to use and when, color combinations you like, etc. Clip pictures and stories about plants, and classify them so that they can be located quickly when wanted.

When the weather is open, walk around your garden to see how your plants are doing. Look for soil that might be drying out, especially on the south side of the house, and water plants in such situations. Remember that plants must have moist soil around their roots every month of the year. Check for places where you could give plants a little protection to avoid damage by snow, sun or wind.

In good weather you can prune grapes and pick up some of the trash that has blown into the garden or been carried in by dogs.

If you have not already done so, investigate the horticultural organizations in your community, and if you find some that are trying to learn about better gardens, join them and help in their programs.

Southwest Zones 7, 8 and 9

If you live in Zones 5 or 6, see the calendar for Intermountain and Plains.

This month the average temperature will be lower than any other. Trees and shrubs will be dormant and need only minimum irrigation. One good watering every 3 or 4 weeks will be sufficient.

You can buy and set out the following annuals, which are available as started plants growing in plant bands or flats: petunia, snapdragon, calendula, pansy, viola, phlox, verbena, sweet pea and African daisy. You can also plant anemones and ranunculus. However, it is too late for stock, which should have been planted last month at the very latest.

By now the soil is comparatively cool and tulips can be planted directly in the ground without refrigeration. Starting the first of the month, gladiolus corms can be planted at weekly intervals through the next 6 weeks— to give continuous spring blooms.

To have a good green lawn within 4 weeks, plant winter rye, provided your location is in full sun.

Nurseries offer bare-root roses for sale beginning early in the month. If you are going to buy them, do it early to assure a good selection and to avoid dehydration, which is a problem in the Southwest because of low humidity. Many nurseries, because of the dehydration difficulty, plant their bare-root roses immediately in containers. Then they sell them with well-established root systems.

It is time to plant bare-root fruit trees, shade trees and flowering trees. Unless you live in the higher elevations, do not plant cherries, apples or crab-apples. There are not enough hours with chilling temperatures for these fruit trees to thrive. For the same reason, do not ask to buy varieties of peach, apricot and plum with which you may have been familiar in cooler sections of the country. Buy only the ones offered locally, which do not need long chilling periods.

For a tree for summer shade, the maple-leaf mulberry heads the list. Other good shade trees include the Texas umbrella-tree, sycamore, Arizona and 'Modesto' ashes, and silk-tree or mimosa. A pecan planted in January will start to bear in about 4 years and eventually provide good shade.

Flowering peaches offer the most spectacular display for spring beauty. They—and redbud—also can be planted now.

When planting trees, if your soil is hard caliche, the holes should be dug 5 ft. across and 5 ft. deep. Then they should be filled with a good soil mixture and thoroughly watered. When a tree is set, it should be 3 in. below the surrounding surface to allow for future irrigation.

Because this is a cold month, be prepared to protect tender plants when freezing temperatures are predicted. Use a frame to hold the protective material away from the foliage. A plant wrapping that touches the foliage will do more harm than good. Heat from a light bulb placed beneath the protection will help.

Prune shade and fruit trees. Evergreens and hedges should be pruned lightly to avoid several months of bare stubs.

Many varieties of camellias are blooming, so this is an ideal time to make selections. January and February are the best months in which to transplant them.

FEBRUARY

Intermountain, Plains, and Southwest Zones 5 and 6

There may be days in February when you can get outdoors and begin to get soil ready for planting. Maybe you can even move a few things. But there is sure to be plenty of bad weather which will give you time to finish indoor work.

Take an inventory of your garden tools, equipment, seeds and plants. Also check the condition of your fences, gates, retaining walls and walks. Make plans now for any of the necessary renewing, painting or repairing.

Send for nursery and seed catalogues. Study them and prepare your orders. If you have dependable local sources for plant materials, give them preference in your buying, for they have already experimented with growing many things for your area. It is fun to enjoy the beautiful pictures and glowing descriptions in the catalogues. But sometimes conditions in your area may be quite different

from those in the state where the catalogue is written. Keep your feet on the ground and check the lists of regional recommendations in this book—also local horticultural authorities—to be certain which plants are good for your purpose and which are not. When you have decided on the necessary things, get your order in at once.

Look over your spruces, pines, junipers, lilacs, cotoneasters and dogwoods for evidence of dormant scale insects. Purchase the necessary spray materials immediately and have them on hand so that you can treat the plants when the weather is suitable. This spraying can be done any time before new leaves have started to emerge, at a time when the temperature stays above 40° for several hours. Try to choose a time when the wind is not strong.

If you stored bulbs of dahlia, gladiolus, canna or tuberous begonia last autumn, check their condition.

When you are planning new plantings, consider some of the excellent but rarely used perennials or shrubs. Your major plantings should always be those that are highly recommended for your area. But after you have filled the important places with these reliable plants, it is fun to try a few others just for the thrill of making a difficult plant grow. You will notice that in any community, certain plants are used over and over by everybody. However, there are always many others that could be used, and will help make a more interesting garden. Why not try some?

One of the best and most unusual things that has happened in this area in recent years is the increased interest in the Japanese-type garden. You might like to develop a part of your yard in this style. We do not need to make gardens in the traditional Japanese way, but we can learn much from them that fits our climate. Their most valuable characteristics include the use of rock as specimens, the use of variously shaped shrubs, and the use of different kinds of groundcovers—both living and inanimate.

Southwest Zones 7, 8 and 9

Annuals for winter- and spring-flowering that were listed in January can still be planted.

Continue to plant gladiolus corms through the middle of the month.

Toward the end of the month purchase geraniums for pots. Keep them in full sun until really hot weather and then change them to shade for the summer months.

Some suppliers of bare-root plants will still be offering roses, fruit trees and shade trees for sale. If January was cool and rainy, the risk of planting bare-root stock this late will not be as great as if the month were dry, windy and warm.

The best time for pruning roses is just before their new leaf buds commence to swell. Ordinarily this is the first part of February. Branches to be saved should be cut back to 1½- or 2-ft. height. Cut back older wood completely to the bud union. After pruning, spray the bushes for both insects and diseases with an all-purpose spray.

Prune deciduous fruit trees, shade trees and shrubs that were not pruned in January. Delay pruning of spring-blooming types, grown primarily for their flowers, until after they have bloomed.

Hedges and evergreen shrubs that require such severe pruning that they have to be sheared back to bare stems should not be pruned until late in the month, for then there will be a minimum wait before the fresh growth of spring covers pruning scars.

Feed winter lawns.

Annuals should be fed with a liquid fertilizer—it is easy to apply and distributes evenly. Before using it, be sure to irrigate beds well so the fertilizer will have the best chance for penetration.

Fertilize camellias with an acid food after they have finished blooming.

Chrysanthemums should be cut back and divided.

Start marigolds and Madagascar periwinkle (*Vinca rosea*) from seed in a greenhouse or hotbed. Also start tomatoes, eggplant and pepper.

If you wish to transplant creosote (greasewood bush) from the desert, dig it during or immediately after a heavy rain and replant at once. Then the chances of survival are good. Do not try bushes over 2 ft. in height. Cut their tops back at least ½.

You can plant any container-grown or balled-and-burlaped nursery stock.

Irrigate trees and shrubs every other week.

Peaches and nectarines should be sprayed for leaf curl with a dormant spray of lime sulfur or Bordeaux when the flower buds show pink. Spray apricots and plums when their buds show color—with a fungicide for brown rot and shot-hole disease.

MARCH

Intermountain, Plains, and Southwest Zones 5 and 6

We often have more disagreeable weather (for humans) this month than we have had all winter. But if snow is piling up in the mountains, to provide us water for irrigation next summer, be glad!

Between storms, as the frost goes out of the ground, it is time to prepare soil where plants will be set out later. In this area it is especially important to work in large amounts of organic matter such as peat, manure, or compost. We also need to add some phosphate. These plant foods are always needed and cannot be supplied efficiently after things have been planted.

Tubers of tuberous begonias should be started indoors now, if you want to be sure of a full season of bloom.

Plants arriving by mail may come when weather prevents planting them outdoors at once. If this happens, you must open the packages to give light and air to the tops, but be sure that the roots are kept covered and moist. Do not let the roots freeze while out of the ground.

Sweet pea seed may be planted about now. The tradition is to aim for St. Patrick's Day, but the seeds will not know the difference a few days before or after.

Bare-root roses should be planted as soon as you can get the plants and when the soil is in suitable condition to dig. Be sure to hill them up with soil after planting, so they will not dry out before they begin new growth.

Any trees or shrubs, deciduous or evergreen, can be set out at this time. So can vines and perennials. Dig the holes big enough to accommodate all of their roots. Backfill with the best soil available and with a good proportion of peat mixed with it. Water thoroughly but not too often.

Do not uncover anything when the first warm days come, for there will be another spell of winter before the weather is really settled. Plants will have more need for mulches and sunshades during the next few weeks than they have had since last fall.

Though it will be possible later in spring to buy almost any kind of annual that you want as a started plant, it is fun to start some seeds indoors now.

You can also sow seeds of some annuals outdoors by the middle of March, if the ground is unfrozen. These are the types that ordinarily tend to be self-seeding, and include calendula, cornflower, larkspur and marigold.

Check your house plants for signs of the start of insect infestations.

While planning new plants for this year, consider a few of the dual-purpose ones. 'Dolgo' crab-apple has beautiful white flowers in spring, followed by brilliant red, medium-sized apples that are excellent for jelly. Currants are moderate-height shrubs that can serve as hedges while providing fruit for jelly. There are many others.

Southwest Zones 7, 8 and 9

March is the end of winter and beginning of spring. Though midmonth is the average date for the last killing frost, there is a possibility of frost damage into April. Be cautious when working with cold-tender plants.

Sow seed of the following annual flowers and vegetables indoors, or in a hotbed, for setting out later: Madagascar periwinkle, marigold, dwarf dahlia, gaillardia, chrysanthemum, gloriosa daisy, tomato, pepper and eggplant. In the outdoor garden sow radish seed.

Buy and set out started petunia plants after all danger of frost is passed.

Poinsettias should be cut back and planted in warm, sunny locations to give them every advantage for outdoor bloom next Christmas.

Resist the temptation to plant citrus that may be offered for sale this month. Let someone else stand the risk of a late freeze. This holds true, too, for other cold-tender plants, such as hibiscus and bougainvillea.

Wait to prune frost-damaged plants until next month when it will be easier to tell which parts are still good.

Watch for signs of red spider, particularly on pyracantha, Italian cypress, arbor-vitae and junipers. Dusty, dirty-looking foliage is a sure sign of this pest. Spray with malathion at 10-day intervals. Once they are eliminated, a strong spray of water every 10 days will prevent recurrence. Do not spray with malathion during the flowering period.

Spray roses and other mildew-susceptible plants with a mildew preventive. Euonymus must be closely watched for mildew when grown in the shade.

Feed roses now to assure good strong flower-producing plants next month. Also give the first feeding of the year to trees and shrubs.

Watch for aphids, which multiply at a rapid rate. Spray once a week until weather is really hot, when they thin out.

There are still some varieties of camellias coming into bloom in nurseries, from which to make selections.

Lawns of winter ryegrass should be fertilized. As the weather warms, feed lawns of clover or dichondra.

Start dichondra lawns from seed. This is much more satisfactory than planting from flats. Dichondra takes lots of care. Learn all about its good points and problems before making the final decision to plant it. Contrary to common belief, it does have to be mowed.

Chrysanthemums should be transplanted this month. Starting new plants from cuttings is much better than making divisions of established plants.

Oleanders can be started by rooting 4-in. long cuttings of last year's wood in water. Change the water every day.

Continue to set out any plants that are container-grown or balled and burlaped.

APRIL

Intermountain, Plains, and Southwest Zones 5 and 6

The most important garden work for this month is to complete all necessary planting and transplanting. Shrubs and trees can be moved now while they are completely dormant. If the procedure previously described is closely followed, they will hardly know that they have been transplanted. Be sure to keep bare roots protected from wind and sun. Do not add fertilizer to the soil at planting time, but wait to fertilize after the plants are growing.

We often have to begin watering this month, though there should never have been any time to stop watering. Whenever the soil around a plant's roots becomes dry, it should be soaked. If the moisture in the soil is right, the plants will jump into new growth as soon as the ground begins to warm up a little.

Help your lawn develop deep roots. The only way to encourage any plants, including grass, to have deep roots is to provide food and moisture down so deep that the roots will have to go down to get it. The early training of a lawn is important. It is often a temptation to start watering and fertilizing a lawn too early in the season. This results in roots massing themselves near the surface. Then, in August when it is difficult to give enough water, the plants will not have deep roots and will suffer.

Now is the time to think about crabgrass

control, rather than in August when it is most conspicuous and has already done its damage. If you encourage the lawn to grow vigorously in April and May, there may not be room for crabgrass seed to start. It must have bare soil with sun shining on it in order to get started.

Watch for juniper galls, those orange-colored gobs of gelatin that form on juniper twigs after the first warm rain. This trouble requires alternate host plants of hawthorn or service-berry trees to complete its 2-year life cycle. Control is difficult but can be done. Check with your local spray authority.

After the season of winter storms and before the rush of spring is a good time to examine trees and shrubs for broken limbs. Cut them off smoothly, close to the larger branch or trunk, so that the wounds will heal quickly.

Most trees can have their general pruning at this time. Exceptions are birch, maple and walnut. If you do major pruning now on spring-flowering shrubs, you will lose this season's bloom; wait until they finish flowering.

Perennials should be set out this month. You may get field-grown plants dug with soil around their roots, or possibly potted plants that have been grown from seeds and cuttings. Select the ones that have proven hardy in your area for the main plantings. Then try a few different things to add excitement.

Southwest Zones 7, 8 and 9

When night temperatures reach 60°, about mid-month, the following seeds of annual flowers and vegetables can be planted outdoors: zinnia, cosmos, celosia, coleus (semishade), four-o'clock, globe-amaranth, sunflower, gourd, castor-bean, cypress-vine, morning-glory (banned in Arizona), melons, squash, cucumber, corn, blackeyed peas, okra and radish.

Early in the month, set out the following, which can be bought as started plants: tomato, pepper and eggplant. Later, add these annual plants: Madagascar periwinkle, marigold and zinnia. Also set out dahlias, caladiums and irises.

The chances of damaging frosts are slight now, so citrus can be planted with comparative safety. Some are more hardy than others. These include red and Marsh seedless grapefruit, navel and juice oranges, mandarin orange, tangerine, tangelo, kumquat, sour orange and calamondin. The last two are ornamentals. Lemon and lime are more tender, and the risk in planting should be recognized. Because citrus are cold-tender, the safest location for them is a southern or western exposure where there is reflected heat.

Plant bougainvillea, lantana and hibiscus. Hibiscus should be set out in tubs or pots so that they can be moved inside during the cold months; or plant them in the ground and consider them as annuals worth their price because of their summer bloom.

Prune frost-damaged plants.

Container-grown roses can be planted.

Lots of leaves will be raked up this month. As new foliage comes out on evergreen trees and shrubs, the 2- and 3-year-old leaves toward the center of the plant drop off. Yellowing and falling leaves from oleanders, for instance, do not mean the plants are diseased or dying; it is a natural process.

As temperatures rise, irrigate more frequently. By the end of April you should be watering once a week, and this schedule should continue through the heat of summer. Irrigation basins around plants should extend as far out as the spread of their branches. If your bermuda lawn has built up a thick thatch, it should be renovated. Good healthy lawns need this attention about once every 3 years. Use either a renovator or a bermuda rake to loosen the thatch. Rake it out. Then cut the lawn low, fertilize it, and start the heavier summer-watering schedule.

Aphids are out in force. Spray at least once a week until hot weather.

Flowers grow so fast now that they can use frequent feedings. Liquid fertilizer applied through a hose spray is an easy way to feed; be sure to soak the soil before applying.

Keep an eye out for mildew, and spray at the least evidence of it.

Use weed-killers early in order to catch weeds before they form seed, but use caution. Avoid soil sterilizers if possible, for their effect lasts for years. Roots not in an area at the time of sterilization can grow there years later and still suffer damage.

Camellias will finish blooming near the end of the month and should be fed.

MAY

Intermountain, Plains, and Southwest Zones 5 and 6

So far this year you have been doing garden work without seeing many results. But now, in May, spring is bursting out all over! It is time to enjoy your garden to the fullest.

Finish the planting of dormant, bare-root trees and shrubs which are still available at nurseries. However, plants sold in containers or pots can be planted throughout the growing season.

Do not fail to set out some annuals. They are the only plants in our gardens that bloom from frost to frost. Get ready to do this at the very end of this month. If you believe that you can predict weather, plant things outdoors early. But if you want to be conservative, wait until after Decoration Day, which is about the time our last killing frosts occur.

As the new shrubs and trees that you have planted begin to put out leaves, various pests will also begin to grow. Weeds are one of the pests. You must start early to cultivate and remove them while they are tiny and easy to eliminate. On lawns and in other difficult areas, the new weed-killing chemicals may be useful. But the old garden hoe is still the best weed eliminator around other plants.

Consider using mulch around some of your plants. It not only helps eliminate weeds, but keeps soil moister and cooler. This may cut down on your garden maintenance and result in better plants. Use grass clippings, leaves, sawdust, etc.

Begin now to make regular inspections to detect the start of insect damage. Look especially for aphids on junipers. (See the chapter on plant diseases and pests.)

Check the soil for moisture, and if it is not thoroughly moist, give it a good soaking. Then wait until it is beginning to get dry before another watering. Do not water on a schedule, but just as the soil needs it.

Get roses ready for their June bloom now. Check the watering, cultivation, fertilizing and spraying. A rose is one plant that usually needs regular spraying.

Plant some white flowers that will be a joy in the dim light of evening. Petunias and nicotiana are two you will especially like.

Continue the crabgrass elimination program that you started in April. There are pre-emergence materials that will control the starting of new plants, and post-emergence chemicals that will kill growing plants with little damage to the lawn.

If your lawn, roses or other plants were not set in really good soil, they may need feeding now.

Southwest Zones 7, 8 and 9

Container-grown trees and shrubs of all kinds are available for immediate planting.

Now that both day and night temperatures are high, new bermuda lawns may be started from seed. After planting, the area must be kept constantly damp to prevent the germinating seed from drying. This may mean watering as often as 4 times a day. Lawns to be started with plugs or runners of hybrid bermudas or zoysia should also be planted this month.

Established lawns of bermuda and zoysia should be watered heavily, fertilized once a month, and mowed at least once a week with the mower set low. If your lawn does not respond to water and fertilizer, the chances are that it is suffering from insect or disease injury. Recently bermuda mite and the Phoenix billbug have raised havoc with these lawns. Evidence of the mite are bunch clusters of grass close to the ground; and of the billbug, grass that can be rolled back because it has been severed at ground level. Use a spray containing diazinon. Repeat applications will be necessary.

Started plants of summer annuals can still be planted. Container-grown perennials which can be set out now include gerbera, columbine, native penstemon, dusty miller, gazania, Shasta daisy and verbena. Feed all established annuals and perennials.

Check peaches and apricots, and if they seem to be overloaded with fruits, thin them out so that fruits which remain will be larger.

Espaliered plants have put out enough new growth to need pruning and training.

Spray pyracantha, Italian cypress, arborvitae and junipers weekly with a strong spray of water to wash off red spiders. If this pest multiplies and a fine dusty web appears, spray with an insecticide.

Chrysanthemums should have their tips pinched back to a 7- or 8-in. height. Then spray with an insecticide and fertilize. Nurseries still have a supply of young container-grown chrysanthemums to set out now.

In higher elevations—above 7,000 ft.— these annuals can still be planted from seed: African daisy, calendula, candytuft, clarkia, babys-breath, marigold, nasturtium, snapdragon, stock and zinnia.

Foliage of spring-flowering bulbs will have withered now, and you must decide whether to leave the bulbs in the ground. Left undisturbed, Dutch iris and amaryllis will bloom and multiply year after year. Daffodils will continue to bloom for about 3 years at a declining rate of effectiveness. As for other bulbs, most gardeners forget them and replant each fall. If you are a thrifty soul, willing to gamble extra work for extra bloom, do this: Dig bulbs now. Remove the foliage. Allow the bulbs to dry for several days. Then treat with a fungicide-insecticide dust and store in a box of peat, sand or perlite, and keep in a cool, dark and dry location until time for fall planting.

Newly planted or transplanted citrus or fruit trees that do not have enough leaves to provide shade for their larger branches or trunks, and thus protect them from sunburn, should be painted with whitewash.

Camellias and gardenias growing in containers tolerate sunshine during winter, but now should be moved into full shade for the duration of summer heat. Geraniums, also, will do better in semishade from now until fall.

JUNE

Intermountain, Plains, and Southwest Zones 5 and 6

This is the month for roses—all types. You can enjoy them all now if you have planted and cared for them properly. But if you did not plant any and regret not doing it, you can still buy some. Nurserymen have them growing and blooming in containers, ready for easy transplanting. Such rose bushes will continue to bloom in your garden all summer, just as though they had been planted there in early spring.

Finish the planting of annuals, both seed and started plants. It is also planting time for frost-tender bulbs, such as gladiolus, dahlia and tuberous begonia. Set them out as soon as possible so that you may have a full season of bloom.

It is too late to plant dormant, bare-root shrubs and trees. However most nurseries have quite a selection of plants growing in cans, and these can be planted at any time.

The best time to do necessary pruning on spring-flowering shrubs is right after they finish blooming. In this way, the least bloom is lost the next season. Learn the characteristics of each shrub, so you can prolong its usefulness by pruning. For most shrubs over 10 years old, the best system is to cut out at ground level about 1/6 of the old stems each year.

Do not cut off the foliage of tulips, daffodils and other bulbous plants until it ripens naturally.

Now we are well into the summer maintenance routine of water, fertilize, cultivate, spray and prune. Carefully doing all of these things at the right time and in the right way is the most important secret of a good garden. When these chores become instinctive, we may have acquired that goal of all good gardeners, a green thumb!

Plants that were set out this spring, or that have been even more recently transplanted, need extra watering attention.

If shrubs or perennials do not seem to be growing vigorously, give them a little fertilizer. Remember that the chemical kinds are quick-acting and of short benefit, while the organic kinds are slower but longer lasting.

About the time cherries begin to ripen, look for leaf slugs on cherries, plums and cotoneasters. Spray or dust them with almost anything—or even throw common dust on them, but do it soon and often.

If you would like your hedge to be nice and dense, trim it frequently. If you want this to be fun, do it without a guiding string!

We repeat: lawns must have regular care. Here are some rules for essential chores. Water only when needed, and then do it thoroughly. Do most of the fertilizing, if needed, between May 1 and August 1. Mow high and often—for bluegrass, set the mower at about a 2-in. height and mow once a week. If these rules are observed, it makes little difference whether you catch the clippings or not.

Southwest Zones 7, 8 and 9

By now most winter- and spring-flowering annuals have passed their prime and should be pulled out. After cleaning up the spots where they were, and digging in peat moss, fill the vacancies with summer annuals.

During hot weather, large palms can be transplanted successfully with a mass of roots no larger than the diameter of the base of the trunk. Transplanting does not stop the growing process, so it does not take too long for them to become re-established.

Container-grown trees and shrubs can still be planted.

Legend has it that summer rains start on San Juan's Day, June 24. They seldom do, but you should take the hint that rains and winds are coming. To be ready for them, thin out excess branches from full-foliaged trees so wind can pass through them without toppling the tree because of too much resistance. Shallow-rooted trees, such as peppers and African sumac, are apt to be felled.

Feed lawns once each month. Watering deeply encourages deep rooting to insulate roots from surface heat. This is a favorable time to start bermuda lawns from seed, or to start bermuda hybrids and zoysia from runners and plugs.

Feed roses, and spray if necessary. Mulching them will protect roots from summer heat and also conserve moisture. Redwood pebble bark is a good mulch because it is heavy enough to resist being moved by water or wind — claims which cannot be made for mulches of manure or peat moss.

Cottony-cushion scale attacks citrus trees and pittosporum. When it first appears, spray with a 50% malathion insecticide.

Again this month pinch chrysanthemums back to an 8-in. height, feed, spray with an insecticide, and dust about the base of plants with chlordane. At the same time cut back poinsettias to develop a bushy plant. Pinch back summer annuals to produce more branching and thus more profuse-flowering plants; feed with a liquid fertilizer after first soaking the soil.

Dust chlordane about the base of century plants to destroy the grubs that feed at their base and destroy them. Also spread chlordane under the branch-spread of the palo verde in hopes of destroying a grub that works on its roots and causes branches to die. Young century plants can be cut from the stalklike root connecting them to the parent plant. Allow the cut to dry and heal and then replant.

If old, inner leaves of shrubs, trees and other plants turn yellow and drop, there is nothing to worry about since this is a natural process. However, if new foliage turns yellow, something is wrong. Usually this yellowing is a sign of a chlorotic condition which may be caused by poor drainage, too frequent watering, or the lack of available iron. If this last is the problem, apply an iron chelate as directed on the package.

Prickly pear cactus is easy to propagate. Cut a pad or group of pads from a plant. Let it lie in the sun for several days to allow the cut to heal. Then plant in the ground to a depth of 3 or 4 in. No special attention is needed from then on.

JULY

Intermountain, Plains, and Southwest Zones 5 and 6

It is hot, and you feel like vacationing. The big spring splurge of bloom in the garden is over. But if you want a good garden this fall and next year, you must keep up the good work and continue the usual garden routines.

Review your watering practices. Do not be fooled by the appearance of the surface of the soil, but dig in and see whether it is still moist—or whether it needs water. If you started early in the season to water thoroughly instead of barely sprinkling, roots will now be deep and the plants can tolerate the hot, dry days with little damage.

Look over your garden for signs of chlorosis. This is usually indicated by yellowing leaves. Look especially at flowering quince, ninebark, barberry and primroses. Iron applied in some form, such as iron sulfate or aluminum sulfate, will usually do some good.

Check for newly formed galls on spruce trees. They look like little green cones. If they are picked and destroyed while still immature, the aphids inside them cannot survive to start more infection.

Rust may be starting on hollyhocks and perennial phlox. Sulfur or a good fungicide will prevent, but not cure, this disease. Faded-looking leaves may indicate the presence of spider mites. Use a good miticide; also hit them hard with a cold stream of water whenever you can.

Some trimming may be in order now, such as broken limbs on shrubs, or climbing roses. Good gardeners often carry their pruning shears while doing other chores and give a snip here and there as the need is noticed. Keep a lookout on roses, lilacs, flowering almonds and plums for sucker shoots that come from the ground. These sprouts are developing from the root onto which the choice named-variety upper part of the plant was grafted. They will have different-appearing leaves and grow more vigorously than the rest of the plant. If left, they will crowd out the choice blooming branches.

You can divide some iris now, and give a start to the new neighbor down the street. It will benefit both you and him. Share some of your accumulated garden wisdom, too.

This is an excellent time to write memos to yourself in your garden notebook—or to start such a notebook, if you do not already have one.

Southwest Zones 7, 8 and 9

It is hot enough so that bermuda lawns started now will grow rapidly.

If you are craving shade, nurseries have well-established shade trees in containers ready for planting. If set out before summer rains, they will be off to a good start before fall.

Camellias should be fed with a special acid food. Buds are just commencing to form, and fertilizing later might cause them to drop.

Pinch back chrysanthemums for the last time. Continue feeding and pest control.

The popularity of gravel yards is often strained after heavy rains because of the weeds that spring up. It is a temptation to use a soil sterilizer. A better and safer solution is to rake off the gravel, lay roofing paper over the entire area, and then cover with gravel. This works well unless there will be a lot of traffic across the gravel which might puncture the roofing paper so weeds can penetrate it. Pea gravel is good for level areas, but on slopes where it easily washes away in rains, use crushed stone of ¾-in. to 1½-in. size. The steeper the slope, the larger the rock.

Acanthus mollis, called bears-breech or Grecian pattern-plant, should be cut back to the ground after blossoming. It will soon send out lush tropical-looking foliage.

Replant amaryllis bulbs immediately after they blossom. Disturbing them at other times may delay flowering for a couple of years.

Roses should be watered, fertilized, and sprayed to control insects. Using a preventive fungicide for controlling mildew is better than waiting for it to appear and then trying to cure it.

Annuals may have to be watered every couple of days if the weather is hot and windy.

The center of *Washingtonia* palms should be sprayed with Bordeaux mixture to protect against heart rot.

When in the market for palms, you will discover a vast range in price for trees with the same number of trunk feet. Some are collected in southern Texas with practically no ball of earth, stacked on semitrailer trucks like logs, and marketed in cities of the Southwest at bargain prices. Delivered during the hot months their chances of living are good. However, they require several seasons of growing before they amount to much. On the other hand, palms may be collected locally, dug with a large ball of earth and moved with big equipment. These are more expensive for an equal number of trunk feet, but within a year they are as good as before transplanting.

The most popular fan palm is *Washingtonia robusta* because of its comparatively small trunk. However, the larger-trunked *Washingtonia filifera* is much more cold-hardy and seldom shows browning leaves. The ornamental date is popular, hardy, and compared to the edible date, is of rapid growth and more desirable for decorative purposes.

AUGUST

Intermountain, Plains, and Southwest Zones 5 and 6

The "August slump" is the greatest concern this month. There is a lack of bloom in the garden, and a lack of ambition in gardeners. Luckily the garden can stand a little neglect right now. It is nature's habit to slow up a little on watering and let plants harden up and ripen their wood in anticipation of the complete dormancy of winter.

To have a better garden in future Augusts, take notes on what is blooming now in other people's gardens in your community. Then you can plant some of these things next spring. Perennial phlox is one of the showy flowers. There are bright annuals of course, including some with handsome foliage. Shrubs with berries, and even evergreens that we plant mainly for winter effect, help out now.

It is time to buy, plant or transplant some favorite perennials. Oriental poppies are dormant and leafless now and easy to move— though difficult at any other time. It is also a good time to move irises.

Tulips, contrary to popular belief, do not need to be lifted and transplanted each year. If they are doing well, leave them alone. If they have "run out," forget them and plant some new bulbs in October.

Save seeds of some of the plants that you especially like. Of course, you can easily buy seeds next spring, but it is fun to grow things from seeds that you have saved yourself.

If you think your garden needs to be pepped up, you can give it a light feeding early this month. However, feeding too much too late in the season is not wise.

Spider mites increase in hot weather and can do a lot of damage now. Check everything periodically for signs of them, and continue to spray.

Do not worry about crabgrass that is now beginning to turn purple in your yard. It has already done its dirty work and will soon be killed by frost. Spring is the time to fight it.

Get out that notebook and make complete records of your successes and failures this season. Note what color combinations were wrong, what new plant failed or was wonderful, what plants have become too aggressive and need their ears pinned back.

For pleasure, straighten your bent back and look around you at the gardens of others. Especially visit parks and botanic gardens where you can meet new and better plants. Though it is sensible to depend on the tried and true for the basis of our garden plantings, the greatest pleasure comes from experimenting with new things.

Southwest Zones 7, 8 and 9

August is not the gardener's best month in the Southwest. The heat is beginning to tell on both humans and gardens. You do well just to mark time.

This is the ideal time to prepare areas

where winter or spring annuals are to be planted. Spread 1 bale of Canadian peat moss to every 100 sq. ft. of bed, along with two 2-cu.-ft. sacks of manure, 2 lb. of ammonium sulfate and 5 lb. of soil sulfur. Spade all of this into the soil to the depth of a shovel, and irrigate at weekly intervals until planting time in late September or early October.

This month weeds take over as a result of heat and summer rains. They have to be pulled, or a weed killer used. In killing lawn weeds you must realize that the term "lawn" is a broad one which includes dichondra and clover as well as grasses. While selective weed killers can be used on grass leaves, they cannot be used on dichondra and clover since these — like most weeds — are broad-leaved plants and that is what weed killers kill.

Special watch should be given lawns because summer rains and heat are favorable conditions for the spread of lawn diseases. Apply a lawn fungicide at the slightest sign of them.

Dates will be ripening this month, and the birds will be the first to know. Protect ripening fruits with sacks if you want them saved.

Roses should be fed and sprayed toward the end of the month to put them in condition to produce more and better bloom in another 6 weeks. Nothing can be done about the cutting bee that cuts perfect circles out of tender rose leaves—to use for its nest. It is too fast to be hit, and does not eat the leaf so cannot be poisoned.

Gladiolus are ordinarily planted from November through February, but some people favor planting them this month over any other time. Set out now, they will bloom in the cool of fall.

Do not be fooled by August downpours. Most of this water washes off into arroyos and there is little soil penetration. It takes an inch of water on the surface to penetrate a foot into the soil. In irrigating, water should go down 2 or 3 ft., so do not skip regular weekly watering because of a rain.

It is in August that root rot first noticeably takes its toll. Actually it has been working on the roots for a long time. The boy next door who has been hired to water during a vacation absence is often blamed for not having watered enough, and is held responsible for the death of certain shrubs and trees. However, they really died of root rot, and could not have been saved even if there had been no vacation.

SEPTEMBER

Intermountain, Plains, and Southwest Zones 5 and 6

When you look at your garden as you return from your vacation, you see it—for a while— as others might see it. This is a good time to put down in your garden notebook the things that you think should be done to improve it and make it more useful and beautiful.

Doubtless many garden chores have been neglected during the summer, so start at the bottom of the checklist and attend to watering, weeds, insects and pruning. Make the place neat again.

Go easy on the watering until frosts come and leaves fall.

When the frosts do arrive and kill the tops of tender plants, do not delay getting the annual bulbs dug and stored for winter. Cannas, gladiolus, dahlias, tuberous begonias and tuberoses all take careful handling to bring them through winter in good condition.

As perennials become dormant, you can transplant them. If it is necessary to move peonies, bleeding-heart and asparagus, fall is the time to do it. Many perennials move best with a ball of earth around their roots so that they are disturbed as little as possible. However, some of the rampant growers like Shasta daisy and hardy aster will need to be divided.

If you are planning to start a new lawn, now is the time to get the area ready. At least half of the lawn budget should go into the preparation of the soil, for future success depends upon this. Sowing can be done any time this month after the soil is ready. Weeds will be less of a problem at this time of year than if you made the lawn in spring, and the weather will continue to get better week by week.

You may think that the war against insects is over for the season, but look in a few places for the very late ones. Aphids may still do considerable damage to the upright junipers, snowballs and dogwoods. Even though leaves are about to fall, the aphids are building up a great population ready for early spring when they will do much damage to the newly unfolding leaves.

In some of the higher altitudes the fall season may be the only time when transplanting can be successfully done. Plants are dormant then, and the ground is not frozen.

Southwest Zones 7, 8 and 9

Prepare beds for winter flowers and vegetables. For details, see August recommendations.

Seed of the following annuals can be sown late this month: petunia, stock, pansy, viola, pink, Iceland poppy, phlox, cornflower, California-poppy, bells of Ireland, dusty miller, forget-me-not, flowering kale, nierembergia, shirley poppy and calendula. Vegetable seeds that can be planted include carrot, broccoli, radish, spinach, cauliflower, kale, Swiss chard, leeks and hardy herbs.

Sweet pea seeds can be planted after midmonth. Irrigate them well after planting, then shade with branches or burlap, and do not water again until they break through the ground. Excess water in hot weather causes a fungus disease and destroys germinating seed in the ground.

Spray chrysanthemums to protect them from red spiders. Continue to feed until they show color. Stake the taller varieties.

This is the time to get busy on lawns. If yours is not to be oversown with winter rye, it should be fertilized. If it is bermudagrass and is to be oversown, start withholding water at the end of the month. If you had no summer lawn, but wish a winter rye lawn, the rye may be planted late this month. Before seeding, soak the ground 6 to 8 in. deep. A few days later rake the surface. Sow the seed at the rate of 2 lb. per 100 sq. ft., with 1 lb. of ammonium sulfate to each 100 sq. ft. Cover lightly with a mulch of ground manure at the rate of 1 yard to 1000 sq. ft. Keep constantly moist while seeds germinate. Start cutting with the mower set high, as soon as the grass is tall enough—usually within a week or 10 days.

Plant colorful flowers in tubs and pots for use on your terrace or around your pool. Petunias head the list, especially the new red, pink and white cascade type, which truly do cascade. Other good flowers are verbena, African daisy, dwarf snapdragon and calendula. For low pots use pansy, viola and alyssum. Geraniums are good but should be in containers small enough to move indoors on cold nights. More permanent plants for containers are boxwood, twisted juniper, kumquat, calamondin, bamboo, sago palms, camellia, gardenia and podocarpus.

The kind of soil you have in your yard may determine the way that you garden. Caliche is a term unknown in most sections of the country, but in much of the Southwest caliche is commonplace. This is a hard limestone formation that sometimes may be broken up with a pick, but more often requires a jackhammer. If you live in a low area, you probably have plenty of soil since it has washed in from high ground for centuries. But in the foothills there is no topsoil

left. You can either excavate flower beds to a depth of 2 ft. and bring in top soil to fill them, or you can use pots and tubs, or build raised planters.

Camellias have well-developed buds by now, so be sure to keep the root area moist at all times. If soil dries out at any time, it can cause dropping of buds next winter. When new buds are large enough to twist off, remove the excess so that only one is left at the end of each stem. That will insure some large blooms, instead of a lot of small ones.

Start geraniums from cuttings. For the right method, see the chapter on starting plants.

OCTOBER

Intermountain, Plains, and Southwest Zones 5 and 6

Leaves begin to show their autumn colors about the time of the first frosts. Let this be a signal to remind you of two things. First, bring in the tender plants that have been outdoors for the summer. Then go to the hills and enjoy the autumn splendor. Aspen and native sumac are especially beautiful.

The big job for October is planting spring-blooming bulbs such as tulips, daffodils, scillas and hyacinths. In this area they should generally be planted at least 50% deeper than is recommended in directions that come from Holland. Also it is wise to plant them in a partly shaded place; they will do better and last longer.

Pot up a few tulips and other bulbs to grow for indoor bloom. For instructions, see the chapter on indoor gardening, under the sub-

ject of gift plants and their care.

If you want to plant some new peonies, or transplant old ones, early autumn is the time to do it. The same applies to bleeding-heart.

When the leaves have fallen from deciduous trees, it is an indication that they have become dormant. It is a good idea to give them a watering that will last them for several weeks.

Do not delay pruning overly heavy limbs of trees. Attention to this may prevent much storm damage if heavy, wet snows come early.

Look around your garden, and those of your neighbors, to see what plants are especially attractive in autumn, especially in leaf color or fruits. Make a note to plant more of these things next spring.

Clean up the garden now for winter. Remove dead plant tops. Trim the edges of your lawn. Prune and shape hedges. Rake up surplus leaves. Do not burn any of the leaves, plant tops and other good organic material unless it is diseased. Save all of this in a compost heap and let it decompose, to be returned to your garden soil as humus. Do not try to be too neat in your autumn clean-up. A few leaves lodging around perennials is nature's way of tucking them in for winter.

Now is the time to plan for improvements in the structural parts of your garden—repair the gate, paint the fence or relevel the stepping stones. This is also a good time to tackle new projects such as a rock garden, a little pool, new steps or a screening trellis.

Do not forget the birds. Start putting out some food for them when the weather is bad. Once you start, keep it up! It will take some time for them to find your feeder, but you should never disappoint them. Next spring, plant more things that provide edible fruits for the birds.

Roses will need to be mounded with earth next month, and at that time the ground may be frozen and difficult to dig. Why not set aside a pile of soil now, and keep it frost-free by covering it with leaves or straw. Then it will be ready when you want it.

Southwest Zones 7, 8 and 9

It is time to buy and set out plants of annuals that will bloom during the winter. One that should be started as early as possible, and certainly before the end of December, is stock. Other annuals that will bloom all through the cold months include calendula, Iceland poppy, sweet alyssum, anemone, pansy and viola. If you are trying to provide color for a spot in winter shade, try forget-me-not, violets and fairy primrose.

If your location is a cold one, select the site for your winter flower bed with care. A bed against a wall facing south is the perfect position, because daytime heat is stored by the masonry and given off at night. Such a position becomes even better if a paved walk or drive is in front of the bed.

You can make desert plantings bloom in early spring by broadcasting seed of African daisy and California-poppy. Buy these seeds in bulk. After scattering, cover them with a light mulch of pulverized manure, and keep the area constantly damp with portable sprinklers until the small plants appear. After that, a heavy weekly sprinkling will be sufficient.

Late in October, spring-flowering bulbs may be planted. These include daffodil, hyacinth, tulip, Dutch iris, ranunculus and anemone. The hyacinths and tulips should be refrigerated first for a couple of weeks.

October 15 is ordinarily a good date for planting a winter rye lawn where there has been bermuda. Contrary to general practice, do not renovate bermuda at this time; renovating disturbs the root system, and later freezing and thawing weakens it for spring growth. Instead, shave the bermuda just as close to the ground as is possible with a low-cutting mower. Then overseed with the rye, using the same general method mentioned last month.

Container-grown chrysanthemums in bloom will be for sale in nurseries this month. Plant in full sun or semishade. This is one of a limited number of perennials that thrive in Tucson.

With cool weather, roses will be at peak again. You can select and plant container-grown bushes in bloom. Roses continue until a killing frost, which sometimes does not come until after Christmas.

Beginning in the middle of October, reduce the frequency of irrigation, in order that plants may harden off and be better able to resist cold when it arrives. This applies especially to tender plants such as citrus and bougainvillea. These should not be planted where they are watered with winter annuals or a winter lawn, since constant watering will stimulate tender growth which will be susceptible to frost.

This is one of the most popular months for planting trees and shrubs.

Poinsettias, to look their best for Christmas, will need staking.

Things in your garden that may need feeding include winter lawns planted in September that may be showing some yellow, and flowers planted at that time.

NOVEMBER

Intermountain, Plains, and Southwest Zones 5 and 6

By now you should be pretty well recovered from summer's routine of water-weed-spray, and can give attention to other things. How about getting some new plants for the indoors, such as a geranium for the window sill, some African violets for the east room, a philodendron for your shady hall? Try potting up some of your smaller outdoor petunia plants to see how they will behave indoors.

If there is not much frost in the ground yet, you can still transplant some of the things you missed out on earlier.

Check again for moisture content in the soil around all roots. Any day now it may freeze up, and then the hot sun of winter can dry out the plants unless their roots have water.

Roses should have soil hilled around their bases.

As the days become crisper, you can do some of the more strenuous things with pleasure. For instance, you may have an old, obsolete shrub that should be removed. Getting rid of undesirable plants is just as important as planting new ones that are needed.

Do everything that can be done to prevent winterkill. This word covers many things. A small part of the damage may be caused by cold temperatures. But by far the most injury results from the opposite of cold—that is, hot, dry weather and sunshine in winter. Remember that most of our ornamental plants have been brought from other parts of the world, where there is more rainfall,

more cloudy weather, more snow cover, and temperatures that are more predictable. Here in the sunshine states we humans love the winter sunshine, but the plants cannot get used to it. While we humans love to live close to the mountains, the plants cannot adjust themselves to the quick weather changes caused by this nearness. Because there has been limited rainfall here for hundreds of years, soils are alkaline and the plants from elsewhere cannot tolerate them.

To prevent winter damage, you should water carefully and thoroughly, erect windbreaks, provide shade for some things, and —when choosing plants to buy—get those that are tolerant of this climate. When watering, soak slowly, so the moisture will reach to the farthest roots. Dig down to make sure how far the water has penetrated.

If you have not started feeding the birds, fix a feeding station now.

Southwest Zones 7, 8 and 9

Plant bulbs of tulips, hyacinths, daffodils, Dutch iris, ranunculus and anemones. Tulips and hyacinths should be refrigerated for several weeks before planting. They do best in full sun, but daffodils will bloom in almost complete shade. Anemones will bloom when it is too cold for most flowers to show color. When buying bulbs of anemone and ranunculus, it pays to get the choice large size sold by dealers handling quality products, rather than buying small bargain sizes.

Started plants of winter vegetables, broccoli, brussels sprouts and cabbage may be set out now. Avoid cauliflower because it becomes badly infested with aphids.

For something unusual and eye-catching, plant flowering kale. It is related to cabbage, but has very decorative and colorful rosettes of foliage and can be planted and used for garden ornament.

Winter rye lawns can still be planted if your plot is in full sun. In shade its ability to get started will be a gamble with the weather.

Container-grown chrysanthemums and roses can be purchased and planted—in bloom.

From now through the spring months, nurseries will have camellias in bloom. If you have the proper location in full shade, and are willing to make adequate preparations, it is possible to have a succession of camellia blooms from early November through April. Because most of the Southwest has an alkali soil condition, and camellias like acid soil, preparation of soil is all-important for success. In solid caliche, dig out the caliche to a depth of 2½ ft. and dispose of all excavated material. To do a good job of separating the bed from surrounding caliche, line it with roofing paper. Then backfill with a mixture of ⅓ red mesa topsoil, ⅓ coarse sand and ⅓ Canadian peat moss. It is better to have more peat moss than less, for this is the one ingredient of a camellia bed that should not be limited.

Gardenias thrive in the same type of location and bed-preparation as camellias.

Contrary to general impression, camellias and gardenias are not cold-tender plants. Of the two, the gardenia is the less hardy.

Trees and shrubs planted in November will not put out any new growth until spring. So all winter they will look as though they are standing still. And they are—above ground. But underneath, their roots are developing, so that by spring they are ready to shoot ahead with no time lost for root establishment. However, foliage of nandina bushes planted now in full sun will undergo a change from green to crimson. These, planted among low-growing junipers, make a pleasing color contrast.

DECEMBER

Intermountain, Plains, and Southwest Zones 5 and 6

If you cannot be sure what your garden friends want for Christmas, give them gift certificates from some good nursery or garden shop. Then each can have just what they most want, at the time best suited to planting.

In planning plantings for your yard, locate an evergreen tree where it can be decorated each year for Christmas. This allows hundreds of passers-by to share the beauty with you.

There are still some places where you can go and cut branches of evergreens to use for decorating at the Christmas season. But do not get anything without first obtaining permission.

Check the bulbs of gladiolus, tuberous begonias, dahlias, etc., that you have stored, to be sure that their temperature and moisture content is all right.

If the ground is frozen, you can cover the garden with a mulch to keep this frost in. Mulch is usually more beneficial for keeping cold in than for keeping it out.

Protect the trunks of young fruit trees and choice flowering trees from rabbits by wrapping them or applying some of the effective repellents. In the higher altitudes, deer may do considerable damage. Sometimes strips of metal foil hung from poles will scare them away.

If you remembered to pot up a few tulips

and other bulbs in October, and put them in a cold cellar or pit, you can bring out a few now and soon have bright color in the house.

Make an inventory of what good the garden did you in the last 12 months. Then make another list of what you have done to pass on these benefits to others. When we give, we always get back more ourselves!

Subscribe to a garden magazine. If you already receive one or more, this is the time of year to read the issues that you were too busy to enjoy earlier. Clip worthwhile stories that you wish to file.

Southwest Zones 7, 8 and 9

Winter and spring annuals can still be planted, and this is the last month in which one of the favorites, stock, can be set out. Since it is late in the season, it is important to use annuals from plant bands, rather than those cut out of a flat or other container. Annuals in plant bands have root systems that will not be disturbed when set in the ground.

It is time to set out delphinium plants; this perennial should be treated as an annual in the Southwest. It puts out beautiful full spikes of flowers in the spring, but will not survive the summer heat except in elevations of 6,000 ft. and more.

Plant hollyhock, canterbury bell and foxglove. These biennials do well the first year, but, like delphinium, will not survive the summer heat at lower elevations.

Set out bulbs such as tulips and hyacinths (both after refrigeration), Dutch iris, daffodils and gladiolus. Lilies planted in full shade will usually perform at least the first year.

If we have not had a killing frost, continue spraying roses, and spray for aphids on stock and other plants.

After a killing frost there will be a lot of cleaning up to do. Cut chrysanthemums to the ground. Pull out remaining summer flowers that you may not have had the heart to take up before.

Early-planted winter rye lawns will need to be fertilized if they are to retain a deep green look. By now, bermuda lawns will be entirely brown and can be dyed green if desired.

Preparations for cold-protection for plants should be made by the middle of December. Areas of tender plants requiring a minimum of water during cold months, should be separated by dikes from winter annuals that will require more watering. If you have any cold-tender plants, drive stakes or make a frame so that protective material may be fastened without touching the plant.

Irrigating once every 3 weeks will be adequate for most trees and shrubs through the end of February.

If you wish a living Christmas tree, the aleppo pine is far and away the first choice for the Southwest. It does well and requires no special care, growing eventually 30 ft. or more high and wide. Second choice is the deodar cedar. It has the accepted pyramidal Christmas-tree shape, but in small tree size it is usually very thin and the branches are not strong enough to hold ornaments and lights. Do not buy a tree in a container so large that it cannot be easily handled. And be sure that it is one that has been growing in a container, and not recently set into it. While the tree is in the house, watch the watering carefully so that there is enough moisture, but not so much as to make the soil soggy. Plant as soon after Christmas as possible.

Bare-root roses and deciduous fruit and shade trees will be on the market in some sections of the Southwest now. The sooner they are selected and planted the better.

THE WEST

*Cacti and other succulent plants look at home
in the sunny, arid Southwest.*

COMBINED SEQUENCE OF BLOOM
FOR INTERMOUNTAIN, PLAINS
AND SOUTHWEST ZONES 5 AND 6

(For descriptions, including hardiness, see appropriate chapters.)

Early Spring

Bulbs: Crocus, Siberian squill, grape-hyacinth, glory-of-the-snow

Annuals: Pansy and viola

Shrubs: Pussy willow

Spring

Bulbs: Tulips, daffodils

Perennials: Bleeding-heart, rock-cress, columbine, primrose, moss-pink, Iceland poppy, bluebell, basket-of-gold alyssum

Shrubs: Vanhoutte spirea, thimbleberry, bush honeysuckle

Trees: Cherry, crab-apple, service-berry, hawthorn

Early Summer

Bulbs: Lilies

Perennials: Tall bearded iris, peony, oriental poppy, Shasta daisy, coreopsis, delphinium, pinks and hardy carnations, gas-plant, foxglove, gaillardia, babys-breath, day-lily, coral bells, hollyhock, lupine

Shrubs: Late lilacs, butterfly-bush

Trees: Horse-chestnut, mountain-ash, golden-rain-tree

Vine: Large-flowered clematis

Late Summer

Bulbs: Canna, dahlia, gladiolus, tuberous begonia

Annuals: Petunia, sweet alyssum, marigold, nasturtium, cornflower, zinnia, verbena, salvia, poppy, snapdragon, cosmos, China aster, nicotiana, geranium, ageratum, stock, larkspur, lobelia, calendula

Perennials: Hollyhock, phlox, poker-plant, goldenrod, golden-glow, chrysanthemum, sunflower, fall aster, sedums, gloriosa daisy

Shrubs: Chaste-tree, tamarisk, bluebeard, rose-of-sharon, hydrangea

Trees: Catalpa

Vines: Trumpet-vine, silver lace-vine

Fall

Colored fruit: Pyracantha, bitter-sweet, cotoneaster, mountain-ash, sumac, barberry, hawthorn, crab-apple, viburnums, elders, privet, coral-berry

Colored foliage: Amur maple, euonymus, sumac, barberry, viburnum, cotoneaster, englemann ivy

Winter

Colored bark on trees or shrubs: Willow, poplar, sycamore, birch, red- and yellow-stemmed dogwoods

Evergreen foliage: Pine, juniper, spruce, fir, mahonia, pyracantha, English ivy, *Vinca minor*, wintercreeper

SOUTHWEST SEQUENCE OF BLOOM
FOR ZONES 7, 8 AND 9

(If you live in Zones 5 or 6, see calendar for Intermountain and Plains.)

January

Flowers: Bougainvillea, African daisy, Calendula, Iceland poppy, pansy, petunia, sweet alyssum

Shrubs: Camellia

February

Flowers: Same as January plus daffodil, Dutch iris, dwarf phlox, hyacinth, gerbera, stock, and sweet pea

Shrubs: Japanese quince, camellia, *Cassia artemisioides*

Trees: *Acacia farnesiana*, flowering peach, redbud

March

Flowers: Add to February's list tulip, carnation, snapdragon, verbena, geranium, wisteria

Shrubs: Camellia, *Cassia artemisioides*, rose

Trees: Citrus, *Acacia farnesiana,* flowering peach, redbud

April

Flowers: Winter-blooming annuals continue. Beginning are foxglove, gazania, columbine, coral bells, iris and amaryllis

Shrubs: Gardenia, camellia, lilac, oleander, *Raphiolepis*

Trees: Palo verdi, flowering peach, citrus

May

Flowers: Petunia, geranium, snapdragon, calendula, Iceland poppy, phlox, delphinium, hollyhock, pansy, verbena, day-lily, amaryllis, gerbera, gazania, bougainvillea

Shrubs: Gardenia, abelia, oleander, pomegranate, *Raphiolepis*, yucca

Trees: Palo verdi, magnolia, silk-tree

June

Flowers: Gazania, nierembergia, zinnia, marigold, Madagascar periwinkle, Shasta daisy, gloriosa daisy, dwarf dahlia, pink, gerbera, lobelia, rose-moss, bougainvillea, passion-vine

Shrubs: Pomegranate, gardenia, hibiscus, lantant, rose, oleander, crape-myrtle, shrimp-plant, *Raphiolepis*, yucca

Trees: Silk-tree, magnolia, crape-myrtle

July, August, September

Flowers: Gerbera, gloriosa daisy, nierembergia, marigold, zinnia, Madagascar periwinkle, verbena, gazania, canna, bougainvillea, passion-vine

Shrubs: Crape-myrtle, hibiscus, lantana, oleander, shrimp-plant, plumbago

Trees: Crape-myrtle

October

Flowers: Chrysanthemum, marigold, zinnia, Madagascar periwinkle, verbena, spider-lily bougainvillea, passion-vine

Shrubs: Oleander, rose, hibiscus, lantana, plumbago

November

Flowers: Chrysanthemum, petunia, calendula, pansy, sweet alyssum, verbena, spider-lily, bougainvillea

Shrubs: Same as October

December

Flowers: Same as November

Shrub: Poinsettia

Regional Calendar of What To Do
Month-By-Month

❧ The Pacific Coast

The Northwest—by Jeannette Grossman, Garden Writer and Photographer, Portland, Oregon

Northern California—by Iva Newman, Garden Editor, *The San Mateo Times;* teacher of horticulture judging, National Council Flower Show Schools

Southern California—by Dr. Robert E. Atkinson, Garden Consultant, *Los Angeles Times' Home Magazine;* Garden Director, KNX radio, Los Angeles

JANUARY

Pacific Northwest

This is a cold and rainy month.

As a tempting foretaste of blossoms to come, cut branches of flowering almond, flowering quince, winter jasmine and forsythia to force their flowers indoors. The method is explained in the chapter on how to pick flowers.

Then prepare for spring by doing the following things.

Have the lawn mower sharpened and see that other tools such as trowels, spades and hoes are clean and sharp.

Listen to the weather reports and be prepared to use dormant spray on deciduous trees and shrubs if a mild, clear spell is in the offing. Sprays are ineffective if rain falls within 24 hours of the application. Before spraying roses, remove all remaining leaves and rotted buds.

List new plants you want to try this year, and order flower and vegetable seeds for spring planting.

Remove fallen leaves from low-growing heathers and groundcovers. Wet, matted leaves, especially the large ones from chestnut and bigleaf maple, may cause small plants to die back or turn brown.

Heavy, wet snow may cause limbs of trees and shrubs to break. Take a broom or mop and lightly tap snow from branches before it gets too heavy.

Avoid walking on the lawn if the ground is frozen or soggy from heavy rains.

Visit plant nurseries toward the end of the month. You will see a surprising number of plants that can brighten the winter garden with bloom and colorful berries.

Young bare-rooted trees are in good supply now, so buy before stocks are picked over. Nurserymen are happy to advise you regarding staking and support for trees of your choice.

Northern California

Rain, frost and possibly some 70° temperatures make January a variable month. Normally, frost is light in the San Francisco area, but about every 10 years there is a big freeze that takes a heavy toll of subtropical plants. A low of 16° is not uncommon in the central valley. The Sierra foothill area may drop to 6° or 10° in low valleys.

Plantings of bare-root materials is at its peak. Roses head the list with fruit, nut, flowering and shade trees a close second. Cane berries, rooted grape cuttings, wisteria, flowering quince, forsythia and other spring-blooming deciduous shrubs are also available at nurseries.

Pruning operations should be scattered over both January and February. Fruit and nut trees should be done in January. Roses should wait until the first of February to prevent a chance of frost damaging new growth. Flowering trees (except cherries, which are not pruned) are pruned while in flower or just afterward.

The main rose task this month is clipping all foliage from climbing and bush plants, to help push them into dormancy. The clipped leaves and any on the ground should be raked up and burned to destroy insect eggs and disease spores that may be wintering on them.

Deciduous trees and shrubs, including roses, should be dosed with a good clean-up spray. Use Bordeaux solution, lime sulfur, or oil at winter strength. Choose a clear, wind-free day, and if possible wait until early morning fog has dried from branches.

Plant pansies, violas and Iceland poppies. Other annuals will flower just as early if you wait until February to set them out.

Make the first planting of gladiolus corms.

On lawns, use a pre-emergence crabgrass preventive after the 15th of the month. Otherwise a 10-day warm spell will cause crabgrass seeds to germinate. Fertilize the grass. Wait to plant grass seed until warm weather is definite.

Southern California

If you have not already set out winter-blooming annuals, now is the time to get sweet alyssum, pansy, viola, calendula, pink, Iceland poppy and snapdragon at garden supply stores.

Perennials for winter color include marguerite, English primrose, English daisy and bergenia.

Plants grown in containers can be planted at any time. But the month of January opens the big bare-root planting season when all manner of deciduous plants are on nature's bargain counter. Best known are bare-root roses. Some plants that you might not expect to find sold this way include grapes, strawberries, raspberries, blackberries, and certain perennials, such as gerbera.

Shade trees are special bargains when planted in January; if you wait to plant them in summer they may cost twice as much. There are a few never sold bare-root because they do not easily recover if dug without soil about their roots. Two of these are crape-myrtle and sweet-gum.

Fruit trees must have a low chilling requirement to thrive here. Only certain varieties of peaches, plums and apples are adapted, but almost all types of apricots do well. Cherries and pears usually do not grow well where winters are mild. Fruiting/flowering peaches such as 'Double Delight' and 'Saturn' have low cold-requirement and give double enjoyment. 'Bonanza' is a new dwarf.

Camellias and azaleas in bloom this month are in their dormant period so you can choose plants in full bloom and plant immediately.

FEBRUARY

Pacific Northwest

There are signs of spring now. Mild periods bring out crocus. Winter-flowering heathers are reaching bloom peak. Three especially fine heathers which bloom from late January until April are 'Springwood White,' 'Springwood Pink' and 'Ruby Glow.' Their low mounds of moss-green foliage are most effective in groups of 3 or more plants of one variety. Use them as groundcovers for slopes, as edging plants for taller, acid-loving shrubs, or to soften the edges of terraces or drives.

Dormant spraying and most pruning jobs should be completed by the end of this month. In cooler Puget Sound areas, rose pruning should usually wait until March. Cut back vines of large-flowered clematis varieties to within 10 to 12 in. of the ground. Summer-blooming shrubs such as French hydrangea and butterfly-bush should be pruned this month. Remove all wood that bloomed last year and about ⅓ of the weakest and twiggiest remaining growth. Thin and prune raspberries, currants and blueberries.

Complete plantings of bare-rooted deciduous trees and shrubs, including roses. After planting roses and cane fruits, mound soil around canes until growth starts, to protect against drying winds.

Sow seeds of the annuals sweet alyssum, clarkia, larkspur and calendula in the bare ground. For early-blooming sweet peas, sow in rich, well-drained soil. In the vegetable garden, a first sowing of green peas can be done. If you have a few feet of ground near your kitchen door, sow parsley and plant a clump or two of chives in order to have these herbs handy for seasoning hurry-up meals.

Start tuberous begonias in damp peat moss.

As for camellias: Buds which are showing color may be cut and brought indoors where they will open in a few days. If you planted a camellia under an overhang to protect its blooms from rain and wind, check the soil to see that the plant is getting ample moisture. If you like rose-pink varieties, consider a recent introduction called 'Brigadoon' with long-lasting flowers starting to open this month.

On chrysanthemums, when green shoots appear, take cuttings from them and discard the old woody clumps.

Lawns should have their first application of fertilizer by the end of February.

If you have noticed showy heads of pink flowers blooming now in Puget Sound and Willamette valley gardens, it is bergenia. The large, leathery leaves are somewhat coarse, but the plant has merit where a bold, easily grown groundcover is needed.

Northern California

This can be the wettest, coldest month in the year. Yet, there is usually one weekend when weather is perfect for gardening. Do not let a false touch of spring lead you into setting out tender plants that can be ruined by sudden frost.

Planting of bare-root trees and shrubs heads the list of important tasks.

Dormant spraying is a must. If you did not get a winter-strength oil spray on deciduous fruit and flowering trees and roses to wipe out scale, do it now before the buds swell.

Pruning is another important task. With roses, wait until the 15th of the month to begin. If you start earlier, frost can damage resulting new shoots and cause imperfect flowering. In the coastal and valley areas, roses never go dormant so pruning should not be as heavy as in colder areas. For the general principles of pruning, see the chap-

ter on roses. However, with reference to our northern California area, a good general rule is to shorten the major canes no more than ¼ to ⅓ of the previous year's growth.

Fruit-tree pruning should be completed as soon as possible, but flowering shrubs and trees should not be pruned until immediately after they have flowered, or while in flower. For fuchsias, wait until March.

Camellias are in bloom, and camellia shows are scheduled. This is also planting or transplanting time since camellias are at their most dormant period while in flower.

Tuberous begonias should be checked for signs of life. If you see tiny pink buds showing in the center of tubers, start them growing.

New lawn seedbeds can be prepared now, but it is too early to sow the seed. Crabgrass pre-emergence killers can still be applied in most areas. All lawns can stand an application of high nitrogen fertilizer to stimulate spring growth.

Start the vegetable season by setting out divisions of artichokes, asparagus and rhubarb available at nurseries this month. Seed of lettuce, spinach, chard, parsley, peas, beets, carrots, radishes and onions can go in. Plants of broccoli, cabbage and cauliflower are available.

Southern California

Sow seed of quick-growing annuals such as sweet alyssum over tulip and daffodil bulbs.

It is time to prune roses, peaches, nectarines and deciduous shade trees. On roses, a good general rule is to prune hybrid teas no lower than 24 in., grandifloras no lower than 30 in. Floribundas should have the old blossoms trimmed off and that is about all.

Prune peaches and nectarines severely because fruit is formed on 1-yr.-old wood; remove ⅓ of the fruiting wood each year.

Apricots and plums bear fruit on spur branches which produce for 3 years, so prune them to replace fruiting wood every 9 years.

After pruning, it is customary to apply a dormant spray which controls many insects and diseases. An oil spray is commonly used against scale insects, and lime sulfur against fungus diseases and red spider mites. Do not use lime sulfur on apricots; use a copper spray instead. Be careful not to get oil on ferns and azaleas.

Fertilize grass lawns and all garden plants, except newly planted roses, camellias, azaleas and any tropical plants where succulent growth might be subject to frost damage. Dress dichondra lawns, and shrubs and flower borders, with composted humus.

Basket fuchsias should be pruned to the edge of the container; cut those in the ground back ⅓. Mulch with a 2-in. layer of peat moss. Repot established fuchsias in a mixture of peat moss and composted sludge.

Buy plump begonia and dahlia tubers.

Frost damage is likely this month. You can prevent a degree or two of it from injuring groundcovers and vegetables by turning on sprinklers and letting them run slowly all night. Do not use this method on trees and shrubs which may be broken by ice. For valuable trees and shrubs, construct a canopy above the plants. It should not touch leaves and does not need to cover sides. This utilizes heat retained in soil and ordinarily lost by radiation into a clear sky. A lighted electric bulb placed under the canopy will give all the protection necessary except under the most severe conditions.

Do not immediately prune plants damaged by frost, but allow them to sprout first.

MARCH

Pacific Northwest

Temperatures are rising gradually. Blustery winds and sudden hailstorms are often followed by a day or two of shirt-sleeve weather.

Rose pruning should be done when swelling buds are plainly visible. In Puget Sound and Basin regions, it should be done between mid-March and the first of April.

Moss in lawns is a common problem. An application of iron sulfate this month rids the lawn of it and does not harm the grass.

Tender annuals and vegetables that are being started indoors now must have sufficient light to prevent weak, spindly growth. Consider some of the newer methods of artificial lighting to insure sturdy seedlings. (They are discussed in the chapter on indoor plants.)

Moles and slugs are becoming active, so start control by baiting and trapping. The strawberry weevil, another Northwest pest, is especially fond of primroses but also likes other perennials and rhododendrons. Apply bait around roots to kill grubs before they emerge as adult leaf-eaters.

This is the best time to plant magnolias, before they start into active growth. Rhododendrons and other broad-leaved evergreens, as well as narrow-leaved ones, can be planted if your soil is light enough to be worked properly.

Should you have a new house, and be planning to plant rhododendrons, heathers and other acid-loving shrubs next to it, beware of excess lime. Plaster and concrete deposits, sometimes left on the ground by workmen, are often the cause of plant fatalities.

Double-flowering peaches and almonds should be pruned severely after they have blossomed. They are the only flowering trees which may be cut freely for indoor decoration.

Some of the loveliest flowering trees and shrubs come into bloom this month. Star magnolia is laden with white blossoms, and everywhere there are clouds of bright pink flowers on blireiana plum. There is fragrance too in the delicate blossoms of the evergreen shrub delavay osmanthus and the showier flower heads of burkwood viburnum. A rhododendron of medium-low growth which deserves special mention is 'Cilpinense.' It has apple-blossom pink flowers. While the buds are nipped by frost some years, the gamble is worth taking.

It is time to divide summer-blooming perennials such as coral bells, phlox and monarda. Plant the strongest divisions from the outside of the clumps; discard old, woody central parts.

Northern California

Weather is unpredictable. One weekend may be clear and warm; the next cool and frosty. Daytime temperatures average in the mid 60's. High winds, 40 to 50 miles per hour for 2 or 3 days at a time, are a problem.

Gardeners in the intermountain areas can take advantage of warm days to spray and prune but should not set out tender young plants.

Shopping at nurseries is a delight this month, for they are loaded with plants in bloom, including camellias, daffodils, pansies, primroses and flowering trees.

The top-priority job is providing plenty of moisture for newly set plants so winds will not cause severe leaf burn.

Do not prune plants that suffered frost damage earlier. When new growth starts, they can be cut back to just above that new growth.

Annuals for summer that can be started from seed in coastal and inland valley areas in open ground include sweet alyssum, forget-me-not, nasturtium, nemesia, salpiglossis, summer-flowering sweet peas, godetia, larkspur, ageratum and salvia. Pegging a piece of cheesecloth over freshly planted seeds prevents wind from drying out the soil and interfering with good germination. Water through it.

Bedding plants can be purchased at nurseries. Among the best buys are cineraria, petunia, stock, snapdragon and annual phlox. Heat-loving plants like zinnia will do better if set out next month.

March is one of the best months for setting out perennials. These are available as transplants and also in gallon cans. The little transplants need another year of growing before they flower while those in cans will bloom like old-timers this season.

Plant summer-flowering bulbs, such as gladiolus, agapanthus, calla, canna, clivia, tigridia and montbretia.

In coastal and inland valley areas, March is the time to fertilize every plant in the garden. April and May are best for intermountain regions. Always have soil moist before applying any fertilizer.

Fuchsias can be pruned back hard now in all but the coldest areas. Those in pots should be repotted immediately after being pruned, using rich, porous compost. Those in the ground should be fertilized after pruning.

Watch geraniums for tiny new growth along branches and cut plants back to strong growth near their base. If the cut-off pieces have not been injured by frost, 4-in. tip cuttings from them can be rooted. Cuttings started last fall can be set out now.

Tender plants such as hibiscus, bougainvillea and Burmese honeysuckle should not be set out until the end of the month.

If you have not started a monthly fertilizer program for your lawn, do not put it off.

Southern California

Seed of annuals, including aster, marigold, petunia, zinnia and celosia, should be started indoors. Do not transplant them into the garden until weather is mild and the soil warm.

Bulbs that can be planted this month include dahlia and tuberous begonia, but keep them in a warm place, embedded in peat moss, until they sprout. Plant gladiolus and iris in the garden now or any time of year; repeated plantings of gladiolus keep blooms coming all year.

Shop for the many flowers in full bloom to give spring color, including marguerite, geranium, English and fairy primroses. Cuttings of fuchsia and carnation made this month can be set out after rooting and will bloom this year.

This is the last month that bare-root roses, fruit and shade trees are available.

Poinsettias lose their leaves and become unsightly now, and should be cut back to only 1 or 2 buds. You can use the stems to produce more plants because they root readily when inserted in the ground. After growth begins, cut back the branches repeatedly to make them bushy.

Because soil never freezes in the mild winters, it lacks the conditioning derived from freezing and thawing. In addition, these soils lack humus. This is a good time to add copious amounts of composted humus to flower beds prior to planting. It should be spaded deeply into the ground for best results.

Prune early-flowering shrubs, such as forsythia, flowering almond and flowering quince, after they are through blooming. Flowering fruit trees can be pruned when in full bloom, or branches may be cut in bud and brought into the house to bring spring indoors.

Grass lawns can be planted any time in Southern California, but spring and fall are preferable for cool-season types, including bluegrass, fescue and bent. After thorough preparation of the soil, including an application of 2 to 3 in. of composted humus mixed in with a rotary tiller, plant the seed. If you cannot water every 2 or 3 hours during the day in the first week, apply ½ in. of mulch evenly over the seedbed. Then the grass can be left safely without watering oftener than morning and evening, except on the hottest days.

APRIL

Pacific Northwest

April is a gala month. Daffodils and polyantha primroses are at their peak. The lovely Yulan magnolia greets the first days of the month with blossoms resting like white porcelain cups on the bare branches. Petals of early-flowering trees fall like snowflakes while a multitude of later ones rush into bloom. Small bells of grape-hyacinth and Siberian squill make a carpet of clear, light blue, while Japanese andromeda presents a

double show with bright new growth and ivory-white bells in drooping clusters. Opening in moist woodlands are western trilliums and dainty yellow violets.

In the Rogue Valley, there are balmy days in the high 60's. But nighttime temperatures sometimes drop to freezing levels, calling for smudge pots to protect pear orchards from damage.

Often there is a dry spell this month. This is a critical time for broad-leaved evergreens which are starting into new growth. So get out the hose and water.

Indoor-started seedlings should be transplanted and pinched back. Give these and tuberous begonias plenty of light, but avoid direct sun on the latter.

To prevent troubles, bait and trap for slugs and moles. Spray or dust roses and also fertilize them. Dust daffodil plantings to control narcissus fly. Cut and burn dead stalks of peonies if you did not get this done last winter; give their new shoots a spraying with Bordeaux solution to prevent botrytis blight.

Mulch trees and shrubs and apply acid fertilizer to established plantings of camellias, azaleas and rhododendrons. Mulch raspberries and other cane fruits with several inches of manure or compost. Also spread a mulch of peat moss or bark dust on the ground between small groundcover plants and heathers. This conserves moisture and discourages weeds.

It is pruning time for both winter- and summer-flowering heathers. On these, and on forsythia, flowering quince and spirea, cut back the branches that have bloomed. Other shrubs to prune this month are abelia and ceanothus.

Seeds of the vegetables that grow best in cool weather should be planted now. These include lettuce, carrots and radishes.

Gladiolus corms can be planted, but wait until next month to plant dahlias.

If your spring-flowering bulbs are not planted near spring-flowering shrubs, this is the time to make notes on where to move them this fall. Here are some good color combinations: Daffodils and forsythia; blue Siberian squill 'Spring Beauty' and pink royal azalea; blue grape-hyacinth and white evergreen candytuft; mollis or Knap Hill azaleas and blue Spanish bluebells.

Good spring combinations that feature perennials used with shrubs are these: Rhododendrons 'Blue Tit' or 'Snow Lady' with an edging of forget-me-nots, pansies or primroses; white Vanhoutte spirea underplanted with white or pale yellow polyantha primroses.

Caution: Be on guard against the gyp artists who start their door-to-door selling this month. They offer super humus, magic lawn rejuvenator and sensational new plants. If you buy these so-called bargains, you usually end up paying a high price for a sad experience. Buy only from established dealers whose prices are comparable to those of competitors.

Northern California

One lovely sunny day follows another in April, though wind may be a problem. Flowering cherry, native dogwood, wisteria, rhododendron, azalea, bearded iris, early tulips, late daffodils, and even a rose or two, provide spectacular color.

Watering heads the list of chores, for no longer is there a chance of a stray shower. Plants are growing lustily, and even a short period on the too-dry side will leave its mark for weeks. Since water is the most expensive item of California gardening, study your watering pattern for a minimum number of hose settings. Look into some of the new watering gadgets which might save time and money.

April is seed-planting time for most vegetables. If you are considering tomatoes, they are slow to ripen in coastal gardens, but more rewarding in inland valleys and intermountain regions where night temperatures are higher.

Annuals started from seed this month bloom in July and August.

Spraying for pests is almost as steady a chore as watering. Timing is important if you are to get the full benefit of the spray material. Have a professional attend to large trees since it takes heavy power equipment to penetrate their heavy foliage.

Earwigs and ants can be a severe problem unless you head them off. Use either a spray solution or a dust containing 10% active chlordane. Thoroughly cover every foot of the garden including the lawn; even shoot it into the crotches of trees. Then go around the outside of the house foundation, along walks and over patios. One good application keeps the garden free for a year.

Aphids can be found on new tip growth on everything from roses and chrysanthemums to camellias. Watch especially tulips, callas and fuchsias. Regular applications of an insecticide are needed.

Citrus can be set out in April. Once a plant becomes established, it can tolerate colder weather, but a muslin frame should protect a young citrus the first 2 or 3 winters that it is in the garden—even in coastal areas.

Camellias generally finish flowering this month. Thin out extradense branch growth. Rake up fallen blossoms, being sure to get every petal. Feed plants with an acid-type fertilizer, and water it in. Mulch. Keep the soil moist through the coming months, for one hour of being too dry will cause bud-drop and poor flowering next winter.

Southern California

Be alert for aphids on roses and other plants whose tender shoots attract them. Spray when they first appear for they increase rapidly.

Fertilize camellias and azaleas, as well as all other garden plants and lawns. Use cottonseed meal to fertilize acid-loving plants.

When you visit your nursery, look for rooted cuttings of carnations and chrysanthemums to set out. Carnation cuttings will be accompanied by the flowers, so you will be able to choose colors you want.

Snails are most active during spring's moist, cool weather. If their damage is noted, apply bait that attracts and poisons them.

This is the best month to plant tropical and subtropical shrubs and trees that need warm soil for root growth. Included are citrus and avocados, hibiscus, bougainvillea, tropical palms, banana and ti plants. Certain tropical plants used as groundcovers do best when planted this month. They are lantana, gazania, most species of ice-plant, verbena and alternanthera. Annuals to set out this month include marigolds, petunia, celosia, rosemoss, salvia, China aster and zinnia.

Citrus and avocado varieties have to be chosen with great care, depending on the area in which you live. For instance, lemons do well in the cold climate near the Coast, while oranges thrive in the warm inland areas. Grapefruit and tangerines require the hot desert climate to produce good fruit.

If you live in a lemon area, you must choose the warmest location in the garden for oranges, and a hot one for grapefruit. In the desert area you would grow lemons and probably oranges in the shade. You can have citrus fruits ripening every month of the year by judicious selection. In cold areas, kumquats may be the only thing you can grow.

Avocados are of 2 types: Mexican and Guatemalan. The Mexican are more cold-resistant. The 'Fuerte' avocado, a cross between these two, does best around Ojai in the San Fernando and San Gabriel Valleys, the Riverside-San Bernardino area, and interior San Diego County. In the coastal area, 'Anaheim' and 'Hass' varieties do well. In Los Angeles and Orange Counties, 'Bacon' and 'Zutano' are best. 'Hass' does well everywhere and is rapidly replacing 'Fuerte' in commercial groves. The ripening time of Mexican varieties, including 'Zutano' and 'Bacon,' is November and December; of Guatemalan varieties, including 'Hass' and 'Anaheim,' July to September; of 'Fuerte,' March through June.

MAY

Pacific Northwest

Warm, sunny days have arrived. Suddenly it is lilac and tulip time. Forests of dark firs provide a sheltering canopy for the snowy blossoms of western dogwood. It is also rhododendron time. If you live in the Portland area, this is the month to visit the test gardens of the American Rhododendron Society. Here azaleas and rhododendrons display an impressive mass of bloom in a landscaped setting of lawns, wide paths, giant firs and a placid lake. Admission is free.

May marks the end of hard frosts, and tender annuals and vegetables can be planted outdoors by mid-month. Dahlia tubers can go in now, too. Wait until mid-May to set out fuchsias, geraniums and tender annuals, such as petunia, zinnia and marigold. By the end of May it is usually warm enough to set out tuberous begonias and tomatoes. Set out rooted cuttings of chrysanthemums and when their new growth is about 4 in. high, pinch out the tips. Be sure to shade all newly set plants from hot sun for a few days.

Continue April jobs of weeding, spraying and baiting. As weather becomes drier, watering becomes more important.

Stake tall-growing perennials, such as delphinium, and spray delphinium foliage with Bordeaux solution to prevent mildew.

As plants finish flowering, many need attention. Cut back trailing kinds such as aubrieta, rock-cress, and basket-of-gold alyssum. On daffodils and other early-flowering bulbs, remove faded flowers but leave the foliage to ripen. On rhododendrons, camellias and lilacs, remove the spent flowers or clusters of flowers.

Pruning jobs this month include cutting back winter-flowering jasmine. Young abelias and photinias should have their tips removed to prevent straggly growth. On flowering quince and wisteria, wood that has produced flowers should be cut back, and new growth should be shortened several times during the growing season.

If you are planning color combinations of flowers for future years, here are some suggestions. While the acid-yellow flowers of doronicum and orange tulips is a good combination, do not plant these colors near pink dogwood, pink *Clematis montana rubens* or red rhododendrons. Avoid yellow basket-of-gold alyssum with pink tulips, and orange and flame azaleas near pink rhododendrons.

If your color taste runs to blue and violet, there is a wealth of those colors this month in wisteria, violas, pansies, forget-me-not, lilacs, ajuga, catmint, aubrieta and bearded irises. There are endless possibilities for using these with pink, red, yellow or orange.

Northern California

There are hints of summer in the air. Some rain is possible. Plants are putting on new growth at amazing speed. Insect pests and garden diseases thrive also, but prompt action can place you in control. Plants in bloom include rose, dogwood, hydrangea, horsechestnut, rhododendron, lilac, ceanothus and ice-plant.

The major job is to finish spring planting! It is too late to set out bare-root plants in most of Northern California. However, plants in containers and those balled and burlaped can be set out if there is ample soil moisture.

Dahlias can be planted now, and in June.

New lawns seeded early this month give a good covering quickly. Temperatures are cool enough so that 1 or 2 waterings daily can keep the surface moist. Water by hand with a very fine spray. You can wash out the seedbed trying to water with your finger over the end of the hose! Wind is so constant in portions of the Bay area that the only way to keep seed from blowing away is to cover newly seeded areas with horticultural cheesecloth.

Clematis is opening its big, showy flowers on container-grown vines in nurseries now, so it is a good time to make a selection.

Cut summer water bills by spreading a mulch this month. It reduces evaporation from soil, lowers soil temperatures and controls weeds. Use ground bark, leaf mold, steer manure or sawdust, keeping it at least 3 in. from the base of the plant or root crown.

Hibiscus should be planted this month. Most of us treat them as annuals since they seem to succumb to the lightest frost. But you can grow them in containers and bring them under cover for winter. Give them a warm, protected spot.

Spray peonies with Bordeaux solution, ferbam or captan for botrytis. Give them plenty of water and a light application of high phosphorus fertilizer.

Southern California

If you have not already done so, set out ageratum, asters, petunias and marigolds this month. But there is no value in setting out zinnias or planting seed of zinnias before the soil becomes thoroughly warmed; later plants invariably catch up with those planted earlier. The same is true of tomatoes and corn.

Bulbs to plant this month include gladiolus, dahlia and tuberous begonia. Sprouted dahlias and tuberous begonia tubers are best, insuring an early start for the plants.

This is a good month to apply weed controls to dichondra lawns. There are many choices available. Some do a better job on grass weeds while others control oxalis and clover. They can be applied with fertilizer to encourage the dichondra to fill in when weeds are gone.

The newest grasses for Southern California lawns are hybrid bermudas. These are fine-leaved grasses which spread very rapidly and make a tight turf that withstands much wear. The main disadvantage is some browning in winter months. They do not grow well in the shade. For a shady lawn area, consider planting zoysia grass which has tight, dense turf like bermuda.

Many perennials can be purchased in full bloom for continuous flowering through summer. The most colorful are pelargoniums, but gerbera, pink and Shasta daisy are all in this class.

Stake delphiniums, since their spikes must be held erect for best display. Pinch fuchsia, chrysanthemum, carnation and any annual you wish to make more compact and floriferous.

Prune spring-flowering shrubs such as spirea, weigela, forsythia, flowering quince and flowering almond.

Continue spraying roses to control aphids but this month use a mildew control also, such as Karathane or Acti-dione. Flower thrips often are troublesome this month and prevent the normal opening of roses.

Thin peaches, plums and apricots when the fruits are about ½ in. in diameter. Leave 1 peach for every 6 in. of branch, and 1 apricot or plum for every 3 in. of branch.

JUNE

Pacific Northwest

June is a balmy month in the Northwest, with cloudless skies and warmer temperatures except in seacoast regions. In Seattle and Willamette Valley regions, a rainstorm may occur. Wind and rain will break bloom-heavy delphinium stalks, so be sure plants are well staked.

This is a big month for roses. All through

the Northwest shows are held, and this is the time to see Portland's famous Rose Festival. In your own rose garden, do not cut long-stemmed blooms from young plants; allow the bushes a year or two to form strong canes. If you are interested in edging your rose beds with a low-growing perennial, some plants with pretty flowers at rose-blooming time are coral bells, pinks, violas and Carpathian harebell.

Main jobs this month are the control of aphids and blackspot on roses, and summer pruning and watering. While overhead watering is relished by broad-leaved evergreens and conifers, avoid wetting foliage of roses and perennials, for this encourages mildew. A strong stream of water aimed at the undersides of conifers will discourage red spider mites. Remove flowering wood from mock-orange, beauty-bush, deutzia and weigela when their bloom is gone. Rub off water sprouts on fruit and flowering trees and keep a diligent watch for suckers growing from the root stock of grafted plants, such as roses and lilacs.

Finish setting out bedding plants and warm-season vegetables, such as tomato and pepper. Give geraniums full sun; they bloom better if the soil is not too rich, and watering is kept to a minimum.

Remove spent blooms on perennials. Wait to pull out forget-me-nots until they have scattered seed, so you will have plenty of self-sown seedlings for next year.

It is time to sow seeds of biennials such as sweet william, pansy, wallflower, hollyhock, foxglove and Canterbury bells. Sowing may be done in boxes, or in moist, open ground.

Lawns should be kept thoroughly watered, with special attention to areas where tree roots compete for moisture.

Primroses appreciate having a little bone-meal scratched around them, and some of their old leaves removed to encourage new growth.

Now that most rhododendrons and other broad-leaved evergreens are out of bloom, take a critical look at their foliage masses and form. Perhaps a feathery, upright-growing clump of bamboo, or the strong silhouette of a pine is needed to relieve the monotony of too many rounded forms. Bamboo is available in cans if you want to plant now. Wait until fall to plant balled pines if the ones available in cans seem too small. *Pinus contorta*, the native coast pine, is a good choice. In selecting bamboo, the invasive habits of some types should be considered. The hardiest are the running types, and root control is usually necessary. This is done by placing underground barriers of galvanized sheeting, or concrete poured to a depth of 3 ft.

Star perennial performers for June are oriental poppies, lilies and delphinium. Lovely as these are, their on-stage roles are brief and then they rest. It is wise to use foreground plantings to hide the bare spots left by these resting beauties. Peonies, *Aster frikarti* and day-lilies are especially good for the purpose.

Northern California

June weather is like that of May but warmer. Fog rolls in each evening to cool coastal gardens, while valley gardeners find plants wilting unless given extra water. Average maximum temperatures for the Bay area are 65 to 72°, for Sacramento 85 to 90°, and in intermountain areas 75 to 82°. Little or no rain is expected.

Watering is the most important job until rains start again in December.

This is the season to change plantings of bloomed-out winter annuals (such as stock, nemesia, Iceland poppy and calendula) for warm-weather flowers. Pull out the old plants, and then immediately soak the soil with an all-purpose insecticide-fungicide. This gets the troublemakers before they can relocate. If you are going to compost the old plants, spray them with the same solution so any pests are prevented from returning.

Fertilize plants frequently, both those in containers and in the garden, since constant irrigation leaches nutrients from the soil. Fuchsias, dahlias, chrysanthemums, roses and all annuals need a monthly feeding. Most of them, during this fast-growing period, benefit from a fertilizer relatively high in nitrogen such as a 10-10-10 (10% nitrogen, 10% phosphorus, 10% potash). If quickly soluble material is used, it is better to fertilize lightly every 2 weeks than heavily once a month. New slow-releasing chemical nutrients and the plastic-coated nutrients are more expensive to use, but they nourish a plant from 60 to 90 days with no leaching. They are especially worthwhile for plants in containers.

Pruning is needed to cut back spring-flowering shrubs after they have bloomed. Then fertilize and water deeply.

Camellias and azaleas have finished blooming. Remove any lingering buds and flowers. Clean the soil carefully beneath plants. Fertilize by watering in a dry fertilizer, or using a liquid fertilizer such as fish emulsion. Do not dig in dry fertilizer since roots are right on the surface. Add or replace mulch to save moisture and keep roots cool.

Roses should be fertilized every 30 days until September 1. They need 5 to 6 gal. of water per plant about once a week in most areas. In San Francisco, where soil is mainly sand, more frequent irrigation is needed.

Bearded iris clumps that have become so crowded that they bloom poorly should be lifted and divided. (See the chapter on perennials for details.)

Lawns of bluegrass should be fertilized every 30 days and watered about twice a week. Set your mower to cut at a 1½- to 2½-in. height.

Established dichondra plantings should be cut with the mower this month to prevent bunching. Cutting 2 or 3 times a year will keep the planting smooth.

New dichondra plantings can be made now using either seed or nursery-grown starts. Soil preparation is the same as for grass. Save yourself a lot of hand-weeding by using one of the preplanting weedkillers after the soil is prepared. It adds to the cost but you will be so sorry if you do not do it.

Southern California

It is not too late to plant asters, petunias, marguerites and zinnias. Even though you planted some last month, you will get prolonged bloom by planting more now. Do not plant asters in the same location in which they were planted last year unless you are sure you have wilt-resistant varieties.

Groundcovers set out this month will cover more quickly than at any other time. Verbena, lantana, dichondra, bougainvillea, ice-plant and star-jasmine are good examples.

Fuchsias can be purchased in bloom. For hanging baskets, use 3 plants to get the fullest effect.

This is the best month for planting palms and bamboos; also tropical fruits, including papaya, sapote, cherimoya, banana and litchi.

Mildew may appear on tuberous begonias. It is easily controlled with sprays of Karathane or Acti-dione.

Watering becomes a major chore this month and should be done regularly and thoroughly to avoid problems. Overhead watering, contrary to the opinion of many, is a good way to water once in a while. It helps control mildew and red spider damage, and washes smog and dust accumulations off leaves. However, it should be done only in the morning, because when plants go into the evening wet, fungus disease may be induced.

Dichondra lawns must be watered twice a week in hot weather, and most grass lawns once a week, except bermudagrass—every 10 days to 2 weeks. In hot desert areas, and where soil is light, these rates must be increased. Leave the water running at least an hour to soak to a depth of 1 ft. Shrubs must be watered at least 2 hours, and trees overnight, letting the hose run slowly into the basin. Mature trees need watering only once a month.

Mulch, applied thickly, can reduce the frequency of watering and control weeds as well. It is especially important with roses, camellias, azaleas and other plants where a high humidity is desired. Camellias and azaleas are very shallow-rooted and can be permanently damaged by allowing the soil surface to dry.

The patio season begins this month. Dress up the area with plants in containers, either flowering or foliage types.

JULY

Pacific Northwest

July brings long, sunny days, and near-perfect weather for gardening. Along the coast, temperatures stay in the cool 50's, climbing inland to the comfortable 70's.

Since this is one of the Northwest's driest months, watering demands top priority. First on this list is lawns, which need thorough, deep watering rather than frequent light sprinklings. Fertilize grass this month to stimulate steady growth and rich green color. Moisture-loving perennials such as ferns, Japanese iris and astilbe need lots of water.

Remove faded flowers from annuals to prevent seed formation. Cut plenty of sweet peas for arrangements; if allowed to set seed, these soon stop flowering. Fuchsias and begonia should be fertilized, sprayed, and given ample water. Chrysanthemums need to be pinched, disbudded, and fertilized with ammonium sulfate every 2 weeks until buds show color.

Roses need water about every 10 days. Dust or spray their foliage regularly. Scratch in a complete fertilizer around bushes and water in.

Make final plantings of dahlias, gladiolus, beans, corn, cucumbers and squash. Winter vegetables, such as cabbage, broccoli and turnips, should go in now.

This is the month to dig and replant crowded clumps of daffodils, bearded irises and primroses.

If you are going on a vacation, do not wait until the last minute to give the garden a thorough watering. Plants such as fuchsia, begonia, and those in containers, will need the care of a coöperative friend or neighbor during your absence.

You may want to consider some of the drought-resistant plants to reduce watering chores and insure more carefree vacations in future years. Many of the gray-foliaged plants add a soft, pleasing texture to dry, sun-baked areas. Some of these are woolly thyme, *Stachys lanata,* snow-in-summer, pinks, dwarf rosemary, sedums, santolina and dusty miller. Taller perennials for dry soils include globe thistle, showy sedum, oriental poppy, coreopsis and yucca. Annuals such as California-poppy, rose-moss, and verbena supply summer color with a minimum of watering. Shrubs that are undemanding of moisture are mugho pine, cotoneasters, sumac, pyracantha, hypericums, manzanita, *Choisya ternata,* barberry, broom and juniper.

Northern California

Days are now warm or hot everywhere, but nighttime temperatures depend upon where you live.

Water, water, water is the rule by which Northern California gardeners live in summer. The amount needed, and frequency of application, depends upon many things, including the type of soil and whether plants are deep- or shallow-rooted. Shallow-rooted things like azalea, camellia and rhododendron suffer when the top few inches of soil are dry. The time of day that you water makes a difference. In early morning and after 8 P.M., you have high water pressure so every watering device works at peak efficiency. Avoid watering when wind is blowing since the sprinkler pattern is disrupted and the water wasted.

To save water, make basins beneath trees and shrubs, extending them as far as the branches reach. Direct water into these where it will wet the soil and root area rather than being wasted on bare ground. Water when the sun is not up, or at least avoid the period from 10 A.M. to 5 P.M. Spread a mulch 2 or 3 in. deep over all cultivated areas to reduce surface evaporation.

Tuberous begonias are beginning to flower. They can be transplanted easily when in bloom. Experienced gardeners wait to replenish plantings until July when world-famous growers in the Santa Cruz area let customers go into the fields and choose their own plants.

Sow perennial seed now. It is an ideal time to sow delphinium; plants from a July sowing may flower this fall, though they will not put out a normal-sized spike of bloom until next spring. Watch for snails and slugs; it is best to spread a bait just before new sprouts are due to appear.

Southern California

Since this is swimming-pool season, it is a good time to consider which plants are best for use in the pool area. Not all are equally good. Broad-leaved plants—if they drop leaves at all—are as bad as deciduous trees. Needle evergreens are fine but somehow do not provide an appropriate setting. The best trees are palms, dracaenas, bananas and yuccas. They never cast their leaves, but usually old leaves

must be cut off. Perhaps the best palm is the Senegal date palm, whose curved trunk can be trained out over the pool to simulate a coconut palm of the tropics. Either the Abyssinian banana (*Musa ensete*) or the edible banana is handsome in a sheltered location, but their leaves shred badly in wind. The Abyssinian banana forms a single stem, and when it flowers, it dies. The edible banana forms many suckers, which continue to grow indefinitely.

The giant bird-of-paradise is another ideal plant; it makes a vertical, tropical accent. The arborescent philodendrons and the tree-fern also lend a tropical appearance; however, the latter cannot be grown in full sun.

Low-growing plants that are excellent near a pool are found in the succulents: *Agave attenuata*, aloes, aeonium and century plant.

This is the time of year when plants that thrive on neglect are especially attractive to gardeners harassed by the chore of continual watering. We naturally think first of California natives which subsist without summer rain. California lilac, matilija-poppy, fremontia and carpenteria are excellent for dry hillsides that cannot be watered.

Succulents that make good groundcovers and require little attention include the many species of ice-plant, several kinds of sedum and echeveria.

Popular desert plants for landscape use are the ocotilla and the many species of prickly-pear (*Opuntia*). The elkhorn euphorbia, species of cereus, and felt plant (*Kalanchoe beharensis*) are also used. Yucca, aloe and aeonium are other good choices.

Dahlias and chrysanthemums should be disbudded this month if you wish to have prize blooms.

If you go away on vacation, soak your trees and lawns before leaving, and add mulch around your roses and shrubs. They can probably go for 2 weeks without any further attention.

AUGUST

Pacific Northwest

The weather is unusual when in some years temperatures soar into the 90's. This situation seldom lasts more than a few days.

Watering heads the list of chores. Humidity-loving plants such as fuchsias and begonias need a light sprinkling each day. Newly planted shrubs and trees will need more water than established plants. If rhododendron leaves begin to curl, this is a sign that they need water in a hurry. Turn on the sprinklers and water foliage as well as roots.

Stake and tie tall-growing chrysanthemums, and disbud exhibition types. Tall, late-blooming perennials, such as autumn asters, should be staked now. Dahlias should have plenty of water and a feeding or two of fertilizer low in nitrogen. Several perennials are dormant for a short period in August, so should be divided and replanted at this time. They include astilbe, bleeding-heart, oriental poppy, Christmas-rose and other hellebores. Dormant bulbous plants, such as hardy cyclamen and colchicum should also be planted this month.

Trees, both deciduous and evergreen, should have their summer pruning early this month. It is important, even on young trees, to encourage an open-branching structure by removing crossing branches and those that tend to grow inward. Pruning cuts made now have a chance to heal rapidly.

Top perennial of the month is phlox. The showy heads of fragrant bloom give an opulent effect to the summer border. Pink varieties are especially pleasing with clumps of steel-blue globe thistle or clear blue veronica. They combine well with edgings of petunias, ageratum or lobelia. White phlox adds a soft glow to the garden at night.

This month the Cornish heaths come into bloom. Three varieties, 'Mrs. D. F. Maxwell,' 'Lyonesse' and 'St. Keverne,' are a mass of pink and white appreciated by humming birds.

Northern California

Warm to hot days with cooler nights are the general rule. Exceptions are portions of the Coast, where hot weeks may alternate with cool ones, and inland valleys where heat lessens after dark. No rain is ever expected in August.

Watering is by far the most important task. Only a garden of native plants can be left without a "sitter" for more than a week. Every day some part of the garden needs extra moisture. Do not rely on surface appearance but check a foot or two deep where the roots are.

If camellias, azaleas and rhododendrons get dry for even an hour, they may drop many of their flower buds. Nightly syringing of the foliage, after the sun goes down, refreshes the plants. Camellias in containers will need almost daily watering. A mulch over the soil will help, as will wrapping the container with several thicknesses of burlap. Start disbudding camellias now. Most varieties have much larger and prettier flowers if all but one flower bud in a cluster are removed. Allow 1 flower bud for each 3 in. of stem. You can tell the flower buds from leaf buds because they are fatter.

Most perennials, such as delphinium, coreopsis, and Shasta daisy, are at the end of their bloom. But if they are cut back, fertilized with a balanced plant food and kept watered, they will produce another crop of flowers this fall.

Madonna lilies are planted now, though other lilies are planted later. If gophers are a problem, set the bulbs in a hardware cloth basket, made deep enough to extend 1 in. above the surface and wide enough to accommodate the bulb and 2 or 3 in. of root.

Citrus need regular watering, about once a week in sandy soil, and more often in hot weather. If they get too dry they will drop their leaves and fruits. Fertilize young citrus once a month. Those in containers should be fed every other week. Watch for, and spray for, aphids, mites and scale. One of the largest growers of dwarf citrus recommends malathion for all 3 of these pests.

Dahlias are at their peak of beauty. Be sure their heavily laden stems are securely staked and tied to prevent breakage. Watch for mildew and at the first sign of it spray with an all-purpose fungicide-insecticide. Basin-out the soil, and water heavily once a week.

Fuchsias are also at their prime. Most fuchsia hobbyists drop nitrogen from the twice-monthly fertilizer program at this time, and use an 0-20-0 fertilizer to keep the flowers coming. The San Mateo County Floral Fiesta and the San Francisco Flower Show have huge fuchsia exhibits this month that are worth visiting.

Southern California

Soil alkalinity often becomes an acute problem in Southern California in August. This is due to the alkaline irrigation water which is added to the soil and continuously evaporates, leaving the salts behind to accumulate like lime in a teakettle. Acid-loving plants are the first to show signs of distress, but eventually all plants are affected, even those that do not show symptoms. Excessive alkalinity first ties up iron, manganese and zinc, and as the pH gets higher, phosphorus, potash and nitrogen also are made unavailable to the plants.

To control alkalinity when planting, always mix a cupful of soil sulfur thoroughly with the soil in the planting hole. After a plant is established, use a soluble acidifier. Iron sulfate, aluminum sulfate and liquid lime sulfur applied to the top of the soil will penetrate and correct alkalinity.

Salts in irrigation water also can be directly harmful. If they occur in sufficient quantity in the soil, they can prevent the absorption of water by the roots. You can leach out these harmful salts by watering heavily. But such watering also washes away fertilizers, so you must reapply them.

Some soils are prone to become compacted, and impervious layers are formed below the soil surface. Drainage must be improved or else the plants will suffer. You can break up the layer by deep cultivation or with an aerating tool.

Lawn insects and diseases often become prevalent in August. Larva of lawn moth (sod webworm) is the most common insect attacking bluegrass lawns. Cutworms are the most damaging to dichondra. Both are easily controlled with insecticides which can be combined with fertilizer.

Crabgrass makes bluegrass and dichondra lawns unsightly because it turns red at this time. For ways to control it, see the chapter on lawns.

Crape-myrtle blooms in August and can be obtained in tree or shrub form at the nursery. Plants with red, white and pink flowers are available.

Low humidity this month damages many plants, but especially camellia buds, tuberous begonias and fuchsia flowers. Sprinkle these plants often to raise humidity and make sure sufficient mulch is present to protect their shallow roots.

SEPTEMBER

Pacific Northwest

The first days of September are much like August. But there is a hint of change in the dry rustle of a leaf as it skitters across the lawn. Sometime during the month the dry summer weather is broken by the first fall rain, and then the delightful days of Indian summer are ushered in. Flowers and lawns put on fresh make-up to greet the quiet, hazy days and dew-laden nights.

In the garden the spotlight shifts from tired annuals to hardy asters and Japanese anemones. Do not overlook *Aster frikarti*, whose 2½-in. flowers of soft blue continue to open from mid-August through October. This showy aster forms a mound of gray-green foliage 2 ft. high. Consider, too, the hardy dwarf asters in named varieties. These make fine edging plants for September and October, and require no staking as do the regular tall types.

A small bulbous plant which blooms this month is the hardy *Cyclamen neapolitanum*. Both a pink and a white flowering form are available. The pretty marbled leaves unfold as blooms fade, providing an attractive groundcover until their summer dormancy. Hardy cyclamen like filtered shade and the leafmold soil of a woodland area. Good companions are the bulb flowers colchicum and autumn-blooming crocus, which flower at the same time.

This is a fine time to plant or transplant many things. If rains moisten the soil enough so that it can be worked, it is a good month to plant broad-leaved evergreens; roots establish themselves in the warm ground and during fall rains. New lawns should be planted early in the month so that they will be well along before cold weather comes. Spring- and summer-blooming perennials can be divided and reset. Daffodils, hyacinths and other spring-blooming bulbs should be planted now, but wait until October to plant tulips.

Order lily bulbs for late fall planting.

Northern California

Some of the most delightful weather comes in September, California's second spring.

There is less fog; days are bright and clear.

Watering is still the most important task. Use a soil auger to check whether the soil around roots of trees and shrubs is moist enough.

Bedding plants to fill your garden with color through winter are at the nurseries. You will find pansy, viola, nemesia, fairy primrose, snapdragon, winter stock and Iceland poppy. There is time to grow these from seed if you hurry, but flowering will start much later. For an attractive border, try nemesia backed by winter stock and snapdragons.

If summer annuals were pulled out to make space for these winter bloomers, it is wise to treat the soil with an insecticide-fungicide dust before planting. Follow label directions.

Perennials may be found as bedding plants at nurseries, and this is an economical way to buy them, for once they are moved into gallon cans the price jumps fantastically.

Sweet peas can be had for Christmas if you use seed of "early-flowering" varieties, plant early this month, water and fertilize carefully, and have luck with weather.

On bulbs for fall planting, watch for early arrivals in order to get some of the largest, as well as some of the new varieties which are frequently in short supply. Even though tulips have been precooled, you will have better results if you buy them early and keep them in the vegetable compartment of the refrigerator until planting time in December. Time to plant most spring-flowering bulbs is October.

Do not fertilize roses after September 1, so new growth will have a chance to mature and harden by dormant-pruning time. Keep up watering.

On chrysanthemums, stop fertilizing any that show color, but keep up the watering program. Check stakes and ties on tall varieties and those with large flowers. Use furrow or flood irrigation, since overhead watering adds too much weight to blossoms. Keep up a regular spray program for insects and mildew.

New lawns are advantageously started this month. Seeding may be done any time in coastal areas, the early part of the month in intermountain areas, and at the end in inland valleys.

Southern California

September is often the warmest month. Cutworms and red spider mites often damage dichondra lawns now. Use DDT or toxaphene to control cutworms, and Kelthane to kill red spiders. Red spiders also infest many other garden plants including trees and shrubs. Kelthane sprayed over the entire garden is usually recommended, although regular overhead irrigation also keeps them under control.

Plant sweet peas, calendula, snapdragon, pansy and stock for fall and winter color. Seed them where they will grow in the garden, or plant in flats and set in a cool, shady location. Either way, protect them with polyethylene plastic film to prevent the soil surface from drying out and to avoid continual watering. The new 'Bijou' sweet pea, a bush type that does not need a lattice on which to grow, will bloom in December if planted this month. Use Spencer sweet peas if you prefer the vine type, but either will provide ample blooms for bouquets. New hybrid snapdragons have extra vigor and a longer blooming season than old types. Both pansies and violas can be obtained in solid colors, most effective when planted in clumps.

Replace summer flower beds of tuberous begonia with bulbs of cyclamen. Summer annuals should be pulled out and replaced this month.

Revitalize soil in flower beds by adding a thick layer of composted humus, and spading it in deeply before doing any planting.

On hydrangeas, prune all stems which have produced flowers. Do not cut the nonflowering stalks; they will produce blooms early next year.

Divide bird-of-paradise any time it is not in bloom. Cut pie-shaped segments out of the plant, but do not disturb the plant lest you retard its flowering.

This month, the Santa Ana winds begin to blow and can cause severe damage to garden plants. Uprooted trees often can be saved if they are righted immediately and pruned severely. Before pulling the tree upright, remove enough soil under the exposed roots to permit them to be set back into the earth without being forced. This space under the exposed roots keeps roots from acting as a pry which could damage roots on the other side and result in the death of the tree. Young trees should be staked to prevent their toppling.

Much damage is caused by low humidity brought on by these desert winds. Leaves dry faster than they can be supplied with water from the roots. Water trees deeply to prevent this type of injury. Citrus trees are especially susceptible and react by dropping their leaves.

Withhold fertilizer from azaleas, camellias, fuchsias, indeed most plants except grass and dichondra lawns.

OCTOBER

Pacific Northwest

Usually there is a noticeable difference between October and September weather. Days are cooler, rainfall is more abundant, and nights are crisp. Seasonal change is also evident as deciduous trees and shrubs glow with the gold and scarlet colors of autumn.

Visit nurseries this month if you want to select plants with fine autumn hues, because some forms color better than others. One Japanese maple may have brilliant leaf color while another is disappointing. Redvein enkianthus and the summer-blooming small tree sour-wood can usually be depended upon to produce glowing scarlet leaves. An excellent large tree for brilliant foliage display is sweet-gum.

October is often a windy month, so check young trees and chrysanthemums to be sure that they are well staked.

Things to plant include spring-flowering bulbs and lily bulbs, also broad-leaved evergreens.

Take in tuberous begonias, geraniums and fuchsias. Dig up dahlias, gladiolus and other tender bulbs. Harvest and store fruits and vegetables.

Lawns should have a final cutting. Make neat edges where grass has grown into beds. Select an overcast day to apply an all-purpose fertilizer to the grass. Rake bare spots, apply sifted compost, and reseed. If heavy traffic on a grass path presents a maintenance problem, consider substituting pea gravel or ready-made concrete blocks.

Clean-up jobs done now save hours of maintenance in spring. Rake up leaves and add them to the compost pile. Do not include foliage of peony or rose, which may harbor disease. Manure is still one of the best materials for use as a fall mulch, since it contains slow-acting fertilizers. Wet beds before applying mulches.

Northern California

October starts warm but ends cool. Some rain may come, but do not count on it.

Watering is still the most important job.

This is the best time to start new lawns. Old ones need generous fertilizing and can have renovating attention.

Annuals for bloom in winter and early spring should go in now as bedding plants; it is too late to start them from seed. Good ones are fairy primrose, snapdragon, stock, viola, pansy, lobelia and calendula. In milder coastal climates, cinerarias are usually good but they are quite frost-tender. Sweet alyssum can be bought as bedding plants, but seed sown in October gives good results. However, if you wish this flower as a groundcover for bulbs, you should start some now in flats for transplanting in November and December after tulips and hyacinths are planted.

Perennials are an excellent buy in flats this month, since the price per dozen will scarcely equal the cost of one in a gallon can next spring.

All of the popular spring-flowering bulbs except tulip and hyacinth can be planted this month. Along the San Francisco peninsula they should be set 2 to 3 in. deeper than the general rule of 3 times their greatest diameter. This is because the upper soil stays too warm for proper root development. Use either bonemeal or superphosphate in the soil below the bulbs, since most Northern California soils are deficient in phosphorus and it is most difficult to get this element down into the root area after the bulbs are planted.

Tulip and hyacinth bulbs should be kept in the vegetable compartment of the refrigerator until planting time, which is late October or early November in the intermountain areas, November and December in valley areas, and December to early January in the San Francisco and Monterey Bay areas.

Japanese iris will be arriving at nurseries toward the end of the month. This iris does especially well all over Northern California.

Dahlia tubers should be lifted and stored.

Cuttings can be made of pelargoniums, fuchsias and hydrangeas. In the case of the first two, this is a safety measure, because every so often a severe freeze hits all of Northern California. Use 2- to 3-in.-long tip cuttings of pelargoniums, and hardwood cuttings of the same length for fuchsia and hydrangea.

Southern California

Chrysanthemums bloom profusely from early October until late fall. You can buy them at nurseries in full bloom and plant them in the garden or in containers. When they finish flowering, cut them back. Next spring they can be divided to make more plants to bloom next fall, and if you want still more plants, cuttings root very easily.

Shop this month for the best selection of daffodil, hyacinth and tulip bulbs. Daffodils, ranunculus and scillas should be given particular prominence because they easily naturalize in Southern California gardens. Tulips must be stored in a refrigerator until late November in order to get even one year of satisfactory bloom.

Tender bulbs such as freesia, wand-flower (*Sparaxis*), cape-cowslip (*Lachenalia*), African corn-lily (*Ixia*), veltheimia and nerine can be grown outdoors in Southern California. They do not need winter chilling to bloom, but respond to periods of alternate wetting and drying. They can be planted all together in a container and set on the patio for continuous bloom through the year.

Do not overlook such minor bulbs as cyclamen, star-of-Bethlehem, and grape-hyacinth.

This is the best time to plant native California shrubs, for they often die when watered if planted at other seasons. Wild flower seeds scattered this month will turn waste places into blazing colors next spring.

Colorful fall foliage, according to many people, is lacking in Southern California. But a tree easily grown here that gives brilliant yellow color is ginkgo. Others whose leaves turn red or yellow are sweet-gum, pistache, red oak, Japanese maple and crape-myrtle.

Bird-of-paradise, the city flower of Los Angeles, starts blooming this month and continues through winter and spring. It is a tough plant but needs full sun for best growth.

Sweet peas, snapdragons, calendulas and stock set out this month will give winter color in a sunny location, while pansies, cineraria and primroses do the same for a shady place.

Continue to water lawns, trees and shrubs until fall or winter rains arrive.

NOVEMBER

Pacific Northwest

This month brings gales, heavy rains and the first heavy frosts. The bare branches of trees are shrouded in wintery fog and braced for a possible snow flurry.

While November dictates a tapering off of garden work, some chores should be done if weather permits. Continue your garden clean-up; rake up leaves and twigs, remove rain-soaked buds and some of the twiggy growth from roses. Dormant spraying can be started. In heavy clay soils dig in compost or manure, leaving the surface rough; this makes spring preparation easier. Give small plants a protective mulch to prevent heaving from frost. Bring in, clean and store ceramic plant containers before heavy frosts damage them.

Continue to plant lilies and tulips. Bulbs of easy-to-grow Dutch iris should also go in.

November need not be a colorless month in the garden. Plants with fruits and berries now have their day. Pernettyas are gay with white, pink, rose or violet berries, and the hawthorns are laden with clusters of showy red fruits. Wintergreen covers the ground with dark foliage studded with cheerful red fruits. Pink flower buds on laurestinus viburnum start to open this month, providing contrast with the metallic-blue berries. Strawberry-tree also displays both fruit and bloom this month with clusters of hanging ivory bells and red "strawberries."

A cheerful foliage plant for the winter garden is *Calluna vulgaris aurea*. A drift of this golden heather is like a patch of sunshine on a dreary winter day. Another gloom-breaker is the sasanqua camellia, which, depending on variety, blooms from late October until after Christmas.

If your soil is well-drained, sweet peas and green peas can be planted this month. November planting usually results in earlier sprouting and stronger plants. Try the following method: Dig a trench 12 in. deep and work in a layer of rich compost. Plant the seed and cover with several inches of soil and press firmly. As the plants grow in spring, gradually fill in soil around them until the trench is almost full.

Northern California

Weather may be warm or cold. Get set for rain though we may have drought instead.

Store dry soil for use in planting bare-root material next month and in January.

Clean up the garden. Fallen rose leaves should be picked up, since many insect pests and fungus spores winter over in the soil. Camellias and azaleas should have all debris removed from beneath their branches; it serves to shelter dread "petal blight."

It is too early to plant bare-root material, but watch for balled-and-burlaped trees and shrubs which arrive at nurseries this month —they are an excellent buy if you want something larger than 5-gallon size. They must be planted at once.

On roses, it is too early to prune and too early to set bare-root plants. However, you can dig holes and store the removed dry soil for use later in planting.

Dig and store "bulbs" of gladiolus, dahlia

and tuberous begonia. For instructions, see the chapter on bulbs.

Lily bulbs arrive at nurseries this month. Be on the alert, for the sooner they are planted the better—lilies never go truly dormant. They have two serious enemies: excess moisture about roots, and rodents. Raised beds and tile drains are the best assurance of fast drainage. Hardware cloth baskets are the best rodent preventative; make them tall enough to extend 1 in. above the soil surface.

Rainy weather brings out snails and slugs. Spray under shrubs and other likely areas with new snail-slug killers, or spread baits.

Southern California

Set out annuals, if you have not already done so. Plant tulips that have been chilled in the refrigerator. Plant lily bulbs, and finish up on other bulb planting.

Shop now for sasanqua camellias, which are in full bloom in the nursery and which transplant easiest at this time. They are ideal for espaliers, hanging baskets and groundcovers.

Harvest dahlia and tuberous begonia tubers this month and store in dry vermiculite after they have been thoroughly dried.

This month you can turn your bermuda lawn into a green winter carpet by overseeding with ryegrass. Cut the bermuda as close as possible or renovate with a vertical mower. Sow with ryegrass and mulch with steer manure. The grass will germinate in 3 days and you will be cutting green lawn within 2 weeks.

Some camellia varieties set buds too heavily and should be disbudded. Remove buds of all sizes so that you can maintain a long blooming period. When only the larger or only the smaller buds are removed, the flowers appear later or earlier as the case may be.

Plant bare slopes with a mixture of ryegrass, purple vetch and birdsfoot trefoil to prevent erosion by this winter's rains. Perennial groundcovers planted now will hold slopes permanently as soon as they have time to grow. Choose deep-rooted kinds for fill slopes. Plant out slopes with vines set in basins, fertilizing the soil in the basin before planting.

Most shrubs can be planted this month to gain an extra season's growth. Winter rains take care of the watering necessary, and the roots grow well in the cool season. Next spring these shrubs will develop much faster than plants set out in spring, because they will have become well established.

Cymbidiums and epidendrums are orchids that can be grown outdoors in the ground in the coastal regions of Southern California. Cymbidiums are forming flower spikes this month and should be staked before the flowers open. Epidendrums bloom the year round and are an unfailing source of flowers for indoor arrangement.

Cattleyas and other epiphytic orchids also grow outdoors but require high humidity and must be brought inside when freezing weather threatens. They can be grown on slabs of tree-fern fiber and hung like pictures throughout the garden in shady spots. Planting the cattleya in a pot or on a slab facilitates bringing it indoors when the weather is chilly.

DECEMBER

Pacific Northwest

This is a wet month. "This is good weather for ducks" is the quip heard as seasoned gardeners go about preparations for Christmas.

English holly is the plant of the month. While red-berried varieties are justly popular, the equally cheerful yellow-berried form deserves wider use. Those with silver or yellow variegated leaves should be located in the garden with careful thought so they will not create a spotty effect.

Pines and other conifers are also in the spotlight. If they need some pruning or shaping, do it this month and use the cut branches for Christmas decorations. Afterward, lay the cut greens over tender young plants for winter protection.

If you wish to buy a living Christmas tree that can go into the garden after the holidays, pick out one at your nursery. Some care is necessary to prevent a living tree from dying indoors. First, spray the needles with an antitranspirant. Set the tree in a container deep enough to permit watering of the root ball.

After the holidays, move it to a sheltered porch or carport and protect the root ball from freezing. Allow a week or so for the tree to adjust to the temperature change, and then plant as soon as possible.

Northern California

Storms, with rain accompanied by wind, are part of normal December weather. In the intermountain areas rain changes to snow.

This is the favorite month to plant tulip and hyacinth bulbs, for they need cool soil and growing conditions to produce good flowers on long stems. Planting depths recommended for other regions are not deep enough here to provide coolness. Allow 8 in. of soil above bulbs in all but shady locations. If buds show color as they emerge from soil, start pouring on extra water and stems will lengthen.

Dormant spraying can be done during let-ups in weather that allow branches to dry off.

Bare-root planting of roses, also flowering

and fruiting trees and shrubs, begins this month.

Shop early for living Christmas trees. Nurseries start getting them around the end of November. Many people now use these just outside the living-room window rather than inside where they may be endangered by warm, dry air.

Southern California

The appearance of red berries on holly, pyracantha and other plants heralds the winter season. English holly does not do as well in Southern California as the Chinese holly. The hybrid *Ilex X altaclarensis* 'Wilsoni' has great vigor, seems to thrive locally, and is used sometimes as a street tree. Burford holly, a variety of Chinese holly, produces berries without a male plant and withstands hot, dry locations better than other types. The dwarf Chinese holly produces no berries, but is popular as a low accent plant because of the beauty of its leaves. Japanese holly has black berries; some varieties have a dwarf, prostrate habit. 'Brilliant,' a cross between English holly and Perny's holly, produces large quantities of red berries and heavily toothed leaves.

Prune berried plants now and use the clippings for Christmas decorations.

The flaming poinsettia means Christmas in California. Pink and white varieties, as well as a spherical type called 'Flaming Sphere,' with its bracts curled and curved backward to resemble a huge chrysanthemum, are also available in pots at this time.

Pre-emergent crabgrass controls should be applied this month to prevent the appearance of crabgrass next spring.

This is the best month to plant conifers. Popular ones for landscaping include stone pine, Japanese black pine and for larger gardens, the Canary Island pine. The best spreading junipers are tamarix, San Jose and shore. Popular shrub types include mugho pine, pfitzer juniper, Hollywood juniper and arborvitae. Yew-pine, often used as a vertical accent, will eventually become a tall tree, as will the fern-pine. Italian cypress, redwood and monkey-puzzle are popular tree conifers, while deodar cedar and Norfolk Island-pine are commonly sold as living Christmas trees. These must be purchased this month, and can be brought indoors for a week, decorated, and then planted out.

Plant the Cuthbertson type sweet pea now for spring blooms.

Flowering/fruiting peach tree varieties are very susceptible to peach leaf curl and must be sprayed with lime sulfur this month to control the disease.

This is the best month to prune deciduous shade trees. Also cut back the fruiting canes of boysenberry and other small cane fruits.

THE PACIFIC COAST

*Flowering cherry trees thrive in all but the
warmest parts of the Pacific Coast.*

NORTHWEST SEQUENCE OF BLOOM

BULBS   J F M A M J J A S O N D

Snowdrop
Crocus
Daffodil
Grape-Hyacinth
Tulip
Anemone
Dutch Iris
Lilies, various
Gladiolus
Tuberous Begonia
Dahlia

ANNUALS   J F M A M J J A S O N D

Pansy
Ageratum
Sweet Alyssum
Calendula
Snapdragon
Sweet Pea
Petunia
Clarkia
Lobelia
Marigold
Zinnia
Rose-Moss
Aster
Salvia

PERENNIALS   J F M A M J J A S O N D

Christmas-Rose
Bergenia
Polyanthus Primrose
Aubrieta
Moss-Pink
Basket-of-Gold
Bleeding-Heart
Wisteria (vine)
Oriental Poppy
Tall Bearded Iris
Peony
Coral Bells
Astilbe
Lupine
Foxglove
Day-Lily
Pink
Delphinium
Shasta Daisy
Japanese Iris
Fuchsia
Balloon-Flower
Asters, various
Chrysanthemum

NORTHWEST SEQUENCE OF BLOOM
(continued)

SHRUBS   J F M A M J J A S O N D

Winter Daphne
Camellia Sasanqua
Heaths, various
Flowering Quince
Camellia Japonica
Laurestinus
   Viburnum
Forsythia
Japanese
   Andromeda
Skimmia
Rhododendrons
Azaleas, various
Vanhoutte Spirea
Lilac
Pernettya
Escallonia
Rose
Abelia
Scotch Heather
Hydrangea

TREES   J F M A M J J A S O N D

Autumn Higan
   Cherry
Flowering Apricot
Blireiana Plum
Crab-Apples
Flowering Cherry
Saucer Magnolia
Flowering Dogwood
Golden-Chain
Southern Magnolia
Silk-Tree

NORTHERN CALIFORNIA SEQUENCE
OF BLOOM

BULBS   J F M A M J J A S O N D

Crocus
Cyclamen
Daffodils, various
Ranunculus
Dutch Iris
Freesia
Tulip
Gladiolus
Amaryllis
Calla
Agapanthus
Lilies, various
Tuberous Begonia
Dahlia

ANNUALS   J F M A M J J A S O N D

Sweet Alyssum
Calendula
Nemesia
Snapdragon
Fairy Primrose
Pansy
Sweet Pea
Stock
Petunia
Lobelia
Rose-Moss
Zinnia
Marigold

NORTHERN CALIFORNIA SEQUENCE
OF BLOOM
(continued)

PERENNIALS   J F M A M J J A S O N D

Primrose, various
Violets
Bergenia, various
Marguerite
Calceolaria
Shasta Daisy
Bearded Iris
Wax Begonias
Day-Lily
Delphinium
Gazania
Geranium
Gerbera
Pink
Fuchsia
Lythrum
Phlox
Aster, various
Chrysanthemum

SHRUBS   J F M A M J J A S O N D

Camellia japonica
Winter Daphne
Poinsettia
Heaths, various
Flowering Quince
Forsythia
Abelia
Ceanothus, various
Azaleas, various
Rhododendrons,
    various
India-Hawthorn
Lilac
Broom
Lantana
Hydrangea
Oleander
Escallonia, various
Rose-of-Sharon

TREES   J F M A M J J A S O N D

Strawberry-Tree
Magnolias, various
Acacias, various
Autumn Higan
    Cherry
Blireiana Plum
Flowering Apricot
Crab-Apples
Flowering Cherry
Hawthorns
Horse-Chestnut
Flowering Dogwood
Goldenrain-Tree
Crape-Myrtle

SOUTHERN CALIFORNIA SEQUENCE
OF BLOOM

BULBS   J F M A M J J A S O N D

Daffodil
Freesia
Hyacinth
Calla
Cyclamen
Amaryllis
Gladiolus
Anemone
Agapanthus
Canna
Dahlia
Lilies, various
Tuberous Begonia
Lycoris

SOUTHERN CALIFORNIA SEQUENCE
OF BLOOM
(continued)

ANNUALS	J F M A M J J A S O N D
Calendula	
Cineraria	
Sweet Alyssum	
Stock	
Iceland Poppy	
Pansy	
Snapdragon	
Sweet Pea	
Marigold, various	
Ageratum	
Rose-Moss	
Petunia	
Zinnia	

SHRUBS	J F M A M J J A S O N D
Azalea	
Camellia japonica	
Flowering Quince	
Chinese Hibiscus	
India-Hawthorn	
Lantana	
Poinsettia	
Strawberry-Tree	
Winter Daphne	
Scotch Broom	
Ceanothus griseus	
Shrimp-Plant	
Oleander	
Orange-Jessamine	
French Hydrangea	
Gardenia	
Camellia Sasanqua	

PERENNIALS	J F M A M J J A S O N D
Bergenia	
Bird-of-Paradise	
Marguerite	
Ice-Plant	
Day-Lily	
Gazania	
Geranium	
Pinks & Carnations	
Verbena	
Wax Begonia	
Alyssum saxatile	
Iris, various	
Delphinium	
Shasta Daisy	
Gerbera	
Ginger-Lily	
Phlox	
Aster	

TREES	J F M A M J J A S O N D
Acacia baileyana	
Hong-Kong Orchid-Tree	
Oriental Magnolias	
Southern Magnolias	
Flowering Cherry	
Flowering Peach	
Weeping Bottle-Brush	
Sweetshade	
Jacaranda	
Tipu-Tree	
Eucalyptus ficifolia	
Crape-Myrtle	
Cassia	

SOURCES FOR SEEDS AND PLANTS

The following mail-order nursery and seed firms issue illustrated catalogues.
Some of the catalogues are free, while a slight charge is made for others.

SEEDS

Geo. W. Park Seed Company, Greenwood, South Carolina 29646

W. Atlee Burpee Company, Philadelphia, Pennsylvania 19132; Clinton, Iowa 52732; Riverside, California 92502

PLANTS FOR OUTDOORS

Armstrong Nurseries (roses), Ontario, California 91764

Gardens of the Blue Ridge (wild flowers), Ashford, McDowell County, North Carolina 28603

Henry Field Seed and Nursery Company, Shenandoah, Iowa 51601

Inter-State Nurseries, Hamburg, Iowa 51640

Jackson & Perkins Company (roses), Newark, New York 14513 and Medford, Oregon 97501

Lamb Nurseries (perennials), East 101 Sharp Ave., Spokane, Washington 99202

Walter Marx Gardens (perennials), Boring, Oregon 97009

Earl May Seed & Nursery Company, Shenandoah, Iowa 51601

Schreiner's (irises, day-lilies), Route 2, Box 297, Salem, Oregon 97303

Sky-Cleft Gardens (rock plants), Camp Street Ext., Barre, Vermont 05641

Star Roses (roses), West Grove, Pennsylvania 19390

Stark Brothers, Louisiana, Missouri 63353

Will Tillotson's Roses (old-fashioned kinds), Brown's Valley Road, Watsonville, California 95076

Vick's Wildgardens, Inc. (wild flowers), Box 115, Gladwynne, Pennsylvania 19035

Wayside Gardens, Mentor, Ohio 44060

Gilbert H. Wild & Sons (irises, day-lilies, peonies), Sarcoxie, Missouri 64862

INDOOR PLANTS

Alberts & Merkel Bros., Incorporated, P. O. Box 537, Boynton Beach, Florida 33435

Fischer Greenhouses (African-violets), Linwood, New Jersey 08221

House Plant Corner (supplies), Box 810, Oxford, Maryland 21654

Johnson Cactus Gardens, Paramount, California 90724

Logee's Greenhouses, 55 North St., Danielson, Connecticut 06239

Roehrs Company, Rutherford, New Jersey 07070

Tinari Greenhouse (African-violets), 2325 Valley Road, Huntington Valley, Pennsylvania 19006

Wilson Brothers, Roachdale, Indiana 46172

HELPFUL READING

DISEASES AND PESTS

How to Control Plant Diseases, by Malcolm Shurtleff, Iowa State University Press

Insects and Related Pests of House Plants, U.S.D.A. Home and Garden Bulletin No. 67, Superintendent of Documents, United States Government Printing Office, Washington, D.C.

The Gardener's Bug Book, by Cynthia Westcott, Doubleday & Company, Incorporated

Keep Your Garden Healthy, by Louis Pyenson, E. P. Dutton & Co., Incorporated

GENERAL

Botany for Gardeners, by Harold William Rickett, The Macmillan Company

Deadly Harvest, a Guide to Common Poisonous Plants, by John M. Kingsbury, Holt, Rinehart and Winston

Taylor's Encyclopedia of Gardening, edited by Norman Taylor, Houghton Mifflin Company

Woman's Day Book of Houseplants, by Jean Hersey, Simon & Schuster

REGIONAL

The New York Times Garden Book, edited by Joan Lee Faust, Alfred A. Knopf

Good Gardens in the Sunshine States, by George W. Kelly, Smith-Brooks Printing Co.

Southwest Gardening, by Rosalie Doolittle and Harriet Tiedebohl, The University of New Mexico Press

Sunset Western Garden Book, by the editorial staffs of Sunset Books and Sunset Magazine, Lane Book Company

Your Florida Garden, by John V. Watkins and Herbert S. Wolfe, University of Florida Press

Your Garden in the South, by Hamilton Mason, D. Van Nostrand Company

LANDSCAPING

Budget Landscaping, by Carlton B. Lees, Henry Holt and Company

Designs for Outdoor Living, by John Burton Brimer, Doubleday & Company

Japanese Gardens of Today, by David H. Engel, Charles E. Tuttle Company

Landscaping for Modern Living, by the editors of Sunset Magazine, Lane Book Company

GARDEN FLOWERS

Anyone Can Grow Roses, by Cynthia Westcott, D. Van Nostrand Company, Incorporated

Rock Garden Plants, by Doretta Klaber, Henry Holt and Company

The Complete Book of Bulbs, by Rockwell and Grayson, Doubleday & Company

The New Perennials Preferred, by Helen Van Pelt Wilson, M. Barrows & Company

The Rockwells' Complete Book of Roses, by Rockwell and Grayson, Doubleday & Co.

TREES, SHRUBS AND VINES

Flowering Shrubs, by Isabel Zucker, D. Van Nostrand Company, Incorporated

Flowering Trees of the World for Tropics and Warm Climates, by Edwin A. Menninger, Hearthside Press

Landscaping with Vines, by Frances Howard, The Macmillan Company

Ornamental Trees for Home Grounds, by Harold O. Perkins, E. P. Dutton and Co.

Trees for American Gardens, by Donald Wyman, The Macmillan Company

Index